ANOMALISTIC PSYCHOLOGY
A Study of
Extraordinary Phenomena
of Behavior and Experience

LEONARD ZUSNE
WARREN H. JONES
University of Tulsa

LEA LAWRENCE ERLBAUM ASSOCIATES, PUBLISHERS
1982   Hillsdale, New Jersey

Lawrence Erlbaum Associates, Inc., Publishers
365 Broadway
Hillsdale, New Jersey 07642

Library of Congress Cataloging in Publication Data
Zusne, Leonard, 1924-
    Anomalistic psychology.

  Bibliography: p.
  Includes index.
  1. Psychical research--Psychological aspects.
2. Occult sciences--Psychological aspects.
3. Supernatural--Psychological aspects. I. Jones,
Warren H., joint author. II. Title. [DNLM:
1. Occultism. 2. Parapsychology. 3. Psychology.
4. Science. RE1409.Z96a]
BF1040.Z87   133.8 '01 '5   80-17345
ISBN 0-89859-068-X

Printed in the United States of America

Contents

iii

Preface

The need for a textbook like the present was felt by the authors as they taught an experimental course on "Psychology of the Extraordinary" during the interim term of 1978. The course, now named Anomalistic Psychology, has since been made part of the regular course offerings in the Psychology Program at the University of Tulsa, joining the growing number of such courses offered on the campuses of American universities. Still, there are no textbooks available to help the instructor teach a course of this type and the student become acquainted with and organize the very extensive literature that there is in this field. This text thus grew from a need for a teaching aid in a course on the scientific approach to all those psychological phenomena that do not fit the current scientific world view by the criteria of most psychologists, as well as paranormal phenomena of other kinds that at least in part can be explained in terms of known psychological principles. Both types of phenomena may be designated as anomalistic. Psychology texts seldom mention them, let alone accord them a systematic treatment. As any psychology instructor who has ever taught an introductory course in psychology knows, it is precisely these phenomena that—in addition, of course, to the topic of sex—are guaranteed to elicit the undivided attention of the class. To the student, telepathy, faith healing, or psychokinesis are eminently psychological topics. The text, unfortunately, has nothing to tell about these fascinating topics and, chances are, neither has the instructor. Thus, on a more basic level, the need for this textbook was created by the student's to learn about psychological anomalies and the necessity to satisfy this need in an academically and scientifically respectable manner. That esoteric beliefs and occult practices have assumed an increasing importance in American culture is a fact that has been documented repeatedly in both the news media and scholarly literature. A recent (1978) Gallup Poll showed that 57% of Americans believe in UFOs and 54% in angels. Among those for whom religion was very important, the percentage of those believing in angels was 68%, but religion had no effect on belief in astrology, in which 29% of Americans believe. Fifty-one percent of Americans believe in extrasensory perception. Significantly, this percentage rises to 64 among those who have been to college. The will to believe is always more prevalent and stronger than the will to disbelieve. A quick glance in the Occult section of any bookstore tells us that the believer literature outweighs the skeptical literature by several orders of magnitiude. To educate American college students to think rationally and critically about phenomena that all too easily lend themselves to supernatural and paranormal interpretations becomes, therefore, an important challenge to the educator.

The area of anomalistic psychological phenomena is broad enough to warrant a full-fledged course and a textbook. The area is indeed so broad that it is possible to write a text with chapter headings and a chapter arrangement that are not too different from those found in an introductory psychology textbook. Anomalistic processes are largely human behavior and human experiences. The order of the chapters and the significant words in chapter headings in the present text are, therefore, intentionally patterned after the typical introductory psychology text. Not every major psychological topic has merited an entire chapter—for instance, learning—but the learning and conditioning processes as well as other topics that usually do have a chapter devoted to them in an introductory text are referred to throughout the book wherever appropriate. There are few psychological topics that have not been touched upon.

The two chapters that are usually not found in an introductory text are the ones on bad science and on parapsychology. Of all the topics treated, parapsychology in name, content, and method is closest to psychology, and there would be a chapter on it in every introductory text had psychologists ever accepted the evidence offered by parapsychologists in support of their claims. The "bad science" chapter shows that much of what is considered paranormal is based on inappropriate or fraudulent application of scientific principles and logic.

We have explained, however briefly, all psychological terms used, so that having had no introductory course in psychology should not be a major obstacle to one's taking a course in which this book is used as a text. Having had such a course, however, will add greatly to both the student's enjoyment and understanding. It will also save the instructor time if he or she does not have to explain a number of elementary psychological concepts to those students who have not had the benefit of an introductory course in psychology. The target groups are, therefore, second- and third-year students enrolled in a course on the "scientific approach to anomalous phenomena," "psychology and parapsychology," "psychology of the extraordinary," and the like. Needless to say, this text would also serve as a supplementary reading source in an introductory psychology course.

We have not tried it, but it would be intriguing to see how *Anomalistic Psychology* would do in adult education and similar courses in lieu of a standard psychology text to introduce the field of psychology in a sort of a reversal of the way psychology and anomalistic psychology are usually handled. In a regular introductory psychology course, it is the psychic anecdote, the precognitive dream, or the astrological prediction of character that provides, by way of "real life examples," the piquant sauce for what to a number of students may appear to be a rather dull fare. When the psychological explanations appear in a secondary role, learning them may seem a less painful process.

Anomalous objects and anomalous processes were largely ignored by the universities before the 1960s. Cultural changes that occurred during that decade brought the believers in such objects and processes out in the open, and courses began to be offered that would have been unthinkable just a few years earlier. The number of universities where such courses are offered has been growing steadily. Anomalous and paranormal phenomena cover a lot of territory, and the nature of these courses is accordingly quite varied. Disregarding such offerings as short-term, experimental courses on black magic, witchcraft, or astrology taught by believers and practitioners, the courses range from introduction to extrasensory perception taught by a believer out of a psychology department to "fads and myths in science," offered by an astronomy department. Most of the topics in the area of the paranormal come under the purview of psychology, and most of the courses are, therefore, offered by psychology departments. As the title of this book indicates, we treat anomalistic *psychology*, not anomalistics in general; hence, we do not examine in detail the Loch Ness monster, ancient astronauts, or frogs falling from the sky.

The characteristics of the instructors who have offered courses in anomalistics have not varied nearly as much as the nature of the courses themselves. In fact, it may not be an exaggeration to state that they have been mostly of two kinds: believers and nonbelievers. Believers offer courses because they want more people to believe with them; non-believers offer them in hopes of showing what the paranormal is really like and that those who have taken the course will henceforth examine claims of paranormality more carefully. We do not think that *Anomalistic Psychology* will suit an instructor who subscribes to a dualistic philosophy and believes in the reality of most if not all of the "core" paranormal phenomena as presented in the believer literature. On the other hand, this is not a debunking book either. We do explain allegedly paranormal phenomena in psychological and physical terms where such evidence for them is quite clear. We do not attempt to discredit nonrational belief systems by showing that they are wrong because some of their articles of faith are based on phenomena that have a naturalistic explanation. Such an approach defeats the purpose of a course in anomalistic psychology. Science is helpless in face of committed belief, and attempts to change such beliefs are futile and are only met with hostility. Neither do we believe that it is the task of science to change beliefs. What we do is to show what the approach of a psychologist to paranormal phenomena is, how it is related to the scientific approach in general, and what the scientific approach has to say about some of the interesting and bizarre phenomena called paranormal. We present additional ways of explaining phenomena that seem to defy nature's laws, ways that, although based on a monistic view of the world, are not irreconcilably hostile to the dualistic view and what it entails in terms of paranormal phenomena. Thus, we do not reject the possibility that the so-called psi phenomena may have a reality about them, although at the present time the nature of that reality is entirely a matter of speculation. We show how a commitment to the scientific method forces inexplicable phenomena to yield, sometimes after exceedingly long periods of time, and reveal their true nature that enables us to subsume them under nature's laws. Although we do provide the user of the text with the information that may change his or her perspective on the world, we are not trying to force upon that person a new value system. We do this not only out of respect for individuals' freedom to choose it themselves, but also because we believe that the kind of philosophy or value system individuals will suscribe to depends on those individuals' personalities. Whether they will choose the demonstrative (scientific, empirical, monistic) world view or the dialectic (rational, dualistic) one will depend on how they choose to solve the paradox of the relationship between their inner world and the outer world, the subjective and the objective, and whether, therefore, they may be described, in William James's words, as tough-minded or tender-minded personalities. That basic attitude is not subject to educational influences.

Acknowledgments

We are indebted to Kathy Jones, Lucy Mylar, and Phyllis Orbaugh for their generous assistance in the preparation and typing of some of the chapters. The administration of the University of Tulsa granted sabbatical leave for the senior author, which greatly expedited the completion of the manuscript. Our colleagues in the Psychology Program supplied ample encouragement. We wish to acknowledge Mr. Lawrence Erlbaum who has allowed us to pursue a project in a new and controversial area of psychology.

We would also like to express our appreciation to the following sources who have granted their permission to use various quotations and illustrations in this volume.

Chapter 2 Quote on page 15 excerpted from *Handbook of Parapsychology,* edited by Benjamin B. Wolman, copyright © 1977 by Litton Educational Publishing, Inc.; reprinted by permission of Van Nostrand Reinhold Company. Fig. 2.1: National Library of Medicine. Fig. 2.2: Leonard Zusne photo. Quote on page 38 excerpted from *Psychological Healing* by Pierre Janet, copyright © *4* 1925 by George Allen & Unwin (Publishers) Ltd.; reprinted by permission.

Chapter 3 Fig. 3.2: From "Bucky Fuller and the Fire Walk" by G. M. Feigen, *Saturday Review,* July 12, 1969; R. Buckminster Fuller photo, used by permission. Fig. 3.3: Adapted from "A Cartography of the Ecstatic and Meditative States" by Roland Fischer, *Science,* 1971, *174,* 897–904; Copyright © 1971 by the American Association for the Advancement of Science. Fig. 3.4: From *Yoga: A Scientific Evaluation* by K. T. Behanan, New York, Dover Publications, 1959; used by permission of Dover Publications, Inc. Quote on page 81 excerpted from *Kundalini: The Evolutionary Energy in Man* by Gopi Krishna. Reprinted by special arrangement with Shambala Publications, Inc., Boulder, Colorado; Copyright © 1967 by Gopi Krihna. Quotes on pages 75 and 82 from Roland Fischer, "Cartography of Inner Space," in R. K. Siegel & L. J. West (Eds.), *Hallucinations,* Copyright © 1975 John Wiley & Sons, Inc.; reprinted by permission of John Wiley & Sons, Inc. Quote on page 84 from *ESP, Seers, and Psychics* by Milbourne Christopher, 1970; reprinted by permission of Harper & Row, Publishers, Inc. Fig. 3.5: From *Illusions and Delusions of the Supernatural and the Occult* by D. H. Rawcliffe, New York, Dover Publications, 1959; used by permission of Dover Publications, Inc.

Chapter 4 Fig. 4.1: From *Perception* by R. H. Forgus & L. E. Melamed; Copyright © 1976 by McGraw-Hill Book Company; used by permission of McGraw-Hill Book Company. Quote on pages 107–109 from "Some Observations Regarding the Experiences and Behavior of the BaMbuti Pygmies" by C. M. Turnbull, *American Journal of Psychology,* 1966, *74,* 304–308; used by permission of University of Illinois Press. Fig. 4.4: Priscilla O'Connor—Artesia Daily Press. Fig. 4.6: Leonard Zusne photo. Fig. 4.7: From "Solving the Mystery of the Oregon Vortex" by Howard E. Jackson, *Fate,* January 1961; reproduced by permission of *Fate* magazine.

Chapter 5 Fig. 5.1: From *Illusions and Delusions of the Supernatural and the Occult* by D. H. Rawcliff, New York, Dover Publications, 1959; used by permission of Dover Publications, Inc. Quote on page 131 from *The Psychology of Anomalous Experience* by Graham F. Reed, London, Hutchinson University Library © 1972 by Graham F. Reed; reprinted by permission.

Chapter 6 Quote on page 153 from "Eyewitness Testimony" by Robert Buckhout, *Scientific American,* December 1974; reprinted by permission of W. H. Freeman and Company, Publishers, Quote on page 154 from *The Principles of Psychology* by William James (1980), reprinted by Dover Publications, 1950 (vol. 1); used by permission of Dover Publications, Inc. Quote on page 164 from *The Search for a Soul* by Taylor Caldwell; Copyright © 1972 by Jesse Stern and Taylor Caldwell; reprinted by permission of Doubleday & Company, Inc.

Chapter 8 Quote on pages 223–224 from "A Critical Look at Astrology," by B. J. Bok, *The Humanist,* September-October, 1975, p. 6.

Quote on page 234 and Figs. 8.1, 8.2 and 8.3: from *From India to the Planet Mars* by T. Flournoy (1900), reprinted by University Books, 1963; used by permission of University Books, Inc. Quote on page 243 and Fig. 8.4 from *Divided Consciousness* by E. R. Hilgard, Copyright © John Wiley & Sons, Inc. Reprinted by permission of John Wiley & Sons, Inc. Quote on pages 244 and 245 from *The Unfinished Autobiography* by Alice Bailey; Copyright © 1951 by Lucis Trust; used by permission. Fig. 8.5: From *The Divining Rod* by A. J. Ellis (1917), reprinted 1957, Government Printing Office.

Chapter 9 Quote on page 267 from *The Child's Conception of the World* by Jean Piaget, New York, Harcourt & Brace, 1929; used by permission of Routledge & Kegan Paul Ltd. and Humanities Press, Inc. Fig. 9.1: From *Panorama of Magic* by Milbourne Christopher, New York, Dover Publications, 1962; used by permission of Dover Publications, Inc. Fig. 9.2: Library of Congress.

Chapter 10 Quotes on page 299, 312, and 313 from *Magic, Supernaturalism and Religion* by Kurt Seligmann, Copyright ©1948 by Pantheon Books, a Division of Random House, Inc.; used by permission. Quote on page 312 from *The Encyclopedia of Witchcraft and Demonology* by Rossell Hope Robbins, © 1959 by Crown Publishers, Inc.; used by permission of Crown Publishers, Inc. Figs. 10.1, 10.2, and 10.3: from *Picture Book of Devils, Demons and Witchcraft* by Ernst and Johanna Lehner, New York, Dover Publications, 1971. Fig. 10.4: Leonard Zusne photo.

Chapter 11 Quote on page 347 from *Cults of Unreason* by Christopher Evans; Copyright © 1973 by Christopher Evans. Reprinted with the permission of Farrar, Straus and Giroux, Inc. and Patrick Seale & Associates.

Chapter 12 Quote on page 371 from "The Role of Neurological Ideas in Psychology" by Donald O. Hebb, *Journal of Personality,* 1951 *20*, 39–55; Copyright © 1951 by Duke University Press; used by permission of Duke University Press.

Chapter 13 Fig. 13.1: From *Learning to Use Extrasensory Perception* by Charles Tart; Copyright © 1976 by University of Chicago; used by permission of University of Chicago Press. Quote on pages 404–405 from *Science,* vol. 148, p. 1541, 18 June 1965; Copyright © 1965 by the American Association for the Advancement of Science; used by permission of the American Association for the advancement of Science and Luis W.Alvarez.

Chapter 14 Quote on page 439 from *Fads and Fallacies in the Name of Science* by Martin Gardner; Copyright © 1957 by Martin Gardner; used by permission of Dover Publications, Inc.

1 Introduction To Anomalistic Psychology

TERMINOLOGY

Our ancestors of not so many centuries ago regarded any psychological anomaly with awe, attributed its origins to supernatural agencies, and endowed its effects with supernormal qualities. Among such anomalies were not only precognitive dreams, cases of miraculous healing, sleepwalking, and automatic behaviors, but all cases of severe psychopathology. The psychotic individual was said to be possessed by an evil spirit, an explanation that was also applied to the neurotic individual suffering from hysteria. Eventually, demons and spirits were given up as explanations of psychopathology, and behavior that in some way deviated from the statistical norm, or what most people regarded as normal behavior, was designated as *abnormal* and treatable by physical and psychological means.

There remained the other phenomena that were also deviations from the norm; but, these were abnormal in another sense that placed them in a different category of abnormality. They were not just unusual because they did not occur very frequently, as the absence of pain sensitivity or color blindness in only one eye are rare (and anomalous) phenomena. These phenomena, in addition, violated certain "basic limiting principles" (Broad, 1962), which are general principles that describe how nature works. They are not laws of nature but, like the principles of logical reasoning, are accepted by almost everybody in Western culture, at least as far as most everyday events are concerned. For example, an effect cannot precede its cause, no one can literally read another person's mind, objects cannot be moved simply by willing them to move, nor can they be transformed into other objects in the

1

same way, and a person cannot be and act in two places at the same time. When these principles appear to have been violated, there is a strong tendency to attribute supernatural causation to the phenomenon.

The labeling of anything as *supernatural* contains the idea that the cause of the phenomenon is known, that it is some supernatural entity—a god, a devil, or a spirit—and that no further inquiry concerning the nature of the phenomenon is necessary. Rich as it may be in emotional meaning to many people, the term supernatural has no standing with science. A scientist who decides to investigate a phenomenon that seems to defy natural explanation, will, as always, attempt first to explain it by establishing a relationship between antecedent causes and consequent effects. If the scientist finds that a table moves during a mediumistic séance because it is attached to a hidden lever operated by the medium, he or she has shown that the phenomenon belongs to the realm of the natural. Second, if the phenomenon defies its subordination to the natural order of things at first, observing the phenomenon repeatedly may lead to the establishment of reliable relationships and a formulation of a general principle or principles according to which the phenomenon operates. Thus, if American psychologists had not obtained positive results in biofeedback research in their laboratories first, the discovery that the functions of the autonomic nervous system can be trained could have come from repeated observations and measurement of the physiological functions of the yogis. As it turned out, both lines of research converged upon the same conclusion, and the mysterious and seemingly supernatural became quite natural. Third, it is possible that a phenomenon may elude any attempts to establish cause-effect relationships for it. This still does not mean that it has a supernatural cause. Chance alone can produce highly meaningful coincidences. Finally, past experience of scientists shows that there is a good chance that an unpredictable event may be an nonevent—that is, that it is not a uniform set of phenomena but a different kind of thing every time it is observed, each instance being only superficially similar to others. Many instances of unidentified flying objects turn out to be neither objects nor in flight, but light reflections, phenomena of temperature inversions, meteorological balloons, or hallucinations.

We refer to all behavioral and experiential phenomena that have traditionally seemed to constitute violations of the basic limiting principles as *anomalistic*. The term *anomalistic psychology* suggested itself to us upon coming across a proposal, made by the anthropologist Roger Wescott (1977), to prefix the term anomalistic to the name of the particular discipline that dealt with what are often called *paranormal* phenomena. The term anomalistic is neutral, whereas the term paranormal suggests influences and effects that lie outside the natural order of things. We use the term paranormal in contexts where such use has been sanctioned by writers who have dealt with the topic.

Two other terms that are used relatively frequently in the following pages are the *occult* and *esoteric* and their derivatives. In one sense, the occult lies somewhere between the supernatural and the paranormal, but the exact meaning of the term is to be sought more in the connotations that specific groups of users have attached to that term and from the particular context within which it is employed. Formally, occult means: (1) that which is mysterious and beyond the reach of ordinary knowledge; (2) secrecy, exclusiveness, and the communication of arcane knowledge to the initiated only; (3) pertaining to metaphysical systems characterized by monistic idealism, which stress the basic interrelatedness of everything in the universe and hence the possibility of action through affinity, or magic, as in astrology and theosophy. Esoteric means designed for or understood only by those who have been properly initiated. In that sense, it overlaps only with the second meaning of occult just given, and can be applied to knowledge that has no paranormal connotations whatever. Although the term is so used ordinarily, some occult groups use esotericism as a synonym for occultism.

Social scientists have stressed different, sometimes contradictory, aspects of occultism. Marcello Truzzi, who has concerned himself with the problem of defining the occult (Truzzi, 1971), states that the common denominator for most perspectives labeled occult "is that they have in some way concerned themselves with things anomalous to our generally accepted cultural storehouse of "truths." That is, we are here dealing with claims that contradict commonsense or institutionalized (scientific or religious) knowledge [p. 637]." Because the basic limiting principles are part of the "cultural storehouse of truths," occult and anomalistic become synonymous in Truzzi's definition.

SCIENCE, THE SCIENTIFIC METHOD, AND THE CONTENT OF ANOMALISTIC PSYCHOLOGY

Because determining what is occult and what is scientific is a matter of deciding whether a basic limiting principle has been violated, the dividing line between them is not all that clear. Some claims that were once distinctly occult have become part of science, hypnotism and the active agents in some of the witches' herbal remedies being examples. Telepathy, precognition, and clairvoyance have always been part of the occult lore, but now these phenomena are being studied by parapsychologists. Is parapsychology therefore an occultism? Not for that reason, because it is not the subject matter that determines whether a discipline is a science, but its methodology, and parapsychologists do use the scientific method. They have nevertheless tried hard to break the connection between parapsychology and occultism that exists in the minds of many because they both deal with some of the same phenomena, such as telepathy.

In his definition of occultism, Truzzi states that its claims are contradicted by both scientific and religious knowledge. They are not only contradicted, but rejected, by institutionalized science and religion. The best example of this is theosophy. Modern theosophy is a body of teachings that labels itself a synthesis of science, religion, and philosophy. It is equally rejected by all three. Theosophy is perhaps the best example of what occultism means in that it represents a body of knowledge that incorporates most of the esoteric teachings and occult practices of the past, does not accept the supernaturalism of religion, but equally rejects the materialistic and deterministic views of science and emphasizes the hidden, occult nature of its knowledge. Much of this knowledge of course, has been made available through numerous publications, lectures, and courses. Some of it, however, has been reserved for an inner circle of disciples, to whom it is imparted after due initiation, as has always occurred in all mystery and initiatory groups throughout history.

Box 1.1—Theosophy

Theosophy is religious and philosophical thought about the nature of divinity (from the Greek *theos* = god and *sophia* = wisdom) that derives a view of the universe, humanity, and its place in the universe from an insight into the constitution and operation of the divine. The insight is arrived at intuitively or is revealed by superior or more advanced beings. Because no clear distinction is made between religious and philosophical modes of thinking and the role of logic is minimized, theosophy is closer to Oriental than Occidental thought. India gave birth to the earliest theosophical speculations, and the similarity between Indian theosophical speculations and certain features in the thought of Western theosophists who knew little or nothing about India is often pointed out. The imperfection of this world and of human beings and the aspiration to achieve the same exalted states of being that characterize the seers and masters who reveal the divine wisdom is a cardinal feature of theosophical systems. Jakob Böhme is the best example of an early Western theosophist. He was influenced by such men as Paracelsus and Cardano, who during the Renaissance combined theosophy with physics or chemistry as well as with such older but related thought forms as neoplatonism, mysticism, hermeticism, and cabalism.

It is the modern version of theosophy that is of importance to anomalistic psychology. It combined into a synthetic conglomerate Indian philosophy, Buddhism, gnosticism, hermetism, cabala, all of the paranormal phenomena and occult practices dealt with in this book, as well as many others, and added a generous portion of modern science, especially the notion of evolutionary development. It became the treasure trove from which the hundreds of groups, organizations, cults, and movements that were to parallel it took their items and, in combination with their own special revelations and terminologies, presented them to the world as their brand of Ancient Wisdom.

The founder of modern theosophy was a Russian adventuress, Helena Petrovna Blavatsky, an extraordinary woman of the 19th century who represented an amazing blend of intelligence, shrewdness, vulgarity, unattractive body, temper, prodigious working capacity, contempt for people, and the ability to control them if they were eager to believe in miracles. She was born Helena Hahn in Russia in 1831. At age 17, she married an official by the name of Blavatsky, 25 years her senior. The marriage lasted only a few months, after which HPB, as she is known amoung the occultists, went traveling in different countries, allegedly in Greece, Egypt, Turkey, and Tibet, among other places, although what she did for the next 25 years is mostly a mystery clad in legend. It is known that for a number of years, she made a living as a medium in Cairo. In 1872, she arrived in New York, met Colonel H. S. Olcott, who immediately fell under her spell and with whom she founded the Theosophical Society in 1875. In 1877, HPB published her first compendium of theosophical lore, *Isis Unveiled*.

The aims of the Society were declared to be: (1) to form a nucleus of the universal brotherhood of humanity; (2) to promote the study of comparative religion, philosophy, and science; and (3) to investigate the unexplained laws of nature and the powers latent in man. *Isis Unveiled* was an incredible collection, totally unsystematic, of the occult lore of all nations, which HPB had presumably gathered during her extensive travels, presented as the secret wisdom of the ages and revealed, as to its true nature, by her. Both acclaim and criticism followed.

The magnum opus of theosophy, *The Secret Doctrine*, in six volumes, replaced *Isis Unveiled* in 1888. A somewhat more coherent work than *Isis*, this work was allegedly written by HPB's consulting the numerous required references in her astral body—that is, by visiting the necessary libraries not in person, but on the astral plane of existence. In *The Secret Doctrine*, HPB makes an important connection with science by claiming the idea of evolution as a cardinal part of her doctrine: Not only do plants and animals evolve over very long periods of time, but so do man, human races, planets, and the deity itself. Evolution is the law of the universe. Many pages of polemic are devoted to this topic in her work. The second important point that was added to the occult lore by HPB was the notion of the Mahatmas or Masters. Unlike the spiritualists who obtained their information from the spirits of the departed, HPB claimed a much more refined and exalted source of information, humans who had advanced far ahead of the rest of humanity on the evolutionary road, had access to knowledge no ordinary human had, possessed marvelous abilities, such as those of materializing objects, teleportation, clairvoyance, and so on, and who usually worked on levels of existence other than the gross physical matter, although they still used their physical bodies when convenient. The Masters were said to control the destiny of humanity by means of messages to world leaders, to fight the forces of evil, and to reside in secret places, not visible to anyone but those specially favored. At first, HPB located the secret brotherhood of Masters in Luxor, Egypt, with Tuiti Bey as the leader. Later, the Mahatmas were transferred to Tibet, and the leadership acquired an Indian complexion. In the fully developed theosophical scheme, the Masters are of all nationalities, and include such personages as Jesus and the Count Saint Germain.

Other ideas that may be found in *The Secret Doctrine*, either in full or in germinal form and elaborated later by theosophical writers, and that are familiar to those who are "into" the occult are: the lost continents of Atlantis and Mu and their civilizations; the nonphysical bodies of man, such as the etheric and astral bodies; astral projection; clairvoyance; karma and reincarnation; vibrations and forces unknown to science; ancient astronauts, and many others. Through all this runs the unifying thread of the idea of evolution as the supreme law of the universe and its implications for humans in terms of the possibility of spiritual advancement and the development of capacities not available to those who do not work towards self perfection.

Madame Blavatsky remained in New York until 1882. In that year, she decided to move the headquarters of the Theosophical Society to the mother country of theosophy, India, where the "vibrations" were better and the Masters closer. Accordingly, the headquarters was established in Adyar, Madras, where it remains to this day. In 1885, during an absence of Madame Blavatsky, the London Society for Psychial Research conducted an investigation of her miracles (over 50 had been listed by her adherents), such as the precipitation from the ceiling of letters written by the Mahatmas. The investigation disclosed that her miracles had been fraud or trickery, performed in collusion with a caretaker couple, the Coulombs. The disclosure had little effect on the Society, however.

HPB died in 1891, and Colonel Olcott, who had been the President of the Society, in 1907. In that year, the Presidency was taken over by Annie Besant, the famous English socialist, social reformer, union organizer, and Indian independence leader who in 1889 suddenly converted from materialism and atheism to theosophy upon reading *The Secret Doctrine*. Her ability as an organizer and propagandizer was responsible for the spread and influence of theosophical ideas in spite of the numerically small size of the Theosophical Society.

The most dramatic event in Annie Besant's life during her Presidency was the discovery, in 1909, of Jiddu Krishnamurti, an Indian boy who she believed would serve as the vehicle for the incarnation of a new world savior. By 1929, Krishnamurti decided that was not to be, and went on his own philosophical way, renouncing the need for reliance on any masters for occult knowledge. Like the Coulomb affair, Krishnamurti's defection had no major impact on the Theosophical Society or on the acceptance of its teachings. In 1980, there are no messiahs or miracles associated with the Society, but the legacy of Helena Petrovna Blavatsky continues to live in Adyar, the American headquarters at Wheaton, Illinois, and other centers throughout the world, the journals of the Society, its books, and especially in the minds of all those who are members of the countless esoteric groups that are offshoots of the theosophical tree.

Anomalistic psychology is concerned with claims that certain psychological phenomena are inexplicable in terms of orthodox science. The explanations offered violate one or another of the basic limiting principles. It is well to remember that the paranormal is defined in terms of *claims* of paranormality. The task of anomalistic psychology is not to separate these claims into those that are genuine and those that are not. Rather, it applies the scientific method to all such claims and shows that either: (1) a given rare or unusual phenomenon can be explained in naturalistic terms; or (2) the phenomenon or some aspect of it cannot be given an adequate scientific explanation at the present, but that such a conclusion does not imply any paranormality. There is, of course, the third possibility that it might be necessary to invoke a new principle of nature to explain an anomalistic phenomenon and, in the process, revoke one or more of the basic limiting principles. Because a revision of what is normal, natural, and scientifically lawful would be called for, we, in addition to requiring compliance with the usual requirements that we impose on scientific methodology, would place the burden of proof that an anomaly took place because of the claimed paranormal processes on those who make the claim. What this amounts to is that as long as an ordinary explanation is possible, that explanation, regardless of how unlikely it is, will be invoked by the skeptic, it being up to the claimant of the paranormal explanation to show that the naturalistic explanation is inappropriate. In addition, we would demand that the weight of evidence presented in favor of the paranormal claim be proportioned to the strangeness of the facts. Demanding that extraordinary proof be produced for extraordinary claims is known as the principle of Laplace (so named after the French astronomer and mathematician Pierre Simon de Laplace, 1749-1827). These requirements may appear to be unduly limiting. They may be not only used but misused to the point where no amount of evidence in favor of a paranormal claim will avail against a skeptic who has already prejudged the issue. To temper the harshness of the principle of Laplace, Théodore Flournoy, for instance, a Swiss psychologist who did a famous study of the rather fantastic feats of a Swiss medium (see Chapter 8), has suggested that both it and another principle, which he calls the principle of Hamlet, be used when investigating paranormal phenomena. The principle of Hamlet simply states that all is possible. This latter principle is not very frequently invoked by disbelieving scientific investigators of occult phenoma.

What the scientist expects is that the methodology used by the paranormal claimant to demonstrate a phenomenon includes the following:

1. The results must be falsifiable. Falsifiability means that negative results will be obtained if the hypothesis is not true. The problem with many paranormal claims is that they are stated in such a language that no matter

what the results of a particular procedure that has been used to demonstrate a phenomenon, these can be used in support of the claim.

2. The results must be replicable. Different researchers should be able to obtain the same results if they use the same procedures under the same circumstances. This has always been a problem in parapsychology, which investigates paranormal claims using the experimental method. It is not as fatal a problem as the physical scientists have tried to show it to be, however, for the behavior of organisms, unlike the behavior of inanimate objects, is subject to so many unknown and unmeasurable variables that replicability is not always achieved even when ordinary, nonanomalous behavior is studied.

3. The proponent of the paranormal claim and the opponent must agree on a procedure for verifying the claim (intersubjective verifiability). It is evident that unless such an agreement is reached, arguments concerning claims and counterclaims will be, in principle, insoluble.

4. The principle of parsimony must be adhered to. The principle of parsimony is a principle in science that states that of two explanations, the one consistent with the fewest assumptions is to take precedence. It does not necessarily mean that the explanation will be the simplest one, although often it is. Some explanations, although simple in their final form, are arrived at through exceedingly complicated reasoning and calculations. What the principle does state is that an explanation that requires many unverified assumptions is not as good as one that requires fewer such assumptions.

TAXONOMIES OF THE PARANORMAL

When anomalistic psychological phenomena are examined in the manner just described, the result is what constitutes the main body of this text. As was indicated in the Preface, it is possible to organize the body of knowledge thus obtained in a manner that is close to that of an introductory psychology text—that is, by areas of human functioning: perception, memory, cognition and imagination, attitudes and beliefs, personality, psychophysiological interactions, and social interactions. Although we have chosen this organization for our book, other ways of looking at paranormal claims are possible and are used here to some extent.

One way is to classify such claims according to whether the phenomenon is claimed to involve: (1) information transmission; or (2) energy transmission; and whether such transmission takes place (3) within the focal person or agent involved in the phenomenon; or (4) between the person and an external body. Informational, intra-agent claims deal with such things as the information that one may obtain about one's previous incarnations and automatic writing and automatic speaking. Informational, extra-agent claims involve clairvoyance, telepathy, precognition, psychometry, and the like. Examples of energic, intra-agent claims are faith healing, yogic feats, and fire walking; energic, extra-agent claims would include forms of psychokinesis, levitation, and the poltergeist phenomena.

It is also possible to look at paranormal claims and occult practices in terms of beliefs, belief systems, and the human groups that represent them. Esoteric beliefs usually involve more than a single claim, and typically constitute whole belief systems that are institutionalized. What is the relationship between esoteric beliefs and occult practices—that is, specific paranormal claims? Generally, specific occult practices are not tied to specific belief systems, but are shared by several of them and thus appear to be rather independent. The connection between esoteric beliefs and occult practices seems to be the connection between theory and practice. This is the view of the sociologist E. A. Tiryakin (1974)—esoteric beliefs underlie occult practices and techniques the way physics underlies engineering. This does not mean that one cannot practice engineering without first going through a formal educational process in physics, or that, historically, physics came before engineering. Amateur engineers have some knowledge of physics acquired through experience, spotty and unsystematic as it is. In the same way, there are healers, fortunetellers, mediums, and psychics who do not seem to be adherents of any of the major belief systems. The theory-application relationship is there nevertheless. If a particular practice does not arise from theory, theory may serve to explain it.

The sociologist Marcello Truzzi has classified occult beliefs into five categories that are based on the degree of subjectivity or objectivity present in the criteria set to validate the claims arising from the practice of the occult beliefs (Truzzi, 1971). The following, with some modifications, is Truzzi's classificatory system:

In some areas of occultism, the criteria for validating claims are similar to those of orthodox science, for example, in parapsychology. Parapsychology can legitimately claim to be a science in that it consists of a body of knowledge and it uses the scientific method to obtain that body of knowledge. Other scientists are reluctant to admit parapsychology to the orthodox fold because the phenomena of parapsychology do not fit the existing scientific view of the world. The link between two minds that presumably are communicating telepathically, for example, besides not being specified or specified in testable terms, violates the basic limiting principle that a direct, nonsensory communication between two persons is not possible. Truzzi labels this type of occult belief *protoscientific occultism*. Parapsychology and UFOlogy, often called parasciences, belong in this category.

A second type of occultism has a somewhat looser connection with the scientific method in that here, the search for evidence is mostly programmatic rather than an actuality. The exponents of this type of occultism will often assert the scientific nature of their beliefs and practices and the desirability and possibility of scientific proof, but will fail to satisfy orthodox scientists in this respect. The nature of their beliefs in such that experimentation is virtually impossible. Their research is almost exclusively one of the ex post facto or correlational kind—both cause and effect have already occurred, and the researcher is merely measuring and correlating what is already there instead of producing and controlling causes to see what effects these might have. This group of beliefs, among which astrology is the prime example, Truzzi labels *quasi scientific occultism*. Pseudosciences is another label attached to them. Comparatively speaking, protoscientific occultism offers the possibility of consensual validation—that is, validation of its claims by way of agreement among researchers, whereas quasi scientific occultism is more individual or private in nature. This shared-private relationship exists also in the remaining two pairs of categories of occultism.

Protoscientific and quasi scientific occultism typically try to avoid the label of occultism or esotericism as well as other "unscientific" terms. Instead of mind reading, for instance, the parapsychologist will speak of telepathy. The believers, practitioners, and members of organizations under the next two headings not only do not mind being called occultists or esotericists, but may even insist on or exult in being so called. This is the core of occultism. Truzzi labels some of these beliefs *pragmatic occultism*. Occultists here do not consider that it is their business to furnish scientific proof that their methods work. To them, they do work. They believe that these methods could be validated by the scientific method, but that in itself is not a very important consideration for them. Practitioners of this type of occultism are indeed practitioners: They practice what they believe, the emphasis being on doing things, be it the production of magic effects, healing the sick, or finding underground water or lost objects.

We have added the category of *philosophical occultism* to Truzzi's classification. In some respects, it is very close to pragmatic occultism. The main difference is that philosophical occultists are not concerned so much with producing practical results in the real world as with formulating a broad world view based on esoteric philosophy and in bringing about results in themselves, results that are usually thought of as spiritual advances on the path to perfection. Their magic is magic of the spirit, the magic of self improvement and of service. But, they are also pragmatists. Although they are even less concerned with the scientific proof of the validity of their methods than pragmatic occultists are, they do validate them in terms of the results that they see their methods bring about in themselves. The main difference between pragmatic and philosophical occultism is again shared versus private validation of claims. The distinction is only one of degree, however, as are any distinctions of what is public and what is private.

Truzzi's fourth and fifth categories of occultism are *shared mystical oc-cultism* and *private mystical occultism*. Because the shared-private distinc-tion runs through all three pairs of categories of occultism, we have sub-stituted the terms *mystical occultism* and *theistic occultism* for Truzzi's labels. The mystical experience is ineffable, and the one who has it must resort to poetic language and to the metaphor to describe it. But even here, there are degrees of communicability and consensus. The mystic does not in-sist that an experience is for him or her alone. The yogin or transcendental mediator will attempt to describe the desirable state that he or she has reached and to give directions to others for reaching it. Enough communi-cability exists for others to follow the directions to agree that this, in-deed, is the way and that the resulting state is as described by the original ex-periencer. This is a personal demonstration of claims, nevertheless, and the possibility of empirical verification is virtually nonexistent. This is the cate-gory of mystical occultism. Theistic occultism is so close to orthodox religions that superficially there appears to be little distinction at all. This type of occultism is associated with some theistic religion, a religion that recognizes a God or a supreme being, such as the Christian God or God's counterpart, Satan. What distinguishes the practitioners of theistic occult-ism from their orthodox brethren is that the former engage in some form of unorthodox practice that is usually recognized as occult, such as magic, communication with the dead, or divination.

THE AUTHORS' BIASES

In spite of his or her best efforts to be objective and nonjudgmental, or perhaps because of them, the instructor of a course in anomalistic psycho-logy will soon be asked, "Do *you* believe any of this?" Having spent considerable time carefully explaining the pros and cons of the issue from the scientific point of view, the instructor is apt to be somewhat taken aback by his or her apparent failure to get across the point that what he or she has been saying all along *is* his or her point of view. The instructor may also be disappointed by the student's apparent failure to see that once a naturalistic explanation of a phenomenon has been accepted, the question of belief should not arise. It is as if the student were assuming that there are two legitimate but independent ways of looking at paranormal phenomena, the way of scientific fact and the way of psychological fact or belief. That such a question is asked in this course but not in others is symptomatic of the whole field of anomalistics. A very significant component of the field is belief. What the student is really asking is, "Do you believe that some of the basic limiting principles can be suspended at least some of the time?" An affirmative reply causes the believing student to assume a friendly attitude towards the instructor, among other things. Whatever the reply, it reveals the instructor's biases. It is important for the student's sake that these biases be stated explicitly before getting too far into the course material. Because the authors of a textbook are coinstructors with the live instructor, but do not have the advantage of a face-to-face interaction with the students, we state our biases here. A further elaboration of our views on what constitutes the paranormal is found in Chapter 15.

On the most fundamental level, we are monists in that we assume that there is only one substance in the universe and that the universe is a single system governed by a single set of laws. We find that the dualistic view presents insuperable difficulties when an attempt is made to explain the interaction of two systems, each governed by a different set of laws. Whether our monism is of the idealistic or materialistic kind is, in our opinion, of no great consequence. Matter passes freely into energy and energy into matter. Likewise, there is no mind-matter barrier, and one passes into the other, both in terms of the evolutionary development of matter and in terms of the functioning of human beings. This allows us to accept the fact of faith healing, for instance, without accepting a supernatural explanation, as well as the possibility of extrasensory perception (by some as yet unknown but natural rather than paranormal means) without assuming that, in a person, the mental is able to separate itself from the physical and function independently of it. In all cases, when faced with an anomalous and seemingly inexplicable phenomenon, we favor its investigation by the scientific method, and will abide by the findings it yields. We favor the rational and humanistic approach to all phenomena of nature. We hold that even the most startling and spectacular of the phenomena that we deal with in the following chapters pale in comparison with the stupendous intricacies found in even the simplest forms of life and that the human brain and its functioning is the most awe-inspiring phenomenon in the universe. Our final bias is that, although the search for answers to the questions posed by the brain and its functioning is the most fascinating human endeavor, it is the process of search and its attending questions and uncertainty that make it worth while and not the finding and holding of what may appear to be the final and definitive answer.

NOTES

Books supportive of occult beliefs occupy whole bookstores. Those that are critical of such beliefs would fit into a small bookcase. An annotated bibliography of these books appears in *The Skeptical Inquirer*, beginning with the Summer, 1979, issue. The most comprehensive of the several available encyclopedias of mythology, occultism, and parapsychology is the profusely illustrated 24-volume work of more than 200 authors, *Man, Myth, and Magic* (Cavendish, 1970). A useful, smaller work by only three authors is the *Encyclopedia of Occultism and Parapsychology* (Shepard, 1978). To learn about the main editor's biases, see the review of this work by Hyman (1979). A handy, sober-minded paperbound compendium of information on anomalistic phenomena of all kinds is *The World Almanac Book of the Strange* (1977).

The number of English-language journals that are dedicated entirely to the publication of research and theoretical articles on parapsychology is very small. They are the *European Journal of Parapsychology*, published at the University of Utrecht, *Journal of Parapsychology*, published by the Foundation for Research on the Nature of Man (both, the journal and the organization were founded by J. B. Rhine, a pioneer in parapsychological research), *Journal of the Society for Psychical Research*, published in London, *Journal of the American Society for Psychical Research*, published in New York, and *Research in Parapsychology*, which publishes reports of presentations made at the annual meetings of the Parapsychological Association. There is no journal that publishes research papers that deal specifically with anomalistic psychology. Such papers are found scattered in many scientific journals, most of them nonpsychological. There is only one journal that consistently represents the critical view regarding claims of paranormality, *The Skeptical Inquirer*. It is published by the Committee for the Scientific Investigation of Claims of the Paranormal. In it, one is most likely to find a naturalistic explanation, based on actual tests and experiments, of recent as well as older paranormal phenomena.

2 Anomalistic Psychophysiology: I

We have still much to learn as to the laws according to which the mind and body act on one another, and according to which one mind acts on another; but it is certain that a great part of this mutual action can be reduced to general laws, and that the more we know of such laws the greater our power to benefit others will be.

If, when, through the operation of such laws surprising events take place, (and) we cry out, "...Such is the will of God," instead of setting ourselves to inquire whether it was the will of God to give up power to bring about or prevent these results, then our conduct is not piety but sinful laziness.

George Salmon, D. D., *A Sermon on the Work of the Holy Spirit* (1859)

The functioning of the body is affected by energy exchanges within the body itself and by other bodies and energies: microorganisms, poisons, penetrating objects, medicines, sunrays, and so on. Although it has always been recognized that psychological states do affect the body also—we blush in embarrassment, sweat in fear, and lose weight worrying—the acknowledgment that psychological states by themselves can directly cause physical disorders has come only relatively recently, with the advent of psychosomatic medicine in the early 20th century. Anxiety or guilt may be the sole or a contributing factor in disorders such as asthma, colitis, or gastric ulcers; even the immunological system can be affected by learning (Ader & Cohen, 1975) and other psychological and sociological factors, so that susceptibility to some infectious diseases is affected (Stein, Schiavi, & Camerino, 1976).

If worries can cause stomach ulcers, why cannot an intense emotion cause the bleeding of other points of the body? It can and it does. What is more, the process can be reversed. From the standpoint of psychology, the cardinal principle of mental healing is that if the cause of a physical symptom is psychological, the symptom may be removed or the condition alleviated psychologically. If mind and body are parts of the same system, a complete separation and independent action of each is not to be expected. The difference between "normal" psychosomatic interactions and anomalistic psychophysiology is one of degree and statistical frequency and not one of kind. There are far fewer stigmatists (persons who develop wounds similar to those of the crucified Jesus) than there are sufferers from stomach ulcers. To have stomach ulcers is respectable, and one can see one's physician about them, who may prescribe a diet of milk shakes. To have your hands and feet bleed every Friday or even on Good Friday only does not fall in the same category of disorders, although it should. The stigmatist is investigated by parapsychologists, journalists, and perhaps the Catholic clergy. If the bleeding is declared to be of a miraculous origin, one may even gain recognition as a saintly person. The difference between the psychophysiologically normal and the psychophysiologically anomalistic is only a matter of statistical incidence. We, therefore, do not consider "normal" psychosomatics, but look at unusual mind-body interactions and call them anomalistic. Of these, we consider only those that, due to their nature or historical accident, have been associated with the occult.

MIRACULOUS HEALING

When help is sought from a god, a supernatural entity, mental powers, or some other noncorporeal agency in alleviating a bodily or mental ill, we speak of faith healing, spiritual healing, or mental healing. The terms have varied with the historical and religious context, but the practice has existed as long as there have been shamans, witch doctors, and medicine men who have supplemented their herbal preparations with magic formulae, rituals, and incantations. It has always been part of all major religions. In Christianity, its culmination was reached in the Protestant denomination of Christian Science. There are no substantial differences among their healing practices as far as their mode of operation and the underlying physiological mechanisms are concern. The differences lie in the philosophies, religious creeds, and beliefs and value systems within which the practitioners of the healing art and their clients operate. As Jan Ehrenwald (1977a) states it:

> Stripped . . . of its esoteric, supernatural, or ideological implications, unorthodox healing is a concatenation of magico-mythical, spiritual, and religious hopes and expectations, aided by suggestion or autosuggestion, so-called placebo effect, and a hypothetical psi factor involved in the interaction between the healer, the healee, and the group in which they are immersed [p. 542].

The psi (telepathy, clairvoyance) factor is so hypothetical, however, that Ehrenwald does not even mention any evidence for its operation in faith healing, even though the ostensible purpose of his paper is to show the connection between parapsychology and unorthodox healing. That telepathic communication might be involved between patient and therapist in psychoanalysis has been a speculation that psychoanalysts, Freud included, have indulged in.

The noted psychiatrist and psychologist Jerome Frank concludes from his analysis of religious healing (Frank, 1961) that all sorts of ideologies and methods show success in healing and that the "healing power of faith resides in the patient's state of mind, not in the validity of its object /p. 60/." He cites Rehder's (1955) experiment on faith healing, which may be considered as the perfect demonstration of this point. Rehder asked a prominent local faith healer to try absent healing on three of his patients, one with gall-bladder stones and a consequent inflammation of the bladder, one who had failed to recover from major abdominal surgery and was extremely emaciated, and a third one who was dying of cancer. The patients were not told that healing was being done. There was no change in their condition. They were then told about the healer, were prepared psychologically for the next several days by having their expectations for a healing success raised, and were informed that the healer would treat them, from a distance, at a certain time of the day. It was known to Rehder, however, that the healer would be doing something else at that time. The second patient was cured permanently, and the other two experienced dramatic temporary relief. The gall-bladder inflammation abated, the patient went home, and did not experience the problem again for several years. The cancer patient was immediately relieved of accumulated water in her tissues, recovered from her anemia, returned home, and was able to do housework until her death, without suffering very much from the symptoms of cancer.

The controversies and polemics that have raged over the genuineness of cures achieved by faith healers and those that occur at religious shrines, such as Lourdes, have been a wasted effort because there is no necessary connection between the acceptance or rejection of them and the belief in miracles or any particular religious creed. It is quite possible to accept the fact of recovery from a severe illness or handicap without medical intervention and at the same time discount claims that the recovery was caused by supernatural forces. Many such cures can be explained by known physiological and psychological facts. Others cannot be so explained. Those who conclude that such cures therefore had a miraculous cause are making a gross error in logic. Unexplained does not mean miraculous or paranormal. Unexplained only means unexplained. Such a lapse in reasoning occurs, unfortunately, not only in connection with faith healing but also in connection with other phenomena that science with its current conceptual tools finds impossible to explain. Yogic feats and unidentified flying objects are two examples.

The healing practices range from healing magic, performed in preliterate societies, ritual magic in more advanced societies, prayer healing (as in Christian Science), appeals to discarnate spirits for healing help (as in Spiritualism and voodoo), to the invocation of ostensibly physical energies and forces, and clothing the healing procedure in a scientific mantle, notably with the help of apparatus. Such ideas as the odic force, orgone energy, bioplasm, and other assorted energies, vibrations, waves, and emanations may be classified as bad science.

Healing Magic

Magic is religion applied, and as such it has existed as long as there have been religious beliefs. Paintings by cave dwellers already show them practicing magic rituals. Those who became skilled in magic, the shamans, seers, and rainmakers, practiced magic for all purposes: to help hunters hunt their prey, bring good crops, harm enemies, or heal the sick. Healing magic was and still is only one of their activities. As mediators between this world and others, they have traditionally claimed various occult powers as well: communication with the dead, astral travel (out-of-the-body experiences), telepathy, clairvoyance, precognition, and psychokinesis.

The main weapons in the arsenal of the magic healer are symbolic: words—spoken or chanted—and symbols—drawn, painted, carved, or gestured. Clements (1932) lists five primitive theories of disease: (1) disease-object intrusion; (2) loss of the soul (called *susto* in Latin American countries); (3) spirit intrusion; (4) breach of taboo; (5) sorcery, and the corresponding therapies: (1) extraction of the disease object (a stone, ball of feathers, etc.); (2) finding and bringing back of the soul; (3) exorcism, mechanical extraction of the foreign spirit, or the transference of the foreign spirit into another living being; (4) confession or propitiation; and (5) countermagic. The therapies are symbolic formulae intended to achieve their effect by magical means.

Repetition of the magic formulae is deemed essential for their effectiveness, as is the exhaustive listing of the parts of the body to be healed or preserved and of the afflictions that need to be set straight. The symbolic activity is reinforced by motor activity: dancing, swaying, whirling, ritualistic movements, or dramatic acting. The movements in some way refer to the affliction to be cured, as by mimicking its symptoms. This reflects the universal principle of magic that like affects like (sympathetic magic). The healing process is typically a lengthy ritual that is marked by increasing emotionality. This, as we will see, is a landmark of other phenomena involving anomalistic physiology: faith-healing meetings, voodoo death, fire walking, and religious conversion. Heightened excitement brings about a host of physiological changes that involve principally the autonomic nervous system and the endocrine system. These, in turn, have their effect on the central nervous system and, therefore, on overt behavior. These changes, whose details are discussed later in this chapter, are the same as those involved in the organism's reaction to physical or psychological stress and emergency. They alter the organism's neurophysiological state, so that ordinary reactions to pain may be drastically modified, physical dysfunctions alleviated, and ideas previously rejected accepted.

Faith Healing

Faith healing requires faith in the healing agency's power to grant a cure, but it also requires faith in the intermediary—the shaman, priest, healer, sacred relic, shrine, or prayer. It also requires that the healer have faith in himself or herself and, furthermore, that there be social reinforcement: The healee's reference group must share the healee's concern about the illness and his or her faith in the healer's or the healing agency's ability to effect a cure.

A direct appeal to the divine has always seemed a less efficacious way of achieving a cure than by directing it to a human intercessor or some object thought to be charged with healing power. It has been pointed out repeatedly by believers in faith healing that faith in the ability of the practitioner to alleviate an emotional condition is also required in psychotherapy, and that there is, therefore, no great difference between faith healing and what goes on between a psychotherapist and a client. After all, psychotherapy is also "only" a talking cure.

There is a difference, of course. Faith in the efficacy of treatment, any treatment, is necessary for it to take place. This applies even to medicines administered by physicians and surgery performed by surgeons. The significant difference between the faith healer and the psychotherapist (unless, of course, the faith healer proceeds in a manner analogous to that of the psychotherapist and achieves effects for the same psychological reasons that the psychotherapist does) is that in one case the faith on the part of client is in the personal efficacy of the therapist, in the validity of the particular therapeutic method used, or in one's own ability to overcome emotional difficulties. In the other case, faith is placed in the possibility of overriding natural laws through supernatural intervention: The wound would be healed instantly, a deformity corrected on the spot, the course of a fatal illness reversed. Thus, instead of a similarity, there is a diametric opposition between the psychological healer and the faith healer. One places faith in the laws of nature; the other, not satisfied with their working, seeks to override them by hypothetical forces that do not belong to the natural order.

The specific nature of the overriding of natural laws varies with the belief system, and the completeness and sophistication of the specifications differ as much as the preliterate, preindustrial tribal group is different from a group of white, American, middle-class Christian Scientists. Psychologically, there is one element that is common to all instances of faith healing, however, and that element is suggestion.

Hypnosis and Suggestion.   Although healing suggestions may be given to a person while that person is in a normal state of consciousness, it is more effective if given under hypnosis or in a hypnosis-like state induced by rhythmic chanting, hand clapping, drumbeat, dance, pusating lights, or drugs. Suggestion and hypnosis have always been part of mental healing, and hypnosis has always been associated with the occult.

Suggestion is the process of communication whereby one person is led to accept uncritically the ideas of another and to act upon them. The suggestion may be explicit or symbolic, and can be given verbally or through any of the sensory channels. If both the giver and the receiver of the suggestion are the same person, we speak of autosuggestion. If the suggestion is to feel drowsy, that one's eyelids feel heavy, that they are closing, that one feels relaxed, and so on, it leads to what is known as an hypnotic state, an altered state of consciousness. An altered state of consciousness is by no means necessary for a suggestion to be effective. Looking solicitously in a person's face and asking if he or she feels all right may send that person immediately to the mirror for an examination or to the medicine chest for a thermometer, even if there is nothing the matter with him or her.

It goes without saying that in hypnosis an altered physiological state also ensues, although there is no agreement on the characteristics of the physiological changes and therefore on the "real" nature of hypnosis. That is a matter of ongoing research and theoretical conjecture. Dissociationism is the latest theoretical formulation on the nature of hypnosis whose author is one of the foremost psychological researchers in this area, Ernest Hilgard (1977). As others, such as C. G. Jung, had done before him, Hilgard stresses the nonunitary nature of consciousness. An individual represents a multiplicity of functional systems that are hierarchically organized but can become dissociated from each other. Thus, a part of us may not know or remember what the rest is doing or has done, although the converse may not be true. Dissociationism can explain several phenomena that have been placed in the category of the occult and paranormal, and we have occasion to refer to Hilgard's theory when we discuss them. Dissociation is also observed in hypnosis. Hilgard realized that even though a hypnotized subject might be holding a hand in a bucket of ice-cold water and not show any signs of pain, or be deaf to the shot from a pistol, he could, by asking the appropriate question, establish that a portion of the subject's consciousness was registering the pain or the sound of the shot. Dissociation could be related to the functional differences between the two hemispheres of the brain and the split in consciousness produced in both animals and humans when the connecting pathway between the hemispheres is cut (callosectomy). There is, at this time, no conclusive proof that this is so, however.

Whatever the nature of hypnosis and regardless of which brain mechanism is precisely involved, hypnosis and suggestion have been an essential part of faith healing from the very beginning. The silly behavior engaged in by hypnotized subjects on the command of the stage hypnotist is well known. Hypnosis, however, affects not only the muscles that are normally under voluntary control, but also those that are not. Even the cardiovascular system and the glandular system can be subjected to hypnotic influence: The hypnotist can start, stop, or alter the digestive process, heart rate, milk secretion, menstruation, and even induce the symptoms of pregnancy.

Hypnosis was used in antiquity on a haphazard basis because a systematic knowledge of how to induce it and of the conditions governing it were lacking. The modern history of hypnosis begins with the 18th-century Viennese physician Franz Anton Mesmer, who both began to use it for curative pur-

Fig. 2.1. Franz Anton Mesmer, first modern hypnotic healer. (National Library of Medicine)

poses and established its association with occultism. Mesmer was a believer in astrology. He believed that celestial bodies exercised a magnetic influence on humans and, to test this proposition, took some magnets and tried making magnetizing passes over a person. That person promptly fell into a hypnotic trance, which Mesmer did not realize, believing the effect to be that of the magnets. Later, he discovered that he could do just as well without the magnets, and decided, incorrectly again, that the effect was produced not by ordinary but "animal magnetism." It took only a short time for the right kind of patient to come and see Mesmer, a patient whose illness was neurotic in nature. Neurasthenic and hysterical patients, as they came to be known in medical psychology later, became the prime targets of "miraculous" cures effected by Mesmer and his disciples, as well as by all those faith healers who came after Mesmer.

Mesmer's unorthdox healing method did not set well with the Viennese medical establishment, and he was forced to leave Vienna, which, however, was not to his detriment. He went to Paris and found a most responsive clientele among the Parisians. Except for the décor and the presence of a contraption called the *baquet*, Mesmer's salon in Paris and the proceedings that took place therein did not differ too much from a modern-day faith-healing situation. In its most refined form, Mesmer's healing procedure consisted of a group of people sitting around the *baquet*, an oaken tub filled with rocks from which metal spikes protruded. The baquet was supposed to emanate magnetic healing energy, and patients let the spikes touch their afflicted body parts to benefit from this beneficial force. Mesmer himself walked around, dressed in a magician's robe, intoning healing suggestions. Soft music played in the background. Under these conditions, hysterical fits would manifest in some of Mesmer's patients: They would convulse, writhe on the floor, or rise and walk around talking in loud voices. This, as was discovered later, was not a necessary component of either hypnotic or faith healing. Neither was the *baquet*. Nonfunctional as it was, this piece of apparatus, by serving as a symbol of Mesmer's scientific background, also served to inspire confidence in Mesmer himself as well as to center the client's attention. Although many healers today work without any physical paraphernalia, those who come from a scientific background are more apt to employ some sort of device or apparatus that supposedly concentrates or emanates healing energy. Wilhelm Reich's universal life energy, "orgone," and his orgone concentrator, the orgone box, are one example.

Mesmer died believing that what he had done involved magnetism rather than suggestion. It was not until 1843 that the English physician James Braid gave hypnotism its name and described its true nature for the first time. Braid decided that Mesmer's procedures were only a means to induce a form of sleep, that the suggestion, a psychological phenomenon, produced some physiological change in the nervous system, and that this change led to certain kinds of cures. He removed hypnotism from the realm of the occult even further by showing that it could be induced by having the subject concentrate on some object, such as a swinging pocket watch, and that magnetizing passes were unnecessary.

Mesmer had disciples. One of them was the Marquis de Puysegur, discoverer of the posthypnotic suggestion. Puysegur, like his master, believed in "magnetism" and went around magnetizing trees, for instance. Persons with assorted illnesses would be cured by standing under such magnetized trees. Experimentation to check on the claims of the purveyors of animal magnetism entered the picture very early. Benjamin Franklin, a member of a commission set up by the king of France to check on the mesmerists' claims, performed the first experiments in hypnotism and thereby, quite unintentionally, some of the earliest experiments in psychology. By having people stand under trees that had been allegedly been magnetized, but in fact were not, Franklin was able to show that cures could be achieved through mere suggestion—that is, inducing belief in the miraculous healing power of the trees.

Christian Science.   Charles Poyen was Puysegur's pupil who introduced mesmerism in the United States during a lecture tour in the 1820s. One of those who heard Poyen was Phineas Parkhurst Quimby. By using Poyen's method, Quimby was able to cure himself of a number of neurasthenic complaints, and began work as a healer in Portland, Oregon. Like Franklin, but without the benefit of experimental verification, Quimby decided that in medicine the curing agent was the patient's faith in the power of the physical remedy and not the remedy itself because both simple and inexpensive as well as complicated and expensive remedies seemed to have the same effect. Quimby then switched from hypnotism to suggestion and an emphasis on the power of the mind and of right thinking. His thoughts on healing, which he wrote down (Dresser, 1921), became a system of philosophy and theology.

Mary Baker Eddy, then Mrs. Patterson, visited Quimby in Portland in 1862 and was cured of the neurasthenic ills that had plagued her for most of her life. She absorbed and transformed Quimby's teachings, and was able to cure herself from the consequences of a fall she suffered in 1866. Over the next 9 years, she conceived and wrote the bible of Christian Science, *Science and Health with a Key to the Scriptures* (Eddy, 1934). The first charter to a Church of Christ (Scientist) was issued in 1879. Christian Science has remained the largest and most successful Protestant denomination centered principally on faith healing.

In developing her doctrine, Mary Baker Eddy dissociated herself from Quimby and his background of mesmerism. She denounced hypnotism, along with "all other isms," as error. Although Christian Science was a

Fig. 2.2. Mary Baker Eddy, the founder of Christian Science. (Radio Times Hulton Picture
Library)

direct continuation of the healing-magic tradition that had found its most
successful form in mesmerism, Mrs. Eddy dispensed with the physical ac-
couterments of both the medicine man and the hypnotist. It was (Ehrenwald, 1977a): "one of the first methodical attempts to the management of
disease by purely psychological—or spiritual—means, [p. 547]." According
to Mary Baker Eddy, ordinary awareness of one's own body, other bodies,
physical matter, or disease is the awareness of a "mortal" mind and is,
thus, in error. The only reality is God or the divine mind, in which there is
no imperfection, disease, or death. In this cardinal doctrine of the Christian
Science Church, Mrs. Eddy was echoing the doctrine of Maya or the illusory
nature of the world as we perceive it, a tenet of one of the isms she denounced—Hinduism. On it is based the Christian Science practice of faith
healing: Disease and imperfection go away if one disbelieves their reality

and believes in the reality of the divine mind only. Medicines and drugs are not to be used because this means relying on physical matter, hence on "error." Instead, one calls upon one of the numerous Christian Science practitioners to receive help through prayer. The rejection of orthodox medicine by Christian Science represents a radical position that differs markedly from that of other faith healers. Some use herbal medicines as well as mind-altering drugs along with faith healing; Oral Roberts is building a $100 million City of Faith hospital in Tulsa that will combine orthodox medicine with faith healing in providing "holistic medicine" to its patients. If one overlooks the testimonials that are routinely presented at Christian Science Church services, Christian Scientists are not interested in keeping a record of cures or in following up on cases, and there is little information on how successful their faith healing is.

Psychophysiological Disorders, Neurasthenia, and Conversion Reactions. What exactly happens in a mind cure? The basic principle is simple: Because body and mind form a unity, the body must be affected by the mind (and vice versa). But this proposition is a philosophical one and empirically unprovable. Although we know much about the factors that play a role in faith healing, how exactly the mind does affect the body when faith healing takes place is simply unknown, just as it is unknown how the two interact in any other situation. We can make philosophical statements about the nature of reality, whether there is only matter, only mind, or both, and how these two interact, but these statements are not subject to verification. Verification is possible only for that realm of knowledge that has included verification as an integral part of its own system, namely science. We can, therefore, make verifiable statements only about that that affects a human body, about the body's responses, and postulate interior, psychological mechanisms that appear to link these two sets of observations.

When it comes to faith healing, all disorders are not equal. Bone fractures, for instance, are one problem that does not readily yield to the ministrations of either a shaman or an Oral Roberts. Broken bones and irreversible organic processes are not on the list of ills cured by the faith healer. Psychophysiological disorders, neurasthenic complaints, and the physical manifestations of conversion neurosis are the prime targets of the faith healer. These cover a very wide range of the most diverse physical manifestations. Other disorders that do not have primarily a mental origin lie somewhere between these two extremes. All bodily phenomena are influenced by one's state of mind, from the healing rate of abrasions to the time of one's death. Research on the psychological factors in cancer, for instance, has rapidly expanded just recently (see, for instance, Achterberg & Lawliss, 1978).

From the point of view of mind-body unity, the term psychosomatic medicine is a redundant misnomer. All physical disorders have a psycnological element. The term psychosomatic designates a category of disorders in which the individual's attitudes and emotions play a major role. Although all of the following disorders may be caused by physical means, they may also arise due to emotional factors alone: acne, asthma, blisters and other skin problems, such as eczema and psoriasis, dysmenorrhea, heart irregularities, hypertension, colitis, gastric ulcers, allergy, warts, squinting, and a number of others. Because these disorders may be caused by conflict, anxiety, worries, or guilt, they can also be removed when the emotional cause is removed. Such a removal may be effected not only by a psychologist or psychiatrist, but on occasion by a skilled faith healer. In distinction from conversion hysteria, psychophysiological disorders involve mainly the autonomic nervous system. They result from prolonged emotional stress, whereas conversion-reaction symptoms are the unconscious, symbolic expression of a conflict.

Neurasthenia is a type of neurosis that is characterized by the individual's complaining about a number of minor ailments: extreme fatigue and lack of energy, various vague aches and pains that may occur in any part of the body, loss of appetite, constipation, insomnia, headaches, sensitivity to noise, difficulty in starting to do anything, a general feeling of inadequacy, and similar symptoms. Excitement is sometimes all that is needed to help the individual overcome the neurasthenic syndrome, and excitement is what is provided in revival and healing meetings. The result: a "miracle" cure. Psychotherapy in general, whether administered by a professional or an amateur (the faith healer), is likely to achieve a remission of the neurasthenic symptoms if the underlying psychological cause of the neurosis is targeted.

Conversion hysteria involves the central nervous system. Its symptoms are the loss of control over or disorder in some major area of the nervous system. The bodily changes are real enough, but no physical cause for them can be found. Conversion symptoms, if not treated, may last for years and lead to irreversible damage, such as the atrophy of a paralyzed, unused organ. Because of the dramatic nature of the dysfunction, this neurosis has been studied more than any other kind. One of the earliest questions asked concerning faith cures was about the relationship between hypnosis and the personality traits of an individual who is susceptible to hypnosis and whose physical ills could be cured by hypnotic suggestion. The question was asked and answered by the founder of neurology, the French physician Jean-Martin Charcot. An 1875 paper by a respected French physiologist, Charles Richet, reassured Charcot that hypnosis was a genuine phenomenon. (Richet, incidentally, was one of the pioneer researchers in parapsychology and was the originator of the term ectoplasm.) Charcot thereupon proceeded to research hypnosis extensively, finding, among other things, that he could suggest to his patients certain bodily symptoms that resembled those found in patients diagnosed as hysterics. The realization of the similarity between the effects of suggestion made by a hypnotist and the seemingly spontaneous appearance of identical symptoms in hysteria was a most important scientific breakthrough that suddenly threw light on something that hitherto had remained in the realm of the mysterious and supernatural—namely, faith healing.

There are three types of symptoms of conversion hysteria: sensory symptoms, motor paralyses, and disordered movements. The first type includes total or partial blindness, deafness, or anesthesia; the paralyses affect one or both arms or legs, fingers, or vocal cords. Disordered movements show a great variety, from tics to epileptic-like seizures. There are, in addition, a variety of organic symptoms: vomiting, noneating, excessive appetite, lumps in the throat, constipation, and a host of others. In this type of neurosis, the anxiety associated with an experienced conflict, instead of being dealt with, is denied and converted into a physical symptom, which serves the purpose of taking the individual's mind off the conflict, reducing the anxiety over the conflict, attracting attention to oneself, and having one's needs taken care of. In short, the neurosis substitutes a physical problem, which seems easier to deal with, for a psychological one, which may seem intolerable and insoluble. The symptom exhibited is usually symbolic of the problem and affects the organs most involved in the conflict. For instance, guilt feelings over physical punishment given by hand may lead to the paralysis of the arm, or anxiety over sex may lead to a paralysis that makes it impossible to engage in sex.

Because the mechanics of conversion hysteria are now well understood and have been widely publicized, the frequency of this type of neurosis has decreased considerably, especially in economically advanced societies. It is found more often in the lower socio-economic classes.

Conversion hysteria is relatively easy to cure. Psychotherapists and faith healers alike can cause the remission of the symptoms, often with dramatic suddenness. The speed of recovery is related to the fact that there is nothing organically wrong with the patient. The nonfunctioning of a limb or an organ is caused by the blocking of nerve impulses. If the block is removed, function is restored immediately. Hypnotic suggestion is one way of removing the block. This was Charcot's discovery. Eventually, he came to believe that, because hysterical patients could be cured of their hysteria through hypnosis, hypnosis itself was a pathological condition, and that only hysterics could be hypnotized. Rival doctors at Nancy disagreed with Charcot, believing that most people could be hypnotized, even if only lightly, and that hypnosis was a form of sleep, induced by suggestion, hence a normal rather than an abnormal condition. The Nancy school of hypnotism proved to be right as far as this went, but in practice both Charcot and the Nancy physicians continued to effect hypnotic cures theoretical differences notwithstanding.

Conversion reaction, besides being a neurosis, is known as a functional disorder, as opposed to an organic disorder. Given the unity of mind and body, the distinction is one of convenience only. Functional disorders are said not to have any demonstrable physical cause. They are "psychological," or caused by mental factors rather than physical ones, such as injury or germs. The distinction was first made in 1908 by Dr. Richard Cabot of the Harvard Medical School, who asserted that the diseases cured by faith healers were functional rather than organic ones, a definition somewhat circular in nature, but one that indicated a trend in medicine away from the neurological formulations of Charcot and towards conceptions of disease that emphasized mental factors. Thus, Pierre Janet, a renowned French physician and psychologist, shifted from a neurological terminology to a psychological one and talked of the lack of psychic energy as the major cause of hysterical disorders. Hysterical patients were deficient in psychic energy. A deficiency in psychic energy also led to a weakening integrity of the total personality, so that some aspects of it might begin to function more or less autonomously. Thus, conscious control of certain bodily functions may be lost, as in hysterical paralysis where the arm or leg is looked upon by its owner as something alien that has a life of its own and does not obey commands from the self. The nonfunctioning of the limb is symbolic of the patient's having narrowed down or limited consciousness by excluding painful thoughts and memories of conflicts. These are still there, but unconscious to the individual.

The Unconscious.   Janet came close to Freud's formulation of the dynamics of the unconscious and the mechanism of repression of traumatic mental contents. The unconscious as an explanatory principle came to play a very important role already in the 19th century. The idea was present in a germinal form even in P. P. Quimby a long time before it became respectable in medical circles. How did mind affect matter in mental healing? Quimby's answer was "spiritual matter," something that lay between matter and mind. Being no philosopher, Quimby failed to see that postulating an intermediary did not explain anything, but begged the question, because the interaction between spiritual matter and physical matter and spiritual matter and mind still had to be explained. Spiritual matter to Quimby was a storehouse of past experiences, which affected the health of the body. Detrimental ideas, habits, notions, or fantasies had a detrimental effect on the body, and cures were achieved by right thinking, which eliminated the offending items from spiritual matter. Although Quimby did not name it so, spiritual matter is not a bad approximation of the unconscious. The important point is that faith healing was effected through it. Although Mary Baker Eddy rejected even the notion of an unconscious, other faith healers came to rely on the idea increasingly, especially in the 20th century.

Invoking the unconscious as an omnibus explanatory principle in faith healing was reinforced tremendously by the work of Sigmund Freud, whose most important contribution to psychology was the elucidation of the mechanism of unconscious motivation. The idea that we may engage in decision making of which we are unaware or that we may be compelled to act without knowing why was not Freud's discovery. It had been around in various forms for some time. Pierre Janet, mentioned earlier, engaged in a controversy with Freud over the question of who had conceived the idea of unconscious motivation by repressed conflicts.

By historical coincidence, the unconscious was coming into vogue at the same time as was the non-mesmeric mind-cure movement, of which Christian Science was an important current. Other patients of Phineas Parkhurst Quimby besides Mary Baker Eddy began to write mind-cure books. The writing turned more philosophical, metaphysical societies were being founded, and eventually the National New Thought Alliance was founded in 1906. Some of the principal expounders of New Thought and other closely related movements, such as Unity, the so-called "positive thinkers" (Meyer, 1965), were Ralph Waldo Emerson, Ralph Waldo Trine, Charles and Myrtle Fillmore, and Prentice Mulford. In the inevitable process of secularization, mind cure as religion turned mind cure as philosophy and mind cure as psychology, eventually flattening into a technique for winning friends, influencing people, and being successful not only in health but in business, love, and life in general. Thinking God's thoughts became thinking positive thoughts, and the mechanism whereby all sorts of wonderful things were brought about was the unconscious. God and the unconscious became almost synonymous. If God was universal mind and people were part of the universe and part of God, then people's minds, including the unconscious minds, were also part of God. Somehow, the fact that a person is unaware of the working of the unconscious mind made it a better candidate for the works of God (who, after all, works in mysterious ways) than the conscious mind.

Quimby asserted that spiritual matter (the unconscious) was a storehouse of all our experiences. Its contents were molded by others and by ourselves. A logical extension of the finding of Franklin's commission on hypnosis that suggestion alone was effective in achieving miracle cures, without hypnosis, was made: One can make suggestions to oneself. The most famous exponent of the idea was the French hypnotist Emile Coué (1923). Autosuggestion was his term. Coué told his patients to repeat to themselves formulae that expressed faith in self improvement, such as, "Every day in every way I am getting better and better,'' or phrases suggesting improvement in specific organ functions. The combination of the right personality makeup and of the individual's having been primed for suggestion through a powerful emotion or excitement can produce instantaneous and dramatic onset as well as remission of functional disorders. Thus, W. Brown (1924) mentions a typical case of a soldier who became temporarily paralyzed when a shell exploded near him but without injuring him. The fear-induced paralysis became permanent (until it was cured by suggestion) through the soldier's belief that he indeed had become permanently paralyzed. The great Charcot sometimes would recommend that a patient of his go to the Lourdes shrine for healing, as the power of autosuggestion that the shrine would heal appeared greater than the patient's faith in ordinary medicine. What Coué was saying, however, was that any disorder, including organic ones, could be cured by autosuggestion, without implying that the cure would be dramatically rapid or that any supernatural forces were involved. It was medicine without medicines. A modern, more sophisticated, research-based version of Coué's method is Wolfgang Luthe's autogenic therapy (Luthe, 1969). It involves the assumption of a posture of relaxation and the repetition of formulae, for 10 minutes three times a day, for instance, that assert desirable mental or physical states that the patient wishes to achieve. Autogenic therapy is a straightforward medical technique with no connotations of occultism. The technique works. The implication of Coué's and Luthe's methods is that although a religious mantle may be helpful or necessary for some individuals to profit from Christian Science or any other religion-related faith-healing technique, the mantle covers the more essential core of self healing that may be all that is necessary for those who do not require the legitimization of healing by a higher authority.

Suggestions and autosuggestions are mostly verbal and therefore conscious. Those that are not verbal may be verbalized. The mode of operation of suggestion or autosuggestion is quite unconscious, however. It works through the unconscious. An excellent example of this is given by Hopewell-Ash (1912), who tells of a woman who after years spent in bed with what appeared to be tuberculosis, saw and heard an angel who told her to get up and be about, which she did, apparently cured instantly of her illness. Although the case may be taken as a proof of divine intervention, there are a large number of analogous cases in the medical and psychological literature that indicate a standard psychological mechanism at work. That the carrier of the healing message is an angel or even God himself is only a function of the person's value system. Symbolic figures appearing in dreams or hallucinations and giving useful and good advice is a common way for the unconscious to communicate with the conscious self. The particular symbolism of the figure varies with the individual, and the situation need not be one of illness. Solutions to problems appear in symbolic form in dreams, visions, and hallucinations, and take a form that is appropriate to the individual's value system and the nature of the problem. That it is useful for the symbolic figure to appear as somebody other than ourselves especially an authoritative other, is clear: Because we have not been able to solve the problem or get rid of the illness through self-conscious effort, our advice to ourselves, even if we appeared to ourselves in a vision, would not carry much weight.

An attempt to achieve cure through prayer is basically an instance of autosuggestion. One Christian Science prayer runs as follows:

> Help us stoutly to affirm . . . that we have no Dyspepsia, that we never had Dyspepsia, that we never will have Dyspepsia, that there is no such thing, that there never has been any such thing, and that there never will be any such thing. Amen.

The difference between this formula and those of Coué's or Luthe's lies only in the choice of certain words that is dictated by the presence or absence of a religious context. The effectiveness of prayer/autosuggestion is enhanced by previous contact with the healer and on faith in his or her powers. In the case of God, there is, of course, no contact of the ordinary kind, but faith in God, if it is present, has already been established through a long process of social conditioning. Even in the case of human healers, a direct, personal contact is not absolutely necessary; one can be led to believe the powers of an Oral Roberts or Kathryn Kuhlman by watching them on television. Healing can occur over a distance. Absent healing was pronounced feasible by Mrs. Eddy because Mind overcomes all obstacles (which are only illusions of our minds), including space, and it has become the main mode of operation of the best-known healers. As their fame increases, the tendency is to abandon direct contact with the ill and shift to an absent healing mode, including the use of substitute prayer sayers who do the praying on a professional basis. Thus, the well-known Oklahoma healer Oral Roberts moved from tent meetings to televised healing sessions to healing by an organization that conducts its business from a Prayer Tower (Fig. 2.3). In spite of the remoteness of Roberts from most of his believers, his reputation alone is powerful enough to attract millions of dollars in contributions to his organization, the Oral Roberts Evangelistic Association, Inc.—$34.3 million in the fiscal year 1976/77. Another famous healer, Kathryn Kuhlman, also came to use the absent healing mode as well as the medium of television. Edgar Cayce added clairvoyant diagnosis and medical prescriptions to the practice of absent healing through prayer. Ambrose and Olga Worrall also combine clairvoyance with absent healing. The question that arises in the mind of the nonbeliever is, of course, whether any actual praying for the welfare of the requester is done after the check or dollar bills have been separated from the request. From the point of view of the psychology of faith healing, that is not the important question. The nonbeliever is wrong in assuming that all faith healing is fraudulent or self delusional. Occasionally, it works—if there is belief in the power of the healer and if the other conditions that are conducive to faith healing are met. Whether someone at a distant site actually says a healing prayer or not

Fig. 2.3. The Prayer Tower on the campus of Oral Roberts University in Tulsa, Oklahoma. (Leonard Zusne photo)

is immaterial as long as there is belief that someone does. Faith healing is self healing.

The New Thought idea of the unconscious as a limitless source of wealth, health, and power and as a channel for God's healing power was not exactly what Freud had said about it. It is true that Carl Gustav Jung, the most prominent schismatic in the psychoanalytical movement, did postulate God as an archetype of the collective unconscious—that is, a universal predisposition to experience godhead—and thus came closer to the faith healers and New Thought philosophers than did Freud, but that came some time after the mind-cure movement had already spelled out its tenets, and there was no direct influence on the part of Jung. What Freud said about the unconscious, however, is important in understanding the operation of mind cures. First, Freud postulated three levels of psychological functioning: the conscious, the preconscious, and the unconscious. The conscious level is the everyday, ordinary level of mental functioning, the level of the "I feel," "I think," and "I believe." The preconscious is all that we know and have learned and experienced in the past but that is not at the moment in the focus of attention. It can, however, be easily summoned upon demand. In one sense, these mental contents are unconscious. That which is in the focus of attention at any given moment may involve a vast amount of past experience that is being utilized to solve a given problem consciously, but without our being particularly aware that we are using not only the information that is immediately given in the problem but also implicitly very large amounts of information acquired through years of schooling and otherwise.

The third level of psychological functioning, the unconscious, is not of a whole cloth either. All of our reflexes and physiological drives are unconscious. We are not aware of the innumerable life-sustaining processes that occur in our bodies, even when we learn to control some of them. The person who learns how to lower his or her blood pressure does not quite know how it happens. This aspect of the unconscious, which Freud labeled the id, functions largely through the autonomic nervous system and its two branches, the sympathetic and the parasympathetic nervous system, as well as through the lower brain centers that govern the life functions: blood pressure, heartbeat, respiration, hunger, thirst, aggression, sex, and various vital reflexes.

Note that all of the organs innervated by the autonomic nervous system are involved in emotional reactions. For instance, we blanch when we are afraid, we sweat, our peristaltic motions cease, our heart rate increases, our hair stands on end, our mouth becomes dry, and we may even lose control over the sphincter muscles that are involved in urination and defecation. Our pupils contract in anger, blood rushes to our face, the adrenals work overtime, and our blood pressure increases.

Box 2.1—The Autonomic Nervous System

The nervous system may be divided in two ways. In one, a distinction is made
between the brain and the spinal cord on the one hand, which are called the
central nervous system, and those groups of cell bodies (ganglia) and nerve
fibers (nerves) that lie outside it on the other. The latter are called the *peri-*

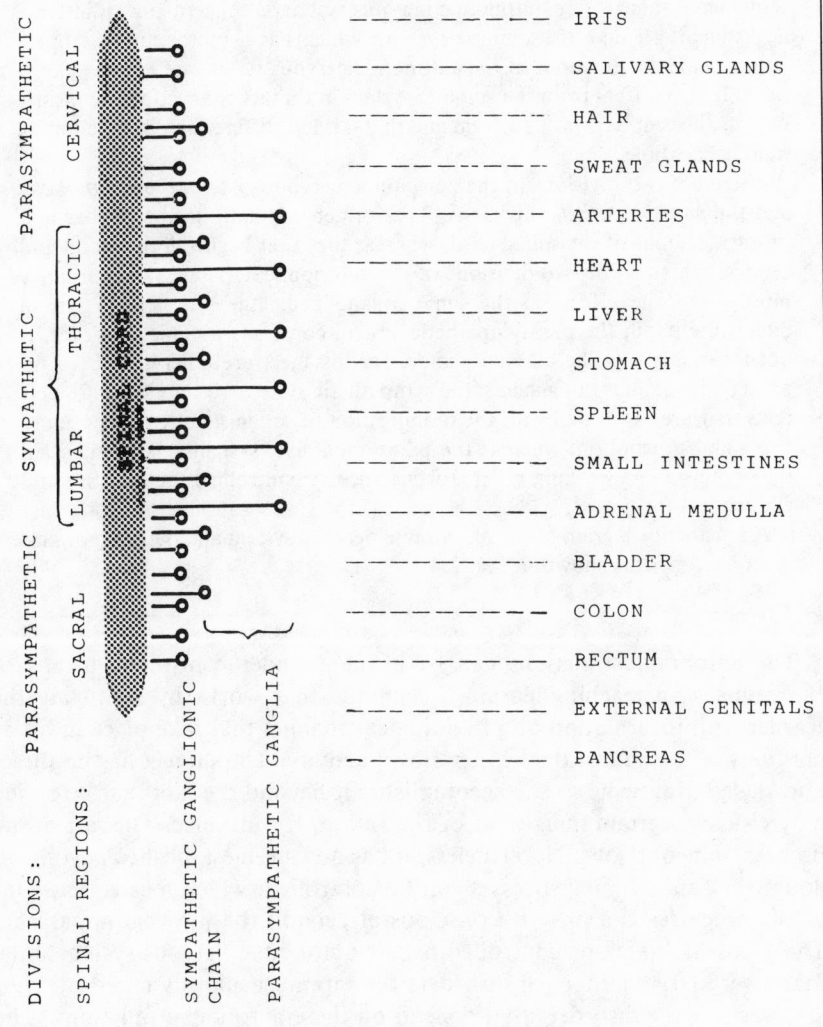

Fig. 2.4. A schematic diagram of the autonomic nervous system.

pheral system. The other way is to divide the nervous system according to the parts of the body it is connected to. The *somatic nervous system* conducts signals from the sense organs to the brain and conveys messages from the brain to the skeletal musculature. Parts of it belong to the central and parts to the peripheral nervous system. The *autonomic nervous system* also includes parts of the central and of the peripheral nervous system, but they are connected to the smooth muscles of the internal organs, the heart, and the endocrine and other glands.

While the somatic nervous system mediates between the organism and its external environment, the autonomic nervous system is concerned with internal adjustments. Unlike the somatic system, which has a motor and a sensory component, the functions of the autonomic nervous system are entirely motor ones. It also differs from the somatic system in that its connections lie mostly outside the central nervous system and that it is less differentiated, functioning more as a whole.

There are two divisions in the autonomic nervous system, the *sympathetic* and the *parasympathetic* divisions. The former originates in the lumbar and thoracic regions of the spinal cord, whereas the latter begins in the sacral and cervical regions. The two divisions of the autonomic nervous system produce mostly opposite effects in the same organ. Thus, the sympathetic system dilates the pupil, the parasympathetic system constricts it. This, however, is not invariably so. The adrenal glands, for instance, are innervated by sympathetic fibers only. In general, the sympathetic system produces all those effects that are associated with the mobilization of organismic resources under stress and in emotion, whereas the parasympathetic system acts to maintain the organism in a working order, for instance by controlling the digestive and elimination functions.

A schematic diagram of the autonomic nervous system and the main organs innervated by it is shown in Fig. 2.4

The autonomic functions can be brought under control by means of biofeedback, a teaching-learning technique that works by supplying the learner with information on physiological changes that take place in his or her body as a result of the learner's own activity. The subject has no direct knowledge of how he or she accomplishes it beyond the fact that he or she may visualize certain images, as of relaxation, for instance. The rest of the process is unconscious. Nevertheless, it has now been established beyond all doubt that autonomic processes can be controlled, which means that conscious processes can have unconscious effects on the physical apparatus. The kinds of functions controlled by the autonomic nervous system show that a very large number of disorders that are miraculously cured by faith are precisely the disorders that depend on these autonomic functions. The mind both makes and cures disorders of its body.

In Freud's system, there is, in addition, that part of the unconscious that pertains to ego functions. In other words, part of the ego is also unconscious. This level of unconscious functioning is, however, vastly different from the simple, nonverbal, vegetative functions of the autonomic nervous system. The ego works with symbols, such as words, and continues to do so even when its functioning is no longer conscious—that is, when the symbolic contents have become repressed. Repression, as already mentioned, results from conflict and intolerable anxiety caused by the conflict. The offending portion of consciousness is then put out of mind but, unlike preconscious contents, is no longer readily available to consciousness. Special techniques, such as free association, dream analysis, or hypnosis, are necessary to bring these contents back into consciousness. Repressed contents are motivating, and may result in behaviors whose cause, without further searching, appears to be unknown. One example already mentioned is conversion hysteria. When suggestion, self suggestion, or insight relieve the anxiety over the conflict that caused the physical symptoms, the symptoms disappear, often with dramatic speed. Depending on the particular environment in which the relief from anxiety occurs, the phenomenon may be termed successful psychotherapy or faith healing.

Reliability of Faith Healing. Control over autonomic processes or psychotherapeutic intervention do not exhaust all instances of faith healing. There are, naturally enough, cases where there is nothing wrong with the subject of a faith cure, and the faith cure is no cure at all. These are the cases of fraud perpetrated by the healer's confederates to attract patients, as well as those people whose disorders are quite literally "all in their minds" —that is, where there are no physical symptoms in evidence, only the say-so of the individual that something is wrong with him or her.

There are two other categories of individuals who account for an indeterminate but probably a sizable number of cases of faith cures,—namely, the cases of spontaneous remission of symptoms and the cases of incorrect diagnosis. Both categories swell the numbers of individuals cured "by faith alone." They are due to the prevailing unconcern with medical verification· that exists both among the purveyors of faith cures and their clients, especially concerning a correct diagnosis before the cure and a follow-up on the permanence of the cure. Spontaneous remission of even the most severe disorders is a phenomenon well-known in medicine. Statistics are available on the percentages of individuals who are expected to remit in their symptoms without medical intervention (e.g., Everson & Cole, 1966), but such statistics are not taken into consideration in the claims made for faith cures. Considering that hundreds of thousands, if not millions, of people are seeking help from faith healers, it is inevitable that in a certain number of them the symptoms should remit spontaneously, even in cases of malignant growth. One such case is sufficient to establish the healer's reputation. On the other hand, even if the healer should die of cancer, as Kathryn Kuhlman did recently, it is not likely to affect the faithful. We discuss the process of attitude change and the factors that prevent attitude changes in Chapter 7. More importantly, unless a correct medical diagnosis of the disorder is made prior to any intervention, any claims can be made for the nature of the disorder and the success in curing it. Where such diagnoses are made, the number of verified cures is reduced drastically in comparison with, for instance, the typical situation of a tent revival meeting and healing session. One example is a study by the psychiatrist Louis Rose (1968) of 97 persons allegedly cured by a famous English healer, Harry Edwards, whose career peaked during and after World War I. Rose found that 80 of the cases were based on unconfirmed claims, incomplete records, and records at variance with the claims. Fifteen additional cases showed relapse, deterioration, or the effect of concurrent medical treatment, and only seven in which the healer appeared to have been responsible for the improvement in the patient's condition. Another example is the Roman Catholic shrine at Lourdes, France. In 1858, Bernadette Soubirous saw there a vision of the Virgin Mary who told her of a spring whose water she was to drink and use to wash clothes. Currently, about three million pilgrims visit the shrine in a year. Of these, some 50,000 are sick or crippled and are seeking a cure. In spite of these numbers, there have been only 63 certified miraculous cures since 1858, eight of them in 1858. This number includes only two cancer cases. It must be remembered that it was not until 1889 that Charcot introduced the notion of hysteria as a pathological category, so that many of the early cures can be probably discounted as not meeting the criteria for certification.

The certification procedure requires that the patient show proof in the form of X-rays, laboratory tests, and medical examinations that he or she suffered from a specific ailment with observable bodily abnormalities before the pilgrimage to Lourdes. It is further required that the symptoms disappear within a few hours after the presumed miraculous cure has taken place. The possibility that the cure was achieved by any medical treatment received by the individual at the time must also be discounted. Finally, the cure must last several years. West's (1957) analysis of the Lourdes miracle cures shows that only 11 cases meet these criteria. If the conditions are met, a tribunal, the *Bureau des Constatations*, made up of local physicians, must certify the results by a majority vote. Then, another tribunal made up of 11 physicians from different countries and selected by the bishops of Lourdes and Tarbes meets several years later and again decides on the matter by a majority vote. If the cure is accepted by this tribunal, the case is sent to the bishop of the patient's diocese, where a canonical commission passes upon it and, in the case of a favorable vote, the bishop then declares a miracle.

The reliability of faith cures varies widely. There is the pathetic sight of the wheelchair-bound individual getting up and walking uncertainly across the stage under the exhortation of a faith healer, only to collapse minutes later after the excitement has worn off. There are also permanent cures. The degree of permanence varies with a number of factors: Faith in the healing agent, the nature of the disorder, and the personality makeup of the patient are the major ones. Thus, a sudden, complete, and permanent remission of the symptoms of a conversion hysteria under the influence of a faith healer is entirely possible, as it is when it occurs in a psychologist's office.

Conditions for Faith Healing. Some of the conditions that are conducive to success in faith healing have already been mentioned: (1) the nature of the disorder; (2) suggestibility; (3) lower socio-economic status; and (4) education. In one study of a contemporary healer, the German psychologist Inge Strauch (1963) observed that subjective improvement was determined by the patient's positive attitude towards faith healing, and that the latter was inversely related to the patient's educational level and critical ability.

Additional conditions include the following:

5. Not only is a positive attitude towards faith healing required, but the world view of the patient must be one that is shared with the healer. If it is not, healing is not likely to take place. The psychiatrist Jerome Frank (1961) notes that "the world-view supporting Lourdes, like those on which religious healing in primitive tribes is based, is all-inclusive and is shared by almost all the pilgrims to the shrine. While cures are regarded as validating it, failures cannot shake it [p. 54]." A spell cast by a witchdoctor does not affect one who does not share the cultural background with the witchdoctor, for instance a European visitor to Africa (cf. the discussion of voodoo death later in this chapter). This situation is not unique to faith healing, but applies to all healing, especially psychotherapy and psychiatric intervention. It has been pointed out (e.g., Torrey, 1973) that if the healer and patient do not share the same world view, neither the witchdoctor nor the psychiatrist are likely to be effective.

6. There must be mutual liking between the healer and the patient. Carl Rogers, (1957) one of the prominent modern psychotherapists, has stressed that intellectual training alone does not produce a psychotherapist, but that accurate empathy, nonpossessive warmth, and genuineness are the qualities that make for successful therapy. The same can be said of the faith healer. On the other hand, if the healer succeeds where the patient's regular physician did not, one of the reasons may be that the healer's personal qualities are such that they attract the patient more than those of his or her own

physician. Some of the switching of medical doctors is also prompted by factors of interpersonal attraction. Seemingly trivial, such factors may play a decisive role in the treatment of a disorder.

7. A patient who enters a standard medical setting for treatment has certain expectations concerning what the doctors and nurses might say and the kind of treatment that may be prescribed. If the actual practice deviates too much from these expectations, the patient is not as likely to respond as when the expectations are met. The same holds true of faith healing. For instance, a faith healer who fails to invoke, refer to, or imply the mysterious, occult, or divine nature of the healing process, or one who tries to explain it in common sense or scientific terms would fail to meet the patients' expectations and therefore fail as a healer.

8. The "atmosphere" in which faith healing takes place is very important. The right atmosphere is one that contributes to the patient's faith in the power of the healer as well as one that heightens his or her suggestibility. The professional healers avail themselves of a whole array of means to achieve such an atmosphere. One that is widely resorted to is the use of large groups and of emotional contagion to suggest the healing power of the healer to those who are still uncertain. Testimonials by those who have been healed, singing, chanting, hand clapping, and shouts of hallelujahs all lead to a change in belief in favor of the healer and heightened receptivity to suggestion. We look at the physiology of overstimulation in connection with religious conversion in the next chapter. The healing session, unlike the practice followed in the medical setting, never starts as soon as the patient arrives. Whereas the medical patient waits in the waiting room simply because the doctor cannot get to him or her, the waiting to be healed by a faith healer is calculated to prime the patient for the process. This happens even when no human healer is involved, for example in a healing shrine. At Lourdes, for instance, when Pierre Janet wrote about it in 1925:

> The patient is not allowed to dispense with preliminaries. He must not straightway touch the relic or drink the healing waters of the sacred spring. There is a probationary period, a propitiatory novena. There are long waits at the gateway of the temple during which the sufferer listens to sermons and repeats prayers. Above all, during these periods of probation, the sick hear a great deal about miraculous cures, and have an opportunity of looking at the numberless votive offerings. In a word, their entry into the temple is a slow one, and their minds are prepared by a special incubation [p. 47].

There is also the factor of the healer's personality. Some healers are obviously more successful than others, and even these latter are more successful than nonhealers. The prime requisite is for the healer to be able to inspire faith in his or her powers. This is a purely personal characteristic that is little enhanced by one's education or appearance. Those who do have the faith may then disregard the healer's obvious shortcomings, failures in achieving cures, and even occasional chicanery or fraud. This is the equivalent of the psychoanalytical phenomenon of transference: The patient endows the therapist with the qualities of a significant and loved person, and then reacts to the therapist as if he or she were that person.

9. Faith healing is usually associated with the notion of a supernatural power as being the real healing agency. A healer who insisted that he or she did it all alone would not be very successful in the business. The supernatural agency may be a god, a spirit, or just some mysterious energy, but it has to be mysterious, inexplicable, not of this world. It is common for healers to refer to themselves as God's "instruments" or as "channels" for the healing energy. The use of the term "energy" among faith healers, occultists, and proponents of esoteric ideas about how the universe functions is very loose and reflects a lack of concern with the scientific view. Except as an abstraction, energy does not exist as such, "pure," but takes on any of a number of forms: mechanical, thermal, chemical, radioactive, and others. "Healing energy" or "vital energy" are not recognized forms of energy, and faith healers have not been interested in specifying further what kind of energy it might be. The occultists teach that it pertains to the etheric plane of existence, one of seven that is next to the gross physical plane, but the existence of an etheric or any other nonphysical planes of existence has not been substantiated by any kind of scientific evidence. The likelihood is very high that "healing energy" is a term that covers the joint effect of suggestion, autosuggestion, and faith (and the corresponding responses of the autonomic nervous system), relaxation, and contact comfort.

10. In the context of faith healing, contact comfort results from massage or touching ("laying on of hands"). One of the authors remembers when, as an adolescent, he was asked repeatedly to massage his mother's back. His mother, who suffered from kidney stones and would experience great pain occasionally, was an emotional person, and, as the pain receded, would refer to his "golden" hands and kiss them, much to his embarrassment. It appears, in retrospect, that the kidney stones played only a secondary role. The pain was triggered as much by them as by the impending separation from her son (by unavoidable circumstances) and a desire to hold him near. Subsequent exchange of letters revealed that the pain and the stones disappeared soon after the actual separation had taken place.

There is considerable agreement among faith healers, although it is by no means unanimous, that touching or "laying on of hands" is an effective means of transmitting healing energy to the healee. Laying on of hands was practiced long before the New Testament was written, but the Christian practice has its authority in the latter. In Christianity, there have been attempts to associate healing power with the upper echelons of the clergy and with royalty. The Royal Touch was the supposed ability of the English kings to cure certain diseases by touch alone. Occult teachings attach great importance to the hands as sources of healing energy (cf. Bailey, 1953), and link them to the yogic chakras or energy centers along the spine that exist on the etheric plane. Although there is no scientific support for healing energy, the chakras, or their connections with the hands, the human touch, especially by hands, has definite symbolic and emotional properties that can be helpful in faith healing. Being touched by a healer means that there is a significant person who cares for you, loves you, and wants to help you. The emotional support rendered by touching hands may indeed work healing wonders, but the work is psychological, not esoteric. The impersonality of Western medicine is emphasized by the fact that there is little body contact between the medical personnel and the patients, and even less contact that is of any emotional significance to the patient. African, South American, and Southeast Asian healers, medicine men, and *curanderos*, on the other hand, may devote a considerable portion of their healing sessions to touching, massaging, or rubbing oil into the body of the patient. The laying on of hands done by some Western healers also may last several minutes. Thus, at least some of the success of faith healing as compared to orthodox medicine may be attributed to the human (and animal) need for and response to sheer body contact. The appearance, in the 1960s and 1970s, of psychotherapies that emphasized feeling and touching is only one example of this need surfacing in a formal therapeutic setting. Touch is the most primitive and basic of all senses, and it can be argued that all other senses are derived from it. The simplest animals lack any sense organs, but they respond to touch; touch is of crucial importance to the normal physical, mental, and social development of the higher primates, as has been amply demonstrated by the well-known work of the Wisconsin psychologist Harry Harlow (e.g., Harlow, 1958).

11. Devious methods may be resorted to to convince the healee of the reality of the alleged healing energy. In earlier times, the magic properties of a witch's brew, for instance, were attributed as much to the magic properties of the ingredients, which were bizarre enough (hence thought to be mysterious and, therefore, powerful), as to the insufferable taste and smell that such a brew must have possessed. Medieval physicians were not below resorting to the same trick. Any "physick" that tasted good was thereby suspect: It had to taste bad in order to be effective, their patients thought (or had been led to believe). In occultism, healing energy is associated with the notion of "ether," a level of matter that is supposed to carry the life forces and give vitality to the body. Some healers "demonstrate" its existence quite tangibly, by using the properties of static electricity. They may go through a ritualistic dance before healing (on a floor that has the correct dielectric properties) or other motions that lead to friction and thus build up an electrostatic charge. When passes are then made around the patient's body, the

combination of hair movements, caused by electrostatic attraction, and the heat radiating from the healer's hand combine to produce a very tangible sensation of radiating energy. If the hands are brought close enough to the patient's body, a mild electric shock results that may be even accompanied by audible crackling. This again may be interpreted as the working of healing energy. Or, in a group that is gathered for faith healing, the healer asks the group to hold hands, then asks if a special feeling in the hands is experienced by all. Because there are always some believers in a group of some size, there will be some agreement to the suggestion. To enhance the feeling, the healer asks everybody to take deep breaths. After several such deep breaths, everybody will agree that there is indeed a tingling sensation in various parts of the hands. What the healer does not supply is the information that deep breathing will promote carbon dioxide exchange in the blood. The increase in oxygen content and a decrease in carbon dioxide content cause an alteration in nerve conductivity, which in turn produces the tingling sensation.

12. A frequent companion of illness and bodily disorder is pain. Although the sensation of acute pain is caused by tissue damage, the psychological component of pain is so large that pain may be experienced even when there is no tissue damage. Chronic pain appears to be largely "psychological" in nature. Pain indeed may be "only in one's mind"; its experience is modified dramatically by psychological factors: sensitivity, past experience, expectations, fears, and attention. Some of the success of faith healers may be attributed to their ability not to cure the disorder itself, but to alleviate the concomitant pain. When pain is relieved by suggestion, which is easily achieved, the patient is all too ready to believe that the disorder itself is gone. A similar effect is produced by the healer's removal of other symptoms of the disorder and by relieving the patient's worry and anxiety about his or her condition. All of this may be experienced by the patient as a sign that a cure has taken place. The patient, by showing signs of relief, joy, and gratitude, prompts the acceptance of healing suggestions by others. The relapse that comes after the healing meeting is not witnessed by them.

13. Symptomatic treatment is well known in medicine. It makes the patient feel better, but is no real cure. It is also resorted to in faith healing. The remission of the symptoms of an incurable disease, for instance, may be achieved hypnotically or through suggestion, but the resulting relief may be interpreted by the patient and by witnesses as divine intervention in a hopeless case. This, like any other temporary victories of the healer, may help swell the ranks of those committed to the belief in the healer's efficacy. A related method that produces similar results is simply to suggest to the patient that he or she is feeling better or well. As an extreme example, we may cite the experience of J. Rosett (1939) who, having been unsuccessful in cur-

ing postencephalitic Parkinsonian patients of their tremors and disordered movements, heard of such cures being achieved in a certain clinic. The patients were being treated by suggestion, and all, by their own testimony, had been cured. There was no visible remission of the symptoms in any of them, however. One patient, according to Rosett, suffered from a severe case of Parkinsonism and could hardly walk. His body and limbs moved uncontrollably, and saliva dripped from his open mouth. Yet, this patient, too, believed himself to have been cured. In an extensive study of the German faith healer Kurt Templer, Inge Strauch (1963) found that during a follow-up period of up to 14 months after the alleged faith cure had taken place, 61% of the 650 patients studied reported subjective improvement, but only 11% showed physical improvement as well.

Psychic Surgery

Psychic surgery, a procedure that has an element of faith healing in it, dates back to precolonial times in the Philippines, for instance, but has received world-wide attention only recently. It is not real surgery and it is not psychic, but some psychological know-how on the part of the healer is involved and some aspects of the procedure have a psychological explanation. The healer, typically an uneducated person with no medical background, instead of attempting to remove a tumor or correct a malformation by prayer or the laying on of hands, goes through the motions of a surgery, with or without instruments. There may be a prayer before the "operation," or the patient may be told to think of Jesus. The "surgeon" may insist that a spirit or Jesus himself is performing the surgery. There may be a scar, some blood (or what appears to be blood), and at the end, a cyst, pus, or a piece of tissue is produced and shown to the patient and witnesses. The healer does not appear to employ hypnosis, no anesthetic is used, and the instruments, if any, are not sanitized.

The center of psychic surgery for some time has been the Philippines. Other psychic surgeons are of Latin American origin, mostly Brazilians and Mexicans. The Filipinos produce their results with tissue taken from small animals and sleight of hand (Nolen, 1975; Rice, 1974). A piece of "cancerous" tissue removed from a woman's breast by the Filipino psychic surgeon Tony Agpaoa was shown by medical tests to be of nonhuman origin, probably from a small animal. After Agpaoa removed a piece of metal and some screws from a patient's hip joint, placed there by a surgeon after an automobile accident, X-rays showed that the metal was still there.

According to John G. Fuller, the author of a book on José Pedro de Freitas, or Arigó (Fuller, 1974), the latter has never been shown to have used fraud. To perform surgery, Arigó would go into a trance, from which he would emerge speaking Portuguese with a heavy German accent and act authoritatively like a real surgeon. He claimed that the spirit of a dead German surgeon, Dr. Fritz, was acting through him. It must be remembered that, in Brazil, spiritualism is so strong that it competes with Roman Catholicism. Fuller's account of Arigó's performance as psychic surgeon reads like a fairy tale until it is realized that: (1) Fuller wrote the book from second-hand information obtained after Arigó's death in 1971; (2) Fuller relied on statements about personal experiences with Arigó made by an enthusiast of psychic phenomena and the biographer of Uri Geller, the spoon- and key-bending Israeli magician, Dr. Andrija Puharich; (3) Fuller is an author, not a medical expert, who (4) is also a flying-saucer enthusiast who contributed two bestselling sensational books on flying saucers in the 1960s.

Although quite different in appearance from "ordinary" faith healing, psychic surgery clearly has an element of faith associated with it. The would-be patient must have implicit faith in magic. The procedure is medically so unbelievable that only those who have some special reason to believe in the "surgeon" or those who do not know any better would submit themselves to the procedure. Because the procedure is basically a sleight of hand operation, coupled with what goes on in "ordinary" faith healing, it holds little interest psychologically. Surgical "incisions" are made with palmed mica slices. A small amount of blood produced in one spot looks like a long, heavy cut when drawn out across intact skin. Alternately, the juice of betel nuts, secreted in a finger pouch, looks very much like blood when released. Instant "healing" of incisions and dissipation of the blood is achieved by using ether—also concealed in a finger pouch or small plastic bag held in the other hand. Curling one's fingers while pushing one's hand into the soft abdomen of a patient gives a very realistic impression of the hand's disappearing into the interior of the body through what the viewer assumes to be a very large cut. Filmed operations do not reveal too much because the "surgeon's" hands are continually covering up the site of the "operation."

The extraction, by suction, of a foreign object from the patient's body in the course of magic healing has always been the practice among shamans. The training of shamans includes teaching how to produce from one's mouth a blood-covered ball of cotton or down (e.g., the Kwakiutl Indians), so that it appears to have come from the treated person's body. Frank (1961) points out that even when the procedure is known, it may not be regarded as a trick by those concerned. To them, the object is a piece of down, but, at the same time, it is also the magical cause of the disorder. Frank suggests that something like the transubstantiation of the bread and the wine in the Christian communion may be believed to take place: Here, too, bread is bread and wine is wine, but they are also the flesh and blood of Christ. The idea need not be articulated to be effective, and it explains the instances of puzzling unconcern about what to an outside observer appears to be all too transparent trickery and sleight of hand.

Incisions and bleeding are part of any surgery. Psychological states have an effect on the cardiovascular system, and this has been demonstrated in the laboratory. Suggestion can affect bleeding and tissue repair, if for no other reason than that the suggested relaxation and calm are states more compatible with the control of autonomic processes than is excitement and emotionality. Being aware of an operation being carried out on oneself, for instance, makes for bleeding and longer healing of the cuts. There are individuals who, through training and peculiarities of their own makeup, have achieved a remarkable degree of control over bleeding and pain in their bodies. One example is the Dutchman Jack Schwartz. Schwartz does not believe that there is anything mystical or occult about his ability, although the appearance of a man calmly stabbing himself with a piece of steel or lying on a bed of nails with little bleeding and no signs of subcutaneous hemorrhage (black and blue spots) is the classic one of the fakir and Eastern wonder worker. Schwartz has been tested at various reputable hospitals, such as the Menninger Foundation (Green, Green, & Walter, 1972) and the Langley Porter Neuropsychiatric Institute (Pelletier, 1974), and there is no doubt that his phenomena are genuine. Schwartz says that he is able to control bleeding and pain by working himself into a state of detachment and depersonalization so that he perceives his body not as *his* but as *a* body. Pain control is discussed in more detail in the next chapter.

MIRACULOUS INJURY

Stigmata of the Crucifixion

Stigmata are the spontaneously appearing scars and wounds that correspond to those received from some important religious figure that the stigmatist identifies with. Although stigmatism is known in other religions, such as Islam, it is usually associated with Christianity, and the stigmata are those of the crucified Christ: nail wounds in hands and feet, spear wound in the side, thorn wounds on the head, and scourge marks on the back. The appearance of the stigmata varies. They range from a reddening or rawness of the skin to deep wounds, and include localized bleeding without a visible wound.

Although stigmata are usually thought of as having been bestowed by God as a recompense upon very pious individuals, the Catholic Church does not require such a belief. Catholic sources indicate, in fact, that there is no reliable list of recognized stigmatists.

The term stigmata is an ancient one; it meant the brands placed on criminals and slaves, and Paul applied it to the wounds of Christ. The first stigmatist of record, however, did not appear until the 13th century. It was St. Francis of Assisi, but his case is not very well known (see Hastings,

1922). Only some 330 persons have been stigmatized since the time of St. Francis, most of them women. Well-known examples from the 20th century are Louise Lateau, Padre Pio, and Therese Neumann.

Cases of stigmatism fall into two categories: self-inflicted wounds, which may be either cases of fraud or of unconscious self-infliction, and those that are caused by emotional states. The Catholic Church calls the latter "natural" stigmata—that is, they are recognized as occurring due to known physiological processes. A distinction is made between those stigmata that do not occur as a sign of God's grace and those that are divinely caused. The former can occur in non-Catholics and non-believers. The genuineness of the latter must be demonstrated by such criteria as additional miracles, divinely inspired visions, and spiritual fruits, such as religious conversions.

The psychological nature of stigmatism is quite evident. There may be a desire to receive the stigmata, as was the case with the nun Lukardis of Aberweimar (Thurston, 1922). Her desire led to the nervous habit, known as neurotic excoriation, of stabbing or scratching her hands and feet with fingernails and toenails and the consequent bleeding of the wounds. In spite of ample proof that the wounds were self-inflicted, both the nun and others continued to believe that the stigmata were of supernatural origin.

Dermographia is a skin condition in which pressure or friction will temporarily raise reddish welts, so that a word may be written on the skin. Although it may be found in otherwise normal people, it is also found in hysterics, stigmatists, and the possessed. The symbols and words of religious or occult significance that are sometimes written on the skins of the latter are easily produced surreptitiously or quite unconsciously by fingernails or pointed instruments.

The location, extent, and nature of stigmata vary according to the stigmatist's idea of what Christ's crucifixion was like, which may come from the Bible, oral accounts, or pictures. There is no indication in the Bible whether the spear wound was inflicted on the left or the right side of the body, for instance. Although in most cases, stigmatists develop it on the left side, some have it on the right side.

The hysterical nature of stigmata is attested to by the fact that they do not occur in isolation but are part of other phenomena that are usually associated with mental disorders. The stigmatist may experience the passion of Christ during Easter week or else bleed every Friday. The trance reenactment of the passion may be very dramatic, with many details. Therese Neumann of the Bavarian village of Konnersreuth suffered hysterical paralysis, blindness, and other symptoms of conversion reaction at age 20 in connection with a fire. She gradually developed a pattern of sudden onsets and terminations of maladies of various descriptions, and in 1922 was declared to be a case of severe hysteria. In 1926, she began to bleed from her eyes and developed the stigmata of crucifixion during Lent of the same year. The stigmata, however, had the typical appearance of wounds seen in ordinary hysterics (Graef, 1951). She suffered from sleepwalking in addition, and developed two extra personalities, those of a 4-year-old child and of a wise saint. Therese's home became the center of unofficial pilgrimages. She was tested in 1927, but only for alleged total abstinence from food (see *Inedia* later in this chapter) and again in 1928. When her family refused permission to have her tested outside her home, the Church forbade pilgrimages to see her. There was a surge of pilgrimages after World War II when thousands came, especially during Easter week. She died in 1962.

Self-induced (through autosuggestion) itching and subsequent scratching of which the individual is quite unaware is likely to occur in suggestible persons if the stimulus is a mental or actual picture of the crucifixion used during meditation and if the main motive is to receive the stigmata. The motive behind that may be an unconscious conflict and a desire to escape from an intolerable situation into invalidism, where one's needs are taken care of. It then becomes a case of hysterical conversion reaction. Although many, if not most, cases of stigmatism can be explained as fraud or consciously or unconsciously self-inflicted wounds, some appear to have an entirely "mental" basis. Given that a person can develop perforating gastric wounds from emotional stress, it should not be impossible, in principle, to develop such wounds elsewhere. Hypnotic experiments give strong evidence that focalized changes in the skin, such as itching, reddening, or blister formation, can be achieved by suggestion alone. The particular psychological makeup of an hysteric is a particularly fertile ground for the much more dramatic changes that occur in stigmatism.

It is quite clear from everyday observation that mental states do control the flow of blood to specific sites in the body: We blush and blanch in anger, fear, and embarrassment, and we can learn to control these events through mental imagery, for instance. Erotic images produce increased blood flow to the genitals with consequent congestion or erection. That mental states can control blood flow in skin capillaries has been amply demonstrated in recent experiments with hypnosis (Barber, 1978). There are certain disorders of the vasomotor system that, although quite rare, can also be brought about psychologically. These are the subcutaneous congestion of the capillaries (erythema) that may lead to severe inflammation, and capillary hemorrhage (ecchymosis). There is also the disorder of hemetidrosis or sweating of blood in which blood appears in the sweat ducts through percolation. Changes in the capillary system can be brought about hypnotically as well as by other purely psychological means. Thus, Moody (1948) reports the case of a patient who first developed red streaks on the back of her hands when intensely reliving the experience of being whipped across the hands. When one of her hands was put in a plaster cast, blood was found on the dressing when the cast was removed the next day. The blood had oozed from ruptured capillaries in the skin on top of the welts. The stigmatist, Louise Lateau, was examined by the Belgian Academy of Medicine. Her stigmata bled even when protected from the possibility of her inflicting the wounds herself.

A combination of a hysterical predisposition, heightened suggestibility brought about by repeated hypnotization, and readiness on the part of the hypnotizer to engage in somewhat drastic procedures with human subjects has yielded, in the past, vivid demonstrations of bleeding and blister formation produced to order by psychiatrists under controlled conditions. Profoundly hysterical individuals are in short supply today, and the use of humans as guinea pigs by scientists is not countenanced. There is, however, no reason to doubt the results of these early experiments, nor that, given the right conditions, a few individuals might be able to produce the same phenomena themselves.

Voodoo Deaths

That a witchdoctor can bring harm, even death, through magic incantations, rituals, or curses is a belief that has been particularly prevalent in Africa, but also exists among the natives of South America, Australia, New Zealand, and the islands of the Pacific. Black slaves took it with them wherever they were taken. In Haiti, it is found in association with voodoo beliefs, especially in the form of voodoo death, and the latter term is applied to all such deaths generically.

That death can be brought about by the mere belief that a death spell has been cast against one cannot be doubted. The form of the spell itself varies from one culture area to another. It may consist, for instance, of being "boned"—that is, of having a bone pointed at one by the witchdoctor as he utters a death curse, or of a doll made in the likeness of the victim that becomes the target of needles stuck into it along with the appropriate utterances of magic spells. The ritual itself is inessential. It is indispensable, however, that the victim believe the power of the witchdoctor to bring about death in this way and, by extension, the power of another sorcerer to cast a counterspell. If no counterspell is cast, the victim may die in a very short time, provided belief in the power of the spell is strong enough.

The sorcerer, the villagers, and the victim all believe that voodoo death occurs through some supernatural agency. It is an occult explanation. Those who have disbelieved such an explanation but have undertaken to study cases of voodoo death, such as the famous physiologist Walter B. Cannon, have found that the mechanism involved in voodoo deaths is no different from the psychophysiological processes involved in faith healing (Cannon, 1942). It is belief that brings about bodily changes. Thus, Whites are usually immune from voodoo death spells, unless they are in some way involved with or identify themselves with the tribal life and customs. If the spell is not expected to work too well, the spell caster may help it along with means other than occult, such as poisons placed in the intended victim's food.

Cannon thought that voodoo deaths occurred because the victim's fear activated the sympathetic nervous system, which is involved in activating the body's emergency system and releases, among other things, increased amounts of adrenalin into the bloodstream. Excessive amounts of adrenalin can bring about a heart attack. The work of Curt Richter has shown, however, that it is the parasympathetic branch of the autonomic nervous system that is to blame (Richter, 1957). The parasympathetic system slows down the internal activity of the body, including that of the heart. When Richter overstimulated his experimental rats and put them in water, their heart rate slowed down, they lost consciousness, and sank. Normally, rats would continue swimming for some 80 hours before sinking. Human victims of the voodoo death spell also show signs of parasympathetic activity: They withdraw, refuse food, and lose interest in the daily affairs of the village.

Sudden, psychologically caused deaths are by no means limited to members of non-industrialized societies. Engel (1971) analyzed 170 cases of death that occurred within an hour of a significant event. Among the eight types of such events, the category of personal danger or threat of injury, real or symbolic, accounted for 46 of the 170 cases. Some of these cases involved curses and were in no way different from voodoo deaths reported from more exotic settings.

Inedia

Inedia, a Latin term meaning prolonged fasting or starvation, is a rare disorder that appears in individuals in association with hysteria and multiple personalities and in conjunction with the allegedly paranormal manifestations in such individuals, such as stigmata. One form of pathological noneating is called anorexia nervosa, thought by some to be a type of conversion reaction. Anorexia patients are typically women in whom the disorder begins at an age between 10 and 15. It has a purely psychological basis. It may begin as a result of an attempt to lose weight, or, in fewer cases, because the individual is afraid of food or eating. It is always a symptom of some deeper conflict within the individual. There is no feeling of hunger, and anorexia patients demonstrably go without food because eventually they reach an extremely emaciated state. Unless treatment is undertaken, some 5 to 15% of them may starve themselves to death.

Hysterical patients who allegedly take no food probably do not suffer from anorexia nervosa as such. One reason for this is that they do not become as extremely emaciated as the classical anorexia patient. Rather, they may present a relatively normal appearance. In addition, the length of time that they (or others) claim they have lived without food or water far exceeds the limit beyond which a person will survive, such as months or years. This is attributed to a miracle or divine intervention. In the occult tradition, the explanation is quasiphysiological: It is said that the individual is absorbing life-sustaining energy through the medulla oblongata, a brain structure that is indeed concerned with vital functions, such as respiration. Because the existence of vital forces different from physical and chemical ones is not recognized by science, this hypothesis has not received any empirical support.

There are no well-documented cases of prolonged inedia. One well-known case of inedia is reported from the 19th century. It is claimed that Mollie Fancher of Brooklyn hardly took any food at all between 1866, when she was 18 and her death in 1910. Her case is remarkably similar to that of the stigmatist Therese Neumann, cited earlier, except that Mollie Fancher did not develop stigmata. As was the case with Therese Neumann, Mollie Fancher's story began with a traumatic accident, followed by others. These served not only as stimuli for inedia, but for other phenomena as well: additional hysterical disorders, such as blindness, partial paralysis, multiple personalities, xenoglossy, and clairvoyance. These were also present in Therese Neumann. While bedridden, Mollie Fancher spent 9 active years writing and working on hobbies, then lost all memory of these years. The additional personalities (four of them) appeared after her amnesia. Because she was a good letter writer, it was suggested to her that her different personalities should get acquainted through correspondence, which they did.

The genuineness of Mollie Fancher's inedia was never really tested. Even the examining doctors apparently relied on second-hand evidence (Thurston, 1930). Somnambulism and amnesia are part of hysteria, and it is entirely possible that Mollie Fancher actually did obtain and eat food in her somnambulistic state and could not remember doing so in her waking state. Because she was bedridden, not much food was required to keep her alive. It also led to the assumption that she did not walk around and, therefore, to relaxed vigilance, although she could very well have been sleepwalking if her paralysis was hysterical, as it must have been. In any event, documented cases of hysteria show that hysterics can live up to 3 weeks without any food.

Therese Neumann was tested specifically for inedia by four trained Franciscan nursing sisters under the supervision of her own doctor. The test lasted 2 weeks. Her weight fluctuated during the fortnight, but was the same at the beginning and at the end of the period. Urine samples were taken twice, the analysis showing "hunger urine" composition. Similar tests were done during the 2 weeks after the examination, but the analysis was normal. It is quite possible that Therese Neumann did not eat during those 2 weeks in 1927, but all attempts to get her to a hospital for observation under more controlled conditions failed, which led to the prohibition to visit her. Therese's claim that she had subsisted only on holy wafers for years was finally shattered when it was discovered that her father was smuggling food to her. Because Therese was somnambulistic and was not constantly observed, she could have obtained food even without her father's help. As in the case of Mollie Fancher, amnesia would have obliterated the memory of such an inconsistency in her behavior.

NOTES

Ader and Cohen (1975) used rats in their experiment, but there is nothing in principle against assuming that the same sequence of events can be set up in humans or that, in general, the immune system is susceptible to environmental influences and that susceptibility to infectious diseases may thus be either lowered or heightened. Ader and Cohen used the classical conditioning paradigm of Pavlov's: an immunologically neutral stimulus, saccharin, was administered simultaneously with an immunosuppressing agent, which also caused taste aversion. Immunosuppression was achieved from there on when saccharin alone was administered.

Frank (1961) examines faith healing within the context of psychotherapy, and relates both to religious conversion and political brainwashing as well as to placebo effects. Chapters 3, 4, and 5 offer an excellent treatment of these subjects.

In Kiev (1974), many anthropologists, as well as psychologists and sociologists write on primitive psychiatry and magic healing in many different cultures. Although the papers are mostly descriptive, there is some analysis of the psychological and sociological factors that are involved in the cures. Chapter 1 in Ellenberger (1970) is an excellent and ample review of therapeutic techniques used in antiquity and in nonindustrial societies today that, by way of magic, ritual, exorcism, and similar techniques, attempt to heal physical and mental ills.

The literature on faith healing is considerable. Many of the works, however, are apologetics written by believers in supernatural causation or memoirs and autobiographies of the healers themselves (Kuhlman, 1962; Roberts, 1972; Worrall & Worrall, 1965) that add little to the understanding of the phenomena involved. Meyer (1965) offers a very well-written and researched account of faith healing in Protestant America, from the time of Mary Baker Eddy to the present. It is particularly valuable because it shows how faith healing develops into more secular endeavors, and the relationship of faith healing and "positive thinking" to psychology, sociology, and business. A shorter review of faith cures in America from 1872 to 1892 is found in Cunningham (1974). In addition to Frank's (1961) book, mentioned earlier, sober and useful presentations of the subject of faith healing may be found in Goodman (1974), Nolen (1975), and Rose (1968). Kripner and Villoldo (1976) offer much interesting material in first-hand experiences with a number of contemporary faith healers. Kripner, a psychologist turned parapsychologist, sets a disconcerting tone for the book by combining the stances of both a scientist who calls for the controlled study of anomalistic phenomena and a defender of the view that the phenomena of parapsychology are real and operate in faith healing. In spite of the disarming strategy of telling readers how healing fraud is perpetrated, the work must be classified as apologetics for the supernatural.

Much was written on suggestion in the second half of the 19th century and earlier in this century. Of the early works, two that can be read profitably even today are Baudouin (1920) and Sidis (1910).

The best work by far on hypnosis in connection with anomalistic psychology is Hilgard and Hilgard (1975). It deals with hypnosis in relation to relief from pain, and discusses in this connection the nature of hypnosis, of suggestibility, and faith healing. Each chapter has an annotated bibliography. The bibliographies are helpful in pursuing several of the topics dealth with in this chapter and the next: the nature of pain and hypnosis, the history of hypnosis, suggestion, acupuncture, and dissociation.

There are several biographies of Mary Baker Eddy. They fall into two categories, those that are "authorized" by the Christian Science Church, or written by Christian Scientists, and those that are not. They differ in the way some of the facts of Mary Baker Eddy's life are presented, such as her relationship to Quimby and hypnosis. An example of a biography of the first kind is Powell (1930), of the second kind, Dakin (1930).

Cabot made the distinction between functional and organic disorders in an 1908 article published in the August issue of *McClure's Magazine* ("One Hundred Christian Science Cases").

Two recent reviews of the history and nature of the unconscious are Ellenberger (1970) and Klein (1977).

A good psychological analysis of the Lourdes shrine and cures is found in Chapter 3 of Frank (1961).

Besides Hastings' (1922) article, which dwells at length on the case of St. Francis, articles on stigmatization may be found in the standard encyclopedias and the *Catholic Encyclopedia*. Graef's (1951) account of the case of Therese Neumann is one that is most readily available and is also a well-researched and a well-reasoned one. Although it is written from the Catholic viewpoint, it suffers less from personal bias than other accounts of the same subject.

3

Anomalistic
Psychophysiology: II

Faith healing is self healing, but the subjects of healing project the healing power outside themselves to a real or imagined entity or force. It is something that is being done to them. They are unaware of the process of self healing set in motion by faith and suggestion. Nevertheless, the process is seen as a triumph of mind (mind, soul, spirit, God) over matter, the effect of the intangible on the tangible. This chapter is also concerned with phenomena that appear to show an interaction between mind and body and that have been traditionally assigned an occult significance. The difference between the phenomena of faith healing and those described here—pain control and the ecstatic and meditative states—is that, in the latter, a deliberate effort is made to achieve the desired state. The effect may still be ascribed to some esoteric power and the purpose of the effort is transcendental, but the effort is a conscious one and is one's own. Whether they are consciously aware of it or not, both the healer and the yogi are engaged in the task of melding the subjective and the objective, mind and body, the I and the non-I. In either instance, the scientist is able to observe changes in their psychophysiological state.

CONTROL OVER PAIN

Tales about painful feats of endurance, such as burials alive and walks over glowing embers performed by Egyptian fakirs, Moslem dervishes, Indian yogis, and Polynesian fire walkers, used to be a regular feature of newspaper Sunday supplements and popular magazines. The Indian yogi's bed of nails is a universally known item and a butt for jokes by Western cartoonists. Insensitivity to pain in the dervish and the yogi is observed in two rather distinct situations. In one, wounds may be inflicted on oneself during a state of euphoria brought about by a prolonged whirling around, orgiastic dancing, or religious frenzy. In the other, the practitioner is calm, collected, or in a state of trance. These conditions suggest that more than one variable is involved in pain control.

One can simply learn to tolerate pain. This requires motivation, training, and practice. At one time, pain-enduring feats in the form of lying on a bed of nails or between swords and pushing needles through different parts of the body were a standard feature of a circus performance. Although most of the practitioners were Europeans and Americans, they bore assumed Oriental names to enhance their prestige through association with the traditional Oriental thaumaturgists. In 1928, a competition between a French and an Egyptian fakir took place in a Paris circus. While Tahra Bey, the Egyptian, did a variety of pain-defying acts, Paul Heuzé, the French challenger, could only thrust a needle through his cheeks, explaining that Tahra Bey's other feats were merely a matter of practice. Another French magician named Karma entered the contest in the last minute and duplicated Tahra Bey's act of lying on a bed of nails as well as on two steel blades. Both he and a committee of doctors and scientists declared that there was nothing abnormal in the Egyptian fakir's performance that required an occult explanation. The contest at the Cirque de Paris spurred circus performances of similar feats in the 1920s and 1930s. Even third-rate performances in obscure places must have impressed the audiences tremendously and reinforced their belief in the occult. One of the authors of this volume (L. Z.) does not remember much of his first visit to a circus at the age of 5 or 6 except for the most vivid image of a pale-skinned performer in an athletic costume and handle-bar moustache pushing a long knitting needle through both his cheeks, his biceps, and lying on the sharp edges of two vicious-looking cutlasses.

Factors That Influence the Experience of Pain

To understand how an individual can seemingly feel no pain when cut with a surgeon's blade, when walking on hot embers, or when a needle is stuck deep into the body, it is necessary to understand something about pain itself. Pain appears to be a simple, direct, and universal experience, and yet neither physiologists nor psychologists have been able to define pain in a satisfactory manner. Pain is not simply a matter of our nerves conducting certain impulses from the site of an injury to the brain: Pain may be experienced when there is no injury whatever. Because this kind of pain may be said to be "all in one's mind," it should not be surprising that one should be able to abolish it by psychological means also. On the other hand, there may be an absence of pain experience when there is tissue damage or excessive stimulation of the sense organs. Overlooking the rare cases of congenital insensitivity to pain, absence of pain in these cases is a rather complex phenomenon.

Pain experience may be diminished or abolished by a number of factors that are reducible to our past experience and hence may be categorized as psychological. Of particular significance to the perception of pain are the early experiences. Working with dogs, Thompson and Melzack (1956) found that the effect of raising their subjects in isolation without the normal stimulation that dogs get from their mother and littermates led to a gross insensitivity to pain. They endured pinpricks and flaming matches applied to the skin, and did not shy away from these stimuli on repeated presentation. The dogs were not insensitive, their nervous systems were working, but the lack of social stimulation in early life had led only to reflex movements without the emotional disturbance that normally accompanies pain experience.

An essential component of pain experience is the meaning—emotional, symbolic, and social—that an individual attaches to it. The endowment of pain with meaning occurs during the developmental period and in the course of social learning. It is well-known that expectations have a profound effect on the degree of distress that an individual will experience when in pain. Objectively measured, the anticipation of pain can be quite literally worse than the pain itself. Expectations are learned not only individually but socially as well. Thus, culture itself dictates to a considerable extent the nature and extent of pain experience. Childbirth in our culture is associated with the possibility of danger to the woman, and fear of it makes childbirth a painful experience. That it need not be is demonstrated by other cultures in which the woman continues to work in the fields until the time of birth, for instance. As she gives birth to the child, her husband takes to bed and goes through the agony of labor, then stays in bed to recover, keeping the newborn with him. The mother returns to work almost immediately.

The placebo effect is intimately related to expectations. The placebo, a physiologically inert substance, can be as effective as a drug if there is expectation that it will work. The placebo effect has an obvious bearing on the relief of pain in faith healing. Clinical studies show that severe postoperative pain can be reduced in some individuals by giving them a placebo instead of a pain-killing drug, such as morphine. Some 35% of the cases studied experienced relief. On the other hand, only 75% of patients report relief from morphine.

The attitude that one takes towards injury is also of crucial importance. The extent of the injury does not appear to bear any relationship to the pain that is experienced. Minor scratches can be quite painful, whereas deep and extensive wounds may be painless. A soldier wounded in battle may not require an anesthetic even after the excitement of the battle is over—if the injury is experienced as a price paid for escaping from death. Most civilians with a similar injury caused by an operation would require an anesthetic because of severe pain. That reward associated with pain may modify pain experience profoundly can be demonstrated experimentally with animals. If an animal receives a strong electric shock, it will react to it with violent movements, cries, and so on. If, however, the shock is used as a signal for food, anticipatory sniffing and salivation may replace the former behavior. Animals trained to expect an electric shock to signal the appearance of food learn to administer the shock themselves.

Attention, Hypnosis, and Surgery.   The soldier's pain experience just described has an additional aspect. Not only is he relatively free of pain in the hospital but he probably did not even notice when the injury occurred. This also happens in other situations where the individual is injured while highly aroused emotionally, as in sports games, automobile wrecks, or religious frenzy. Whenever our attention is strongly focused on a single item, the lack of focus on injuries also defocuses our pain experience, even to the point where pain is not noticed.

One way of redirecting a person's attention is through hypnosis and suggestion. Some individuals (about 20%) can be made to fall in an hypnotic sleep that is deep enough to render them completely anesthetic, so that even major surgery can be undertaken. One of the first to perform such operations was the Scottish surgeon James Esdaile, who did 261 of them. In an era that did not know chemical anesthetics, hypnosis not only alleviated the patients' suffering, but also drastically reduced mortality and led to better healing of the wounds, a phenomenon that is also often reported in connection with faith healing. Here is how Esdaile (1846/1977) describes one of his cases:

May 11th.—Meeroolla, a policeman; aged twenty-eight, strong and healthy looking. He has got a fatty tumour of the right mamma, which he begged me to remove today. I desired him to lie down, and let me carefully examine it, and commenced mesmerising him. In ten minutes he was fast asleep; in five minutes more I transfixed the tumour with a hook, drew it up off the muscles, and cut it out, without disturbing him in the least, and he did not awake till half an hour afterwards. He declares that he felt no pain till he awoke, and remembers nothing after my hands were placed on his stomach, which was in about five minutes from the commencement [p. 206].

Ether and chloroform were introduced in medical practice in 1846 and 1847, respectively. Because chemicals were much more convenient to use than hypnosis and worked with everybody, hypnosis was not given a chance to establish itself as a surgical anesthetic. The medical profession has been traditionally suspicious of it because of its occult connotations and because it has been used for entertainment. It has, however, recently been coming back in use in the United States, particularly as a treatment for pain in chronic, intractable, or terminal cancer cases.

The Central Nervous System

The central nervous system consists of the brain and the spinal cord. The brain is divided into the *forebrain*, the *midbrain*, and the *hindbrain*. The midbrain and the hindbrain together are called the *brain stem*. Those portions of the central nervous system that are mentioned in this book in connection with anomalistic phenomena are shown in Fig. 3.1.

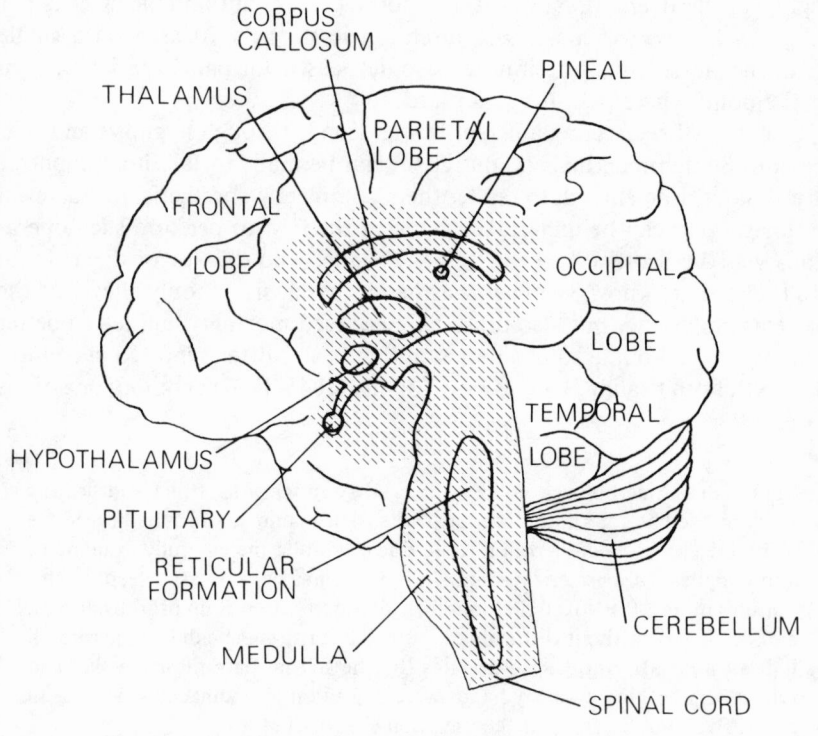

Fig. 3.1. The forebrain and the brain stem of the human brain.

The shaded portions in the Fig. show the inside of the brain in its midplane.

The brain is divided into two distinct halves, the right and left *cerebral hemispheres*. The are connected by a thick bundle of nerve fibers, the *corpus callosum*. The *frontal, parietal, occipital*, and *temporal lobes* are regions of the outer covering of the brain, called the *cortex*. Each hemisphere has the same four cortical lobes. The cortex is only one-quarter-inch thick, but its area is much larger than the surface of the brain because of the extensive folding.

The frontal lobes serve all voluntary motor functions, they control sequential acts, and they are involved in foresight or the anticipation of the future. The main function of the parietal lobes is the processing of body sensations. The occipital lobes are concerned mainly with vision, and the temporal lobes process auditory information, smell, and the understanding of speech. The cerebral cortex, the thalamus, and the hypothalamus form the forebrain. The *thalamus* is the main relay station of the brain. Nerve fibers from the spinal cord and the lower centers of the brain connect here with nerve fibers from the cortex. The *hypothalamus* controls the autonomic nervous system functions (see the insert in Chapter 2) as well as the master endocrine gland, the *pituitary*. It also controls the hunger, thirst, and sex drives, and is of enormous importance to the total economy of the body. The *pineal body*, of uncertain function, is located on the floor of the middle or third ventricle of the brain.

The cerebellum and the medulla are parts of the brain stem. The *cerebellum* serves the function of motor coordination. It integrates signals from the joints, muscles, and the inner ear. The *medulla* is the upper portion of the spinal cord. It contains nerve centers for breathing, heartbeat, and blood pressure.

The *reticular formation* is located within the hindbrain, but its upper fibers extend into the midbrain and the hypothalamus. It connects to the thalamus and the cortex, and is related to general arousal, attention, sleep, and waking.

Not shown in the drawing because of its size and complexity is the *limbic system*, located in the forebrain. It is primarily involved in emotion, hence sometimes is called the "emotional brain," but it also serves other functions, such as learning.

The Neuroanatomy of Pain. The control that psychological factors exercise over pain can be viewed as an interaction of the various anatomical and functional systems of the brain (see Box 3.1). Past experiences are represented in the brain as some type of biochemical change that takes the form of electrochemical activity when the experience is reactivated in memory, thinking, and emotion. This activity can modify other activities, such as the activity of pain pathways in the brain. This can be seen in animal experiments where the stimulation of the animal's cerebral cortex may stop nerve impulses caused by a painful stimulus before they reach the site where pain is experienced. In humans, a lesion in the thalamus, a structure that acts as a relay station for sensory nerve fibers before they reach the cerebral cortex, brings marked relief in those suffering from severe pain. Prefrontal lobotomy, an operation that severs the connection between the frontal lobes of the cerebral cortex and the rest of the brain, is sometimes used in cases of incapacitating anxiety as well as in cases of intractable pain. The consequences of this operation illustrate the working of the sensory and affective components of pain. Prefrontal lobotomy does not abolish pain. The patient still feels it and may complain, for instance, about skin punctures or burns, but is no longer concerned about the severe pain that was the occasion for the lobotomy. The patient is aware that the pain is there, but it does not bother him or her any more. The psychic surgeon or faith healer does not, of course, perform any kind of nerve surgery to achieve a remission of pain. It is clear, though, that the activity of the brain itself can block or modify its own activity, so that the outcome can, for all practical purposes, resemble that of an actual surgical operation.

Although the neuroanatomy of the pain pathways is roughly known, it is also known that the interactions among various nerve tracts and brain structures is very complex and not completely understood. One example of what might be the outcome of such complex interaction is seen in the practice of trephination by East African bush doctors. Trephination is the opening of a hole in the skull to alleviate or remedy some morbid condition, such as incurable headaches. The operator cuts through the scalp and drills a hole in the skull, all without any anesthetic, but also with little or no pain. There is a copious flow of blood, but no complaint about pain from the patient. How this is accomplished is still a mystery.

Acupuncture

The ancient Chinese medical art of acupuncture—the insertion and twirling of fine needles in certain points of the body to alleviate pain, as well as to remedy various disorders—has aspects, in addition to its medical or physical ones, that warrant its discussion here. The origin and underlying philosophy of the practice are mystical and the effect has a large psychological component.

According to traditional Chinese philosophy, the universal principle is *ch'i*, or vital energy. This principle manifests itself in opposites and alternations between opposites: hot-cold, male-female, day-night, and so on. The positive member or phase of each pair of opposites is called yang, the negative yin. Yang is activity, the male principle, the sun, heat, or summer. Yin is rest, the female principle, the moon, cold, and winter. Yin and yang are in a constant state of dynamic exchange, one passing into the other. Health depends on a balance of yin and yang, and the purpose of acupuncture is to restore the balance. This is accomplished by inserting needles in points that lie on certain lies on the body, called the meridians. The meridians are lines along which *ch'i* flows, but they do not correspond either to the course of blood vessels or the nerves, which is one of the reasons for the reluctance of Western medicine to accept acupuncture. Another reason is that *ch'i* resembles too much the discredited notions of animal magnetism, vital energy, and similar universal explanatory concepts that have a strong flavor of mysticism, occultism, and the supernatural. Nevertheless, acupuncture works. Why it works is another question, but the lack of a satisfactory answer does not preclude its widespread application in China, in the same way that not knowing exactly how aspirin works has not precluded its having become one of the most widely used medicines in the West.

Several possibilities have been suggested to explain why acupuncture works. They include the placebo effect, suggestion, hypnosis, mass conditioning, and a physiological theory called the gate theory of pain. A placebo is any physiologically inert substance, such as a weak salt or sugar solution, that acts like one that is physiologically active (a drug) through the power of suggestion. It is clear that a placebo acquires its power through the subject's belief that it is an active medicine. The belief itself does not convert the placebo into a drug. The chemistry of the placebo involves a very recently discovered substance that is manufactured by the organism, the endogenous morphine compounds or endorphins. Endorphins have properties identical to those of opium-derived analgesics, such as morphine, and act as the body's own analgesics. They are generated in the nerve pathways whose electrical stimulation can suppress pain. Substances that counteract the effects of narcotics, such as naloxene, abolish the pain-suppressing effect of the endorphins. An experiment conducted by Howard Fields and Jon Levine (Fields, 1978) at the University of California in San Francisco demonstrated very clearly that the release of the endorphins can be triggered by a placebo. They studied pain experience in persons who had just undergone tooth extraction. Some of them received naloxone, the others a placebo. Naloxone worsened the pain in comparison with the placebo group, and Fields and Levine concluded that the placebo acted by releasing the brain's endorphins. Not everybody responds to placebos, and the group that received the placebo treatment was divided into reactors and nonreactors. The researchers then gave naloxone to both groups and observed a dramatic difference: Naloxone worsened the pain only in those who responded to the placebo. That is, naloxone completely reversed the action of the placebo. Fields and Levine concluded tentatively that the effect must have been one of endorphin suppression by an anti-narcotic agent, endorphins that were generated by the placebo, that is, suggestion. These researchers also noted that the effect of acupuncture is partially canceled by naloxone, which suggests two possibilities: that endorphins may be released by physical means, and that narcotics, natural and externally administered, are only part of the complete picture of pain suppression.

The mass-conditioning factor, absent in the West, may be a factor in China. It may prime the population as a whole and make it receptive to the idea that acupuncture works. During and after the Chinese revolution, when chemical anesthetics were in short supply, Mao-Tse-Tung recommended the use of acupuncture. Mao's authority and the expectation that the method would work because it is *the* method lie behind the successful use of acupuncture in China. It is aided to a considerable extent by the stress that Chinese hospitals place on relief from anxiety and the inspiration of confidence in the patient, as well as by the use of sedatives and mild spinal anesthetics in the case of major operations.

On the individual level, the expectation that acupuncture would reduce pain may produce behavior on the part of the patient that to others suggests that pain has been reduced when in fact it has not. That is, acupuncture may not alter the threshold for pain at all, but it may alter the individual's willingness to report pain. These two situations may be indistinguishable for all practical purposes, but they are crucial to the understanding of pain and acupuncture. One line of evidence comes from work on hypnosis done by psychologists who hypothesize that hypnosis has less to do with a special state of consciousness than with successful role playing. Martin Orne (1959) has shown that, when properly rewarded, college students can withstand intense pain without flinching and otherwise pretend that they are hypnotized. They do it so successfully that a professional hypnotist finds it difficult to tell which ones are in a "real" hypnotic trance and which ones are only role playing. It is evidence such as this, as well as other factors, that make one discount the hypnosis theory of acupuncture. Although only about 20% of the population can be hypnotized deeply enough for surgery, in China, some 90% of the patients undergo surgery without analgesics. In addition, to achieve a satisfactory hypnotic state, preliminary work with the patient is necessary, whereas acupuncture works without any special training of the patient. Finally, patients who are operated upon with acupuncture analgesia speak spontaneously, eat, and engage in other voluntary activities, something that the hypnotized individual rarely does. There is further experimental evidence that acupuncture and hypnosis belong to two different orders of things. MacHovec and Man (1978) compared the effects of true acupuncture, placebo acupuncture (needles in sites other than the correct ones), group hypnosis, and individual hypnosis in four groups of Western medical patients. Of the four treatments, correct-site acupuncture and individual hypnosis proved to be the most effective treatments. The rates of improvement with these two treatments, however, were different, suggesting a difference between them.

There is another line of evidence that suggests that the pain suffered during an operation with acupuncture (or hypnotic analgesia) is perceived but is not reported (or remembered in the case of hypnosis). Using special experimental and statistical procedures, it is possible to separate an individual's sensitivity to pain from the decision-making processes that make that individual say either "yes, I feel pain," or "no, I don't feel anything," depending on the circumstances. Thus, Clark and Yang (1974) failed to find a sensory or physiological change when acupuncture was used to reduce the pain caused by a heat stimulus. What they did find was that subjects raised their criterion of when to report pain in response to the expectation that acupuncture would work. Because the only objective evidence of pain was the subjects' reports, the higher criterion for reporting pain that the acupunctured subjects set themselves made it appear as if acupuncture was relieving pain when in fact, as shown by the sensitivity index, their sensitivity had not changed at all. Clark and Yang (1974) suggest that: "until the role of suggestion on the readiness of the subject to report pain after acupuncture has been determined, speculations concerning the physiological mechanisms involved are premature [p. 1097]."

One instance of physiological speculation concerning the mechanism of pain has been the gate control theory of pain of Ronald Melzack and Patrick Wall. According to Melzack (Melzack, 1971; Melzack & Wall, 1965), the effects of acupuncture are produced in a crude form by other processes in which pain is used to alleviate pain. For instance, applying freezing cold to a leg raises the pain threshold for a toothache by 30%. The weaker pain stimulus not only distracts the subject's attention from the stronger pain, but acts as a nerve block. In acupuncture, the needles stimulate large peripheral nerves (A nerves), which produce a jamming effect in the spinal cord so that pain impulses coming from the site of the operation by way of smaller nerve fibers (C fibers) do not reach the brain and pain is not experienced. The A fibers operate to close a physiological pain gate. Although the theory is plausible, the existence of a physiological pain gate is yet to be demonstrated.

Fire Walking

The fire-walking ritual may be found in all parts of the world, but especially in Asia and the Pacific Islands. Both the purpose of fire walking and the explanation of the fire walker's immunity from fire are occult. The walk is performed as a magic ritual for better crops, as a purification rite, or to demonstrate one's innocence. In many instances, it has degenerated into a simple exhibition of the prowess of the walker.

Fig. 3.2.   A Bora Bora fire walk. (R. Buckminster Fuller photo. Used by permission.)

The fire walk takes several forms, the most prevalent ones being a walk on glowing embers or hot stones (Fig. 3.2). A shallow trench is dug, 15 to 40 feet long, 3 to 4 feet wide, and 9 to 12 inches deep. Wood is burnt in the trench. The fire walk begins when only glowing embers remain. The stone walk trench is wider and deeper to accomodate the stones. When the wood has burnt, the embers are swept away, leaving the exposed hot stones to walk on. In a fire-walking experiment in which the temperature of the embers was measured (H. Price, 1936), it was found to be 430 °C at the surface and 1400 °C inside the layer of embers, which was several inches thick.

There are always preparatory ceremonies that precede a fire walk, such as fasting, prayers, sexual abstinence, and, just before the walk itself, singing, chanting, and dancing. The fire walkers then walk rapidly through the length of the trench. Their feet may be examined at the end of the walk, but the walk may be performed more than once by the same person. Usually there are no burns or blisters, but not invariably. The injuries may vary from small burns in a few participants to severe ones in almost all. In one recent fire walk done in India, 10 of the 15 participants were severely burned, although previous such walks had occurred without any injuries (Freeman, 1974).

Various explanations have been advanced for the seemingly miraculous immunity of the fire walkers from burns. These include mass hallucination, chemicals applied to the soles of the feet, the use of pain-deadening drugs, callous feet, autohypnosis that induces analgesia and a biochemical modification of the skin surface, hydration, and the spheroidal state. Although some of these factors may be involved some of the time, none of them in itself is the complete explanation.

Mass hallucination on the part of the spectators may be effectively excluded as an explanation because the fire walk has been photographed and witnessed many times by a number of different investigators. The fascination with the phenomenon and a willingness to accept an occult explanation, on the other hand, has contributed to some of the wildly exaggerated reports and to contradictions among the observers.

Chemicals on the soles and the ingestion of narcotics may be used occasionally, but not as a rule. Although narcotics may deaden pain, they do not prevent burns or blisters.

The autohypnosis hypothesis may be correct to the extent that the fire walkers must not be afraid to take the walk. The preliminary rituals and activities achieve not so much an effect of purification as one of inspiring confidence in the walkers and a belief that they will not be hurt. Whether such a mental state would lead to some modification of the physiological state of the soles of the feet is doubtful, although that possibility has not been scientifically tested.

Callous feet appear to be a factor in stone walking, practiced mostly in the Pacific islands where the natives walk barefoot, but not necessarily in the case of ember walking. There have been instances where the walker's feet were found to be rather soft and flexible.

Hydration, or increasing the water content of body tissues by the ingestion of water, may be a factor, although it is hard to reconcile it with the fact that moist feet are more apt to pick up hot ashes and produce burns. Nevertheless, the fire walkers in the state of Orissa, India, do stand in holes of muddy water just before doing their walk. Elsewhere, dry feet appear to be a prerequisite for a fire walk.

The spheroidal state is the state assumed by water poured on a very hot metal surface: The water gathers up in rounded masses, the Leindenfrost drops, separated from the hot metal by a layer of vapor that is a poor conductor of heat. The temperature of the water in the drops is several degrees below the boiling point. The formation of Leidenfrost drops explains why it is possible to dip one's hand in molten lead with impunity if the temperature of the lead is considerably above its melting point. It has not been demonstrated, however, that this is what takes place in fire walking. A physicist who had studied Leidenfrost drops walked over a bed of hot coals of his own making, armed with nothing more than his faith in the principles of physics (Walker, 1977). That this is not a conclusive proof that it was Leidenfrost drops that saved him from burns is evident from the remainder of our discussion of fire walking.

Several experiments on fire walking were performed in the 1930s (G. B. Brown, 1938; Indian fire-walk, 1935; H. Price, 1936). They are still the best available. In these experiments, both Indian fire walkers and European volunteers walked along a 20-foot trench. Although the Europeans did suffer slight burns and formed blisters, some of them could walk the entire length of the trench. In the 1937 tests (Brown, 1938), the Indian fire walker Ahmed Hussain was badly burned. The famous Indian fire walker, Kuda Bux, also developed blisters when fire walking in Rockefeller Plaza, New York, in 1938. The investigators who organized these experiments concluded that no magic or occult powers were involved in fire walking. Price (1936) thought that fire walking could be explained by the short contact time between foot and embers, the low heat conductivity of wood embers, and confidence and steadiness in walking. He discounted or minimized the role of some of the other factors already discussed, such as the chemical preparation of the feet, the spheroidal state, or the need for special preparations.

One of the factors that is not stressed in reports on fire walking is that fire walking is walking, not standing still on embers or stones. There is no recorded instance of anyone's ever having attempted to just stand on red-hot stones or glowing embers for any length of time. The walkers walk rapidly, and it may take them only five or six steps to traverse a 20-foot long trench, for instance. As anyone who has felt the temptation to challenge the flame of a lit candle knows, it is possible to pass one's finger through the flame repeatedly and not get burned, provided one does not linger too long in the flame. It takes a couple of seconds for the skin temperature to reach the point where damage will begin to occur. Rapid walking through the embers, moving one's feet so that no one point is in contact with the embers for more than just a fraction of a second, should not allow the skin temperature to rise enough for burns to occur, even after several steps have been taken. Whatever heat accumulates from the four to six steps taken is dissipated on the cool grass or loose earth around the pit before the walker takes another walk.

Stones offer a larger contact surface with the feet than do embers, and having callous feet may be a significant factor in stone walking. The magician Milbourne Christopher reports, however (Christopher, 1970), that in 1901, S. P. Langley, a physicist and secretary of the Smithsonian Institute, tested a stone used in the Raiatea Island (near Tahiti) fire walk that he had brought to Washington. He found that the porous basalt rock was a poor conductor of heat. He could hold one end of the stone while the other had been heated to a red heat. More recently, the surgeon G. M. Feigen was taken across these rocks in a fire walk on Bora Bora island (which is near Raiatea) and suffered no pain or injury except for a burn caused by his having stepped on a wood cinder (Feigen, 1969). In the Japanese Shinto firewalking ceremony of *hi watari*, ceremonial throwing of salt on the embers and the method of raking the embers so that a thinner and cooler alley is left between the two higher side heaps make it possible for spectators, including women and children, to take the walk following the priests. The priests, walking first, reduce the heat further by crushing the embers with their feet.

Physical factors play an important role in fire walking. Psychological factors are involved indirectly. For instance, Freeman's (1974) report on the 1972 fire walk in Orissa indicates that the injuries suffered by two-thirds of the fire walkers may have occurred because of a conflict in the village community that affected the fire walkers' attitudes, because the same individuals had performed the walk repeatedly in previous years without a mishap. Fear as one attitudinal factor translates into sweating, including the sweating of the feet, which may cause hot ashes and small cinders to adhere to the skin and cause burns. Fear also affects the way we walk. Inexperienced volunteers who are uncertain about their ability to do the walk and become apprehensive as they feel the heat radiating from the trench, attempt to jump or run, dig their heels too heavily into the embers, and get burned as a consequence. Confidence in oneself manifests itself in a confident posture and a confident walk. Confident walking, in turn, leads to the least damage in fire walking.

THE PSYCHOPHYSIOLOGY OF HYPO- AND HYPERAROUSAL

The functioning of the nervous system is characterized by a degree of arousal, or the relative balance between excitatory and inhibitory processes in the neurons. The state of the nervous system induced by stimulation is known as excitation. When excitation in one part of the nervous system interferes with excitation in another part, this is know as inhibition. The level of arousal of the nervous system is determined by the degree of predominance of excitatory over inhibitory processes. The notion of level of arousal is applied both to the brain as a whole or to any of its parts.

Sleep

Walking consciousness is associated with the aroused state of the cerebral cortex. The cortex is kept in the waking state by stimulation from the structure in the brain stem known as the reticular formation. Inhibitory processes originating in the reticular formation lower the arousal level of the cortex and reduce the input from sense organs preparatory to falling asleep.

Brain-wave analysis is the only positive way of distinguishing between the different stages of sleep. It shows that sleep is not a uniform state. Several stages of sleep are distinguished, from relaxation and drowsiness to deep, dreamless sleep. In addition, there is the level of the so-called paradoxical sleep that is so different from the others that proposals have been made to consider it a special state of altered consciousness, distinct from sleep. Whereas the stages of ordinary sleep are characterized by a progressive slowing of brain activity, the brain in paradoxical sleep is as active as in the waking state. It is also the state in which dreams occur. In spite of the cortical arousal, there is no behavioral arousal: The cortical signals are blocked and never reach the muscles. Thus, neuronal and behavioral arousal do not always go hand in hand.

Sleep in itself has not had any particular occult connotations except as a facilitator of such events as the torments by succubi and incubi (see Chapter 8) and the soul's leaving the body during sleep. Dreaming has had such connotations, especially that of prophecy. The interpretation of dreams is also taken up in Chapter 8.

Ecstasy and Meditation

Levels of cortical arousal do have a direct bearing upon quite a number of phenomena presumed to be of an occult nature. The Swiss physiologist Walter Rudolf Hess distinguished two types of subcortical arousal, which he called ergotropic and trophotropic arousal (Hess, 1964). Heightened activity level of the sympathetic branch of the autonomic nervous system leads to ergotropic arousal, more active internal states, and a correspondingly more active behavior, whereas trophotropic arousal is associated with the activity of the parasympathetic nervous system and leads to a decrease in sensitivity to stimulation and lessened behavioral arousal. It is the extremes of both ergotropic and trophotropic arousal that are associated with mysticism, religious notions, and certain occult phenomena.

The psychophysiology of arousal has received two important treatments, one from the Russian physiologist Pavlov earlier in this century, the other more recently from the American psychologist Roland Fischer. Although Pavlov and Fischer deal with the same phenomena, they differ in their terminologies. Pavlov's focus is on the physiology of conditioning and the

Electroencephalography

Brain activity is electrical activity. The state of the brain and the kind of activity it is engaged in may be inferred from the recording of the electrical activity of the brain, called the *electroencephalogram* or *EEG*. The EEG is a pen tracing, on a moving paper tape, of fluctuations in the voltage generated by the brain, the *brain waves* or *rhythms*. They can also be displayed on the screen of an oscilloscope, and looked at or photographed with a camera.

The electrical potentials generated by the brain are extremely low, measured in millionths of a volt. The signals are picked up by placing electrodes on the scalp, and are amplified by an amplifier before they are recorded or displayed. The signals may be also fed into a computer for statistical analysis.

Brain waves differ in wave frequency and amplitude. These are determined by the kind of activity the nervous system is engaged in. Table 3.1 lists the major known types of brain rhythms.

TABLE 3.1
Major Types of Brain Rhythms

Name of Rhythm	Frequency per Second	Condition of Organism
alpha	8-12	Awake, relaxed, eyes closed; meditating
beta	18-30	Awake, aroused, mentally active
gamma	30-50	Awake, aroused, mentally active
delta	.5-4	Deep sleep
theta	5-7	Awake, under stress; emotion
kappa	8-12	Awake, solving problems (?)

The alpha waves were the first specific brain-wave rhythm identified. They are produced when the subject relaxes, closes the eyes, and does not engage in strenuous thinking, such as problem solving. Light in the eyes, loud sounds, doing a problem in arithmetic, or being aroused in any way blocks the alpha rhythm. The alpha rhythm does not reach the 8-12 cycle frequency until the individual is about 12 years old. Some individuals, even as adults and in a state of relaxation, do not show the alpha rhythm.

The beta and gamma rhythms characterize the EEG of an awake, alert, and aroused organism. They are fast, low-voltage waves.

Delta waves are slow and have a large amplitude. They characterize deep, dreamless sleep, as well as unconsciousness induced by an anesthetic or a concussion. The presence of delta waves in a waking individual indicates severe brain damage. When dreaming sets in, the sleep waves are replaced by a rhythm that resembles the waking beta rhythm.

Theta waves originate in one brain structure, the hippocampus, and are more prominent in children and adolescents than in adults. Alpha and theta waves show alternation: When the alpha rhythm is blocked in arousal, the theta rhythm becomes stronger, and vice versa.

Kappa waves appear to be associated with intense mental activity, such as doing mental arithmetic or making difficult discriminations.

Other characteristics of the brain waves besides their frequency and amplitude are used to assess aspects of brain functioning, including the presence of tumors, lesions, epilepsy, cognitive and perceptual functioning, and the functional relationships among the various portions of the brain.

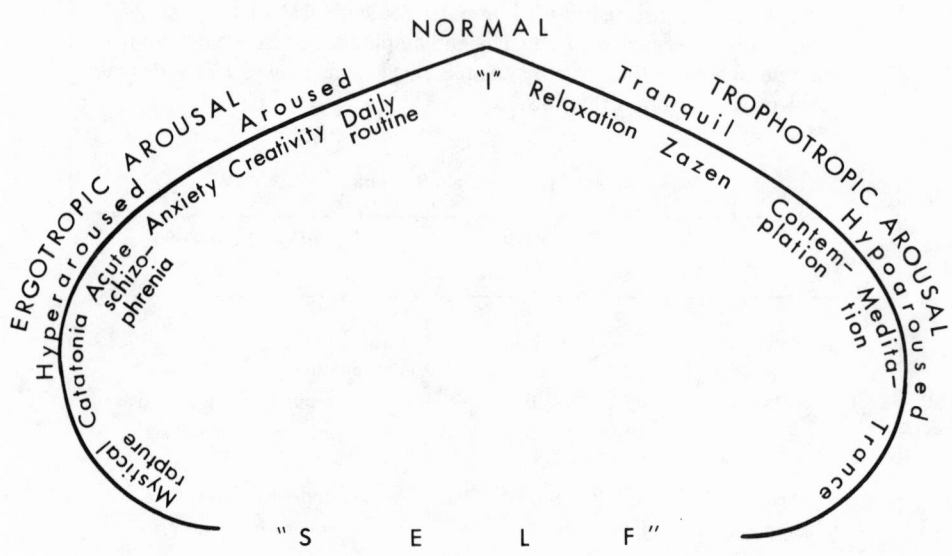

Fig. 3.3. States of consciousness mapped on continua of ergotropic and trophotropic arousal. (After Fischer, 1975. © 1975 by the American Association for the Advancement of Science. Used by permission.)

observable physiological and behavioral responses of animals and men under stress; Fischer is concerned with systematizing the variety of subjective experiences associated with both stress and tranquility. We consider Fischer's views first.

Fischer (1971, 1975) has placed the normal state of consciousness and the different levels of ergotropic and trophotropic arousal on a continuum, shown in Fig. 3.3. At the center of the continuum is the normal state of awareness, ordinary perception, and all the mental and motor activities that involve saying "I" and the awareness of oneself as an independent entity, separate from everything else. Conscious experience, according to Fischer, is the interpretation by the cerebral cortex of any particular state of subcortical arousal. Thus, normal levels of arousal are interpreted as an ordinary state of consciousness, such as one may experience while reading a book, eating, or being engaged in any daily, routine activity. One-half of the arousal continuum represents those experiences (cortical interpretations) that accompany increasingly lower levels of arousal—relaxation, contemplation, and meditation. The other half describes states of mind that arise from increased levels of arousal—from creativity to anxiety, psychotic states, and ecstasy.

Movement along this continuum in either direction is accompanied by a systematic change in the relationship between the objective and the subjective in the individual's relationship to reality. This change is an increasing dominance of the subjective aspect—imagination, hallucinations, visions, and other phenomena of the inner world—and a decrease in the objective aspect, that is, movement. To an outside observer, the most conspicuous feature in the behavior of an individual who is in a deep meditative state or religious ecstasy is the absence of behavior. In daily routine, the interpretation of our experiences is aided by voluntary motor activity—we check out what we see, hear, and otherwise experience, by touching and other motor acts and thus confirm to ourselves that what we perceive in fact exists. With both increasing (ergotropic) and decreasing (trophotropic) levels of arousal, the willingness and ability to check experience by behaving decreases, and perceptions become hallucinations. Those who experience the out-of-the-body state (Chapter 5) invariably report that attempts at motor activity—speaking to or touching persons or moving objects—produce no results.

Ergotropic arousal (hyperarousal) is thought to be related to the secretion of the hormone noradrenalin (Brodie, 1958). It is correlated with a decrease in a measure of brain-wave activity, the variability of EEG amplitude (Goldstein, Murphree, Sugerman, Pfeifer, & Jenney, 1963). Whether natural or drug induced, it leads to increased sensitivity, creative ideation, then acute schizophrenic states, and culminates in the ecstatic rapture of the mystic. It is not necessary to go through all of these stages to reach the last: There are individuals who travel freely between ordinary consciousness and the creative state, or back and forth between ordinary consciousness and the creative state, or back and forth between I consciousness and ecstasy. Some, on the other hand, may get ''stuck'' in the uncreative state of schizophrenia, overwhelmed by and unable to process the amount of information that impinges upon them.

Brodie's (1958) findings indicate that trophotropic arousal (hypoarousal) may be related to the secretion of serotonin, a substance that is involved in the transmission of nerve impulses from neuron to neuron. The decreasing level of arousal is reflected in the decrease of the frequency of brain waves as one passes from normal waking activity to relaxation and meditation.

Meditation is characterized by increasing withdrawal of attention from the external world and a concentration on emptying the mind of all sensory contents and thought. The EEG frequencies decrease from a range of 13-26 (beta waves) in the waking, aroused state, to a range of 8-12 (alpha waves) in relaxation and Zen meditation, to a range of 4-7 per second (theta waves) in the yogic state of *samadhi* or deepest meditative state.

Hyperarousal, Conversion, and Possession

I. P. Pavlov performed experiments and analyzed the behavior and physiological changes in animals under stress—that is, when hyper-aroused—and noted the effects stress had on the process of conditioning. He generalized his findings to humans, as there were obvious parallels to be observed in human life situations, and extended his observations to states of hypoarousal. When subjected to prolonged overstimulation, protective inhibitory processes are set in motion by the brain—that is, nervous processes begin to inhibit themselves so as to protect the brain from damage. Pavlov called the initial phase of such activity the "equivalent" phase. Normally, weak stimuli elicit weak responses and strong stimuli elicit strong ones. In the equivalent phase, all stimuli elicit responses of the same strength. If presented at this stage, any idea, for example, may appear as good or as valuable as any other. In the next, the "paradoxical," phase, weak stimuli cause stronger responses than do strong stimuli. Small, inconsequential events may produce a strong emotional reaction, whereas misfortune may lead to a response of indifference. In the "ultraparadoxical" phase of protective inhibition, ideas that were previously valued are rejected, and those that were not are now accepted. For instance, a person may reject the previous life style, turn against former friends, and accept religious or political ideas that were previously rejected and ridiculed. Pavlov stated that it is in this ultraparadoxical phase that feelings of possession arise. The individual may begin to feel that the object that at this moment happens to be at the center of concern is entering and taking possesion of him or her. It may be a god, Jesus, a demon, or, if the object of concern is sex, an imagined sexual assailant. In the ultraparadoxical phase, all critical reasoning ceases, and ideas and commands are received, accepted, and believed unquestioningly. Ideological conversions take place.

Transmarginal inhibition, protective inhibition brought about by prolonged overstimulation, is a state in which a person is amenable to influences to which he or she was previously not amenable. Sufficient intensity and duration eventually breaks down even the strongest. The means whereby this state can be brought about may be self-imposed or imposed from outside. They include powerful mental conflicts, prolonged fasting, extreme fatigue, other forms of severe physical and psychological stress, or prolonged, high levels of stimulation of any of the senses. Rhythmic hand clapping, drumming, music, dancing, whirling, singing, chanting, supported by a mounting emotional excitement from a congregation has been the typical background for sudden religious conversions and possessions since the earliest times and across all cultures. In Christianity, preachers such as John Wesley were adept at adding the element of mental anguish by vivid depictions of the torments of hell. Many of those who listened to Wesley changed from a state of indifference to one of ardent support of religion as a result of a sudden conversion. Wesley (1872-1878) took such conversions to be demonstrations of supernatural intervention and of events that were invisible to the eyes of flesh.

Pavlov believed that a process of protective inhibition also took place when stimulation was reduced far below normal levels. In meditation, although sensory input is reduced, there is a high level of excitation in the one point in the brain that corresponds to the object of meditation. This point of intense arousal is comparable to the arousal that involves larger brain areas in the case of overstimulation. Pavlov theorized that this point would be subject to the process of protective inhibition, including its three phases and the feeling of possession in the ultraparadoxical phase. For instance, before reaching the final goal of mystic union, many mystics report that, quite against their will, they are tormented by thoughts of lust, anger, or despair, and undergo various terrible temptations, which would correspond to the paradoxical phase of protective inhibition in which the positive and negative values of stimuli and ideas are reversed. William Sargant (1959) relates that:

> somebody interested in magical possession and in the raising of devils, but of very stable personality himself [told him] how he had found it possible, only after long and painfully learned periods of intense mental concentration, and by emptying of the mind of all other matters, and by special breathing techniques, to look across a room, continuing to picture in his mind the particular devil or spirit he wished to raise. Sooner or later, after perhaps many hours of quiescent but active mental contemplation, the desired spirit or devil would appear before him. Its face and the details of the bodily features could all be seen without loss of consciousness. It might even be heard talking [p. 17].

What Sargant's informant describes is at the core of mysticism where very similar methods are taught as a means of achieving union with God or Brahma. Although he never reached the stage of actual possession, many others throughout the ages have reported such possession.

A state of quiescence is reached by transmarginal inhibition regardless of whether one follows the path of over- or understimulation. The brain's self-protective devices lead to the same result in both cases. Contemporary research shows that even though the ergotropic and trophotropic arousal states are mutually exclusive, ergotropic arousal carried to the extreme results in what is called ergotropic rebound—that is, a direct passage from the extreme of ergotropic arousal to the extreme of trophotropic arousal (Gellhorn, 1970). This rebound is a protective device, associated with the appearance of a particular brain-wave rhythm, the theta waves, and appears to be identical with Pavlov's transmarginal inhibition. Behaviorally, this condition manifests itself in a collapse, prostration, fainting, and similar signs of complete exhaustion. It is observed, for instance, in individuals who are induced through hypnosis or a "truth drug" (barbiturates) to recall a very traumatic experience that is related to their present pathological condition. The terror of experiencing the event again and the accompanying autonomic nervous system hyperactivity may lead to sudden collapse and a state of quiet. In African tribal rituals, rituals associated with beliefs exported from Africa to Haiti and Brazil, and ritual observances in southeast Asia, the excitement brought about by dancing, whirling, drumming, and chanting that lasts for hours leads to a collapse in some of the participants and the feeling that they are possessed by some discarnate entity. In evangelistic Protestant sects, such as the snake-handling cults of eastern United States, the handling of snakes or religious conversions takes place only after a calculated build-up of excitement through music, singing, hand clapping, and excited preaching. In the final phase, some of the participants fall to the ground in a state of nervous exhaustion. This is explained as the work of the Holy Ghost and described as "wiping the slate clean for God."

John Wesley, probably the most effective preacher ever in his ability to cause a state of high excitement in his listeners, followed by conversion, created tension among them by convincing them that they would go to Hell if they were not first saved. He might point out that there was always the possibility of meeting a fatal accident after the meeting and thus dying unsaved and therefore condemned to Hell's tortures, which he described eloquently. The urgency of saving oneself was strongly impressed by Wesley on his audience, served to further heighten the level of arousal, and led to the ultraparadoxical state with the accompanying physiological and behavioral signs—groans, moans, shouts, gesticulation, convulsions, falling to the ground—and acceptance of Wesley's brand of religion, if not on the spot then upon returning home. Wesley's success was all the more spectacular when he preached to individuals who were already under considerable stress, such as criminals who were condemned to death or individuals debilitated by disease. The first time Pavlov observed transmarginal inhibition in dogs was during the great flood in Petrograd when water entered his laboratory and rose in the cages that contained his dogs. They were rescued from drowning, but only at the last moment. The stressful experience was found to have wiped the dogs' slates of conditioned responses clean: Old, established responses could no longer be elicited.

Regardless of the time, place, or culture, similar physical and physiological stresses lead to similar neurophysiological reactions. Only the interpretations of the experience vary according to the symbolic conventions of the particular group of which the stressed individual is a member. In this case, group membership is not determined entirely by one's birthplace, parentage, or formal initiation rites. If one is interested in a particular belief system, sympathizes with it, or identifies oneself with it, group membership is thereby established and the specific content of the ecstatic experience will be the same as that of other members of this reference group, even though the individual's "official" cultural background may be quite different. Belief is what counts. It counts in faith healing, voodoo deaths, and voodoo possessions. Maya Deren, an American, went to Haiti to observe and film Haitian dancing. She became not only an interested observer, but also a participant in voodoo ceremonies. As she danced to the beat of the drums, she became possessed by the love goddess Erszulie. The drumbeat became part of her. The foot that stomped the ground with the beat of the drums could not be stopped, and a "white darkness' began to move from the ground up her leg in a great tide that seemed to both absorb and explode her (Deren, 1970, p. 260).

Deren felt that the possession was induced by the rhythmic sound of the drums. Drumming, chanting, and hand clapping are all rhythmic sounds, and rhythmic sounds and lights are known to have a direct effect on the rhythmic activity of the brain, the brain waves. The so-called photic driving consists of flashing a light at a rate that is close to the rhythm of one of the brain wave rhythms, such as the alpha rhythm (10 Hz). The alpha rhythm of the person who is exposed to such flashing light will be driven by it—that is, it will assume the frequency of the light flashes. In individuals who suffer from neurological disorders that are characterized by a disorganization of brain rhythms, such as epilepsy, photic driving may lead to the onset of an episode of the disorder, such as epileptic fits. It is significant that epileptic fits have been considered to be of supernatural origin. Epileptic fits were watched with awe by the ancient Greeks who called it the "sacred disease." Although Hippocrates (who lived in the fifth century B.C.) called his contemporaries' attention to the fact that it was caused by a malfunctioning brain and was, therefore, a natural and not a sacred phenomenon, fits have been given paranormal attributions at all times and in all cultures. Even today, fits and convulsions that result from overexcitement in a religious revival meeting are interpreted as being of supernatural origin rather than an extreme effort of the organism to protect itself from damage. The best way to make protective inhibition unnecessary is to maintain an attitude of calm detachment and to avoid emotional involvement with the proceedings or its principals, such as becoming fearful or angry. Emotional non-involvement makes it possible to maintain a stable mental state in any situation of emotional contagion, be it a voodoo ceremony, a revival meeting, or political rally.

Another illustration of Pavlov's stages of protective inhibition may be found in the Biblical story of Saul, his persecution of Christians, and what happened to him on the road to Damascus (Sargant, 1959). Saul appears to have brought about the ultraparadoxical stage in himself through hate and anger:

> But Saul, still breathing threats and murder against the disciples of the Lord, went to the high priest and asked him for letters to the synagogues at Damascus, so that if he found any belonging to the Way, men or women, he might bring them bound to Jerusalem. Now as he journeyed he approached Damascus, and suddenly a light from heaven flashed about him. And he fell to the ground and heard a voice saying to him, "Saul, Saul, why do you persecute me?" And he said, "Who are you, Lord?" And he said, "I am Jesus, whom you are persecuting" [Acts, Chapter 9].

Following the high degree of excitement, Saul develops hysterical symptoms: "Saul arose from the ground; and when his eyes were opened, he could see nothing; so they led him by the hand and brought him into Damascus. And for three days he was without sight, and neither ate nor drank." Three days of fasting must have weakened Saul even further and increased his anxiety and susceptibility to new ideas, so that total acceptance of the very ideas that he had previously tried to suppress followed:

> Ananias departed and entered the house. And laying his hands on him he said, "Brother Saul, the Lord Jesus who appeared to you on the road by which you came, has sent me that you may regain your sight and be filled with the Holy Spirit." And immediately something like scales fell from his eyes and he regained his sight. Then he rose and was baptized, and took food and was strengthened.

Further indoctrination followed: "For several days he was with the disciples at Damascus. And in the synagogues immediately he proclaimed Jesus, saying, "He is the Son of God."

The Inner World

The descriptions of their experiences by two Christian mystics, St. Teresa of Avila and St. John of the Cross (Stace, 1960) show quite clearly that they took opposite paths to the same goal, St. Teresa the path of ecstasy, St. John the path of meditation. Roland Fischer calls the final state that is reached traveling along either the ergotropic or the trophotropic path the Self. Traveling along either path leads to the loss of the categories of space and time. It was noted earlier that in both hyperarousal and hypoarousal both the willingness and the ability to check one's experiences through motor acts decreases. Space and time speak of the external world. These decrease in importance as the mystic, instead of looking outward, turns his or her gaze increasingly inward. This inward-directed gaze gradually loses the gazer or the I-ness component, and the distinction between the observer and the observed, the subjective and the objective, is lost. The second sentence of the classic treatise on yoga, the *Yoga-Sutras of Patanjali (Patanjali, 1947)*, states that yoga is the suppression of the transformations of the thinking principle. The ultimate goal of the yogi is a union with the Oversoul and therefore the obliteration of the subjective-objective distinction. St. Teresa of Avila states (Stace, 1960) that during union with God "all the faculties . . . fail and are suspended in such a way that . . . it is impossible to believe that they are active [p. 180]." In ecstasy and in the *samadhi* state of yoga, there is pure, contentless contemplation of the ground of one's being, the Self. This has always been the goal of mystics of all times and all religious persuasions.

According to Fischer (1975):

> Thus the mutual exclusiveness of the normal and the exalted states, both ecstasy and *samadhi*, allows us to postulate that man . . . exists on two levels: As *Self* in the mental dimension of exalted states; and as *I* in the objective world. In our terminology, the *Self* of exalted states is that which sees and knows, and the *I* is the interpretation, that which is seen and known in the physical space-time of the world out there. The mutually exclusive relationship between the "seer" and the "seen," or the elusiveness of the *Self* and the *I*, may have its physiological basis in the mutual exclusiveness of the ergotropic and trophotropic systems [p. 211-212].

The consequence of this conceptualization of the inner world is that it brings the subjective and the objective together in a relationship that makes it unnecessary to postulate realities separate and different from ordinary reality, and at the same time does not deny the existence of states and phenomena that have been made part of such realities at one time or another: creativity, out-of-the-body experiences, and religious conversion among others. Fischer sees these as instances of I-Self communication. Fischer (1975) calls the point of contact between *I* and *Self* as they communicate, the boundary condition between *I* and *Self*, the soul, "and only those whose *I* and *Self* can communicate with each other become conscious of it [p. 223]."

The subjective, psychological side of the exalted states is their all-important aspect. It has to do with a person's view of himself or herself. If an exalted state were only a physiological event, it would have no more significance than, say, an orgasm. Agehananda Bharati, an Austrian who became a Hindu mystic, points out (Bharati, 1976) that in some ways an exalted state and the orgasm are comparable: They are both peak experiences, they are sought for their own sake, but they are not related to any significant behavior changes. What makes them vastly different is that the exalted states provide new information. There is little information content in an orgasm. After a *samadhi* or ecstasy experience, the mystic sees himself or herself as a new person, has a new perspective on existence, has left the old world behind him and has entered a new one; the mystic knows more, there has been growth. The mystic's inner self has changed in ways that could not have been predicted from a previous life. These are specifiable psychological changes nevertheless: change in self-image, self-esteem, security, ego strength, self-confidence, egocentricity, and the like. How exactly meditative practices bring about these changes is as yet unknown. Speculations along these lines from within the ranks of the mystics are abundant, but do not concern us here. Changes in self-image are measurable changes, however, and psychologists have recently begun to measure such changes that are due to the practice of meditation. A consideration of these efforts would also lead away from the main subject matter of this book.

Hypoarousal, Hyperarousal, and the Occult

Both the occult tradition and orthodox religions have ascribed the possession of special powers to individuals who have been able, through discipline, training, ascesis, or saintly living, to reach the ecstatic or *samadhi* states and remain there at will. Such individuals are often in the religious life—yogis, nuns, and monks—but not exclusively. Some are anonymous private citizens. Bucke (1959) has collected a number of case histories of such individuals.

A corollary of Fischer's conceptualization of hypo- and hyperaroused states, which Fischer himself does not stress, is that the byproducts of these states that have been variously described as powers, gifts, or *siddhis* belong to the same order of things as all others and can be accommodated within it using the conceptual tools that are used to analyze consciousness, hallucinations, and physiological arousal.

It is the nature of the subjective experience in altered states of consciousness that gives rise to the idea that one possesses such powers as the ability to travel outside one's body, to see things that are far away without being there, to foresee the future, or to move objects without physical intervention. The psychology of meditation and of altered states of consciousness has recently become a new field of psychology, and both research and theoretical studies in this area are multiplying rapidly.

On the way to the ultimate goal, ecstatic or meditative, but before reaching it, the individual may feel that special occult powers have been acquired. These are called the *siddhis* in Sanskrit, and both Hindu yoga manuals and Buddhist meditation instructions warn the practitioner against becoming too interested in them and losing sight of the goal. The *siddhis* are telepathy, clairvoyance, psychokinesis, levitation, the ability to move outside one's own body, to become very large or very small, know one's previous incarnations, invisibility, and so on. Considering that both the ergotropic and the trophotropic path to the Self lead to a feeling that the boundaries of the I have been exceeded, that the individual's true self has been revealed and that it is one with the universe, that one can be outside one's body and move about in a fourth dimension, as it were, it is not surprising that the notion of having acquired special abilities that complement the special state of mind should develop.

The main factor in this belief is the sense of realness of the experience. It is as real as, or even more real than, everyday reality. Persons in an ecstatic trance may have such a strong feeling that they are rising in the air that they may try to hold on to things in order to prevent it from happening. There is an absolute sense of certainty concerning the validity of all features of the experience. This certainty is of a different kind than that which comes from having accumulated a large number of facts about a problem or of having reached the correct conclusion because one has followed a logical line of reasoning. It is a direct, intuitive feeling that the experience is true, truer than anything one has experienced before, and that its truth will stand up under later scrutiny. Although the Christian Bible repeatedly demonstrates the power of conviction that comes from revelations received in altered states of consciousness, St. Augustine's *Confessions* is perhaps the first documented instance in which the self-validating sense of truth received in prayer, adoration, contemplation, and ecstasy is made into a philosophical tenet that becomes part of Christian theology.

Unfortunately, a feeling of realness, however convincing, is no evidence of physical reality. Dreams and hallucinations may appear to be very real, yet have no correspondence to anything in this world. The argument that dreams, hallucinations, or trance states may indeed be the "really" real world and that this world is an illusion or a dream does not stand up against the pragmatic test of action; the conviction acquired in an altered state of consciousness that one is now invulnerable, for instance, will not pass the pragmatic test of standing in the way of oncoming automobiles on a freeway. The argument that even death is an illusion is a moot one because death effectively prevents the proponent of the argument from continuing the discussion.

Is there nothing else than this to the alleged paranormal powers associated with states of hyper- and hypoarousal? The answer to this question hinges on whether parapsychology can satisfactorily answer the questions it has asked itself about the reality of telepathy, clairvoyance, precognition, and psychokinesis. We take up this question in our discussion of parapsychology in Chapters 12 and 13.

The Psychophysiology of Meditation and Yoga. If the word "occultism" were used in studies of word association, it is quite likely that the most common association to it would be "India," and the association to that, "Hinduism" or "Yoga." Although Westerners have known about yoga for a long time, the common associations to it have been those of mystery, mysticism, magic, bizarre practices, and a generally uneasy feeling that the yogis had somehow been able to overcome the laws of physics and physiology.

Scientific tests of yogis did not begin until the 1920s. One of the first researchers was a French cardiologist, Dr. Thérèse Brosse (1946, 1954), who studied the yogis' control of the heart and breathing with electrocardiographs and pneumographs. Her findings were that there were indeed physiological correlates of the yogic phenomena. Her conclusion that the yogis could stop breathing for hours or stop the heart completely were unwarranted. In the breathing control test, the yogi was out of sight, buried in the ground, and her EKG record was probably contaminated by signals from the thorax muscles, which were strained by the yogi in performing the so-called Valsalva maneuver in an attempt to stop the heart (Bagchi & Wenger, 1957).

Such studies were very rare, however, one of the main reasons being that it was expensive, time consuming, and difficult to obtain yogi subjects who were willing to be tested. With the phenomenal increase in interest in Eastern philosophies during the 1960s and since the introduction of meditative disciplines in the West, particularly the United States, the subject problem has been alleviated, and a number of physiological studies of meditators have been performed.

The following studies may be cited as representative of the field. Sugi and Akutsu (1964) found that in Zen meditators oxygen consumption decreased by some 20% and carbon dioxide production decreased as well. These signs of reduced metabolic activity as well as additional ones have been observed repeatedly in meditators and yogis. Anand, Chhina and Singh (1961b) took physiological measurements of the yogi Ramanand while the latter was confined in an airtight steel chamber instead of being buried in the ground in the usual manner. Air samples were periodically extracted from the box. The yogi reduced his oxygen consumption and carbon dioxide production to a marked degree, surviving under conditions in which an untrained person would have perished. R. K. Wallace (1970) recorded a decrease in oxygen consumption of 16% and in carbon dioxide production of 15% in 36 practitioners of transcendental meditation. The level of lactate in the blood, another index of the rate of metabolism, fell four times faster in these meditators than in a person just resting, even though the blood flow in the arm increased. Both events are related to a decrease in sympathetic nervous system activity. Hypoarousal of this system leads to a relaxation of the walls of blood vessels and hence to an increase in blood flow, as well as to hyposecretion of the hormone norepinephrine, which is known to stimulate lactate production. Skin resistance to electric current, the galvanic skin response (GSR), increased up to four times during meditation, a measure of restful, non-emotional state, and the brain-wave pattern showed a marked increase in alpha waves, characteristic of the relaxed state of the nervous system, as well as an increase in theta waves in the frontal lobes of some subjects. Wallace's findings concerning the brain-wave changes were not new and have been repeated since. Okeima, Kogu, Ikeda, and Sugiyama (1957) and Kasamatsu and Hirai (1966) recorded the EEG activity of Zen monks and found a predominance of alpha waves, even though the meditators' eyes were only half closed. (Just closing the eyes leads to an increase in alpha waves.) Moreover, more experienced meditators showed a slowing down of the alpha rhythm from about 9-12 to only 6 or 7 cycles per second. Anand, Chhina, and Singh (1961a) found a similar EEG pattern in meditating Indian yogis. It is important to note that even though EEG changes and hypometabolism also occur in sleep and hypnosis, the rate and degree of these changes in meditation as well as other dimensions of the EEG and metabolic processes suggest that the meditative state is a different and independent one.

Yoga and the Occult. Yoga instructions, such as those of Patanjali (1947), state that one of the methods of stilling the mind is breath control (*pranayama*). *Pranayama* is based on the mystical assumption that an individual's physical breath is part of universal breath (*prana*), and that health and bodily harmony is achieved by breathing, which is attuned to the universe. The physiological effect of deep and rapid breathing is a decrease of carbon dioxide content in the blood and an increase in the amount of oxygen. Dizziness and a trance-like state may be associated with hyperventilation, but that is not aimed for in yoga. Rather, the breathing rhythm is made to follow a particular pattern that, in addition to serving as a focuser of attention, leads to the physiological changes previously described. Although the purpose of rhythmic breathing is a metaphysical one, the yogi does learn an efficient technique of breath control that can be and has been used in demonstrations that appear miraculous, such as allowing oneself to be buried alive for hours. The yogi cannot do so indefinitely, though, and cannot survive if not released. An imitator of a famous fakir, Blacaman, died on a theater stage in Argentina after having been buried for only 15 minutes. Stories of burials alive lasting weeks and months have been reported from earlier times, where uncontrolled conditions, wild exaggerations, and a willingness to believe the unbelievable contributed to the stories. Fakirs have been shown to use tunnels to escape and live in comfort above ground until the time came to return. Another device used has been to be buried under or near a tree and to use hollow tree roots for air vents. Besides, there is a considerable amount of air in loose earth, so that if the burial takes place without a box or coffin, the air supply available to the fakir is grossly underestimated. Even a small, airtight container has more air than is usually believed necessary for survival. Two and one-half cubic feet of air are sufficient to keep a person alive for an hour if the person does not move. This amount is good for even longer periods if the person is a yogi who has learned the art of breath control. In July of 1926, the fakir Rahman Bey stayed a full hour in a metal box that was submerged in a swimming pool, then challenged Harry Houdini to duplicate his feat. Houdini, who did not believe trance or any occult powers were involved, experimented secretly on himself and found that the feat could indeed be performed without trickery or yoga. On August 5, 1926 Houdini was sealed in a galvanized iron box with a glass top and submerged to the bottom of the Shelton Hotel swimming pool in New York by 800 pounds of iron and the additional weight of eight swimmers. He stayed in the box for 90 minutes.

Asana or posture is the most obvious aspect of yoga practice (Fig. 3.4) The purpose of the posture is to place the body in a stable and comfortable position. The cross-legged position is one that comes easy to an Indian through cultural conditioning, but it is not required. Postures do have both a symbolic meaning and a magic function. The cross-legged lotus posture, for instance, is related to the lotus symbol in Hinduism and Buddhism. The lotus, like the human, has its roots in the mud (the physical), its blossom (head) in the air (the mental or spiritual), and its stem (middle portion, the viscera) in water (the emotional). The upright position of the spine is important in connection with the development of the *kundalini* power (see the following paragraph), the upturned palms receive an inflow of energy, and so on.

The development of occult powers is particularly associated with what is known as the raising of the *kundalini* fire. The *kundalini* fire is said to be an occult energy that resides at the base of the spine and is normally dormant. Located on the spinal cord are the seven (or eight) *chakras* or energy centers. These are identified by some with nerve ganglia that are also located on both sides of the spinal cord. The *kundalini* fire is said to rise from the lowest *chakra* at the base of the spine to the highest in the head and, in the process, to awaken the yogi to higher spiritual realities and confer occult powers. The rising is said to occur along three pathways, the *sushumna* (the spinal cord), the *ida* (lunar nerve or left ganglionic chain), and the *pingala* (solar nerve or the left ganglionic chain). The three are often pictured in a form that resembles the two serpents coiled around a winged staff, the symbol of medicine in the Western tradition.

Bharati (1976) avers that the physiological and anatomical correspondences are not the work of Hindu yogis, but are recent additions by Western occultists. Yogic instructions were prepared a long time ago when no one knew anything about the internal structure of a human being. Dissection ran counter to Indian cultural values, and it was not practiced even in medicine until relatively recent times. In addition, what the yogis do, according to Bharati, is not to concentrate on their own internal organs, but on an imagined body outside themselves, the *lingasarira*, which is given a very simple and schematic internal structure. The chakras are not nerve ganglia, but imaginary rungs or way stations on the imaginary ladder of the spine against which the practitioners check their progress. The whole process of razing the *kundalini* fire occurs only in imagination. The goal is, however, the exalted state of *samadhi*. Here is how one practitioner of *kundalini* yoga describes the *kundalini* experience (Krishna, 1971):

> The illumination grew brighter and brighter, the roaring louder. I experienced a rocking sensation and then felt myself slipping out of my body, entirely enveloped in a halo of light . . . I was no longer myself . . . a small point of awareness confined in a body, but instead was a vast circle of consciousness in which the body was but a point, bathed in light and in a state of exaltation and happiness impossible to describe [p. 61, 66]

Fig. 3.4. A yogi in the lotus posture. (From Behanan, 1959. Used by permission of Dover Publications, Inc.)

Note the similarity between this passage and Maya Deren's description of her possession by the goddess Erszulie earlier in this chapter. Fischer (1975) describes the *kundalini* experience as an instance of trophotropic arousal that rebounds to ergotropic arousal and an out-of-the-body experience. He also gives a physiological interpretation to a "bad" *kundalini* "trip" experienced by the same mystic, Gopi Krishna, as a result of which Krishna felt exhausted, extremely fatigued, apathetic, and with body heat regulation out of control. Krishna learned that if *kundalini* is raised through any other nerve but the *sushumna*, there was grave danger to health and even life, especially if the fire was raised through the *pingala* on the right side of the spine. Krishna then tried to concentrate on the *ida* on the left side of the spinal cord and imagine a cold current rising in it, in which he succeeded. Fischer (1975) notes that:

> many neurons of the heat-dissipating system are located in the anterior part of the hypothalamus, with their descending pathways passing down the brain stem in or near the central gray and setting up connections with respiratory and cardiovascular mechanisms of the brain stem and spinal cord. Localization of thermoregulation within a hemispheric site is not possible, because the relevant fibers are all crossed. But around the spinal cord the fibers are not yet crossed . . . Krishna's description allows us to speculate . . . that he indeed may have been able to reinstate thermoregulation after a bad Kundalini trip that was induced on the right side (spreading contralaterally into the left or dominant hemisphere). Since during ergotropic hyperarousal it is physiologically appropriate to spend significantly more "space" in the nondominant hemisphere . . . a Kundalini ecstasy with left-hemispheric predominance may have been the physiological factor involved in this bad trip [p. 229].

That yogis, lamas, and holy men living in the upper elevations of the Himalayas are able to control their body temperature to a degree that appears miraculous, such as standing naked for hours in subfreezing temperatures or meditating in caves with little or no clothing, has been alleged both in the occult literature and by travelers in those areas. It must be noted that walking barefoot on snow or ice is not, by itself, a sign that deliberate thermoregulation is taking place. It may be simply a matter of having a thick skin on the soles and being inured to low temperatures, as is the case with some of the South American Indians who live at high elevations. Some Tibetan Buddhists, however, have undertaken training in extreme asceticism with respect to cold. To graduate from such training, one undergoes such tests as sitting naked in the snow on a river bank and drying, by body heat alone, pieces of cotton dipped in the icy water. These ascetics claim that the ability to withstand cold is due to a mystical force called *tumo*. *Tumo* warms the semen and lets its energy circulate through the body through minute channels, the *tsas*, thus warming the entire body.

Although thermoregulation through *kundalini* yoga exercises may be beyond the ability of most, the regulation of skin temperature may be achieved in a relatively short time by most. Thermoregulation can be achieved through hypnosis, autogenic training, or biofeedback. There is no mystery or occult power involved, although it may appear so to the uninformed. As early as 1920, J. A. Hadfield of London University (Hadfield, 1920) was able to reduce the temperature of a suggestible subject's arm from 95° to 68°F by suggestion alone. More recently, Maslach, Marshall, and Zimbardo (1972) trained college students to concentrate, under hypnosis, on the skin temperature in their hands, and were able to produce temperature changes than ran in opposite directions in the two hands simultaneously and were of the order of some 5°F. Autogenic training (Luthe, 1969-1973), which is a form of autosuggestion, enables one to raise the temperature of the hands by 9°F in only 10 minutes (Surwit, 1978). In biofeedback training, the trainee is provided current and continuous information on the course of a physiological process, such as skin temperature, which the trainee attempts to influence by mental activity alone. Biofeedback training also leads to substantial changes in skin temperature (e.g., Keefe, 1978).

Biofeedback is a technique that came into prominence in the 1960s. It had been almost an article of faith among psychologists that processes under the control of the autonomic nervous system were not susceptible to training with the usual reinforcement techniques. This opinion was held in the face of the well-known fact that everyone learns routinely to control the sphincter muscles (which control waste material elimination) and that sexual responses, such as penile erection, can also be influenced by voluntary mental activity. It has now been demonstrated in numerous experiments that, if an autonomic process is continually monitored and the monitoring is presented to the subject so that the subject is continually informed of the response that his or her body makes to any mentation that is engaged in to modify the response, such as particular thoughts or mental images, one can learn to control a variety of such autonomic responses: perspiration, dilation and contraction of skin capillaries (temperature control), blood pressure, heart rate, or brain-wave patterns. It is not absolutely necessary that the learner be attached to any sophisticated electronic device that provides the feedback information. Individuals differ widely on how sensitive they are to their own internal processes, and some individuals are by nature quite sensitive in this respect. If a vegetative process is made the subject of a meditative technique, one can learn to become more sensitive to it without any special feedback apparatus. This is what lies behind some of the rather amazing demonstrations of control over bodily processes by the hatha yogis. Hatha yoga is a yogic discipline in which self-development is furthered by developing complete physical control of the body. Stupendous hatha yoga feats, such as the reversal of the peristaltic motion of the lower end of the gastrointestinal tract, are only the result of gaining control of a function that is controlled by the autonomic nervous system by means whose essence is illustrated by the biofeedback procedure.

One of the bodily functions that is normally not under voluntary control but can be brought under such control is the heart rate. It can be slowed down considerably below the normal rate, for instance. Claims to the contrary notwithstanding, the heart cannot be stopped completely. The yogi can diminish the strength of the wrist pulse, yet the EKG shows that the heart continues beating at the normal rate. Anyone claiming to be able to stop his or her heart completely should be examined for the presence of hard rubber balls in the armpits: Pressing the arm down on such a ball will make the wrist pulse imperceptible.

Levitation is one *siddhi* that the yogi is said to acquire. There have been no bona fide demonstrations of a human body floating unsuspended in midair. Even those who, instead of the air, have sought the support of the somewhat denser medium of water, have failed. The magician Milbourne Christopher (1970) describes one attempt to walk on water that he himself witnessed:

> In 1966 . . . the newspapers announced that Lakshamanasandra Srikanta Rao, a hatha yogi who in the past had eaten nails, needles, razor blades, and glass, and who had walked on fire, would walk on water in Bombay. Some of the five thousand spectators paid as much as $70 for the choicest seats. An oblong concrete tank, twenty feet long and six feet wide, had been built for the occasion and filled with water. The white-bearded mystic ascended the steps to the edge of the basin. There he paused and prayed. With complete confidence he stepped on the surface of the water. As the huge audience gasped, Rao sank immediately to the bottom [p. 249-250].

It is clear that Lakshamanasandra Srikanta Rao not only failed the water-walking test as such, but also the pragmatic test of the reality of his inner certainty. What has been demonstrated is that at some point in the course of relaxation, such as is involved in progressing to the deeper levels of meditation, a feeling of lightness or of floating may be experienced. Of a group of 30 subjects studied by Horton (1918-19), eight reported illusions of levitation. One of them even had to hold on to her chair for fear of floating away, and another jumped up and discontinued the exercise because of the powerful impression of soaring.

The illusion of levitation is a standard act of stage magic. It was introduced on Western stages from the Orient in the early 19th century. The trick consists in making the actual means of support invisible to the spectators. The means is a rod or a narrow bracket that faces the spectators end-on and blends with the background in shape and color. Figure 3.5 is a photograph taken in 1936 by *Illustrated London News* of a levitation act performed in the open. An iron rod is fastened in the ground. It rises, draped by a piece of cloth, to the level of the fakir's hand, where it makes a right angle and enters his clothing, providing an invisible means of support. The trick is easier to accomplish on a stage because the supports are easier to conceal. Also, the support can be suspended from the ceiling, which cannot be done outdoors. Most importantly, the spectator is confined to a single point of view, that of a seat. This, in combination with the camouflaging, makes for a rather two-dimensional appearance of the entire stage, so that the trickery that goes on in the third dimension is not easily detected.

Fig. 3.5. A yogi in the lotus posture. (From Behanan, 1959. Used by permission of Dover Publications, Inc.).

Recently, students of Transcendental Meditation taught by Maharishi Mahesh Yogi, the most popular yoga movement in America, that up to that time had stressed the non-religious, non-occult aspect of meditation and its use to achieve peace of mind, stability, and efficiency, were offered the chance to learn how to levitate (at the cost of over $1000). Photographs taken of those who had allegedly mastered this skill (live demonstrations have not been offered) showed them sitting cross-legged a few inches off the floor. An analysis of the photographs shows that they were taken while the subjects had propelled themselves upward momentarily, using their hands. Maharishi has also offered to teach invisibility (for an additional fee), forbidding, however, public demonstrations of the feat. Videotape recordings (supplied by Maharishi) of fading persons notwithstanding, the yogic *siddhi* of invisibility must be relegated to the same category of beliefs as the one that comprises the Emperor's new clothes.

At the core of the Oriental levitation and other myths is a cultural factor that is not recognized by those who, in the West, have accepted the trappings of Oriental mysticism without becoming familiar with its cultural and linguistic conventions. Agehananda Bharati, the Austrian-Hindu mystic mentioned earlier, tells of his once hearing of an Indian mystic who allegedly levitated at night on a regular basis (Bharati, 1976). He decided to see it for himself. He and some 50 people sat through a good part of the night waiting for the swami to levitate, but nothing happened and he fell asleep. In the morning, others who Bharati had noticed had also fallen asleep, asked him how he had liked the swami's levitation this time. The swami was said to have levitated at least 4 yards above the ground from sunset to sunrise. Because Bharati had not seen him do it, he was somewhat upset. It was not until some time later that he realized that statements about levitation and other demonstrations of unusual powers are not statements of fact, but statements made by adherents and believers from within the swami's ingroup as part of their confession of their belief in him. Levitation, omniscience, and magic powers are ascribed by the devotees to the saint. Empirical demonstrations have no place in this scheme of things, and objections from someone who fails to see the man rise 4 feet in the air are met by the irrefutable argument that the observer is not pure enough, spiritually advanced enough, or that he is simply preventing himself from witnessing the marvels by his disbelief. In the West, this type of argument is a familiar one in the area of parapsychology: Disbelief on the part of the researcher interferes with the manifestations of extrasensory perception in the research subject. When Bharati met the same swami a year later, under different circumstances, and was able to talk to him alone, the swami stated quite seriously that he neither levitated nor performed any of the other feats ascribed to him (Bharati, 1976): "It is the *bhaktas* (devotees) who say these things [p. 107]," he said.

Transcendental Meditation centers on the repetition of a word, the mantram (a magic formula or invocation), which is given individually to each meditator who enrolls in a Transcendental Meditation course and which may not be revealed to anyone else. The occult aspect of the mantram is that it is supposed to set up beneficial vibrations, or, in the case of a personalized mantram, resonate with the meditator's true being, thus facilitating the achievement of the goal of meditation. A very well-known non-secret mantram is "aum" or "om." The occultists have a most detailed explanation of how each sound in that word is related to the various planes of existence, the soul, and so on. To use a mantram is to use a creative force, to engage in white magic. It is not unreasonable to assume that the beneficial effects of an individual mantram, if any, would arise, first, from the meditator's knowledge that it is secret and that it is his or her own and, second, from the principle of cognitive dissonance reduction. An investment of over $100 to obtain an individual mantram constitutes not only a monetary, but also a heavy psychological, investment. One does one's best to make sure that the mantram works or, rather, that any dissonance created by the realization of the discrepancy between the amount of money invested and the results obtained be minimized. For instance, the motivation of the meditator may be strengthened by the monetary payment, leading to better meditation results than would have been achieved without it.

The conclusion that can be drawn from the discussion of yoga and the occult is that there is no need to invoke magic or paranormal powers to account for the yogic phenomena. The traditional belief that occult powers are conferred on the diligent practitioner of meditative techniques arises from the meditator's subjective experiences during meditation. Once the meditator has allowed that he or she has acquired such powers and makes statements to that effect, these powers will be ascribed to him or her by force of cultural tradition. Such a tradition could very well have begun when one or more of the alleged powers was confirmed, for instance, by a prediction coming true, although in an entirely coincidental fashion. The belief is further reinforced by those who, after having progressed some distance on their way to self-development, drop out and begin to exploit the fascination of the public with the uncanny and the occult for their own profit and satisfaction, as by exhibiting the fruits of yogic training—breath control or pain endurance, for instance.

The use of the skills acquired in yogic practice brings up the question of ecstasy and morality and of the relationship of these two to yoga and mysticism. Occultists insist that the "misuse" of occult powers, such as exhibitionism or their use for selfish ends, will degrade the individual who so misuses them and will even lead to their loss. This in spite of their belief in the existence of black magicians, who by definition are using occult powers for selfish purposes. The assumption is made that, because yogis, swamis, and gurus all appear to be "good" and saintly persons, their goodness and saintliness is the result of their yogic and mystical practices, one consequence of which is also the acquisition of paranormal abilities, and that the use of such abilities for selfish purposes is tantamount to denying the validity of all of one's previous efforts. The fact is that there is no necessary connection between ecstatic experiences, *samadhi*, and morality. This point is made forcibly by Bharati (1976). He stresses that the sum and substance of mysticism is to achieve the exalted state and to do so repeatedly. Having achieved this state, however, does not imply that the individual is also made a better person. He or she may be, or he or she may not be. Chances are that, to begin with, it will be the moral person who will engage in meditation. If that person is not moral, it is possible that the exalted state may indeed also exalt him or her morally. On the other hand, if a morally reprehensible person achieves ecstasy, he or she may still be a morally reprehensible person after the experience; Bharati cites examples of mystics who, in spite of apparently having had ecstatic experiences, are not very admirable persons. It was mentioned earlier that Bharati makes the point that the experiences of exalted states and of orgasm are in some ways comparable. What the individual does between any two such experiences has much more to do with that person's morality: He or she may become a saint or turn criminal between two *samadhis* or orgasms, but these in themselves have nothing to do with his or her behavior. Like any experience of achievement in any area of life, the ecstatic experience may engender some changes in a person's behavior towards others, but, otherwise, it does not lead to (Bharati, 1976): "moral splendor, scientific grandeur in the mystic, or any extra-mystical excellence [p. 99]."

This notion is particularly underscored by the fact that the ecstatic and meditative states may be brought about by means other than yogic exercises, for instance, certain drugs. Bharati (as well as Fischer and others) feel that there is no qualitative difference among these states, regardless of the particular means employed to achieve them. What does vary is the specific content of these experiences. The content depends entirely on the particular setting, environment, circumstances, and belief system within which the experience occurs. The object of the mystic union will be God, Christ, Brahma, Shakti, Krishna, or any other idea that is dictated by the mystic's cultural experience. Given this, the acquisition and use of the *siddhis*, regardless of whether they are deemed to be real or not, is not particularly related to the moral status of the mystic.

NOTES

Good explanations of pain and of the factors that modify the pain experience are to be found in Arehart-Treichel (1978) and Melzack (1961). The best recent reference on pain that brings pain in relation to anomalistic psychology is Hilgard and Hilgard (1975). It considers both the nature of pain and its control through hypnosis and acupuncture.

Acupuncture, complete with charts of the meridians and acupuncture points, is presented by a practicing Western physician in Moss (1964). There is a good analysis of the placebo effect in Chapter 4 of Frank (1961), and Chaves and Barber (1976) review the existing literature on the use of hypnosis and acupuncture in surgery. Some of the literature for and against the gate-control theory of pain is listed on page 46 of Hilgard and Hilgard (1975).

An informative and enjoyable account of fire walking may be found in Milbourne Christopher's 1970 book on the natural history of the occult. One of its chapters is a likewise enlightening account of burial alive.

The foremost representatives of the newly established field of the psychology of consciousness are Robert Ornstein, who has written a text in this area (Ornstein, 1972), edited a book of readings (Ornstein, 1973), and composed what is probably the first monograph on the psychology of meditation (Naranjo & Ornstein, 1971); and Charles Tart, who stresses altered states of consciousness (Tart, 1969) and has done considerable experimental work on marijuana intoxication and in parapsychology.

Even though it was first published in 1937, Behanan's book on yoga (Behanan, 1959) is still the best exposition of yoga. Himself a practitioner of yoga, Behanan presents the yoga philosophy and practices for their intrinsic worth, stripped of supernatural claims. An extensive review of physiological studies of yogis and meditators may be found in Funderburk (1977).

William Sargant's (1959) work on religious conversion, political brainwashing, and their physiology in terms of Pavlov's concept of transmarginal inhibition is an excellent and unique presentation of this material. There are references to the phases of inhibition throughout the various papers, lectures, and open letters in Pavlov (1941), the amplest being in an open letter to Pierre Janet.

John Wesley's *Journal* (Wesley, 1872-78) is a fund of first-hand information about religious conversions. Although religious conversion is also a contemporary phenomenon, there is not much documentation of it that is comparable to Wesley's *Journal*.

Agehananda Bharati's view of mysticism (Bharati, 1976) is like a breath of fresh air taken after emerging from the sultry, sticky atmosphere of traditional writings on mysticism. Bharati's qualifications are a unique blend of being born a European, being a member of a Hindu monastic order and a practitioner of Tantric yoga, a thorough knowledge of Sanskrit, and academic training in anthropology and experience as a professor of anthropology in America.

Evelyn Underhill's book on mysticism (1955) is probably cited more often by both occult and academic writers than any other contemporary work on the subject. The doctoral dissertations of Berkowitz (1977) and L. J. Scott (1977) may be cited as examples of psychological research on the effects of meditation on self-experience.

On the fraud aspect of Maharishi's levitation program, see Randi (1977).

4 Perception and the Paranormal

Things are not always what they seem.
Phaedrus: Fables IV.ii.

In a 1978 episode of the NBC television show, *Project UFO*, the witness to a UFO landing is taken to see a psychologist, not for therapy, but to be shown that the senses can be deceived. He is given a demonstration of the autokinetic illusion (the apparent movement of a stationary spot of light in a dark room) and of the vertical-horizontal illusion. The witness remains unconvinced that what he saw was only an illusion, as well he might be. Although these two phenomena do demonstrate that our senses sometimes play tricks on us, they are in no way directly relevant to seeing a complex flying machine in all detail, and the psychologist's attempt must have appeared pathetic to many viewers of the show. To point out that what we see does not always correspond to what there is to see objectively is one thing. To relate this fact to the witnessing of UFO's, ghosts, or miracles is another. This cannot always be done. Nevertheless, misperception does play a significant role in extraordinary phenomena, and a look at the perceptual process helps to shed light on some aspects of extraordinary phenomena.

PERCEPTION AS INFORMATION PROCESSING

We approach perception and misperception from the information-processing point of view. From this point of view, *perception* is the process whereby individuals extract information from their environment. *Information)* is anything that reduces uncertainty. It is contained in any kind of stimulus that produces a response or adaptive action in the individual. A *stimulus* is energy change, or patterned energy, at a sense organ. We first remind ourselves of how psychology views the perceiving individual or organism (O) in relationship to information-bearing energy or stimulation (S) and the individual's behavior or response (R) to stimulation. Stimuli act upon organisms, organisms respond to stimuli. Light shines in the eye of the child, the pupil of the child's eye contracts. The driver of a car sees a certain light turn from yellow to green and he or she applies a foot to the brakes of the automobile. A psychologist's client looks at an inkblot and says that it reminds him or her of a dead, dry bat that has been flattened by a truck. The S-O-R formulation states not only that stimuli act on organisms who produce responses, but also that the relationship between stimulus and response is mediated by the organism, or that the organism has its own contribution to make to the S-O-R relationship, which might make it less than direct and straightforward. This, indeed, is the case in all instances of perception. We are concerned primarily with the description of the contribution of the O to the S-R relationship. This contribution is in the nature of a variety of internal states and processes within the organism that make for a relationship between stimulus and response that is far different from what it would be if the sense organs were connected to the muscles and glands in a straight and direct manner, in the way wires connect two telephones. "There is many a slip 'twixt the cup and the lip"—that is, beteen the stimulus cup and the response lip, and this is what leads to misperception. We now examine briefly the way in which psychologists have modeled this "slipping" that occurs between stimulus and response in the course of perception.

Several different models have been proposed to describe the internal processing of information in perception. They may be all considered variants of D. E. Broadbent's (1958) model. Broadbent, a British psychologist, was responsible for putting attention back in psychology after decades of neglect. The details of the models differ, but we are not concerned with a comparative evaluation of these models. The communalities of these models are more impressive than their differences.

Their first common feature is that several different stages or phases in the perceptual process are assumed. It is also assumed that these stages follow each other in time or else are ordered from hierarchically lower stages to those higher in the hierarchy. A second common feature is that there is incorporated somewhere one or several feedback loops. Linear models—that is, models in which one stage in the perceptual process is assumed to follow another in a direct, undeviating fashion—have been found inadequate to cope with a number of important perceptual phenomena. Feedback loops that shunt information from the mainline unto a side line or temporary storage, backward towards an earlier stage, or forward to a later stage so that mainline processing is modified before the first response occurs are able to handle the explanation of these phenomena and have become in-

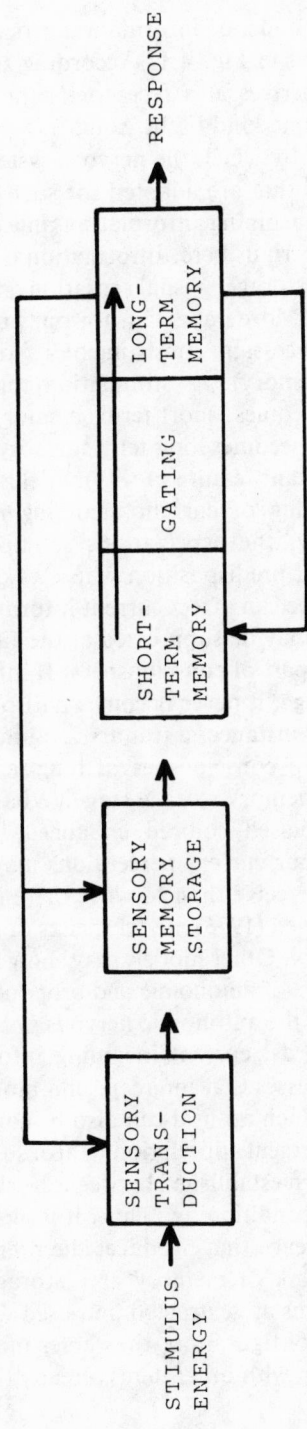

Fig. 4.1. Information-processing model of perception. (After Forgus & Melamed, 1976. Used with permission of McGraw-Hill Book Company.)

93

dispensable. A current model of information processing within the central nervous system is shown in Fig. 4.1. According to this model, patterned stimulus energy, as it arrives at a receptor (sense organ), is immediately modified, as energy of one kind (light, sound) is transformed into another (electro-chemical energy by which the nervous system operates) by the sensory transducers or cells that are adapted for such energy transformation. This preprocesssing of incoming information and the associated losses of information do not concern us here. Information is next stored, very briefly, in a sensory memory storage. Visual sensations, for instance, outlast the stimulus for this reason. More important for our purposes are the next two stages of information processing, consisting of a short-term and a long-term information storage (memory). As stimulation continues, information in the sensory register becomes short-term memory that lasts about 30 seconds. If rehearsed, it becomes long-term memory of indefinite duration.

To us, the most important feature of this model is the effect of long-term memory on the processing of current incoming information. What the perceiver knows already, the expectations set up by repeated past experiences, or any kind of predisposition whose essence is memory that incorporates past experience can affect current information processing *at any one point*. Information may be suppressed at the first point of processing, so that it never becomes part of consciousness. If information is suppressed in sensory memory storage, it never becomes part of conscious experience. It is easy to see how, for instance, a traumatic stimulus may be suppressed and never become part of consciousness if long-term memory control intervenes at the sensory memory-storage stage. What is added to long-term memory is in some way biased, colored, enhanced, impoverished, or otherwise modified. In fact, our current perceptions may correspoond more to what we would like to perceive than to what there is to perceive.

The Forgus and Melamed (1976) model speaks of information and information storage or memory. Other models may show feedback loops that are thought to be in the nature of autonomic and proprioceptive arousal—that is, stimulation coming from the autonomic nervous system and from the internal organs. In other words, current incoming information is thought to arouse unconscious processes that intercept and modify that mainline processing of information. Such arousal can also be conceived to be the result of past experience. For present stimulation to arouse emotional responses, a connection must have been established between the stimulus and the arousal in the past by means of conditioning. Thus, it is again memory (albeit unconscious) of past experience that produces the present state of arousal.

We usually do not think of memory as a storage bin from which individual unconnected items are extracted and used. The items are recorded in memory in a certain configuration, they enter memory storage to make up a certain configuration with other items already there, and are extracted for use in these configurations. In other words, learning and thinking are inextricably involved in the perceptual process. *Learning* refers to changes in behavior of considerable duration that are due to experience. Because learning involves sensory stimulation, the basis for learning is perceptual and involves some minimum amount of information processed. *Thinking* is symbolic problem solving. When we manipulate symbolically coded information about objects and events (rather than the objects or events themselves) in order to solve a problem, we are thinking. Thinking presupposes learning, but thinking is also often involved in the perceptual process: We may not only perceive but also think about what we perceive. As a result, our percepts are modified. Thus, although stimulation leads to perception, which leads to learning, and learning leads to thinking, thinking in turn may affect the way we learn, learning modifies the organism through memory, and the modified organism may affect the perception of stimuli.

For the purpose of discussing misperception as an element of extraordinary phenomena, we divide the perceptual process into stages, not in order to model the possible neural mechanisms responsible for it but only for the purpose of providing headings under which to subsume related events. These stages are: attention, expectancy, and decision making. The labels of the stages are arbitrary and their number a matter of convenience. More stages and both similar and different labels have been used by others. Our concern is more with the reality of the events described than with modeling the flow of information within the perceiver.

ATTENTION

For a stimulus to be perceived, it must be attended to. As an aspect of perception, attention may be compared to a searchlight that perpetually scans the environment and picks out some feature or another of it, one at a time. A characteristic of attention is that it, like a searchlight, can focus on only one thing at a time. The impression that we may be attending to several different things simultaneously comes from our ability to shift attention rapidly from one object to the next so that the transition is not noticed and we seem to be taking in a lot of different things at the same time.

What makes us select one object over another, pay attention to one but not another feature of an object or event? The *determinants of attention* are external and internal. The *external determinants of attention* are stimulus properties that attract attention automatically, without learning. Thus, the newborn child's attention is first attracted by movement and contrast (such as between dark and light areas, colors, or sizes), later on by change and novelty, and, towards the end of the first year, by "interesting" things that make the child wonder what they might be. Attention elicited by these factors used to be called involuntary, which was contrasted with voluntary or directed attention. This distinction is not very useful. "Voluntary" attention may not be so voluntary after all because, while directing our attention to an object, we may be entirely unaware that we are doing so. The main distinction between the two kinds of attention is that directed attention is determined by internal, rather than external, factors. These bear a variety of names: interest, motivation, predisposition, set, past experience, cultural bias, perceptual selectivity, and others. These have the greatest interest to us in connection with the perception of extraordinary events.

Absentmindedness and Concentration

We begin with an anomaly of attention that is quite familiar and hardly qualifies as anything "extraordinary." Although absent-minded professors are the exception rather than the rule, the stereotype of the bushy-haired, bespectacled professor dressed in tweeds who mumbles to himself as he carries a sack of trash to his office, having deposited his briefcase in the garbage can, is a very familiar one. The problem that the professor has, however, is not that his attention is habitually scattered. On the contrary, he is able to concentrate his attention exceedingly well. The object of his attention is something internal, a thought, a problem. On this, the absent minded professor concentrates a very narrow and a very intense beam of his attention, and both the scope and intensity of his attention to external things and events, especially those that he considers distractions, are quite reduced. At any rate, to the ordinary observer, the professor's behavior will appear amusing. It will also appear to be highly anomalous.

We do not need to take any additional steps, only a different kind of person, a person with a different set of values and motives, to observe what is virtually the same phenomenon except that it would never be called absentmindedness. Instead, it may be called *concentration*, and it may be associated with such practices as meditation and contemplation. Although some esoteric schools that cater to Western customs, tastes, and habits of thought insist that concentration is not essential and that it is all right to get distracted, most traditional esoteric systems that advocate meditation or contemplation emphasize the need of concentrated attention on the subject of meditation, if meditation is to succeed. Training manuals are written in which concentration exercises are described for the pupil to practice, so that the scope of his or her attention is reduced and its intensity is enhanced to the exclusion of everything else. In the training exercises, the subject matter may be a very mundane thing, a match box, for instance, yet even here the aim is to achieve oneness with the subject, to become it, so that it can be perfectly understood. In both yoga and Christian mysticism, the goal of meditation and contemplation is union with godhead.

Can one train one's attention to the point where, at will, one can become completely absorbed in a subject, understand it perfectly, so that one may indeed be said to have become one with it? Perhaps. The question that is raised by the psychologist, however, is whether it is training that leads to this desirable state of affairs. The reason why the term concentration is hardly ever mentioned in contemporary textbooks of introductory psychology is that, first, concentration is one form of attention, and attention itself was off the books for a good number of years because it had been treated extensively earlier (in the 19th century) by psychologists who relied on self-observation. Because this method produced no great results, both the technique and the subject appeared fruitless to the behavioristically oriented psychologists of the first half of this century. Attention was reintroduced in the textbooks in the 1950s, soon after researchers were able to show that a specific neural mechanism underlay it, and thus made it amenable to nonintrospective experimentation. The second reason is that concentration has been thought to be simply a function of motivation. The old adage about chess playing improving one's concentration was shown to be true—in the reverse. It is not chess playing that enables one to concentrate; only those who can concentrate will play chess. But why should some concentrators play chess and not others? The answer is that some are interested in playing chess or, more generally, are motivated to do so, and motives of this sort are generally learned. In other words, one learns to play chess, finds it rewarding, continues playing it, and, in the process, proceeds to show the picture of concentration that so characterizes chess players. It is no doubt true that one can learn to direct one's thinking so that it would be more apt to stay on a given subject, but underlying this process there must be interest or motivation to engage in the exercise in the first place. The classic complaint of the college student, "I just don't seem to be able to concentrate on my math," is most often due to a lack of interest on the part of the student—there is no motivation in the student to learn it.

In some contemplative belief systems, concentration plays a very important role. In fact, it may be given the role of the ultimate foundation of existence. George Berkeley, the 18th-century English bishop and philosopher, guaranteed the reality of a world "out there" because a Permanent Perceiver, God, was constantly perceiving it, thus ensuring its reality in spite of the fact that mere humans could only register their sense impressions and could never know by their own powers whether their perceptions were anything more than an illusion. Berkeley did not speculate on the possibility and the consequences of God's attention wavering, however slightly. Others have. Lewis Carroll repeated the Berkeleyan argument in an oft-quoted exchange between the Tweedle brothers and Alice in *Through the Looking Glass* (Carroll, 1960). Alice, says Tweedledee, is "only a sort of thing" in the Red King's dream. "If that there King was to awake," adds Tweedledum, "you'd go out—bang!—just like a candle! [Ch. 4]" In some esoteric belief systems, it is said that the world exists only because a supreme being is constantly creating it by keeping every minute detail of it in the focus of its unfaltering attention. Should the concentration of this supreme being falter, at least part of the universe would disappear instantaneously. This, of course, is an article of faith, and not subject to proof or disproof. What can be demonstrated is that when people concentrate completely on an object and thereby fail to deploy their attention to other objects, their perception of the total situation will suffer. This is not unlike the case of the absent-minded professor. If the observers happen to be highly interested in some unusual sight, such as a presumed strange flying object, their report of what they saw may fail to reflect the presence of clues in the environment that might have told them that what they saw was, say, the reflected glare of automobile headlights rather than an alien spaceship. The technique of attracting the spectators' attention to some interesting or conspicuous feature of the magic act in order to divert their attention from another, less conspicuous but crucial one is the main principle of stage magic, and is called misdirection. The proposition that concentrated attention on one item impairs attention to others has been demonstrated experimentally. As an illustration, the experiment of Erdelyi and Appelbaum (1973) may be cited: members of a Jewish organization failed to notice a number of neutral stimuli if among them were placed either the star of David or the swastika.

The Time-Gap Experience

Our routine activities, even very complex ones, tend to become automatic. One such activity, for instance, is driving. Those who drive themselves to and from work along the same route, day after day, year after year, find themselves slipping into reverie, daydreams, or problem solving while driving along the accustomed route. They avoid obstacles, stop and go at stoplights, and otherwise perform all routine driving activities while being mentally "somewhere else." They may "wake up" with a jolt after a mile or two and realize that they have driven all this distance without having been aware of doing so. It may be a frightening experience, first, because of the danger involved, and second, because the time that it took to drive the distance seems to be lost.

The experience of time is an entirely subjective phenomenon. We have no sense organs to register the passage of time. Time is measured by the passage of events, which means that the driver in the foregoing example has been unaware of the events that happened between two points in the route. To be exact, part of the driver was aware of the pertinent objects and events or else he or she would not have been able to navigate the distance successfully. On the other hand, his or her self-conscious self was engaged "elsewhere" and was not aware of all these things. In other words, the driver was paying attention to some image or thought totally unrelated to driving, allowing those portions of the nervous system that normally do not register very clearly in consciousness to take care of the driving.

How is this related to extraordinary phenomena? Witnesses to extraordinary phenomena, real or hallucinated, are often called upon to relate the events leading to and following the phenomenon, as well as those that happened at the same time. If the phenomenon has absorbed all of the witnesses' attention, their accounts may be quite distorted because they may omit important events surrounding the event. They may deny that these events ever happened, even when confronted with contrary evidence, because to them, they never did. Yet, these events may be such as to throw a very different light on the nature of the phenomenon that to the witness appeared to be so extraordinary.

Selective Attention

The capacity of the nervous system to process information is limited. It therefore acts selectively to admit some and to exclude other information. How this happens, what the mechanisms involved might be are questions that are being actively investigated by many researchers. Although we have learned a lot about selectivity in attention, a lot more remains to be learned.

We already touched upon models of perception. The question of attentional selectivity is but one aspect of modeling the perceptual system: Is it a matter of reduction of informational pathways from the sense organs to the brain? Are there neural filters that filter out surplus or unwanted information? Where are they located and how are they tuned? We do not try to review the literature on the subject, which is very large indeed. For our purposes, it is sufficient to know that innumerable experiments have established the fact that a phenomenon does take place that, for a lack of a better term, may be described as selectivity, tuning in, selective perception, or filtering. We know about some of the conditions that lead to a person's picking out a particular feature of stimulation and ignoring others. Some of the conditions pertain to the stimulus and may be described as physical or mechanical. Selectivity, however, also has very much to do with meaning, which makes it so much more difficult to model the perceptual process. Meaning resides in the perceiver. How does it happen that the meaning of a message may be used by the perceiver to filter it out so that it is actually not perceived? To explain this phenomenon, the most often resorted-to explanatory mechanism is the feedback feature of the perceptual process discussed earlier. This kind of selective filtering is most relevant in connection with the psychology of the extraordinary, regardless of which particular model of attentional selectivity we may want to subscribe to.

Around 1947, the so-called New-Look in perception arose, stimulated by the experimental work of a few psychologists, among whom Jerome Bruner and Leo Postman were the most prominent ones. The main contribution of the New-Look psychologists was to show experimentally that internal determinants, such as needs, values, motives, and emotions, affected our perceptions. They showed, for instance, that hunger would make a person see food objects in vague pictures (Levine, Chein, & Murphy, 1942), that being poor made you see coins larger than they actually are (Bruner & Goodman, 1947), that valued words had lower recognition thresholds than neutral ones (Postman, Bruner, & McGinnies, 1948), that in reversible figure-ground configurations, the rewarded portions were perceived as figure an punished ones as ground (Schafer & Murphy, 1943), and that taboo words had higher recognition thresholds than neutral words (McGinnies, 1949). Many additional studies have been performed since the original ones. Some of the findings have been negative or at least debatable. The phenomenon of selective attention remains firmly established nevertheless.

One of the most controversial areas of New-Look research concerned the changed recognition thresholds for words with an emotional or value investment. Before Broadbent (1958) proposed his model of perception, a pre-perceiver or censor had to be postulated to account for the word-threshold phenomenon, and psychology does not take kindly to little men sitting in people's heads doing things that the hosts are not aware of. The combination of perceptual feedback loops and of learning and reinforcement enabled psychologists to maintain the existence of the word-threshold phenomenon and to provide an acceptable explanation of it (cf. Eriksen, 1951a, 1951b, 1954). To invoke the learning concept, for instance, words that pertain to a person's value area will tend to be read and heard by that person not only more often but also under reinforcing conditions. This leads to that person's showing lower recognition thresholds for such words. Stated otherwise, these words acquire the ability of attracting the person's attention more readily. The valued word stands out like a figure against the ground of non-valued words. Thus, words, sounds, pictures, symbols, or anything else that a person values will tend to be selected, perceived, and emphasized, and other items of information, especially those that are undervalued or disliked, will be slighted or ignored.

In Chapter 7, we describe selectivity in information pickup caused by beliefs. The selectivity is quite literal and physical; if the information is such that it might clash with a person's beliefs, causing anxiety, the person's perceptual filtering system may quite literally prevent that person from picking up the information. The person is "biased" not only in the social-psychological sense, but also in the technical sense of, say, a biased electronic tuning system. In practice, this results in the occasional very frustrating experience of debating a person who hears and remembers only what that person wants to hear and remember. Given the same information, two people, one a believer the other a nonbeliever, may interpret it in two diametrically opposed ways because some of the information has been selectively and effectively filtered out.

Negatively valued objects and events will not always or necessarily be pushed into the background or suppressed. It depends on the role the object or event plays in the individual's belief systems. Some features of the environment, although undervalued, may actually be accentuated by an individual because accentuating or discriminating such features serves to support the belief systems. Thus, it is a well-known phenomenon that racially prejudiced individuals are better able to discriminate racial features (Semitic, Negroid) than can unprejudiced individuals. They also exaggerate the differences between Whites and Orientals or Whites and Blacks, for example, if they are prejudiced against these racial groups. This has been demonstrated in a number of studies (e.g., Secord, Bevan, & Katz, 1956). This feature of social perception is most pertinent to the case of witnesses' descriptions of the physical appearance of the occupants of UFOs. Such descriptions, although conveying little information about the occupants, may speak volumes about the witnesses' bias, prejudices, and attitudes.

Fatigue, Drugs, Abnormal States, and Attention

The inability to concentrate when very tired is well-known to any student who has been trying to burn midnight oil over half-a-dozen textbooks in preparation for several examinations the next day. Attention wanders away from the figure of the textbook to sundry items in the perceptual ground—the hardness of the chair, the discomfort of bodily posture, the itch under the left shoulder blade, the noisy crickets outside—that now vie with the textbook as perceptual figures worthy of at least as much attention. As in the case of stimulus overload (Chapter 2), the fatigued individual is also more susceptible to suggestions and hallucinations. Hallucinated scenes may become the perceptual figure to the fatigued individual. For these reasons, care must be taken by interviewers in establishing whether their informants, witnesses to some extraordinary event, were fatigued at the time of the event.

Hallucinogenic drugs, such as LSD and mescaline, are known to enhance perceptual processes. Reports from people taking these drugs speak of extremely vivid ("psychedelic") colors, colorful, flowing geometric patterns, enhanced textures, louder noises, more beautiful music, a reduction in concern for pain, and a drastic slowdown in the experience of time. These are only some of the perceptual changes brought about by these drugs. Hallucinations, a direct consequence of taking hallucinogenic drugs, are discussed in Chapter 5.

In a way, it appears if the drug taker's ability to concentrate has been heightened, and things appear in their real values, free from the vagaries of a wandering attention. Actually, the person under the influence of LSD, for example, finds it difficult to concentrate. It is very difficult to administer an intelligence test during a hallucinogenic episode because the subject finds the taking of the test very unmotivating. The drug's action seems to be one of lending the quality of a first experience and the clarity and vividness that comes with novelty of sensory impressions. This quality of novelty is so absorbing that there is a great reluctance to pay attention to concurrent external events. The sensory enhancement effect is not one of concentrated attention, but rather the result of an impairment of the nervous filtering system, which no longer serves the function of selecting and attenuating sensory input, but allows a much larger amount of unchecked signals to pass unhindered.

Some types of schizophrenia have a biochemical basis, and there is considerable similarity between the hallucinatory states produced by drugs and those occurring in schizophrenia. For instance, there is the experience of increased intensity of sensations in schizophrenia. This is coupled with inability to pay consistent attention to any one item of experience. The separation of the relevant from the irrelevant, figure and ground, becomes more difficult. There is ample experimental evidence that attests to the fact that schizophrenics are more distractible than normals in the performance of various tasks. It goes without saying that reports of people about extraordinary experiences cannot, in general, be accepted if these people are known to have been under the influence of drugs or to suffer from one of the more severe forms of mental disorder. One of the main reasons for this is not that such individuals are temporarily "crazy," but because the attention aspect of their perceptual processes is impaired to an extent that their observations are no longer reliable.

EXPECTANCY

Paying attention to some item of the environment does not guarantee that it will be perceived correctly. One reason is that we have certain expectations concerning environmental objects and events, and these expectations may modify and distort perception. Stress and high expectations sometimes combine to render even an expert observer vulnerable to perceptual distortions. For instance, on March 3, 1968, a mature woman with an earned Ph.D. degree and engaged as a science teacher saw what she thought were three luminous UFOs flying in formation. She observed them with a pair of binoculars and later gave a detailed report on her sighting to the U. S. Air Force; her description included the characterization of the UFOs as "inverted saucers." It was determined later that the sighting coincided with the time that a Soviet space satellite booster rocket had entered the atmosphere, had burned and broken down into fragments. An independent observer who had also seen the fragments thought that the trajectories of the objects were such as to indicate intelligent control. The woman science teacher was deeply interested in UFOs, had seen one several years earlier, and carried a binocular on her walks in anticipation of a repeated sighting (Klass, 1974).

In general, expectancies serve a very useful purpose. By and large, objects and events behave in predictable ways. We come to expect them to continue behaving in these ways. When they do, we derive a certain amount of satisfaction from the fact and are further reinforced in our belief. Most importantly, expectancies reduce the need for us to be constantly on the alert for any possible changes in the way our environment is going to behave. If objects did not present constant, predictable aspects and events showed no inherent cause-effect relationships, the amount of information that we would have to process would immediately overwhelm and immobilize us. Predictability provides security and reduces work, but there is a price to pay. When events do not occur as predicted and objects present novel, unpredicted aspects, our expectancies may actually lead us to misperceive the world.

Expectancies may be of a permanent nature, having been set up by repeated experiences that begin at birth. They may also be of a relatively short duration and subject to change. Such expectancies are set up by explicit verbal instructions or commands or by implicit cues present in the environment that interact with the perceiver's value system. For instance, in an experiment, the experimenter tells the subject that at certain randomly determined intervals the lights in the laboratory will blink and that the subject should report such blinks, which the subject dutifully does, except that the lights are actually burning steadily. Or, in an experiment to determine the thresholds for perceiving form, a subject shows unusually high thresholds—that is, the subject requires greater amounts of light before identifying a form. The reason: The subject's previous experience has led him or her to be wary of hallucinatory experiences, hence he or she decides to make positive identifications only when absolutely sure so as to avoid the stigma of seeing things that are not there. These two examples could also have been described in terms of the *suggestion*, explicit or implicit, given the perceiver, or of a changeable response bias that exists in the perceiver because he or she anticipates an event to occur with a certain degree of probability and/or because the correct responses may be rewarded and incorrect ones punished. Short-term expectancies are more profitably discussed under these two headings. Expectancy in the present context is therefore, expectancy that has been set up by past experience, that is relatively permanent, and relatively impervious to current, contradictory information.

Expectancy is very much in evidence in the case of ventriloquism, a type of entertainment that never fails to fascinate because of the suggestion of the inexplicable, the paranormal, the extraordinary. Normally, we can establish the direction from which sound comes with a fair degree of accuracy. In the case of ventriloquism, there is an apparent shift in the direction of the sound source, even though physically there is none. Past experience tells us that sounds issue from moving mouths, that speakers assume a certain posture and facial expression when speaking, whereas listeners do it differently, and so on. Because the tone of voice also changes in a predictable fashion between the ventriloquist and the dummy, the net result is an unmistakable shift in the direction from which the voices come. The phenomenon of ventriloquism has been employed in situations that are not entertainment, but that concern the deadly serious business of keeping believers in line, impressing foe and friend alike with the ostensibly magic powers of a shaman or witchdoctor who makes trees and stones speak, and other situations involving extraordinary, occult phenomena and esoteric beliefs. Ventriloquism has obvious relevance to stage magic, mediumistic phenomena, UFO sightings, and other seemingly miraculous events.

That no elaborate means of deception are necessary for the ventriloquistic phenomenon to take place is evident from one of the most common items of modern living, the TV set. The sound does not come from the picture tube, let alone the particular mouth of each speaker who appears on the screen. Yet, the sound does not seem to come from the loudspeaker off to one side of the screen, but from each person's mouth, vehicle, and so on. In this sense, the TV loudspeaker is the ventriloquist and the mute images on the screen are the dummies. The placement of the actual sound source is unimportant as long as it is not clearly off to one side, but even that is eventually ignored; the sound comes from where you expect it to come. It makes no difference whether the loudspeaker of a movie projector is placed behind the projection screen, in front of it, to one side of it, or with the projector, in back of the spectators. In the latter case, hearing the sound come from the screen rather than from behind one's back is helped by the fact that, without the aid of vision, it is impossible to distinguish the directions of two sound sources, both of which are in the meridian plane—that is, straight front and back of the listener. The main factor is, nevertheless, the expectancy of a lawful relationship between the direction from which sound comes and the location of the sound source in the visual field.

Expectancy can affect not only the directionality of sound, but phenomena that would appear to be entirely the function of neural activity, such as the perception of color. Tree leaves are green and donkeys are gray, even when both are cut out from the same green material and illuminated by red light so that both appear gray. This was the nature of one of the earliest experiments performed to demonstrate the effect of subjective factors in perception (Duncker, 1939). Perceivers required more green to match the color of a gray comparison disc to the color of the leaf. Other researchers, modifying Duncker's procedure, have achieved essentially the same results (Bruner, Postman, & Rodrigues, 1951; Harper, 1953). Duncker referred to the phenomenon as memory color. Memory of what the usual color of an object is (and the expectancy of what it therefore should be) undoubtedly accounts for a great many cases of incorrectly remembered colors.

One of the most dramatic demonstrations of the influence of past experience on current perception that one can obtain readily under controlled conditions is the well-known rotating trapezoidal window illusion of Adalbert Ames. A window is painted on stiff, flat material and cut in the shape that it would have for an observer looking at it from, say, inside a house with the window opening outward—that is, a trapezoidal shape (Fig. 4.2). When this trapezoidal window is rotated about a vertical axis, it does not appear to rotate through 360°, but to flip-flop beteen the ends of a 180° arc. The apparent flip-flopping makes the window's behavior appear consistent with our past experience with windows (and doors): When they open, either in or out, their nearest edge appears to be longer than the farthest edge. Seeing the trapezoid actually rotate would make the window appear to behave in an inconsistent manner because every so often, the longest edge would also be the farthest edge. So, perceptually, we make the window behave the way it ought to. The illusion is extremely strong, and will not weaken or disappear after numerous observations. If an object is attached to the window such that it is seen unmistakably as rotating, at certain points the object and the window appear to go in opposite directions. The object, such as a cardboard tube, may be seen as cutting through the window, wrapping itself around the window, or performing some other strange contortions. The Ames window demonstrates that it is quite possible to see a rectangle where there is a trapezoid to see, to see oscillation when there is rotation, and to see two solid objects penetrate each other when in fact nothing of the sort is actually happening. This is not to say that the Ames window as such explains any occult phenomena. What it does prove is that we do see the world through glasses heavily tinted by past experience, and that we are completely unaware that the glasses are even there. People who live in environments in which there are no rectangular doors and windows do not experience the Ames window illusion nearly as strongly as those who do (Allport & Pettigrew, 1957), and they are as unaware of their counterbias as we are of our bias.

Another demonstration of Ames' that does directly explain at least one form of allegedly paranormal phenomena is the Ames distorted room, which is routinely illustrated in introductory psychology textbooks (Fig.

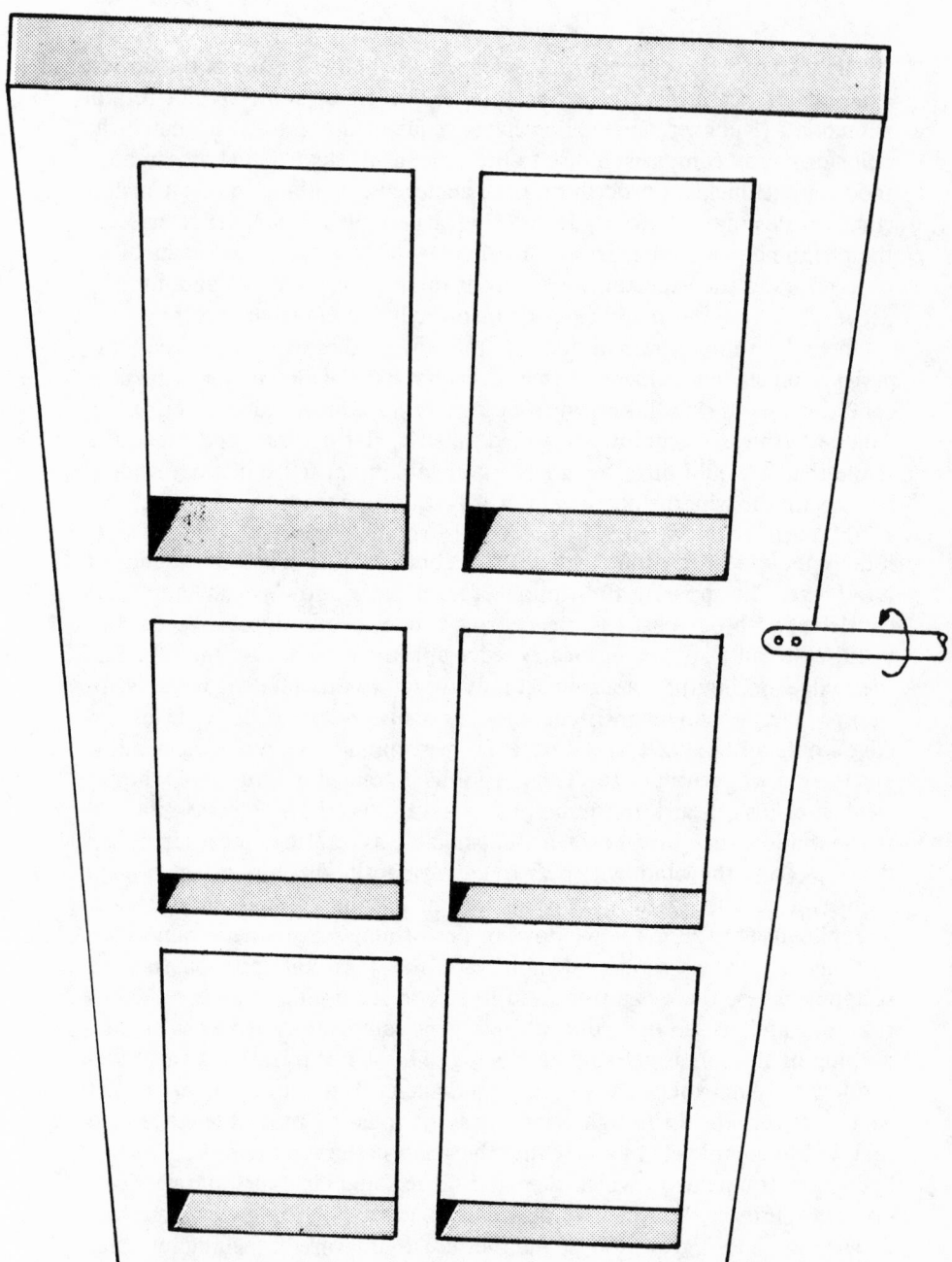

Fig. 4.2. A trapezoidal window used to demonstrate the effect of past experience on

4.3). Parallel lines, such as those that mark the boards of the floor or rows of bricks of a wall, seem to converge as they recede into the distance. In the Ames room, what would normally be parallel lines are made to expand with distance. The convergence of the perspective and the built-in expansion cancel each other out, and the room appears to be normal. If objects that have not been tampered with are placed inside the room, they will appear smaller or larger as a function of their distance from the observer. The observer looks inside through a peephole. Lacking the necessary depth cues, the perceiver sees, in an almost miraculous fashion, the growing and shrinking of a person, for instance, as that person walks along the back wall of the Ames room.

The effect does not require a peephole, only conditions where the perception of slant is distorted so that distance and size perception are also distorted. This is made advantage of in a number of places billed as "vorteces" or "power fields" of a mysterious nature and within which, among other things, people seem to grow and shrink somewhat depending on where they are standing inside a building that, by good fortune, is located right in the middle of the "vortex" (and of a well-traveled tourist route). The building is just a naturalistic and somewhat weaker version of the Ames room, and the phenomenon is due to our assumption about size-distance relationships, fortified by life-long experience with parallel lines and right angles (See Fig. 4.7).

The size-distance relationship and the intimately related phenomenon of size constancy—that is, seeing familiar objects as being of about the same size regardless of distance—are something that most people take for granted, assuming perhaps that being able to tell the size of an object at just about any distance is an innate capacity. As it turns out, it is largely learned. If one's culture does not provide the opportunity to experience the same object at widely varying distances, size constancy may be seriously undermined. How easily the resulting misperception is then attributed to supernatural causes is illustrated by an incident involving a member of a pygmy tribe, reported by the anthropologist Colin Turnbull (1961). The tribe lives in a dense forest and never sees objects more than a few yards away. Turnbull (1961) took the pygmy Kenge in his car to an open plain:

> Kenge looked over the plains and down to where a herd of about a hundred buffalo were grazing some miles away. He asked me what kind of *insects* they were, and I told him they were buffalo, twice as big as the forest buffalo known to him. He laughed loudly and told me not to tell such stupid stories, and asked me again what kind of insects they were. He then talked to himself, for want of more intelligent company, and tried to liken the buffalo to the various beetles and ants with which he was familiar.

Fig. 4.3. The Ames room. *Above*: Viewed through a peephole, the two stuffed dogs appear to be of unequal size whereas the windows seem to be about the same. *Below*: The same two dogs viewed through the top of the room appear identical and the room distorted, as they really are.

He was still doing this when we got into the car and drove down to where the animals were grazing. He watched them getting larger and larger, and though he was as courageous as any Pygmy, he moved over and sat close to me and muttered that it was witchcraft . . . Finally, when he realized that they were real buffalo he was no longer afraid, but what puzzled him still was why they had been so small, and whether they *really* had been small and had so suddenly grown larger, or whether it had been some kind of trickery [p. 305].

Even in the educated Westerner, size and other constancies break down if the necessary clues are missing. The size and distance (and therefore the rate of movement) of unfamiliar silhouettes and spots of light in the dark, for instance, may be grossly misjudged. In the absence of perspective, shading, texture, color, and other depth clues, and not knowing what the object is, correct estimation of whether an object is a small one and near by or a large one and far away is impossible. Given that UFOs are often observed at night, that they are often nothing more than a spot of light, and the additional fact that they are unidentified by definition, the rather fantastic estimates of the size and velocity of UFOs that are sometimes turned in should come as no surprise.

DECISION MAKING

As the perceptual process progresses (it must be remembered that it may take only a fraction of a second's time), the perceiver may engage in some decision making, especially if the information available is incomplete or doubtful. Before the final percept is formed, a decision is made as to what the percept should be, its identity, or whether there should be a percept at all. The decision-making process may be described in precise statistical terms. The perceiver, however, is unaware that any decision making is going on.

Even when the information available is very scanty, a hypothesis will be typically formed concerning the identity of what is perceived. Also typically, the identification will be made in terms of what is already known—known objects or known processes. When American Indians first saw the locomotive, there was nothing in their experience to enable them to label the contraption appropriately, so they labeled it in terms of what they were familiar with already: iron and moving horses—thus, the "iron horse." When people saw lights in the sky, they labeled them "flying saucers": Vague spots of light tend to appear circular, and, because the circles sometimes became ovals, they presumed the objects had to be discs rather than spheres. Before the days of the frisbee, one disc-shaped object that sometimes was seen in flight was the saucer.

Poorly understood perceptual phenomena may be misidentified not only in terms of what is known, but also in terms of what is valued, such as some idea from an esoteric belief system that one subscribes to. Many people see the so-called "floaters" in their eyes; this is cellular debris that floats in the vitreous humor between the lens and the retina or between the vitreous humor and the retina and casts shadows on the retina, especially when viewed against the sky. Less well known because it is less noticeable is another entoptical phenomenon (an event inside the eye that may be seen by the owner of the eye) that may be observed along with the floaters. It is the many bright particles that move rapidly along curved paths. Because bright light, focusing the eyes on infinity, and a particular combination of wave lengths (blue-violet is the best) is necessary for observing the phenomenon, some theosophists (C. W. Leadbeater, Annie Besant) pronounced the rapidly moving particles to be "vitality globules," related to the yogic concept of *prana* (breath) and the notion of the life-support functions of human's "etheric body" (Powell, 1925). Feeling no need to check the scientific literature or to conduct some very simple experiments of their own, and somehow assuming that the phenomenon was impervious to scientific investigation, Leadbeater and Besant attached an occult label to a perfectly ordinary biological phenomenon—namely, the entoptical perception of the circulation of the blood in the retinal capillaries (Zusne, 1963). The bright spots happen to be images of red blood corpuscles. The phenomenon is obscure and the literature sparse, but the correct information on its nature was available a long time before the theosophists made their pronouncement. The simple procedure of straining and observing the acceleration of the movement of the bright spots would have shown them that what they assumed was outside their bodies was in fact very much inside them.

People see all kinds of things in clouds, smoke, fire, water spots on the ceiling, or the random decorative spots in the Formica top of their breakfast table—faces, animals, castles—especially if they are good imagers. Strictly speaking, what they see is not images but misperceptions, because a physical stimulus is present, and parts of it are seen as something they are not. These misperceptions are illusions of a special kind, called *pareidolia*. The principle underlying the use of the famous Rorschach ink-blot test is that verbalized pareidolia will reveal the subject's unconscious life, wishes, and desires as these are projected upon the diffuse, ambiguous blots. In other words, given an unstructured stimulus and the proper incentive (such as instruction or self-instruction), people will attribute structure to it that reflects their personality dynamics. In 1978, a New Mexico housewife, Maria Rubio, noticed that the skillet burns on one of her tortillas resembled the traditional representation of the face of Jesus Christ, complete with a crown of thorns (Fig. 4.4). Mrs. Rubio decided that it was a sign that Christ would

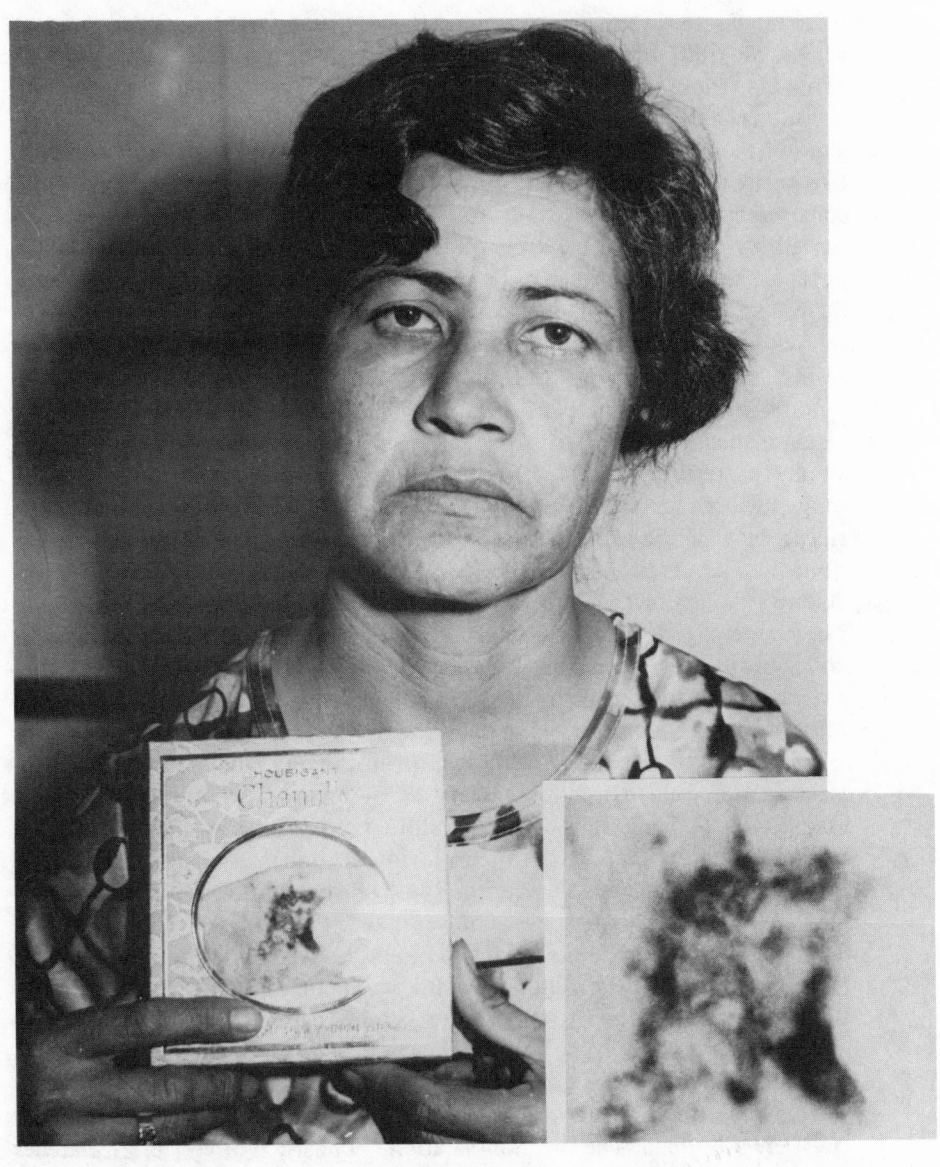

Fig. 4.4.   Pareidolia at work. Mrs. Maria Rubio and her tortilla image. (Priscilla O'Connor, Artesia Daily Press)

return to Earth. In spite of admonitions that if you fry a lot of tortillas, you will get all kinds of things and even discouragement from the Archbishop of Santa Fe, thousands of pilgrims have streamed to Lake Arthur to make devotions to the glass-framed tortilla image. Regardless of whether the subject is a person being tested with the Rorschach test in a psychologist's office or a child who sits in the grass watching the clouds, once a percept is constructed, it becomes more and more difficult to destroy it and see something different in the same physical configuration. Thus, if two cloud puffs are seen as the cheeks of Santa Claus, it becomes more difficult to see them as the two humps of a camel, and vice versa. Patterns that have a religious or supernatural meaning are particularly powerful in this respect.

Pareidolia are the basis of all those divination practices that involve the visual inspection of patterns formed by random processes, be it tea leaves, smoke, patterns formed by randomly falling objects, the shapes assumed by molten wax or metal that is poured in water, or, indeed, skillet burns on tortillas. Because the process underlying the formation of the pattern is random, it is assumed that it is, therefore, more malleable by paranormal influences. When meaningful configurations do emerge, they are assumed to carry a message from a supernatural being or entity or to have been produced by unspecified occult forces.

In addition to the personality of the perceiver, other factors that determine verbalized responses to pareidolia are the particular form and modality of the stimulus (it can be auditory, for instance) and the nature of the instructions or self-instructions given. What happens when the stimulus is vague, ambiguous sound, or even random noise, such as would be heard on an unused radio channel or when playing an unused magnetic tape? One answer may be found in Konstantin Raudive's book *Breakthrough*, published in 1971 when the author was 62 years old, three years before his death. The breakthrough, Raudive claimed, was to have been able to record the voices of the dead. By running a blank magnetic tape on "Record" or by taping from an unused radio channel, and then playing the tape many times, Raudive thought he began to hear voices that spoke in German, Russian, Latvian, and other languages that Raudive happened to know himself. He also believed that the voices came from people whom he used to know but were now dead. The "communications" consisted of very brief snatches of conversations and short phrases that did not have much relation to each other. Often, words from several different languages were used in the same phrase. Many of them were distorted. Unbelievably, a small group of Raudive's friends, as well as some outsiders, agreed with Raudive's interpretations of what it was that could be heard on the tapes.

Raudive's "breakthrough" did not receive much publicity, and years later there still has not been any attempt to replicate his work or follow up on it. Not only did it all sound somehow too simple and easy, but it must have been recognized that Raudive's method was simply an invitation for stray voices and voice-like sounds that fill the ether and the air to be recorded on the magnetic tape, later to have ideas from one's world of daydreams to be projected upon them. In other words, the tapes were private, individual, auditory Rorschach cards. Many of Raudive's personal life circumstances and his psychological background were such as to make the recording of the voices of the dead (his mother's voice played a particularly prominent role) an especially apt development—it was a man's last grasp at fame and glory in the decline of his life, made that much more poignant by unconscious intimations of his own imminent passing.

In the laboratory, the formulation of hypotheses concerning poorly defined objects and the influence of these hypotheses upon perception was dramatically illustrated by Jerome Bruner and M. C. Potter in 1964. These researchers showed defocused slides to three groups of observers. The slides were gradually brought into sharper focus, but not completely. Eventually, all three groups saw the slides at the same level of blur and were asked to identify the objects shown. One group of observers started viewing the slides under conditions of heavy blur, the second group began with slides at medium blur, and the third group first saw them lightly blurred. Even though all three groups eventually saw all slides at the same degree of blur, the heavy blur group made the most errors of identification and the light blur group did best. In a subsidiary experiment, one group of observers saw slides coming out of medium blur to the point of clarity used as the stopping point in the main experiment, whereas another group saw the same slides being defocused from that point to the level of medium blur. Even though both groups saw the slides over exactly the same range of blur, the group that saw the slides go out of focus did considerably better in identifying the objects than did the group that saw them come into better focus. The explanation of this difference offered by Bruner and Potter is that regardless of the level of blur, all observers immediately formed some hypothesis as to the identity of the object. Those who saw the slides more blurred at first were more apt to form incorrect hypotheses. They also tended to maintain these hypotheses, however, even when additional contradictory information was being provided by the slides coming into sharper focus. Because it took less time to go from, say, light blur to the final point, observers in this condition, even when they did form an incorrect hypothesis at first, had less of a chance to get attached to it and changed it when additional information was provided by the increasing clarity of the image. Thus, hypothesis testing is not just a matter of weighing the evidence for and against it. The formulator of the hypothesis also makes an emotional investment in the hypothesis, and the longer the person maintains it, the heavier the investment and the more difficult it becomes to change the hypothesis in favor of a different one. This principle operates in the area of attitudes and beliefs in general (cf. Chapter 7) and of the occult and paranormal in particular.

THE DETECTION OF FAINT STIMULI

We now consider decision making in situations involving very faint stimuli. The perceiver's task is to decide whether to say "yes" (I perceive the signal) or "no" (I don't perceive the signal) when he or she may not be quite certain one way or the other. This is what happens when sensory thresholds are measured in a psychophysical laboratory. The implications have consequences for such phenomena as subliminal perception, which is regarded by many as a feat verging on the paranormal, if not, in fact, paranormal, telepathy, and extrasensory perception in general.

Suppose we use the following procedure to establish a person's loudness threshold for a tone of a given frequency: We present the tone at very low levels of intensity many times, the different intensities arranged in a random order. We signal the onset of each sound signal with a light. The sound is so faint that on a number of trials, the person will not be able to hear it. In this way, we can establish the sound intensity level at which the person is just as likely to say "yes" (I hear it) as "no" (I don't hear it) and call this the person's loudness threshold for the particular frequency. Suppose also that after giving 100 trials, we add a series of 10 trials with no sound. Chances are that the subjects will say "yes" on one or more of these trials because they have become used to saying "yes" quite often. Expectancy leads them to say "yes" when, in fact, there is nothing to hear. We will also find that if of the 100 trials only 10 are filled, the subject would probably not say "yes" to any of the 10 blank trials added at the end. In general, the chance that the subject will say "yes" when there is a signal relative to the subject's saying "yes" when there is none (or only random noise) will increase with increasing signal frequency and decrease with decreasing signal frequency. The result: The computed sensory thresholds in the two cases will be different. Does this mean that the person's sensitivity has changed? Not really. What has changed is the subject's willingness to say "yes."

Another factor that has analogous effects on sensory thresholds is reward and punishment. Keeping signal frequency the same but varying the *pay-off function*—that is, the schedule of rewards for correct responses and/or of punishments for incorrect ones—also leads to differences in measured thresholds. High rewards without punishment leads to a person's saying "yes" quite often, even in the absence of signal, whereas punishment leads to saying "no" even when there is signal. It is thought that in any given instance, the person tested is using a certain *response criterion* to decide when to say yes and when to say no. The response criterion is a variable one, affected both by the probability of stimulus presentation and the pay-off function. In other words, a person's sensitivity may not vary, but the criterion for saying that a signal is being perceived does. A high criterion, for instance, will give the impression that the person's sensory threshold is very high—that is, that the person is very insensitive, when in fact there may be nothing wrong with his or her sensitivity. It is just that the person has decided not to give a positive response very often.

It is possible, by comparing the hit rate (saying yes when there is a signal) and false-alarm rate (saying yes when there is no signal), to obtain two measures, one a measure of pure sensitivity that does not depend on the response criterion, and another one that shows the subject's *response bias*. The response bias does vary with signal probability and with pay-off. Hence, a high threshold may mean nothing more than that the subject used a high response criterion and that his or her true sensitivity is the same as that of another person with a lower threshold. If stimulus intensities are adjusted to accord with individual thresholds, the result may be the impression that perception is taking place unconsciously—that is, that stimuli below the sensory threshold are being perceived or that *subliminal perception* is taking place.

Subliminal Perception

Subliminal perception is sometimes attributed to the unconscious, especially as the unconscious is conceived in psychoanalysis. Because of the enormous importance that the unconscious plays in personality dynamics in psychoanalytical theory, subliminal perception is seen as being in some way compelling, so that the subliminal message is implicitly obeyed. This faulty logic led to experiments in the 1950s to test the possibility of subliminal advertising. The first experiments were done by movie-theater owners and other individuals who lacked the necessary sophistication to design the proper experimental controls (McConnell, Cutler, & McNeil, 1958). They caused a great furor anyway, not only because of the feared power of advertisers, but also because of evil-intentioned people who might be out to influence our minds without our being aware of it. The whole issue may be dismissed by stating that signals that are truly below an individual's sensory capacity to perceive will not be perceived and therefore acted upon. On the other hand, signals, however faint, will be perceived by someone some time because people differ in sensitivity. Given a large enough number of people, such as a movie audience, some people will perceive messages flashed on the screen that may be imperceptible to others. But, why should those who can read the message to drink brand X soft drink, for instance, rush out into the lobby and order large quantities of this beverage? They do not (unless it is hot and brand X is the only brand available), and the assumption that they will or should arises from a semantic confusion between unconscious motives and subliminal (and therefore unconscious) stimuli. The compelling nature of unconscious motives derives from reasons that have nothing to do with the perceptibility of faint signals. Unconscious motives are motives that some time in the past were conscious but became repressed and unconscious because of their traumatic nature. Subliminal signals are just that and have no necessary motivating power, although they could have. For them to trigger unconscious motives, the association would have to become established first.

There is some research (see Dixon, 1971) that shows subliminal instructions to be effective in influencing verbal behavior, perceptual thresholds, dreams, and other processes. The effectiveness of the instructions is due to the same reason that posthypnotic suggestions are effective: The fact of the instructions is not remembered, hence the individual does not consciously oppose them. The prime mechanism in this case is suggestion and not the subliminal nature of the suggestion. Everybody is susceptible to suggestion, some people more so than others. Research also shows that the kind of suggestion that is effective is the kind that does not run counter to a person's well-established habits. In other words, if the suggestion is to eat popcorn, the response, unconsciously, is likely to be, "Why not?"—unless, of course, the person has a conditioned aversion to popcorn. Even then, the combination of suggestibility and subliminal suggestion does not guarantee success. Each individual's true sensitivity is different, and the measured threshold varies from time to time as the individual's response bias changes. Thus, there is no guarantee that a message of a given strength will be the right thing for everybody in an audience; for some, it will be too weak to be perceived, for others it may be above the threshold and may create actual resistance as a person begins to think about the message and its implications.

Signal Detection and Parapsychology

A second implication of the existence of response bias is for the field of parapsychology, specifically the phenomenon of mind reading or telepathy. When, in a telepathy experiment, the sender of a mental message and the receiver are in the same room or, in general, within sight or located so that they can hear each other, the transmission of faint messages, intentional or not, is all too possible. In the older telepathy experiments, both the sender and the recipient were, as a rule, present in the same location without much by way of an effective barrier between them. This applied to both human experiments and mind-reading animal acts. For this reason, much of the older parapsychological literature on telepathy is virtually worthless. In the newer and more sophisticated experimentation, the physical separation, soundproofing, and so on, of the persons involved is routine. The problem of response bias raised by modern psychophysics persists, however. As long as the experiment in telepathy can be described as another experiment in signal detection—one individual presenting faint signals, the other making decision as to whether there is or is not a signal present—the experiment can and should be analyzed by breaking down the recipient's performance into a measure of sensitivity and a measure of response bias. If the former is zero or near zero and the latter is large, even performance that is statistically significant as computed by the standard statistical procedures cannot be considered as showing the presence of telepathy (sensitivity), but instead is due to other factors (response bias). This problem, as well as pertinent experimental evidence, is discussed in more detail in Chapter 12.

Sensory Hyperacuity

Sensory hyperacuity is not a phenomenon that one often finds discussed in psychology textbooks. For one thing, its identity may often be hidden by other labels. It has to do with the detection of faint stimuli and with paranormal phenomena. In themselves, cases of extremely acute vision, hearing, smell, or taste are nothing unusual. Sensitivity, like any other biological variable, is distributed normally in the population. It follows the bell-shaped distribution, which of necessity will include some people who are very insensitive as well as some who are extemely sensitive. Some people, for instance, can hear what other people are thinking. Thinking is often accompanied by muscular movements of which the thinker is not aware. The entire speech apparatus, including the tongue and the larynx, moves. Even though the movements are extremely slight, some people are able to pick up the air vibrations produced by these movements. For people with auditory hyperacuity, the challenge "Guess what I am thinking about!" does not suggest mysterious mental powers, but only careful listening. The Australian Aborigenes are said to be able to see the four Galilean moons of Jupiter with the unaided eye. They are also able to find water by smell from a long distance in desert country with no visible signs to aid them. In the 1960s, the reporter Lowell Thomas was led to the remains of a pilot and gold miner, Harold Bell Lasseter, lost in the Australian desert in 1926, by an Aborigene named Nosepeg who, at the age of 9, had seen Lasseter buried among the sand hills a long way west of Alice Springs. Nosepeg had not been back there since then, but he led Lowell Thomas's expedition unerringly to Lasseter's unmarked grave in the middle of an undifferentiated desert landscape, guided only by his extremely fine senses and perfect visual recall.

Although these facts may seem nothing short of the miraculous to the Westerner, the Aborigenes themselves claim no paranormal causation in any of this. To them, it is "all in a day's work." The difference between the Westerner and the Aborigene is that the Westerner does not need extremely sharp senses in order to survive, whereas the Aborigene does. The point is that a highly developed sensory acuity can be achieved with the proper motivation and proper training. In the Western world, motivation to learn to perceive differences that to most people are imperceptible is not related to survival, but to activities that are much less vital. They may even be trivial. The more prosaic instances of highly developed sensitivity may be found in the experts on taste and smell, such as wine, coffee, or tea tasters. That a person should be able to tell the difference between wine at the top and the bottom of the bottle, or between wine made from grapes grown in the south and the north ends of the same vineyard sounds almost incredible. One acquires this ability, nevertheless, through the process of *perceptual learning*. Perceptual learning is learning to perceive, to discriminate. By being repeatedly exposed to the same stimulus, the learner will begin to distinguish features of the stimulus that previously passed unnoticed. By tasting different varieties of wines and associating tastes with labels or names, the wine taster eventually is able to respond to differences between stimuli so unremarkable that others fail to perceive them. The same process of perceptual learning is at least partly responsible for the very acute senses of members of some of the nonindustrial societies.

"Dermal Vision"

Dermal vision, dermo-optical perception, cutaneous sensitivity to light, aphotic digital color sensing, extraretinal photic sensitivity, paraptic color discrimination, fingertip sight, eyeless vision—the profusion of terms suggests that the nature of this phenomenon is not really understood. It has to do with sensation, and it has to do with stimuli that are faint because light stimuli must be faint to whatever skin sense is responsible for their perception, if indeed the response is to light. Thus, the question of whether one can "see" with one's skin may just as well be discussed under some other heading, such as clairvoyance; laboratory demonstrations of eyeless sight very easily become demonstrations that are indistinguishable from those of telepathy and clairvoyance. If it is decided that this is the nature of the phenomenon, then, of course, all that can be said about parapsychological experimentation would apply to eyeless vision also.

"Clairvoyance" means seeing clearly something that is not available to ordinary sight. In that sense, dermal vision is a special case of clairvoyance. What has distinguished the instances of dermal vision from other instances of clairvoyance is that serious attempts have been made to identify the physiological mechanism responsible for this ability without necessarily alleging that the phenomenon is in any way paranormal. The lines between straightforward laboratory research in physiological psychology, parapsychological investigations, and public demonstrations of dermal vision with few controls and proven instances of trickery are hard to draw in the case of dermal vision, however. It is an excellent example of a topic in anomalistic psychology where different belief systems, research methods, theoretical explanations, practitioners from different specialties, public gullibility, fraud, exhibitionism, and demonstrable physical phenomena all converge to produce a tangle of claims and counterclaims that is brightly lit by the glare of publicity.

In 1898, a Russian psychiatrist published a report on a woman, Sophia, who could read with her fingertips while blindfolded. No further study of her or of similar cases followed immediately. In 1920, the French novelist Jules Romains wrote a small book describing his own experiments with "dermal vision." The public appreciated Romain's literary output more than his excursion into experimental psychology. In the 1950s, one of the most prominent Russian psychologists, A. N. Leontev, shone a green light on a blindfolded person's palm and simultaneously applied electric shock to the hand. After a number of trials, a conditioned hand withdrawal to the green light alone was established. (It must be noted that light, even when filtered through heat-absorbing filters, will convert to heat upon striking the skin. For this reason, the experiment remains ambiguous.) Again, there was no surge of interest in the phenomenon. The Russians persisted. In 1962, a Soviet physician working in the Siberian town of Nizhnii Tagil discovered that one of his patients, a woman by the name of Rosa Kuleshova, could see print with her fingertips and could identify colors and pictures with the skin of her fingers alone (Ivanov, 1964). The woman had a history of blindness in her family, suffered from epilepsy, and later, under the press of publicity that developed around her, showed symptoms of schizophrenia. At first, Rosa Kuleshova used her fingers to "see." She touched her fingers to the printed page or handled the objects she was asked to identify. She performed successfully also when the target was covered with cellophane. Eventually, she saw dermally with her elbows, toes, and other skin areas and by simply holding her hands above the target, not touching it.

With many scientists focusing their attention on a Siberian nobody, Rosa got caught up in the whirlwind of fame, began to give performances in the public and on television, and—was caught cheating. If she had been the only person to show dermal vision, this would have ended the flap. But there were others. Numerous persons, especially children, applied to be tested for dermal vision, claiming to perform feats greater than those of Rosa Kuleshova, such as reading what was on a sheet of paper covered by several thick books. Even Rosa offered to identify targets by sitting on them. Most of the dermal seers were unmasked as conscious or unconscious frauds. What the testers were forgetting was that they were witnessing a well-established and widely practiced trick of a particular kind of stage magician, the "mentalist." One of the mentalist's standard tricks is to find a chink in the blindfold, however minute, and obtain the information very directly by peeking down the nose; no amount of taping of the eyelids or padding the blindfold prevents the individual from seeing through the space between the blindfold and the nose. When the target is covered, as with books, the trick is to read the target before it is covered, memorize the information, then reproduce it later as if by direct reading. The Russian dermal-vision children were doing just that.

The testing of subjects went on in laboratories in spite of the trickery. It was soon becoming clear that dermal vision, whatever its nature, was an ability that could be trained. Training, however, did not lead to reading *Pravda* or the *New York Times*. It led to an improvement in the ability to discriminate and identify colors of colored papers sandwiched between a piece of cardboard and a piece of transparent plastic and taped around the edges. It will be remembered from previous discussion that perceptual learning does lead to the discovery (discrimination) of features of the environment that previously passed undetected. If there is any difference at all between squares of different colors, handling them many times while being told their color should lead to an improvement in the ability to discriminate colors by touch.

One of the first to perform experiments on dermal vision in America was the psychologist Richard P. Youtz. He first tested a woman who, many years earlier as a student, had shown dermal vision. Pat Stanley was tested with the color sandwiches just mentioned and showed both discrimination and identification of colors far beyond the chance level. She did not do well with colored wood sticks and pieces of colored sponge (Youtz, 1968). Individual differences in dermal vision are great, and Pat Stanley was an exceptional case. When Youtz undertook the training of a large number of female college students, he found that about 10 percent of them showed dermal vision in a rudimentary form after some 20 hours of training. Some individuals did qutie a bit better than that, others showed little improvement. Even Pat Stanley did not perform consistently, which Youtz attributed to fatigue and, mainly, to variations in the temperature of her skin. It is temperature that Youtz invokes to explain the phenomenon of dermal vision.

Youtz and other American psychologists currently favor the theory that dermal color discrimination is based on differential heat exchange between the colored surface and the skin rather than the action of light on some unknown photoreceptors in the skin (Makous, 1966). It is not clear whether it is the relative amount of body heat that is reflected from colored surfaces that is the effective clue or whether what is perceived is the depth at which rays reflected from the surface are reabsorbed by the skin.

Reading fine print or identifying pictures is a different matter, though. First, the charge of fraud or trickery cannot be easily dismissed. Martin Gardner (1966) a well-known debunker of occult claims and scientific charlatansim, has suggested, for instance, that the sole explanation of dermal vision is the "peek down the nose." Ordinary blindfolds, even when they envelop the entire head and in combination with cotton, coins, or adhesive plaster over the eyes, do not exclude the possibility of peeking. The magician who drives a car while blindfolded finds a way to see through the blindfold. So do dermal-vision subjects. The shape of the nose plays a certain role here. If you intend to peek, it pays to have a turned-up nose. People with turned-up noses have a distinct advantage over people with straight noses—they can peek down their noses better. One wonders if the spate of dermal readers who turned up in the 1960s did so in Russia rather than in some other country because, among other things, the East European ethnic type features a short and upturned nose. The blindfold problem is avoided by interposing an opaque screen between the subject's head and their hands, such as a large bib, boxes into which the subjects put their hands through tightly fitting cloth sleeves (as Youtz did), or fitting a metal box with vent holes around the subject's head.

Second, the phenomenon of reading fine print or identifying pictures inside closed books looks very much like standard clairvoyance performance. The possibility that dermal vision may be an occult phenomenon after all has not been dismissed. It is significant that a number of reports and research papers on dermal vision have been published in parapsychological journals and newsletters. The behavior of subjects in dermal-vision experiments is very similar to the behavior of subjects in telepathy and clairvoyance experiments, and the methodological problems and statistical issues are identical to those shared by all parapsychological experiments: The residue of only one or two "star performers" after repeated tests given to a large pool of unselected subjects, the waxing and waning of the ability in these performers after their selection, and the improvement of performance with training are only a few of the features shared by dermal-vision and parapsychological experiments.

INDIVIDUAL DIFFERENCES IN PERCEPTION

The end product of information processing in perception is the percept, which may or may not lead to an overt response (behavior). The percept is like the figure-ground phenomenon. It has thing-like qualities: It has definite boundaries and form whereas ground has not; it stands out among other things and against the ground; and it has identity. The segregation of the perceptual experience into figure and ground is an innate process; it is present at birth and does not have to be learned. Like any other innate process, it can be modified through learning, however. Hence, individuals do differ in the way the figure-ground segregation is accomplished. Although everybody sees, hears, or smells perceptual figures on ground, some people are better at segregating or differentiating figures that may be obscured or masked by ground. In addition, what in a given case may be figure to one individual may be noise to another. Under conditions of insufficient information flow, as in darkness, with little observation time available, or under otherwise "noisy" conditions of observation, including emotional a-rousal—conditions that often exist when paranormal phenomena are reported—individual differences in figure-ground perception may put a very different slant on the interpretation of the nature of such phenomena.

Individual differences in figure-ground perception show up most dramatically in the performance on tests with embedded or camoflaged figures, as illustrated in Fig. 4.5. Young children take more time to find the camouflaged figure than do older children, who take more time than do adults. Overly long search times for the embedded figure also indicates brain damage. Also, women, by and large, take more time than do men. In addition to the groups of individuals just mentioned, there are individuals who simply do not do as well as others. We return to them shortly. Lesser ability to disembed figures from a camouflaging context is correlated with lesser ability to extract conceptually main points from a verbal context. Performance here parallels performance on embedded figures: Children are not as good as adults, and brain-damaged individuals are not as good as intact individuals.

The psychologist Herman Witkin (Witkin, Lewis, Hertzman, Machover, Meissner, & Wapner, 1954) introduced the terms *field-dependent* and *field-*

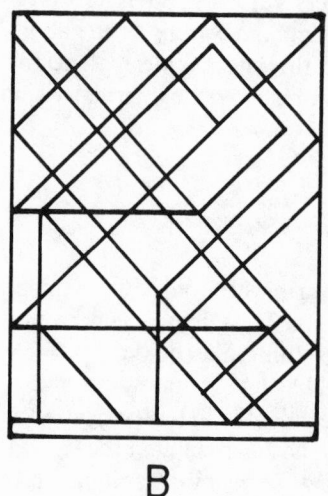

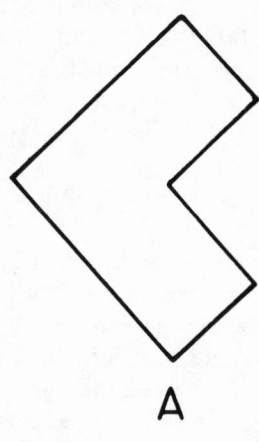

Fig. 4.5. An embedded-figure problem: Find figure A in figure B.

independent to characterize the performance of individuals on the embedded-figures test. "Field" in this connection refers to the immediately visible visual field that the individual is faced with at the moment. The field-dependent individuals rely too much on this field, which interferes with their perception of that that may be obscured by the field and yet is the more important part of it. Performance on embedded figures correlates well with performance on a set of tests of a different nature. Witkin devised the tilting-room-tilting-chair test and the rod-and-frame test. These also reflect the relative dependence of the individual on the visual environment. In the tilting-room test, the subject sits in a chair inside a room that can be tilted. The chair can also be tilted independently of the room. Because the outside cannot be seen, a person must go by the feel of the gravitational pull on the body to determine whether they are tilted, or else depend on the visual clues

Fig. 4.6.   The rod-and-frame test. The rod and frame move independently of each other. In a dark room, only the phosphorescent rod and frame are visible. Instructed to set the rod vertically, a field-independent person would adjust the rod as shown and disregard the tilt of the frame. (Leonard Zusne photo)

present in the room, which is what the field-dependent person does. Field-dependent persons may thus judge the room and themselves to be upright when in fact they may be tilted as much as 30°. The field-independent person goes by the feel of the gravitational pull and may be able to establish the correct vertical direction in spite of the misleading visual clues supplied by the room.

The rod-and-frame test consists of a rotating square frame and a bar that is of the same width as the frame material and that rotates about an axis that passes through the midpoint of the square (Fig. 4.6). Both the frame and the rod are presented so that no clues as to the true up-and-down direction are visible, as by painting the frame and the rod with phosphorescent paint and placing them in a totally dark room. For the field-dependent person, the orientation of the frame (the visual field) will determine their judgment of whether the rod is vertical or not because the feel of the gravitational pull on their own bodies is not sufficient for a correct judgment.

Our relative insensitivity to the sensory signals that come from our muscles and joints and are triggered by changing direction in the gravitational pull is capitalized upon by a certain type of tourist attraction, of which there are a number in this country. They all feature a room or building within which "strange" or "unknown" (occult!) forces are said to be operating ("force fields," "vortices"), leading to such phenomena as balls rolling and water running uphill, old brooms balancing at an angle to the horizontal, and other similar occurrences that seem to indicate that the laws of gravitation have been superseded. A photograph taken inside the so-called "House of Mystery" in the Oregon Vortex (Gold Mill, Oregon) is shown in Fig. 4.7. Although the building is crazily tilted and the lack of reliable reference lines disorients the observer quite readily, a photographer, by using short plumb chains hanging from the ceiling as reference lines and drawing the appropriate coordinate axes on the photographs is able to establish that nothing out of the ordinary is taking place. Water still runs only downhill, even in the Oregon Vortex. The more field-dependent person, however, is easily led to believe that some very unnatural phenomenon is taking place in the Gold Hill House of Mystery.

One other dimension along which people differ perceptually has to do with whether they will enhance or reduce the salient features in the objects they perceive. First, there is the general tendency that, given the right conditions, an object will be remembered as resembling the prototype or ideal form of the class of objects to which it belongs. This is known as *assimilation*. Thus, if not sufficient time is allowed for viewing or if the same object is copied and recopied a number of times from previous copies, an irregular blob may begin to resemble a circle, for instance, or, if the object is a square with some imperfections, the imperfections may eventually be omitted. This tendency towards a "good" form is also seen in such processes as the retell-

Fig. 4.7. Interior view of the House of Mystery in the Oregon Vortex. The bottle appears to be rolling uphill. The dashed lines are the true vertical and horizontal, established by using a plumb line hanging from the ceiling. They show that what appears to be an uphill gradient is actually a downhill gradient. (Reproduced with permission from *Fate* magazine.)

ing of a story. The final version of the story may not only be different from the original version, but different in a certain way: Its structure is "better"—it is simpler, more regular, more symmetrical, better proportioned, and it therefore sounds "better." This assimilative tendency is seen both in the reported shapes of unusual objects, such as UFOs, and the form of the reports of their sightings if repeated a number of times by the same person or when passed from mouth to mouth.

In addition to the general tendency to assimilate, there is the tendency either to accentuate existing differences or to minimize them. Individuals who do the former have been called *sharpeners*, the latter type *levelers* (Holzman & Klein, 1954). Sharpeners perceive stimuli more accurately. Levelers, on the other hand, tend to confuse stimuli in the middle range of differences because they tend to assimilate them to the mean type. Sharpeners also do better on embedded figures than do levelers. One could

expect that in seeing any human-like figures that are assumed to be the occupants of a UFO, the leveler would be more apt to describe them as human
in form, whereas a sharpener would be more apt to stress their green skin,
pointed ears, or huge eyes, for instance.

NOTES

The finding of Lasseter's grave in the Australian desert is depicted in one of
Lowell Thomas's *High Adventure* television programs. Additional details
were kindly supplied by Mr. E. J. Connellan of Narwietooma, near Alice
Springs, Australia.

5 Anomalous Imagery and Hallucinations

As for the bodily temper of man and his Brain . . . a very little distemper of the brain . . . is enough to represent Spirits, Angels and Devil, Sights and Stories of Heaven and Hell to the Fancy . . . which sober kind of madness and delineation (is) little understood vulgarly.

Burton's *Anatomy of Melancholy,* 1621

Imagery and hallucinations are similar in that both refer to perception-like experiences in the absence of direct and simultaneous external stimulation. They differ in that imagery is mostly known by imagers to be subjective events, whereas hallucinators usually do not realize that the images originate within themselves and believe them to be external realities. The qualifiers "mostly" and "usually" are added for the reason that, sometimes, an extremely vivid image may be briefly mistaken for reality, and that the hallucinator may, on occasion, still know that he or she only "sees" things, as happens in cases of drug-induced hallucinations and even in some hallucinating psychotics. The reality character of the hallucination is such, however, that even those who know they are hallucinating are guided in their behavior by the apparent reality contours of the hallucination.

Anomalous imagery and hallucinations account for a good number of experiences that may be described by the experiencer as having esoteric significance or paranormal cause. The relevance of anomalous imagery and especially of hallucinations to the occult and paranormal needs no special elaboration. Until the 19th century, most hallucinations were endowed with occult significance, and the hallucinator was often thought to be divinely inspired. Hallucinations sometimes even affected the course of history. Joan of Arc heard voices and had visions of angels who told her to lead the French army against the English. She brought them a decisive victory at Orléans at the crisis of the Hundred Years' War. On a less exalted level, the connection between the occult and hallucinations in everyday life may be exemplified by the student, known to one of the present authors several years ago, who used to talk a lot about extrasensory perception. It was through extrasensory perception, he said, that various historical figures would communicate with him. The late President Truman would appear to him on his television screen, for instance, with the set off. President Truman would tell him about other historical personages, such as President Roosevelt, and even take him on tours of interesting places—the Moon, for instance.

HYPNAGOGIC AND HYPNOPOMPIC IMAGERY

What is one to make of seeing a face like the one in Fig. 5.1? Is it a ghost, an evil spirit, a demon, a discarnate entity, or the crazy neighbor next door who has found a means of invading your mind? Lacking other information, these ideas are more likely to come to a person than "hypnagogic imagery," which is what this face is. "Faces in the dark" is one type of imagery that occurs in

Fig. 5.1.   "Face in the dark." A hypnagogic image painted immediately upon awakening. (From Rawcliffe, 1959. Used by permission of Dover Publications, Inc.)

the *hypnagogic state*, a state between wakefulness and sleep. The state that occurs after sleeping and prior to waking is called the *hypnopompic state*, which is very similar. In one study (McKellar, 1975), it was found that about 63% of a sample of nearly 200 university students experienced hypnagogic imagery at least occasionally. Only about 21% reported hypnopompic imagery.

When imagery does occur in either the hypnagogic or the hypnopompic state, it does so without warning and, for the most part, cannot be controlled voluntarily, although on occasion a pleasant hypnopompic imagery that might be the continuation of a dream sequence may be consciously guided when the imager realizes that "I am in a dream." The contents of hypnagogic and hypnopompic imagery may be quite vivid and realistic, and the distinction between imagery and hallucination may become blurred.

The most frequent kind of hypnagogic imagery is visual and auditory. Visual imagery ranges from points of light and geometric figures to faces and complex scenes. "Faces in the dark" is the most frequent theme. These are faces of unknown strangers that may change every few seconds. They are seen most frequently by children, often causing fear. Hypnagogic visions are typically in color, both their form and color are often distorted, unnatural, or surrealistic, and they are in the nature of unrelated color slides having no connection with each other or with preceding or ongoing mental processes of the imager.

The most frequent auditory image is hearing one's name called. Because one's name is the most significant auditory stimulus to a person, it often awakens the person completely. If being called is associated with a preceding dream that reflects one's concern about the fate of a close person, the combination may be interpreted as a prophetic dream. However, a simple count of the frequency with which people have an auditory image of being called and nothing happening as a consequence would make one at least pause before attributing paranormal significance to this experience.

Hearing music is another frequent form of auditory hypnagogic imagery. One may hear snatches of familiar music being played by a full orchestra or else a new and original piece. Some composers, such as Wagner, have utilized auditory hypnagogic imagery to write some of their works. In other words, the imagery can be creative. This is not always or necessarily so. In this respect, there is a resemblance between the hypnagogic state and the sense of creativity, beauty, originality, or deep insight sometimes experienced under the influence of the hallucinogenic drug LSD. Upon reaching the fully awake or undrugged state, the insight or creative idea does not seem so great any more. One of the authors of this volume remembers vividly the seemingly brilliant witticism that came to him one morning before waking. He mulled over it, enjoying it greatly, firmly resolved to write it down immediately upon getting up. When that time came, the only thing left was an amazement that such a trite joke should have ever occurred to him let alone appear worthy of being written down.

Hypnopompic imagery often anticipates coming events of the day, such as those associated with getting up, dressing, eating, or seeing a spouse off to work. Thus, one may hear the alarm go off before it actually does, hear a call to get up even when no one is calling, or get up to answer the door when in fact no one is knocking. Under the proper circumstances, this characteristic of hypnopompic imagery may lead to the belief that one is dealing with precognition. The imagery is vivid enough to blend with actual events, so that later on, a complete story of a paranormal experience may emerge in which the hypnopompic portions are not so identified.

The preceding discussion suggests that hypnagogic and hypnopompic imagery has certain features that make it easy to place interpretations of paranormality upon it. First, the images are spontaneous, vivid, and sometimes fear provoking, so that they may be interpreted as attempts "from the other side" to contact the living, or as apparitions or evil spirits. Second, visual imagery often takes the form of colored geometric forms. If such forms are used in a telepathy experiment and the experiment is conducted late at night to make the telepathic recipient more relaxed, hypnagogic visual imagery may be interpreted as the reception of a telepathic message. Third, the very frequent auditory image of one's name being called can be interpreted as a premonition, especially is coupled with a preceding significant dream. The tendency of hypnopompic imagery to anticipate the day's events also has the effect of calling for an interpretation in terms of precognition.

Very few experimental studies of hypnagogic imagery have been conducted. In one such study, done by Foulkes, Spear, and Symonds (1966), it was found that individuals who were good imagers were less rigid, more self-accepting, better poised socially, and more creative than individuals whose imagery was infrequent or poor. The researchers suggested that low imagers had very strong impulse control and strong defenses against subjectivity, such as images, feelings, and impulses. Although these do show up in dreams, the hypnagogic state retains enough ego control to suppress their manifestation. The impression that hypno imagery (of the kind that lends itself to occult interpretations) might be a special boon granted to a select few arises from the fact that not everybody reports it. There may be several different reasons for this, but the most significant ones are that many people either do not recognize hypno imagery for what it is or forget it as soon as sleep or waking takes over. Similarly, not all people remember their dreams, yet objective measures show that everybody does dream. There is no reason to assume that hypno imagery is different in this respect.

THE SENSE OF PRESENCE

The feeling that one is not alone, *the sense of presence*, is not unusual among ordinary, healthy people. Aggravated cases may be found in mental illness and they may be referred to as hallucinations. There are usually physical clues that help create the sense of presence, but of which the subject is unaware. Silence and darkness are appropriate backgrounds on which a "presence" may be projected. The child's request for light in the bedroom or for at least an open door or the adult's whistling in the dark are unconscious devices that serve two purposes: They mask slight stimuli that otherwise might be interpreted as signs of somebody's being present, and they serve as a focus of attention, preventing one's diffuse fears from concentrating and being projected outside oneself. It is the unnoticed faint stimuli—faint creaks, clicks, rustling, air currents—that, when they occur against an appropriate background, create the impression of somebody's being there. Fatigue accentuates the effect, as when otherwise sober-minded individuals, finding themselves alone and tired, may panic because they believe that someone is stalking them. The Canadian psychologist Graham Reed suggests that if such an experience occurs to a traveler in a particular region, a legend of some mysterious being haunting that region may become attached to it and provide the necessary setting for future visitors to also sense a presence there. An example that Reed (1972) cites is the "giant specter" of Ben Macdhui, a 4300-foot peak in Scotland:

> This particular legend is of quite recent origin, dating back only to the late 1920s when a story related by a veteran climber and respected scientist reached the newspapers. Professor N. J. Collie, F. R. S., had recalled that on one occasion he had been alone on the summit of Macdhui when he felt he could "hear" footsteps in the snow as if somebody or "something" was accompanying him. The feeling became so overwhelming that he fled from the peak. Since then the invisible "thing" has stalked many lonely walkers over the snowy, featureless top of Macdhui and among its vasts cliffs and desolate lochans [pp. 44–45].

HALLUCINATIONS

Horowitz (1975) classifies imagery and hallucinations into four groups according to vividness (e.g., hallucinations), context, (e.g., hypnagogic imagery), interaction with perception (e.g., the *déjà vu* experience, discussed in Chapter 6), and content (e.g., the autoscopic hallucination). Although this is a useful classification for systematic purposes, we discuss just those few types of hallucinations that pertain to occult phenomena, without breaking them down into types.

Hallucinations, like imagery, are perception-like experiences that occur in the absence of a corresponding objective reality, but that are believed by the hallucinator to be objectively real, occurring "out there." Thus, hallucination is not misperception. It is not determined by external objects or events, although the hallucinatory process may be superimposed upon them, such as when real objects appear distorted, increased or decreased in size, or animated. That a particular experience is an hallucination rather than the perception of something objective may be confirmed by witnesses who can testify that nobody else saw or heard anything like what was described by the hallucinator. This becomes problematic if the hallucinator happens to be alone at the time of the hallucination. Unless the content of the experience is obviously bizarre, illogical, or physically impossible, it may be difficult to relegate the report to the category of "mere hallucination." But, even bizarreness or physical impossibility are no guarantee that the report of a sole witness to an event will be classified as an hallucination. UFOs and their occupants have been seen by so many people, including several of them simultaneously, that a report of little green men alighting from a flying saucer and incinerating a Wisconsin village is not very likely to land the bearer of such a tale in a psychiatric hospital. Likewise, hallucinations whose contents are religious or revelatory are apt to be dignified by the term vision and taken quite seriously, whereas, an hallucination of a secular nature, even though it is as physically impossible as the religious one, is apt to remain unnoticed except by psychiatric personnel. Finally, the fact that a phenomenon has been witnessed by many people does not exclude the possibility that it was an hallucination after all. There are collective hallucinations also. These are discussed separately later in this chapter.

Hallucinations often occur in psychotic states, but they are by no means associated with mental illness alone. Hallucinations may also be caused by sensory deprivation, high fever, sexual abstinence, hallucinogenic drugs, toxic states (for instance, the *delirium tremens* caused by ethanol), extended fasting, partial strangulation, and suggestion. With the exception of suggestion, all of the other causative factors have this in common: They involve some form of biochemical malfunctioning of the body. Suggestion is a different type of causative factor, and there is some question whether one can truly produce hallucinations through suggestion.

It must be stressed that it is largely in the Western cultures that hallucinations have been associated with mental illness and therefore perceived as an undesirable state. Even here, there have been exceptions in that certain subcultures have not shared this association with the larger society. For instance, the medieval witches induced hallucinations of flying, animals, the devil, and so on, through the use of hallucinogenic preparations (belladonna, deadly nightshade, mandrake, toadskins, i.e., bufotenin), taking them to be objective experiences. In other cultures, hallucinatory states may be sought intentionally for purposes of religious revelation, divination, decisions upon a course of action, healing, determination of guilt, or achieving status within a social hierarchy.

The contents of hallucinations can vary over a very wide range of subjects for a given individual. The range of content is prescribed by the hallucinator's past experiences, and these are heavily influenced by the culture. For this reason, a Crow Indian or an Aborigene from New Hebrides would be quite unlikely to hallucinate pixies, fairies, or gnomes clad in medieval European garb. Such people, may, however, be told during the course of an initiation not to report back until they have seen a particular guardian spirit, for instance. The LSD user in the Western culture will also hallucinate only that to which the culture has exposed him or her. However fantastic a given hallucination, upon examination, it will be seen to contain only elements from the hallucinator's past experience.

Hallucinations may be visual, auditory, olfactory, gustatory, haptic, kinesthetic, or organic. Visual hallucinations range from simple light phenomena to the seeing of life-sized, life-like persons engaged in various activities. Objects usually appear to be three dimensional and solid. They cast shadows, people do not walk through walls and furniture, but around them, and the entire vision may not appear any less detailed, vivid, or substantial than ordinary perceptions. Sometimes, however, the hallucination may be less substantial and may appear to be larger or smaller than natural size. Micropsia and macropsia—the seeing of objects as being of a size smaller or larger than their natural size—in hallucinations may have given rise to stories about diminutive people, such as fairies or leprechauns, or of giants.

Auditory hallucinations most often include the hearing of voices, usually single, but sometimes multiple. They appear to come from very specific locations—animals, trees, furniture, or parts of one's own body—and may belong to some identifiable person, anonymous strangers, or nonhuman agencies, such as spirits or beings from other planets. Where do these voices originate? As is the case with any hallucination, auditory hallucinations also arise in the brain, specifically, in the right hemisphere. Self-consciousness is, to a large extent, the ability to distinguish between experiences that arise from within and those that are caused by outside agencies. According to the psychologist Julian Jaynes (1976), humanity as recently as 4000 years ago did not have self-awareness. Its two hemispheres functioned independently, the right hemisphere talking and giving orders to the left hemisphere, which proceeded to execute the orders, believing them to have come from an outside agency—a god, for instance. Jaynes believes that this is still happening in the less-advanced peoples today, and that at least a partial loss of self-awareness takes place in schizophrenia. The schizophrenic, as is well-known, may hear voices telling him or her to do things. These voices are attributed not to one self, but to outside agencies, such as God, angels, devils, demons, or some other entity. It is recognized that in schizophrenia there is a blurring of the boundaries of self, and that, for this reason, signals from within and without may be confounded. In 1977, police learned, after arresting New York's "Son of Sam" killer, that he had murdered six women on the instigation of a voice that came from a dog.

The hallucinations associated with the other sense modalities are more intimately linked with mental illness and epilepsy. We do not discuss the details and variations of these hallucinations associated with psychopathological states. However, the connection between psychopathology and occultism needs to be elucidated, and all of Chapter 10 is devoted to that subject. At this point, we consider special cases of hallucinations that may also occur in otherwise normal people who do not suffer from any organic abnormalities. These particular kinds of hallucinations have been interpreted as having occult significance or an occult origin.

Pseudohallucinations

Pseudohallucinations differ from sensory ones in that they are recognized by the hallucinator to be "inside," in the subjective space. Pseudohallucinations differ from hypnagogic and hypnopompic imagery in that the latter occur in the state between sleep and waking, whereas pseudohallucinations occur when the individual is awake. They also differ by being related to the hallucinator's current situation, most often involving people, where hypno images may bring anything.

Pseudohallucinations are often called visions. This implies that they are not dismissed as mere flights of fancy, but that meaning is attributed to them. The mediums, clairvoyants, and other psychics do not claim that their prophetic or clairvoyant visions are in any way objective. They do claim, however, that they are valid and that it takes a "gift" to see them. If their report is honest, it must be assumed that the vision referred to is a pseudohallucination. Beyond this, and as far as occult phenomena are concerned, it does not make much difference whether the experience is a pseudohallucination or a sensory one.

It can be argued that the behavior of hypnotized individuals who, under suggestion, behave as if they were seeing a hallucination, involves pseudohallucinations. In fact, it can be argued that even the unhypnotized individual who misperceives things because the particular misperception has been suggested by another person is experiencing a pseudohallucination. The "reality" of the hypnotic state and therefore the nature of the hypnotized person's subjective state (Is the person actually perceiving things that are not there? Is it a pseudohallucination? Does the person only go along with the hypnotizer and act as if he or she experienced the suggested phenomenon?) has been a hotly debated issue in hypnotism, and the answer depends on the particular theoretical explanation of hypnotism advocated.

Collective Hallucinations

The same hallucination may be experienced by two or more persons. If the event is entirely subjective, as all hallucinations are, how do two or 200 people manage to coordinate and synchronize their subjective lives? Recall our discussion of the role of expectation and misperception in the preceding chapter. It is expectation that plays the coordinating role in collective hallucination. Although the subject matter of individual hallucinations has virtually no limits, the topics of collective hallucinations are limited to certain categories. These categories are determined, first, by the kinds of ideas that a group of people may get excited about as a group, for emotional excitement is a prerequisite of collective hallucinations. The most common causes of emotional excitement in groups are religious, and, indeed, phenomena related to religion are most often the subject of collective hallucinations. Second, the categories are limited by the fact that all participants in the hallucination must be informed beforehand, at least concerning the broad outlines of the phenomenon that will constitute the collective hallucination. This may take the form of a publicly announced prophecy, for example, or someone suddenly looking up and saying, "Lo, in the sky!" or words to that effect. Things in the sky, or at least overhead, are the most commonly seen collective hallucinations: radiant crosses, saints, religious symbols, flying objects, sometimes all these in combination. Once the general type of hallucination is established, it is easy to harmonize individual differences in the accounts. This may take place during the hallucination or in subsequent conversations.

Even in cases of emotional contagion that so often takes place in crowds moved by strong emotions, there will be always some who will not see the hallucination. It is uncommon for them to speak out and deny it. They usually keep quiet, doubtful perhaps of their worthiness to have been granted the vision for which so many of their fellows all around them are fervently giving thanks. Later on, influenced by the accounts of others, they may even begin to believe that they saw it too. The "reliable eyewitness," who, as it turns out upon closer examination, did not see anything unusual at all, is an all-too-frequent experience of the investigator of phenomena seen by many.

Collective hallucinations have always occurred, perhaps more frequently in the past than now because of the interrelated factors that more people used to be uneducated, scientific thinking did not exist or had not yet spread widely enough, and there was a greater readiness to attribute anything inexplicable to supernatural, occult, paranormal, or divine causes. Religious visions, individual and collective, were abundant. One of the better known and more recent cases is the multiple collective hallucination that occurred at Limpias, Santander, in 1919 in which some church paintings of saints appeared to move, step out of their frames, and even drip blood as hundreds watched. Several mass hallucinations of moving and bleeding images of saints occurred in various places in Italy towards the end of the 19th century and the first decade of this century. In 1917, three Portuguese children from the village of Fátima were tending their sheep when they saw a bright flash. In a meadow, lit by a radiant light, they met a little woman who told them she was from heaven and asked them to return every month. On October 13th, a public miracle would take place. In the meantime, crowds that grew from 50 to several thousands witnessed the children's monthly conversations with what was presumed to be the Virgin Mary. Although the witnesses never saw her, they did see various other phenomena, such as explosions in a tree. On October 13, 1917, 70,000 people gathered to witness the public miracle. Although the children reportedly saw the Virgin, the crowd, at least many of them, witnessed a "solar phenomenon" in which the sun in the shape of a fiery disc began to move and approach the Earth. Although it had been raining before, after the fiery phenomenon, both the ground and the spectators appeared to be dry. The Fátima miracle is one instance where collective hallucination may have mingled with some celestial event along with more than a suggestion of UFO-like phenomena, long before the advent of the UFO age.

What was said about the dubious status of pseudohallucinations can also be said of collective hallucinations. Suggestion is the primary causative factor in both, and thus it may be asked: Because the 70,000 witnesses at Fátima were neither drunk nor under the influence of drugs, presumably not fatigued, feverish, or famished, what did they really see? Did they see an hallucination, or did they think they saw something, in the same way that the experimental subject may report seeing a light when there is none to see, only because the experimenter said there would be a light to see once in a while? The final answer to these questions has not been obtained yet.

The Autoscopic Hallucination

Seeing oneself the way one sees another person is *autoscopy*. What one sees is one's *double* or *Doppelgänger*. Meeting oneself in person is a most unusual experience. It is like a living proof of the dual nature of humans, soul and body, and the experience has always been part of the occult and religious beliefs of humanity. The double is part of folklore throughout the world. It is still part of religion in preindustrial societies. Witchdoctors and witches send their doubles on errands, and the *Doppelgänger,* under the name of the etheric or astral double, plays a prominent role in modern theosophical beliefs.

Experientially, there are varieties of the autoscopic hallucination. R. A. Moody (1975), for example, makes a distinction between autoscopy and the *out-of-the-body experience* (OBE, or looking at one's inert or sleeping body from an external point of view), relating the latter only to instances of a close brush with death. It is quite probable that the experiential varieties of autoscopy arise from clues supplied by the environment and the particular subjective state of the experiencer at the time of the OBE. We consider the varieties of the autoscopic hallucination as forms of essentially the same phenomenon.

Being mentally ill or under the influence of hallucinogenic drugs is not a prerequisite for experiencing the autoscopic hallucination. Startling, bizarre, and frightening as it may be, it can happen to anybody. It does not have to have any occult connotations either. For instance, a beginning university teacher lecturing to his or her first class may suddenly begin to experience the first stage of a full-fledged OBE: There is a feeling of an increasing distance between oneself and the droning figure at the lectern who seems to have no business being there lecturing anybody on anything. There may even be a full-fledged OBE, with the instructor watching himself or herself from a vantage point several feet away or above the behaving body. There are many instances in the history of literature of the double experience described by famous writers: Dostoevski (in his story *The Double*), Oscar Wilde, Edgar Allan Poe, Guy de Maupassant, and others. Even granting that there was something pathological in the makeup of the writers just mentioned (Dostoevski, for instance, had epilepsy, and the *Doppelgänger* experience occurs more frequently in epileptics, so that Dostoevski may have seen the double himself), there are examples of others whose mental and physical health was eminently good: Goethe once met himself riding a horse. Celia Green (1968) reports a very large number of case histories of OBEs, all of which occurred to seemingly normal individuals.

In terms of frequency, autoscopic hallucinators seem to fall into two categories. About 60% of individuals who report it experience it only once. The number of people who have experienced it twice, three, four, and five times is very small, but those who have experienced it six or more times constitute about 21% (Green, 1968). It is possible to self-induce the autoscopic hallucination deliberately, and the latter group of individuals would appear to have learned to do so.

The autoscopic hallucination can occur in any person, but does it occur in all? The answer is obviously no. At least, many people who could have had it have not reported it. There are individuals who have been declared clinically dead, revived, and have brought back stories of seeing themselves lying in bed or on the operating table and being ministered upon by physicians and nurses while they themselves float at the ceiling observing the scene (Moody, 1975). There are other such cases, however, in which the individual, upon regaining consciousness, has nothing to report. Although no comparison of these two groups of individuals has been made, the difference between them may well be the difference in the ability to visualize—those who report nothing may be poor visualizers.

Where there appears to be a memory of what happened while the individual was unconscious or under anesthesia, the memory can be explained naturalistically. Although vision does not function under anesthesia, other senses may be. Their impressions are recorded by the brain unconsciously, however. Under the proper circumstances, the brain is able to reconstruct a visual scene from auditory, kinesthetic, olfactory, and organic information as well as information available from past experience. That memory of what happened during anesthesia is recoverable has been recently demonstrated in several experiments. Levinson (1967), for example, tested the recall of specific statements made concerning the condition of a patient as the patient was being operated upon under deep general anesthesia. Ten patients who had been previously tested for susceptibility to hypnosis were exposed to the statements (regarding the color of their complexion and the need for oxygen) and interviewed a month later. They recalled nothing in their normal state, but under hypnosis, four of them reproduced the crucial conversation. Four others became so anxious reliving their operation that they woke up from the hypnosis, and two did not remember anything.

What conditions appear to be correlated with the autoscopic hallucination? First, age has something to do with it. It is experienced more often by people between 15 and 35 than by those who are older. The reason for this has not been researched, but one possibility is that the peaks for different types of creativity and imagination lie within these two decades. Both imagination and imagery tend to decline in middle age. We mentioned that the ability to visualize may underlie the difference between people who do and those who do not remember anything of what happened during a brush with death. John Palmer, a parapsychologist, suggests that the overwhelming majority of OBE experiences can be explained as hypnagogic states (Palmer, 1978), which have to do with imagery.

Sometimes, stress seems to facilitate the phenomenon. There are reports of individuals who have dissociated themselves from their bodies when undergoing intolerable torture. The OBE is just as likely to occur without stress, however. The first, spontaneous experience may take place while the individual is taking a relaxing stroll along the beach. A factor that is more important than stress is that the individual be in some way concerned with and attentive to the problem of his or her own identity, selfhood, existence, or self-preservation. Stress, then, would be secondarily related to these primary concerns. Carl Gustav Jung (1957), for instance, mentions the case of a woman who experienced the out-of-the-body state while a splinter was being taken out of her finger. She suddenly saw herself sitting in a meadow beside a brook, picking flowers, and remained in that state until the splinter had been removed.

The different forms of the autscopic experience that have been reported in the literature seem to be related to the degree to which the experiencer perceives the double as a separate, independently functioning entity with a mind of its own. This, in turn, is related to the intensity of the selfhood experience that triggers the autoscopic phenomenon. Thus, at one end of the continuum, walking by oneself may trigger a feeling of strangeness, of suddenly not knowing who you are or where you are, a perception of your body as something different from "you," and perhaps a sensation of tension between your body and the you that is trying to separate from it. It may be accompanied by a fear that you might not be able to return to your body, and then a quick return to a normal state. At the other end, there is the experience of near death, when a person may be unconscious while being operated upon on a vital function or lying in an automobile wreck and temporarily losing the vital signs, as in death. The autoscopic experience then includes seeing the inert body as it is handled by medical personnel or rescuers, the realization that one is dead, the experience of great calm and happiness, entering a new and wonderful place of existence, and perhaps ineffectual attempts to interfere with the efforts of those who are trying to resuscitate the body (Moody, 1975). In between these two extremes of stress and peril to one's individuality, there are intermediate states that may ensue as a result of fatigue, traumatic dreams, psychological stress, physical trauma, or philosophical reflections on personal identity. These conditions may lead to the experience of being outside one's body, looking at it from the outside, but having only a "disembodied consciousness,"—that is, no additional body, at this point of view. Green (1968) calls this the "asomatic case." By contrast, the experience may take the form of a duplicate of oneself, which is the case of the double of *Doppelgänger* (the "parasomatic case"). The double may appear in different degrees of completeness, from a simple, amorphous ovoid to a complete person, either identical in physical appearance and dress, or dressed differently and behaving quite independently of the "original." The English poet Shelley, when walking alone on a street in Italy, came across a cloaked man whose face was hidden by a hood. When the figure was within a few feet from Shelley, it raised its hood and Shelley recognized that it was himself. A most dramatic flourish was added when the figure said, in Italian, "Are you satisfied?" (Reed, 1972).

Modern occultism borrows its explanation of the phenomenon of the double from modern theosophy, and modern theosophy got it from Oriental sources—Hinduism and Buddhism. According to this view, humans exist on seven planes, or have seven bodies, only one of which is the physical body we all know. The other bodies exist on other planes of less dense matter. One such plane is the astral plane. The astral body may separate from the physical body while the person is still alive, go to other places, obtain information, or even produce changes on the physical plane. The doubles we occasionally see are thus our own astral bodies. The astral bodies of other people may also be seen on occasion. The connection between the physical and the astral body is said to be maintained by a silver cord. This cord used to figure prominently in the description of autoscopic hallucinations. Green (1968) notes that it is very seldom mentioned nowadays.

Psychologists fail to see the need for a paranormal explanation of the autoscopic hallucination. Even on a superficial level, there are enough problems to reject such an interpretation out of hand: The mode of appearance of the double varies according to the historical period and cultural differences and preferences; the inconsistent, Earth-bound way in which individuals about to pass to "the other side" describe their experiences and attending circumstances, a way that more than anything reflects their past experiences and expectations; and the logical inconsistencies (for instance, why should an astral body require a suit or dress, socks, shoes, etc.?) all point to the source of autoscopic experience—one's own mind. More fundamentally, the implicit mind-body dualism of the occult explanation clashes with the monistic position of science.

It is true, nevertheless, that in spite of the fascinating nature of the phenomenon, psychologists have devoted very little interest to it. Perhaps it has been thought that it was not important enough, or that the term "hallucination" already sufficiently explained it. It is quite possible, though, that, because the autoscopic experience may begin under a variety of different circumstances, the experience itself is not all of the same cloth. Thus, even though the double may be a true sensory hallucination in the case of a psychotic patient, it may be a different type of imagery with non-psychotic individuals. For instance, it could be a projected body image. The body image is an idea of what one's body looks like, how it is made, or how it appears to oneself and others. Because the body is a most familiar object, the idea is a familiar and a fundamental one. It exists not only in humans, but also in animals. When an ape, without any prior learning experience, "apes" a human, it does so because the bodies of both humans and apes are built on the same plan and the ape has a perfectly good image of this plan. Well-established ideas can be projected or, rather, they project themselves (unconsciously)—that is, they may appear to have acquired independent existence outside our minds. For instance, certain strangers may appear to us to resemble our parents even when in other people's opinion they do not. The parent's image is projected upon a stranger when the appropriate clues are present. The externalization of the body image may therefore be nothing but a projected body image. It is perhaps even incorrect to speak of an autoscopic hallucination because some types of the ecsomatic (out-of-the-body, Green, 1968) experience do not involve an image of oneself—they may be mental states that signal the possibility of a projected idea, but are not yet projections themselves. The initial stage of strangeness and feeling of imminent separation may be achieved by repeating to oneself a number of times, "Who am I?" or "What am I doing here?" and assuming an attitude to match the question. Schizophrenics are said to be strangers to themselves, and the feeling of strangeness and separation that is most often experienced first in puberty was once thought to be a sign of incipient schizophrenia (*dementia precox*, as it was called then). The exercise just described does not lead to a mental disorder of any kind. It is imagery, but it is not hallucination.

All reports of ecsomatic experiences that have been analyzed to obtain some coherent picture of them (Green, 1968; Moody, 1975) have been self-reports of subjective experiences obtained by way of mailed questionnaires. The most dramatic reports are obtained from individuals who have been declared clinically dead, have revived, and have been able to tell about what happened while they were "dead." Moody's (1975) informants were not all that uniform in their accounts of what they experienced; still, Moody presents a "theoretically complete model experience" that has the following components: The patient experiences great physical discomfort, hears the physician pronounce him dead, hears an uncomfortable buzzing sound, and is drawn into a long tunnel. He then notices that he has a new and different body with new capabilities, such as being able to pass through solid objects, and sees his old body prostrated, with those trying to help him gathered around. He meets dead relatives and a being of bright light who helps him review his life panoramically and leads him to "the other side." The patient is suffused with joy, peace, love, and the wisdom of the ages. He then comes to a barrier and is made to turn back and occupy his old body because the time for him to die is not yet.

There are several major problems with such accounts. A number of Moody's cases were obtained by him when individuals contacted him after hearing him talk about such experiences. How many others had read descriptions of what happens after death in the occult literature is not known, but there must have been several such persons. Moody believes that it is the common elements in the accounts he has collected that speak for the reality of the phenomenon, but the communality may have been achieved partly due to reasons that have nothing to do with the hypothesis of the survival of bodily death.

The pattern of experiences, such as described by Moody, is not unique to life-threatening situations. It is quite similar to the experiences of the mystic and the drug user. The patterns and designs that are seen in hallucinations, for instance, are variations of a very few basic themes, and these are found in hallucinations seen by people under the influence of hallucinogenic drugs, in a delirium, in hypnagogic and hypnopompic states, in sensory deprivation, as well as when they are in mortal danger. It was established quite some time ago that the basic form types seen in hallucinations are gratings or lattices, cobwebs, tunnels, and spirals. These are typically seen in vivid colors and are intensely bright (Siegel, 1977). The tunnel, the spiraling tunnel, and falling through a tunnel is an image known well enough for it to have become an almost standard visual device for writers and filmmakers to indicate the passage to a different time (time travel) or state of existence (as in *Alice in Wonderland*). On the basis of experiments with hallucinogenic drugs and other evidence, Siegel (1977) concludes that there must be a nervous mechanism that is the source of "a universal phenomenology of hallucinations (p. 132)."

Another problem is that because the individuals did revive, they obviously were never dead to begin with. The fact that cases of presumed clinical death are relatively numerous only indicates that the medical profession is making quite a number of diagnostic errors. In the case of emergencies, this is understandable because the physicians and nurses are more concerned with saving the victim's life than with making sure that the person is indeed dead. The definitive criterion of death is a flat EEG record. No one showing such a record has ever been revived to tell anything about the experience. The concern of the resuscitation team with life-saving procedures leaves them little time to attach the patient to an EEG machine or to pay attention to and remember, let alone record, the precise details of what went on or who said what to whom. Their alleged amazement at the subject's ability to recount what happened while they were "dead" can be therefore attributed largely to their inability to verify these statements against facts.

All of this would seem to indicate that the only real proof (to a dualist) of the separation of an individual into two entities would be provided by a simultaneous photograph of them. Given the easy acceptance of such transparent fakes as fairy photographs (by such famous people as Sir Arthur Conan Doyle, for instance), and the ingenuity of the current crop of "mental photographers" in producing images without light, even this method offers no guarantees. Current attempts to photograph the double have yielded negative results. They have been made by the parapsychologist Karlis Osis of the American Society for Psychical Research. An alternative method used by Osis is to have an individual who claims to be able to produce an astral projection at will to obtain information from another location where it is placed so that it can be read only by looking down at it from the ceiling. Success is claimed for these experiments, although its degree does not appear to differ from the degree of success obtained in telepathy and clairvoyance experiments with pictorial materials. It seems that of two individuals, both of whom are equally convinced of their own ability to obtain information by way of the out-of-the-body phenomenon, the one who also considers oneself to be clairvoyant or telepathic, shows better performance than the one who does not. The magician Milbourne Christopher (1970) recounts in detail a field experiment with the Reverend Dr. Gilbert N. Holloway in which the latter, in spite of his total confidence in his ability to go astrally anywhere in the world and describe any location whose address was given him, failed to do so for Christopher. Although his descriptions of two dwellings were minutely detailed, most of the descriptive items were wrong, and those that were not were either easy inferences or so general that they could have fitted any number of dwellings.

The OBE experiment most often cited in the parapsychological literature is one done by Charles Tart (1968). A young woman, Miss Z., who reported having OBEs two to four times a week during sleep, was studied for four nights in a sleep laboratory. She was encouraged to have OBEs and, during them, to look at, remember, and report a five-digit number placed on a shelf several feet above her bed. Although she experienced OBEs each night but the first, she was able to see the number only on the fourth. She gave the number correctly. Tart, however, does not attach much significance to this fact for two reasons. One is that, according to Tart, Miss Z. could have read the number telepathically or clairvoyantly rather than by flotation towards the ceiling to look at it from above. Second, the possibility that she could have obtained the number through ordinary sensory means was not excluded. For instance, when light fell on the number, it was reflected from the shiny surface of a wall clock located above the shelf. Miss Z. was attached to an electroencephalograph and could not get out of the bed without disrupting the connection. She could, however, have read the number while the light was still on and she was being attached to the EEG equipment or later on by means of a flashlight reflection, because she was not being constantly observed visually. The significance of the experiment lies in the fact that Miss Z. reported OBEs, and these correspond in time with a very unusual EEG pattern, one that was neither a typical waking or sleeping pattern ("flattened EEG with prominent alphoid activity"), no rapid eye movements (which would indicate dreaming, and no galvanic skin-response changes (which would indicate emotional arousal). This, of course, does not mean that any kind of mind-body separation took place, only that a correspondence between a form of altered state of consciousness and a particular brain-wave pattern was established.

Isolation and Hallucinations

One of the most significant discoveries in the behavioral sciences made in the 1950s and 1960s was the necessity of varied stimulation for normal growth and development and the normal functioning of both animals and humans. When the variability of stimulation drops below normal levels, organisms engage in behaviors that increase such variability. Humans, if they are not allowed to do so by manipulating their physical environment, will produce their own stimulation internally—that is, they will hallucinate.

There are different types of isolation (Brownfield, 1965): isolation achieved through confinement to a limited space, by means of seat belts, walls, or sealed cabins, for instance; isolation through removal or cutting off of normal, ordinary stimulation, social or physical, as in solitary confinement or experiments on sensory deprivation; isolation through separation from persons, places, or objects that have special significance for the individual, as through the death of a loved one; and isolation from normal stimulation that is achieved when stimulation is monotonized and eventually ceases to be effective. Hallucinations are triggered mainly by the first two types of isolation, but not exclusively so.

One of the surprising discoveries in the early sensory-deprivation studies conducted at McGill University in the 1950s was the hallucinations experienced by subjects who had been deprived of normal visual, auditory, and tactual stimulation. Having caught up on their sleep and having run through their reportoires of memories, daydreams, problems, and free associations, subjects began to see lights, geometric patterns, wallpaper border-like designs, as well as more complicated visions that came and went spontaneously (Heron, 1957). Although it has been suggested that the visions were hypnagogic or hypnopompic imagery rather than true hallucinations, there is no doubt that such spontaneous imagery does occur.

The content of hallucinations and of imagery is to a considerable extent determined by past experience and the present situation. There is nothing in the sensory deprivation experiment to suggest to the subject paranormal or occult ideas, and such ideas are seldom reported. There were, nevertheless, some reports in the McGill studies of experiences that in other contexts have been considered to be of occult significance. For example, a couple of the McGill subjects felt at one point as if they were two overlapping bodies lying side by side, one felt that his mind was like a "ball of cotton" floating above his body, and another felt "detached" from his body. These experiences are not unlike the autoscopic hallucinations already discussed. Hallucinations of occult and religious significance do occur quite often when the individual is already primed to have them or when isolation and imminent threat to life occur together. Hallucinations associated with isolation that have occult significance are thus to be sought in anecdotal reports and case histories rather than in scientific experiments. What the experiments do show are the conditions that are favorable to hallucinatory experiences with an occult content. Thus, complete sensory deprivation does not increase the vividness or the frequency of hallucinations. Rather, some stimulus input, such as diffuse light, is necessary for hallucinations to occur. This is to say that laboratory-like conditions need not be present in natural settings and that partial sensory reduction, monotonization, and other forms of isolation will be hallucinogenically effective. Also, stimulus reductions in one sense modality, such as vision, may produce hallucinations in another, such as hearing.

Perhaps the best-known first-person account of self-imposed isolation is that of Admiral Richard Byrd (Byrd, 1938), who spent 6 months alone in a confined space in the Antarctic during polar night. Of interest here is the fact that Byrd experienced hallucinations and an "oceanic" feeling of at oneness with the universe that characterize many accounts of experiences under the influence of LSD. *A Woman in the Polar Night* is a similar account by a woman, Christiane Ritter(1954), who hallucinated monsters, felt at one with the moon, and saw her past life in a vision. Byrd and Ritter isolated themselves voluntarily. Individuals lost at sea experience equally mystical visions, but of a somewhat different nature, probably due to the constant threat of imminent death, poor nutrition, physical exertion, and exposure to the elements (Merrien, 1954). Depending on the experiencing individual's ego strength, he or she may see a vision of a "savior" or a "destroyer," the former type of vision being more common for individuals who believe in their ultimate rescue throughout their ordeal and the latter being experienced by those who do not survive (and whose hallucinations are reported by those who do). The solitary sailor Joshua Slocum, who became sick and whose boat was tossed by a gale, saw the pilot of Columbus' ship *Pinta* take over the helm and guide the boat through the storm. Slocum had conversations with the pilot, and subsequently saw him several times during storms (Slocum, 1900).

Both written tradition and current practices of the world's religions show the recognition of the necessity for isolation in order to achieve creative religious insights, divine revelation, or spiritual rebirth. Such experiences are often accompanied by visions of divine figures or symbols. Hermits, recluses, and anchorites, in addition to seeking solitude, have enhanced their hallucinatory experiences through fasting, self-mortification, immobility (such as the pillar-top sitters of Asia Minor), and possibly the consumption of hallucinogenic desert plants. The Christian Bible gives a number of instances of religious revelations, accompanied by visions, having occurred during prolonged isolation from social contact and with reduced sensory stimulation, such as by spending 40 days and nights on Mount Sinai (Moses), in the desert (Jesus), 3 years in the desert of Arabia (Paul), or the whole life in the wilderness (John the Baptist). The Hindu or Tibetan Buddhist guru either meditates in the desert, an isolated mountain cave, or else retreats from sense impressions through yogic exercises. Members of Christian holy orders live in the seclusion of the monasteries and retreat into even deeper isolation by dwelling in hermitages, maintaining vigils, and otherwise enhancing isolation through means that tend to increase their susceptibility to hallucinations: fasting, fatigue, or monotonous rituals. Materially primitive tribes impose isolation on their young men as part of their maturity rites. The hallucinations experienced are thought to be of supernatural origin and of high value to the individual who, as a result thereof, becomes a different and a better person.

Flying an airplane, driving an automobile, watching a radar screen, or doing work on an assembly line may seem like activities radically different from meditating in a cave, yet these can also be instances of isolation, especially when done alone and when the task is repetitive, monotonous, and prolonged. Being confined to a small space enhances the monotony effect. Jet fighter pilots, flying at high altitudes and in level flight, have reported hallucinations, such as the "break-off" phenomenon, milder forms of which may be a simple feeling of loneliness, depression, and of being "broken off" from people and the Earth, and more severe forms of which may result in the pilot's suddenly finding himself or herself outside the aircraft and being pushed by it. It is believed that at least some cases of pilots' sighting "flying saucers" may have been hallucinations induced by the monotonous conditions of flight.

NOTES

The most useful reviews of the hypnagogic and hypnopompic states have been provided by McKellar (1972), Rawcliffe (1959), and Reed (1972), and the best treatment of hallucinations is the collection of papers edited by Siegel and West (1975).

Brownfield's (1965) small book on the effects of isolation is a compact but comprehensive, as well as readable, treatment of hallucinatory experiences that occur under conditions of sensory deprivation or monotonization.

6 Psychology of Anomalous Memory

A man's memory may almost become the art of continually varying and misrepresenting his past, according to his interests in the present.

George Santayana. *Persons and Places,* I

"Living backwards!" Alice repeated in great astonishment. "I never heard of such a thing!" "—but there's one great advantage in it, that one's memory works both ways." "I'm sure mine works one way," Alice remarked. "I can't remember things before they happen."

Lewis Carroll, *Through the Looking-Glass and What Alice Found There,* Ch. V

Psychophysicists and communications engineers use the notion of the ideal observer. An ideal observer is one who records events with utter faithfulness. There are no distortions in the recording system, and the record is a perfect replica of the event. No such recording system, biological or artificial, exists in reality, but the ideal observer is a useful abstraction, a standard that the actual performances of real observers may be compared with. The memory systems of living organisms are real recording systems. Their operation may be described as marred by internal noise, distorting, faulty, incomplete, and prone to adding items that were never recorded at all. Still, the idea prevails that, with the exception of those few instances where human memory might admittedly fail, it operates by and large like that of an ideal observer, and performance standards are set for it accordingly. Eyewitness testimony is still considered better than circumstantial evidence, even though psychologists have been demonstrating the unreliability of the memory of witnesses for the past 60 years or more.

The malfunctioning of memory has a bearing on occult phenomena. There are two ways in which faulty memory creates or contributes to the impression that the phenomenon in question is of an extraordinary nature. First, it does so whenever the substance of the phenomenon is witness testimony, notably reports of ghosts, apparitions, "physical" phenomena of the mediumistic séance, and events associated with unidentified flying objects. Even when these phenomena are recorded on film or magnetic tape, which is seldom, the record is typically so poor or ambiguous that witness reports remain the principal source of information presented. All the problems that are associated with the testimony of witnesses in a criminal court, for instance, are also involved where a witness testifies that he or she has just seen the landing of little green men from Mars. Second, faulty memory in its various manifestations may in itself be taken as evidence for esoteric notions, such as when the *déjà vu* phenomenon is taken as evidence for reincarnation.

As far as anomalistic phenomena are concerned, the fallibility of human memory is it most significant feature. Most people do not realize how extremely fallible human memory can sometimes be. There is another factor of human memory that, although recognized, is not always connected to paranormal phenomena involving memory. It is the existence of individuals, usually children or youths, whose memory capacity is far beyond that of even the best intellects. When an adolescent who cannot tell you how to add two single-digit numbers can nevertheless tell you the day of the week for any date hundreds of years back and ahead; when 10-year-old Henry Stafford calculates correctly 365^{12} (a 36-digit number) in less than a minute; when Zerah Colburn at age 8 computes 8^{16} in his head without pausing; when Shakantula Devi extracts the square root of a 720-digit number in a few minutes; or when child Mozart remembers every note in a long symphony—this is evidence in favor of the position that there is no reason to call for supernatural explanations of phenomena of human memory regardless of how impossible they may appear to the average person, because human memory is clearly capable of imaging, retaining, and using amounts of information far beyond what is normally expected.

MEMORY SYSTEMS

Before discussing anomalies of memory, we briefly review some facts about memory and memory storage. The review parallels and overlaps the discussion of the processes of perception in Chapter 4.

Three memory systems are distinguished: the sensory-information stage, short-term memory, and long-term memory. There can be no memory unless some change in energy level (stimulation) has affected the sensory apparatus and the sensory apparatus has produced the information that becomes stored in the memory-storage system. The duration of memory in the *sensory-information storage* is very brief. It lasts only a little longer than the energy that impinges upon a sense organ and triggers its activity. Thus, a brief flash of light lasting 1/1000 of a second, for instance, will always be estimated to have lasted longer because the electrochemical activity that a brief burst of light sets up in the cells of the retina, the rods and the cones, will continue for some time after the flow of energy has ceased.

Repeated or continuous stimulation is given an interpretation, or meaning, by the brain, and it is in this form that it passes into the *short-term memory* storage. Short-term memory contains the meaning of stimulation.

Unless they have some unusual or salient feature that forces itself upon our attention, meaningless items are not likely to be remembered. Short-term memory lasts only seconds or a few minutes. It also has a very limited capacity, about seven items or bits of information. While we have it, it is very clear and vivid and can be reproduced at will. However, unless an item that circulates in short-term memory is rehearsed, it soon will fade away.

What is referred to as memory in everyday speech is *long-term memory*, the material that has been recorded somewhere in the nervous system so that it lasts indefinitely. Long-term memory has a virtually limitless capacity. Anomalous retention refers to problems with this kind of memory storage. The problems arise from the nature of long-term memory. It is dissimilar from both the sensory-information memory and short-term memory because it is neither a copy or reproduction of the item that caused it originally, nor is it only an interpretation of what it means. It is a reconstruction or, more precisely, a recreation of past experience. Long-term memory is an active process of searching, upon a clue, of the memory storage for the salient features of a past experience and then reconstructing it, piece by piece. This happens even when the long-term memory is an image. Chances are that this image is not an exact copy of the original scene, as becomes evident when that scene is revisited. One is often surprised to find that, even though the scene has not changed objectively, one's memory image of it has: The remembered building or room may actually be quite a bit larger or smaller, or the relationship between rooms or the location of objects quite different from the memory image. Long-term memory is an active, creative process, not at all like a photographic image. It is unlikely that it even resides in any specific brain structure, a possible reason why it has been so difficult to establish what the physical counterpart of long-term memory is.

It was the work of the English psychologist, Sir Frederic Bartlett, that established the dynamic nature of memory (Bartlett, 1932). Bartlett showed with some simple experiments that memory, instead of being a thing, was a process, the process of remembering. It was not a static property or the reactivation of memory traces left by experience, a view commonly held up to that time. When the material to be remembered is more complex than digits or nonsense syllables, repeated reproduction of the material, Bartlett showed, leads to certain predictable changes, such as simplification, condensation, increased symmetry, increased familiarity, in general something better than what it was before. This tendency applied to all kinds of materials, not just the reproduction of drawings. Stories are notorious for getting better in the retelling, better in the sense of being more entertaining, having a "better" form, not in the sense of being closer to truth. Bartlett's work has been replicated since by other researchers, and his view of memory as an active, creative process of remembering prevails among psychologists today.

Bartlett also stressed the role of attitudes in remembering. In remembering, attitudes play the same role as attention and expectation do in perception: They filter and color the information that is being put together. The information is not arriving from outside, but is found in long-term memory storage. Because attitudes reflect a person's values, it is clear that reconstructed memories will not be unbiased, objective records of the past, but will be tinted (and tainted) by the subject's attitudes. As the psychologist Graham Reed (1972) puts it in writing about anomalies of recall: "what we remember is to some extent what we think we ought to remember. [p. 72]."

Measures of Retention

When retention is measured, the conclusion that is reached whether the individual tested remembers anything or not depends on the particular method used to measure retention. This has a direct bearing on conclusions reached concerning the occult nature of what is remembered.

Technically, *recall* means unaided remembering. No clues are given, and the individual produces a report, account, drawing, and so on, "out of his or her head." The essay test in which no aids are allowed is an example of measuring retention by the method of recall in the educational setting. When applied to single items, and in particular in relation to testing memory with emphasis on perception, the term *identification* is used. An item is identified when the subject can give its name.

When naming is not required, we speak of *recognition*. Saying, "Yes, I've seen that person," is recognition, whereas to state that "This is Jim" is identification. It is clear that in the recognition test, there remains the uncertainty of whether the testee indeed remembers or just says he or she does. Not until indentification takes place does the tester know for sure. It is evident that the way in which a witness is questioned has a great deal to do with the kind of conclusions that will be reached based on the witness's replies.

In the educational setting, the most common method of measuring retention is the recognition method, specifically in the form of the multiple-choice test. In comparison with the essay test, the multiple-choice item offers the student some aid in that one of the alternatives he or she is looking at is the correct answer, so that, if the student remembers the textbook or lecture, he or she should be able to recognize it. The recognition method is a more sensitive method than the recall method. It may show retention where the recall method does not. Thus, a student may be able to recognize the wording of a multiple-choice alternative as something he or she has seen before, whereas he or she might be completely unable to write anything on the subject. One example of the difference between recall and recognition within an occult context is the *Déjà vu* experience, discussed later in this chapter, in which the sense of familiarity (recognition) is not supported by recall of how familiarity was ever acquired.

A third method of measuring retention, the method of relearning, is less well known because it is not used to measure students' achievement. It is, however, a method that is more sensitive than either recall or recognition. This method may show retention where the other two methods fail to do so. In the relearning method, the number of trials it takes an individual to learn certain materials is compared with the number of trials it takes the person to relearn the same material some time later. If the number of relearning trials is smaller than the number of original learning trials, something has been retained. For our purposes, the significant aspect of this method is that the testee may be totally unaware that he or she remembers anything, and yet the relearning method shows that there is retention. As we show, relearning experiments demonstrate that *xenoglossy* (the use, in an altered state of consciousness, of a foreign language that is unknown to the individual in his or her normal state) requires no occult explanation.

MEMORY AND OCCULT PHENOMENA

Faulty Memory

The general term applied to faulty memory and memory distortions is *paramnesia*. Both cryptomnesia and the *déjà vu* experience, described later in this chapter may be classified as instances of paramnesia.

The attention of a person under extreme stress is focused primarily on his or her own well-being. When fear or distress are extreme, the entire stressful situation may later be forgotten, and we speak of psychogenic *amnesia*. Where the functioning of memory has been studied under controlled conditions, it has been found that subjects are less able to remember details or notice information presented on dials and other kinds of displays. Visions, apparitions, ghosts, spiritualistic séances, and UFOs are stressful experiences, and reports of such experiences must be studied with great caution. Even expert witnesses are not free from omissions and distortions caused by stress.

Expectations, sets, attitudes, prejudices, and values in general color our memories to such an extent that black can quite literally become white in remembering. In a classical study, Gordon Allport had students describe what they had just seen in a picture that featured a White person and a Black person engaged in a discussion during a subway ride. The White person was holding an open straight razor in his hand. In the retelling, one-half of the students switched the razor blade to the hand of the Black man (Allport & Postman, 1945). Buckhout (1974) covered a person completely with a black bag and had him visit a number of classes at Washington University. When asked to describe the nature of the person inside the bag later, the students did so willingly, including precise details that were not available from a visual inspection of the bag-covered person—for instance, the person's race. Eyewitnesses to flying-saucer landings report seeing occupants of the saucer not necessarily because there are occupants (or even because there is a saucer), but because a flying machine is expected to contain fliers. The occupants are, for the most part, dissimilar enough from humans to conform with the hypothesis of their extraterrestial origin, but similar enough to conform to the only prototype of higher intelligence that the witness is familiar with, the human being.

Incorrect assumptions about cause-effect relationships often translate themselves into incorrect memories. If it is assumed, incorrectly, that a more intelligent brain requires a larger skull to contain it, science-fiction writers, illustrators, makeup artists, and witnesses to UFO landings will draw, describe, mold, and remember aliens with extra large heads to hold all that intelligence, evidence from the animal world, let alone the history of computer development to the contrary notwithstanding.

There is a human need for ego enhancement, to feel important, to do important things, or to be part of important events, even as only an eyewitness. This need is so strong that a person may assert that he or she was a witness to an important or historic event that took place near where they live even though they may not have known at the time that the event was happening. A field study was once conducted by a journalist who fabricated a story about a naked woman, inhabitant of a small town, who got stuck to a freshly painted toilet seat. The journalist distributed the story through a newspaper wire service. On visiting the town and interviewing its citizens about the incident, the journalist found many who claimed to have witnessed or played part in it. There were refusals to accept the truth even after the true origin of the story was made public. Similar incidents are reported in connection with UFOs—that is, witnesses are found to UFOs that exist only in the rumors spread by the perpetrators of a hoax. Nevertheless, the reports of the witnesses are not necessarily lies or fabrications; they may actually "remember" that the events they describe did take place.

When there is an intention to deceive, eyewitness testimony is all but worthless. One should only be reminded of what happens during a performance of stage magic, where it is not even assumed that the phenomena, as they appear to the spectators, are "real." A well-performed trick of stage magic is undetectable, often even by experts—that is, other magicians. Eyewitness testimonies of what was seen in situations where deception is the rule but the assumption is that the phenomena are genuine, as in the mediumistic séance, are that much less reliable. The credentials of the witnesses, who may be characterized as "unimpeachable" because of their social or professional standing, are irrelevant in such cases. Tests of eyewitness reliability were performed quite early in the history of the Society for Psychical Research in London, with devastating results. An SPR member, S. John Davey, pretending to be a medium, conducted several mock séances, afterwards asking the sitters to write down what they saw. They gave incorrect reports of very common happenings, and reported things that never happened. They consistently failed to observe crucial events, such as the manipulations performed on a slate (Davey was producing spurious "spirit" writings), even though the slate was only 3 feet away from the sitters. They failed to detect anything even when they were told that trickery would be used (Hodgson, 1892; Hodgson & Davey, 1886-1887). Theodore Besterman performed similar tests with SPR members several decades later (Besterman, 1931-1932), with comparable results. Besterman did not use any tricks, merely asking the participants in séance-like situations to describe what they had witnessed. Their responses were scored according to the difficulty of the question and the precision of the answer. The best report was only 61% correct, the average being 33.9%. Thus, even when trickery and sleight of hand were not involved, the reports of two-thirds of the observers could not be trusted. As Buckhout (1974) puts it:

> Eyewitness testimony is . . .based on a theory, constructed by a human being (often with the help of others), about what reality was like in the past; since that theory can be adjusted or changed in accordance with personality, with the situation or with social pressure, it is unwise to accept such testimony without question [p. 31].

Cryptomnesia

In *cryptomnesia*, the memory in question is not faulty or distorted as such. What is lacking is the recognition that it is a memory. Cryptomnesia usually involves seemingly original ideas that are not or the telling of old stories as if they were new. In one situation, the person who has cryptomnesia is the originator of the idea, but does not remember that he or she had stated it once before. A typical example is the researcher who struggles with a problem, finds a brilliant solution, then discovers that he or she had thought of the very same solution weeks earlier, perhaps even twice (Reed, 1972). Another situation is one in which the originator of the idea is another person, yet the one who thinks of it believes that it is his or hers. Unconscious plagiarism, with consequences that may be either humorous or annoying, occurs ever so often in academic circles. The composition of melodies that have already been composed (and performed) is another example. The clairvoyant dream of the type where one sees the location of an object that has been misplaced earlier is explicable in terms of cryptomnesia.

Cryptomnesia is involved in the alleged remembering of past lives (reincarnations). Although the individual seems to have knowledge of historical facts to which he or she has never been exposed, it may be found, upon closer examination, that such an exposure has, in fact, taken place, except that the individual does not remember it, even when faced with the evidence. This was the case with Virginia Tighe, the subject of the celebrated case of the "reincarnation" of Bridey Murphy, which is described later in the section on age regression.

It is quite probable that long-term memories are never lost, only that their retrieval may become difficult and require special methods. Such methods include hypnosis and drugs, as well as such naturally occurring conditions as shock or high fever. The memories need not be particularly significant or unusual. They can be, in fact, nonsense materials. When the material learned is meaningless to the learner and a long time passes between the original learning and subsequent reproduction, the result may be quite spectacular and tends to evoke occult explanations. William James (1890/1950) tells one such story:

> In a Roman Catholic town in Germany, a young woman, who could neither read or write, was seized with a fever, and was said by the priest to be possessed of a devil, because she was heard talking Latin, Greek, and Hebrew. Whole sheets of her ravings were written out, and found to consist of sentences intelligible in themselves, but having slight connection with each other. Of her Hebrew sayings, only a few could be traced to the Bible, and most seemed to be in the Rabbinical dialect. All trick was out of the question; the woman was a simple creature; there was no doubt as to the fever. It was long before any explanation, save that of demoniacal possession, could be obtained. At last the mystery was unveiled by a physician, who determined to trace back the girl's history, and who, after much trouble, discovered that at the age of nine she had been charitably taken by an old Protestant pastor, a great Hebrew scholar, in whose house she lived till his death. On further enquiry it appeared to have been the old man's custom for years to walk up and down a passage of his house into which the kitchen opened, and to read to himself with a loud voice out of his books. The books were ransacked, and among them were found several of the Greek and Latin Fathers, together with a collection of Rabbinical writings. In these works so many of the passages taken down at the young woman's bedside were identified that there was no reasonable doubt as to their source [p. 681].

Although James' story is only an anecdote, psychological research shows that bits of a foreign language can be retained for a long time without the person's knowing the language or without the person's being aware that he or she is the possessor of such memories. In an heroic experiment, Burtt, an English psychologist, read to his son passages from the *Oedipus Rex* tragedy by Sophocles in the original Greek (Burtt, 1941). He read to his son the same 20-line selection every day for 3 months beginning at the age of 15 months. Every 3 months, a different selection was used, and that procedure continued until the subject had reached the age of 3 years. Young Burtt was not exposed to Greek at any time after this age. At the age of 8 ½, his father tested him for the retention of what had been essentially nonsense words to him. The father compared the number of trials it took his son to relearn seven of the original 21 stanzas with the number of learning trials for three stanzas from the same work that the subject had been never exposed to. There was a saving of 27%. Similar tests were given at ages 14 and 18. There was a saving of 8% at age 14 and none at 18.

Therese Neumann, the Bavarian stigmatist whose ability to speak Aramaic when reexperiencing Christ's passion during Holy Week, was mentioned in Chapter 2. Before divine inspiration or an occult explanation of xenoglossy may be considered, several more parsimonious alternative explanations need to be looked at first. One is fraud. Because Therese's father was discovered secretly supplying her food during the long period of time when she claimed to have lived without food, the possibility that he may have furnished her with some Aramaic phrases cannot be discounted. Second, some of the researchers who heard her use Aramaic knew the language themselves. Therese was not tested for auditory hyperacuity during the 3-week examination she underwent in 1927. Endowed with hyperacusis, a person can quite literally hear what another person is thinking, even though that person's lips are closed and the ordinary ear hears no sound. Third, Therese could have picked up some Aramaic on her own, possibly in circumstances similar to those described by James. The unconscious use of it would then place the phenomenon in the category of cryptomnesia.

Memories of Previous Lives

The teaching that we live more than once is part of Hinduism and Buddhism, as well as other religions, past and present. Modern theosophy, which is based to a considerable extent on Hinduism and Buddhism, as well as most other esoteric belief systems, accept the doctrine of reincarnation as an integral part. The ability to remember past lives with continued practice is promised in the yoga systems, but individuals who do not practice yoga and lay no claims to any particular spiritual achievements also seem to remember their past lives.

Karma and Reincarnation.   The core of the doctrine of reincarnation is the principle of cause and effect applied to the moral sphere. In Hinduism and Buddhism, it is known as karma. Karma is the law of ethical causation: We reap what we sow. Karma is not limited by time or space; neither is it applicable to individuals only: There is also the karma of groups, families, and nations. The doctrine of reincarnation follows necessarily from the idea of karma. One is born into a particular life with a personality, nationality, and family environment determined by actions in past incarnations. Liberation from the round of rebirths may be achieved only by liberating oneself from the belief in a separate, individual self and from the attachment to the consequences of action.

One problem with the doctrine of reincarnation is that although the nature of the physical world is relatively well understood, at least well enough to formulate a few laws about cause-effect relationships, the same cannot be said about the moral world. There is no agreement on what the nature of the moral world is. For this reason, even within a single belief system, such as Buddhism, not much may be said about the mechanism of the law of retribution, except that eventually everybody gets their just deserts, even if it takes another life or lives.

If Christianity accepted the doctrine of reincarnation, it would be said that it is the soul that reincarnates. St. Thomas Aquinas, the foremost philosopher and psychologist of Catholicism, taught that even though the essence of the soul is single, the soul is endowed with powers or functions. The powers of the immortal aspect of soul are self-awareness, reason, and will. Thus, there is room for a record or memories of past lives in the soul. Buddha never made it explicit what it is that reincarnates. The existence of a personal soul is denied (the doctrine of *anatta*, or no soul), at least in one of the two major schools of Buddhism, the Theravada or Southern school. Nevertheless, the doctrine of reincarnation is a cornerstone of Buddha's teachings. Modern theosophy, combining the teachings of ancient and medieval occultism, such as those of the Gnostics, the Cabala, and Hermetism, with those of Hinduism and Buddhism, views humans as sevenfold beings, consisting of an "upper" triad and a "lower" quaternary. The lower quaternary consists of the physical body, the etheric body, the astral body, and the life principle. The physical body is on the "densest" level of matter, the others occupying a place on increasingly "subtler" levels. The lower quaternary dissolves upon death, first the physical body, then gradually the others. The upper triad consists of Mind, Intuition, and Oversoul, or, in Hindu terminology, Manas, Buddhi, and Atma. This triad does not perish at death and provides the vehicle for remembering past incarnations. The theosophists' answer to the question of why we do not remember our past lives while we are incarnated is that such memory is hindered by the upper triad's connection with the lower quaternary. The "denser" levels of matter on which the latter exists make such remembering difficult. Only the refined or spiritually advanced individuals are able to overcome this obstacle and remember their past lives at will.

Whatever details of the particular formulations of the doctrine of reincarnation, they all imply a thoroughgoing dualism or pluralism. The body is one thing, the soul another. Each obeys its own set of laws. Although the brain does record the life's experiences, it belongs to one life only, dies with the rest of the body, and its memory is thereby lost. But the record lingers on nevertheless because it has also been made on a different level of existence, in bodies that are not physical. This permanent remnant provides for continuity of a given identity, even though the occasional incarnations each bear a different name and appear to have no connection with each other. The connection becomes apparent when the brain in a given incarnation responds to the record of past lives brought along by the immortal carrier of individual identity.

It so happens, however, that scientists, including psychologists, by and large subscribe to a philosophy of monism. Psychologists do not study souls, but the behavior of organisms, with some concession to mental processes. If the assertion is therefore made that it is possible to remember past incarnations, it is greeted with definite disbelief. If memories pertain to the brain and the brain dies, so do the memories.

Hypnotic Age Regression. A comely young woman writhes in the pains of labor, even though she is not pregnant: She is giving birth in a previous incarnation. She is reliving the tragic fate of the Jewess Rebecca in 12th-century York. A man talks in the language of 19th-century British sailors as he participates in the battle of Trafalgar, and is killed in action. These scenes occur in a film called *The Bloxham Tapes*. It is about the work of the British hypnotherapist Arnall Bloxham on hypnotic regression beyond the point of birth.

Detailed case histories of individuals remembering their past lives did not appear in the literature until the late 19th century, and a systematic collection and investigation of such cases did not begin until the 1960s. In adults, memories, or what appear to be memories, of past lives occur in altered states of consciousness—dreams, under the influence of hallucinogenic drugs such as LSD, in meditation, and under hypnosis. Because dreams and hallucinations confound memories with other processes, case histories that are presented in the literature are based mostly on reports by those who claim to have gained memory of their past incarnations through meditation or in hypnotic age regression. To these must be added the special case of memories of past incarnations in young children, which is discussed later in this chapter.

Hypnotic age regression is an established phenomenon. But, can we regress to where we have never been? The position from which it is argued that we can states that we *have* been there before—in a previous life. Thus, hypnotic age regression, on this theory, can be carried back beyond the present life into lives past because personal identity continues from life to life. The experiences of Bloxham's clients and of others are taken by some as evidence for reincarnation. Even if the reincarnation doctrine is not accepted, the phenomenon is still a very interesting one and needs to be examined and understood.

Hypnotic age regression has been practiced for some time. It goes back to the last two decades of the 19th century when a high level of interest in hypnosis coincided with the appearance of modern theosophy and its teaching of reincarnation. One early practitioner of hypnotic age regression was Colonel Rochas (1911), who not only regressed his subjects to their previous lives, but also managed to progress them into their future lives, about which more is said later. The purpose of age regression may be therapeutic—reliving, for instance, a childhood trauma as a child would live it, in order to integrate the experience into waking consciousness—or scientific—for instance, to study developmental processes in thinking (Reiff & Scheerer, 1959). One hypnotic phenomenon that is crucial to hypnotic age regression as well as to the alleged remembrance of past lives in the regressed state is *hypermnesia* or improved recall. Under hypnosis, people remember better, especially events from some time ago and from the remote past. When the hypnotist suggests that the subject is now younger and reliving a particular episode in earlier life, the subject's behavior impresses everyone with its realism. The question of whether the subject has actually regressed to an earlier age or is playing the role of a younger person as seen through an adult's eyes has been investigated experimentally by a number of researchers. The answer is that there is an actual regression, even though it is not a stable or permanent phenomenon: There are fluctuations between regressed and nonregressed states in the subject. When in the regressed state, however, not only do the subject's speech and other behavior patterns conform to the suggested chronological age, but also the appropriate autonomic processes, even when no specific mention is made of them to the subject. Thus, for instance, Gidro-Frank and Bowersbuch (1948) and True and Stephenson (1951) obtained the Babinski reflex (dorsiflexion of the big toe and fanning of the toes when the sole of the foot is stimulated) when subjects were regressed to an age below 6 months. (The Babinski reflex usually disappears by the end of the fourth month.) A change from the Babinski to the plantar reflex (curling of the toes) observed in older infants was obtained as the subjects were regressed gradually to a later age. The reflex was not suggested and could not be produced by the subjects voluntarily. Kupper (1945) obtained irregular brain-wave rhythms and even spiking in the electroencephalogram when a subject was regressed to an age when he had experienced epileptic seizures. Spikes or irregular, high-voltage peaks in the brain-wave record are associated with epilepsy and are observed before and during epileptic fits.

Many observers of hypnotic phenomena feel that some occult force is at work because behavior under hypnosis is in such marked contrast with ordinary behavior. This impression has been part of the hypnotic scene ever since Franz Anton Mesmer began making passes over some of his clients in 18th-century Vienna. Given the strangeness of hypnotic phenomena, the possibility of age regression, and a belief in the dual nature of humans, the scene is set for obtaining "proof" of reincarnation by regressing individuals beyond the point of birth. The crux of the matter is that, because suggestion is part of hypnosis, suggesting that the subject go beyond the point of his or her own birth and examine his or her previous lives achieves precisely that result—the subject all too willingly proceeds to do just that. This, however, is no proof of reincarnation. The cases that have been thoroughly investigated show beyond the shadow of a doubt that one is dealing with hypnotic hypermnesia coupled with the subject's unconscious wish for exhibition, for romance to liven up a drab life, for fantasy as an ego defense mechanism, and similar psychological needs, all reinforced by the hypnotist's own beliefs in the reincarnation doctrine. That suggestion is the immediate cause of fantastic memories is further demonstrated by a logical extension of age regression, which is age progression. Rochas (1911) introduced age progression when he suggested to his clients that they were now older and asked them to relate experiences that had yet to occur. In more recent times, the work of M. V. Kline (1951, 1953) and other investigators (e.g., Rubenstein & Newman, 1954), shows that, although age progression can be achieved, it is nothing but unconscious role enactment along the lines suggested by the hypnotist, utilizing information that is available to project one's behavior into the future.

The contemporary awareness of and interest in hypnotic age regression as a means of learning about past lives started in 1952 with the celebrated case of Bridey Murphy. In Pueblo, Colorado, a housewife by the name of Virginia Tighe (Fig. 6.1) was speaking in Irish brogue when under hypnosis, relating incidents from her previous incarnation as an Irish woman in Cork, Ireland, in the year 1806. The story was serialized in the *Denver Post*. William J. Barker, assistant editor of the paper's Sunday supplement, and Morey Bernstein, the hypnotist, later wrote a book about the case (Bernstein, 1956), in which Mrs. Tighe bears the name of Ruth Simmons. It created a sensation. The book was at the top of the bestseller list for weeks. The repercussions ranged from rock-and-roll records about Bridey Murphy and in increase in demand for jobless hypnotists to a teenage suicide in Oklahoma committed in order to investigate the reincarnation theory in person. Bernstein searched for evidence of Mrs. Tighe's story by checking

Fig. 6.1. Virginia Tighe also known as Ruth Simmons, the protagonist of *The Search for Bridey Murphy*, in 1956. (United Press International photo)

on the names of places and persons mentioned by her, but he uncovered very little. It appears that neither Bernstein nor anyone else thought of asking Mrs. Tighe herself about her earlier life and what she remembered from it. Reporters from the *Chicago American*, however, did begin to check out leads in Mrs. Tighe's childhood city, Chicago. It became gradually clear that she, instead of remembering her 19th-century existence in Ireland, was remembering what she had learned as a child from a Mrs. Anthony Corkell, an Irishwoman whose maiden name had been Bridie Murphy and who had greatly impressed the child with her stories about things Irish and also taught her the Irish jig that Mrs. Tighe would dance in her hypnotic trance. Additional influence (and memories) could be traced to an Irish aunt of whom Mrs. Tighe had been very fond of as a girl and who told her tales from Ireland. Her attachment to the aunt, which was reciprocated, arose from her being rejected by her parents (no psychologist or psychiatrist ever managed to interview Mrs. Tighe). Thus, out of a frustrating life situation grew a particular love of Ireland and everything Irish. Virginia Tighe learned to a perfection the Irish brogue, which she, as a girl, used to advantage in high-school dramatics.

The language aspect of age-regressed recall of past lives deserves a special mention. It has already been shown that a person can learn bits of foreign languages without knowing it, as well as recall them a long time afterwards without having any conscious knowledge of the language or a memory of where the fragments were learned. Such learning can be quite mechanical, as when young Burtt learned the Greek stanzas (see the section *Cryptomnesia* earlier in this chapter), and require many repetitions before anything is retained. Retention, in turn, may not show up except when the most sensitive method of measuring retention, the method of relearning, is used. Learning unusual materials is greatly facilitated if the learner has an emotional attachment to the person with whom the material, such as a foreign language, is associated. This is seen in the case of the German peasant girl in William James' story (see the section *Cryptomnesia* earlier in this chapter) and Virginia of the Bridey Murphy case. This principle applies also to animals. It is well known that a parrot will learn to speak only from a person to whom it is attached, the master, and not from a stranger. In the appropriate psychological situation, memory of the material may then manifest itself in spontaneous recall.

When remembering a past life, subjects under hypnosis either relive an incident with all the accompanying emotions, or else tell the hypnotist about their lives in general terms, covering long time periods. In the former case, the language used may be the appropriate one for the place and the period, but its use is restricted: the cries, groans, moans, and other nonverbal utterances that accompany the experience of birth, death, torture, or injury are supplemented by short utterances, such as exclamations, command, or questions, rather than long declaratory sentences. In the second situation, the narrative is in the person's native language, and thus the subject's knowledge of the language used in that particular reincarnation is not tested. The shorter bits and fragments are learned either intentionally or accidently, but cryptomnesia ensues as to their source. The languages are mostly well-known Indoeuropean languages (for Western subjects), or else mythical one, such as those of Atlantis or of some distant planet, so that there is no possible way of checking on their authenticity. When the language is real but exotic, it can often be traced to a concrete instance of its learning by the subject prior to the age-regression experience. Harold Rosen describes one experiment in age regression in which the subject spoke words in a third-century Italian dialect, Oscan (Kline, 1956). When hypnotized again and asked to recall the source of his knowledge of this obscure language, the subject told of his having once looked at an Oscan grammar. Apparently, this brief encounter with the grammar enabled him to register in his memory a few words and phrases.

Additional light on the xenoglossy phenomenon is shed by observations of hysterics whose symptoms, such as the stigmata of the crucifixion, are given a supernatural interpretation. It is the easily hypnotizable subject who will tell of past lives and speak in foreign languages. The relationship between hypnotizability and hysteria was noted earlier (Chapter 2). It is, therefore, not surprising that both types of individuals would show some common anomalistic behaviors, such as xenoglossy. The stigmatist Therese Neumann, mentioned in Chapter 2, a little-educated Bavarian peasant, "knew" Greek, French, Aramaic, and other languages. Her vocabulary in any language was very limited, however, amounting to just a few words in French, for instance. She insisted she recognized Portuguese, but did not understand or speak it. Her Greek phrases revealed a recent translation of Biblical statements rather than Biblical Greek. She did not begin to use any of the languages suddenly, but learned them gradually. In all cases, her access to the language—through specific instruction, reading, or listening—could be demonstrated. This included Aramaic, her most puzzling and most "occult" language, because Aramaic was the language of Jesus.

Therese was not proficient in Aramaic (or in any of the other languages), using only a few words. These words appear to have been not so much genuine Aramaic words as Bavarian dialect words distorted to sound like Aramaic, a sort of pig-Aramaic. Where did Therese learn the sound of Aramaic? Several of her examiners knew it, and one priest who was also a university professor specifically taught her how to say Christ's last words on the cross as well as other phrases in Aramaic. The assertion that Therese spoke "colloquial" Aramaic rather than the Aramaic known to scholars (Teodorowicz, 1940) only reveals an attempt to prove her xenoglossy genuine, because her "Aramaic" did not sound very genuine. Given that there were several Aramaic dialects, some differing considerably from standard Aramaic, and that the sound of any language spoken thousands of years ago is irretrievable, Therese clearly had considerable latitude in sound selection to make her utterances pass as Aramaic.

When the hypnotist suggests remembering past lives, the subject complies. What is not particularly stressed in these cases is that even though anybody will readily relate incidents from their "past lives" under hypnotic suggestion, most people's accounts are rather dull and unimaginative. It takes a combination of hypnotic suggestion, vivid imagination, and a psychological need to produce accounts that will receive publicity. The stories of past lives produced by Mrs. Tighe, Jane Evans (Arnall Bloxham's subject who remembered living in the 12th century as a Jewess), and other publicized individuals are either a combination of cryptomnesia and imaginative storytelling under suggestion or the latter alone. The individual may adroitly combine elements of information obtained earlier into an interesting, creative pattern and be amnesic about how the information was originally obtained, or just weave a story out of his imagination. The fabrication by mentally disturbed individuals of stories that are readily disproved or are manifestly untrue is called *pseudologia phantastica*, or simply pathological lying. The term suggests mental illness and unacceptable behavior. When the individual is not under psychiatric care and the fabrication is not readily detected, it may pass, under the proper circumstances, for a remembrance of past lives. Individuals with hysterical tendencies are known to appear as very sincere and to be good actors. Still further down the line, there are individuals who are imaginative, creative, and will produce stories of past incarnations under hypnotic suggestion, but who also realize that the material was available to them and that the stories well up from their unconscious in relation to a psychological need and because of their particular psychological makeup, such as easy dissociability (see Chapter 8). There is a good illustration of such a case in the person of the well-known novelist, Taylor Caldwell. It had been suggested to her that her fictional work owed much to her memories of past incarnations because she often seemed to have detailed first-hand information on subjects that she consciously had no knowledge of and would also occasionally write as if in a trance, with no conscious effort. Caldwell wished to prove that the material came from her unconscious rather than being a remembrance of past lives. Age-regressed hypnotically, Caldwell managed to describe 11 of her past incarnations that spanned thousands of years. Jess Stern, who had expressed the belief that it was past incarnations that were the source of Caldwell's information, wrote a book describing the experience (Stern, 1973). The results were inconclusive, mainly because of the interplay between Stern's willingness to believe in reincarnation and Caldwell's opposition to the idea. Caldwell herself remained unconvinced (Stern, 1973):

I had warned Jess that I am a novelist, and that perhaps some or most of the material had lain fallow in my subconscious, and was only the creative power waiting dormantly in my mind for expression through future books. I wanted to believe that. I still believe it. I still heartily reject the idea of reincarnation [p. 284]

Taylor Caldwell's story illustrates the operation of certain psychological factors in the belief of reincarnation. That the memories about past lives are in fact made up of information obtained during the individual's present life is suggested by the fact that, first, the lives take place either in cultures that the individual is likely to have some information about or else in civilizations that are only mythical, such as those of Atlantis or Mars, and about which no one therefore has any factual information. Thus, of Taylor Caldwell's 11 lives, four were in England and set in the late 18th century or later, one on the legendary lost continent of Lemuria, and one on a planet called Melina. Tenth-century Latvian warriors, 15th-century Samoyed shamans, or 19th-century Mthethwa kings are unheard of as vehicles for incarnating souls. Second, ordinary people tend to have reincarnation memories of ordinary lives. Although one of the incarnations of Taylor Caldwell was as a servant girl, she was a servant girl to the writer George Eliot. A real servant girl is not likely to come up with a reincarnation as a servant girl to George Eliot because, in spite of her fame, she is not likely to have ever heard the name, let alone know, for instance, that George Eliot was a woman (Mary Ann Evans), which Caldwell as a writer naturally did.

Another psychologically interesting point is Taylor Caldwell's view of life and its relation to the belief in reincarnation and the nature of the 11 lives she describes. Her statement in Stern's (1973) book that:

I shudder at the very thought of being born again into this world. Life to me, practically from infancy, has been a monstrous, painful, agonizing affair, and the idea of repeating such an existence—even in a better way—is horrifying to me. I think I'd prefer total oblivion [p. 10]

is a literate, Western affirmation of the Buddhist concept of *dukkha*, suffering or unpleasantness as the universal characteristic of existence and of the consequent desire to escape from it into nonbeing or nirvana. Buddha's teaching, however, is inextricably linked to the notion of reincarnation. Repeated incarnations and repeated pummeling by experience and suffering lead to a desire to escape into nothingness, nonexperiencing. Most of the 11 lives Miss Caldwell describes are full of suffering and end in suicide or violent death. Miss Caldwell's concern with the idea of reincarnation may thus be seen as arising from a "Buddhist" temperament. The Buddhist temperament that experiences life as suffering is the very soil in which the seeds of the idea of reincarnation will flourish.

Reincarnation Memories in Children. Being an adult and being in an altered state of consciousness are two sources of serious problems for the reincarnationist who would like to use materials obtained from adults under hypnosis, drugs, or in meditation as evidence for the doctrine. Adults have a memory bank of enormous size to draw upon, and the dynamic interplay among its parts is something that psychologists have not yet been able to understand completely. Memory storage and retrieval of innumerable items interact complexly with the dynamics of a fully developed personality in the adult. Thus, memories of past lives obtained from adults in an age-regressed state, for instance, are described even by those who accept the reincarnation doctrine as only "suggestive" or reincarnation rather than as evidence for it.

In this respect, very young children are better sources of information because the previous experience and altered state of consciousness factors are absent. Among the more than 1600 cases suggestive of reincarnation collected by Dr. Ian Stevenson of the University of Virginia Medical Center, there are a number of cases with children as protagonists. In a typical case, a child begins to make statements about a previous incarnation soon after he or she begins to talk, and continues to do so through middle childhood, with the memories gradually fading. The memories include persons, places, relationships, and life incidents that are allegedly verified when the child's family travels to the place of its previous incarnation and talks to its "former family" there. The child may also exhibit behaviors that are suggestive of reincarnation, such as behaving like an adult of the social class and calling that characterized the previous incarnation.

Like most reports of cases of reincarnation, the childhood cases also come from cultures in which most people believe in reincarnation. Reincarnation takes place either immediately or shortly after the death of the person whose body the child claims to have occupied previously. It takes place in the same culture and within a short distance from the place where the individual alledgedly lived before. In almost every case, the two families involved get together and exchange information before an investigator is able to talk to them. Stevenson has only 15 cases on record in which he or another investigator were able to interview the family of the child's previous incarnation first (e.g., Stevenson, 1974).

Child cases have their own problems. Children's utterances, especially at an early age, may be interpreted in different ways: calling someone "uncle," for instance, does not necessarily mean that a blood relationship is understood. This is a particularly acute problem for the researcher who has to work through an interpreter and in a culture whose forms of address may be more intricate than the researcher's. Children also live within a family that, consciously or unconsciously, may provide the child with the necessary information. Parents, upon discovering that their child looks or acts somewhat like a deceased relative, may reinforce the child's behavior, coach the child, and convince the child that he or she is someone else. Parents are typically present when the child is interviewed, and the results of coaching, as well as of actual prompting, are sometimes well in evidence. Parental chicanery, the readily malleable imagination of a child, and the researcher's methodological naivete and a bias in favor of the reincarnation hypothesis all combine to render the child cases as useless as evidence for reincarnation as are those discussed earlier.

Conclusions.   Reincarnation as a moral view of the world has much to recommend itself. It satisfies the human hunger for justice, at least in those countless individuals who do not have enough strength or power to obtain justice themselves and are reassured by the doctrine that karma will catch up with those who have done them wrong, if not in this life then in another. The doctrine of reincarnation is a belief, however, a belief in universal moral justice. The belief may be a very satisfying one and it may pass the pragmatic test of truth in that, for some people at least, it makes life easier to live or makes the believer a more attractive human being. The demonstration of the carry-over of long-term memories from previous incarnations with the methods of science is a matter of a different order. Beliefs as value systems are not subject to empirical verification. To make a science verify a belief means forcing upon science an activity that is not in its province, and any such attempt is doomed to failure. When science is asked to test empirical propositions concerning human behavior, the results are what we have described in this chapter. As an attempt to reconcile the subjective and objective sides of life, the search for a scientific proof of reincarnation is understandable. As an attempt to make science, it fails.

Déjà Vu

The French term *déjà vu* means literally "seen before." It refers to the not uncommon experience of seeing, for instance, a place for the first time and yet feeling that it is very familiar, that one has been there before. The feeling of recognition with respect to a place or event that in reality has not been seen by the person before is found in epileptics and psychiatric patients, but it is not in itself a sign of abnormality. In one survey done some years ago (McKellar, 1957), it was found that of a group of 182 students at a Scottish university, 70% had had the *déjà vu* experience.

Although the psychologist sees nothing but a memory failure (paramnesia) in this phenomenon, others have given it paranormal interpretations. Reed (1972) states that the three most common ones are the following:

1. The precognition explanation. The subject's first experience of the place was not physical. He or she foresaw being there some time in the future, and now it appears familiar to him or her.

2. The telepathic explanation. The feeling of familiarity arises because the subject has seen the place before vicariously or telepathically through the eyes of another person.

3. The reincarnation explanation. The subject has been there before, but in a previous life. This is perhaps the most widely used explanation.

Although *déjà vu* is classified most often as an instance of paramnesia, it can be viewed also as an anomaly of perception. The close relationship between perception and memory has already been alluded to. The eminent French psychologist Pierre Janet, for instance, has argued that the *déjà vu* experience is a case of disturbed perception. It is a matter of how the subject perceives the present situation, not a matter of whether the person remembers something incorrectly (which he or she does not) or fails to remember something (which he or she does not do either). The paranormal interpretations assume there was an original experience of the place or event and concentrate on the place or event, whereas the salient feature of the *déjà vu* experience is the subject's *feeling*, triggered by the perception of the environment, that he or she has seen it all before.

How does such a feeling become attached to a particular experience? As a general principle, a feeling or emotional tone accompanies most cognitive activities. Our recall of the cognitive activity may fail, however, yet the emotional component may remain in awareness, so that when the appropriate stimuli are present, they elicit the feeling, but not necessarily the memory of the situation in which the feeling was originally produced. Often the stimulus is a smell. A smell in itself is a clue that elicits a feeling rather than one that provides discrete bits of symbolic information. It is significant that smell signals end up in those portions of the brain that are concerned with arousal and emotion, the limbic system, and do not project to the cortex as other systems do. The dissociation between cognition and affect can be demonstrated experimentally. As early as 1941, Bannister and Zangwill showed hypnotized subjects pictures, induced posthypnotic amnesia, then showed them the same pictures again a few days later in their normal waking state. Most subjects did not recall having seen the picures, but they did report a strong feeling of familiarity, a feeling they could not explain.

Although the Bannister and Zangwill experiment may explain the *déjà vu* experience when the subject has in fact had the visual experience before, it does not explain it when the subject demonstrably had not had it. The most dramatic *déjà vu* cases are reported in relation to places the subject has never been before, such as a distant place abroad. As to that, another feature of the dynamics of memory that has already been discussed can be invoked. If memory is remembering—that is, an active reconstruction of what has been—this it is possible that repeated reconstructions may distort the final product to such a degree that, if the original is presented, it may no longer be recognized. For instance, the scene in question may be a room in a dwelling. Rooms, in spite of differences in detail, have many important features in common. A room that is remembered and whose image is reconstructed a number of times in memory, eventually may come to resemble another room, seen for the first time, but now experienced as if already seen some time in the past. Thus, objects and events in a *dejà vu* situation need not be identical to anything actually experienced before in order to be perceived as identical. If the perceptual organizing activity experienced now is sufficiently similar to one experienced before, the particular end product of this activity, an object or event, may be experienced as identical to that in the original situation, although in fact it is not.

The seeming recognition of scenes not witnessed before, which has just been explained in perceptual terms, can also be explained in learning terms. The process is called stimulus generalization. A very simple experiment demonstrates this process. A hungry animal will salivate at the sight of food. A tone of a certain frequency is sounded every time food is presented. Eventually, the sound of the tone alone will produce salivation, without the food's being present. This is known as conditioning. It will also be observed that, if the tone has a frequency of, say, 3000 Hz, tones that are somewhat higher or lower will also produce salivation, although not quite as readily. One may say that the animal experiences not only the 3000-Hz tone as familiar, but also other tones that are not too different from it. This is known as stimulus generalization or conditioned generalization. At street intersections that have a left-turn lane, the green left-turn arrow comes on before the red light turns green for the through traffic. As anyone who has been waiting at such an intersection for the red light to turn green knows, the green arrow will elicit automatic driving responses in those drivers who are not turning left at all. Such responses are then voluntarily inhibited. The green arrow, being similar to the green light in color, but not in shape, elicits a momentary feeling of familiarity, one could even say a *déjà vu* experience, and the associated conditioned behavior. It is a simple case of conditioned generalization. Streets, houses, buildings, and interiors have a great deal of communality, and there is no reason why conditioned generalization should not take place with respect to these larger complexes of stimuli, thus producing the *déjà vu* experience.

Another reason why we sometimes experience a sense of familiarity is that when an item that should be familiar to us from past experience, where it has always appeared in a particular context, is presented in a different context, the sense of familiarity may remain even though identification (and the recall of the original learning situation) fails. One's regular waiter in a favorite restaurant is an example. His face is quite familiar in the context of the restaurant and when the waiter is dressed in his uniform. Because this is the only situation in which we meet him, we may fail to identify him when we see him walking along the street dressed in street clothes, yet feel immediately that he should be familiar to us. The same process also operates in the *déjà vu* experience with regard to places and events.

NOTES

An excellent recent work on the reliability of eyewitness testimony, which includes very interesting experimental work done by the author, is Buckhout (1974). The first psychological work on eyewitness testimony was Münsterberg (1915). A more recent book is Wall (1965).

There is a chapter on anomalies of recall and another one on anomalies of recognition in Reed (1972). In addition to discussing such anomalies of memory as *déjà vu*, Reed gives an excellent presentation of other anomalies that do not necessarily have esoteric connotations but may be called clinical abnormalities.

Although the chapter in which he deals with the subject is short, Hilgard's (1977) analysis of hypnotic age regression is a most useful one, especially because he deals with hypnosis as part of the larger concept of divided consciousness. Hilgard presents experimental data, including some very interesting cases of hypnotic age regression, theories of age regression, as well as a critique of regression beyond the point of birth. Good summaries of the Bridey Murphy case may be found in Chapter 26 of Gardner (1957) and in Wallechinsky and Wallace (1978). The latter work also gives accounts of the reincarnation cases of Arnall Bloxham's subject Jane Evans and of Taylor Caldwell, but the reader must be warned that not all the information and quotes in this volume are accurate. Kline (1956) has written a whole book analyzing the Bridey Murphy case from the scientific standpoint.

The best-known investigator in the area of reincarnation is Dr. Ian Stevenson, who heads the Parapsychology Division of the Department of Psychiatry of the University of Virginia Medical Center. He has reported on a large number of cases from his extensive collection in publications other than the book mentioned in this chapter (Stevenson, 1974). His other publications in this field are listed in the bibliography appended to his recent survey of research and theory on reincarnation (Stevenson, 1977). For a critique of the reincarnation hypothesis, including extensive critique of Stevenson's child cases, as well as a unique, new subatomic particle view of reincarnation, Reyna's (1973) book is recommended. It is particularly valuable in that it shows the culturally determined pitfalls that beset the in-

vestigator of reports of reincarnation memories by children. A similar critique is óffered by Chari (1978), an Indian reincarnation researcher at
Madras Christian College. It is particularly telling because it arises from an
"insider's" intimate knowledge of the cultural background against which
he views the child reincarnation cases.

7 The Psychology of Extraordinary Beliefs

> *The great world,* the background, *in all of us, is the world of our* beliefs. *This is the world of the permanencies and the immensities.*
>
> William James, letter to Helen Keller,
> December 17, 1908

> *All reason is against it, but all belief is for it.*
>
> Samuel Johnson on the existence of ghosts.

Human experience is varied and most of us find it necessary to make decisions regarding a wide variety of personal, social, and political issues. The complexity and diversity of our lives require elaborate and complicated processes to sort, compartmentalize, select, evaluate, and respond to many sources of information. One of the concepts that psychologists use to represent the process by which this is accomplished is called an attitude. The focus of this chapter is on attitudes, and in particular, a component of attitudes, beliefs, and their role in explaining the events and concepts that comprise the psychology of anomalies.

ATTITUDES AND BELIEFS

In a way, beliefs are the essential feature of anomalistics in that everyone has unusual and weird experiences. So, the basic issue of the paranormal and also what differentiates the occultist from the skeptic concerns the meaning attached to such anomalies. Many paranormal phenomena do not involve any external physical occurrence at all. Rather, they are experiences, or more often, verbal accounts of someone else's experience, and what one makes of them depends largely on what one believes.

An illlustration may help to clarify this point. At the age of 8, the junior author of this book had a premonition. Aware that his grandmother was ill, he was worried about her, as any child might be. While thinking of her, he had a disturbing fantasy. He imagined seeing a certain uncle racing towards him in a pick-up truck, with a cloud of dust from the dirt road rising in the background. The uncle had come to tell the family that the grandmother was dead. Several weeks later, this was precisely what happened. At this point, the reader has a choice: You may take this to be yet another miraculous manifestation of the paranormal and perhaps proof that the junior author was foolish for becoming a psychology professor rather than a mentalist; you may decide that it was coincidence; or you may suspend judgment in lieu of additional evidence. In any case, you will have relied on your beliefs about reality and the nature of proof to make your decision. Incidentally, the following factors may also help you to decide: The grandmother had cancer and had not been expected to live for some time; the junior author's family lived in the country and did not have a telephone; the certain uncle was frequently out of work and habitually drove his pick-up fast; normal 8-year-old children are capable of rational thought. You may still want to classify this incident as an instance of the occult, and that is precisely the point. What we take to be extraordinary depends on our attitudes and beliefs, and this is the topic to which we must now turn.

Attitudes have been an important subject since the early days of scientific psychology, and even though several theoretical questions remain unanswered, a great deal is known about attitudes, how they are formed, how they change, and how they relate to other aspects of behavior.

Definition and Description of Attitudes

Although many different definitions of an attitude have been proposed, most emphasize the idea that an attitude is a predisposition to respond favorably or unfavorably towards a class of objects (Oskamp, 1977). Allport (1935) enumerated several features often contained in definitions of an attitude that help to illustrate the term. For example, an attitude is often defined as a set-that is, a general orientation with which the person responds as whole, and as a readiness to act-which emphasizes that an attitude is a potential to behave in a certain way that may or may not be manifested, depending on the circumstances. In addition, the relative permanence of an attitude is often stressed. This is not to suggest that an attitude can never change once formed, but rather, that the typical state for many attitudes, particularly those of greatest importance, is stability over relatively long periods of time. Finally, attitudes are often defined as learned entities-that is, they are conceptualized as tendencies acquired during the lifetime of an individual that are based on that individual's experience rather than being genetically or physiologically determined. Although physiological responses are important in the emotional arousal and behavioral manifestations associated with attitudes, they are not ordinarily thought of as comprising the most essential characteristic of an attitude.

For purposes of discussion, an attitude may be described in terms of its component parts (e.g., Krech, Crutchfield, & Ballachey, 1962). First is the *cognitive* component or *belief*, which refers to what an individual believes to be true or false with regard to a particular object. For example, many people believe that ESP (extrasensory perception) is possible and that it occurs on many occasions for many different people, whereas other may believe that ESP is not possible, as it would constitute a violation of natural physical laws. All such ideas regarding the existence of ESP, the conditions under which it might occur, the kinds of individals who might possess ESP, etc., are beliefs and, taken together, comprise the cognitive component of an individual's attitude towards ESP. People, of course, hold beliefs towards many other referents as well, including political candidates, capital punishment, rock music, etc. In fact, one can have an attitude about any person, place, thing, or idea.

The second component of an attitude is called the *affective* or *emotional* component. This refers to the feelings or emotions associated with what an individual believes about a particular referent. Continuing with the previous illustration, one person who believes that ESP is possible might feel good about it by focusing on the potential for the expansion of human consciousness, increased empathy and understanding among diverse groups of people, greater personal power, or perhaps some futuristic vision in which mechanical means of communication would no longer be necessary. On the other hand, another person might also believe that ESP is possible, but might be troubled by its implications, such as the frightening prospect of someone reading your mind against your will and the resultant loss of privacy, or the military and divisive uses to which such an ability might be put. Or, the reverse might also occur, such as an individual who believes that ESP does not exist and yet is disappointed versus someone who is confident that it is not possible and is relieved. Thus, the affective component concerns the feelings that accompany and color what we believe and that make beliefs personally relevant and emotionally important.

The *behavioral* or *action* component of an attitude denotes what an individual does with respect to a given belief—in other words, the ways in which persons act on their beliefs and feelings. For instance, one person who believes in ESP may do nothing about it. Another believer may not only believe in ESP, but also be active in a variety of ways in promoting ESP as a bonafide phenomenon. Such a person might avidly read periodicals reporting scientific investigations of ESP, or participate in one of the several societies whose purpose concerns advancing parapsychology, or less formally, the individual may simply make ESP a central part of conversations with others: Asking each new acquaintance whether or not that person believes in ESP, whether the person has had such an experience, how many times, under what conditions, etc. Some skeptics are also quite active regarding their beliefs, as was exemplified by the work of the famous stage magician Harry Houdini in exposing what he considered to be the fraudulent claims of psychics (Houdini, 1924). In any case, the behavioral component includes the actions an individual engages in with respect to their beliefs towards a given referent.

In addition to the three components of an attitude, psychologists also find it useful to distinguish what is called an *expressed opinion*. The expressed opinion refers to what individuals are willing or able to reveal about their beliefs to others, suggesting that what they say about what they believe and what they actually believe may be different, at least in some circumstances. The reason for drawing this additional distinction is that considerable evidence indicates that people are often motivated (consciously or unconsciously) to distort their expressed opinions. One example is the proverbial politician who changes his or her platform depending on the characteristics of the audience to which he or she is speaking. Of more relevant concern are the ways in which subjects may distort their answers when responding to questionnaires or interviews regarding their beliefs. For example, *social desirability* (Crowne & Marlowe, 1964) refers to the tendency of some respondents to answer in a "socially appropriate" manner, rather than genuinely. Someone possessing an unusual attitude, such as believing in ghosts, may hold the belief secretly for fear of public ridicule, and may even deny their existence if asked. The tendency of people to deny being superstitious even while engaging in a blatantly magic ritual is another example of social desirability. On some occasions, subjects in psychological studies will adopt what are called *response sets*, such as tending to agree with most questions, regardless of their content, or avoiding extreme responses, independent of content. Psychologists have learned that despite relatively sophisticated measurement devices, it is not always possible to determine precisely what an individual believes. Even polygraph examinations can be faked. This does not mean that people are always deceptive or intent on faking their answers or that human nature is inherently dishonest. It simply suggests that, under some conditions, in both psychological research and everyday experience, some individuals are less likely to reveal their own private feelings and thoughts and are instead inclined, with or without awareness, to give their beliefs and behavior a more socially acceptable appearance. This is particularly so for controversial subjects such as the occult. Thus, one practical implication of this type of behavior is that care must be exercised when assessing an individual's beliefs in the paranormal.

Functions of Attitudes and Beliefs

An attitude or belief may serve several different purposes for the individual holding the attitude. For example, Katz (1960) has enumerated some belief functions including value expression, ego defense, need satisfaction, and understanding. *Value expression* refers to the process of identifying ourselves to ourselves and to others. Attitudes fulfill the social need of defining who we are, what we are like, what we do, etc. For someone who believes in astrology, this might involve telling others one's birth sign and requesting the same information from them. Often a discussion then ensues concerning the personality dispositions supposedly associated with each sign or the validity of astrology, or an informal game in which the unidentified astrological sign of one member of a gathering is guessed at by others. Indeed, in some circles, this has become so common that exchanging information regarding astrological signs has all but replaced the more conventional social amenities. Discussing beliefs with others serves two purposes. First, it provides something of interest to discuss and, second, it defines personal identity. One important consequence of this process is that others respond to our expressed beliefs as we respond to theirs, and this often determines who our friends will be because we prefer others who share and validate our view of the world. Of equal importance is the value expression function as it relates to how we think about ourselves. For example, one of the reasons that beliefs tend not to change is the fact that they are experienced as very basic and integral parts of who we are. To change our beliefs, we must, to some extent, change how we conceptualize ourselves, and this we generally avoid. Thus, a serious challenge to one's basic beliefs can be a shattering experience because what is being threatened is not an abstract set of ideas, but rather, the image we hold of ourselves.

The *ego-defense* function refers to the role of attitudes and beliefs in enhancing self-esteem. In particular, certain strongly held beliefs create the impression that one's own view is superior to that of others, and consequently that one is somehow better—i.e., more insightful, intelligent, moral, or patriotic. For instance, a believer in telepathy may contend that disbelievers are narrow-minded, mechanistic, or unimaginative. By the same token, disbelievers may hold that believers are illogical, impressionable, and perhaps "fuzzy-headed." The history of science contains numerous cases in which individuals whose unorthodox theory was rejected by the scientific establishment nevertheless believed themselves to be enlightenened and superior to their detractors. In apparent attempts to salvage their self-esteem, such persons have sometimes engaged in paranoid attacks on "disbelievers." Unfortunately, the history of occult phenomena contains many such examples as well. In any event, some beliefs protect and bolster one's sense of self-worth by providing the means to derogate those whose beliefs are different.

The *need-satisfaction* function refers to a perceived contingent relationship between a belief and a personal need. For example, individuals might join an occult group because they believe that the goals of the organization would be of benefit to them, or one might believe in the power of astrology due to an expectation of increased personal success.

For our present discussion, the most important purpose of an attitude is the *understanding* or *knowledge* function—i.e., interpreting, clarifying, and making sense of the world. Psychologists have long recognized that understanding is a strong human motive (Heider, 1958; Kelly, 1955). Science is one manifestation of this need to explore, understand, and explain. Moreover, this need is probably inherent to human nature and not just the situations in which people find themselves. Thus, similar to the facts and theories of science, beliefs serve to create a sense of order, predictability, and control. For example, holding an attitude towards a particular referent can reduce what is an otherwise enormously complex set of ideas and stimuli down to manageable proportions by providing a structure, simpler categories, and predisposed responses. In the world of extraordinary phenomena, for instance, it would be extremely difficult, time consuming, and perhaps even impossible to thoroughly process and respond to each and every facet and nuance of occultism. Instead of responding anew to each potential stimulus, we generalize via the cognitive structure of our beliefs, thereby simplifying the entire process. Although you may know very little about numerology, if you know that it is a form of divination, and if you believe in divination, or if you do not, your response to numerology is determined. Thus, beliefs provide answers to questions falling into rather broad categories. All such patterns of responding derive from beliefs and these beliefs are ordinarily present even prior to actually experiencing the phenomenon in question. The point is that our attitudes serve to delineate, sort out, screen, classify, and hence to simplify ideas, making it possible to more easily attend to and support some ideas and issues while avoiding, rejecting, opposing, or ignoring other types.

Also, beliefs may serve as explanations that not only connect and summarize seemingly unrelated events, but also create a sense of predictability and control. Considerable research from diverse areas of psychology has substantiated the idea that unpredictability and lack of control are generally negative experiences that we actively seek to avoid, and research indicates that the dread of otherwise noxious stimuli can largely be removed if the onset of these stimuli can be predicted (Averill, 1973; Seligman, 1975). In addition, we take comfort in believing that things do not just randomly happen without specific cause or explanation. In fact, explanations relying on such concepts as chance or randomness are generally unsatisfactory even if they are perhaps true (e.g., Lerner & Simmons, 1966). We do not like to feel vulnerable to capricious and unexpected forces, and consequently, when we encounter what appears to be a random occurrence, we tend to believe an explanation that makes us feel less vulnerable, able to predict such events, and hence to control or avoid them. Thus, we may believe that the source of a traumatic event is "fate," or "God's will," or interference from outer space, or whatever. Such ideas are preferable to chance explanations because they create psychological distance from random misfortunes (e.g., a victim's fate is not necessarily the same as ours, whereas random misfortunes could happen to us) and they imply that something can be done (e.g., God's will may be alterable by piety whereas chance cannot be influenced). That such control may be illusory in these examples is not the point at issue. If such explanations are believed, they will influence the ways an individual thinks, feels, and responds to the event, whether or not they are true or verifiable. Thus, our beliefs function as mechanisms that increase our sense of certainty and perceptions of predictability and control.

Because beliefs can and do operate without external verifications, it may be tempting to conclude that people who strongly believe in the paranormal are illogical and dogmatic whereas confirmed disbelievers are attuned to facts and reason. However, beliefs are personal entities and, as such, they are always to some extent irrational. For example, many scientists cling to outdated theories even after considerable contradictory evidence has been produced. Also, to firmly assert without corroborating evidence or argument that something that is improbable cannot be true is as illogical as believing in something that is patently false. In this sense, all beliefs are functionally equivalent in that they serve the same purpose for the person who holds them. This is not the same as saying that all beliefs are true or accurate reflections of reality. But, all beliefs do have personal validity and therefore they are as important and useful to the "primitive" witchdoctor as they are to the most expert of scientists or the most logical of philosophers.

THE OCCULT IDEOLOGY

Prevalence

It is common for people to view the beliefs of other societies as "superstitious" and backward, while thinking of their own culture as enlightened. Such ethnocentric tendencies create the expectation, even in intellectual circles, that occultism is a belief system of relevance only to medieval times and the nontechnological societies of today. However, observers of the psychic scene have noted their impression of an "occult renaissance" in the United States with the number of adherents to extraordinary ideologies being substantial and growing (e.g. Truzzi, 1971). In fact, research indicates that belief in the paranormal is widespread and generally has been at least since the earliest available studies were reported.

Several early studies suggested substantial levels of belief among students. For example, Conklin (1919) reported that 53% of the "superstitions" used in his study were endorsed by college students, and Gould (1921) found that 54% of the students in his sample believed in and said they were influenced

54% of the students in his sample believed in and said they were influenced by similar ideas. Caldwell and Lundeen (1931) presented 200 "superstitious" ideas to high-school students and found that the subjects were familiar with half of the items, expressed belief in 20%, and said they were affected by 23% of the items. At about the same time, Maller and Lundeen (1933) found that junior high school students accepted as fact 75% of the "superstitious" ideas with which they were presented.

Many of the older studies seem to have been based on the assumption that paranormal beliefs represent failures of education that would be eventually eradicated by expanded training in science and mathematics. From the current perspective, this assumption appears to be condescending in tone, and at the same time, perhaps overly optimistic regarding the potential for scientific education to eliminate paranormal beliefs and practices. More recent studies among college students support this conclusion. For example, Jones, Russell, and Nickel (1977) found that 58% of a sample of students accepted as true half or more of a list of paranormal phenomena and that 26.6% claimed to have experienced a paranormal phenomenon. Polzella, Popp, and Hinsman (1975) reported that 79% of their sample of college students indicated a definite or probable belief in parapsychology (i.e., clairvoyance, precognition, psychokinesis, and telepathy) and 44% of the subjects indicated that they had experienced one or more of these phenomena. An interesting set of contrasts was obtained by Bainbridge (1978a) who had a sample of college students rate (on a scale of zero to 100%) the chances that several controversial ideas were true. Even though Darwin's theory of evolution was rated as the most likely to be true (average rating of 69.8%), it was closely followed by several concepts with considerably less empirical verification, including the idea of intelligent life on other planets (69.2%); the theory that ESP exists (64.4%); biorhythm theory (61.8%); and von Däniken's ancient-astronauts theory (50.9%).

**Box 7.1—Differential Subscription
to Paranormal Phenomena**

In addition to the question of prevalence, an interesting issue in surveys of belief concerns the differential rates of endorsement among various paranormal phenomena and practices. Table 7.1 presents data obtained in the spring of 1974 from a sample of 92 college students regarding their belief in various extraordinary concepts. Endorsement refers to those subjects who indicated a probable to strong belief in each of the items listed, excluding those who were uncertain or opposed to the occult interpretation of the phenomenon.

As indicated, not all paranormal and improbable ideas receive equal support from believers as the endorsement percentages vary from a low of .0%

for phrenology (character analysis of bumps on the head) to 63.0% for extraterrestrial intelligence (i.e., the belief that intelligent life exists on other planets). On the other hand, 13 of the 44 items included in the survey were endorsed by one-quarter or more of the sample with endorsement approaching or exceeding 50% on four items. Also, 91.3% of the sample endorsed at least one item, or, put another way, only eight of the 92 (8.7%) respondents were skeptical or disbelieving across the full range of ideas. Whereas only 3.3% of the subjects endorsed half or more of the items, 33.7% endorsed one-quarter or more and 64.1% indicated a belief in at least 1/10 of the items. The average rate of endorsement was 17.7%, or approximately eight items.

In accord with other studies, these data indicate that most of the more popular ideas fall into one of two categories—ESP and UFOs—whereas the lowest endorsement rates occur for "common superstitions" (e.g., black cats, Friday the 13th, etc.) and older occult and pseudoscientific practices (e.g., phrenology, palmistry, etc.). Interesting also are comparisons between the endorsement rates for similar or related items. For example, horoscopes and Zodiac signs received identical endorsement rates whereas subscription to astrology was somewhat higher. Similarly, ESP elicited a substantially higher rate than did any of the four types of ESP: telepathy, clairvoyance, precognition, and psychokinesis.

Table 7.1
Endorsement Rates for Various Paranormal Phenomena

Rank	Item	• Endorsement
1	Extraterrestrial Intelligence	63.0
2	Extrasensory Perception	46.7
3	Unidentified Flying Objects	45.7
4	Yoga	44.6
5	Telepathy	39.1
	Premonitions	39.1
7	Prophetic Dreams	35.9
8	Prophecy	34.8
9	Loch Ness Monster	34.8
10	Faith Healing	33.7
11	Clairvoyance	30.4
12	Precognition	26.1
13	Astrology	25.2
14	Bigfoot (Sasquatch)	20.7
15	Levitation	18.5
	Psychokinesis	18.5
17	Exorcism	17.4
18	Ghosts	16.3
	Horoscopes	16.3
	Witches	16.3
	Zodiac Signs	16.3
22	Reincarnation	15.2
23	Lucky Numbers	14.1

24	Black Magic	13.0
25	Ouija Boards	12.0
26	Divination	10.9
27	Voodoo	9.8
28	Communication with the Dead	8.7
29	Alchemy	7.6
	Poltergists	7.6
31	Fortunetelling	6.5
32	Divining Rods	5.4
	Friday the 13th	5.4
	Omens	5.4
35	Graphology	4.4
36	Black Cats	3.3
	Numerology	3.3
	Palmistry	3.3
	Rabbit's Foot	3.3
	Tarot Cards	3.3
41	Teacup Reading	2.2
42	Walking Under Ladders	2.2
43	Divination by Moles	1.1
44	Phrenology	0.0

Recent surveys of adults indicate similar patterns of findings. Although ordinarily less detailed, these surveys have the advantage of being based on samples that are larger and are selected using scientific sampling procedures, so that they are more representative of the entire population. Evidence that certain beliefs in the extraordinary are increasing is available from a comparison of two studies reported by the *Gallup Opinion Index* (Jan. 1974, pp. 20-23). A 1966 sample of American adults indicated that 34% believed in life on other planets resembling human beings, and 48% believed that UFOs are real rather than imagined, even though only 5% claimed to have sighted what they believed to be a UFO. Interestingly, by 1973, these percentages had increased to 46%, 54%, and 11%, respectively. Also, 94% of the latter sample reported having heard or read something about UFOs, an unusually large "awareness" percentage in opinion polling, and 70% of the respondents who believed in the existence of life on other planets also believed that UFOs are real, suggesting that acceptance or rejection of the various concepts related to UFOs are interrelated. It is interesting to note that belief in life on other planets is almost as common as belief in life after death, a basic religious tenet for many Americans. Also, *Current Opinion* (1974, vol. 2, p. 10) reported almost identical data for Canadian respondents. Forty-one percent of this sample believed in life on other planets, 53% believed that UFOs are real, and 12% reported having sighted a UFO.

In the area of astrology, a 1975 survey (*Current Opinion*, 1976, vol. 9, p. 100) indicated that 76% of the sample knew their astrological sign and 22% believed in astrology, whereas 33% of an Australian sample said they were interested in astrology (*Current Opinion*, 1974, vol. 2, p. 57). An interesting comparison of the relative extent of various paranormal beliefs is available in a recent Gallup Poll (A Vote for Sasquatch, 1978). For example, 54% of the informants believed in angels, over one-half endorsed UFOs and ESP, 40% believed in devils, more than 25% in astrology, and approximately 10% expressed a belief in witches, ghosts (66% of whom claimed to have seen one), and unusual creatures (e.g., Sasquatch and/or the Loch Ness monster). A somewhat different perspective is provided by a survey study conducted by Greeley (1975) that focused on the experience of paranormal phenomena rather than simply belief. For example, it was found that respondents reported having the following experiences at least once: *déjà vu* (59%); ESP (58%); clairvoyance (24%); and mystical experiences (35%). Rates for having experienced these phenomena several or more times were 30%, 32%, 10%, 11%, and 17%, respectively.

Such beliefs are common in England as well. For example, a 1973 poll (*Current Opinion*, 1974, vol. 2, p. 57) of adult respondents indicated that nearly half of the sample believed in prophecy and telepathy: 46% and 45%, respectively. The rates of endorsement of other phenomena were as follows: faith healing, 38%; life after death, 37%, horoscopes, 22%; ghosts, 18%; lucky charms, 16%; UFOs, 15%; communication with the dead, 12%; and black magic, 10%. Curiously, the lowest rate of belief was reserved for hypnotism, 4%, the one phenomenon from this list that enjoys a wide degree of supportive scientific evidence.

Several conclusions regarding the extent of extraordinary beliefs may reasonably be drawn from these and related studies. First, the extent of belief is widespread and persistent, often surpassing half of the sampled subjects, depending on the specific paranormal concept involved. Although it is difficult to make comparisons between studies using different questionnaires, because the wording of survey items can influence the response rate, it would appear that the extent of belief has remained steady or possibly increased from the time of the earliest studies to the present. Two studies (Levitt, 1952; Nixon, 1925) were conducted on the same college campus and used comparable inventories, but were separated by a period of 25 years. An examination of the respective data indicates that although there were decreases in belief in some areas, such as phrenology and lucky numbers, there were corresponding increases in other areas (e.g., astrology, palmistry). Similarly, two different studies (Bosher, 1973; Tuch, 1968) may be interpreted as suggesting that, over time, there has been a shift away from what might be called traditional simple "superstitions" (e.g., black cats, lucky numbers, etc.) perhaps towards more cognitively sophisticated and complex phenomena (e.g., ESP, astral projection). Also, the two studies (Ralya, 1945; Warburton, 1956) that directly compared responses of respondents in two different countries (the United States and England) indicated only a few differences. Although more data would be required to reach a final conclusion, it may be that the principal difference in paranormal beliefs between societies and within a given society over time, is the specific types of belief endorsed and not the proportion of individuals who endorse them. Finally, it is likely that the studies just cited tend to underestimate the magnitude of extraordinary beliefs. One reason is social desirability. In addition, most studies have exclusively dealt with rather familiar and common paranormal beliefs. Thus, they fail to account for beliefs relevant only to specific groups and subcultures, as well as beliefs that are totally idiosyncratic. For example, Rosenthal, Hendersen, Hobson, and Hurt (1969) used a scale specifically designed for southwestern regions of the United States, where beliefs associated with magical child-care practices are prevalent among lower socio-economic groups and ethnic minorities. These investigators reported endorsement rates as high as 81% (depending on the belief and ethnic group) for various ideas exemplified by the following: Stretching and groaning in an infant is caused by the baby's being handled by a menstruating woman; thrush may be cured by having a man who has never seen his father blow into the baby's mouth. Thus, if specific regional and ethnic beliefs were included in prevalence studies, as well as idiosyncratic ideas, the rate of extraordinary beliefs would appear much higher.

Belief Structure

Because a single attitude may be said to have several components and because one may hold attitudes towards virtually any place, person, thing, or idea, the question arises as to how attitudes and their component parts are related. One answer to this question is that attitudes and their components seek a state of internal balance or consistency. Imagine someone who strongly believes in ESP, and who, while talking to his or her best friend discovers that the friend is very skeptical about the possibility of ESP. Undoubtedly, the uncovered disagreement would create a certain amount of tension. If the tension is sufficiently strong, the person may change his or her beliefs in ESP so that it coincides with that of the friend and the tension is removed. Alternatively, the person may decide that the skeptical friend is not such a good friend after all. In either case, the individual's two beliefs (about ESP and the friend) become consistent by virtue of the change. Similarly, many people who believe in the existence of ESP also believe in psychokinesis (i.e., the ability to move inanimate objects by mental powers), because the two phenomena are similar in nature and effect, they have similar underlying assumptions, and they have similar implications for science. In fact, it might be difficult to believe in one and not the other. Psychologists use concepts such as balance, symmetry, congruity, and consistency to refer to this effect (e.g., Festinger, 1957; Heider, 1946; Osgood & Tannenbaum, 1955). The unifying characteristic among these concepts is the idea that the various factors involved in attitude phenomena (e.g., behavior, feelings, beliefs, etc.) seek a state of balance because inconsistency is a disturbing psychological condition.

There are limitations to the consistency principle. For example, people must first be aware of an inconsistency in their beliefs. Many of the studies investigating the consistency effect have used experimentally induced attitudes in laboratory settings rather than the attitudes people hold regarding actual social and political issues. When the relationships among attitudes towards actual and ongoing issues are assessed, less support for the consistency formulation is found (e.g., Converse, 1964). To the extent that people do feel pressure to maintain consistency among their beliefs, however, an important phenomenon emerges in which the structure of the entire attitude system may determine the nature and content of the component parts. Beliefs are not simply isolated entities or a conglomeration of individual parts that exist independent of other aspects of our experience. Instead, beliefs may be characterized as fluid points in a dynamic organization that may change in content and strength due to changes elsewhere in the system. A pattern emerges from individual beliefs constituting what might be called a belief system, ideology, or world view. Consequently, one of the reasons it is difficult to change a person's attitude on a controversial topic such as ESP is that such attitudes comprise only a portion of a larger system, which may include the person's attitudes towards other paranormal topics, science, religion, the nature of life, and the nature of truth.

Attitudes towards the paranormal often resemble the inclusive and interrelated systems of belief previously described. Many people adopt positive attitudes generally and such orientations tend to remain constant regardless of the specific manifestation of the paranormal involved. At this point, it is useful to differentiate between the professional occultist and the amateur believer. Whereas professional occultists may be somewhat specialized in specific areas of the paranormal, nonprofessional believers often are not. Evidence from several studies indicates that beliefs in the paranormal are both internally reliable as well as consistent over time (e.g., Fishbein & Raven, 1962; Jones et al., 1977; Tuch, 1968), and that tests of paranormal beliefs reflect actual behaviors (e.g., Zapf, 1945). More directly, Bainbridge (1978b) compared belief in von Däniken's ancient-astronauts theory with items measuring subscription to several related phenomena, including extraterrestrial UFOs, the existence of extraterrestrial life, UFOs as illusion, personal and generalized ESP, astrology, Eastern (e.g., Zen) practices and disciplines, and biorhythm theory. The results indicated significant correlations (i.e., statistical degree of association) for all of the comparisons. Thus, what one believes to be true regarding one aspect of the paranormal and the occult is generally related to beliefs in other areas.

**Box 7.2—The Occult Ideology as
Internal Consistency**

One index of the extent to which occult beliefs combine to form a constrained and coherent ideology is the average degree of association among responses to various aspects of occultism. Table 7.2 presents data obtained from 102 college students in the fall of 1976. Subjects indicated the extent to which they accepted as true each of the 11 items on a five-point scale with response alternatives ranging from Strongly Agree to Strongly Disagree. All pairwise combinations were then correlated. A correlation is an index of the statistical degree of association. Coefficients may vary from -1.0 to $+1.0$ with positive coefficients reflecting direct association and negative coefficients, inverse association. The closer the coefficient is to 1 in either direction, the greater the degree of predictability from one variable to the other, whereas coefficients at or close to zero indicate no statistical association. As Table 7.2 indicates, the extent of association is strong and 42 of the 55 comparisons (76.4%) are significant correlations or strong trends in that direction. The coefficients vary from .04 to .64 with a median correlation of .24.

One of the interesting features of this data is the relationsips among occult items that have widely different subscription rates. For example, teacup reading, which was endorsed by only 2.2 % of a previous sample (see Table 7.1), is significantly correlated with all other items on this list except the two pertaining to ESP. Thus, with a few exceptions, how one responds to ancient occult ideas and practices, such as witches and teacup reading, is related to how one evaluates more modern and "scientific" concepts, such as UFOs.

**Table 7.2
Intercorrelations Among Occult Beliefs and Practices**

	1	2	3	4	5	6	7	8	9	10
1. UFOs	--									
2. Black Magic	.27[c]	--								
3. Witches	.43[c]	.64[c]	--							
4. Necromancy	.47[c]	.20[a]	.39[c]	--						

5.	Loch Ness Monster	.45^c	.34^c	.33^c	.20^a	--					
6.	Ghosts	.42^c	.30^c	.34^c	.56^c	.38^c	--				
7.	Astrology	.10	.21^b	.08	.29^c	.22^b	.28^c	--			
8.	Reincarnation	.20^a	.06	.08	.36^c	.04	.40^c	.31^c	--		
9.	ESP	.29^c	.04	.05	.21^b	.24^b	.26^b	.24^b	.24^b	--	
10.	Plant ESP	.20^a	.07	.17	.20^a	.08	.21^b	.01	.26^b	.18^a	--
11.	Teacup Reading	.22^b	.64^c	.51^c	31^c	.38^c	.52^c	.24^b	.22^b	.06	.12

^{a} p < .10.
^{b} p < .05.
^{c} p < .01.

Beyond statistical considerations, there is an important implication of the fact that occult beliefs may be organized as larger cognitive systems. Many believers apparently see applications and implications of the paranormal in virtually every domain of existence. Thus, the occult ideology has been used as an instrument for influencing the outcome of endeavors ranging from functioning more effectively to making significant decisions to the loftiest exercises of explaining the essence and enigmas of life and how the universe and everything in it operates. Although there is variation in the experiences by which people arrive at their paranormal beliefs, there are also basic commonalities. The script often includes a thorough and ardent immersion into one paranormal theme: reading its books, joining its organizations, etc., only to become bored or disenchanted with the original idea, followed by involvement in other themes, and perhaps eventual synthesis of previous beliefs and practices into new theories and rituals. Astrology enthusiasts shift to witchcraft whereas spiritualists become psychics replacing those who have gone on to other themes. Although disbelievers might conclude that such shifting loyalties results from the lack of substance in the various occult systems, believers apparently see this tendency as flexibility and a recognition that there are many routes to the ultimate metaphysical truths in life (e.g., Balch & Taylor, 1977). It is also common to find the paranormal ideologue deeply involved in some of the faddish medical and psychological therapies, cults and marginal religious groups, and pseudosciences and technologies. For some, the degree of involvement becomes a lifestyle permeating virtually every facet of the individual's behavior. Although some people may only toy with occult ideas or compartmentalize them from other aspects of their lives, for others, the occult is their principal source of identity, activity, and social involvement. The primary reason for such extensive involvement in paranormal ideas and activities probably reflects the believer's basic committment to metaphysical and subjective interpretations of reality, which are discussed further in Chapter 11.

Characteristics of Believers

Considerable research has been conducted in an attempt to determine what kind of people ordinarily subscribe to paranormal concepts. A consistent picture of the believer would help to explain how occultism develops as part of an individual's world view. Unfortunately, the results of those studies are quite varied, in part due to differences in methods, instruments, samples, and assumption. In addition, there are some indications that the profile of believers has changed in recent years and what may have been true of "superstitious" people 10 years ago may not apply to contemporary occultists.

One finding frequently cited in discussions of paranormal beliefs is a sex difference, with females typically yielding higher belief scores than males (e.g., Emme, 1940; Garret & Fisher, 1926; Greeley, 1975; Nixon, 1925; Scheidt, 1973). Explanations for such differences have usually focused on the greater tendency of males to be interested in and be better informed about scientific matters, although occasionally "superstitiousness' has been attributed to females generally as though irrational versus rational thinking was inherent to one's gender. The latter explanation was probably based on stereotypes of the sexes, rather than basic personality factors, and several recent studies have failed to find significant sex differences in paranormal beliefs in either direction (e.g., Bainbridge, 1978b; Jones et al., 1977; Polzella et al., 1975; Tuch, 1968). Several factors might explain these inconsistencies. For example, females may have, at one time, been stronger believers than males, but the relationship may have changed due to changes in the typical interests and activities differentiating the sexes. An interesting solution was proposed by Conklin (1919) who found that females were indeed more "superstitious" than males in areas of greater concern to females (e.g., social relations), whereas males were more "superstitious" in typically masculine endeavors (e.g., sports). Also, Greeley (1975) has reported results suggesting that the relationship between psychic experiences and gender may simply be due to the greater tendency of females to report emotional experiences.

Another common finding has been the relationship between paranormal beliefs and such factors as rural and small-town residence and lower socioeconomic status (e.g., Gorer, 1955; R. Gould, 1921; Lundeen & Caldwell,

1930; Rosenthal et al., 1969; Ter Keurst, 1939). Recent survey data also shows stronger belief in less urbanized regions of the United States, such as the south and midwest, and among small-town and rural residents (e.g., Gallup, Opinion Index, 1974, pp. 20—23). Presumably, these patterns derive from the relatively less extensive educational base of poor and rural populations and perhaps also from the strong influence of fundamentalist religious views among these groups (see Chapter 11). Again, such differences are not always found (e.g., Frank, 1930; Jones et al.,1977; Wagner, 1928) and some studies suggest a reversal of this pattern for certain specific beliefs, such as ESP (e.g., Greeley, 1975).

One possible explanation is that extraordinary beliefs are not enhanced by any single social characteristic, but rather by combinations of such characteristics that place an individual in a position of social marginality. For example, Warren, (1970) has demonstrated that UFO sightings are associated with what is called status inconsistency. Status inconsistency is operationalized as a discrepancy among indices of achieved social status—e.g., income, education, and occupation. An example of discrepancy would be to rank rather low on income while occupying higher status on education and occupation. Warren found that the rate of reported UFO sightings increased as a direct function of the degree of inconsistency. Theoretically, the social marginality reflected in such inconsistencies could lead to a greater reporting of UFO sightings because of social alienation. The theory holds that inconsistency creates a relative lack of social predictability and psychological stress. These processes lead to social alienation from established social institutions, such as science, and a corresponding interest in those unconventional ideas that help restore the individual's sense of equity and position.

Significant differences in paranormal beliefs have been found among different age groups, given sufficient variability among the subjects, with age inversely related to level of belief (e.g., Blackowski, 1937; Dudycha, 1933; Garret & Fisher, 1926). Among younger respondents, age is also related to educational level, which has historically been associated with paranormal beliefs as well. For example, it is usually reported that the amount of information regarding paranormal phenomena increases from elementary through high school to college levels, whereas extent of belief and influence of paranormal ideas decreases (Blackowski, 1937; Caldwell & Lundeen, 1931; Dudycha, 1933; Frank, 1930; Lundeen & Caldwell, 1930; Maller & Lundeen, 1933). Survey data also show belief to be stronger among young as compared to older adults (Greeley, 1975). An obvious explanation for this effect is that increasing age and education levels are associated with less credulity and greater exposure to the various areas of science that offer alternative explanations for paranormal phenomena. Less obviously, increased education would also be associated with greater exposure to influential teachers who might be less likely to endorse paranormal ideas. One method for partially disentangling age and level of education is to examine the effects of educational experiences on changes in beliefs—i.e., to assess differences in belief before and after specific educational experiences. As is discussed later in this chapter, the results of such studies are somewhat inconsistent, although the basic pattern suggests significant reduction of belief as a function of coursework. Also, it could simply be that both age and education contribute to an individual's receptiveness to paranormal ideas.

Another correlate of paranormal belief is intelligence, or more precisely, I. Q. scores, as individuals with lower I. Q.s have often been found to be stronger believers in paranormal and occult phenomena (e.g.,Caldwell & Lundeen, 1932; Emme, 1940; Garret & Fisher, 1926; Gilliland, 1930; Killen, Wildman & Wildman, 1974; Wagner, 1928). It has also been reported that believers score lower on a test of reasoning ability (Polzella et al., 1975) and earn lower college grades (Bainbridge, 1978b). The usual interpretation of this relationship is straightforward; lower intelligence renders an individual more vulnerable to the circular and ephemeral arguments put forth in defense of paranormal ideas. However, in a recent attempted replication of this relationship, not only did the typical finding not emerge, but a significant correlation in the opposite direction was obtained (Jones et al., 1977). In other words, belief in the paranormal was associated with college students who were higher, rather than lower in intelligence. Also, a recent survey of persons who claim to have experienced psychic events found them to be better educated than those not reporting such experiences (Greeley, 1975). It may be that the historical relationship has changed (at least among college students), perhaps due to the antirationalism and antiscientific attitudes typical of many intellectually superior students during the 1960s and 1970s.

Several of the earlier belief studies also found a negative relationship between information about the paranormal and extent of belief (Lundeen & Caldwell, 1930). However, the usual manner in which information was assessed was by asking subjects to indicate how many "superstitions," from an available list, they had heard of. A better test of the relationship between information and belief in the paranormal would involve constructing an instrument that directly and objectively measured how much a subject knows. This was done in a study, by the authors of this volume, that was conducted in conjunction with a college course entitled the Psychology of the Extraordinary, covering many of the topics contained in this book. It was found that, initially, the students in the class were, as a group, very favorably disposed towards the occult, but knew very little about it objectively. The statistical relationship between beliefs and knowledge was not significant however. In addition, it was found that students who had attempted to produce a paranormal phenomenon were significantly more knowledgeable than students who had not previously engaged in such attempts, whereas students reporting an experience that they interpreted to be paranormal in nature were not more knowledgeable than the remainder of the class. By the end of the term, belief scores had significantly decreased and knowledge had significanlty increased giving the appearance that increased knowledge led to decreased beliefs. However, the amount of change in these two variables was statistically unrelated, suggesting that the relationship between information about the paranormal and belief is either complicated by additional factors or the two are, in fact, unrelated. As with the education studies discussed later in this chapter, there is also some questions as to what kind of information or knowledge most affects subscription to occult and paranormal beliefs. For example, with regard to belief in von Däniken's ancient-astronauts theory, Bainbridge (1978b) found that familiarity with the ancient-astronauts idea, scores on an objective astronomy quiz, as well as such factors as college classification and the number of courses in relevant disciplines (e.g., astronomy, ancient history, physical science, etc.) were not related to belief, whereas self-reported low grade-point averages were.

Belief in the paranormal has also been related to various personality characteristics. The most prodigious undertaking of this sort was the study by Adorno, Frenkel-Brunswik, Levinson, and Sanford (1950) on the authoritarian personality, in which they found that certain highly prejudiced persons were more prone to "superstition" because of their home backgrounds. The childhood experiences of authoritarians tend to be punitive, harsh, and arbitrary, and the theory holds that such training leads to the belief that one's fate is in the hands of external forces that come to include any external power whether real or imagined. Other personality, emotional, and adjustment relationships with paranormal beliefs include the following: neurotic tendencies (Hunt, 1944); emotional maladjustment, fear of catastrophies, and dread of unknown peril (Maller & Lundeen, 1933); external locus of control (i.e., the tendency to see personal outcomes as under the control of external forces; e.g., Jahoda, 1970; Jones et al., 1977; Polzella et al., 1975; Scheidt, 1973); insecurity (Tuch, 1968); affiliation motivation (i.e., the tendency to want to be with others; Littig, 1971); inadequate mental adjustment, poor social and personality adjustment (Ter Keurst, 1939); conservatism (Boshier, 1973); fantasy and preference for science fiction (Bainbridge, 1978b); and life change (i.e., the experience of numerous changes, both positive and negative, such as the death of a loved one, a job promotion, etc.; Jones et al., 1977). Also, Greeley (1975) found that individuals who frequently experience what they take to be psychic phenomena reported greater family tension and emotional lability.

Results such as those just described have often been used to characterize the occult believer as female, unintelligent, misinformed, poorly educated, authoritarian, and emotionally unstable. However, there are several reasons for exercising caution when interpreting these data. For example, studies of intellectual, demographic, and personality correlates of believers often produce as many nonsignificant as significant findings (e.g., Jones, Russell, & Nickel, 1976) and in a few cases the findings are reversed. Also, many of the variables compared to belief in the paranormal are themselves correlated, so that it is difficult to determine which of several possibilities is responsible for the basic relationship. Finally, even the significant correlations tend to be of such a magnitude as to raise some doubts about the degree of contribution of these variables to the formation of belief in the paranormal.

Some conclusions may be warranted, however. First, as previously suggested, because much of the inconsistency results from comparing studies separated by several years in time, a genuine change may have taken place in the characteristics of those who subscribe to the paranormal, perhaps as a result of shifts in social values and conditions. For example, Lofland (1977) has observed that converts to a "world-saving" religious cult changed from being predominantly marginal, disadvantaged, and religiously oriented people to recruits from higher socio-economic and secular groups in the space of little more than 10 years. Thus, the diversity of results may reflect the spread of occultism to sectors of the society not previously involved. In fact, such a conclusion has been suggested by Bainbridge (1978b) and Marty (1970).

Second, despite the inconsistencies, there is an underlying theme to these results that may suggest that some configuration of personal factors contributes to the development of such beliefs. In particular, it would appear that variables related to feelings of uncertainty, the belief that one's fate is controlled externally, and social marginality may represent the composite dimension that often facilitates the development of paranormal beliefs. Directly, this would include such factors as authoritarianism, externality, life change, and emotional instability and indirectly, might also include such factors as education, social class, age, and status inconsistency. It may be that the experiences related to these variables predispose an individual to paranormal beliefs by alienation from conventional sources of truth and an increase in readiness to believe in mysterious external forces, thereby increasing the probability that extraordinary ideas will be accepted and internalized. It is also clear, however, that these are not sufficient causes in most instance and that paranormal beliefs may also occur for other reasons.

World View and Esotericism

There are basically two different and opposed views of humankind and the world. The two world views have existed ever since people began thinking about what it means to be human and the relation of humanity to the rest of nature. One view places an emphasis on and values the subjective side of life, inner experience, and thought, whereas the other stresses that that is tangible, objective, and deals with empirical facts. *Rationalism* and *empiricism* are two broad terms that describe these views or attitudes. William James (1907/1978) described rationalists as "tender-minded, intellectualistic, idealistic, optimistic, religious, free-willed, and dogmatic," whereas empiricists are "tough-minded, sensationalistic, naturalistic, irreligious, fatalistic, and skeptical." J. F. Rychlak (1968), a personality theorist, speaks of the "dialectic" and the "demonstrative" traditions. In the dialectic traditions, one philosophizes, speculates, argues, believes in the power of the mind to arrive at the truth alone and unaided, using logic and introspection, and holds to the principle that truth is demonstrated by self-consistency. In the demonstrative tradition, the truth of an observation is validated by other observations, and these observations are not of oneself, but of external objects and events. Concerning the nature of humanity, people are viewed as persons in the dialectic tradition and as organisms in the demonstrative tradtion. Although we may find more philosophers, poets, and religionists subscribing to the people-as-persons model and more scientists, engineers, experimentalists, and other tinkerers subscribing to the humans-as-organisms model, one can find individuals representing both views within the same field of endeavor. B. F. Skinner in psychology, for example, represents the demonstrative tradition, and Carl Rogers or Abraham Maslow the dialectic one, although they too are psychologists. Twenty-five hundred years ago, Democritus and Plato each represented one of these views within philosophy.

Although there are some individuals who would be more or less completely oriented in one direction or another, most people's views probably represent some combination of the two, including some nearly balanced mixtures. There are notable examples in the history of thought of such mixtures, as well as of the tension created by them, and of attempts to resolve it. René Descartes is both the father of a thoroughgoing philosophical dualism and of a materialistic, monistic view that considers the living organism an automaton. Gustav Fechner, who conducted some of the first bona fide psychological experiments, founded psychophysics, and wrote the algebraic equation that bears his name and that relates sensation to stimulation, also subscribed to panpsychism. Isaac Newton was both the mathematician and physicist for which he is known as well as a secret mystic and Rosicrucian. William James created the most important American philosophical system, pragmatism, in order to solve the problems presented by the two world views.

As has been suggested, single beliefs do not ordinarily exist in total isolation from the other attitudes that an individual holds. Thus, the importance of the concept of a continuum of world views ranging from the predominately objective to the clearly subjective is that it may add a perspective to the understanding of how extraordinary beliefs come about. Much of the previous research on this questions assumes that such beliefs are the product of somewhat narrowly defined social and personality dimensions and often those dimensions of rather negative social value. In addition, one of the central criticisms of previous theorizing about extraordinary beliefs is that scholars have failed to consider the possibility that they are both normal as well as a result of common styles of thinking and making sense of the world. The world-view concept assumes that one's beliefs with regard to occult and other extraordinary ideas are but one of the outward manifestations of a more basic orientation towards knowledge and understanding. Furthermore, the world-view concept is less value laden as both ideal orientations represent widely accepted and time-honored strategies for acquiring knowledge and understanding.

The World-View Scale. In order to explore the relationship between world view and beliefs in the paranormal, a psychological scale was created by the authors. Originally, statements were written so as to reflect subscription to either an objective or subjective world view within several domains of belief including: theories of human behavior and motivation (e.g., "Most people don't understand their own motivations and intentions."); the value of science and an objective point of view (e.g., "The progress of civilization was created by advancements in science."); the value of a subjective orientation (e.g., "Self-awareness is the most important goal in life."); conceptions of reality (e.g., "Nothing exists beyond that that is physically observable."); and so on. Approximately one-half of the items reflected a subjective orientation, whereas the other half were written to contain objective views.

These items were then tested by applying a standard scaling analysis; subsequently, a new, shorter version of the Scale was administered to college students whose responses were subjected to factor analysis, a statistical procedure that reduces a large number of data to a few underlying, independent dimensions or factors. The factor-analytic procedure yielded 14 factors. Those factors representing the subjective point of view were religious subjectivism, symbolic—artistic subjectivism, mysticism, antitechnology, and escapism, whereas those reflecting an objective orientation were labeled as scientific objectivism, behavioral objectivism, antisentimentalism, antipracticality, naturalism, empiricism, academic objectivism, and determinism. Two factors were uninterpretable.

The validity of the Scale was assessed by several means. For example, if the Scale is valid and measuring what it was intended to measure, one would expect students majoring in the science and engineering fields to yield more objective world views than those in, for example, the arts and humanities. A comparison of World-View Scale scores and college majors in a large sample of college students indicated that this was the case. Another procedure used to assess the validity of the Scale involved asking a group of college students to name the person who, in their opinion, is the most important figure who ever lived throughout all of history. Those listing scientists and inventors (e.g., Einstein, Newton, Edison, etc.) scored significantly more in the objective direction on the World-View Scale than those listing artists (e.g., da Vinci, Michaelangelo, etc.) or religious figures (e.g., Jesus), as would be expected.

Another approach to validity was to compare World-View Scale reponses to scores on existing scales that measure similar or related constructs. For example, World-View Scale scores correlated significantly with inside/outside perspective on psychology (Oleski & Munz, 1978) among a group of upper-division psychology students. This means that those holding an objective view tended to prefer materialistic-objective theories and methods in psychology, whereas subjective orientations were more closely associated with ideal-experiential approaches to understanding behavior. Additional results from other studies indicated that objective world views were associated with more theoretical and economic values, whereas subjective orientations were more closely associated with social and religious values on the Study of Values test (Allport, Vernon, & Lindzey, 1951). Also, objective world views were associated with being tough-minded, imaginative, trusting, and casual, whereas subjective orientations were related to being tender-minded, suspicious, practical, and possessing greater personal control on the 16 PF personality inventory (Cattell, Eber, & Tatsouka, 1970). Thus, the scale appears to be measuring at least some of the concepts that it was originally intended to measure.

World View and Belief in the Paranormal.   The important question is how does one's view of humanity, life, and the world, as reflected in World-View Scale scores, relate to subscription to beliefs in the paranormal. Two hypotheses might be generated based on what appear to be underlying characteristics of occult beliefs. There is the tendency towards reification of the subjective or the acceptance of subjective interpretations as factual reality, something akin to taking myths literally. Although subjectivism involves greater attention to symbolic interpretation of one's subjective experience in an attempt to answer such questions as the meaning of life, ordinarily, a distinction can be made between the essential truth of such interpretations and the factual reality of the interpretation. In esotericism, this distinction is blurred. This characteristic would lead us to expect occult beliefs to be associated with subjective world views, with the magnitude of subscription to occultism increasing with increasing subjectivism. The second theme is the prevalence of scientific thought, terminology, and methodology to be found in some esoteric writings where, in a sense, they do not belong. The reason for this, previously suggested by others, could be that the esoteric believer has somehow lost faith with his or her subjective interpretation of the universe, or perhaps is looking for something beyond conventional subjective views. Thus, the trappings of science, as opposed to its substance, are incorporated (sometimes haphazardly) into the subjective view to help support what otherwise may be an only partially satisfying, comforting, or explanatory philosophy. This characteristic would lead us to expect occult beliefs to more frequently occur among individuals occupying intermediate or mixed positions on the World-View Scale—i.e., those who subscribe to both a subjective and an objective view. Esoteric beliefs should not be related to predominately objective orientations, however.

In order to test these divergent hypotheses, a large sample of college students completed the World-View Scale and the Belief in the Paranormal Scale (Jones et al., 1977). Belief in esoteric phenomena and practices was greatest for those holding subjective and intermediate views and decreased as one moved towards the objective end of the continuum. Statistical analyses indicated that paranormal belief was negatively correlated with objective orientations and positively with subjectivism for males, whereas among females, such beliefs were reliably associated only with subjectivism. This pattern of findings, although not perfectly consistent, suggested that occultism is linked to both subjective and mixed orientations.

Because these findings were preliminary, only modestly significant, and revealed unexpected differences between males and females, a second comparison between World-View and esotericism was conducted. Another sample of college students completed the World-View Scale and an inventory created specifically for this study that contained 21 types of esoteric beliefs and practices, such as ancient astronauts, ESP, UFOs, astrology, levitation, water witching, and reincarnation. Subjects were asked to respond to each of these items on a seven-point scale, indicating the extent to which they believed that each of the 21 phenomena were real and not simply the product of natural forces or misperception. For this comparison, a clearer picture of the relationship between world view and occult beliefs emerged. Occult beliefs were primarily associated with the adoption of subjective orientations, but in this case, less support for the hypothesis that occultism involves the mixing of objectivism and subjectivism was obtained. Also, the pattern of correlations between occult beliefs and world view were consistent for males and females, with occult beliefs negatively associated with objectivism and positively correlated with subjectivism.

Thus, preliminary evidence points to the role of one's conception of life and the universe as a possible predisposing factor in the development of esoteric beliefs. In one sense, it is not surprising that individuals who focus on the religious, symbolic, and subjective side of human existence are more likely to endorse paranormal ideas. There is a basic similarity in content and structure between subjective orientations and esotericism. To a degree, both emphasize experience over analysis, both focus on meaning rather than process, both are more committed to interpretation as opposed to empirical observation. It is even likely that esoteric beliefs derive from a basically subjective world view and that both orientations serve the same or similar psychological needs, although data are not available to substantiate this speculation.

DYNAMICS OF BELIEF IN THE PARANORMAL

Origins of Paranormal Beliefs

Having established that paranormal beliefs are common and linked to other aspects of experience and personality, the question becomes: How are such beliefs acquired? This may be viewed from two perspectives: How do such ideas originate in the first place, and, once in existence, how are they adopted by other people? Unfortunately, a complete answer to the first question is largely lost in antiquity in that many contemporary beliefs are simply cultural descendants of older occult and metaphysical ideas that have been transmitted from one generation to the next for centuries. The second issue is more accessible to research and analysis.

Significant Others. Although individuals can and do hold totally unique beliefs, most of our attitudes initially derive from our interactions with other people, particularly certain significant others. Psychologists use the term *internalization* to represent the process by which children come to adopt the general orientation and attitudes of their parents and older siblings. For example, parents are more likely to accept and reward behaviors of their children that are consistent with or are manifestations of their own beliefs, whereas punishment and nonacceptance usually accompany verbal expressions and behaviors that are incompatible with parental views (e.g., Rappoport, 1972). This process is so natural that it takes place with or without the awareness of parents. In addition, children may identify with and model parental behaviors even when rewards and punishments are not directly applied (e.g., Bandura & Walters, 1963). In this manner, beliefs that were originally external to an individual become assimilated and are no longer standards enforced by others, but rather, become the individual's own frame of reference for evaluating what is right or wrong, true or false, etc. Thus, one original source of beliefs is the immediate family situation in which one is raised and, in particular, one's parents. Accordingly, parents specifically and society in general pass on a set of values thereby creating continuity and stability in a society. Obviously, children do not incorporate every belief of their parents, as is suggested by such concepts as the generation gap. However, even allowing for such differences, parental beliefs remain the best predictor of the beliefs of children in many cases (e.g., Jennings & Niemi, 1968).

Research also suggests that the internalization of others' views is an ongoing process that continues throughout an individual's life. For example, as the family wanes as an important source of our beliefs, it is replaced by other groups, significant individuals, and institutions, such as the peer group in adolescence, classmates, teachers, ministers, work colleagues, the media, and so on (e.g. H. Hyman, 1969). In fact, beliefs eventually become an important determinant of attraction for others. Studies have indicated that the proportion of attitudes similar to our own that another person holds is related to how well we like that person (Byrne, 1971). One explanation of this is that we prefer others who believe the same things that we do because it tends to validate and reinforce our own point of view. In other words, it is disturbing to encounter someone who disagrees with our attitudes because it suggests that we could be mistaken. They may have reasons or explanations for differing that we have never considered or were unaware of, thus risking embarrassment or the necessity of changing our beliefs. This probably accounts for the tendency to avoid other points of view and to rationalize away and derogate beliefs that are different. Because we like and perhaps interact most with people who agree and agree with people we like, an illusion is often created that everyone agrees with us and this, in part, explains how some beliefs, even if preposterous or manifestly false, can be held in the face of concrete, objective, and reliable contradictory facts.

Two early studies suggested indirectly that paranormal beliefs are acquired from interactions with others, as is the case for other types of belief. For example, Maller and Lundeen (1932) found that subjects who accepted many "superstitions" indicated that they had been strongly influenced by peers, whereas disbelief and abandoning previously held "superstitions" were attributed to parents. On the basis of interviews, Emme (1940) reported that peers and parents were equally influential for those subjects who strongly endorsed the paranormal beliefs and practices contained in his inventory, whereas subjects who rejected the same beliefs indicated that their parents had the greatest influence on their disbelief. Generally, less influence was attributed to educational experiences, media presentations, personal reading, and other sources. Thus, someone may adopt the extraordinary ideas of occultism because, in all probability, family, friends, or significant other persons in the believer's life tend to support, reinforce, and validate that view (Balch & Taylor, 1977).

It is important to recognize that people do not ordinarily conceptualize their beliefs in the objectified and unemotional terminology of psychology. Rarely are beliefs even thought of as beliefs. Instead, they comprise an individual's sense of reality and truth. This is particularly so for beliefs acquired early in life, beliefs in which there is a substantial emotional investment, and beliefs shared with others. The impact of friends, associates, and others on our beliefs is explored further in Chapter 11.

Formal Persuasion.   Another way in which extraordinary beliefs may be acquired is from the influence of deliberate and active attempts at persuasion on the part of professional occultists (i.e., someone who makes a living from occultism) and others, including the generally sympathetic presentations of the paranormal found in the media. Although there have been no studies directly addressing this issue, the literature on attitude change suggests several ways in which this might occur.

The research on attitude and belief change may be summarized by looking at the major elements of situations in which attempts to change existing beliefs are made (for reviews, see McGuire, 1969; Oskamp, 1977).First, the identity and characteristics of the person attempting to change the attitude of someone else are important. Not surprisingly, experts typically create greater attitude shifts in the intended direction, as do likable, trustworthy, objective, familiar, attractive, and powerful communicators. Less obviously, similarity of the communicator increases the probability of attitude change whereas dissimilarity reduces it or results in change in the direction opposite to the communication. For example, an astronomer would be more likely to convince us that UFO sightings represent extraterrestrial visitors than would someone who is not an expert. The expertise dimension is apparently manipulated with some regularity by professional occultists and in a variety of ways. For example, an unearned university degree or a degree from a mail-order diploma mill may be claimed, affiliation with prestigious institutions may be implied erroneously, or more simply, the occultist may claim that his or her "special powers" have been authenticated by a prominent group of university or museum scholars when in reality they have not (e.g., Randi, 1978a).

Characteristics of the message and the style in which it is presented also influence the probability of attitude change. Although not all aspects or presentation styles have been found to influence the probability of attitude change, some clearly do so. For example, indications of the communicator's intent to persuade and obvious bias or self-interest generally reduce influenceability, particularly when the committment of the audience to the issue is strong. Perhaps for this reason, mediums, fortunetellers, and diviners often claim to be passive recipients of their supposed paranormal abilities with nothing to gain from practicing them (e.g., Randi, 1979). Novelty also increases attitude change and this may, in part, explain the tremendous power of esoteric ideas to fascinate, intrigue, and attract the general public. It is not known whether professional occultists are aware of and consciously use these tactics of persuasion that influence the receptiveness of an audience. However, several observers have argued that occult presentations are often deceptive and subtle persuasion attempts (R. Hyman, 1977) and there is considerable anecdotal evidence (e.g., Evans, 1973) that many professional occultists are dynamic and charismatic personalities who, therefore, would be expected to be effective propagandists.

Certain characteristics of the audience also have predictable effects on the probability of attitude change. For example, low self esteem, less knowledge, lower intelligence, and less ego involvement in the topic generally increase the likelihood of attitude change, whereas counter attitudinal arguments and well-integrated attitude systems generally reduce the probability of change. Although research examining the relationship between personal characteristics and belief in the paranormal has been somewhat inconclusive, it may be the case that these factors contribute to some manifestations of belief. For example, Evans (1973) has argued that two factors often implicated in the development of allegiance to occult groups and hence in belief are the relative lack of scientific knowledge among adherents of such groups and philosophical alienation, resulting in the need to find a viable alternative system of beliefs.

Despite a general tendency among many people to feel that their attitudes are rational appraisals of the issues involved, and despite the general skepticism regarding advertising and other formal attempts at persuasion, in some circumstances, our attitudes may be manipulated by others without our awareness. This is so partly because it is difficult to resist along every dimension that has been found to increase the probability of attitude change. Also, once a public-attitude commitment has been made, regardless of how strongly and regardless of the reasons for doing so, people are more likely to behave consistently with that commitment.

Recent events have suggested the importance of media presentations in the development of paranormal ideas. Although the actual effect of the media have not been systematically studied, it has been noted that "UFO flaps" (periods of frequent sightings of unidentified objects) are often preceded by new books or movies on the topic (e.g., Klass, 1974). In fact, initial reports by news sources often stimulate public interest, resulting in greater numbers of people scanning the skies for UFOs and, consequently, increased sightings. It is, of course, for the very reason that there is widespread public interest that the media extensively covers seemingly unusual events. The problem is that subsequently developed alternative explanations are, by their very nature, mundane and less exciting and thus receive less coverage, if any, often leaving the erroneous impression with the public that something truly remarkable has taken place when it has not. For example, many UFO sightings on closer inspection prove to be sightings of the planet Venus. However, stories covering the true origin of the sightings are rarely, if ever, accorded the same degree of media coverage.

Personal Experiences.   Another mechanism that apparently leads to the acceptance of paranormal beliefs is personal experience. For example, two studies (Jones et al., 1977; Polzella et al., 1975) found that college students who reported having experienced some form of occult phenomenon scored significantly higher on scales measuring endorsement of beliefs in the paranormal than students not reporting such experiences. However, at this point one may ask, why doesn't a personal experience prove to the individual that the occult interpretation is false, assuming, of course, that most paranormal phenomena have alternative, mundane explanations? Part of the solution derives from the influence of expectations, existing beliefs, anomolous learning, and misattributions on judgments of extraordinary events.

Expectations and Existing Beliefs.   Many beliefs are self-generated. One of the ways in which this occurs is the *self-fulfilling prophesy*, which refers to the effects of our own beliefs and expectations on subsequent experiences in which what we expect to happen usually does (Rosenthal & Jacobson, 1968). For instance, someone who believes that Friday the 13th is an unlucky day may indeed experience greater misfortune on that day due to increased anxiety associated with feeling vulnerable. High levels of anxiety naturally lead to decrements in the performance of skilled activities, especially those at which we are not well practiced, and consequently to more mistakes and grief. Furthermore, believing that Friday the 13th is an unlucky day has the effect of increasing attention to any mishaps that might have occurred regardless. Because such selective attention is not present on other days, it creates the impression that the belief has been objectively confirmed. Thus, by affecting how we behave, attend, and remember events related to the paranormal, our existing beliefs shape our experiences in such a way to reinforce what we believed in the first place.

Empirical demonstrations of this effect on paranormal beliefs have occurred in several psychological studies. For example, Jones et al. (1977) asked subjects whether they had ever experienced a paranormal phenomenon. The 26.6% of the sample answering affirmatively more strongly believed in the paranormal than subjects who had not reported a paranormal experience. Previously unreported data from the same study included responses to a question regarding whether the subjects had ever attempted to produce a paranormal experience. Eighty-five percent of the subjects reporting an experience indicated that they had also attempted on one or more occasions to create one. The vast majority of experienced phenomena fell into the category of parapsychological processes (e.g., telepathy, precognition, etc.), and the same was true for the paranormal attempts, with one exception. The exception was divination using a ouija board, which has become common as a popular parlor game. Thus, with one exception, subjects' experiences were of the type that they had attempted to create, suggesting that they would be expecting miraculous occurrences at these times and might therefore be more likely to notice, misinterpret, or selectively recall unusual events tending to confirm the original expectation. Although this research was correlational in nature and consequently the direction of causality cannot be determined, it is reasonable to assume that positive attitudes towards the paranormal lead to attempts to create it and anticipation that it will occur, which, in turn, occasionally result in at least apparently successful confirmation. Thus, new paranormal beliefs may develop from the expectation created by existing beliefs.

This line of reasoning is further supported by two additional studies conducted by Jones et al. (1977). College students were told that their personality characteristics had been determined from their birthdates using a new, "more advanced" form of astrology. They were also told that a test of the usefulness of this new astrological system would be for the subject to assess the accuracy of his or her personality descriptions. The subject was then given a facsimile of a computer print-out, which contained the subject's name, birthdate, and 10 characteristics that were extremely vague but mildly flattering statements that may be construed as being applicable to anyone. The following serves as an example: "You are sometimes shy when first making a new acquaintance, but eventually you open up to your new friend." The list of 10 statements was identical for all subjects. Subjects were then asked to indicate the extent to which the 10 statements were truly descriptive and accurate for them. Results indicated a significant correlation between belief in the paranormal scores (acquired previously) and the extent to which the subject accepted the veracity of the 10 personality statements. Similarly, Bainbridge (1978b) found significant correlations between acceptance of a bogus biorhythm assessment and belief in several paranormal phenomena. Students of personality assessment will recognize these procedures as versions of the so-called "P. T. Barnum effect" (e.g., Snyder & Schenkel, 1975), in which many people accept as genuine almost any set of generalized and flattering self-descriptions alleged to have been derived systematically. The important point for our consideration is that subjects previously possessing a tendency to subscribe to extraordinary beliefs were the same subjects who said the statements were most pertinent to them. Thus, the believer may be more likely to have a confirming experience because mundane and explainable events are labelled as extraordinary.

Another study reported by Jones et al. (1977) attempted to determine whether believers would be more likely to "facilitate" the production of a paranormal phenomenon, given the opportunity. Subjects were given a piece of string with a paper clip attached to one end. They were instructed to hold the string at arm's length (allowing the paper clip to hang free) and to attempt to move the paper clip by concentration. Subjects were further told that this was a test of their psychic ability and that although nothing might occur at first, to continue concentrating until told to stop. Each subject was then allowed 2 minutes to move the object while an experimenter observed the amount of movement against a calibrated background on the table in front of the subject. The experimenter could easily judge maximum deflection of the paper clip because, on the table, there was a series of concentric circles that were at radius intervals of 1 inch each. This ancient procedure, known as radiesthesia (Chapter 8), has long been a method for easily creating an occult experience and silencing disbelievers because movement will inevitably occur due to the muscle tension that accompanies holding the arm in an outstretched position. However, it can also be easily demonstrated that such movement may be produced by slight muscle contractions that remain unobservable. Results indicated a significant correlation between prior belief and the amount of observed deflection indicating that, whether consciously or otherwise, believers were more likely to ensure the production of an unusual event. Also, a recent experiment indicated that general belief in psychic phenomena was associated with estimates of greater success on a psychokinetic task (Benassi, Sweeney & Drevno, 1979). Because believers have also been found to attempt occult experiences more frequently, it is not surprising that a confirming instance eventually occurs. It should be stressed that the nature of this and many other tasks related to extraordinary phenomena, although simple, are sufficiently elusive that it is conceivable for a person to be physically moving the object without ever being aware that he or she is doing so.

These studies as well as others pertaining to conversion to paranormal cults (e.g., Balch & Taylor, 1977) suggest that persons who adopt occult and metaphysical interpretations of reality tend to do so eagerly, often defining themselves as "seekers" of unusual, mysterious experiences and profound wisdom. Thus, the effect of existing occult beliefs involves not only the more or less passive influence of greater receptiveness to paranormal views, but also active attempts to discover and experience phenomena already taken for granted.

Anomalous Learning. Another way in which personal experience can lead to occult beliefs and behaviors is through an occasional spurious temporal connection between the behavior and positive outcomes. Psychologist B. F. Skinner identified the process of *operant conditioning* by demonstrating the influence of consequences in the learning and retention of certain behaviors. Once a particular behavior has occurred, its place in the individual's repertoire of behavior will largely be determined by whether the behavior operates on the environment in such a way as to produce a positive, neutral, or negative consequence. Behaviors resulting in favorable outcomes lead to increases in the frequency and strength of the behavior.

This process is often what occurs in learning. In most instances, the connection between the behavior and the environmental consequence is a natural and predictable one, such as when one receives praise for performing a socially defined good deed. However, Skinner (1948) has also demonstrated that even when the connection is entirely spurious, changes in behavior will result. Thus, when pigeons were reinforced with food on a totally arbitrary basis, the result was an increase in whatever behavior was occurring immediately prior to the administration of the reinforcement.

Skinner and others have applied this kind of analysis to "superstitious" behavior in which some ritual is performed because at some time in the individual's learning history it has preceded positive outcomes. For example, Gmelch (1978) has documented the "superstitious" rituals of baseball players (e.g., not stepping on the base line, uniform number preferences, talking to the ball, etc.), which, in most cases, originated from behaviors preceding an outstanding performance or achievement. As Jahoda (1969) has noted, this model probably applies best to origination of those paranormal beliefs and practices pertinent to individuals rather than the culturally shared and transmitted ideas. However, the concept of operant conditioning reveals two important aspects regarding paranormal beliefs and behaviors.

First, because conditioned behaviors are strengthened by intermittent schedules of reinforcement (i.e., when the behavior in questions is followed by the favorable outcome only part of the time), occasional spurious connections between the behavior and its apparent consequence are sufficient to maintain the erroneous belief, regardless of how it originated. Thus, operant conditioning explains in part the persistence of such behaviors. Second, it reveals the power of many "superstitious" behaviors even when the person who engages in the behavior has doubts or is not fully convinced of the truth of the extraordinary interpretation. For example, it is not uncommon to find that those who commit "superstitious" acts will admit that there is "probably nothing to it" and yet they will persist in the behavior "just in case."

Misattributions.   Ayeroff and Abelson (1976) have demonstrated that subjects in telepathy experiments who are given more control of the situation (e.g., choice of symbol deck) and who were allowed to discuss with their partners their ideas on telepathy, believed they had performed significantly better at the task than subjects with less control and no opportunity for discussion. Also, it was found that, independent of experimental condition, senders believed that their joint performance was better than receivers did. These beliefs were unrelated to actual telepathic hit rates (of which subjects were uninformed), which were not significantly different from chance-level expectations. Also, Benassi, Sweeney and Drevno (1979) demonstrated that estimates of success on a psychokinetic task were affected by such factors as a positive introductory set, number of practice trials and active involvement with the task, independent of actual performance. These data have been interpreted as supporting Langer's (1975) *illusion of control* theory, which holds that when behaving in situations in which chance is determining the outcome, individuals will interpret the situation as if skill were at work, resulting in the illusion that skill is being exercised. This is particularly so when some form of control, even if irrelevant to the outcome, is involved (e.g., choice of symbol deck). Thus, personal experiences may be interpreted as proof of the paranormal leading to belief in paranormal explanations because coincidences are misinterpreted as significant occurrences and chance effects are misjudged as resulting from skill. Similarly, early theorists of magic emphasized the role of erroneous causal attributions as when one confuses analogy with causal explanation (see Chapter 10).

Changes in Paranormal Beliefs

Because paranormal beliefs may be based on criteria that are not open to empirical verification, they should be highly resistant to change even if the light of contradictory evidence, as are religious and other strongly held convictions. But the questions remains as to how such beliefs persist in the context of a modern society, which generally endorses scientific values and theories, and in view of the evidence for the existence of paranormal phenomena, which frequently varies from the improbable to the fanciful. *Education Studies*   One approach to this question is to examine the effects of educational experiences on changes in beliefs—i.e., to assess differences in belief before and after specific educational experiences. Unfortunately, results from such studies are quite varied. Some studies indicate that general science-education courses alone result in lower belief scores (e.g., Caldwell & Lundeen, 1931; Smith, 1930; Valentine, 1936), but some studies suggest that the instruction must be specific to the paranormal (e.g., Zapf, 1945) whereas other studies find no significant changes even with specific instruction regarding the paranormal (McBurney, 1976; Singer, 1977). The authors of this volume did find significant decreases in the level of belief following a course surveying the psychological aspects of occult phenomena, but these changes were unrelated to the amount of information that the students acquired from the course. In addition, a student's major area of study has been found to effect belief changes in response to education (Gilliland, 1930) and several studies have revealed that such changes as do occur are usually selective—that is, changes will occur in some, but not all beliefs (e.g., Lehman & Fenton, 1929; Lord, 1958; Zapf, 1945). However, there is evidence that such changes are stable and persistent for long periods of time (Kennedy, 1939a).

The inconsistency of these findings may simply reflect the strength of esoteric beliefs. Perhaps change will occur under very specific circumstances, which may not have been achieved in all cases. Alternatively, the failure of courses containing the subject of occultism to result in significant reductions in belief has occurred primarily in those studies in which a special course treating exclusively occult and esoteric themes was created as opposed to those in which occultism was included as a portion of a more broadly defined course on psychology or science. Such specific treatment of the paranormal tends to attract students who are strongly committed to the occult point of view and who would consequently be more resistant to alternative arguments and evidence.

Box 7.3—The Will To Believe: An Illustration

Several years ago, the junior author of this book attempted a bogus demonstration of telepathy in a General Psychology class. The somewhat clumsy and transparent technique was obtained from the instructor's resource manual that accompanied the widely used psychology text that had been adopted for the course. The manual recommended that the demonstration be used in conjunction with lectures on methodology, ordinarily the most boring topic to students in the course and, consequently, the one requiring the instructor's greatest efforts to retain student interest. The idea was to lecture on the scientific method as it applies to the study of behavior, then to claim telepathic skill, attempt the demonstration (hopefully with success), and then to ask the class: Does this prove the existence of ESP? It was expected (perhaps naively) that the answer would be a resounding "No" followed by a recitation of the methodological flaws of the demonstration, such as the need for better controls, the need for replication, and so on. All went remarkably well until, following the successful demonstration, the class overwhelmingly endorsed the authenticity and methodological rigor of the attempt! Even more surprising, when the now abashed professor lamely admitted the ruse and revealed the procedure for creating it, many members of the class argued to the contrary and persisted in contending that it was a genuine instance of telepathy and not a trick. One member of the class even offered the creative explanation that "Maybe you have ESP but don't know it!"

This is not an isolated incident. The same trick, as well as others, has been performed before a variety of audiences including non-student adults, and it never fails that at least some members of the audience will profess their belief that genuine telepathy has occurred, even after the trick has been exposed and explained. Similar experiences have been reported by others as well (e.g., Jahoda, 1969).

This demonstrates the strength of the will to believe, at least with regard to telepathy. For example, there is nothing to prevent the believer from acknowledging that even though this instance of apparent telepathy was fraudulent, others are genuine. Nevertheless, for some reason, many believers persist in asserting that self-confessed fraud is a less reasonable hypothesis than the idea that telepathy is real and could somehow magically occur even when one claims to have presented a sham demonstration. Apparently, the will to believe leads enthusiasts to accept at least a little fraud and trickery on the part of professional psychics due to the contention that psychic powers are difficult to control and therefore one has to cheat every now and then in order to complete a performance. This, of course, may simply be a rationalization for continuing to believe every time some psychic is exposed for cheating.

Perhaps the insistence that telepathy has taken place in these demonstrations·stems from the fact that people do not like to be fooled, particularly about matters of importance to them. Therefore, it may be easier, or at least more comforting, to believe that "real" telepathy is at work, as opposed to accepting the fact that one has been tricked, especially by what turns out to be such a simple, and apparently easily detectable, procedure. But even this explanation suggests that the power of one's belief in telepathy determines the judgments one makes about it. Also, these demonstrations exemplify the tendency of untrained observers to accept even highly compromised procedures as adequate tests of the paranormal, and, as every magician knowns, the ease with which it is possible to create what appears to be an instance of the occult.

Laboratory Studies.   As suggested earlier, existing beliefs in the paranormal dramatically alter the manner in which an individual processes information related to the occult. In an experiment examining this effect (Russell & Jones, 1980), subjects were presented one of two bogus abstracts of a fictitious journal article describing a series of experiments that purported either to prove or disprove the existence of ESP. The two versions of the abstract were identical except for the alleged results of the experiments and the author's conclusion based on those results. Subjects for the experiment consisted of college students who believed in the paranormal (believers) or who did not (disbelievers) as determined by the Belief in the Paranormal Scale (Jones et al., 1977). After reading the abstract, subjects completed items assessing their emotional arousal, agreement with the conclusions drawn by the author of the abstract, and recall for the details presented in the abstract. As expected, results indicated that both believers and disbelievers were emotionally aroused after reading the abstract that contradicted their beliefs, but were not so aroused when they read the belief-consonant abstract. Surprisingly, however, although disbelievers agreed with the conclusion of the abstract significantly more frequently when it was in agreement with their original beliefs than when it was not, there was little difference in agreement for the believers, regardless of whether they had read the ESP-proven or ESP-disproven abstracts. Furthermore, original belief and recall were related only in the ESP-disproven condition, with greater belief being associated with reduced accuracy in recall. Analysis of individual recall items indicted the reasons for these anomalies. Several of the believers who read the abstract purporting to challenge the existence of ESP had distorted the outcome of the studies reported so that it agreed with their initial view—i.e., that ESP was supported. In other words, for these believers, there was no reason to disagree with the counter belief message because in the interval between reading the abstract and completing the recall test, they had reversed the conclusion (and hence the meaning) of the abstract. Thus, both believers and disbelievers showed negative emotional arousal when confronted with information that appeared to contradict their beliefs about ESP, but only believers manifested a distortion whereby the meaning of the information presented to them was altered.

These results were interpreted as an example of the *selective-learning* process (e.g., Greenwald & Sakamura, 1967) in which the learning and retention of attitude-relevant information is theorized to be most likely to occur when that information is in agreement with prior beliefs. Also, these data are consistent with the study reported by Otis (1979) in which it was found that persons attending the movie "Close Encounters of a Third Kind" were more likely to agree that there are flying saucers from out space and intelligent beings observing Earth than were persons attending movies unrelated to UFOs. Thus, selective exposure, attention, and retention of confirmatory information helps to ensure the persistence of extraordinary beliefs.

In another experiment, (Jones & Russell, in press) college students were again classified as believers or disbelievers. Subjects witnessed one of two contrived attempts at telepathy, one of which apparently succeeded whereas the other clearly failed. In both demonstrations, chance-level performance was defined for the subject audience prior to the attempt and the experimenters were able to exactly control the level of performance by the use of marked cards. The successful demonstration was created by the "receiver's" deliberate performance at 60% accuracy (a highly significant outcome), whereas in the failure condition, the "receiver" appeared to have guessed correctly on only 20% of the trials, exactly at chance level. Following the demonstration, subjects responded to a series of questions regarding what they believed to have taken place and then were given the opportunity to test their own telepathic abilities after which (and following feedback concerning how well they had performed on the telepathy task) they indicated the extent to which they believed they possessed ESP.

Two of the analyses from this experiment are of particular interest. First, responses regarding whether ESP occurred during the demonstration indicated that disbelievers responded to this question differently depending on the outcome of the demonstration observed, whereas believers did not discriminate between the two conditions. Thus, both believers and disbelievers indicated that ESP had occurred when it appeared to, whereas only believers said ESP occurred in the condition that failed. It should be noted that in the failure condition, believers were not only more likely than disbelievers to indicate that telepathy had occurred, but also their responses revealed that believers on the average attributed success to the ESP attempt even when objectively the performance was at chance level.

Second, actual individual ESP scores (number correct) were correlated with self-reported ESP ability ratings for believers and disbelievers separately. For disbelievers, the two were highly correlated, but not for believers. The disbelievers apparently based estimates of their own ESP ability on performance outcomes, whereas believers did not. Incidentally, analyses performed on the individual ESP scores failed to yield differences associated with the level of belief and, on the average, were not significantly different from chance-level expectations. Moreover, because not even a single subject indicated that he or she thought the demonstrations could have been rigged, the results may not be attributed to differential suspiciousness between believers and disbelievers. Apparently, the demonstrations were persuasive and the subjects were inclined to believe that they were legitimated. This again suggests the tendency of naive observers to uncritically accept the veracity of those claiming psychic ability. Also, these results are consistent with those of Zusne and Jones (1978) who found that failure at a controlled telepathy task did not reduce believers' endorsement of either the general phenomenon of telepathy nor their beliefs in their own abilities.

It may be argued that a single failure should not result in changes in believers' convictions that ESP is possible because the failure could be explained in a variety of ways other than the possibility that ESP does not exist. Likewise, believers may not base their judgments of their own ability on one poor showing in a controlled experiment because they probably have experienced what they believe was telepathy on many occasions, albeit in uncontrolled situations. Thus, it is easy to understand how believers in ESP can argue, as they frequently do, that the "sterile" or "hostile" atmosphere of controlled experiments renders elusive extrasensory abilities useless. However, this line of argument does not apply to the findings that actual outcomes were distorted or reinterpreted such that they became consistent with the believers' original point of view. Unfortunately, the designs of these experiments do not allow for the determination of how the distortions occurred. However, these data do suggest that beliefs in the paranormal are sufficiently important to the individual holding them that disconfirming information elicits strong negative emotions and perceptual or memory distortions that remove the potential threat by changing the information to support rather than contradict original beliefs.

When Prophecy Fails: A Field Study. Festinger, Riecken, and Schachter (1956) reported an extensive field study examining the effects of belief disconfirmation that actually took place in a natural setting. Several of the investigators joined or made contact with a small group of UFO and occult enthusiasts who had predicted a great flood that would bring the end of the civilized world. The spiritual leader of the group (Mrs. Keech) had for some time received "messages" (in the form of automatic writings) from spirit-beings called the "Guardians" located in outer space. Based on interpretations of the messages, in which several group members participated, a prediction was made regarding the specific date and time at which the world was to be deluged and the "true believers" were to be saved by being taken away in flying saucers to "another plane of existence." Because a specific prediction had been made, something doomsayers usually avoid, considerable interest was generated among the media and others despite the group's initial attempts to keep their activities and beliefs secret.

When the prophecy failed, those faithful who had waited out in the cold for the saucer that never came were initially disappointed and discouraged. But, before the night was over, they decided among themselves that the prophecy had been a test and, thus, the deluge was averted because of their faith and efforts. Remarkably, the group rejoiced at what was now judged to be confirmation of the prediction, and they abandoned their secrecy in frantic efforts to convince others of its accuracy. By contrast with their previous reticence with the press, they granted interviews and appeared willing to discuss with virtually anyone their unusual beliefs and ideas. Instead of losing faith in their leader or the "Guardians," most members of the group appeared to have strengthened their belief as a consequence of this experience. Indeed, their faith and interest in proselytizing remained steadfast and the group even endured a second, more public disconfirmation of its beliefs.

The strengthening of belief as a result of disconfirmation is an example of what is known as *cognitive dissonance* (Festinger, 1957). Dissonance theory holds that people avoid attitude-discrepant information but given forced confrontation with such information, a negative emotional state arises in which they feel the need to alter some aspect of their related beliefs. Dissonance theory assumes that inconsistent beliefs are psychologically motivating, resulting in changes in the less important of two inconsistent beliefs. In this case, it was apparently easier to alter beliefs about what had taken place (i.e., that the prediction had been disconfirmed) than it was to abandon the complex social and psychological needs being fulfilled by the group's belief in the Guardians, Mrs. Keech's messages, the other planes of existence, and so on. Perhaps more importantly, these results demonstrate the strength of resistance to belief change among highly committed individuals and groups, particularly when a public stand has been taken on an issue.

One implication of the results of the laboratory and field studies just discussed is that believers are more deeply involved and committed to their

beliefs than are disbelievers (at least among the samples tested). This in turn
suggests that, given the amount of widely disseminated material advocating
paranormal interpretations and the relative paucity of debunking or alternative information, it would be relatively easy for a disbeliever to become a
believer (because the discrepant information appears to be at least processed
and retained), but very difficult for a believer to become a disbeliever
because even the most thorough debunking effort is apt to be misperceived
or remembered incorrectly. However, it should be noted that the results of
these studies parallel findings reported for the disconfirmation of religious
beliefs as well (e.g., Bateson, 1976) and thus may be pertinent to challenges
to many strongly held beliefs in addition to beliefs in the paranormal. Indeed, one field study has been reported in which over 100 members of an
evangelical religious group who had spent over a month in a bomb shelter in
anticipation of a nuclear attack, emerged to proclaim that their faith had
prevented the holocaust (Hardyck & Braden, 1962). Even so, the tendency
to distort contradictory information found in these studies suggests how
beliefs in the paranormal can continue despite the existence of evidence to
the contrary, and that exposure to contradictory information may even
have the effect of reinforcing paranormal beliefs.

Psychological Functions of Paranormal Beliefs

Singer (1977) discusses several reasons why belief in the paranormal might
come about, including extraordinary personal experiences, ordinary experiences misinterpreted as unusual, generalizing from altered states of consciousness to ordinary reality, and inability or unwillingness to solve a problem using conventional concepts and methods. He also suggests that one
reason, rare among skeptics, for the adoption of paranormal beliefs is an informed and rational review of the evidence, such as when one assesses the
data and arguments for and against ESP and decides that the former
outweighs the latter.

However, Singer particularly emphasizes the role of such beliefs in personal functioning—that is, the value of such beliefs to the person who holds
them. For example, belief in the paranormal may provide a mechanism for
making decision where a more rational appraisal is difficult or too costly (as
in astrology), while simultaneously providing a source of external blame for
decisions that go awry. Some people may be drawn to the wonders of occultism because of the lure of self-improvement or enhanced personal functioning, whereas others may find virtue in anything that appears exciting
and new. Singer notes that occultism may serve as an alternative to the loss
of faith in traditional value systems and as such may function as a personal
religion for many people. As we discuss in Chapter 11, occult and related
beliefs also have definite social-psychological functions. Some people are

simply raised into this point of view, others may see in it a source of personal identity and social contact, whereas still others may be drawn by occultism's counterculture and antiestablishmentarian ties and use it as a means to express their opposition to traditional values and institutions. Finally, according to Singer, occultism may become the vehicle for the expression or solution of deep-seated psychological conflicts and anxieties. For example, relational problems may manifest themselves in disturbing fantasies or visions, and attributing even occult and supernatural qualities may help to demystify and reduce the anxiety associated with dreaded inevitabilities, such as death.

Although Singer's list of the psychological needs from which magical beliefs derives is probably not complete, it is a representative sampling. Underlying this and probably any other listing of psychological motives for occultism are two distinct themes suggesting that believing in the paranormal satisfies specific manifestations of two human motives.

First, paranormal beliefs appear to operate so as to reassure the believer that there is order, meaning, and control in what may otherwise appear to be a chaotic and capricious world. Many of the historical correlates of occult beliefs suggest a person in need of reassurance regarding his or her identity and social standing. For example, demographic and experiential correlates, such as poor education, rural residence, marginality, and social-economic disadvantages might reasonably be expected to lead to feelings of alienation and disaffection for which occultism may offer a partial remedy by emphasizing the possibility of altering the course and consequently the rewards of one's life. Similarly, the magical properties of the occult world may provide comfort for those suffering from emotional and other kinds of problems by appearing to offer obtainable solutions and by providing a wealth of external culprits to take the blame for one's own failures and inadequacies.

Conversely, allegiance to occultism at least partially derives from the implication of all paranormal and pseudoscientific ideas that there is some special meaning to life, something that transcends the ordinary and mundane reality of the physical world. Although sudden change, inconsistency, and uncertainty create psychological discomfort and motivation to seek certainty and control, unending repetition is boring. Thus, beliefs in the paranormal hold out the promise of something beyond, something not yet experienced, and as a result create interest, excitement, and relief from the dissatisfaction of the sameness of everyday living.

Therefore, belief in any or all manifestations of the paranormal may satisfy what are very basic but seemingly inconsistent human tendencies—to seek understanding, meaning, and stability while hoping for change, mystery, and excitement. Along with other major value systems such as religion, the function of occultism is thus to secure the past and the present and at the same time promise something in the future beyond what is immediately available and obvious.

This discussion treats only one perspective (i.e., individual, psychological reasons for occultism) from which paranormal beliefs may be examined. There are other reasons for the adoption of paranormal beliefs, such as social processes (see Chapter 11). Perhaps the most useful conclusion that can be drawn from the literature on occult beliefs concerns the powerful impact that existing beliefs towards the paranormal can have on subsequent responses to anomalistic events. In the case of the believer, this may amount to a search for confirmation of the occult ideology through active attempts to produce or confirm the existence of paranormal phenomena and resist alternative explanations and evidence. The strength of such endeavors no doubt derives from the integral role that occult beliefs occupy in the thinking of the believer and the basic psychological functions satisfied by such beliefs.

8

Personality in Occultism: Determinants and Dynamics

"The fault, dear Brutus, is not in our stars, but in ourselves."

William Shakespeare, *Julius Caesar*, I, ii

"Who in the world am I? Ah, that's the great puzzle!" And she began thinking over all the children she knew that were of the same age as herself, to see if she could have been changed for any of them. "I'm sure I am not Ada," she said, "for her hair goes in such long ringlets, and mine doesn't go in ringlets at all; and I'm sure I can't be Mabel, for I know all sorts of things, and she, oh, she knows such a very little! Besides, she's she, and I'm I, and—oh dear, how puzzling it all is!"

Lewis Carroll, *Alice's Adventures in Wonderland*, Ch. II

One definition of personality is that it is the behavior pattern that is characteristic of a given person over a more or less extended period of time. Personality is the most complex idea in psychology, however, and there are a large number of theories of personality, each subscribed to by a substantial number of psychologists. Each presents a different set of ideas about the origins of personality, its nature, development, varieties, dynamics, and measurement. In this and the following chapter, the term "personality" is used in the sense of definition just given.

Introspectively, much of a person's personality is the subjective experience of the quality of one's thoughts, perceptions, emotions, motives, and memories. It is the experience of one's self, and it is fundamental to all the rest of one's mental life. The experience of self is an entirely subjective process. It is not, however, perceived simply as a process that is somehow exuded by the brain. Inner speech, talking to oneself, and self-instruction begin around the age of 5, when the child has mastered his or her native language. In middle childhood, our inner dialogues become such a common, ongoing affair that the idea of an inner person and of that person's autonomous existence forces itself upon us. The mere fact of self-observation leads almost inevitably to the consideration of the inner self as something separate and distinct from the body. This idea is reinforced by what appears to be instances of the independent functioning of the inner being, such as dreams. Sometimes, we may not even experience ourselves as ourselves. We may have the delusion that we are somebody else, that our thoughts are not ours but somebody else's, or that the boundary between the self and the not-self is melting or has disappeared altogether. Although

212

such delusions are found mostly among the mentally ill, they may be present in some form also in those who are not. The result of the experience of self as opposed to non-self is that attempts are made to reconcile the two or at least show what the relationship between them might be. The territory of such endeavors often overlaps that of occultism. In the following discussion, we analyze some attempts to classify personality types in occultism, occult interpretations of the experiences that occur in cases of depersonalization or dissociation—that is, the breakup or loosening of personality boundaries—and some of the occult interpretations that have been attached to personality functioning in the altered state of consciousness of paradoxical sleep or dreaming.

OCCULT PERSONALITY DIAGNOSES AND GUIDES FOR ACTION

The earliest and the simplest personality theories were type theories: All people are divided into a few categories based on some classificatory principle, such as physique, body fluids, or behavior. The four classic temperaments—sanguine, choleric, melancholic, and phlegmatic—were based on the teaching of the ancient Greek philosophers about the four elements that everything was made of (air, fire, earth, and water) and the four humors that corresponded to them: blood, yellow bile, black bile, and phlegm. Carl Gustav Jung's division of personalities into extroverts and introverts and each of these into four subtypes is also a type theory.

The Seven-Ray Typology

The Hindu scriptures show what is probably the oldest type theory of personality. It is based on the universally sacred and magical number seven. The Hindu scripture *Satapatha Brahmana* describes the building of a fire altar (Müller, 1897). The structural elements and the dimensions of the altar are tied to Hindu cosmogony and the Hindu view of the constitution of humans. These passages come as close as anything in the Hindu scriptures to a sevenfold typology. Another relevant Hindu septenary is the seven Rishis. These, depending on the level of discourse, are the seven wise men, the seven archangels, the seven primeval emanations, and the like. The seven Rishis figure prominently in the conception of the seven "rays" in modern theosophy. Helena Petrovna Blavatsky, founder of the Theosophical Society, made the modern version of theosophy a comprehensive, eclectic religious and philosophical system that drew heavily on Hindu and Buddhist cosmogony, religion, philosophy, and psychology. She seems to have been the first to use the phrase "the seven rays" (*The Secret Doctrine*, quoted in Wood, 1952):

There are seven Forces in Man and in all Nature . . .The Seven Beings in the Sun are the Seven Holy Ones. It is they who send the seven principal Forces, called Rays . . .There are seven chief Groups of [exalted beings], which groups will be found and recognized in every religion, for they are the primeval Seven Rays. Humanity, Occultism teaches us, is divided into seven distinct Groups [p. 2].

The idea of the seven rays was considerably elaborated by theosophical writers who followed Blavatsky, such as Wood. It was also in theosophy that a number became associated with each ray or governing principle and hence with all their "lower" manifestations, including types of people. Godhead, the One, becomes the Three (the Trinity), which in turn become the Seven; the three "higher" principles—Atma (1), Buddhi (2), and Manas (3)—manifest themselves on the "lower" levels of existence as the three "lower" principles, Sattva (5), or natural law, Rajas (6), or natural energy, and Tamas (7), or matter. The two sets of three are united by a seventh, harmonizing principle, represented by Maya, the illusion of outward appearances, to which is assigned the number four. The qualities of the seven rays, according to theosophy, are as follows:

First Ray: the ray of will, power;

Second Ray: the ray of love, wisdom;

Third Ray: the ray of higher thought activity;

Fourth Ray: the ray of harmony (through conflict);

Fifth Ray: the ray of truth, knowledge, lower mind;

Sixth Ray: the ray of devotion;

Seventh Ray: the ray of order, magic, physical matter.

In addition to Wood, Hodson, another theosophical writer, also detailed a sevenfold human typology (Hodson, 1956). Alice Bailey, a theosophist who went on to found her own school of arcane knowledge, wrote many volumes on occultism, several of which centered on the theme of the seven rays, and the sevenfold human typology became even more elaborate. (e.g., Bailey, 1950).

There exists a well-known psychological test, the *Study of Values* (Allport, Vernon, & Lindzey, 1951), which measures the strength of interests on the first six of the dimensions just listed: political, social, economic, artistic, theoretical, and religious. The test was based on the typology of a German psychologist, Eduard Spranger (1928), but neither the authors of the test nor Spranger seem to have been aware of the Hindu typology or the theosophical teaching of the seven rays (Zusne, 1965). In turn, the theosophical authors mentioned seem to have been unaware of Spranger's work. Yet, there is a remarkable similarity between Spranger's descriptions of the personality traits of his six types (and therefore of the value areas in the *Study of Values*) and those of the theosophical writers. Thus, Spranger (1928) describes "the purely political type" as one who "makes all value regions of life serve his will to power . . .anyone who lives in this one-sided sphere of life considers truth and falsehood equal if only they serve the system of power [p. 190]." Wood (1952) states that "in the man of will on the first ray, self-government is the dominant note. If you belong to this ray your sense of self will be strong [p. 70]." Bailey (1950) asserts that the first ray "has been spoken of as the ray of power, and is correctly so called . . .Those on this ray have strong will power, for either good or evil. . . Vices of the ray. . . [include] desire to control others [p. 201]." By and large, the correspondences between rays and attitudes are: first, political; second, social; third, economic; fourth, artistic; fifth, scientific; and sixth, religious.

It is significant that although it is missing in Spranger and in the *Study of Values*, a seventh type has been suggested by the psychologist H. A. Murray (1951), author of the *Thematic Apperception Test*, that appears to match the characteristics of a person "on" the seventh ray of theosophy. Murray's suggestion has been in no way influenced by theosophical thought, however (Zusne, 1965).

There are now hundreds of published studies that have included the use of the *Study of Values* in the area of personality as well as in other areas of psychology where personality factors play a role. To the extent that this instrument has proved itself a reliable and valid tool of personality measurement, it also reflects favorably on the ability of some Hindu religious authors and some theosophical writers to identify areas of human endeavor and broad types of human personality through empirical but non scientific observation that have stood the test of time.

Astrology

Astrology claims to predict events on Earth, including individual human behavior, from observation of the stars and the planets. It is the oldest science. Western astrology originated around 3000 B.C. in Mesopotamia where the observation of the motions of the planets and the charting of the starry sky was combined with the religious notion that each star was also a deity. The ancient Greeks learned about Mesopotamian astrology in the fourth century B. C. They modified it by associating the Mesopotamian star-gods with their own deities. Besides, the Mesopotamian astrologers had used astrology mainly to ascertain the propitious time for important state affairs and to predict the future of kings and rulers. They did not cast individual horoscopes for ordinary people. This aspect of astrology was added by the Greeks towards the end of the second century B. C. The Greek astronomer and astrologer Ptolemy, who lived in Alexandria in the second century A. D., was the Greek authority on astrology. His system, contained in the famous work *Tetrabiblos*, the astrologer's bible, is still in use in the Western world, virtually unchanged in spite of the tremendous advances in astronomy and changed views of the universe that have taken place since Ptolemy's time.

The basis for a belief that celestial bodies influence earthly events or determine human character is not difficult to establish. Even to a Mesopotamian of 5000 years ago, it must have been quite clear that the movement of the sun, a celestial body, was responsible for the day and night cycle, as well as for the quality of life and life itself. The moon caused tides, affected mood, and seemed to affect plant growth. Other celestial bodies, by extension, were given credit for similar influences, because their appearance gave no clue to the incomprehensibly vast distances between them and Earth. Forces that produced natural phenomena and were responsible for birth, death, and sickness, the gods, were always located in inaccessible places, such as the heavens. Thus, the Mesopotamian deities and the stars were made identical. The Greeks, in turn, identified celestial bodies and constellations with their gods and mythological figures.

The influence of astrology spread to the rest of Europe and penetrated all aspects of life. The all-pervasive influence of astrology continued into the 17th century, the century of the rise of modern science, as well as into the 18th century, and waned only in the 19th. Although today, millions of people believe in astrology, it may be considered only a widespread popular superstition. A few highly placed and otherwise educated individuals may cherish a personal belief in it, but astrology is not used to time the affairs of state, it is not used in science, it finds no application in business, at least not officially, and it has no status in public affairs, all of which used not to be true. Individuals in their private lives, however, continue to believe in it in spite of repeated empirical proofs that there is no correlation between stellar and terrestrial events or between the position of the stars and planet at the time of birth of a person and that person's personal characteristics. Because the belief exists nevertheless and is widespread, it is necessary to examine the reasons for it.

Astrology's Claims.   Of the two claims of astrology—that of predicting the future and that of determining a person's character from the position of the sun, moon, and the planets in relation to the constellations in the zodiac at a criticial time point, such as the time of birth—we examine only the latter. Because the causal mechanism is purportedly the same, the arguments used apply equally to astrological divination.

The key to astrology, and its problems, as well as to its popularity, lies in the fact that it is a form of magic. The basic principle of magic is the principle of correspondence, which is most readily seen in sympathetic magic; for magic to work, there must be a similarity, analogy, correspondence, or "sympathy" between the object of magic and the means whereby the magic effect is to be achieved. Like affects like, and "as above, so below." Applied to celestial influences, the latter form of the principle of correspondence is quite clearly in operation. The planet Mars appears reddish, and red is the color of blood. Blood is spilled on the battlefield, one sees "red" when angry and blood rushes to the face, and red is also the color of fire, which is also associated with war and "fiery" temperaments. Thus, Mars becomes the planet that governs war and aggression and, by extension, virility, masculinity, dominance, and the metal iron because it is used in war. The bright glow of Venus in the evening or morning sky is beautiful, so the planet Venus becomes associated with beauty and the goddess of beauty, Venus, as well as with her other characteristics: love, sex, and sensitivity. The fancied resemblance of constellations to earthly objects also works to establish the principle of correspondence here. If fishes live in water and a constellation resembles a fish, that constellation comes to be considered a water sign. Water, because it moves and because it is the main constituent of sweat and tears, is associated with emotion, hence the Pisces-emotionality correspondence. Because the sun entered the constellation Pisces at about the time of the rise of Christianity, the correspondence between it and the Christian symbol of the fish is seen as a significant one, and religious fanaticism is seen as governed by the watery fish sign. The astral influence of Capricorn, the goat, is tenaciousness; the children of Leo (the lion) are proud (hence the collective term "a pride of lions"), forceful, and born leaders; those whose sign is Taurus (the bull) are plodding, patient, and stubborn, and so on. In ordinary magic, the principle of correspondence is made operative by the magician. In the absence of a magician to make the astrological correspondences operative, the "celestial harmony of the spheres" is invoked as the effective agent.

Arguments Against Astrology.   Because astrology is based on the belief in magic, arguments against it along non-magical lines are in a sense superfluous. For the most part, the believer will deny the presence of the element of magic in his or her thinking and use other explanations. There are three types of arguments against astrology's other explanations: arguments of logic that demonstrate the absurdity of astrology's claims, arguments from physical evidence about the behavior and nature of celestial bodies and physical nature in general, and arguments from the results of statistical studies in which correlations between horoscope data and personal characteristics have been computed.

The known influences exerted by the sun, moon, and the planets are of two kinds, gravitational and radiative. The stars are so remote that the gravitational effects of people's bodies and of objects and walls of a delivery room are greater than of any of the stars. Although starlight is perceptible, it is so faint that no effect has been attributed it by anyone. The gravitational and radiative effects of the sun and the moon are considerable, and extend not only to such phenomena as the tides, but also the behavior of animals. The effects of the sun spots and of the phases of the moon on mood in humans are within the realm of possibility, but these are not the kind of influences that astrology is concerned with. These influences are said to be occult influences, specific to each planet and constellation. The problem is that science has yet to establish that such influences or energies do in fact exist. A greater problem is the question of why should the influence that determines personality be present only at the birth of the individual and not at the time of conception or any other time during pregnancy. A technical problem that plagues astrology is the precession of equinoxes. The point in the sky at which the Earth's axis is pointing describes a complete circle in 25,800 years. Its position has thus shifted about 30° in the last 2000 years, or a full house of the zodiac, so that a person who was born under the sign of Capricorn 2000 years ago, for instance, would be born under the sign of Aquarius today. Even though astrologers are aware of the problem, they are sharply divided on how to solve it. The consumer of popular astrology knows nothing about the problem, and popular astrology is still based on the way the sky looked 2000 years ago.

Recent discoveries of periodicities in the physiology and behavior of plants and animals have been used by astrologers to reinforce their claims that celestial events influence those on Earth. Some of the biological clocks do seem to coincide with astronomic cycles, such as the day-night cycle or the phases of the moon. This in itself has no real bearing on the issues in astrology because it has been known for quite some time that the sun and the moon exert physical influences on earthly events. What is overlooked by the astrologers is that although some periodicities in living organisms are related numerically to astronomic periodicities, there are so many different astronomic and biological cycles that it is not at all difficult to find matches. Superimposing and shifting the graphs of two cycles with respect to one another will show overlaps over some portion of the two cycles, especially when they are not too disparate in length. It is this portion of the graph that is offered as proof of cosmic influences. The menstrual cycle in women corresponds approximately to the length of the phase cycle of the moon. Each woman's menstrual cycle begins on a different day, however, so that it is only for those women for whom it begins on a certain day that there will be correspondence (still entirely coincidental) with the phases of the moon.

All of these arguments are in a sense irrelevant. They attack the astronomical explanations of astrology when the main concern of astrology is not astronomic but psychological. Because its main concern is the prediction of human character and behavior, it follows logically that the proof or disproof of astrology lies in its ability to predict human behavior when other methods fail to do so or to predict it more reliably. If it is shown that astrology does not do so, there is no need to further disprove its astronomical assumptions. If, on the other hand, it does a creditable job of predicting behavior, even the falsity of its astronomical assumptions will not damage its position as a useful method of predicting human behavior.

A number of statistical studies have been done either to demonstrate a correlation between astronomic variables and behavior or to show that there is none. When the proper statistical tests are properly applied, the relationship cannot be demonstrated. In 1937, Farnsworth failed to find any correspondence between artistic talent and either the ascendant sign or the sun in the sign of Libra for the birth dates of 2000 famous painters and musicians. Bok and Mayall (1941) found no predominance of any one sign of the zodiac among scientists listed in a directory of scientists, the *American Men of Science*. Barth and Bennett (1973) did a statistical study on whether more men who had chosen a military career had been born under the influence of the planet Mars than men who had chosen non-military careers. They found no such relationship. Very large numbers of birth dates were used by McGervey (1977), who tabulated the number of scientists and politicians (a total of 16,634 scientists and 6,475 politicians) born on each day of the year, and found no astrological sign favoring either one of the callings. Although from the point of view of the "scientific" astrologers, the study was inconclusive because the rising sun and planetary influences were not taken into account, at least the influence of the sun (the sun sign) was assessed. Popular astrology with its innumerable newspaper columns of daily predictions is certainly based on the sun signs alone because it cannot and does not consider the birth dates of individual readers. In another recent study, Bastedo (1978) tested statistically whether persons with such characteristics as leadership ability, liberalism/conservatism, intelligence, and 30 other variables, many of them attributed to astral influence, would cluster on certain birth dates—that is, according to the astrological sign that governs the appropriate characteristics. The results for a 1000-person, cross sectional, stratified cluster sample taken from the San Francisco Bay area were entirely negative.

The list of studies in which astral events have been found to have no relationship to personality characteristics or behavior is longer, but the studies cited are fairly typical. For an example of research with equivocal results, we may turn to the best-known researcher in statistical astrology, the Frenchman Michel Gauquelin. Gauquelin is the author of papers and books on the subject and is a critic of the incompetent use of statistics in astrological research. He points out quite correctly (Gauquelin, 1978) that unless the person doing research in the area of statistical astrology is competent in statistics, astronomy, and demography, the results will not have much validity. The field of demography bears on such research because one has to be aware of and include corrections for such factors as seasonal variations in the rate of birth for the entire population from which the study sample of subjects has been selected. In a review of two works on statistical astrology, one old and one recent (Krafft, 1939; Van Deusen, 1976), Gauquelin (1978) demonstrates that neither one of them produces any evidence in support of astrology in spite of the authors' belief that they do.

Gauquelin's initial studies, begun in the 1950s, showed no correlation between astrological signs and other traditional astrological predictors and occupation, personality, criminality, and other behaviors. He used the birth dates of 25,000 famous people and found none of the relationships claimed by astrology. In examining a sample of 576 members of the French Academy of Medicine, however, Gauquelin found that the position of the planets Mars or Saturn at birth—having just risen above the horizon or being halfway across the sky—occurred much more frequently than statistically expected (Gauquelin, 1970). Eventually, Gauquelin found evidence of the influence on occupational choice of other planets, planets that were large and relatively close—Venus, Mars, Jupiter, Saturn, and the Earth moon—but not for Mercury, a small planet, or Pluto, Uranus, or Neptune, which are far away. The occupations in which the influence of the first type of planet is felt include, according to Gauquelin, scientists, doctors, athletes, actors, politicians, playwrights, soldiers, and journalists. Gauquelin also claims to have discovered that many people are born under the same planetary alignments as their parents (Gauquelin, 1962), and he thus speaks of "planetary heredity." All this is not standard astrology, for Gauquelin cannot detect any effect of the traditional zodiac signs on behavior, and the planetary influences appear to be physical in nature rather than based on the principle of correspondence. Gauquelin's own statistical assumptions have been severely criticized, but this issue has not been settled yet.

Carl Gustav Jung, the Swiss psychiatrist who founded analytical psychology, showed an interest in the occult throughout his professional life, although his interest did not stem from an acceptance of occult phenomena as objectively real. Rather, he believed them to be manifestations of unconscious processes. Jung once conducted a statistical study of astrology that is often cited in support of astrology (Jung, 1973). He investigated the natal horoscopes of 400 married couples and calculated the frequencies of aspects (oppositions and conjunction) of the sun, moon, Mars, and Venus. Both the opposition and conjunction of the sun and the moon are held by astrologers to be significant in governing marriage relationships, and the planets Venus and Mars, representing the female and male elements, govern love relationships. Jung sought to establish whether these particular aspects were found in the horoscopes of married couples more often than would be expected by chance. Even after various recombinations of the individuals in the pairs and rather complex statistical manipulations, Jung (1973) was forced to conclude that "not only do the frequency values [of the various aspects] approximate to the average with the greatest number of married pairs, but that any chance pairings produce similar statistical proportions . . .[E]verything seems to indicate that in the case of large numbers the differences between the frequency values for the marriage aspects of married and unmarried pairs disappear altogether [p. 59]." Jung went on to note that although the Venus-Mars aspects showed no trend whatever, the highest frequencies were obtained for the following sun and moon aspects: conjunction of sun and moon, for a group of 180 couples, moon-moon conjunction for another batch of 220 couples, and Moon-ascending sign conjunction for a third batch of 83 couples. Although the absolute numbers were small (18, 24, and 8, respectively), statistically non-significant, and in each batch a different conjunction was the most frequent one, Jung believed that the results were significant—not statistically, but in terms of their meaning. Astrology predicts that it is these astrological aspects that govern marriage, and they indeed turned out to be the most frequent ones. The probability against this happening is very high. Jung calls this a synchronistic even—a meaningful but uncaused coincidence (see Chapter 13). According to him, the improbable coincidence would not have occurred had he not showed much interest in astrology. He refers to J. B. Rhine's ESP experiments (Chapter 12) and the regularly observed phenomenon that it is the researchers who believe in ESP who produce significant positive results whereas nonbelievers do not. Thus, Jung places statistical research in astrology and parapsychological research on the same footing: The phenomena do not exist in an objectively verifiable manner, but they do exist psychologically. It is a matter of meaningful (that is, entirely psychologically determined) coincidence. This interpretation of astrological relationships is a matter quite different from stating that Jung's study lends support to astrology. It decidedly does not.

Psychological Factors in the Belief in Astrology.   Given that there is no evidence for the validity of astrological claims, how is one to explain the widespread belief in astrology? Horoscopes are carried by two out of every three newspapers in the United States, and, according to the Gallup Poll, three out of every four adults know their astrological sign and one out of every four is a believer in astrology. This amounts to between 30 and 40 million adults, more than there are adherents in any one religious denomination.

The reasons for the belief in astrology are largely psychological. As far as astrology as a method of divining the future is concerned, it is preferred to other methods because it is extremely old (and therefore venerable) and because the preparation of a horoscope is a technical affair of some complexity, involves some familiarity with celestial mechanics, the consultation of tables, and other paraphernalia that make it appear "scientific." In addition, there is solace in the availability of impersonal rules for making personal decisions. The opportunity to shed the responsibility for making one's own decisions all the time is welcomed by many, especially when it can be assigned to such irreproachable agencies as "subtle influences," "cosmic energies," and other forces that are only a step removed from God. The fact that the predictions do not always come true is of little consequence; first, as the unfailing appearance of the predictions of psychics for the next year clearly show, we have a remarkable ability to forget and ignore failures in prediction. Besides, astrology offers an ironclad safeguard against failure in prediction in the famous maxim that "the stars incline but do not compel." Hence, should a prediction fail to come true, one can still believe that the conditions were ripe for the event to occur as predicted and that it was only owing to some potent factor, such as somebody's free will, that precluded the prediction from coming true this time.

The Delphic oracle, as well as other oracles before her and after, have often resorted to an unfailing principle to guide their formulations of predictions and personality diagnoses: Make it vague, ambiguous, general, and favorable. The key to the effectiveness of such statements is that contrary to what one might expect, their recipients believe that they were prepared expressly for them. As is demonstrated by the Chinese fortune-cookie case—one's name need not be on the message. The belief in the magic of correspondence, the "sympathy" or "attraction" between the cookie and the hand that picks it is all that is necessary. The principle of the personalized generality is one of the major factors that underlies the widespread belief in astrology. The formula of success of the circus showman P. T. Barnum was always to have something for everybody. The psychologist Paul Meehl (Snyder & Shenkel, 1975) applied the term "the P. T. Barnum effect" to the ready acceptance by people of general personality descriptions as accurate for themselves. C. R. Snyder has particularly studied the P. T. Barnum effect in connection with astrological personality descriptions (Snyder, Larsen, & Bloom, 1976; Snyder & Shenkel, 1975) by having personality descriptions rated by experimental subjects. Although the descriptions sounded as if they had been taken from an astrology magazine, they were bogus descriptions that used general but favorable terms to describe a person's traits and behavior. Most of Snyder's subjects thought the description fitted them uniquely, especially if they were led to believe that the description was prepared for them based on a psychological test they had just taken. In several studies, Snyder found that the average rating of accuracy of his bogus personality descriptions was 4.5 on a 5-point scale, where 5 was "excellent agreement." When a French psychologist advertised himself as an astrologer in the newspapers and sent out the same mimeographed, ambiguous horoscope to those who requested one, he received more than 200 letters of thanks for his accurate and insightful work. The need to be "special" apparently leads to a selective reading of such horoscopes, so that only those statements that apply to the reader are attended to and the rest are ignored. Snyder also discovered that the more precise was the information required to prepare a personality description, the higher was the rating of the accuracy of the description. Some individuals received the same horoscope, with the comment that it was "generally true of people." In this group, some were not asked for any birth information, some were asked to supply the year and month of their birth, and some were asked for the year, month, and day of birth. The first group rated the accuracy of the horoscope as 3.24 on a 5-point scale, the second 3.76, and the third 4.38. Because the preparation of a natal horoscope requires also the hour and minute of birth, one can surmise an implicit belief in the total accuracy of such horoscopes on the part of the requester. One consequence of such a belief is that the person's faith in the astrologer and the astrological procedure increases. This happens even when the description is not personalized in any way, for instance, when a person happens to read the personality description that belongs with an astrological sign and finds that it fits him or her or some other person known to him or her and born under the sign. Given the limited number of personality descriptions (12) and the unlimited number of persons who read them, such coincidences are bound to happen. The scientifically natural question of whether the same description does not also fit a whole lot of other persons who are not born under this sign is not asked.

In 1940, the Harvard psychologist Gordon W. Allport drafted a statement entitled "Psychologists State Their Views on Astrology." He did it at the request of his colleague, the astronomer Bart J. Bok. The statement was endorsed by the executive council of the Society for Psychological Study of Social Issues and released for publication. It is a statement that most psychologists would subscribe to today. It is given in full here (Bok, 1975).

Psychologists find no evidence that astrology is of any value whatsoever as an indicator of past, present, or future trends in one's personal life or in one's destiny. Nor is there the slightest ground for believing that social events can be foretold by divination of the stars. The Society for the Psychological Study of

Social Issues therefore deplores the faith of a considerable section of the American public in a magical practice that has no shred of justification in scientific fact.

The principal reason why people turn to astrology and to kindred superstitions is that they lack in their own lives the resources necessary to solve serious personal problems confronting them. Feeling blocked and bewildered they yield to the pleasant suggestion that a golden key is at hand—a simple solution—an ever-present help in time of trouble. This belief is more readily accepted in times of disruption and crisis when the individual's normal safeguards against gullibility are broken down. When moral habits are weakened by depression or war, bewilderment increases, self-reliance is lessened, and belief in the occult increases.

Faith in astrology or in any other occult practice is harmful insofar as it encourages an unwholesome flight from the persistent problems of real life. Although it is human enough to try to escape from the effort involved in hard thinking and to evade taking responsibility for one's own acts, it does no good to turn to magic and mystery in order to escape misery. Other solutions must be found by people who suffer from the frustrations of poverty, from grief at the death of a loved one, or from fear of economic or personal insecurity.

By offering the public the horoscope as a substitute for honest and sustained thinking, astrologers have been guilty of playing upon the human tendency to take easy rather than difficult paths. Astrologers have done this in spite of the fact that science has denied their claims and in spite of laws in some states forbidding the prophecies of astrology as fraudulent. It is against public interests for astrologers to spread their counsels of flight from reality.

It is unfortunate that in the minds of many people astrology is confused with true science. The result of this confusion is to prevent these people from developing truly scientific habits of thought that would help them understand the natural, social, and psychological factors that are actually influencing their destinies. It is, of course, true that science itself is a long way from a final solution to the social and psychological problems that perplex mankind, but its accomplishments to date clearly indicate that men's destinies are shaped by their own actions in this world. The heavenly bodies may safely be left out of account. Our fates rest not in our stars but in ourselves. [p. 9]

It is not at all certain that Allport's sober and humane statement influenced anybody to abandon a belief in astrology. In 1975, among signs of an unusual increase of interest in the paranormal and occult, including astrology, a statement was issued that did produce a considerably stronger response in society than did Allport's (Bok, Jerome, & Kurtz, 1975). The statement was signed by 186 leading scientists, 18 of them Nobel-Prize winners. It summarized the arguments against astrology presented in this chapter and affirmed the position of scientists that astrology has no foundation in scientific fact. Although the statement was given wide publicity and elicited much response from astrologers, astronomers, scientists, and laypeople, there is no indication that the statement has been directly responsible for any decrease in the number of those who believe in the magic of correpondence between events above in the sky and human destiny on Earth.

PHENOMENA OF DIVIDED CONSCIOUSNESS

When a person suddenly asserts that he or she is somebody different from what he or she used to be, speaks in a different voice, and shows skills and knowledge of people, places, and events that apparently have been unavailable to him or her, the thought that first comes to mind is that the person's primary personality must be temporarily in abeyance and that the body must have been taken over by somebody else. We may then speak of possession and attempt to drive the possessing spirit out. Under different circumstances, we may decide that the controlling entity is the spirit of a dead person, and speak of mediumistic trance and spirit controls.

The idea that these phenomena may be entirely our own creations seems so improbable that the thought may not even arise. They are, nevertheless, just that. "The unity of consciousness is illusory," [p. 1] says E. R. Hilgard (1977), a prominent psychologist and one of the outstanding contemporary investigators of phenomena involving divided consciousness. Our attention is not always directed at one thing only. In arguments or debates, we not only attend to what our opponent is saying, but also to our own thought process that is preparing a rebuttal to be delivered as soon as the opponent stops speaking. The professional piano player may continue executing a complex piece while engaging in a lively conversation at the same time. Whether our attention jumps back and forth quickly between two objects or whether two mental processes may be occurring simultaneously are questions that are being currently investigated.

The situation becomes baffling when we realize that, sometimes, we may not be at all aware of any of the activity that is going on in one of the channels of attention. It is a common experience to begin to daydream while continuing to read a book. One may realize later that one has read a paragraph or page without remembering any of the material. It is as if one's mind worked along two different channels at the same time with amnesia following. The forgotten material may be retrieved, however, using such techniques as hypnosis. This example of an everyday case of divided consciousness has all of the characteristics of the most spectacular instances of this phenomenon. There is no dividing line.

If the unconscious portion of attention becomes associated with motor activity, such as speaking, writing, or drawing, we may not only not remember having done any of it, but we may also fail to recognize the voice or the product of our hands as our own. The concealed portion of attention may then be described as dissociated or split off from the rest of consciousness. It is this capacity of the human consciousness to dissociate, for one of its aspects to acquire functional autonomy, that leads to paranormal and supernatural interpretations of such behaviors as automatic writing or painting, speaking with tongues, dowsing, possession states, trance, and mediumship.

It was Pierre Janet, the French psychologist we discussed earlier in connection with hypnotism, who introduced the notion of dissociation (Janet, 1889). Janet's concept of dissociation was that some ideas split off from the main personality and exist in the unconscious as a separate personality to which access can be had through hypnosis. The American psychologists Morton Prince and Boris Sidis followed Janet, but Prince became convinced that the split-off portion of consciousness was not somehow lying dormant in the unconscious, but was as active as the rest of the individual's consciousness. He therefore called it coconscious (M. Prince, 1914).

The evidence for a divsion in consciousness first came from clinical observations on the so-called split personalities, but was later supplemented by experimental observations. An experiment on the classical dissociation pattern was conducted by Morton Prince in 1909. The main personality A of Prince's female subject was unaware of her personality B even though B was aware of A. A could not be hypnotized but B could. B's hypnotic trances were followed by amnesia. Prince hypnotized B and instructed her to add some figures that were written inconspicuously on the sides of a sheet of paper, but only during the time that A was present and engaged in a different and unrelated task. The task was to write familiar verses on the same sheet of paper. As soon as A had completed writing the verses, her personality shifted to hypnotized B personality, which loudly announced the result of the computation. Although A had been unaware of doing anything but writing verses, the hypnotized B personality could tell where the numbers had been written, how the computation was done, and what A had been doing during that time. Much of the later experimental work on dissociation has been done with Prince's experiment as the model, with the assessment of the degree of interference between the conscious and unconscious task as the main objective. The rationale of these experiments is that the degree of interference would also indicate the degree of dissociation. Because complete noninterference is hardly ever found, some controversy has arisen over the reality of dissocation. It must be pointed out that total dissociation would be assumed only by those who take an extreme position on the subject. In addition, even when there is task interference, there may be complete unawareness in one sector of consciousness of the activity of the other, which is the most significant feature of dissociation from any point of view.

Very recent experimental work that dramatically demonstrates divided consciousness has been done by E. R. Hilgard (1977). Hilgard, in a classroom demonstration, hypnotized a subject, instructing him that he would cease to hear. Loud noises near the subject produced no response. When a student in the classroom suggested that a portion of the subject's consciousness could be registering something because there was nothing wrong with the subject's hearing, Hilgard agreed, and presented this idea to the subject in a quiet voice, asking to lift a finger if indeed part of him could still hear anything. The subject's finger rose. He immediately asked to be awakened in order to find out what was happening because he had felt his finger rise (the subject was blind). Hilgard awakened him, but in the awake state, all the subject could remember was what had happened just before he was hypnotized, and that while he was "deaf," he had amused himself by doing problems in his head until he felt his finger rise. In experiments on hypnotic pain control, Hilgard has obtained similar evidence for the existence of what he calls the "hidden observer." For instance, a girl was hypnotized and the suggestion was given that she would feel no pain when her left hand was immersed in ice-cold water. A further suggestion was given that her right hand would not be subject to hypnosis and would write down the degree of pain actually experienced in terms of a number between 0 and 10. Although the girl's verbal report indicated no pain (0), her right hand kept recording increasing levels of pain—5, 6, 7, 8.

When phenomena of this nature occur outside a scientific setting, they easily elicit paranormal interpretations. Each appears to be living proof of mind-body duality. The notion of the possibility of a bodiless mind is so deeply entrenched in our thinking that even the terms associated with divided consciousness reflect it: A spirit possesses your body the same way you possess it; in ecstasy, you are literally beyond yourself (from Greek *exstasis, existanai*—to put out of place); in trance, one "passes over" to another psychic state (from the Latin *transitus, transire*—to go or pass over). Once body-mind duality is accepted, the further assumption that they are separable comes almost automatically. The assumption of the plasticity of body and mind leads to several possibilities. One is for human awareness to be associated with bodies lower on the scale of evolution, such as animals or even plants and inorganic matter. According to the Hindu doctrine of reincarnation, a bad karma may bring on an existence in an animal body. Such descending plasticity is exploited mostly in fairy tales, legends, and fantasy fiction, however. A number of belief systems allow for the presence of animal characteristics in humans or the possession of humans by the spirit of an animal. Paranormal explanations of phenomena of divided consciousness resort to horizontal plasticity—that is, the assumption that souls, etheric bodies, or some other incorporeal form of human individuality can exchange places, occupying a vacant body or displacing the rightful occupant of a body. If, in the latter case, the occupying entity is a demon, god, or spirit, possession is said to take place, and the type of plasticity is one of the descending variety with a human body as the target vehicle.

Possession States

A person in a state of possession may announce, in a changed voice, that he or she now bears a different name, speak in a manner appropriate to the possessing entity, speak in a foreign language or some unknown language, behave in an unusual manner, sometimes violently, shriek, groan, fall to the ground, and utter curses, profanities, and blasphemies, especially if the person's normal self has been one of a pious member of a religion.

Possession states have always existed in all cultures. What has varied is their use and interpretation. There are records of possession states in ancient China, Egypt, Greece, and Palestine, among other places. In the ancient world, spirits were blamed for any and all untoward events that people could not control: sickness, fires, lightning and thunder, storms, and earthquakes. Not surprisingly, mental disorders were also thought to be the work of evil spirits. Possessions were attributed to both good and evil spirits, the distinction being made on the basis of the possessed person's behavior. There are several accounts of possession in the Bible, the best known being the story of Jesus who drove out "unclean spirits" from a man. The spirits took abode in a herd of swine, who ran down a slope and perished in the sea.

The psychological and psychiatric interpretation of possession states is that these are a form of dissociation. Clinically, possession states are either psychoses that belief and tradition have shaped to take the form of a permanent possession, or they are cases of more or less severe hysteric neuroses. Why does a portion of one's psyche split off and begin to act like some mythological entity,—a demon, for instance? The awareness of inacceptable impulses, such as to harm someone, to reject one's upbringing or religious background, and the resulting conflict and guilt feelings leads to the repression of this impulse, which becomes unconscious. In their milder manifestations, repressed contents may show up in slips of the tongue or dream images. The ego may also be protected from the awareness of the conflict between opposed motives by the person's engaging in any of a number of ego defense mechanisms that protect the person from feelings of anxiety over the conflict. One of these ego defense mechanisms is projection. In projection, one's own inacceptable impulses are projected outward onto an object or person. The various forms of the devil become an easy choice because of the long tradition that has associated evil and evildoing with the devil, Satan, demons, evil spirits, and other supernatural entities in virtually every culture. The projection of one's inacceptable feelings and impulses onto an external entity absolves one from responsibility for such feelings and impulses ("The devil made me do it!").

Projection and divided consciousness will not always result in demonic possession, however. The split-personality case and the medium's "guide" are cases analogous to the possession state: One portion of the divided consciousness enacts the role of a personality that the principal personality would like to be like, or it may show characteristics that are greatly disliked by the main personality. Still, the specific behaviors associated with possession are lacking here. This does not make the possession states a qualitatively different condition. It is just that society, culture, and individual experience dictate which particular form personality dissociation will take.

The main treatment for possession, both in antiquity and the Middle Ages, was exorcism, a combination of various rituals and techniques for ridding the individual of the possessing entity. In Christianity, the techniques were at first rather mild, consisting of the laying on of hands, prayer, treatment with holy water and such concoctions as a "spew-drink of lupin, bishopwort, henbane, garlick, ale, and holy water." As the preoccupation of medieval people with salvation and other matters not of this world grew, the system of demonology grew more elaborate. The Satan was supposed to have fallen because of his pride; hence, it was reasoned that one way to drive him out from a possessed body was to insult his pride. This was accomplished by reading lengthy lists of the worst possible insults and curses, all addressed to Satan.

Even epileptic fits were considered to be the handiwork of demons, in spite of the fact that Hippocrates, the father of medicine, had centuries earlier declared that epilepsy was a natural, organic disorder. Because mental disorders do not always remit when treated with insults or holy water, church authorities resorted to stronger means to make the possessed person's body as uncomfortable a dwelling place for the devil as possible. This included scouring, immersion in hot water, starving, and other painful methods. In the 15th century, demoniacal possessions were considered to be of two kinds, those in which the victim was being punished by God for his or her sins, and those in which the possession was willful, the person being an accomplice of the devil. The distinction between the two categories became blurred, however, and as the concern about the devil's other enterprises, such as the work of the witches, grew, all cases of mental disorder were lumped under the general rubric of heresy and witchcraft. The one sure way of saving a person from the clutches of the devil was to end his or her life, such as by beheading or burning at the stake. In the 15th, 16th, and 17th centuries, large numbers of people were so executed, even though their only crime had been to have fallen victim to a mental disorder.

Sex is an important aspect of possession state. It played a major role in medieval possession because of the suppression and repression it suffered owing to the association made between sexuality and the devil. This applied particulary to women. Women were presumed to tempt men sexually, and because sexuality was of the devil, woman was the devil's instrument. Witches traditionally are of the female sex, and the medieval manual of witch hunting, the *Witch Hammer*, was a *malleus maleficarum*, not *maleficorum*. Sexual repression affected women most. As a consequence, so did hysteric reactions. Even at the turn of this century, Sigmund Freud had difficulty convincing the medical profession that men could also be hysterical. Sex-related hysterias broke out regularly at convents. For instance, a series of notorious incidents of demoniacal possessions with clearly visible sexual components broke out in France in the first half of the 17th century: at Aix in 1611, at Loudun in 1634, at Louviers in 1647, and at Auxonne in 1660. The Loudun case is best known because Aldous Huxley wrote about it (Huxley, 1952). Although it was the nuns who were presumed to be possessed, it was a priest whom the nuns had accused of bewitching them, Father Grandier, who was burnt at the stake. This pattern was repeated in several other cases.

Enlightenment and the advent of science gradually abated the fanaticism associated with possessions and witchcraft, and mental disorders were taken out of the province of the devil and other evil entities. The belief in the occult, supernatural origins of possession states has not died out, however. Because the basis of these states is certain fundamental psychological realities, the states themselves have not disappeared. A low educational level and a cultural background that favors belief in the supernatural increase the probability that it will be very difficult if not impossible to convince a person that the entire possession drama begins and ends in the mind of the individual possessed.

Belief in possessions and religious beliefs have always gone together. The association is universal. The voodoo religion of Haiti centers on possession. The "divine horsemen" described by Maya Deren (1970) are gods who "ride" the people whom they possess like horses. To be possessed is the principle aim of an adherent of this religion. The Roman Catholic Church has always recognized possession by the devil, and a minor order of clergy, the exorcists, has existed since the third century. The exorcism ritual currently in use, the *Rituale Romanum*, was written in 1614, but the ordination of special priests—exorcists was abolished in 1972. Exorcism rites are still performed, although rarely, and treatises on the devil and demoniacal possession and exorcism are still being written (e.g., Richard, 1974; Rodewyk, 1975). Although such compendia now recognize that hysteria and epilepsy are natural phenomena that may have the appearance of a possession, "genuine" cases of demoniacal possession are still being recognized. The release of the film, *The Exorcist*, in 1973 (based on a 1971 novel by W. P. Blatty) was somewhat of an embarrassment to the Catholic Church, especially because of the enormous success of the film. Although both the film and the book were based on a real case, the facts of the case had been incomparably less spectacular than the events portrayed in the film. The filmed portrayal of the devil was more in accord with mythology than Catholic theology, the Church was shown as being heavily involved in exorcism, which it is not, and the exorcist was presented as a powerful magician, which is not at all the role assigned the exorcist by the Catholic Church. Worst of all, the exorcism ritual was shown in full. Since the 17th century, the actual exorcism rite, which is quite elaborate, has been performed out of sight of the possessed to avoid suggestion, which is precisely what happened when the rite was presented for public viewing in the film. There was a dramatic increase in the number of people who, after viewing the film, sought the help of an exorcist or a psychiatrist. It is significant that the real protagonist of the case, an 11-year old boy, became possessed only after the exorcism rite had been performed on him in the open. He had been only the center of poltergeist (see Chapter 13) phenomena before.

Special forms of possession states are found in cases of mediumship and psychic healing. Although these are continuous with those of demoniacal possession, they did not appear until after the introduction of hypnosis in Europe by Mesmer in the 18th century. The combination of increased rationality and scientific and medical advances led to a shift towards new forms of divided consciousness, which included fugues (amnesia and flight from former environment and the associated conflicts), multiple personalities (first reported in 1815), and spirit guides (since the 1840s), all of which were in better accord with the emerging new view of humanity and the universe. A direct confrontation between the old possession view and the new, "naturalistic" view occurred in 1775 (Ellenberger, 1970) when Mesmer, who was then still a physician in Vienna, showed that he could cause and cure convulsions through "animal magnetism" just as well as a certain Father Gassner, a well-known priest and exorcist, who accomplished it by way of the Catholic ritual. The test, ordered by the Prince-Elector of Bavaria and aimed at stopping the practice of exorcism, which he considered to be unenlightened, led to the end of Father Gassner's career as an exorcist and marked the conclusion of an era.

Some psychic healers deliberately induce dissociation in themselves in order to allow an alleged external entity to take control of them in order to do healing work. For instance, the Brazilian healer Arigó discussed earlier (Chapter 2), would go into a room by himself prior to a healing session, then emerge with a changed demeanor, his personality taken over by a dead German physician, complete with a German accent.

Mediumistic Dissociation

Arigó's case is in essence no different from the case of the spiritualistic medium who goes into a trance and begins to speak in a changed voice, assuming the identity of a "spirit guide." The spirits, controls, and guides of a medium are the products of the medium's own psychological dynamics. On the one hand, they personify the medium's hidden impulses and wish life. On the other, they are also shaped by the expectations of the medium's sitters, the medium's experience, the cultural background, and the spirit of the times.

In the West, mediumship arose after the 1840s as part of spiritualism. In one sense, mediumship is continuous with tribal shamanism. The shaman, too, mediates between the living of this world and the denizens of another world, although these denizens are most often spirits and gods, not the souls of the dead. In other respects, however, mediumship is different. Mediums tend to be women whereas shamans tend to be men. The prevalence of women is historically determined by the role that women had assigned to them in the 19th century. Spiritualism offered them an opportunity to break out of that role in a socially acceptable manner. Another difference is the distinction that is made between the "physical" mediums and "mental" mediums, a specialization that does not appear among shamans. The physical medium specialized in physical manifestations of alleged other-worldly influences—levitation, psychokinesis, ectoplasm, visible spirit forms, and spirit noises. The mental medium acts as a transmitter of information from "the other side": she speaks or writes what she is "told" by the spirits, or else her vocal apparatus is used by them directly. The physical manifestations of a mediumistic séance, insofar as they really exist and are not hallucinated or misperceived by the sitters, are mostly magic tricks. The mental phenomena, unless they are only an act that is put on by the medium, are of interest in the present context because they represent manifestations of a divided consciousness.

The origin of the term trance suggests passage to another mental state. The supernatural interpretation is that the soul leaves the body during trance. There are degrees to which such "leaving" is accomplished, and the states to which the term trance may be applied vary widely in degree of dissociation and the specific forms and circumstances of manifestation, ranging from the state of being profoundly absorbed in one's daydreams to the cataleptic trance of profound hysterics. All trance states are characterized by relative immobility and unawareness of the immediate surroundings, but that too is a matter of degree; the sleepwalker moves about in a trance, and the medium may be at least partially aware of her environment.

The means whereby the trance state may be attained vary. They may involve sensory overstimulation, hyperventilation, drugs, hypnosis, and self-hypnosis. The medium most often goes into a trance using some method of self-induction. The facility in doing so increases with practice. In addition, the medium is apt to have had early experiences that have increased her readiness to engage in daydreams, imagery, and fantasy. Loneliness, which in very sensitive individuals leads to daydreaming, talking to oneself, and the creation of imaginary playmates, is not an uncommon characteristic of the childhood lives of mediums. It is also the lonely, the imaginative, and the autistically oriented individual who is more likely to be attracted to spiritualism. The "true" medium is one who dissociates readily. Proneness to dissociation, repeated practice, and the expectant and supportive atmosphere of the séance room combine to make the medium's performance what it is: a smooth and reliable passage into the trance state and the impressive welling up of autonomous portions of her divided consciousness that are taken as the manifestations of the spirits of the dead.

The intellectual and creative level of the utterances or writings of different mediums varies considerably. Occasionally, the medium produces no more than gibberish, or the language may be that of a child. A medium's guide or control—a spirit that serves as a contact between the medium and other spirits—is often a child, which reflects the regressive nature of the personality dynamics of many mediums. On the other hand, a few mediums exhibit a high level of intellectual and creative skills in trance, which far surpass their abilities in their normal state. They may create whole new languages, show acting ability of a professional caliber, write poetry or prose, and paint with consummate skill.

The mode of communication between the spirit world and the sitters that the medium may choose varies. The medium may repeat what her guide or a spirit contacted directly may be telling her. She may repeat it in her own voice in reply to a sitter's question. Alternately, either the guide or another spirit may assume control over the medium and speak or write through her, in which case the voice, handwriting, and behavior may show the characteristics of another personality. A visible appearance and the sound of voices coming from places other than the medium herself is a sign that trickery is being resorted to.

The cases where the medium is presumably controlled by a spirit are no different from cases of possession or multiple personality. The basic phenomenon is the same, only the circumstances and interpretations differ. Mediumship, however, is never only hysterical dissociation, dissociation without hysteria, trickery, automatic speech or writing, unconscious motivation, role playing, suggestion, or autistic thinking. It is some combination of these, which makes it impossible to classify it as a single psychological category. Like the opera, which combines several of the arts, mediumship combines several psychodynamic mechanisms into a unified performance. This performance, like operatic performance, may sometimes

reach great heights, as was the case with the medium Hélène Smith (Flournoy, 1900/1963). Although the case is an old one, it may be taken as a
classical case of mediumship because of the exceptional richness of the
material and the fact that the case was thoroughly and objectively studied
by a psychologist over a period of 2 years. The psychologist, Théodore
Flournoy, even gave Miss Smith hand-grip, pain-sensitivity, and finger-
tremor tests, and measured her respiration rate during trance.

Hélène Smith (Catherine-Elise Müller's better known pseudonym) was a
young French Swiss woman. She had a pleasant personality, was bright,
and worked in a large store before she became a medium. She came in contact with the local spiritualists and, because of her ability to dissociate and
go into trance states, soon became their star medium. Hélène Smith,
however, never performed in public or for remuneration. Her association
with the spiritualists furthered the satisfaction of her own needs, which were
to escape from her humdrum existence into a more exotic world. She had
always been powerfully attracted by anything Oriental.

In her trance, Hélène Smith engaged in automatic writing and painting,
automatic speaking, had auditory hallucinations, and gave somnambulistic
performances—that is, dramatic enactments of fantasy scenes, with accompanying visual and auditory hallucinations. Her guide was a spirit called
Leopold, which, according to the medium, was a cover name for the true
identity of Joseph Balsamo, or Count Calgiostro, a notorious 18th-century
adventurer and charlatan. Nevertheless, Leopold represented the positive
side of Hélène's personality. In one sense, Leopold was an independent and
different personality from Hélène's (described by Flournoy, 1900/1963):

> He speaks for her in a way she would have no idea of doing, he dictates to her
> oral and mental questions, converses with her, and discusses various ques-
> tions. Like a wise friend, a rational mentor, and as one seeing things from a
> higher plane, he gives her advice, counsel, orders, even something directly op-
> posite to her wishes and against which she rebels. He consoles her, exorts her,
> soothes, encourages, and reprimands her; he undertakes against her the
> defence of persons she does not like, and pleads the cause of those who are an-
> tipathetic to her. In a word, it would be impossible to imagine a being more in-
> dependent or more different from Mlle. Smith herself, having a more personal
> character, an individuality more marked, or a more certain actual existence.
> [pp. 78-79]

On the other hand, the personalities of Leopold and Hélène penetrated
each other on occasion. Ellenberger (1970) divides multiple personalities into four categories. The most frequent is the case of the successive dual personalities that are one-way amnesic: Personality A knows about itself but
not about personality B, whereas personality B has memories about both A
and B. Another type of successive dual personality is the type that is

amnesic both ways. In a third type, the two personalities also alternate, but know of each other's existence. The rarest case is the case of simultaneous dual personality. This was the relationship between Leopold and Hélène Smith. They would alternate speaking, or Hélène Smith's handwriting would alternate with that of Leopold's. Flournoy found that Leopold had had his origin in Hélène Smith's childhood. In an incident that she had completely forgotten, she had been rescued from being hurt by a vicious dog by a man of striking appearance. This figure became Hélène's ideal self, the focus of her romantic daydreams, a personification of all that she could not achieve in reality.

In addition to Leopold, Hélène Smith exhibited alternate personalities that, strictly speaking, could be termed possessions, because they were the personalities of historic individuals, Marie Antoinette for one. The medium's behavior during one of her Marie Antoinette possessions was truly regal, and she spoke and wrote with the appropriate peculiarities of 18th-century French. At another time, she declared that she was a reincarnation of a 15th-century Indian princess, Simandini, asserted that Flournoy had been her husband in that life, and spoke Sanskrit, even though in her normal state the only language she purportedly knew was French. She also produced some Arabic writing. After her Hindu episode, she traveled to the

Fig. 8.1. A painting of a Martian landscape and buildings by the medium Hélène Smith. (From Flournoy, 1900/1963. Used by permission of University Books, Inc.)

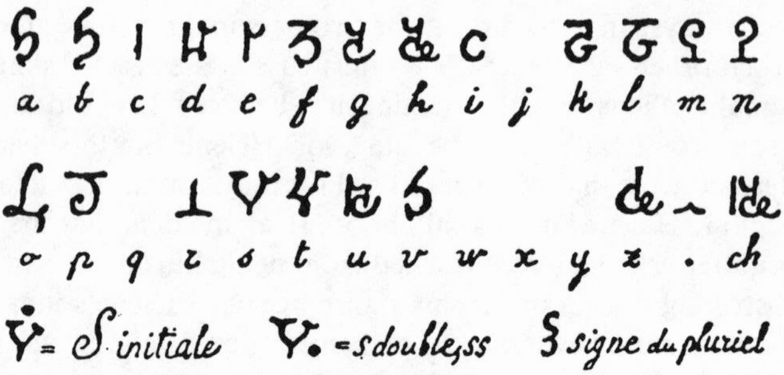

Fig. 8.2. The alphabet of the Martian language. The Martian letters were produced by medium Hélène Smith, the alphabet was constructed by her investigator, Théodore Flournoy. (From Flournoy, 1900/1963. Used by permission of University Books, Inc.)

amès   mis   tensée   ladé   si — amès   ten   tivé   avé
Viens   un   instant   vers moi,   viens   près d'un   vieil
men — koumé   ié   ché   pélésse — amès   somé   têsé
ami   fondre   tout   ton   chagrin: viens admirer   ces
misaïmé — ké   dé   surès   pit   châmi — izâ   méta   ii
fleurs,   que   tu   crois   sans parfum,   mais pourtant   si
borêsé ti   finaïmé —   iâ   izi dé   séïmiré
pleines de senteurs!...   Mais   si   tu   comprendras !
Come towards me a moment, come near an old friend to melt away all thy sorrow; come to admire these flowers, which you believe without perfume, but yet so full of fragrance! But if thou couldst understand.

Fig. 8.3. A transliterated passage of a Martian text written by the medium Hélène Smith, with French and English translations. (From Flournoy, 1900/1963. Used by permission of University Books, Inc.)

planet Mars, described and painted its landscapes, cities, and inhabitants, and spoke and wrote fluent "Martian" when under the control of Martian "guides." Flournoy was able to prepare the complete Martian alphabet and grammatical rules.

Although Flournoy did believe that Hélène Smith was telepathic, he denied that any of her other phenomena had anything to do with the occult. He never witnessed Hélène's psychokinesis that she was alleged to exhibit. Her various personalities—Leopold, Simandini, Marie Antoinette—were just that, multiple personalities that satisfied her deep yearnings for the exotic, the Oriental, and the romantic. This went hand in hand with her profound dissatisfaction with her ordinary, unexciting life. Her handwriting did change noticeably from one personality to another, but there was no similarity between her handwriting as Marie Antoinette and Marie Antoinette's actual handwriting, for instance. Concerning her linguistic ability, Flournoy knew that her father had lived in different countries and knew eight languages. She herself detested the study of languages. Nevertheless, Hélène Smith quite early in her life exhibited a trait that must have been at work in her use of foreign languages in her trance states, namely cryptomnesia. In her work as a clerk, she would amaze her coworkers and employers by being able to recall upon demand, information about items of merchandise, such as stock numbers, but without being able to say when or how she had picked up that information. Flournoy was able to show that her Martian language was an artful fabrication. Although it sounded decidedly foreign, frequency analysis of words and letters and an examination of the syntax convinced Flournoy that the language had all the basic structural characteristics of French, Hélène Smith's native tongue. In a subsequent investigation, Flournoy reported that the source of a short phrase that Hélène Smith had written in Arabic during her Hindu cycle probably came from her having seen an identical phrase inscribed in a book owned by a Genevan physician. She had retained a visual image of the script and, in due time, copied it from memory in an uncertain hand. Flournoy could not establish the source of her information about her Indian incarnation, but he suspected that her Sanskirt was probably a case of cryptomnesia. It was not until much later that the Indian parapsychologist C. T. .K. Chari (1963) was able to show that Hélène Smith's Sanskritoid language was based on a few genuine Sanskrit words, which she must have picked up from some books shown her by her spiritualist friends, amplified by others that bore a resemblance to Sanskrit, but were actually productions of the medium's creative unconscious during her trance states.

After 2 years of observation, Hélène severed her connection with Flournoy, outraged by the suggestions made in his book that her phenomena were somehow not "real" but originated in her mind. She died in 1930. W. Deonna (1932) reported after her death that in her last years, Hélène Smith had developed still another possessing personality, namely that of the biblical Mary, sister of Martha, and in this role engaged in spirit painting, with New Testament stories as subjects.

Automatisms

Automatisms are motor behaviors that may accompany states of divided consciousness and therefore may not be under the conscious control of the primary personality. The individual appears to be performing automatically or, in the proper circumstances, as if under the control of an external agency. The degree of the individual's awareness of what he or she is doing varies considerably, however. The individual may be only partly unaware, as when doodling while talking on the telephone, aware that the hand is writing something, for instance, but unable to control it, or totally unaware that the body is performing any unusual motor acts.

The fact that in automatic writing the person's handwriting may resemble that of someone dead, that an automatically executed painting may be signed with the name of a dead artist, or that the automatically speaking voice declares itself to be that of a deceased person, a god, or a demon has led to the belief that automatisms prove mind-body duality, the existence of discarnate spirits, or the reality of supernatural entities. Automatisms are often part of possession states, multiple personalities, and mediumistic trance states.

Glossolalia.   Glossolalia, or the gift of tongues, refers to spontaneous utterances, usually made within some religious context and by deeply religious persons who feel that it is a sign that they have been particularly blessed. The utterances are often incoherent, the tongue is strange, but not invariably so, and the inspiration for it is felt to have come from outside the individual. In other words, the cause is thought to be supernatural or paranormal. A Mormon elder, for instance, may erupt in the following (Cutten, 1927): "O me, sontra von te, para las a ta se, ter mon te roy ke; ran passan par du mon te! O me, santrote krush krammon palassate Mount Zion kron chow che and America pa palassate pa pau pu pe! Sontro von teli terattate taw! [p. 74]." An English interpretation of this 45-word passage required 127 words. Edward Irving's (1792-1834) preaching caused many a congregation member to speak with tongues. His unorthodox religious views, known as Irvingisms, led to his excommunication from the Church of Scotland. Although some of the Irvingite glossolalia was gibberish, some utterances were relatively coherent passages. Thus, when Irving referred to the Church as being barren, a voice from the congregation rose, saying (Cutten, 1927): "Oh, but she shall be fruitful, oh! oh! oh! she shall replenish the earth! Oh! oh! she shall replenish the earth and subdue it—and subdue it! [p. 85]." Tongue speaking that occurs in a religious setting and is done in a recognizable language normally does not contribute any original thought. It is more in the nature of a chorus, the words and phrases coming from a well-rehearsed repertoire of scriptural stereotypes, marked by alliteration and repetition.

Glossolalia is found in all cultures and in all historical periods. In Christianity, glossolalia has had a particularly prominent place because of its sanction by Paul and the events of Pentecost (Acts 2:1-13). The Holiness and Pentecostal Churches of today are the major carriers of the tongue-speaking tradition in Christian Protestantism, where it forms the center of the religious experience.

Speaking in tongues quite often begins as incoherent sounds and exclamations that only gradually evolve into words and sentences. The relationship of tongue speaking to the immaturity of the brain and brain impairment is quite evident. Children are known to engage in a form of spontaneous tongue speaking. It is a form of play in which, as in all play, the child is making the world over in his or her own image. Creating one's own language creates a sense of the mysterious, enhances one's feeling of competence, and, as a form of self-expression, is fun besides. The counting-out rhyme of enee menee minee mo, for instance, is a vestige of an invented children's language. The child, however, is neither hysterical nor in a state of divided consciousness. Thinking and self-analysis do not dominate the child's life as yet and, while the child engages in "tongue speaking," these processes are to some extent suspended. The emotional excitement of religious meetings serves to facilitate the separation of thinking and speech. In that sense, at last a partial division of consciousness occurs. Although speech and thinking are normally related, speech can function quite independently of conscious mentation. The ability to produce speech sounds and words is an innate ability in humans. It remains even when the thinking and reasoning functions of the brain have been temporarily suspended, as in panic and shock, when an individual may be able to repeat a sentence when somebody else says it, but without being able to understand what is being said (echolalia). Echolalia is also present in persons with severe brain damage, as, for instance, in the microcephalic individual, who may be otherwise so severely impaired that speech is virtually absent. As long as the ability to produce speech sounds is intact, even severely retarded individuals are able to repeat their own speech sounds (autoecholalia). This ability is an essential feature of speech development in normal children. The frequent alliterations and repetitions found in glossolalia (prou pray praddey; pa palassate pa pan pu pe; teri terattate taw; terrei te te-te-te; vole virte vum; Cutten, 1927) suggest that the brain is functioning here in a state that is comparable to that of an immature or brain-damaged individual.

What glossolalia appears to represent is a form of emotional expression. Whereas some people may dance and jump for joy, others may speak, but not in ordinary words, for these do not convey the emotional experience that is being lived at the moment. The utterances *have* to be meaningless because their purpose is not to convey semantic but emotional meaning. Exclamations like yahoo and tra-la-la are emotional utterances that have become part of the language. The variety of verbal emotional utterances that is afforded by standard language is very limited; hence, one may feel compelled to resort to one's own language-making capability that is a source of a much richer trove of verbalizations that express gratitude, bliss, or ecstasy.

Automatic Writing. The connection between automatic writing (also known as autonography) and the paranormal was made by the Fox sisters, who reported strange rappings in 1848 and attributed them to the spirits of the dead, starting thereby the spiritualist movement. Kate Fox produced very large amounts of automatic writing at the request of a physician and his wife. Automatic writing became a standard means of communication with the dead. In addition to writing by hand, other forms of writing have been employed. One of them is the *planchette*. The planchette is a heart-shaped surface, about the size of a hand, that moves freely on three points over a writing surface. Two of the points are casters, the third a pencil. The planchette first appeared in the 1850s as an improvement over the method of spirit communication used by the Fox sisters, which had consisted of calling out the alphabet and matching letters with the raps.

The *ouija board* (from the word "yes" in French (*oui*) and German (*ja*), which is more euphonic than yes-yes) was successor to the planchette. It was invented by Isaac Fuld of Baltimore and patented in 1892. It created such a controversy over whether it was a scientific instrument (as the spiritualists claimed it to be) or just a toy that it required a decision of the United States Supreme Court to solve it. It was declared a toy, and is still being sold as such by Parker Brothers. During the recent upsurge of interest in the occult, its sales have increased spectacularly (2,000,000 boards sold in 1969 alone, for instance). Like the planchette, the ouija board is a small, three-pointed frame that moves over a board surface. It works not by writing words but by spelling them out as the frame approaches successively the letters of the alphabet and the words "yes" and "no" printed on the board. The patent description of the board states that "a question is asked and by the involuntary muscular action of the players, or through some other agency, the frame will commence to move across the table." The "other agency," of course, implies spirits.

To the amazement of both the person whose hand is on the planchette or ouija board platform and the observers, comprehensible messages may be written or spelled out, although the operator may not be paying any conscious attention to the hand that does the writing or be aware that the hand is doing anything at all. Matching raps and letters of the alphabet or even movements of the platform on a ouija board and alphabet letters is a slow process, and automatic writing can be done faster. Some preliminary training may be necessary. The psychiatrist Anita Mühl (1930), who used automatic writing as an alternate method for tapping the unconscious in psychotherapy, recommends placing the subject's forearm in a sling, so that it hangs about an inch above the table. The subject is next distracted, such as by reading a book. As the subject continues reading, a pencil is placed between his or her fingers. At first, not much happens, except perhaps that the subject may draw a few lines. Questions that can be answered by a yes or no are next asked in a whisper and, by way of suggestion, the subject's wrist is raised when the question is asked, and lowered, ready for writing, until an answer is given.

Even with training, not everybody will produce automatic writing. In an unselected sample of subjects, about one in 10 will (Hilgard, 1977). In her clinical practice, Mühl asked her clients the following questions before deciding on the use of automatic writing: Does the subject talk or walk in sleep? Does the subject write in the air or on the table with a finger? Has the subject ever had a feeling of unreality or of watching oneself do things? Does the subject operate a ouija board? Does the subject doodle while telephoning? Does the subject ever say things and be surprised by having said them? It is clear that questions of this type constitute a test of dissociability. If the answer to any of these questions is yes, the subject is likely to be able to do automatic writing.

The contents of automatic writing often reveal matters that the conscious individual is entirely unaware of, in the same manner that dreams and free association reveal unconscious contents of the subject's psyche. Automatic writing allows repressed ideas to emerge in a manner that does not cause anxiety to the individual. Because repressed ideas are unacceptable or alien to the overt personality, automatic handwriting often differs from the person's normal handwriting, reflecting the "foreign" nature of what is written. In fact, the author of the writing may be perceived as an intruding entity or alien spirit that guides one's hand or dictates what is written. It was this relationship of automatic writing to unconscious motivation that led to its introduction in clinical practice early in this century. Mühl's (1930) account of it presents a good picture of this use of a motor automatism. One of the reasons why it has not found a wider use is that, like hypnotic susceptibility, the ability to engage in automatic writing varies widely in the population, to the point that it is absent in a large percentage of it. Another reason is that automatic writing has always been associated with spiritualism and the paranormal, more so than hypnosis, and the use of it has not appeared respectable enough to many psychotherapists.

The degree of dissociation that may be present between the primary personality and the dissociated portion of it that does the writing is sometimes astounding. One may, for instance, engage in a conversation with one's own hand. The British parapsychologist, S. G. Soal, on discovering that he had the ability for autonography, proceeded to have a question-and-answer session with his hand, the hand informing him that it was being guided by the spirit of a Victorian poet named Margaret Veley (Rawcliffe, 1959). Because Soal did not believe that spirits were involved, his conversations are a fascinating example of the kind of game that one can play with oneself in which one portion of the self attempts to establish the truth while another portion does its best to deceive. Soal presumably knew nothing about Margaret Veley, but his autonographic ability suggests that he could well have been cryptomnesic. Soal himself thought that he had obtained the information telepathically or clairvoyantly.

It is not certain whether the source of information and the motivation for automatic writing resides in a person's unconscious or in a portion of the mind that is at the time unavailable to consciousness. It is entirely possible that both aspects of the mind are involved. It was mentioned earlier that, according to psychoanalytical theory, the psychological person functions on the conscious, preconscious, and unconscious levels. Repression refers to the process of avoiding anxiety over a conflict situation by making certain aspects of consciousness unavailable to it. These aspects are said to be repressed and made part of the unconscious, retrievable only indirectly by such methods as dream analysis and free association, and when they make themselves known through slips of the tongue and symbolic behavior. According to the dissociation theory, and without denying the truth of the psychoanalytical view, parts of the conscious and preconscious mind may be made unavailable to consciousness by another means, amnesia. The amnesic barrier is not crossed, but the ideational contents on either side of the barrier become known as attention focuses on the one or the other. It is state-dependent awareness, the state in each case being determined by a shift in the focus of attention from one personality to the other (the "hidden observer"). Thus, as the state of attention changes, so does the field of awareness. The relationship between repression and dissociation as diagramed by Hilgard (1977) is shown in Fig. 8.4.

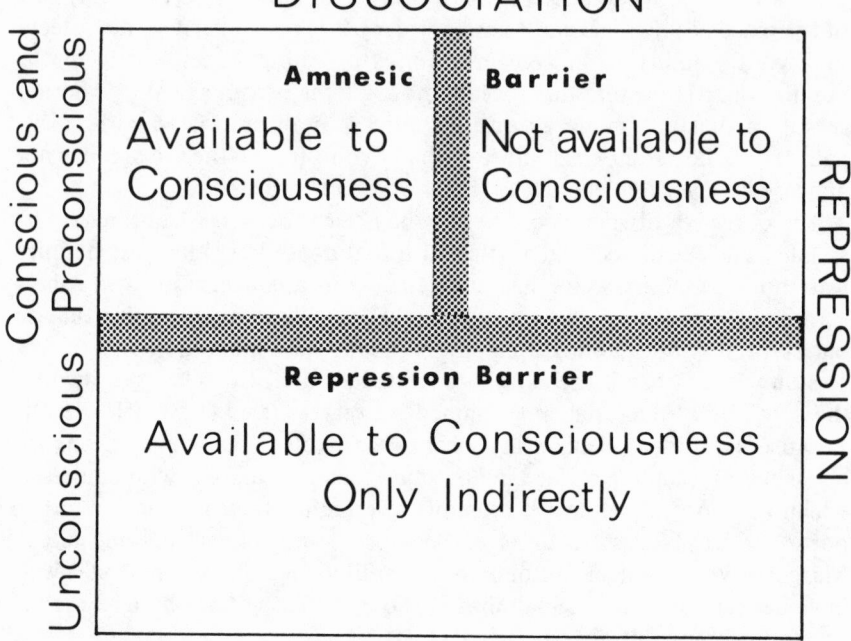

Fig. 8.4.   Division of consciousness in dissociation theory and in psychoanalytical theory. (From Hilgard, 1977. ©1977 John Wiley & Sons, Inc. Used by permission of John Wiley & Sons, Inc.)

It is thus quite possible that, depending on the psychodynamic history of the individual, the particular method used to elicit the automatism, and the socio-cultural circumstances in which the method is applied, either repressed contents, the working of the "creative unconscious," or conscious contents on either side of the amnesic barrier would manifest themselves in the automatism.

Serious laboratory studies of automatic writing began in the 1920s, but very slowly. When Clark Hull began his hypnosis studies at the University of Wisconsin, Ramona Messerschmidt (1927—28) did an experiment testing the degree of interference between a conscious and an unconscious task. The conscious task was reading, the unconscious one addition. Both were performed at the same time. The unconscious task was suggested during hypnosis and executed, upon a cue, as a posthypnotic suggestion. It was not until 15 years later that another similar experiment was performed, and it was only after 1958, when Hilgard's hypnosis laboratory began operation, that systematic studies of automatic writing were conducted. They followed the task interference pattern of the Messerschmidt study, the main object being to establish the degree of dissociation present in automatic writing and the degree of awareness of the writing process by the subject. Two published studies are those by Stevenson (1976) and Knox, Crutchfield, and Hilgard (1975). Hilgard reviews this and some unpublished work from his laboratory in his book on divided consciousness (Hilgard, 1977). He summarizes the results of the two experiments just cited as follows:

> First, the subjective ignoring of the subconscious automatic task while a conscious task is being performed is very real to some highly hypnotizable subjects; second, the interference is increased by the effort to maintain one task as subconscious, and this effort is a function of the difficulty of the task. Mutual interference between conscious and subconscious tasks are found; the division between the tasks depends on the strategies available for their integration [p. 147].

Hypnotic experiments, including those involving automatic writing (Hilgard, 1977), "suggest rather strongly that processing of information may go on at some level while being deflected from consciousness through an inhibitory process [p. 148]."

Although laboratory experiments confirm the reality of automatic writing, statements like the preceding quotes from Hilgard, though true and accurate, do not begin to describe the automatic writing performance of some individuals outside the walls of the laboratory. In all cases, beginning automatisms are repetitious and not very interesting. However, with time, the level of writing skill acquired by a given person may far exceed the skill of this individual in the normal state, and the content of the writings shift from personal to impersonal or supernatural. In these cases, a marked division in consciousness is invariably present in the form of an alternate personality, and the authorship of the writing is attributed to that alternate personality. Automatic writing practiced diligently often leads to possession states or multiple personalities, which confirms the existence of a common underlying mechanism for all of these manifestations. A classic documented example of one such case is that of Ludwig Staudenmaier (1922). Staudenmaier's autobiographic account is valuable because of his insight into the nature of his problem. Even though several different spirits claimed to control his writing, Staudenmaier (1922) realized that it was he who was doing the writing: "Nevertheless, I absolutely had the impression of having to do with a being utterly alien to me. At first I could tell in advance what was going to be written, and from this there developed in time an anticipated 'inner' hearing of the message [p. 71]." Eventually, Staudenmaier's voices acquired increasing independence and could be described as possessions or multiple personalities. He produced three of them. Fully aware that he was not dealing with supernatural entities or departed spirits, Staudenmaier nevertheless failed to integrate these aspects of his personality, and continued to struggle with them to the end of his life.

Most of the highly developed and interesting automatic writings fall into two categories: (1) moral and religious precepts, accounts of the world to come, or complete religious, metaphysical, or theosophical systems built on a cosmic scale; and (2) historical romances dictated by the spirit of some deceased spirit or hallucinated by the writer. Two prominent examples, those of Alice Bailey and Mrs. Curran, also known as Patience Worth, illustrate the two categories of automatic writing.

Alice Bailey (1890-1949), at first active in the Theosophical Society, went on to establish her own school of occultism, the Arcane School, as well as a number of associated organizations, such as the Lucis Trust and Lucis Publishing Company, for the propagation of the teachings of the Tibetan Master Djwhal Khul, which she had received via clairaudience and telepathy. Alice Bailey's childhood had been unhappy. At age 15, she had a momentous experience (Bailey, 1951):

It was a Sunday morning. . . This Sunday, for some reason, I had not gone to Church. All the rest of the house-party had gone and there was no one in the house but myself and the servants. I was sitting in the drawing-room reading. The door opened and in walked a tall man dressed in European clothes (very well cut, I remember) but with a turban on his head. He came in and sat down beside me. I was so petrified at the sight of the turban that I could not make a sound or ask what he was doing here. Then he started to talk. He told me there was some work that it was planned that I could do in the world but that it would entail my changing my disposition very considerably . . . He said that if I could achieve real self-control I could then be trusted and that I would travel all over the world and visit many countries, "doing your Master's work all the time.'' Those words have rung in my ears ever since . . . Having said what He had come to say, He got up and walked out . . . I did not know what to make of it all [pp. 35–36].

After a stint as a missionary in England and India and an unhappy marriage, Alice Bailey became acquainted with theosophy, joined the Theosophical Society, and, at age 35, according to her account, realized that a portrait that was hanging in the offices of the Theosophical Society was a portrait of the turbaned individual who had come to see her 20 years earlier, the Master Koot Hoomi, *her* Master. Four years later, in November of 1919, Alice Bailey made her first contact with yet another Oriental master, the Master Djwhal Khul. The sequence of events given by Alice Bailey cannot be verified. It is quite probable that the experience described in the preceding quotation occurred later and was projected backward into her youth, which then would make her case not unlike the Hélène Smith–Leopold case presented earlier in this chapter.

Alice Bailey's encounter with the Master Djwhal Khul was somewhat unusual (Bailey, 1951): ''Then I heard a voice which said, 'There are some books which it is desired should be written for the public. You can write them. Will you do so?' Without a moment's notice I said, 'Certainly not. I'm not a darned psychic and I don't want to be drawn into anything like that' [p. 163].'' The Tibetan persisted, and the result was 19 volumes of writing produced over the next 30 years, plus five additional volumes written by Alice Bailey ''herself.'' The 19 volumes were a complete system of esoteric teachings for the ''New Age.'' Although Alice Bailey was intimately familiar with theosophy and had H. P. Blavatsky's *The Secrete Doctrine* to use as a model, her work is different and original enough to qualify as a monumental achievement of the creative unconscious. She insisted that she did not do automatic writing (Bailey, 1951):

. . . the work I do is in no way related to automatic writing. Automatic writing, except in the rarest cases . . . is very dangerous. The aspirant or disciple is never supposed to be an automaton. He is never supposed to let any part of his equipment out of his conscious control. When he does, he enters into a state of dangerous negativity. The material normally then received is mediocre. There is nothing new in it, and it frequently deteriorates as time goes on . . . .

In the work that I do there is no negativity but I assume an attitude of intense, positive attention. I remain in full control of all my senses of perception and there is nothing automatic in what I do. I simply listen and take down the words that I hear and register the thoughts which are dropped one by one into my brain. I make no changes in what I give out to the public from that which has been given me except that I will smooth the English or replace an unusual word with one that is clearer, taking care, always, to preserve the sense as given [pp. 163–164].

This passage is informative in that it shows the way in which the recipient of a revelation perceives the mental activity she is engaged in. It also shows that even though Alice Bailey was very much aware of spiritualism and the role that automatic writing played in it, she was completely unaware (as evidenced also by the rest of her writings) of what psychology knew about personality dynamics. It also shows a lack of insight into the workings of her own mind. The same pattern—a supernatural voice that commands one to write down a revelation, automatic or semiautomatic writing, an activity that, however, is perceived as being merely an amuneunsis for a more exalted entity, and the production of a weighty tome or a body of writings that usher in a new doctrine that replaces or supplements an older one—is seen in a number of other instances of revelatory writing: the Revelation to John, the *Urantia Book* (Urantia Foundation, 1955), *Oahspe* (Newbrough, 1950), Emanuel Swedenborg's work (see Box), and others.

Box 8.1—Emanuel Swedenborg

In Emanuel Swedenborg (1688–1772), scientific and inventive creativity combined in a unique way with creativity in automatic writing along theological lines. Until he was 57 years old, Swedenborg was making important contributions in the areas of mining engineering, astronomy, physics, neuroanatomy, physiology, philosophy, and technical inventions. These contributions place him among Sweden's outstanding men of learning. He conjectured that the planets had originated from the sun, reached conclusions concerning atomic structure that are close to those of modern physics, localized mental functions in the cerebral cortex, established the function of the cerebro–spinal fluid, and made suggestions that resemble the neuronal theory 100 years before its formulation by Ramón y Cajal. As assessor at the Royal College of Mines, Swedenborg contributed to the improvement and development of the Swedish mining industry. Among his inventions were a method for determining longitude by observations of the moon, new methods of dock construction, and plans for a submarine and an airplane. He wrote many books and papers on these subjects.

In 1745, however, Swedenborg experienced illumination. A vision and a divine call told him to abandon science and to take up the interpretation of the Bible. A change in his thinking had already taken place in that during the last 10 years, he had been concerned mostly with the mind–body relationship. He had also become interested in dreams, and had begun a dream journal. He discovered that he could shut off all sense impressions when he wanted to concentrate. The creative process of these moments was accompanied first by the impression of a mysterious radiation, then by visions of a flame that Swedenborg took for "a sign of approbation." The control of his writing shifted from his primary, conscious personality to the spirits whose voices he heard and who guided his pen. The spirits were those of the biblical patriarchs Isaac, Jacob, Abraham, and Moses. Later, Swedenborg began to doubt the authenticity of the dictating voices, but established contact with others whose truthfulness and goodness he could judge by himself, such as Jesus Christ. Swedenborg's automatic writing was accompanied by other phenomena of dissociation, such as visions and travel to the world beyond for visits with the spirits. He also became clairvoyant. His most celebrated clairvoyant vision was that of a great fire in Stockholm. He had the vision in the presence of a number of witnesses who testified that it occurred at the same time as the fire. Both Swedenborg and the witnesses were a long distance from Stockholm, however, and there was no way of learning about the fire at the time. Immanuel Kant dedicated an entire work to Swedenborg's paranormal abilities, *The Dreams of a Spirit-Seer* (1766/1900).

Swedenborg's writings amounted to some 20,000 pages. His descriptions of his visits to the next world made him famous throughout Europe. Rather than his scientific work, it was his spiritualistic and theological writings that earned him recognition. His best known work is *Heaven and Hell*, published in London in 1758.

Swedenborg did not preach or found any church. The New Jerusalem Church (later called the Swedenborgians) was founded in 1784 by a few of Swedenborg's adherents. Although it numbers only a few thousand members, it is widespread, and has influenced some well-known individuals. William James' father was a Swedenborg enthusiast, and William James' own interest in psychic research was owing partly to his father's Swedenborgian interests.

A famous instance of literary collaboration between divided personalities is the case of Pearl Curran (1883–1937), a St. Louis housewife. Mrs. Curran had been operating the ouija board. Haltingly at first, a spirit began to spell out messages for Mrs. Curran. On July 8, 1913, the spirit introduced herself formally (Litvag, 1972): "Many moons ago I lived. Again I come—Patience Worth my name [p. 2]." First through the ouija board and later through automatic writing and speaking, Mrs. Curran, under the name of Patience Worth, produced a voluminous literary output: aphorisms, poems, several short stories, seven novels, and one play. The literature was not great, but it received favorable reviews, even from well-known literary figures, such as Edgar Lee Masters, who said of her poems that she was producing "remarkable literature." In contrast to the bland, humdrum personality of Mrs. Curran, that of Patience Worth was a vivid one. She was sharp witted, fluent, very observant, somewhat flirtatious, but also religious and given to sentiments. She reported variously as having lived in 17th-century Dorset, England, and later in America, as well as being a free-roaming spirit. The various accounts of Mrs. Curran's background purporting to show that, as Mrs. Curran, she could not have produced the literary works of Patience Worth are inaccurate. As a child, Mrs. Curran was a precocious learner.

Her education was good enough to enable her to teach at various public and private schools. She had received extensive tutoring as well as extensive voice and piano training. She played the piano at a church, which happened to be a spiritualist church headed by her uncle, a medium. As to the purportedly 17th-century English that Mrs. Curran used as Patience Worth, English experts testified (Jastrow, 1935/1962) that it did not belong to any particular historical period but was a mixture of contemporary English, poetic terms, some dialect expressions, including some misused and misunderstood would-be Scottish words, and even some of her own invention. The trigger for the appearance of Patience Worth could have been the death of Mrs. Curran's father just 2 months earlier. The background, the ability, and the occasion were thus given for the dissociation, when it occurred, to take the particular form it did in Pearl Curran.

The case of Pearl Curran illustrates the general case of the individuals who, either under hypnosis or in a state of dissociation and behaving as alternate personalities, show talents they normally do not possess. Writing talent is only one of them. Some draw or paint, either as themselves or guided by the hand of some great master of the past. Although automatic painting may show some stylistic similarities to the paintings of the master represented, they are usually of much poorer quality. Singing and playing an instrument can also be automatic, as can the composition of pieces of music. A well-publicized recent case is that of Rosemary Brown, a widowed kitchen worker, who found herself tutored in piano playing by the spirit of the composer Franz Liszt. Mrs. Brown, who came from a family with a history of psychism and who thought she had very definite psychic abilities herself, saw the figure of Liszt, complete with white flowing hair and black cassock. He introduced her to other famous composers—Beethoven, Schubert, and Chopin, among others—all of whom she saw in person. The general level of her experience may be judged by her reporting that Schubert no longer needed glasses, that Beethoven had regained his hearing, that Chopin dressed in modern clothes and had become addicted to television, and that Liszt, in accompanying her on her trips to the grocery store, would express his concern over the rising prices of bananas. Rosemary Brown wrote hundreds of pieces of music dictated by the various composers. They were passable works, entirely in the styles of these composers, but appeared to be simply reworkings of existing pieces. After a publicity flare-up over her in 1970 and 1971 (she even wrote an autobiography), Rosemary Brown's star sank as rapidly as it had risen, although she continued producing music under the dictation of her masters.

One feature common to many cases of automatic writing is that the writing is perceived to occur under dictation. A voice is heard, and the writer writes down what he or she hears. If the voice is produced by our own brain, how is it that we are not conscious of it and attribute it to an external source? The answer is speculative, but well within the realm of possibility. There is a distinct functional asymmetry between the two hemispheres of the human brain. The difference in functioning cannot be observed except under special experimental conditions or when the main bundle of nerve fibers that connects the two hemispheres (corpus callosum) is severed. Normally, the two hemispheres communicate and their functions are unified by the individual's self-awareness; whichever function is exercised, it is felt to be "my" function. Julian Jaynes (1976) has speculated that this may not always have been so, that earlier than the second millenium B.C., humans possessed a bicameral mind—that is, one in which the functioning of the two hemispheres was not integrated under the common concept of an "I"—that self-consciousness was lacking, and that the functioning of one hemisphere could be perceived by the other as an external effect. He speculates that thinking in the right hemisphere could be heard as an external voice by the left hemisphere and that such voices were identified with the voices of gods whose commands had to be obeyed. He sees remnants of this condition today in cases of schizophrenia where the patient's own thoughts may be perceived as external voices that command that person. The separation between the hemispheres need not be physical. Environmentally produced changes in neural organization can facilitate or impede the passage of nerve impulses. In a schizophrenic, such changes may duplicate the conditions that were the rule in humanity's earlier state of evolution. The term dissociation implies a severing, a blocking, and hence noncommunication. Thus, it is possible that the relationship between repression and dissociation diagramed in Fig. 8.4 represents a breakdown in communication between the two hemispheres of the brain, a splintering and weakening of I-consciousness, as a result of which the individual finds it easier to attribute his or her own inner speech to an external source.

Ideomotor Movements.   Unawareness of one's own behavior occurs not only under hypnosis and other states of dissociation, but is also part of the normal mode of functioning; we are unaware of how we walk or speak, or that muscle tension is building up in the neck leading to an eventual headache, or that our lips or voice box move when we think. Lip and laryngeal movements in silent thought are in direct correspondence with the content of thought, as are otherwise imperceptible muscle movements of other kinds. These have less to do with divided consciousness and more with the fact that body and mind form a unity and that internal, subjective processes find expression in unconscious muscular contractions. William Carpenter, an English physiologist, coined the term *ideomotor action* in 1874 to designate all behaviors that do not depend on volition but are nevertheless caused by ideas, such as those resulting from suggestion, expectations, hypnosis, or those that show in the use of the ouija board, the divining rod, the pendulum, or the phenomenon of table tipping. In the use of the pendulum, the divining rod, or the tilting table, involuntary, unconscious muscular movements are imparted to the object, which appears to move as if impelled by some external force. This gives rise to the notion that these practices are associated with the paranormal and the occult.

Rhabdomancy, or divination by rods or sticks, has been practiced since antiquity, but mainly to point out persons guilty of crime, to predict the future, or to help decide on a course of action. The first description of the use of the forked twig to detect metal ores is found in the work *De re metallica*, by Georgius Agricola, which is a treatise on mining published in 1556. Agricola's (1556/1912) description of the rod, its use, and his warnings that it is useless could have been written in much more recent times (quoted in Ellis, 1917/1957):

> There are many great contentions between miners concerning the forked twig, for some say that it is of the greatest use in discovering veins, and others deny it. Some . . . first cut a fork from a hazel bush . . . Others use a different kind of twig for each metal . . . All alike grasp the forks of the twig with their hands, clenching their fists, it being necessary that the clenched fingers should be held toward the sky in order that the twig should be raised at that end where the two branches meet. It is said that the moment they place their feet on a vein the twig immediately turns and twists, and so by its action discloses the vein . . . The truth is, they assert, the movement of the twig is caused by the power of the veins . . . [The movements of the forked twig] give rise to the faith among common miners that veins are discovered by the use of twigs, because whilst using these they do accidently discover some; but it more often happens that they lose their labor . . . Therefore a miner . . . should not make use of an enchanted twig, because if he is prudent and skilled in the natural signs he understands that a forked stick is of no use to him, for as I have said before, there are the natural indications of the veins which he can see for himself without the help of twigs [pp. 38–41].

The usual manner of holding the forked twig, described by Agricola, is shown in Fig. 8.5.

The early use of the forked twig was to locate ores, whereas today it is mostly underground water. Underground water is found most frequently in the form of saturated strata, rather like in a wet sponge than a vein. The incorrect use of the term "vein" in reference to water is a remnant from the days when locating mineral veins was the main purpose of rhabdomancy. Because rhabdomancy is basically a form of divination, it can be applied to detect all sorts of things besides just ore and water. Divining rods have been used to locate oil deposits, discover buried treasure, locate lost landmarks and reestablish property lines, detect criminals, analyze personal character, cure disease, locate lost animals, find buried archeological remnants, and

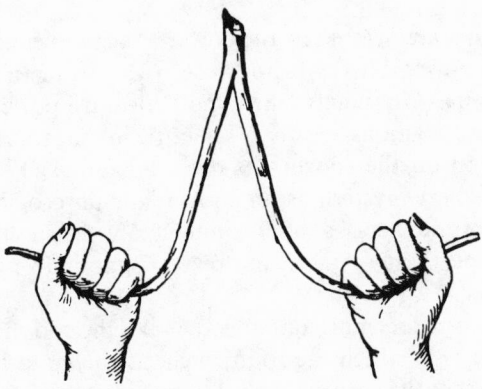

Fig. 8.5. The traditional method of holding the divining rod. (From Ellis, 1917/1957.)

sex unhatched chicks. The connection between the "power" of the ore vein or underground stream of water and the rod, tenuous as it has always been, is nullified when the rod–object attraction idea is extended to include every imaginable substance. In other words, the use of the rod is magical. Attempts to impart respectability to it by naming it radiesthesia, for instance, do not change the situation. The term radiesthesia suggests that some sort of emanations are being emitted by any and all objects that are being searched for with the rod and that the diviner is somehow sensitive to such emanations. The only "emanation" that is common to all objects and substances and is recognized by science is gravity, but that is decidedly not what the radiesthesists are talking about.

Hyman and Vogt (1967) tested the hypothesis of the anthropologist Bronislaw Malinowski that magic is resorted to when there is uncertainty about the outcome of an important natural event but when action must be taken nevertheless. Applied to water witching (or dowsing, as it is called in England and the New England states, New York, and Pennsylvania), the prediction was made that there would be more water witchers per capita in areas where water was difficult to find and where the problems involved in finding good underground water were greater than in areas where water was easy to find. A survey of a representative sample of 3017 counties from across the United States confirmed the hypothesis.

The magic nature of dowsing is also suggested by the folklore that surrounds it. Some dowsers speak to the rod while water witching, which amounts to prayer or magic incantation—for instance, "Please indicate a vein of good drinking water. It should flow at a rate of . . . and not be more than . . . feet deep." Only the person who has the "power" can find water, and the power is inherited. Many believe that only men have the power, although in fact there are female dowsers. Many of the explanations of how dowsing works that are offered by the dowsers themselves are supernatural, such as that the power derives from Moses (who struck a rock and made water flow from it). Alternately, the hypothetical psi power (ESP) may be invoked. Some explanations are quasi-scientific in that some form of radiation and its action on the rod or the diviner is invoked. The forces and radiations invoked are mysterious, unknown, and unrecognized by science, however. Many of the theories can be quite involved, especially those stemming from Europe. Many American dowsers simply do not have any explanation to offer.

The water witcher does not consciously make the rod move. There are, however, four ways in which the rod, if held as shown in Fig. 8.7, can be made to move so that the person who is holding it is not aware of it (Hyman & Vogt, 1967). First, because the rod is held very tightly, a very slight easing of the grip will cause the rod to rotate. Second, rotating the wrists slightly towards each other will make the rod dip, whereas a slight turning of the wrists outward causes the rod to turn upward. If the rod is gripped very tightly, the movement can be very powerful. The third and fourth way consist of pulling the hands slightly apart or pushing them slightly together. These movements produce a greater tension in the rod than in the hands gripping it. The result may be such a violent movement of the rod that the bark of a freshly cut twig may come off where the hands are holding it.

In an interested and attentive onlooker, the performance of a dowser creates the same muscular tensions, albeit on a smaller scale. An invitation to try the rod for oneself and the assurance that it will work constitute additional suggestion, and the muscular tension pattern is repeated in an enhanced manner as the novice begins dowsing. Concentration on the task and expectation serve to recruit the excitation and minute contractions of separate muscle fibers until a larger muscular contraction occurs and the rod, in one of the four ways mentioned, dips at the exact spot where it had previously dipped for the diviner. The beginner is convinced that it was some external force that moved the rod (Hyman & Vogt, 1967).

Field and laboratory tests of the ability of diviners to locate water have been sparse, although the literature on the divining of water and minerals is quite large (Ellis, 1917/1957). In field tests, the problem is the cost of drilling the wells to verify the diviner's performance. Another difficulty consists of establishing a baseline against which the diviner's performance may be compared—that is, how many successes does a person without the "power" have in the same location? The problem of establishing a baseline under field conditions has not been solved. In a 1949 experiment conducted in Maine under the auspices of the American Society for Psychical Research (reported by Hyman & Vogt, 1967), 27 diviners failed completely to estimate either the depth or the amount of water to be found in a field free of surface clues to water, whereas a geologist and an engineer successfully predicted the depth at which water would be found in 16 sites in the same field, although they failed to predict the amount. Vogt and Hyman (1959) conducted an experiment in a large indoor area using filled and unfilled water containers under a surface. On this test, water witchers achieved only chance results, as they have in all other laboratory experiments.

No arguments or negative evidence ever convince a believer in dowsing, however. Hyman and Vogt (1967) offer some of the reasons for this tenacity of belief. If there is very little scientific information on where to drill for water, if it is believed that the dowser will not find water in an inconvenient site, if there is a pressing need to find water, and if the property owner or farmer has no better chance of finding water than the dowser, the dowser will be called upon. In all cases, an overriding consideration is the cost involved: a $5 to $25 fee for the dowser, compared to thousands of dollars for drilling a hole. The geologist's recommendation, when it comes, is apt to be vague and uncertain in comparison with the clear and unambiguous directive of the dowser, "Drill here."

Many water witchers continue to operate for the reasons stated and because they may succeed occasionally by chance or because success in a given area may be virtually assured to anyone. The use of the dowser is thus reinforced by the same rule that says that the occasional jackpot will keep the slot machine's arm pulled through hundreds of non-reinforced trials and because, as is the case with the annual predictions of the psychics, success are remembered whereas failures are forgotten. There are water diviners who show a remarkable degree of success in finding water in areas where others fail to do so. This is no proof, however, that their ability is some paranormal "gift" or that mysterious forces are involved. The successful dowser develops skill over many years. What a dowser learns is what the Australian aborigene has learned to locate water in the desert where there are no visible signs to indicate its presence. The dowser learns to pick up clues, both gross and extremely slight ones, that indicate the presence of water: changes in ground color and texture, type and appearance of vegetation, air temperature changes, as well as topographic and geological clues. The dowser, like the aborigene, may have developed extremely acute hearing so that, if there is indeed an underground stream of water, he or she can hear it running. Similarly, the dowser may have developed an extremely keen sense of smell, of the kind that allows the aborigene to smell water from a very long distance. A dowser is, in fact, an excellent observer who, in addition to using available clues consciously, may use subliminal cues unconsciously. In all cases, it is these clues that provide the necessary changes in muscular tension to make the divining rod move. The rod will move for most people, if held properly, but that in itself is no sign of dowsing ability, as many would-be dowsers believe. It takes keen senses, observational ability, and long practical experience to become a successful dowser.

It is estimated that there are some 25,000 dowsers in the United States. Members of the American Society of Dowsers have been meeting at Danville, Vermont, annually. In 1978, the 18th annual meeting was held. The activities of that meeting were no longer confined to an exchange of information among water witchers. The meeting featured psychic healing, exorcism, lectures on a "new" theory of illness that attributes it to "entities," out-of-the-body experiences, body auras, universal grids, treasure hunting, book stalls with books on occultism, and vendors selling dowsing hardware, from small $1 plastic rods to electronic black boxes that, according to *Time*, (October 9, 1978) "discharge toxic vibrations from your mind, emotions, and etheric body." Like spiritualism and ufology, dowsing has become the magnetic core that attracts other occult practices and esoteric beliefs.

Dowsing for water or divining for anything else may be accomplished not only with rods, sticks, or twigs, but also with other objects that respond to unconscious ideomotor behaviors. The most widely used alternate device is the pendulum, which is, in fact, a much older device than the rod and is found in both Europe and China. The pendulum is often a ring that is suspended from a hair, thread, or string, but it can be any other suitable small object. Like the rod, the pendulum is also used to divine just about anything. The Romans observed its swinging over a board with letters of the alphabet written on it, the spiritualists had it swinging inside a glass. When swinging over a map, its direction, size of excursions, and type of swinging may be used to dowse for water or oil, locate missing persons, or find buried treasure. The practice is called *radiesthesia*, a mixture of pseudoscience, dowsing, and the occult.

At the beginning of the 19th century, quite a number of scientists believed that the pendulum possessed remarkable investigative powers. It would swing one way for one substance or object and another way for a different one. It did not matter what the object or substance was. Theories about the new and mysterious force were generated, ascribing to it expansive and compressive characteristics, and active and passive perturbance. The French chemist Michel Eugene Chevreul was also at first deceived by the movements of the pendulum, which seemed to occur without any movement of the hand that held it. He persisted in his experiments and discovered that no physical forces save those inherent in the hand muscles were involved and that the entire phenomenon reduced itself to self-suggestion. Chevreul at first held an iron ring over mercury. As the pendulum was swinging over it, he inserted a glass plate between the mercury and the ring. The movement died. When the glass plate was removed, it started up again. Not satisfied, Chevreul blindfolded himself and had another person insert the glass plate, without his knowledge. This time nothing happened. Chevreul decided that as long as he did not know the cause of the movement, it occurred. He failed to reproduce it once he had discovered its cause. He thought the discovery might be of some interest to psychology and the history of science. He wrote a letter to Ampère in 1833 describing his experiments. He became interested in the phenomena again in the 1850s when spiritualism and table tilting appeared on the scene. He thought the pendulum, table tilting, and the divining rod were the same phenomenon, all due to suggestion and self-suggestion (Chevreul, 1854).

It is impossible to keep the pendulum from swinging, even when the hand seems to be perfectly still, but the direction of the swing can be affected by visualizing the particular path the pendulum is to follow: If a circle is visualized, the pendulum will describe a circle. Although radiesthesists accept the idea that the pendulum swings because of minute muscular movements of the arm, wrist, and fingers, they believe that these movements are caused by the radiesthesist's sensitivity to the emanations, waves, or fields associated with the object of interest. The various "forces" invoked to explain radiesthesia are concepts that are based either on electromagnetism or extrasensory perception. No attempt is ever made to demonstrate the reality of these forces, however.

Table tilting (table tapping, table turning) is also a phenomenon that belongs with swinging pendulums, dipping twigs, and traveling planchettes. Two or more people sit at a light, round table, place their spread-out hands along the edges of the table, and wait. If the sitters think along similar lines or have similar expectations, the slight ideomotor tensions in the arm muscles of the sitters translate into movement, such as a circular or tilting movement, or raps of the table legs against the floor. Although in a given instance, hours may pass before there is any movement, in others it may begin promptly, and a circular movement of the table, for instance, may reach the point where the sitters are compelled to get up and move or even run around in order to keep pace with the table.

The practice originated within spiritualism where it was assumed that the movements of the table were the attempts of spirits to communicate with the living. By the use of suitable codes, table movements were translated into messages, in a manner analogous to that used with the ouija board. Although the practice is not as widespread today as it used to be, the belief in spirits moving the table persists. That it is the sitters who make the table turn was demonstrated by the famous physicist Michael Faraday soon after the spiritualist séances began in the last century. Faraday (1853) accomplished this by cementing several layers of thick paper with a soft cement to the top of the table and measuring the degree of displacement in the layers of paper after the table had rotated. He found that the uppermost layer, which was in direct contact with the sitters' hands, had shifted more in the direction of the table's rotation than the lowest layer. This indicated that instead of following the table's movements, the sitters caused the table to move. Faraday also attached levers to the table, which activated a pointer telling him whether the upper layer of papers was turning clockwise or counterclockwise. One direction meant that the table was turning before the hands, the other direction that it was the hands that moved before the table did. When the participants did not see the lever, the results were the same as in Faraday's first experiment. When the pointer was exposed to the participants' view, the table did not turn at all. Thus, muscular feedback was apparently inoperative in the table tilters and they perceived the table as being turned by an external force, whereas visual feedback, by sensitizing them to their own muscular efforts, also served to inhibit these efforts, and no motion occurred.

Dreams

Traditionally, dreams have been interpreted in relation to what they might be saying concerning the future. Like many other events and things whose appearance seems random or uncertain, fluid, easily modified, and therefore subject to guidance by unseen forces—smoke, tea leaves, or the toss of dice—dreams have been used as a means of divination (oneiromancy). Prophetic dreams have always been part of every culture. These dreams refer to the fate of a tribe or nation rather than the fate of a single individual. The message is seldom a direct one. It is usually clothed in a symbolic or allegoric form, but the precognitive nature of the dream is quite apparent to the dreamer, who then proceeds to seek an interpretation of the dream.

Because the future is unknown to mere human beings, it has been assumed that significant dreams are sent by God or gods, angels, or, if the dream is bad, by the devil or evil spirits. Scriptural references reflect this belief and support it. Even today, many individuals find it hard to believe that people could be the authors of their own dreams, and seek their source in the supernatural, such as God, the occult, such as travel outside the body (on the astral plane), or the paranormal, such as telepathy.

Traditional dream interpretation has been based on the universal principle of magic and occultism, which postulates a correspondence between things "below" and those "above," which in the case of dreams amounts to reasoning by analogy: Seven lean cows mean seven years of scarce food, seven fat cows mean seven years of abundance, finding money means tears, seeing a snake means meeting a deceitful person, and so forth. The "above" in dream interpretation is the fate that is written "in the stars," God's decision to bring about certain changes, or any other form of preordained or prescribed future. This is communicated in a veiled form to the dreamer. The interpretation of the dream links the supernatural cause "above" to the natural effects "below." The dream is thus a medium of communication between the denizens of this world and entities that rule another, "higher" world. The traditional dream books are based entirely on the rule of correspondence. As far as this kind of interpretation goes, it has no basis in fact, coincidental correct predictions notwithstanding. Considering that everybody dreams every night, one should expect by the laws of chance that quite a number of dreams of the money–tears variety will come true.

Although Sigmund Freud's monumental work, *The Interpretation of Dreams*, (1900/1953) introduced an entirely new view of what dreams were and how they should be interpreted, this view influenced only a relatively small number of people. The majority either do not give much thought to the origin or interpretation of dreams or else continue in their belief of supernatural causation and interpretation. Freud's view was that: (1) dreams are symbolic; and (2) that both the symbols and the dream content originate in the dreamer's psyche, specifically the unconscious. Freud distinguished between primary and secondary processes in thought. Primary processes were impulsive and irrational. When biological drives are not gratified but are repressed, they stir up hallucinations of the possible satisfiers of these drives. Freud thus saw dreams as normal hallucinations that served the purpose of wish-fulfillment. Freud's followers and Neo-Freudians modified Freud's original position somewhat by referring to dreams as being drive-related rather than wish-fulfilling and by allowing for symbolic problem-solving in dreams, though not of the logico-verbal kind, but problem-solving that is intuitive and apprehends the solution in a global fashion. Regardless of the specifics, Freud (1900/1953) saw the dream as the entry to the unconscious: the dream is both a product of the unconscious and a means of exploring it. The involuntary, spontaneous, impulse-driven quality of dreams (primary process thinking) distinguishes them from secondary process thinking, or rational, logical thinking. This quality places dreams in the category of dissociated experiences. So does the fact that a remembered dream qualifies as a hallucination—it is a remembrance of a non-physical experience, with the locale of the experience being different from the place where the dreamer's body lies—and the fact that in the so-called lucid dreams, the dreamer is aware that he or she is dreaming. If the dream content wells up from the unconscious representing a repressed conflict, the dream involves both dissociation and repression (see Fig. 8.4).

Contemporary research on dreams stresses dream interpretation less and is more concerned with external influences on dream content. It is obvious that dream images are not only symbolic or fantastic, but often repeat real experiences from the past, show an event that is physically correct and contemporaneous with the dream, or even one that comes true in the future. The question is, therefore, can past, present, or future events influence dream content? That past experience does so is beyond doubt; often the first dream of the night as well as the last one is about very recent experiences, such as the events of the previous day. Various dream adventures often take place in locales that are replicas or modified versions of locales experienced in childhood, especially places where one has lived a long time or has vivid memories about. These influences have no direct bearing on the paranormal. There is also no doubt that present internal stimuli (e.g., bladder pressure) and external stimuli (e.g., getting cold because the blanket has been kicked off or a limb becoming numb) also affect dream content. Hypnotic suggestion leads to the subject's experiencing a dream immediately upon being told to do so, to the subject's experiencing dreams of a particular content during the night, or to the subject's talking about his or her dreams aloud while asleep. To this may be added the fact that dream content may be suggested not only hypnotically but by any emotionally significant external source, such as an authority figure. This is highly significant. To realize that it is the patient of a Freudian psychoanalyst who has Freudian dreams, that patients in Jungian analysis have Jungian dreams, and that those who believe in telepathy have telepathic dreams means realizing that the relationship between a dream and its interpretation is an interactive, relativistic one, and that dreams do not have an objective, absolute quality: A dream and its interpretation interact and affect each other.

It has been supposed that perhaps extrasensory influences could affect dream content also—through telepathy, clairvoyance, or precognition. Telepathic dreams would allow the dreamer to become aware of, say, a picture or a book that an awake person was looking at while the dreamer was dreaming. Clairvoyant dreams would allow the dreamer to report, upon waking, what had transpired at some distant site, and precognition would lead to dreams that depicted some event yet to come. Scientific tests of this hypothesis became possible as a result of the scientific advances that were made in the study of sleep and dreams in the 1950s. One was the introduction of the electroencephalograph to assess the depth of sleep and the association of different brain-wave patterns with different levels of arousal. Another was the very important and useful discovery that rapid eye movements during sleep were associated with dreaming (Aserinsky & Kleitman, 1953). The distinction between rapid eye movement (REM) sleep and non-rapid eye movement (NREM) sleep and the association of REM sleep with a particular brain-wave pattern allowed researchers to identify the exact time when a subject was in a dream state and when the subject was not. This made it possible to wake the dreamer immediately after each dreaming episode and to obtain a report of the dream before it was forgotten. As a rule, most dreams, unless they occur just before waking or unless the person awakens after the dream, are forgotten very soon after waking. As a result of the combined EEG–REM techniques, more has been learned about sleep and dreaming since 1950 than in all the time before that date. It also led to the parapsychological study of dreams in dream laboratories.

When subjects in telepathic dream experiments report the contents of their dreams, their descriptions, even when they appear to refer to the target object, are never exact replicas of the target. This does not necessarily mean that the experiments are failures. It may only reflect some general principles that govern any external influence upon dreams. In assessing such influences, several factors must be taken into account. In sleep, sensory thresholds are heightened, yet some stimulation spills over the thresholds, as it were, and enters the dreamer's consciousness anyway. What the dreamer then perceives is not a complete, but a spotty, abbreviated picture of reality. There is enough information to perceive it as reality, but not enough to perceive it as reality of the ordinary kind. Hence, the dreamer makes attempts to restructure it in various ways in order to establish the meaning of the dream images. This aspect of stimulation mixes with memory images that, because logical thought processes are partially in abeyance, are used in ways that differ from those of the waking consciousness—that is, the logic of temporal and spatial separation may not be followed and the sequentiality and locality of events may become mixed in various illogical, bizarre ways. Conflicts or problem situations are then enacted against this fluid, changing perceptual background provided by memory, current organismic states, and environmental stimulation. Another factor is that the external stimulus that triggers a dream may not merely constitute the first link in the following dream sequence. It may be incorporated in that sequence, transformed by it, and appear in a place that is chronologically different from the time the stimulus was actually applied. For instance, sounding the conductor's whistle at a distance and simultaneously applying a whiff of ammonia to the nose of a dreamer may lead to the person's dreaming that he or she is boarding and riding a train and that there is a collision with an oncoming freight train, which derails, spilling deadly chemical fumes from overturned tank cars. These considerations should alert the researcher not to expect a faithful reproduction of a painting, for instance, that a sender is looking at in a dream telepathy experiment (assuming, of course, that telepathy is, in fact, at work). What they also imply is that the evaluation of experimental results is made that much more difficult because the subject's responses cannot be evaluated strictly in terms of whether the subject was right or wrong and that statistical criteria must be employed to decide on the probability that the dream images had any relationship to the telepathic or clairvoyant stimulus.

The most extensive program of parapsychological dream research has been carried out since the mid-1960s at the Maimonides Medical Center in New York under the direction of Montague Ullman, chairman of the

Department of Psychiatry, and Stanley Krippner, a psychologist and director of the Department's Dream Laboratory. The research has been published in over 60 articles and a popular book (Ullman & Krippner, with Vaughan, 1973). The basic design of the experiments has been the same. The dreamer and receiver of the telepathic message is connected to a brain-wave and eye-movement recorder. The subject sleeps in a soundproof room. After the subject falls asleep, an art reproduction is selected from a large collection randomly, placed in an envelope, and given to the agent (sender of the message). The agent does not open the envelope until he or she is locked in a separate room some distance away from the receiver's. A third person, the monitor, monitors the receiver's brain waves and eye movements and signals the agent when the receiver enters a REM period of sleep. The agent then begins to "transmit" the picture. After 10 or 20 minutes of REM sleep, the monitor awakens the receiver and asks that person to describe the dream. The description is tape recorded. The same picture is used throughout the night during the several REM periods. In the morning, the receiver is shown the picture with a number of others and asked to rate the level of confidence that he or she has that any of the pictures corresponds to the last night's dream content. The dream transcripts are also given to three judges who rate their confidence that the dream content matches the target picture. The ratings are then analyzed statistically.

The pattern of results has been basically the same as in any other telepathy experiment, and it has been repeated by other investigators. The results have varied from insignificant to fairly good from experiment to experiment, as well as from receiver to receiver and with the same receiver from time to time. As in other telepathy experiments, targets with emotional content appear to be more effective than neutral targets, and motivation, directed attention, and expectation all play a role in determining the results. Because the telepathic dream experiment is analogous to the ordinary telepathic experiment on card guessing, the issues involved are the same and are discussed in Chapter 12. The issue of whether dream content can be influenced by paranormal means thus hinges on the overall evaluation of experiments in telepathy. It must be mentioned here that one of the factors that must have led to statistically significant results in at least some of the experiments in the Maimonides dream laboratory was the manner in which the receiver was primed prior to going to sleep (Ullman & Krippner, 1978). It had been found that if the receiver had no prior knowledge that an attempt would be made to influence his or her dreams, no such influence could be detected. This led to preparing the receiver through experiences that were related to the content of the picture to be telepathically transmitted during the night. Thus, when the picture was Van Gogh's Corridor of the St. Paul Hospital, which depicts a lonely figure in the hallway of a mental hospital, the receiver: (1) heard Rosza's *Spellbound* played on a phonograph; (2) heard the monitor laugh hysterically in the room; (3) was addressed as "Mr. Van Gogh" by the monitor; (4) was shown paintings done by mental patients; (5) was given a pill and a glass of water; and (6) was daubed with a piece of cotton dipped in acetone. The receiver was an English "sensitive," but it is obvious that no psychic sensitivity was required to figure out the general content of the picture and to produce an appropriate report, whether any dreams were actually seen or not.

Before laboratory studies of dreams became possible, numerous dream surveys had been made. By the admission of the parapsychologists themselves, surveys that utilize case material sent in by unknown individuals in response to an advertisement, for instance, are useless as scientific data base. There are thousands of recorded cases of telepathic and precognitive dreams. Corraboration and documentation of such cases can be obtained only in a fraction of the total, but the main problem associated with "spontaneous case materials" lies elsewhere. The memory of a dream, like any other memory, is apt to become distorted if not recorded immediately upon waking. Information about a future event may have been obtained prior to the dream, but is forgotten after it, and the exact circumstances of what was said to whom and when may not be recalled correctly either. The sequence of events is apt to get changed as are clock times, so that a "better" story emerges. This phenomenon was already discussed in connection with anomalies of memory (Chapter 6). There is also the problem of coincidence. The fact was mentioned that everybody dreams every night, and about a great variety of things, so that the amount of dream material that is produced every night is extremely large. That some of it coincides with ongoing or future events should therefore come as no surprise; the laws of chance predict that. Furthermore, some future events may be brought about by dreams themselves. A dream foresaging an accident may be so upsetting to the dreamer that anxiety in the waking state may bring about precisely the kind of behavior that leads to accidents. Most importantly, it is only the dreams that are perceived as coinciding with reality that are brought to the attention of those who collect them. For every such dream, there must be at least one that did not come true. These are never reported, because they happen all the time and are of no further interest. The effect of publishing only the positive cases in survey reports and the like is to convey the impression, however, that there is an overwhelming amount of material that speaks in favor of telepathic and precognitive dreams. If these dreams were ever combined with all the other dreams that are just as vivid and detailed as the prophetic ones but that just miss being staged in real life, it would become quite obvious that, numerically, the case for the telepathic and precognitive dreams is not very well supported at all.

Two dream phenomena may be mentioned because of their connection with the occult, the *incubus* nightmare and the *mutual dream*. The incubus nightmare usually takes the form of a cat-like creature that sits on the sleeper's chest, looks terrible and feels worse because it seems to crush the victim's lungs and drain the very life out of the victim while that person feels paralyzed, unable to move. Although most dreams begin in a REM phase of sleep, the incubus nightmare begins in NREM sleep and coincides with a markedly slow breathing and heart rates. These may become so slow that they trigger alarm responses in the brain, as if the sleeper were close to death. The longer the condition lasts, the more probable is the incubus nightmare and the more intense it is. It usually occurs during that phase of the sleep cycle when bodily functions are at a low ebb. It may be associated with sleepwalking. As the nighmare starts, the sleeper may cry out, the heart rate increases twice or three times, breathing becomes much faster, and the person enters a REM phase of sleep with such dream images as a cat creature pressing him or her to death.

In medieval times, the terrifying animal was identified with an evil spirit as well as with sexual intercourse: The incubus (in Latin, the one lying above) would torment women whereas a succubus (one that lies below) would torment men. Sleep research has indicated that the nightmare is caused by temporary but critical malfunctioning of the vital functions of breathing and heartbeat. It is possible that it is related to the same factor that causes infant crib deaths, the activation of the diving reflex. The diving reflex is of no particular use to humans at this stage of their evolution, but it is present in and used by diving animals, such as water birds and seals in whom reflexive holding of breath is essential. It is possible that the incubus nightmare is triggered by the spontaneous operation of this reflex.

Reports of mutual dreaming—that is, dreams that are shared by two people (Donahoe, 1975)—are reports of so-called astral travel or else refer to telepathic and clairvoyant experiences that involve two people's dreams as the objects of these perceptions. A third possibility is that these are cases of *folie à deux*, a "folly"—that is, a delusion or hallucination that is shared by two people. The astral travel hypothesis is entertained by the occultists and requires the acceptance of the reality of a level of existence different from the ordinary physical/psychological level, namely that of the astral plane where people are presumed to go while they are dreaming. Although the assumption of a special dream world would explain mutual dreams, the idea is difficult to test scientifically, and no such test has been attempted. The telepathy hypothesis stands or falls with the hypothesis of the reality of telepathy itself. The probability of the existence of telepathy is discussed in Chapter 12. A shared delusion, or *folie à deux*, usually develops between individuals related by blood, but not necessarily. About one-fourth of the cases involve people who are not related by blood, namely spouses (Gralnick, 1942). They must be in close and prolonged personal contact, however. Not enough cases of mutual dreaming have been reported in the literature, however, to decide in favor of the *folie à deux* hypothesis.

NOTES

For a recent bibliography of astrological experiments and tests, surveys of belief in astrology, and critiques of astrology, see Bastedo (1978).

The two articles that follow the Objections to Astrology statement (Bok, Jerome, & Kurtz, 1975), Bok (1975) and Jerome (1975), present the basic terms of astrology, an explanation of how a horoscope is prepared, a history of astrology, as well as the reasons why it should not be believed. A good, short introduction to astrological terms and computations may be found in Shadowitz and Walsh (1976).

The nature of the controversy over Gauquelin's statistics in assessing the influence of planets on occupations can be gathered from a series of papers that appeared in *The Humanist* in 1976: Gauquelin (1976a, 1976b), Jerome (1976), the Committee Para's reply to M. Gauquelin (1976a, 1976b), and Zelen (1976). Lawrence E. Jerome, an engineer and science writer, has recently published a book (Jerome, 1977) debunking astrology.

On the anthropological approach to possessions, see Raymond Prince (1968). A detailed review of multiple personalities was provided in 1944 by Taylor and Martin. Ellenberger's (1970) book on the unconscious also provides a good overview of the topic of multiple personalities and lists all previous reviews. Hilgard (1977) discusses briefly the most recent cases of multiple personalities. The appropriate references may be found in that volume.

In spite of its date, Cutten's (1927) historical and psychological review of glossolalia is still a good source. A more recent psychological analysis of glossolalia is Samarin (1972).

On automatic writing, see Mühl (1930) and Hilgard (1977, Chapter 7). There have been no books published on this topic besides Mühl's. A brief but useful review of automatic art may be found in volume 2 of *Man, Myth, and Magic* Cavendish, (1970). The entire body of Kate Fox's automatic writing was published by the son of the physician and his wife for whom she had done the writing (Taylor, 1932).

Alice Bailey's life is described in her very readable autobiography (Bailey, 1951). It traces the development of a teacher of occultism that has many parallels in the lives of other such teachers, H. P. Blavatsky and Annie Besant, for instance. It not only reveals Alice Bailey's way of thinking about herself and about occult phenomena, but also constitutes an historic document that records, from an insider's point of view, the tensions, rivalries, and problems within an occult organization and one of the innumerable instances of schismatic splits that plague such organizations. Litvag's (1972) book is a recent thorough review of the case of Patience Worth/Pearl Curran.

A complete history and bibliography of water witching from the beginning of the 16th century through 1916 may be found in the 1957 reprint of A. J. Ellis's 1917 pamphlet. The most complete journal article on water witching is the 1967 article by Hyman and Vogt in *Psychology Today*. Additional tests of dowsing and radiesthesia are described by Christopher (1970).

9 Personality in Occultism: Mind Externalized

> *Glendower.* I can call spirits from the vasty deep. *Hotspur.* Why, so can I, or so can any man; But will they come when you do call for them?
>
> Shakespeare: 1 *Henry IV* III.i.

SOUL, MIND, AND THE REIFICATION OF THE SUBJECTIVE

We assume that animals are aware but not self-aware. Even that is a matter of degree: the behavior of an amoeba or flatworm shows sensitivity to environmental stimuli and no more, whereas certain items of behavior in the apes are not inconsistent with the notion of some rudiments of self-awareness. Early humans probably did not differ from the apes in self-awareness. According to Jaynes (1976), self-awareness may have developed quite recently, in the historical times. Whatever the precise course of development of awareness into self-awareness and the phylogenetic level at which it may be said to begin, awareness and self-awareness constitute a continuum and a matter of evolutionary development.

The significant next stage in the development of self-awareness was that when humans became aware of their awareness, they began to objectify it, to project it, and to give it names—psyche, thymos, atman, soul, mind. At various times and places, these terms have carried different connotations as our concept of ourselves, of nature, and of our place in nature changed. In the West, the transformations of the soul begin with the ancient Greeks. By the fifth century B. C., the Greeks recognized almost all of the ways in which Western people have come to consider the soul: as the principle of life, as the cause of emotions and intelligence that perished with the body, as an immortal entity that survived bodily death, or just as another manifestation of the atomic structure of the universe. The one interpretation lacking was that of an immortal entity that could be rewarded for its good deeds or punished for its sins after the body's death. This Christian interpretation was added during the first few centuries of our era. The salvation of the immortal soul remained the main preoccupation of Europeans for the next 1000 years.

A shift from otherworldly concerns to an interest in this world and in human beings as human beings occurred during the Renaissance. In the 17th century, however, a development took place in Europe that finds no parallel in other times or other civilizations. It was the rise of science as a field of human activity distinct from speculative philosophy. The advent of science also brought about a gradual change in the idea of the soul. Science brought about the "naturalization of the soul" (Kantor, 1963). This happened as follows: St. Thomas Aquinas (1225-1274) had taught Christians to think of an immortal soul, as well as of the faculties of the soul that manifest themselves in life as intelligence, emotions, the will, and the like. Scientists and the thinkers of the Age of Enlightenment emphasized this second aspect of the soul. Even though the term soul was retained for some time, the general context within which the term was being used was soon making it clear whether what was meant by soul was its imortal aspect with all of its theological connotations or soul as the bearer of certain psychic or mental potentialities. In the English language, the term mind was soon substituted for soul in the latter sense. The soul, in the guise of mind, lost all theological and supernatural connotations. It became part of nature.

The various esoteric beliefs reflect this historic soul-mind split in that those that incorporate more of the transcendental or religious element are more apt to use the term soul with its connotations of immortality and philosophical dualism, whereas those that are more empirical in their beliefs are more apt to refer to mind. In the 19th century, the spiritualists, in order to avoid both the theological connotations of the term soul and the materialistic, "nothing-but" connotations of the term mind, applied the term "spirit" to the various alleged manifestations of those who had died. Although everybody seems to know what that term means, it is quite imprecise nevertheless, and, in addition to the various interpretations of Christian theology, can refer to the immortal soul, a mental projection of a living person, or a representation of an individual in matter that is "subtler" than ordinary physical matter, such as etheric or astral matter. The particular meaning depends on the particular belief system to which the user of the term adheres. In all instances, it reflects the need for assurance that existence does not cease with the cessation of the physical body, as well as the fact that self-awareness very easily, almost automatically, translates into a belief that it can transcend the physical substrate from which it arises and function independently of it. Anything that says "I" thinks of itself as an autonomous entity. It will wish to demonstrate to itself that it is autonomous in the same way as the brain from which it arises and all other objects of the physical world are autonomous.

The reification of the subjective, the attribution of physical qualities to that that is merely the experience of a state or a process, is a universal phenomenon and unavoidable. It is not a permanent state of affairs, however, for there is both an evolutionary and a developmental trend to pass from a denial of the subjective to its recognition for what it is. Like the Jaynesian ancient (Jaynes, 1976) who externalized his own inner voice, attributing it to gods, and lacked a developed self-consciousness, the young child externalizes, reifies subjective events, such as dreams. Jean Piaget, (1929), who has studied the characteristics of the intellectual development of children extensively, presents an interview with a 5½ year–old child as follows:

> Do you ever have dreams?—*Yes, I dreamt that I had a hole in my hand.*—Are dreams true?—*No, they are pictures* (images) *we see!*—Where do they come from?—*From God.*—Are your eyes open or shut when you dream?—*Shut.*—Could I see your dream?—*No, you would be too far away.*—And your mother?—*Yes, but she lights the light.*—Is the dream in the room or inside you?—*It isn't in me or I shouldn't see it* (!)—And could your mother see it?—*No, she isn't in the bed. Only my little sister sleeps with me* [p. 94].

Those who feel the commanding need to reconcile the objective and subjective sides of life show an almost child-like tendency to reify the subjective. A good example of this tendency is Colonel Albert Rochas d'Aiglun who, among other things, was responsible for starting the practice of hypnotic age regression in order to study reincarnation. One of his works (Rochas, 1899) is significantly titled *The Externalization of Sensitivity*. In it, he speaks of the "objective nature of light emanations perceived in the hypnotic state," expresses the belief that, under hypnosis and suggested anesthesia, pinpricks administered to the hypnotic subject are not felt by the subject unless the pinprick is administered to an inanimate object that the hypnotic subject has "projected" sensitivity unto, refers to the ancient belief that it is the sense organs that emanate energy instead of receiving energy from the outside, talks of "cerebral radiation," shows drawings of red and blue light emanating from the ends of a magnet as well as alleged emanations involved in telepathy, and so on. Ludwig Staudenmaier, who was mentioned in the preceding chapter in connection with possession states, even though sounding eminently objective and level-headed with regard to his own experiences of possession, spirit voices, and automatisms (Staudenmaier, 1922), and even though denying that any supernatural forces are involved, is quite serious in giving specific directions for intensifying one's subjective visions, hallucinations, and willed imagery to the point where it would be possible, according to him, to make an objective record of it, such as by photography. In other words, imagination, if intensified sufficiently, would quite literally project outward and become sensible.

From a particular perspective, the tendency to reify the subjective may be called the transcendence wish, the wish of the subjective, the mental processes, or, rather, their unified representation in the idea of the self, the I, to transcend the boundaries and limitations of the physical body and to function independently. Theosophy supplies humans with additional bodies besides the physical in which to do the transcending, such as the ethereal, the astral, and the mental bodies. Once the transcendence wish turns into assumed reality, nothing is impossible. Mind transcends body and meets other transcended minds (as in telepathy), other personalities (spirits of the departed), or goes to places distinct from that at which the body is at the moment and sees places, things, and events (clairvoyance) or even one's own body (the out-of-the-body-experience).

Very few psychologists or psychiatrists have concerned themselves with the transcendence wish or with the question of life after death, spirits, and apparitions because, officially at least, these are considered to be matters of fantasy, superstition, or of concern to the religionist. It is therefore of interest to see how the matter of spirits was dealt with by Carl Gustav Jung, one psychiatrist who took such things as spirits, occultism, and alchemy seriously because to him they represented significant psychological realities to be dealt with psychologically. Jung (1910) considers a psychological explanation of apparitions in terms of universal psychological principles because apparitions are and always have been a universal phenomenon. Jung postulates a psyche that is not an indivisible entity but a "more or less divided totality," proof of which are dreams, waking visions, mental disease, and split personalities. Jung calls these fragments of the psyche autonomous complexes. Some of them function quite independently of the ego—that is, we are seldom or never aware that they are part of ourselves. When we are aware of them, they appear to be independent entities—that is, we project them and deny their connection with our own psyche. From this viewpoint, "spirits" are unconscious projected complexes. Some of the autonomous complexes belong to the personal unconscious, and, in religious contexts, are viewed as manifestations of the soul, the soul complexes. The loss and restoration of the soul is a common idea found in shamanistic religions and used to explain physical and mental disease and magic spells. Other complexes belong to the collective unconscious (see the section *Contemporary Research on Discarnate Survival* later in this chapter). These are spirit complexes. Because the contents of the collective unconscious are not the personal property of the individual but belong to all of humanity, they are experienced as strange, foreign intrusions, often fearful images. Relief is felt when the spirits are exorcised or the apparition is gone. Jung explains the spirits of the dead in the following way: The emotional attachment to a person represents an investment of psychic energy. When the object of the attachment dies, this energy informs only an idea or image of the dead person. When the attachment has been strong, the image acquires a life of its own and becomes a spirit. Jung refused to speculate on whether spirits have an objective existence—that is, whether psychic projections may become externalized. Jung's reluctance is understandable because, in trying to answer this question, one comes face to face with insurmountable problems. If we assume that the subjective can become something objective, we immediately return to the starting point, for the question of how this happens has still not been answered. If, as an alternative, we assume that in the course of evolution matter becomes first conscious, then self-conscious, we can theorize further that, logically, self-consciousness should keep evolving further and become independent of the material base from which it arose. If so, it would be necessary to postulate that such qualitative changes are also accompanied by changes in the laws that govern this new kind of matter. Unfortunately, postulating a new system (or world) that is not governed by the laws we are familiar with makes it impossible to investigate it because we can approach it only in terms of our own system. In the face of this dilemma, scientific statements become impossible and preferential decisions are made that are governed by considerations other than scientific. The spiritualists constitute a world-wide movement that represents the transcendence wish. In spite of the averred intention to prove life after death scientifically, their activity has been governed more than anything else by this wish rather than scientific thinking.

SPIRITUALISM

Spiritualism is the belief in communication with the dead through a living intermediary, the *medium*. As a religion, it began in the 19th century, and is still in existence today. *Psychical research*, which began after spiritualism had already taken hold, was an attempt to investigate scientifically both the phenomena that took place during a mediumistic *séance* and other, related phenomena that occurred outside the séance room: telepathy, clairvoyance, precognition, levitation, apparitions, haunted houses, and poltergeists. Although some of the psychical investigators were prominent scientists, not all of them were, and not all of the investigations were conducted applying strict scientific controls. Systematic experimentation was absent. *Parapsychology* was in a sense the heir to psychical research in that it investigated the same phenomena, but there was one crucial difference: The principal method of investigation was experimentation. The experiments concerned telepathy, precognition, clairvoyance, and psychokinesis. All other phenomena—communication with the dead, ghosts and hauntings, and precognitive hallucinations—were classified under the heading of "spontaneous phenomena" that could not be experimented on and that, although of interest, could not form a scientific data base. In fact, the question of survival after death was eventually declared to be in principle untestable.

Spiritualism, psychical research, and parapsychology represent aspects of another attempt to reconcile and bring into a relationship the subjective and objective sides of life, specifically science and religion. As R. L. Moore states in his history of spiritualism and parapsychology (Moore, 1977): "Over the past 175 years spiritualism and then psychical research have offered Americans a reasonable solution to the problem of how to accomodate religious and scientific interests [p. *xii*]." Reasonable or not, the solution has appeared acceptable to millions of people, not just Americans, but Latin Americans and Europeans as well. These are people who are not necessarily members of some spiritualist church or parapsychological researchers, but people who have found their belief in an afterlife confirmed by the phenomena of the mediumistic séance, people who read the accounts of apparitions and hauntings and believe them at least halfway, and those who operate the planchette or ouija board, frequent séances and fortunetellers' parlors, and are in general "into" the occult. Spiritualism and psychical research appeal to so many because, for one thing, they are not limited to one kind of phenomenon, as mental healing is, for instance. Rather, they cover a whole gamut of related occult phenomena. Most importantly, however, they seem to give a satisfactory answer to a major philosophical question by providing, in an age of science, "scientific proof" of the existence of human personality after death.

Belief in continued existence in another form after death, communication with the spirits of the dead, and visible apparitions or ghosts of the dead have always been part of humans' religions and folklore and of occult lore. It was the increasing dominance of scientific, naturalistic thinking that was to culminate in the 19th century's optimistic faith in the omnipotence of science that led to the rise of spiritualism in the middle of that century. It did not arise as an attempt to save religion from destruction by science. The striking difference between spiritualism and occultism was that spiritualism insisted on bringing the occult out in the open. Spirit communications, apparitions, and the rest were to be examined empirically, using the methods of science. It was not an attempt to bring back superstition and irrationality but, quite the contrary, it was animated by the desire to make religion rational, to put scientific foundations under the belief in an afterlife, and to make the spirit world part of the natural order. Inherently, however, it was still a form of occultism because, under the guise of scientism, it was seeking a transcendental solution to the eternal paradox of the subjective and the objective, mind and body, the physical and the non-physical.

Apparitions of the dead have been reported from all historical periods and from all societies. These apparitions have been explained in terms of an additional or duplicate body, made up of a substance subtler than physical matter, which leaves the physical body upon death but continues to serve as a vehicle for the individual's memories and personality. Scientists, including the majority of parapsychologists, reject this view and consider the apparitions of the dead to be hallucinations that have no external reality.

Prior to the mid-19th century, apparitions of the dead or revenants were the most commonly reported form of contact with "the other world." In the 17th century, ghost stories were being collected systematically to combat religious skepticism. Contacts with the dead through mediums were rare, however.

In early 1848, two sisters, Margaret and Kate Fox, aged 15 and 12, declared that the rappings they had been hearing in their Hydesville, New York, cottage, were coming from an intelligent entity. Their older, married sister Leah was soon encouraging the public to come and see the girls in their home, and by 1849, they were already demonstrating the rappings to paying audiences. When it was realized that there was money to be made from spirit rappings, suitably translated into messages by the use of codes, the movement to communicate with the dead began. It spawned periodicals, lectures, and séances, and by the end of 1850, organizations were being founded, both secular and religious, under the banner of spiritualism. No unified spiritualist church emerged, but there was one unifying theme that all spiritualists subscribed to, which was the empirical foundation of spiritualism and the openness of the spiritualist phenomena to scientific investigation. It was a religious faith founded upon physical phenomena and a belief in science, an attempt to solve the mind-body paradox in the middle ground between science and religion, hence an occultism.

In the preceding chapter, the distinction between physical and mental mediums was mentioned and the trance states of the latter were discussed. It was the physical medium and her phenomena that constituted the basis for the objective verification of the existence of a spirit world, and the Fox sisters produced the first of such phenomena. The spiritualists insisted that there was not distinction between the natural and the supernatural, that everything was matter, except that some forms of matter were too "subtle" for the senses to perceive, such as the matter spirits were made of, but that the spirit world could be investigated like any other material phenomenon nevertheless. This position naturally led to a heavy emphasis on the "physical phenomena" or "manifestations" of mediumship.

What a mental medium said could or could not be true, and the verification of what she said was often impossible. Spirits that answered questions were a different matter. Their statements could be verified. Noises and movements of objects were observable physical phenomena that, if they were not caused by anything demonstrably physical, had to be attributed to the action of the spirits. In 1860, the *Spiritual Magazine* was already listing the following physical phenomena of the séance room that were taken as evidence for contact with spirits of the departed: table rapping and tipping, spirit writing and drawing, luminous phenomena, spirit music in the form of musical instruments that played untouched by a human hand, the touch and sight of spirit hands, and spiritual impersonation, or the reproduction by the medium of the behaviors characteristic of a dead person. Later on, the phenomena of materialization were added: teleportation, or the producing of objects (apports) from remote places; the production of ectoplasm, a white, mysterious substance emanating from a bodily cavity of the medium; wax castings of spirit hands or their fingerprints; spirit photographs; and the levitation of objects and persons. The more rambunctious spirits did everything a rambunctious person might do, including the withdrawal and replacement of gentlemen's pocketbooks and the insertion and withdrawal of articles from ladies' bosoms. To produce these manifestations, the spirits required darkness and the use of a spirit cabinet, a sort of an operating base that could be an actual cabinet or just a curtained-off corner of the séance room.

It did not escape the notice of the professional stage magician that at least the most blatant phenomena were tricks because, among other reasons, many of the less adroit practitioners of the séance room were being exposed as tricksters. Neither did it pass unnoticed that such exposures did nothing to abate the public's enthusiasm for the mediumistic spectacle, and it was soon incorporated by the magicians in their repertoire. Whatever the medium could do, they could also do. Their performances were not always billed as stage magic or entertainment. Many advertised themselves as intermediaries between the spirit world and this one, then proceeded to give the public a rousing performance. Such performances were in full swing in America in the 1860s. The Davenport brothers were at the top of their profession and acquired international fame. Because they billed themselves as mediums and not as magicians, attempts were made to expose them. It was easy to do and was done many times, such as by simply lighting a match near the stage. What the light of the match revealed was the upraised arm of a Davenport brother shaking the tambourine, for instance, a tambourine that a second ago appeared to be floating freely in the air. Such exposures did little to turn the public away from them. Those who believed in spirits continued to attend the magicians' performances, refusing to believe what their eyes saw. This is an extremely important psychological aspect of psychical phenomena that is relevant not only to them but to anything touching on the occult. Even public confessions of fraudulent mediums or of a professional magician pretending to be a medium does nothing to shake the belief of those who have the need to believe. As early as 1851, Mrs. Culver, a relative by marriage of the Fox sisters, signed a statement before witnesses that she had signaled Kate Fox when to make the raps, that Kate had shown her how she made the raps, and that, when her wrists or feet were being observed, she would crack her ankle and knee joints to produce the raps. The flood of spiritualism continued undiminished. In October of 1888, Margaret and Kate Fox confessed before an audience of 2000 people that the rappings had been produced by them deliberately, first by bumping an apple on their bedroom floor, then by cracking their finger and toe joints

MUSIC HALL.

THIS EVENING,

AND EVERY EVENING DURING THE WEEK EXCEPT WEDNESDAY, ALSO ON WEDNESDAY AND SATURDAY AFTERNOONS,

THE WORLD-RENOWNED

DAVENPORT BROTHERS

Will appear after a most extraordinary and successful tour of four years in Europe, in their unique and startling wonders, mysterious displays, and unaccountable manifestations.

Fig. 9.1. A handbill announcing the appearance of the Davenport brothers in Boston after a 4-year European tour. (From Christopher, 1962. Used by permission of Dover Publications, Inc.)

(*New York World*, October 21, 1888), Margaret proceeded to demonstrate how this was done. Even this did not affect the course of spiritualism, let alone end it. Even today, many accounts of the Fox sisters leave out their confession of fraud and present the rappings as genuine manifestations from the spirit world. When the world-famous magician Harry Houdini once performed a stage trick that seemed explicable only in terms of occult powers, but proceeded to state to the audience that it had been just a trick, someone later tried to persuade him that he must have genuine psychic powers or else the feat would have been impossible for him to accomplish. The magician S. J. Davey once produced certain spirit phenomena and obtained testimonies from unimpeachable witnesses that the phenomena could not be explained by trickery. When Davey confessed that he was a magician and that the performance was fraudulent mediumship, the witnesses refused to believe him (Hodgson & Davey, 1886-1887). The French photographer Buguet made fake spirit photographs using dolls and lay figures. During his court trial for fraud, numerous witnesses testified that Buguet had given them photographs of their departed relatives, and refused to believe Buguet when he explained how he had manufactured the photographs (Fodor, 1933).

These examples are not isolated instances, but typify the attitude of very large numbers of people. It is based on ignorance, poor observation (many of the phenomena were so poorly staged that by today's standards it is almost unbelievable that anyone should have been deceived by them), a general penchant to find easy solutions to life's problems by relegating them to the mysterious and the supernatural, and the psychological mechanism of dissonance reduction—once a considerable emotional investment in and commitment to a belief has been made, changes in the belief will be resisted to the point of ignoring all evidence against it. This attitude is virtually unassailable and impermeable to any sort of contrary evidence. Individuals with this attitude will admit that, for instance, a medium is occasionally or even often fraudulent or that certain paranormal phenomena may be duplicated by ordinary means, but they will maintain that as long as there is any residual of instances where trickery of any other natural explanation has not been shown to operate, the explanation for that residual must be paranormal and that the genuineness of the entire class of phenomena must be upheld. It is basically an unscientific attitude. When scientists detect that a source of information is repeatedly unreliable, they, without necessarily concluding that it is always unreliable, will seek to substitute a more reliable source for it. It is a matter of efficiency or, philosophically speaking, pragmatism. If a source of information is unreliable, it does not "work." By this criterion, William James, the author of the philosophy of pragmatism, failed to apply his own principle to the matter of mediumistic phenomena. Even though James was quite aware of the practices of fraudulent mediums and had contempt for them, he allowed that the proposition that all mediums are frauds could not be sustained if it were proven that there was at least one medium who was not. That medium was James' (1897/1960) "white crow": "If I may employ the language of the professional logic-shop, a universal proposition can be made untrue by a particular instance. If you wish to upset the law that all crows are black, you must not seek to show that no crows are; it is enough if you prove one single crow to be white [p. 41]." James believed that he had found his white crow in the person of the Boston medium Mrs. Piper. On pragmatic principles, James should have abandoned the investigation of mediums when sufficient evidence had accumulated that their phenomena could be explained for the most part as tricks. He did not. Although no source of information can be assumed to be reliable all the time, on pragmatic principles, we ought to choose that that has the higher degree of probability of yielding correct information. To James, Mrs. Piper may have appeared to be the sought-after white crow. To others, she was half gray, at best.

It is significant that Mrs. Piper was not a physical, but a mental, medium. Although both spiritualists and the investigators of spirit phenomena agreed that the physical phenomena of the séance room could be treated like any phenomena of the physics laboratory, the evidence for the paranormal origin of a mental medium's statements is of a different order. When the evidence consists of words, of their interpretation, and of verbal memory, a white crow may only appear so—because of the particular angle from which one may be looking at it. From other angles, it may appear just as black as any others. Thus, even if James did not believe that spirits controlled Mrs. Piper, but that she obtained information telepathically, he should have noticed, as had E. M. Sidgwick, a psychical researcher of the Society for Psychical Research of London, that Mrs. Piper's own personality showed through the personalities of her spirit controls and communicators; that the latter were ignorant of subjects that Mrs. Piper was ignorant of, but that they were not ignorant of when still alive; that her first control, a French physician by the name of Phinuit, knew only as little French as Mrs. Piper herself and not very much at all about medicine, and that nothing could be discovered in France about his birth, life, or death; that the spirits covered up for mistakes in blundering ways that were not at all characteristic of the persons when alive; or that the communications received from her control spirit G. P., or George Pellew, were denied by George Pellew's family to have any connection with him. George Pellew was a control spirit that replaced Dr. Phinuit and was supposed to be the spirit of a deceased friend of Richard Hodgson's, an investigator of the London Society for Psychical Research. The information contained in G. P.'s communications was such that it was thought impossible for Mrs. Piper to obtain it except through paranormal means, and it converted Hodgson to a belief in spirits.

Psychical Research

Thirty-two years passed after the Hydesville rappings before formal scientific research on spiritualist phenomena began. Both Kate and Margaret Fox had been investigated, as well as innumerable other mediums, for that was the main purpose of spiritualism. The methods used could not pass scientific muster, however, and many questions about spirit phenomena remained unanswered. In 1882, the Society for Psychical Research (SPR) was founded in London. Parapsychological research may be considered to have started on that date.

In the 19th century, physicians and psychiatrists were equating mediumship with mental disorder that was reducible to some form of organic malfunctioning. Psychical researchers, many of whom were scientists, assumed that paranormal capacities were involved. They further assumed that these capacities were not supernatural but quite "normal," and attempted to investigate them. In the course of doing so, they made contributions to psychology that were relevant to the explanations of the paranormal offered by neurologists and psychiatrists. It was in the form of theories and hypotheses concerning the functioning of the human mind on levels that are at least temporarily inaccessible to conscious experience. F. W. H. Myers, the most active member of the SPR, wrote a two-volume work (Myers, 1903) that James hailed as the only scientific attempt to explain spiritualism. The key concept in Myer's work was the subliminal self, or the unconscious, which Myers used to account for mediumistic phenomena, the automatisms, possessions, telepathy, and the like. The term telepathy itself was coined by Myers. Even though Janet was also speaking of the unconscious and so did Freud later, all three were attributing rather different functions and qualities to it. At any rate, for a time at least, both psychiatrists and psychical researchers were moving in the same direction.

The founders of the SPR were learned men, most of them educated at Cambridge, who represented a variety of fields: philosophy, physics, and literature, among others. The fact that many of them were wealthy was important because it meant that the Society could carry on its work in research and publicaton and that some of its members could devote full time to its work. The most important ingredient, however, that went into the SPR mixture besides scientific respectability and financial support was the personalities and beliefs of the founders of the SPR. These are pivotal in understanding the reasons for the coming into being of the organization and the nature of the results of their investigations.

Frederick Myers, one of the most active and important founding members of the Society, was a philosophical writer. He loved life passionately, shrank back at the thought of extinction, and felt that there was a unity hidden behind the diversity of this world, a unity with which he hoped to make contact some day. Myers believed in afterlife even before 1882. Henry Sidgwick, a philosopher, although convinced of the necessity of remaking social and religious creeds in accordance with science, would not accept even agnosticism and believed that a proof of discarnate survival was vital to the maintenance of morality. Edmund Gurney, after attempts to find his life's work in music and other fields, found it in the SPR as its Secretary. With superabundant energy, in just 4 years Gurney produced a two-volume collection of case materials concerning apparitions of people who, at the time of their appearance, were near death (Gurney, Myers, & Podmore, 1886). Alfred Russel Wallace, a coproponent with Charles Darwin of the evolutionary theory, already believed that spirit communication was a fact, and proclaimed so in public. So did W. Stainton Moses. Richard Hodgson, an Australian investigator who in the mid-1880s conducted an investigation of the miraculous phenomena of Madame Blavatsky, the founder of the Theosophical Society, and declared her to be an impostor, was very good at uncovering the mechanics of fraud. When mysterious phenomena occurred to him personally, however, he was ready to believe them. He experimented with hallucinogenic drugs, and must have been primed for the acceptance of spiritualist phonomena by such drug-induced experiences as disembodied hands touching his face. There was a passionate need in Hodgson to find proof of psychical belief, which he, like James, thought he had found in Mrs. Piper.

In these and other men associated with the early days of the SPR, the conflict between advancing science, abetted by the newly promulgated theory of evolution, and traditional religion was also staged on an individual basis. They felt the conflict between the monistic view of humans as organisms and the dualistic view of humans as persons in a particularly acute manner because these two views were nearly equally balanced in them. Their biographies clearly indicate this. To those who played the most significant roles in the work of the SPR, psychical research was not just an avocation that was "in" for men of their education and social standing. It was something they had to do as part of their quest for answers to the paradoxes posed by the two views of humanity, and the motivating force came from the near-equal strength of these two views in them. They could have accepted either the scientific or the religious view, but as soon as they began to lean towards one, the other made itself felt. Thus, in spite of repeated findings that the physical mediums were frauds, they did not declare the field to lack validity but proceeded to examine more mediums. On the other hand, even though there were repeated instances in which the SPR investigators could not find any naturalistic explanation for some of the phenomena observed and were ready to admit the work of spirits (even though others would not), the Society did not unequivocally endorse the spirit–world hypothesis. The net result after several decades of research and investigation is still one of uncertainty. Also, the biographies and autobiographies of prominent workers in the field of psychical research and parapsychology (Gauld, 1968; Rhine & Rhine, 1978; Turner, 1974) all show religious crises in their lives. Their religious family backgrounds clashed with the knowledge acquired in their education. The conflict, repeated in different forms, was solved by adopting a third view that rejected the traditional forms of both science and religion.

Some of the positive results obtained in the investigation of mediums were obtained by physical scientists of the highest standing, such as Sir William Crookes. Advocates of the survival hypothesis do not tire of stressing this point. The fact is that William Crookes, among others, although very good at physical experimentation, was rather weak on drawing inferences and on theorizing. Besides, he was gullible. He endorsed several mediums in spite of their demonstrated trickery. Having witnessed a single séance with Kate Fox, he became convinced that the Fox sisters' phenomena were genuine. He actually believed that he had touched a ghost (Katie King, the daughter of Sir Henry Morgan, the buccaneer), listened to her heartbeat, taken her pulse (75 beats a minute), and that the lock of hair he had taken off her actually came from a ghost and not a living person (Medhurst, 1972).

Being a scientist, even a highly respected one, does not exempt one from the affliction of gullibility. By now, it has become an article of faith that physical scientists are probably the least qualified people to test for genuineness of a medium or anyone professing supernormal powers. The professional trickster or magician are simply no match for the physical scientist, who has been trained to observe phenomena provided by nature, not those contrived by humans to look as if they were natural. The use of a stage magician as a consultant in all such investigations is a must, but magicians were only gradually given such a role in psychical research. Thus, the seeming guarantee of the genuineness of a phenomenon just because it has been observed by a prominent physical scientist counts for little when it comes to psychical phenomena. It is further undermined when the scientist also happens to be a firm believer in another form of reality. Sir Oliver Lodge, an SPR member and psychical investigator, was one such individual. In spite of overwhelming evidence that pointed to mediumistic fraud, such as was found in the case of the notorious Neapolitan medium Eusapia Palladino, Lodge refused to change his favorable opinion. Hereward Carrington, another SPR investigator and a popular writer on psychical subjects, shared Lodge's attitude. It was these investigators who kept reporting favorably on mediums whom other teams of investigators were finding to be clearly fraudulent. Contemporary believer literature typically selects these favorable reports to bolster the believers' case and ignores the others. For instance, such literature highlights the 1898 and 1908

SPR investigations of Eusapia Palladino that were favorable to her, and ignores the 1895 seances with her at Cambridge, also organized by the SPR, which found fraud, as well as the 1909 American sittings in which repeated and conclusive evidence was found that Eusapia Palladino produced her phenomena using tricks.

The SPR conducted many investigations of mediums. Their discovery that only natural phenomena were involved in a given case of house haunting or that a medium had obtained information by natural means or had resorted to trickery to produce her phenomena was nothing new. Similar findings had been made by others before the Society had been founded. What was new was that the investigations were conducted by individuals with a scientific background who presumably used scientific methods of observation. In addition to the case in which H. P. Blavatsky was unmasked by Richard Hodgson, the case of Eusapia Palladino was perhaps the most famous case that involved the SPR, because in her time Palladino was the most famous medium of Europe. She was investigated repeatedly by psychical researchers, and her case was held to be the test case of spiritualism: If she were shown to be a fraud, the entire case for spiritualism would supposedly collapse. She was exposed in test séances conducted in America in 1910. Her table levitations were accomplished by her foot, which she extracted from her shoe while the examiners believed they had their feet firmly on hers, and she used her feet to produce other physical phenomena as well. The disheartening part of her story is that her unmasking did not undermine the believers' belief in her in the least, and even today she is considered by many to have been a genuine medium and the greatest of them all.

Earlier in the 19th century, the most famous medium had been Daniel Dunglas Home, who was endorsed by William Crookes himself. Home was never publicly exposed. The reason for this was that he never performed in public and was never formally investigated. Although Home did not perform for money, he led a very comfortable life. He had such an appealing personality that people would ask him to stay in their homes for extended periods of time as their guest. He eventually married a daughter of a Russian count. Home's performances always occurred in private and under the exact conditions specified by him, which included darkness, small numbers of witnesses, and involved the use of the devices of the stage magician: diversion of attention, sleight of hand, slipping his foot out of his shoe to ring bells, tug at garments, and so on. The most celebrated of Home's feats was his floating out one window and floating in through another, except that the feat probably never took place. Three witnesses of high repute presumably saw the feat. The witnesses, however, never actually saw Home leave through a window: they heard a window open, then, upon seeing Home's silhouette in the window of the room they were in, assumed he had gone outside and floated in again. The witnesses' room was dark, the only light available being the light of the moon. The few witnesses who saw Home perform in private and were not mesmerized by his personality and their own desire to believe, saw Home perform his feats using the usual methods of the stage magician (Christopher, 1970).

Mediumistic phenomena are basically stage magic performed under the special conditions of the séance room. These conditions, which make magic performances so much easier, include darkness or semidarkness, the readiness of the medium's sitters or clients to believe her, and the fact that it is the medium who determines how the séance should proceed, for instance, prohibiting anyone to look under the table lest the spirits be "offended." Controls instituted by investigators and their disbelief are a standard excuse for the failure of the phenomena to materialize because, again, the spirits are "offended." The use of devices, accomplices, and trickery to liberate a hand or a foot from the investigators' control in order to produce the phenomena has been amply described by professional magicians (e.g., Christopher, 1970; Gibson & Young, 1953) and debunkers of the occult (e.g., Rawcliffe, 1959). It must be emphasized that even when the phenomenon is palpably physical, it is still mostly psychological factors at work—distraction, misdirection, play upon the distraught state of mind of the sitter who longs to see the loved one who has just died, and capitalization on the fact that one sees what one wants to see.

As technology advanced, the perpetration of mediumistic fraud became more and more difficult. Investigators had already noted that as controls became stricter, the phenomena ceased to manifest themselves. With the introduction of the film camera and of the infrared film, darkness no longer could obscure the doings of the medium, and by 1930, physical manifestations of the spirit world were on their way out as subjects worthy of researchers' attention. Naturally, the fraudulent medium can take advantage of technological advances as well. This works against the medium, however, because in this age of electronic surveillance devices and holograms, it would be impossible to convince any even modestly informed person that the standard physical phenomena of the séance room are produced by anything but known physical methods and apparatus, even if they are not immediately detected. The cessation of physical phenomena on the mediumistic scene is routinely explained by spiritualists as a result of the spirits having turned their attention away from them and towards spiritual healing. We saw in Chapter 2 that the unity of body and mind of necessity involves the mind in the course of any bodily ill and its recovery therefrom. Because the operation of the mind cannot be separated from the operation of spirits (or any other immaterial entities) in principle, the statement that spiritual healing proves the existence of a spirit world is irrefutable. The assumption can be and is rejected by science on the principle of parsimony, which states that the explanation consistent with the fewest assumptions is preferrable. The Franciscan friar, William of Ockham (ca. 1300-1349), to whom the first formulation of the principle is attributed ("Ockham's razor"), had precisely the invisible world of demons and angels in mind when he stated that "multiplicities should not be posited without necessity."

In addition to the investigation of mediums, other noteworthy work of the SPR included the publication of a monumental collection of 702 stories of apparitions of a living person, to another living person, just before the former's death or injury. The labor that went into this work, *Phantasms of the Living* (Gurney, Myers, & Podmore, 1886), was largely wasted. None of the stories had been written down immediately after the events had happened. Some of them had been recorded only years later, which made them useless as scientific evidence on that count alone. Memory is fallible, and it is much more fallible when it involves matters that affect the individual personally and emotionally, as matters pertaining to the occult do. By the admission of the authors themselves, there was only a small number of "fairly conclusive cases" among the ones recorded, and, as already mentioned, modern parapsychologists have excluded spontaneous case materials as scientific data.

Concerning the psychic anecdote, the story about a ghost, apparition, or meaningful coincidence, one point cannot be stressed too strongly: There is no such thing as a reliable, objective informant, regardless of how upright, socially eminent, or educated the informant might be, because that person is so intimately involved in it. Retrospective falsification, the mixing of imagination and memory, is the rule in these stories rather than the exception. Dreams are remembered as actual physical events, a dream that comes after a significant event is remembered as having come before it and therefore as being prophetic of it, and the story itself gets better and better in the retelling, with significant but inconvenient details being omitted and other details added. The latter, although not having any basis in reality, nevertheless make for a better story, one that is simple, symmetric, and convincing. To this day, the occult literature is replete with stories similar in kind to the following story about Judge Hornby, told in 1884 by Gurney and Myers, 9 years after the incident had happened. Taken as it is, it is utterly baffling and seems to demand an explanation in spiritualistic or occult terms—that is, until someone decides to investigate the facts of the case and shows what really happened in the case. Sir Edmund Hornby was, at the time of the incident, the former Chief Judge of the Supreme Consular Court of China and Japan at Shanghai. One night in January, 1875, a newspaper editor known to the judge entered his bedroom, ignored the Judge's request to leave, sat down on the foot of his bed, and asked for information for his paper concerning a judgment made the previous day. The time was 1:20 in the morning, acording to the Judge. The Judge finally gave in to the request for fear that an argument might wake up his wife. He then told the visitor that this was the last time he would allow any reporters in his house, to which the man replied, "This is the last time I shall ever see you anywhere." After the visitor was gone, Lady Hornby awoke, whereupon the Judge told her about the visitor. He repeated the story to her the next morning. That day, he also learned that the editor whom he had seen the night before had died about 1:00 in the morning. The inquest showed that he had died of a heart disease. In his notes, there was found the following statement: "The Chief Judge gave judgment this morning in this case to the following effect," followed by some illegible shorthand. The Judge stated in a newspaper article that appeared years later, "As I said then, so I say now—I was not asleep, but wide awake. After a lapse of nine years my memory is quite clear on the subject. I have not the least doubt I saw the man—have not the least doubt that the conversation took place be-tween us." In a later issue of the newspaper, it was disclosed, however, that the editor had died at 9:00 in the morning of the day in question, that no inquest was held on his death, that there was no record of the judgment that figured so prominently in the story, and that Judge Hornby was not married at the time. Thus, what had probably been a vivid dream had turned, in the Judge's mind, into reality wrought with occult implications.

Psychical Research in America.   The American counterpart of the SPR, the American Society for Psychical Research, was organized in 1885. The moving force behind the ASPR was William James. The group of sponsors

---

Box 9.1—William James (1842–1910)

William James, America's foremost philosopher, is also considered by many to have been America's foremost psychologist. He began his academic career as a professor of physiology, taught physiological psychology, became a pro-fessor of philosophy, only to have his title changed again to professor of psychology. When he spoke as a philosopher, he spoke disparagingly of psychology, and vice versa. He did the same for any other position that he took: When he spoke for empiricism, he regretted not being a rationalist, or, when presenting the advantages of pluralism, he longed for the simplicities of monism. Throughout his life, James continued to present these two sides of his nature, which also reflected the way he saw humanity and the universe. Although they often seemed to intermingle, there was in fact a constant alter-nation between two seemingly contradictory but actually complementary points of view. Any time James appeared to be making a statement in favor of one view, he would turn around and show why the opposite view might be preferable.

James's main philosophical contribution, the philosophy of pragmatism, arose from an effort to solve the paradoxes that he saw in himself and in life—the opposition between rationalism and empiricism, free will and determinism, the philosopher and the scientist, the "tender-minded" and the "tough-minded" individual, the subjective and the objective. He held that it was incorrect to hold a distinction between subject and object, between the knower and the known. Neither the knower nor the known are things but relations in pure experience. He accepted empiricism in that he agreed that knowledge is acquired through experience, but it was a radical empiricism in that the dualism of subject and object was rejected.

Given James's Janus-like nature, it was natural for him to become interested and involved in psychical research. His father's life-long concern with questions of religion and the meaning of life was an additional influence. James's attitude towards science arose from his own inability to acquiesce in any solution to a problem that was based on a single point of view, and he constantly chided scientists for not being open-minded, for ignoring facts that could not be conveniently accommodated somewhere within the framework of science, and for their seeming objectivity that often amounted to not much more than bias. Thus, when the SPR was founded in England, James immediately saw its relevance to his own problems and hastened to establish a similar organization in America.

In addition to organizing the ASPR, James became personally involved in a number of enterprises related to spiritualism, mediumship, religion, and the paranormal. In the 1890s, he opposed bills before the Massachusetts legislature that required that mental healers pass an examination in medicine. James himself had paid a mental healer "ten or eleven visits." Even though the healer had not helped him, he believed mental healing should be allowed to continue because of the light it might throw on human functioning. He would not accept the idea that all human ills had a physical cause and were to be cured physically. His position and testimony before the State House of Representatives did not endear him to the medical profession. He wrote quite a number of articles on psychical research, both for popular magazines and for the *Proceedings* of both the SPR and the ASPR, discussed subjects like mediumship and the soul in his main psychological work, *Principles of Psychology*, referred to matters concerning psychical research in his correspondence, both briefly and at length, and delivered public lectures on the subject. The physical phenomena of mediums James wrote off as despicable fraud. His wondering about whether there was anything left in a medium's performance after the phenomena had been accounted for in terms of physical causes and coincidence stopped (almost) after he came across Mrs. Piper, a Boston medium, in 1885. He maintained an interest in her until his death. Mrs. Piper did not produce any physical manifestations. In her trance, however, she would produce information about the private lives of James' family members that he thought no one could have possibly known, and thus saw himself forced to accept the genuineness of Mrs. Piper. He did not believe that her information came from the spirit world, however. He thought, and Mrs. Piper at one time at least agreed with him, that she obtained her information telepathically. Richard Hodgson, the SPR investigator, also fell under the spell of Mrs. Piper, to the point that James thought Hodgson was quite obsessed with her. When Hodgson died suddenly in 1905, messages purportedly coming from Hodgson via Mrs. Piper began to arrive. James wrote a lengthy report on Mrs. Piper's Hodgson control (James, 1909/1960), concluding that the material received was "vastly more leaky and susceptible of naturalistic explanation than is any body of Piper material recorded before." Once again, James refused to make the final leap.

Fig. 9.2.   William James. (Notman photo; Library of Congress)

James's openness to new ideas, his caution of not generalizing beyond available facts, and his penchant for seeing both the subjective and objective side of any issue may appear to many individuals as an ideal worthy of emulation in matters concerning the occult and the paranormal. It is, however, a matter of one's personality; those in whom the tough-minded and tender-minded attitudes are nearly equally balanced, as they were in James, see it that way. Those in whom they are not will continue to favor the simpler solution of belief or disbelief.

and founding members was as distinguished as the one across the ocean, and included astronomers, psychologists, physiologists, and philosophers. Psychologists were particularly well represented. The ASPR differed from the British Society in two respects. One was that none of its members engaged in psychical research full time. The ASPR also lacked funds. This resulted in an initial dearth of publications and the absorption of the ASPR into the SPR in 1889. The other difference was that the motive that had drawn together the founding members of the ASPR was not a desire to give religion a scientific support or to prove the existence of spirits. Although none of them rejected the idea of spirits outright, they were much more cautious and skeptical than their English counterparts. They did not come to psychical research with preconceived ideas as to what they should find, not even James. Their approach at its most sanguine was still pragmatic. After all, they counted among their members the two men who were responsible for the creation of the philosophy of pragmatism, Charles Santiago Peirce and William James. When James thought he had found his "white crow" in Mrs. Piper, even that confession was in the nature of a temporary "let's pretend," as he once had pretended that he had a free will just to see if that hypothesis would work.

In 1907, the SPR dissolved its American branch, and James Harvey Hyslop made the ASPR a branch (Section B) of his American Institute for Scientific Research. Section A of that organization, which was supposed to study abnormal behavior, never came into existence, and only psychical research continued under Hyslop's direction until his death in 1920. Although Hyslop was the most prominent American psychical researcher during this period, he did not do much to advance psychical research. He was succeeded upon his death by Walter Franklin Prince, a minister and also a Ph.D. in psychology. It was also the year when William McDougall, then England's most prominent psychologist, arrived to teach at Harvard University. Among McDougall's beliefs that found little acceptance among his peers in America was a belief in a spirit world and a vital principle in humans that could separate from and act independently of the body. McDougall was almost immediately made President of the ASPR, with Prince as its principal research scientist.

The major event in the life of the ASPR during the 1920s was the investigation of the case of Mrs. LeRoi G. Crandon, better known as "Margery." Margery, a physical medium, emerged in the wake of an increased interest in spirits following World War I. In December of 1922, the magazine *Scientific American* offered a $2500 prize to anyone who could produce a "psychic photograph" or "visible psychic manifestation of other character" to the satisfaction of a specially constituted committee. The idea was that of J. Malcolm Bird, an associate editor of the magazine, who was also a psychical researcher and convinced spiritualist. Those who agreed to serve on the committee were Prince, McDougall, Hereword Carrington, and Daniel Comstock, a professor of physics, and the magician Harry Houdini. By mid-1924, Bird had discovered Margery. Under the control of her deceased brother Walter, Margery rang bells, moved tables, exuded ectoplasm, and received messages. The latter were unimportant, the most significant part of Margery's performance being physical manifestations, which were quite entertaining because Walter proved to be a wit and a prankster. The spirit capers of Walter were the ideal grist for the journalistic mills of the 1920s. After a few sittings with Margery, Houdini discovered fraud and, because the other committee members were reluctant to concede it, left the committee (Gibson & Young, 1953). Eventually, they too announced that there was nothing supernatural involved in Margery's performance. *Scientific American* printed their report and closed the contest. Several other investigations followed, however, with inconclusive or negative results. When in 1932 it was discovered that the spirit fingerprints left behind on a piece of wax (spirit fingerprints had become a specialty of Margery's) were those of Margery's dentist, very much alive, rather than of Walter, the Boston Society for Psychical Research published a report on it, describing Margery as the most ingenious and persistent fraud in the annals of psychical research.

Contemporary Research on Discarnate Survival.   Speculation, the seeking of proof, and beliefs about what happens after death have always been part of human society, and it is very unlikely that these speculations and attempts to find proof will cease in the future. The need to remove the uncertainty about what happens afterwards is too powerful. The approaches and methods used in data collection do change, however, following the lead of science. Currently, they are fitted to match the methodology used in social and behavioral sciences.

The physical, materialist model of an objective, measurable universe was the science model of the 19th century, and both psychological and psychical research tried to emulate it. The unconscious furnished the pivotal point around which speculation about people's mental life turned among both psychologists and psychical researchers. In the atomic age, speculations on the nature of the psychical turn on the interface between matter and energy, subatomic particles and quantum physics furnishing the models. In an age when psychology's concerns have been shifting from the human being as an organism to the human being as a person and a member of groups, large and small, the concerns of the psychical researcher have also shifted away from physical manifestations and towards the experiencing person who, it has been discovered, hallucinates things that seem to pertain to an afterlife just before he or she dies. The method used to research these experiences is the survey method of the social sciences, an analysis of the contents of the statements of persons who are experiencing death, and, on occasion, an analysis of their statistical structure using both descriptive and inferential statistics.

The psychiatrist Elisabeth Kübler-Ross, (1968) finds a basis for her belief in life after death in her interviews with many terminally ill patients and persons who, after having been declared clinically dead, revive. Moody (1975) analyzed the statements obtained from interviews with 150 individuals who had been declared "dead" and who revived, but avoided drawing conclusions concerning the possibility of an afterlife. Osis and Haraldsson (1977) conducted three survey studies, two in the United States and one in India, in which deathbed observations were gathered from doctors and nurses. The contents of statements made by 877 individuals were analyzed and evaluated statistically, including 163 cases of individuals who had recovered from apparent death. Osis and Haraldsson concluded that their data supported the afterlife hypothesis. Although they observed the expected cultural differences between the American and Indian samples (for instance, whereas a number of those Christian informants who saw religious figures just before death saw Jesus, none of the Hindus did, and neither did the Christians see any Hindu deities; Indians saw female figures very rarely, in accordance with their cultural bias), the main features of the experiences of both cultural groups were similar and resembled those reported by Kübler-Ross and Moody. These included the vision of living and dead persons, particularly relatives, and of mythological and religious personages in about 80% of the cases, which is about three times the incidence of hallucinations in the general population. "Survival-related" figures (dead persons and religious and mythological figures) predominated. Medical, demographic, and psychological factors appeared to be unrelated to the hallucinations. In 70 to 80% of the cases in which the dying person saw a human or religious figure, the purpose of the figure was to take the dying person away to another mode of existence. This occurred independently of the person's religious affiliation. Only about one-third of the reporting doctors and nurses were aware of whether a patient believed in an afterlife or not, however. Osis and Haraldsson note that 12 individuals who were known not to believe in an afterlife also saw apparitions. Belief did determine whether the apparition was of the "take-away" type or not in that more believers experienced the "take-away" type than those on whom the belief information was not available. The reaction of the majority of dying patients to impending death was serenity, peace, and religious emotion.

Although the type and frequency of deathbed hallucinations may be different from other kinds and may not be necessarily caused by drugs, fever, or a schizoid reaction to stress in the form of an escape into a pleasant fantasy from the shattering realization of impending death, data such as those produced by Osis and Harraldsson do not compel an interpretation in favor of the survival hypothesis. In our discussion of out-of-the-body experiences in individuals who seemingly die and are revived (Chapter 5), we noted that their experiences are not unique but have characteristics common to hallucinations experienced in other situations. Except for the features that are dictated by the specific nature of the experience of dying, such as the take-away personage, the visions of the dying are not unique either. There are, in addition, serious methodological problems with the surveys conducted by Osis and Haraldsson. The fact that only 20% of the individuals contacted in the American sample returned the questionnaire makes the data very questionable. This is further aggravated by the fact that none of the interviews were conducted in person by either Osis or Haraldsson, but were memories of doctors and nurses of events, some of which must have happened many years ago. This may also account for the differences between the descriptions of near-death experiences of the resuscitation type in the Osis and Haraldsson sample and those given by Moody. Osis and Haraldsson's cases fail to report the tunnel experience, for example, mention the panoramic recall of their lives less frequently, and do not seem to have any problem in describing their experience due to its ineffability, which Moody finds frequently to be the case.

It was noted earlier that when the material phenomena of the mediums failed to deliver a physical proof of survival, the activity of the spirits shifted to the realm of faith healing where it is difficult, if not impossible, to prove that, when an unusual reversal in the course of an illness takes place, spirits are not involved. The situation with survey data that are verbal descriptions of subjective experiences is similar: It is impossible to disprove the survival hypothesis with such data. What is possible is to offer an alternative interpretation that does not imply a body–mind duality, the existence of disembodied entities (which is suggested by Osis and Haraldsson), and that is therefore more parsimonious than the hypothesis of life after death.

In spite of the problems mentioned, there is a residual of similarity in deathbed and near-death experiences, whether they are reported from America of from a country that is in many respects its cultural opposite, India, and regardless of whether the individual who has the experience actually does die or does so only seemingly and may be resuscitated from the "dead." The other significant feature of these experiences is that they are modifiable in terms of the individual's past history and cultural background. The predisposition for a type of experience is there, but its particular form of manifestation is subject to learning. This is what Carl Gustav Jung called an archetype of the collective unconscious—a predisposition, impressed upon all humans because of their having shared the same universal experience over extremely long periods of time, to react to and apprehend the world in certain common ways. The deathbed experience may be considered an archetype, but it is not necessary to invoke this concept. Whether the individual is aware of it or not, the body as a biological system reacts to physical changes in itself, changes that presage death. Given the unity of body and mind, the reaction of the body to impending death must trigger off a corresponding subjective reaction that takes a visual–symbolic form and shows a common core from person to person and from one culture to another. Thus, the "take-away" personage arises logically from the recognition that, for the first time, one will be completely alone. This is such an elementary fact that the recognition may be said to be biological in nature and thus unconscious. The unconscious also produces the loving–guide image, which is thus a compensatory act of the psyche asserting our nature as social beings, totally dependent on others for our physical and psychological welfare. Who the "take-away" figure will be depends, however, on our personal history and cultural conditioning.

There is a current hypothesis that mediumship phenomena could be explained in terms of a sort of "super-ESP" whereby the medium obtains information through ESP either from the living sitters, other living persons, or from discarnate personalities, combines it and manifests it through her own personality. This hypothesis belongs in the same class as the hypothesis about spirit intervention in faith healing, about the existence of entities separable from the body (souls, spirits, discarnate personalities) to explain deathbed experiences, or the hypothesis that out-of-the-body experiences involve the splitting up of the individual into two parts. Because nothing is known about the laws under which ESP operates, it may be invoked to explain anything, including apparitions; e.g., a person has a precognition of his or her own death, which he or she dramatizes in an hallucinated form. In examining the current hypotheses of discarnate survival, namely that of the "survivalist" hypothesis (the entire personality continues to exist in some other mode), the continuity hypothesis (some aspect of the personality continues to exist), and the super-ESP hypothesis, Gauld (1977), who opts for the latter two as the viable alternatives, concludes, however, that they are currently at an impasse: "Each can produce some sort of explanation of the other's most cherished data." Gauld's article is particularly instructive in that it shows what the inevitable conclusion will be when even a person who would like to accept the survival hypothesis examines the evidence objectively, closely, and allows logic to take its course. After eliminating certain types of weak evidence for survival and limiting evidence only to cases of "apparent recrudescence of the personality of a person who has suffered bodily death," Gauld asserts that "without doubt we have evidence for survival." However, as his examination of the evidence progresses and arguments both for and against the three hypotheses are weighed, the case for survival becomes a very slippery affair. In the end, Gauld is left with the ESP hypothesis, which he favors in spite of cogent arguments against it. He then examines it and concludes that: (1) "the super-ESP hypothesis is silent on the laws and characteristics of ESP, so that we have no means of saying for certain whether or not it has been at work," and that (2) the models of ESP that say ESP is something like ordinary sense perception or that it is something like the transmission of information along a communications channel are "grossly implausible." He feels that ESP is a priori knowledge of matters of fact that is indifferent to the distinction between the present, the past, and the future and hence not subject to causation. This is quite true, although the conclusions drawn from this may not be necessarily those drawn by Gauld. Gauld does two things: He wants to make ESP the explanatory concept of mediumistic pheomena, and, at the same time, exclude ESP from being subject to the laws of physical nature. This automatically excludes both the question of discarnate survival and of ESP from the purview of scientific investigation and makes them entirely a matter of belief, on a par with the belief, for instance, in the dogma of the bodily assumption of Mary. Even though this dogma deals with an ostensibly physical fact, as a physical fact, it is in principle unprovable. Neither is discarnate survival or telepathy, as has been recently argued by the individual who has been responsible for starting parapsychological research, J. B. Rhine (1974b). The difference is that, in matters of faith, physical proof is neither expected nor offered, whereas the psychical researcher and the parapsychologist both expect and attempt to offer proof of what is in substance a matter of belief. Of this, more is said in Chapters 12 and 13.

PSYCHOMETRY

Psychometry refers to the "reading" of history of an object and of the people and events associated with it by individuals who claim to have the ability to do so. The term *psychometrics*, with which psychometry is sometimes confused, has no occult connotations whatsoever. It is a field of psychology that deals with the measurement of individual differences by means of psychological tests.

The assumption that underlies psychometry is that inanimate matter —clothing, articles of personal use, furniture, buildings, the ground— somehow record and retain and therefore can trigger off an impression of the characteristics of humans and human events that have been associated with them: A comb may tell not only the color of the hair that is on the head of the person who uses it, but also what is inside that head, such as personality disposition; a shoe that belongs to a lost child may tell where the child is; a murder weapon may tell the "sensitive" who the murderer was, and so on. The mechanism whereby an object serves as a gateway to its owner and the owner's condition is never stated, however. There is talk about influences, emanations, impressions, and vibrations, all suggesting some kind of energy transfer, but what kind of energy is transferred and how is left unspecified. Needless to say, science recognizes no energies or mechanisms whereby an individual's personality, experiences, or other events may become invisibly impressed upon any object that has not been appropriately prepared (e.g., photographic film or a magnetic tape). What is quite apparent is that psychometry, like the belief in an afterlife, is another instance of the wish to transcend the limitations of the physical body, to make objective (reify) that that is subjective, and to be able to pass back and forth between the objective and the subjective, thus demonstrating both their duality and reality.

The modern founder and promoter of psychometry was Joseph Rhodes Buchanan, a self-appointed "professor" and "doctor" of very dubious academic qualifications. A scientific crank and shady practitioner of strange arts, he would have occasional run-ins with the law. In the 1840s, Buchanan developed the practice of assessing personal influences that clung to an object by placing the object against the forehead of a "sensitive." In 1885, he published a *Manual of Psychometry*, modestly subtitled "The Dawn of a New Civilization," wherein he also offered the service of "psychometric readings" at two and five dollars each. A specialty that developed among Buchanan's followers was the psychometrizing of signatures held to the forehead. Others generalized his method to other fields, such as geology; placing a rock from, say, the Carbon Age to one's forehead evoked visions of tropical forests, reptiles, and so on. Crime detection could be simplified enormously because detectives and witnesses could be dispensed with. History and archeology held the greatest promise: The exact history of a culture could be read by just holding one of its artifacts to one's forehead.

Psychic archeology is by no means a curiosity of the 19th century. In 1920, an archeologist by the name of Bond published an account of how, by using information supplied by way of automatic writing by a "sensitive," John Alleyne, he was able to excavate previously unknown parts of the Glastonbury Abbey in England. The hand of John Alleyne was presumably being guided by the builders of the abbey. Bond's tale shows clearly that he had been a strong believer in the occult even before he undertook psychic archeology. It is also clear that the information allegedly provided by discarnate spirits and not otherwise available could have been gathered from available historical records and from on-site observations and deductions. At least some anthropologists and archeologists avail themselves of the sevices of "sensitives" even today (Long, 1977). Other practicing psychometrists make themselves available to law enforcement agencies. Some, such as Peter Hurkos and Gerard Croiset, have thereby gained international fame. Unfortunately, there is little officially documented evidence available concerning the solution of cases that have involved the cooperation of psychics and the police. The reports in the believer literature are sensational. Enquiries with police officials, however, reveal that the involvement of the psychics has not been very helpful, and that second-hand reports are often in gross error, tending towards an exaggerated positive view of the psychic's abilities (cf. Hansel, 1966, Chapter 14).

Neither anthropological-archeological psychometry nor psychometry used in crime detection is conducted under controlled conditions, because the main purpose of the procedure is to achieve practical results and not to test the validity of the claims of the psychic. As is the case with dowsing, the psychic picks up considerable information from the sensory clues that are available, but of which the archeologist or police detective may not be aware at the time. They also use information that is already available on the case and, like Sherlock Holmes, may make some "elementary" and correct deductions that may not appear quite as elementary to the principal investigators. There is also considerable "fishing" for information, which is used to good advantage. All factors considered, psychometry works no better than other methods. All "sensitives" make mistakes. They are partially wrong many times, and entirely wrong some of the time. However anomalistic their method, their results do not surpass those obtained by ordinary methods of detection. This may be asserted of any results obtained in connection with paranormal phenomena when these can be evaluated statistically and compared with some standard, as is evident when we examine the results of parapsychological research.

A variant of psychometry is provided by the type of anecdote that tells how a person, by being at a certain place, usually rich in history, at a certain time, usually an anniversary, is suddenly transported from the present time to the time that is significantly associated with the site and experiences historical events as they occurred then. The idea is that locations, buildings, and grounds that are historically pregnant also serve as a species of three-dimensional auditory and visual record that may become activated at certain times and under certain circumstances, allowing an appropriately sensitive person to reexperience the historical events recorded. The best-known example is the vacation visit of two English schoolteachers to Versaille in August of 1901. The teachers, Charlotte Anne Moberly and Eleanor Jourdain, were walking towards the Petit Trianon, lost their way, and suddenly found themselves in the Versailles as it looked in 1789, with people in the historically appropriate costumes, including Marie Antoinette herself. They described their adventure under pseudonyms in 1911 (Moberly & Jourdain, 1955). The book was a success, saw several editions, and was eventually published under their own names. Moberly and Jourdain spent the time between the adventure and the completion of the manuscript researching French historical documents to verify, to their own satisfaction, that their observations had been historically accurate. It is clear from their account, however, that their experience, real as it must have appeared to them, was a creation of their own minds. Miss Moberly was very well acquainted with French history of the 18th century. The historical researches of the two women over the years must have served the purpose of verification as much as it served the purpose of providing missing information with which to fill the gaps in their story and to restructure it retrospectively. It is significant that they did not talk to each other about the incident until a week after it had happened. Apparently, the experience (which may have been only Moberly's) did not appear as extraordinary at the time as it turned out to be in retrospect. It cannot be believed, as they aver, that they each prepared a preliminary account of it without consulting each other. It took them another 9 years to prepare the short manuscript of *An Adventure*. There must have been a large amount of retrospective falsification of memory. The terms used by the two women to describe their feelings while walking through the 18th-century grounds of the Versailles reveal that the current stimulation was triggering off images of paintings, tapestries, and stage sets that they had seen before and was combining them with the real scene; they felt as if they were in a dream, an unnaturally oppressive, dream-like atmosphere pervaded everything. They wrote (Moberly & Jourdain, 1955): "Everything suddenly looked unnatural, therefore unpleasant; even the trees behind the building seemed to have become flat and lifeless, like a wood worked in tapestry. There were no effects of light and shade and no wind stirred in the trees. It was all intensely still."

Even though superficially, the basic pattern of the Versailles adventure is that of psychometry on a grand scale, it does not involve either the use of subtle clues, logical inference, or even ESP. Rather, it was an hallucinatory experience that grew from a fascination by a particular historical period and factual information about that period that was translated into an imaginary overlay on an actual scene bearing the remnants of that period, plus considerable retrospective falsification nourished by information acquired after the fact, plus possibly an instance of a *folie à deux* (cf. Chapters 8 and 10). Other instances of quasi psychometric time travel bear the same hallmarks as the adventure of Charlotte Ann Moberly and Eleanor Jourdain.

NOTES

Moore's (1977) In Search of White Crows is an outstanding survey of the history of spiritualism, psychical research, and parapsychology. It reflects on the cultural, sociological, and psychological aspects of the beliefs involved, the interactions between individual psychologies and the social, economic, and cultural trends of the time, and, without categorically denying the possibility that there is anything to the phenomena described, casts an occasionally bemused look at the psychical events of the 19th and 20th centuries.

Chapters 14, 15, and 16 in Hansel's (1966) devastating but irrefutable critique of ESP are given to strange experiences, spiritualism, and mental mediums. They may be considered required reading for anyone interested in learning the down-to-earth facts about these subjects.

Spiritualism is no longer socially significant in America and England, but it is in Brazil, where there are four major spirit religions and several minor ones. Of the four major ones, three stem from the African Yoruba tradition, imported with the Black slaves in mid-16th century, and one from the writings of Allan Kardec, a French spiritualist (who called his brand of belief spiritism), whose writings became immensely popular in Portuguese translation in the mid-19th century. A brief history of Brazilian spiritualism and a description of present-day practices may be found in Chapter 4 of Krippner and Villoldo (1976).

The first "spirit photographs" were taken in 1861. Photographing the ghosts of the departed became a popular feature of spiritualism and a source of income to the photographer who offered to produce photographs of dead relatives on demand. The history of spirit photography, along with numerous reproductions, has been written by Gettings (1978). Although Gettings believes that a small number of the photographs, especially the earlier ones, are genuine spirit photographs, he holds that the majority of them are fraudulent. Gettings's book is also interesting because in it Gettings furnishes proof that the famous "Cottingley Fairies" photographs were faked. In 1917, 16-year-old Elsie Wright took a picture of her 10-year-old friend, Frances Ealing, in the woods, surrounded by several fairies. Sir Arthur Connan Doyle, who had begun to write a book on fairies, published the photograph in his book, endorsing its genuineness. In 1977, Gettings came across a drawing of fairies by Claude A. Shepperson for a book published in 1915. There can be no doubt by looking at Shepperson's drawing that the fairies were a copy of his vignette, cut from cardboard and positioned in the grass in front of Frances Ealing. By looking through the photographs in Gettings's book, one cannot help but be constantly amazed that anyone should ever have been taken in by obvious double exposures of photographs taken during the deceased person's lifetime, phosphorescent paintings, flat pictures, people masquerading as ghosts, and an occasional light reflection or light seeping through a faulty camera that looks like part of a person. The Cottingley Fairies affair is also treated by Jastrow (1935/1962), who classified it as a hoax, even though there was no direct proof of it. It is an excellent illustration of the fact that allegedly occult phenomena may remain classified as occult for a very long time and used as proof of esoteric beliefs because no natural explanation is immediately available. It took 60 years for the evidence to surface in the case of the fairy photographs.

The term "ectoplasm" was coined by the French physiologist Charles Richet, whose life span (1850–1935) coincides with the age of spiritualism from its beginning to its decline. Richet earned the Nobel prize in physiology in 1913. He did not find it incompatible with physiology to pursue psychical research (which he called "metapsychics"), do experiments on telepathy, believe in mediums like Eusapia Palladino, and in the genuineness of ectoplasm, although this substance, when examined, has turned out to be nothing more esoteric than gauze, cotton, or paper secreted in the medium's mouth, nose, ears, secret compartments of such objects as combs, or even the vagina.

A good discussion of the physics and the psychology of the physical manifestations of the medium is given by Rawcliffe (1959, Chapter 20). Chapter 21 of this work presents the doings of Eusapia Palladino and her misadventures in America. Similar accounts are given by Jastrow (1935/1962), Hansel (1966), and Christopher (1970). The latter work has a delightful chapter on the history of 19th-century table tilting. Hereward Carrington's *The Physical Phenomena of Spiritualism* (1908) is a monumental work on fraudulent 19th-century spiritualism.

An account of the Colombo affair and Richard Hodgson's investigation of H. P. Blavatsky's miracles may be found in a number of sources. A brief but adequate one is in Edwards (1977). A more detailed one may be found in Williams (1946), which is an excellent biography of Madame Blavatsky.

All of James's contributions to psychical research are in the collection compiled and edited by Murphy and Ballou (1960).

Harry Houdini describes in detail his role in the Margery case and his unmasking of Margery and her husband as frauds in Gibson and Young (1953). Chapter 4 of this work presents contemporary documents, verbal exchanges, including Houdini's testimony before the United States House of Representatives, and many drawings illustrating how Margery performed her tricks. In describing the behavior of J. M. Bird, Houdini offers a good illustration of the effect of belief on how one confronts unpalatable facts. Tietze (1973) has written a book describing the Margery case.

Recently, a group of eight psychical researchers at the Toronto Society for Psychical Research have produced a wholly imaginary "spirit" who, nevertheless, communicates with the group by means of raps and table movements. The seances with Philip, the name given to the imaginary spirit, are described by two of the researchers, Owen and Sparrow (1976).

A sober, objective, and exhaustive review of the theories of discarnate survival, the arguments for and against, and the evidence available, especially evidence provided by the mental medium, has been written by Gauld (1977). An extensive (242 items) bibliography is part of the article. Alcock (1979) has written a very useful paper on near-death experiences, offering a critique from the psychological point of view.

A summary of the adventure of Moberly and Jourdain is provided by Wallechinsky and Wallace (1975), and a critical appraisal of it by Jastrow (1935/1962).

10 Psychopathology And Magic

Giving up witchcraft is in effect giving up the Bible.

John Wesley

He who believes in the Devil, already belongs to him.

Thomas Mann, *Doctor Faustus*

Fascination with anomalous behavior is as old as humanity, and attempts to explain it are an integral part of human history and the age-old struggle for knowledge. Historically, anomalies have been an ideological battleground for a series of conceptual conflicts between competing systems of explanation. On the surface, the issue has been how to explain the unusual and discontinuous aspects of experience, but the deeper, more enduring debate has focused on how the universe and, in particular, humanity was to be conceptualized. At first, the struggle was between traditional beliefs and naturalism; later, it was between rejuvenated paganism and Christianity, and more recently, religion and science have defined the essence of the controversy.

A point of contention in this debate has frequently been abnormal behavior or what is now termed *psychopathology*. Psychopathology and magic have been inextricably linked historically. Only very recently have naturalistic explanations of human behavior (whether normal or aberrant) gained any sort of popular acceptance. Although the history of thought contains numerous examples of ideas proposing natural, physiological, or psychological determinants of disordered behavior, throughout much of human history, anomalous behavior has been presumed to have supernatural origins, and at times, little distinction has been made between insanity, demon possession, witchcraft, and magic.

PSYCHOPATHOLOGY

Psychopathology refers to those behaviors variously described as insanity, lunacy, mental illness, psychological disturbance, and so on. Unfortunately, psychopathology is not a unitary concept whose nature is completely understood. In fact, there is wide diversity of opinion as to exactly what

296

behaviors can be reliably associated with the conditions of psychopathology, and comparable disagreement regarding its root cause. Like its theoretical predecessor, physical illness, psychopathology is an overly inclusive term that, at times, has been used to refer to behaviors varying from the overt symptoms of brain pathology to inadequate psychological functioning and even immorality.

Definition

Despite such conceptual diversity, however, there is general consensus regarding certain features of psychopathology. For example, it is now assumed by theorists that unusual behaviors that may be designated as psychopathological are naturally occurring phenomena created by natural causes,—that is, psychopathology emerges from the interplay of the same behavioral determinants responsible for all behavior, whether anomalous or commonplace. Also, psychopathology is generally accepted to be multidetermined, stemming from genetic, neurological, experiential, intrapsychic, and situational forces, or various combinations of these. Although differing theories will emphasize differing aspects of causation, it is now generally acknowledged that no single determining factor will be found and that quite different theories may subsume at least a portion of the phenomenon of psychopathology.

Psychopathology is regarded as a psychological state or pattern of behavior that deviates from some ideal condition of adjustment, maturity, well-being, and so on, although often, the exact criteria of the ideal state are left unspecified (Coleman, 1972). Also, it is widely acknowledged that the perspective from which judgments about abnormality are made may influence what is considered to be abnormal. For example, someone experiencing severe marital problems might label himself or herself as "disturbed," whereas a psychiatrist might not, but another person who claims to be Napoleon reincarnated might maintain that his mental status is intact, whereas a psychiatrist would tend to disagree. Psychopathological behavior is ordinarily considered to be a negative and detrimental state in which the person displays a disturbance in some aspect of experience, such as cognition, feeling, communication, conduct, and so on, which interferes or prevents an effective or satisfying life style. Finally, a central defining principle of psychopathology is that the person involved either has or appears to have little or no voluntary control over the occurrence of the problematic behaviors (Page, 1975).

Regardless of the specific orientation one adopts towards the issue of psychopathology, however, it is clear that unusual and detrimental behavior is an integral part of the human condition. Every known language has at least one term for disordered behavior (Page, 1975), and despite tremendous differences between societies regarding what is considered acceptable and "healthy" behavior, there are basic commonalities in manifestations of psychopathology across societies, although cultural differences do result in different constellations of "symptoms" and different rates of seriousness and frequency (Meth, 1974). Also, it is clear that such disorders have existed throughout history in one form or another (Arieti & Bemporad, 1974). What has typically changed historically and differed across cultures have been the principles used to explain and understand abnormal behavior.

The Supernatural Connection

The close conceptual relationship between abnormal behavior and magic probably derives from the irrational and involuntary appearance of psychopathology. Under certain conditions, some people behave in such a bizarre and unusual manner that it gives the impression that they are no longer in control of their faculties and are instead controlled by external, possibly evil forces. For example, the "disturbed person" may exhibit any of the following: seeing visions or hearing voices not discernible to others; verbalizing fantastic tales of accomplishment, blame, disease or nonexistence that defy possibility; showing signs of mutism, paralysis, insensitivity to pain or other physical conditions without evidence of underlying organic pathology or cause; appearing disoriented, unaware of personal identity, unable to think or reason, to be more than one person; remaining motionless and apparently unresponsive to external stimuli; engaging in wild, impulsive, frantic, violent, self-destructive, and other apparently pointless bursts of behavior, and so on.

Often, the link between abnormal behavior and extraordinary forces is even more direct, such as when a person claims to hear the voice of devils, spirits and the like, or directs responsibility for his or her own (usually socially unacceptable) actions on the influence of external forces such as demons, space creatures, computers, etc. Both severe (psychosis) and mild (neurosis) forms of psychopathology may involve apparently supernatural causes. One remarkable pattern of abnormality that easily lends itself to supernatural interpretations is the phenomenon of *folie à deux* in which one person incorporates the pathological behavior (e.g., delusions) of another person (Gralnick, 1942). In one study of over 100 such cases, it was found that sister–sister and husband–wife combinations were the most common, but other relationship pairs can also result in *folie à deux*. It is more common in persons who have known one another for some time. On the surface, *folie à deux* may appear to be magically contagious and it may also appear to involve some form of telepathy because the manner in which one person acquires the beliefs and behaviors of another cannot always be observed directly and thus may not be known. However, it is assumed that the adoption of pathology occurs by the ordinary psychological processes of observation, imitation, and learning.

In everyday experience, how one acts is basically predictable as individuals abide by the subtle but pervasive social customs and norms that prescribe certain types of responses for certain situations. By contrast, disordered behavior is by its very nature unpredictable and unresponsive from the perspective of ordinary social expectations, and this, too, may contribute to the impression of irrationality and external control. Thus, from prehistoric times until the 18th century, the predominant view of psychopathology has apparently been supernatural both among popular and scholarly observers, and to some extent the residual of this ancient perspective may be found even today.

THE ORIGINS OF MAGIC AND DEMONOLOGY

Ancient and Nonliterate Concepts

Among ancient civilizations, the belief in magic was closely related to the world view of *animism*, or the belief that all objects are alive in the sense of possessing a spirit. The influence of animism on the magical thinking of ancient peoples was extensive. The universe was populated with numerous spirits and forces. Although friendly spirits were believed to exist, there were more objects to fear than to trust. The all-inclusive concept of spirits in ancient civilizations has been described by Seligmann (1948):

> From time immemorial, man has felt himself to be confronted with evil supernatural beings, and his weapon against them has been the use of magical rites. Spirits lurked everywhere. Larvae and lemures lived beneath the earth; vampires escaped from the dead to attack the living; Namtar (pestilence) and Idpa (fever) plagued the cities. Night was ruled by the demons of evil, of the desert, of the abyss, of the sea, of the mountains, of the swamp, of the south wind. There were the succubi and incubi, carriers of obscene nightmares; the snare-setting Maskim; the evil Utuq, dweller of the desert; the bull demon Telal; and Alal the destroyer. People's minds were dominated by malign demons who demanded sacrifices and prayers. . . . Not only were the demons to be feared; but also within man himself lived dangerous powers. If magic was a protector, it was likewise a destroyer, a formidable weapon in the hands of criminals who used it to attain evil ends. The sorcerer believed himself to be beyond laws and religious commandments, casting spells and reciting incantations to kill at random [pp. 1-2].

The animistic world view gave rise to many ancient magical practices and occultisms including astrology, divination, numerology, the idea of transmigration of souls, etc., and in general was indistinguishable from the religious beliefs of many peoples of the ancient world.

Also with animism arose the view of abnormal behavior that was to dominate for centuries, that of *demonology*. Not recognizing the multitude of experiential and neurological influences that can result in bizarre and unusual behavior, ancient people have generally incorporated explanations for abnormal behavior into their larger world view by positing the existence of spirits that take command of the disturbed person's soul or mind, resulting in the outward behavioral manifestations of psychopathology. References to mental disorders among the writings of early Chinese, Egyptian, Hebrew, Greek, and other civilizations make it clear that the demonological view was the common answer to the problems posed by psychopathology (Coleman, 1972). The types of behaviors exhibited determined the type of spirit believed to be in possession of the afflicted person. For example, if the person's actions appeared to have religious or mystical significance and if they were not recalcitrant, good or friendly spirits were presumed to be in residence, whereas evil spirits were attributed to those whose behavior was unmanageable and destructive. A form of this view persisted during the Homeric period in Greece where it was believed that angry gods took away the mind of the afflicted (Kisker, 1972).

The magical–demonological approach to explaining disordered behavior was the product on intuitive and mystical systems of knowledge combined with hit-and-miss empirical observations of nature by nonliterate and ancient societies (Alexander & Selesnick, 1966). Among such people, simple and obvious cause-and-effect relationships were recognized and correctly identified (e.g., overeating causes discomfort), but where complexity and subtlety disguised the true nature of an ailment, magical thinking filled the void by ascribing the cause to the malevolent intentions of other people or superhuman beings.

By possession or entrapment of the soul, the evil sorcerer or spirit directly caused the outward manifestations of disease and disturbance and, accordingly, a central concept of ancient treatment for both physical and psychological aberration was various procedures designed to free or drive the evil spirit from the afflicted person. For example, contemporary scholars have speculated that one ancient treatment called *trephining* (i.e., creating an opening in the skull of an afflicted person) was for the purpose of releasing the spirits presumed to be the cause of the affliction. Other procedures that emerged from the dawn of civilization, but that are better documented included exorcism (e.g., prayer, incantations, noisemaking, bribery, and appeals) to coax the evil spirit out of the afflicted, and physical abuse (e.g., torture, flogging, starvation, purgatives) to make the body of the afflicted such an unpleasant place that the demon would become discouraged and leave. The idea that there is something malignant inside the deviant person that requires harsh treatment to remedy proved to be an enormously persistent one. An important sequence of events that was apparently repeated several times throughout history concerned the fact that although treatment of abnormal behavior originated with medicine men and shamans, it was eventually taken over in many societies by priests because of the religious connotations of the concept of spirits (Coleman, 1972). This factor is probably responsible in part for the eventual tendency to view the disturbed person as a religious sinner.

There is some evidence that concepts of abnormality among the nonliterate societies of today are generally analogous to those of the ancients. For example, Clements (1932) suggested that there are five dominant concepts of disturbance (both physical and behavioral) among nonliterate societies, including spirit possession, loss of soul, taboo violation, sorcery, and object intrusion. Similar to ancient ideas about abnormality and magic, these views assume an animistic world view and supernatural causation.

The role of magic has been fundamental to the views of some societies. The human need to understand is pervasive, but its expression is dependent on and shaped by the cultural, philosophical, and ideological realities in a given place, at a given time. Explanations cannot transcend available or conceivable concepts; therefore, among nonliterate societies, magic emerges as a scientifically inaccurate but genuine attempt to understand the influence of nature.

For example, Tylor (1931) suggested that magic derives from the underlying belief in *animism,* or the idea that all objects possess a spirit that causes the characteristic actions of the object. Water flows, winds blow, trees grow, and so on, because of a pantheon of gods, spirits, and supernatural forces residing therein. Tylor theorized that animism resulted from a confusion between analogy and causality—that is, analogous objects and processes were assumed to contain a causal connection. In animism, that part of the universe not understood is anthropomorphized by attributing to it known qualities. Thus, to understand the behavior of inanimate objects, the concepts of human experience (e.g., human motives, emotions, attitudes, etc.) are applied.

Borrowing from Tylor, James Frazer (1931) identified the principle of *sympathetic magic* as the belief that like affects like. In its various forms, sympathetic magic comprises both the explanation and the remedy for many threatening processes, such as disease among tribal societies. Things looking the same (similarity) or once connected (contiguity) are assumed to contain a degree of sympathy or causal influence. Thus, an evil sorcerer may be believed to be able to use an object formerly belonging or relating to an intended victim, such as a piece of fingernail, a lock of hair, or an image, as a means of inflicting harm. The object is subjected to abuse with the expectation that the same effect will befall the victim. Correspondingly, the principles of sympathetic magic can be invoked to ward off or remedy such evil influences.

Jahoda (1969) has suggested that it is important to distinguish between errors of logic and irrationality. The concepts of animism and sympathetic magic, although scientifically erroneous, are nevertheless useful to the groups to which they are relevant both as an instrument of destruction and a cure, as well as a system of explanation. As these beliefs are deeply entrenched in the world view on nonliterate groups, sympathetic influence can actually occur due to the effects of suggestion, for example. Similarly, Tylor argued that these concepts are functional where believed because, for example, in some cases the desired effects are brought about by deliberate human actions, they are often used for natural processes that would take place regardless, failures are rationalized as poorly constructed magic or the effects of more powerful magic, and only occasional successes are adequate to maintain the belief. Although these theories of the origins of magic have been expanded and altered by more recent anthropological work, they do suggest how magical ideas might arise from the predominant world view of a given society.

Naturalism

Demonological assumptions and harsh treatment have not always dominated, however. For example, the practitioners at the medical temples of Asclepius in Greece (c. 800 B.C.) employed rather humane forms of treatment for psychopathological behaviors, such as prayer, kindness, suggestion, relaxation, and recreation, although their theory of abnormality was decidedly demonological (Kisker, 1972). It was also widely believed in Greece that certain forms of abnormality, such as epilepsy, were divinely inspired possessions to be valued rather than feared.

A serious challenge to the concept of spirit possession was posed by the ideas of Hippocrates (460–367 B.C.), the Greek physician who, because of his innovations in medical thinking, is often called the father of medicine (Alexander & Selesnick, 1966). Hippocrates rejected domonological interpretations, even the positive ones, and taught that disease is the consequence of an imbalance among what were believed to be the four basic humors of the body: blood, black bile, yellow bile, and phlegm. In addition, Hippocrates anticipated the homeostatic theories of today as well as promoting the idea that disease as well as disordered behavior resulted from the functioning of natural physiological processes and that the brain was the most important organ in determining human experience. Accordingly, this approach has become known as *naturalism*. For example, Hippocrates rejected the traditional view that epilepsy was a "sacred disease," insisting that it, too, resulted from an underlying pathology of the brain. The rationalism of the classical Greek era produced several other advances in naturalistic thinking.

But the influence of mystical explanations also remained strong. For example, although Plato (427-347 B.C.) acknowledged the role of physiological processes and recommended humane treatment, he also taught that some forms of abnormality were mystical,—for example, "delirium," which he believed to be caused by the gods. On the other hand, whereas Aristotle (384-322 B.C.) endorsed Hippocratic concepts, he specifically rejected the possibility of psychological factors (e.g., emotional conflicts) in the development of psychopathology. Subsequent Greek and Roman physicians and scholars expanded Hippocratic concepts, but traditional and superstitious ideas proved to be too entrenched. Except in Arabia where enlightened practices continued for some time, the "Dark Ages" in psychopathology and medicine probably began with the death of Galen (131-200 A.D.), the last of the great Roman physicians. The influence of naturalism proved to be relatively brief in the Western World and disappeared almost entirely before reemerging during the Renaissance. For hundreds of years, Europe returned to the supernatural explanation of demon possession to understand and treat unusual behavior.

Strange Behavior and Magical Beliefs

One consequence of the demonological concept, particularly during the Middle Ages, was the development of supernatural explanations for virtually any anomalous, strange, and possible pathological behaviors. One such pattern is known as *lycanthropy*, or the belief that one can change into a wolf or other animals. There are numerous examples of individuals who imagined themselves to be wolves and imitated their actions (Coleman, 1972). Although possibly the result of psychopathological states, such claims appeared authentic at the time because the animistic idea that the soul of one entity could invade and control the body of a person was taken for granted. Although prominent much later (in the 18th century), the belief in *vampires* or the living dead who rose from the grave in the flesh to prey on the living at night was taken seriously in Russia, Poland, Hungary, and Greece (Seligmann, 1948). Again, the belief was rooted in the concepts and theories of the time. It was widely believed, for example, that the dead experienced hunger and that blood was the essence of life. On very rare occasions, individuals claiming to be wolves or vampires are still encountered in the practice of clinical psychology and psychiatry. In modern cases, the delusional nature of such claims appears to be more definitive because they lack the supportive influence of popular beliefs. Similarly, other medieval beliefs in ghosts, poltergeists, devils, possessions, and so on, were not psychopathological aberrations in the modern sense, but rather, commonplace ideas about how nature worked. The role of psychological factors, such as abnormal behavior, was to legitimize and reinforce what was already believed. The widespread belief in vampires might be strengthened by the assertions of the disturbed person who actually claimed to be one, but they did not cause the belief.

The so-called dancing manias of the Middle Ages, which were apparently instances of mass hysteria or suggestion, were also influenced by supernatural conceptions about behavior. Called the *St. Vitus dance* in most of Europe, participants would dance for hours, eventually resulting in delirium and frenzied actions, and finally exhaustion. Some participants would later report vivid hallucinations during the dance, such as seeing faces or being dowsed with blood, whereas others would report no memory for the event or insensitivity to what was happening around them while dancing (Page, 1975). In Italy, similar episodes of frantic dancing were called *tarantism* due to the erroneous belief that the compulsion to dance was caused by the bite of a tarantula. The dancing manias took on special significance because they were interpreted as instances of demonic possession, probably due to the fact that the participants acted as if they were possessed and out of control. More likely, such episodes were probably attempts to resurrect the pagan rituals of antiquity, which had been suppressed by Christianity. Such explanations were, of course, generally unavailable to the medieval mind, however.

In the discussion of occult beliefs (see Chapter 7), the influence of existing beliefs and expectations on responses to anomalous and even mundane events was stressed. An important point to keep in mind about most of human experience is that such expectations have historically not been restricted to individuals or subcultural groups. Instead, supernatural concepts have typically been dominant among both intellectual and popular circles. The conceptual context of demonology is particularly relevant to the phenomenon of witchcraft, the topic to which we now turn.

WITCHCRAFT

For hundreds of years, particularly in 17th-century Europe, witchcraft was thought of as demonstrable reality and taken for granted by almost everyone. The period of the witch persecutions was a dramatic and appalling spectacle, a human tragedy based on incredible ignorance and fear on both the side of the persecuted and the persecutors.

Characteristics of Witchcraft

Beliefs about witchcraft varied from country to country and across time. Eventually, the activities of witchcraft came to include virtually any alleged form of magic or sorcery. There is no doubt that some people actually believed themselves to be sorcerers and witches and actually practiced diabolical rites. But beliefs about what actions constituted witchcraft varied from innocent pagan customs to the impossible. For example, at one time or another, witches included those persons who allegedly possessed or manifested the following characteristics and behaviors: riding a stick at night; changing into animal forms; the evil eye; the use of charms, incantations, superstitions, words, images, spells, baneful herbs, magic potions, poisons, and ointments; evil works against men, beasts, property; influencing nature, creating supernatural things, necromancy, conjuring ghosts, raising spirits, causing crop failures, natural disasters, and bad weather; prophecy, astrology, fortunetelling, soothsaying, and divination by means of lots, stars, entrails, air, images, bones, figures, fire, water, calculation, numbers; being wise and revealing secret things; bloodsucking and the use of blood in ceremonies; juggling or curing diseases through magic; pacts with the devil to do evil, calling demons, consorting with demons and devils, possession of a familiar, witches teat, or devil's mark; lewd lusts and behavior at nocturnal sabbat orgies; killing by poison or with the help of demons, killing and eating babies; delivering one's children to the devil, etc. (Robbins, 1959).

Ostensibly, one important clue to witchcraft was attendance at a *sabbat* (see the insert later in this chapter), which, although they may have been actually practiced by some as a sort of alcohol-induced free-for-all, was believed by many to be the celebration of the devil's power and an incredibly licentious and evil orgy involving all manner of perversion, from illicit and indiscriminate sexual relations between humans and incorporeal beings and humans and animals, to the grisly habit of eating cooked babies. The sabbat was also believed to be the initiation rite for witches at which the devil marked his accessories with the sign of evil fidelity called the devil's mark. Another supposed clue to witchcraft was the possession of a *familiar*, believed to be the incarnate form of a demon (e.g., as a goat, bird, cat, etc.), which aided the witch in his or her evil activities. Similarly the belief that witches could fly, change into animals at will, afflict persons, crops, and animals with spells, and even control the weather were commonplace assumptions accepted as both true and frequent.

For roughly three centuries, the idea of witchcraft gripped Europe in what often amounted to a reign of terror. Although magic, sorcery, and witchcraft had been practiced from the beginning of human history, the wholesale and institutionalized persecution of witches occurred mostly between 1450 and 1750 and mostly in Western Europe, although one period of witch trials occurred in the New World at Salem, Massachusetts, in the 1690s. Contrary to popular opinion, the witch persecutions were less a product of the Middle Ages than of the social and political ferment of the Renaissance. There was no compelling reason for the persecutions during the Middle Ages when the authority of the Church and the feudal lords was absolute. The peak of the witch persecutions was around 1600. Roughly 200,000 accused men, women, and children (sometimes as young as 3 or 4 years) from various stations of life were executed, most by being burned. The victims and the methods of the witch persecutions varied from one location to another. In England, the victims were primarily women from the lower classes, whereas in Germany, the educated and wealthy were often the principal targets of the inquisitors (Robbins, 1959). It is also generally acknowledged that the victims of persecution were often simply social deviants or minorities of various kinds, including the insane and feeble-minded, gypsies, Jews, polygamists, scientists, Protestants, Calvinists, or anyone not devoutly Catholic. However, despite the initial victimization of Protestants, the Reformation did little to slow the growth of witch hunting, as Protestants also created their own brand of fanatical orthodoxy.

Prior to the middle of the 14th century, witchcraft was often equated with simple sorcery, the remnants of traditional pagan beliefs and practices (Seligmann, 1948). It was not really a religion so much as the rural belief, stemming from animism, that nature was alive with spirits who could be controlled or at least influenced by the performance of magical rites. Although opposed by the Church for theological reasons, ecclesiastical authorities were not united in their opposition, and thus punishment for witchcraft was haphazard and lenient by medieval standards. During the 14th century, however, the Church began to define witchcraft as *Christian heresy*—a treason against God—and although the alleged indicators previously listed were considered to be manifestations of witchcraft, it became essentially a crime of thought, loyalty, motives, and attitude. The objection was not so much to magic, or more precisely miracles, for miracles wrought by God were, of course, accepted by the Church. Rather, the definition of the offense centered on miracles accomplished with the aid of demons or the devil. Even *white magic*, the use of magical powers to do good, became a form of witchcraft. Church authorities (and later civil authorities as well) began to authorize the existing inquisition to prosecute sorcerers. For example, in 1484, Pope Innocent VIII issued a papal bull that authorized the systematic persecution of witches. In 1486, the *Malleus Maleficarum* (The Witches Hammer) appeared and became the theological and procedural text for prosecuting witches. Witch persecutions eventually spread beyond the Inquisition and throughout Europe.

Witch Hunting and Persecution

Because of the ideological nature of the crime and the incredible fear and fanaticism associated with its persecution, any sort of reasonable or logical rules of testimony and evidence became irrelevant at the witch trials (Robbins, 1959). For example, several criteria were established to determine witchcraft. But proving these imaginary crimes was understandably difficult and therefore more practical means for determining who was a witch quickly emerged. For example, any scar, blemish, mole, etc., was easily determined to be a *devil's mark* (i.e., signifying a child of the devil) or witches' teat (i.e., the location where the witch suckled her familiar), and such spots could naturally be found on most accused witches. No indignity or indecency was spared as suspected witches were stripped, shaved, poked, and probed to discover the infamous mark or other clues of guilt. The shaving of pubic hair was pursued with particular vigor, ostensibly because it was a common location for a witches teat. The practice of *witch pricking* involved sticking the accused witch with pins to determine whether or not blood would flow, its absence being interpreted as a sign of witchcraft. Because capillaries are distributed unevenly about the body, and peripheral blood flow is affected by emotional states, it was ordinarily possible to find at least one location on each potential witch that resulted in the incriminating lack of blood. Even the failure to flinch or cry out would be interpreted as demonic. But scar tissue is insensitive; also, apparently some accused witches recognized their doom and suppressed reactions to end the ordeal (Spanos, 1978). Any commonplace incident or spurious temporal connection could be interpreted as a sign of witchcraft. A woman quarrels with her neighbor, the neighbor's cow dies mysteriously, and the woman is suspected of being a witch. To curse someone was particularly dangerous because cursing was interpreted as an attempt to summon demons. In many cases, the accused was simply a poor, disagreeable old woman who was disliked in the community.

Moreover, there was an almost inevitable verdict of guilt for those simply accused (Robbins, 1959). This occurred for two reasons. First, as already suggested, there was a definite double-bind quality to the determination of who was a witch. If one method failed to prove guilt, a second one was tried, until the foregone conclusion was "proven" and thus the accused witch was "damned if she did and damned if she didn't." Some of the procedures themselves were logical fallacies and provided absolutely no legal protection for the accused. Lawyers for the accused (a pretext that was eventually dropped from most witch trials) had to be careful not to defend the accused too vigorously, lest the court decide that such tactics represented a defense of Satan. Protestations of innocence were of course simply branded as satanic lies and, in fact, in the Salem witch trials, accused witches who confessed were, although punished, eventually freed, whereas the witches executed by hanging were those accused who professed their innocence to the end (Hansen, 1969). Even publicly acknowledged reputations of absolute piety and purity were likely to be interpreted by the judges as masquerades calculated to fool them.

Common sense and rules of evidence were overruled for the witch trials because according to the *Malleus Maleficarum*, accepted by both Catholics and Protestants, deception and lying in the prosecution of the Devil and his emissaries was not only allowed but was necessary to combat the evil deceptiveness of Satan. Judges often promised freedom and rewards for confessions of witchcraft, but these promises were euphemisms for freedom from the miseries of life or the reward of the pyre. Character witnesses for the accused were not allowed, but testimony was accepted as genuine from individuals who were otherwise barred from judicial proceedings, including children, felons, excommunicates, etc. The essence of the procedural irrationality and inevitable doom of the accused during the witch trials is exemplified by the *water ordeal* practiced in England. Suspected witches were bound and thrown into a pond or river. If they floated, they were found guilty and hanged; if they sank, they were pronounced innocent, posthumously.

Second, most accused were found guilty because quite often they confessed, revealing in infinite detail the nature of their crimes and implicating others. However, witch confessions were ordinarily extracted under the conditions of unimaginable torture and privation in which the prospect of confession and subsequent immolation at the stake became a welcomed relief from ceaseless and agonizing punishment. Even here, the paradox of the presumption of guilt was practiced. If the torture became too severe and the accused died before confessing his or her guilt, the blame was laid to Satan, who was said to sneak into the cells and kill his minions to prevent their suffering or disavowing their loyalty to him. Even though the persecutors helped to create and perpetuate the myth that the accused were hideously depraved creatures capable of any outrage or blasphemy, the real depravity clearly resulted from the maniacal and sadistic methods used to extract confessions. Every conceivable form of torture, sadism, and deprivation was used, including all manner of beatings and whippings, dunking, the rack, the water ordeal, the ladder, the strappado, the vise, Spanish boots, sexual abuse, starvation, burning, dismembering, disemboweling, vivisection, insults, recriminations, tirades, deprecation, and so on. And even the corpses of the hapless victims were subjected to further humiliations.

There is considerable evidence (e.g., Robbins, 1959) to suggest that the most extreme forms of torture were reserved to the last, at which time the witch, having ordinarily confessed his or her own guilt, would be made to implicate others. Also, in many cases, the names of accomplices were supplied by the judges or other authorities and there is clear evidence in some instances that convicted witches privately recanted their confessions and accusations, indicating that such was the only way to cease the horrible torture.

Robbins (1959) lists several characteristics of the witch persecutions that contributed to both the atmosphere of uncertainty, fear, and fanaticism, and the inevitability of proving guilt. For example, much of the trial procedure was carried out in secret; gossip, hearsay, and unverified accusations were accepted as testimony; and specific charges were nebulous and often withheld from the accused. In addition, accused witches were rarely found innocent, at best the verdict would be not proven, and the accused in question might be vulnerable to subsequent prosecution at a later date. In such an atmosphere of fear, uncertainty, and pain, it is not surprising that many of the accused confessed to acts and attitudes of which they were innocent.

Box 10.1—The Sabbat

One of the difficulties encountered in trying to understand witchcraft in its historical context is differentiating between magical rites that might actually have been practiced and those that were simply assumed by people of that period to have been practiced. An example of this problem is the witches' sabbat. On the one hand, it is clear that many of the alleged characteristics of the sabbat were products of the imaginations of superstitious peasants and the irrational fears of the Christian persecutors (Seligmann, 1948). The witches were naturally described as flying to the sabbat on sticks and brooms and, with the aid of the right potion or brew, they would change into animal forms. Another common belief about the sabbat was that witches would bring their children to the demons either to be eaten or rebaptized by Satan. The sabbat was also ostensibly the initiation rite for prospective witches. In a ceremony described by several authors of that era, the new witch was required to renounce allegiance to God, be marked with the devil's claw, be baptized in dirty water, and give up something, often a child. Additional levels of initiation included denial of the Christian sacraments, inscription of the witch's name in the *Book of Death*, promises of gifts for the demons, and promises of future performance of vile and evil acts (e.g., killing children, bringing misfortune to others, recruiting new witches), promises to abstain from Christian practices, and so on. In exchange, the devil would offer to sustain the witch and provide happiness after death.

Many scholars contend that celebrations and feasts that became known as sabbats were held, often in secrecy, but these may have been observances of pagan beliefs that extolled the virtues of nature but were held surreptitiously because of the opposition of the Christian authorities. In the bacchanalia of old, it had been customary to wear animal skins and masks, which may have contributed to the belief that the celebrations were attended by the Devil and demons in the form of animals. Drinking, dancing, carousing, and frenzy were also common and this may have resulted in the characterization of the sabbat as an evil orgy. Sabbats supposedly took place at night in forest clearings and other locations near large dying trees. It is possible that flickering or wind-

Fig. 10.1   Sorcerer exchanging the Gospels for a book of black magic. From R. P. Guaccius'
Compendium Maleficarum, Milan, 1626.

swept flames created moving shadows of the bare branches, resulting in illusions of apparitions and incorporeal beings, especially among less sober groups. Shouts and cries from participants and strange, unidentifiable noises from the forest may have suggested the presence of wailing demons. The behavior of any domesticated animal that happened to be about might easily have been judged as the actions of a familiar. Thus, heightened expectations could have resulted in the perception of magical events.

If the sabbat was practiced in any form, it is conceivable that participants could have misperceived what actually happened and reinforced one another's belief in the magical nature of the event. If so, it is even easier to imagine how a superstitious populace that did not attend, but heard rumors and exaggerated tales, could attribute a multitude of mysterious and evil characteristics to them.

The Cultural-Ideological Context

The persecution of witchcraft was the product of complex social and ideological forces. For example, many authors agree that the persecution of witchcraft arose from the conservative and reactionary impulses of the medieval establishment. The Church and the feudal lords were trying to retain control over the peasantry (Seligmann, 1948). The rural concept of a pervasive and personified spirit of nature (which became the idea of the Devil) threatened and challenged the ideological power of the Church. Indeed, Robbins (1959) has argued that the Church invented the crime of witchcraft as a means of perpetuating enforced orthodoxy begun by the Inquisition. This line or argument holds that the Inquisition had been relatively successful at suppressing other kinds of religious crimes and therefore needed a new target. Similarly, the nobility needed an excuse to perpetuate its oppression of the masses as Western civilization slowly evolved from feudalism towards capitalism. Moreover, once the persecutions had begun, they generated a self-interested economic bureaucracy that was vested in its own self-preservation. Ecclesiastical and secular scholars were needed to interpret and develop laws pertaining to witchcraft, numerous judges and inquisitors were employed; even executioners, jailers, torturers, etc., were paid piece-work wages for every successful confession or prosecution. The property of condemned witches was parcelled out among the persecutors.

That segment of the general public that escaped accusation also had a stake in the proceedings. Charges of witchcraft became a social solution for jealousy, hate, and prejudice; vendettas against neighbors, relatives, enemies, and violators of social norms could be carried out with the acquiescence and assistance of the authorities. Also, the witch trials and executions took on a carnival atmosphere and became the principal source of lustful and pagan entertainment in an otherwise excessively religious, strict, and punitive environment.

Even the persecuted peasantry gained, in a sense. Witchcraft served as an instrument for ideological rebellion when open revolution was impossible. The serf found refuge in the fantasy of witchcraft, which resurrected the essential characteristics of the deities of old. Open revolts against Church and State had proven useless, and yet the desire to escape the misery of incredible oppression remained and found expression in witchcraft. Pagan sexual rites intended, through sympathetic reasoning, to stimulate the fertility of nature evolved into the forbidden and lustful sabbat (Seligmann, 1948).

Belief in witchcraft and the persecution of witches was an enormously complex social and ideological struggle, and as a consequence, a variety of opinions have emerged regarding its meaning and causes. For example, one school of thought holds that the phenomenon of witchcraft was simply religious heresy and exclusively in the minds of the persecutors and thus represented an unjustified and hideous attempt at religious repression and thought control, a violent and vicious enforcement of religious orthodoxy and dogma. In his introduction to *The Encyclopedia of Witchcraft and Demonology*, Robbins, (1959) forcefully expresses this point of view:

The record of witchcraft is horrible and brutal; degradation stifled decency, the filthiest passions masqueraded under the cover of religion, and man's intellect was subverted to condone bestialities that even Swift's Yahoos would blush to commit.

Never were so many so wrong so long. Witchcraft destroyed the principles of honor and justice; it opened wide the rosters for the Hall of Shame [p. 3].

At the other extreme, some have argued that witchcraft was real, at least as regards the intentions and motives of the accused. For example, Hansen (1969) writing on the minor flare-up of witch persecution imported to the New World at Salem, argues that many of the witches did indeed think of themselves as Satan's helpers as a consequence of hysterical ruminations, and actually held hostile attitudes towards the neighbors and kinfolk whom they attempted to harm with magical incantations and diabolic rites. Witchcraft was apparently practiced by certain members of colonial society with malevolent intentions and with, in some cases, the desired effects via hysterical suggestion. In this view, the much maligned authorities such as Cotton Mather were responding to an outbreak of hysteria in their midst in the context of 17th century understanding of medicine and behavior. Thus, witches are characterized as the targets of sincere if overzealous attempts to solve a real social problem, rather than the victims of ideological tyranny, and thus as largely responsible for their own persecutions.

A third perspective, adopted by Seligmann (1948) emphasizes both sides of the witchcraft controversy. Although acknowledging that the driving force behind witch persecutions was an attempt by the feudal establishment to forestall social and ideological change, and also noting that witch confessions were invariably elicited under conditions of incredible torture, Seligmann, (1948) also recounts the potential benefits of practicing the witches' sabbat and the general idea of witchcraft that accrued to the otherwise powerless and oppressed medieval peasant:

It was not a perversion, but a primitive and innocent custom. At the sabbat he was free to do as he pleased. He was feared also; and in his lifelong oppression, this gave him some dignity, some sense of freedom. Here he could give himself to excitement without the interference of the Church, that wanted to regulate even human emotions. If this was Satanic, the peasant thought, I shall cling to Satan.

The sabbat and the witch existed because there were non-conformist people in Europe who, oppressed though they were, clung to the defeated gods of the past, their brethren in oppression. Today we tend to overlook the fact that the new religion was alien to Europe, whereas the old peasant customs were rooted in the very soil where they had always lived. Most of the resentment which religion was earning had sprung from the feeling that it was something foreign and that it had come from a remote land, from the east [p. 177].

But the phenomena of witchcraft also arose from the tyranny of the oppressors in this view. For example, Seligmann (1948) goes on to argue:

> Persecution produced resistance and also leaders for such resistance; and Satan, who represented nature, freedom, hatred of the established order, became a political figure. Witchcraft was considered a penal offense in legislation ordained by Catholics and Protestants alike, and by the leaders of the state. Wherever the voice of freedom was heard or an original idea was expressed, the authorities detected the activities of Satan [pp. 177–178].

Witchcraft and Psychopathology

Beyond the turmoil of the times, there were psychological components to the witchcraft mania. Zilboorg (1935) has explained how this might have come about by examining the text of the *Malleus Maleficarum*. The infamous Witches' Hammer was written by two Benedictine monks who, although appointed by Pope Innocent VIII as inquisitors to prosecute sorcerers and witches in Germany, had met with a general resistence by the local populace and clergy. Their motive then was to produce a document that would serve as the theoretical rationale for their work, or more likely a rationalization. The *Malleus Maleficarum* was zealously and polemically written and consisted of three parts. The first part presented an argument for the existence of witches and held that anyone disbelieving in them was either wrong or a heretic. The second part contained sort of clinical case histories of witchcraft and its persecution, and part three discussed the legalities of examining and punishing witches and delivering the condemned from the Devil (usually by burning).

One thesis of the *Malleus maleficarum* that was of utmost legal importance was the concept of consent or intentionality. As previously mentioned, witchcraft in part derived from the concept of demonology, the ancient theory that disordered behavior resulted from possession of the afflicted by demons. The difference between the ancient theory of demonology and that of the witch persecutions was subtle but important. Although demonological interpretations had often contained a linkage between psychopathology and moral behavior, the connection was not necessarily due to the intentions of the possessed. For example, primitive and ancient peoples believed that insanity might result as the punishment by the gods for doing evil. But the insane did not intend to be possessed; rather, it was the animistic price to be paid for offending the gods or engaging in immoral behavior. With the invention of the theological definition of witchcraft came the idea that one could intentionally enter into a pact with evil, personified by Satan, and thus the phenomenon of insanity was believed to be the result of a direct and self-conscious decision to become possessed with the devil's power and identity. Witches gave in to the devil's influence because they were sinful and full of malice and in order to gain special powers, whereas *magicians* were even more diabolical and actually bartered away their souls in return for the power to summon and command the devil to accomplish evil and magical ends. But this was a technical distinction that mattered little with regard to the fate of the accused. The important point is that possession became officially an act of willful intention and thus the culpability of the insane for their affliction was increased. The *Malleus Maleficarum* strongly emphasized two main points: One could become a witch only by entering a pact with the devil by one's own free choice; and the idea that the devil cannot act alone and has no power beyond the complicity of a willful agent. The latter contention was considered important to bolster the theological notion of free will.

The second feature of this argument was more complex but nonetheless critical. The *Malleus Maleficarum*, even though acknowledging the ideas of medicine and psychopathology espoused by the Greeks and others, generally equated disease and ailments with witchcraft. Certain "obviously" organic pathologies such as epilepsy and leprosy were considered to be natural and thus the province of the physician. Everything else, such as psychological disorders and even organic states not known at the time to be

Fig.10.2 Mass execution of citizens of Haarlem as disciples of the Devil, under Fernando Alvarez de Toldeo, Duke of Alba, after the conquest of Haarlem in 1573.

physiological, were considered to be supernatural and hence, a matter of heresy that was to be dealt with legally. Two criteria, suddenness of onset and chronicity, both of which are common in psychopathology, were especially indicative of witchcraft. Moreover, the *Malleus Maleficarum* was explicit and emphatic regarding the inclusion of what today would be thought of as psychological problems as symptomatic of demonological possession, including anesthesias, contortions, and convulsions (often symptomatic of hysteria), sexual dysfunction (e.g. impotence), sexual perversions, carnal lust, and prostitution; hallucinations, visions, apparitions, and some dreams (often symptoms of functional or organic psychosis); mutism (often associated with schizophrenia); drunkeness and melancholy (i.e., depression). It was also anti-erotic and anti-hedonic and tended to ascribe a demonic cause to all human passions and desires in favor of an ascetic–mystical view of nature. If some unusual behavior could not be unambiguously classified as natural with the crude and superstitious medicine of the day, it was supernatural by default. Thus, by definition and by ignorance, the *Malleus Maleficarum* functioned as a classification of disordered behavior, as a nosology; only the disease was sin, heresy, apostasy, to be in league with the Devil, and therefore demonological pathology.

Psychiatric historians (e.g., Alexander & Selesnick, 1966; Zilboorg & Henry, 1941) have thus generally explained witchcraft as a combination of repressive religious orthodoxy and rampant outbreaks of psychological disorders. Accordingly, witch persecutions are seen as essentially persecutions of the insane and neurotically afflicted. For example, claims of accused witches to having performed impossible feats such as *transvection* (i.e., flying through the air) may have resulted from the fantastic delusions common to severe psychoses such as schizophrenia (Bromberg, 1954; Zilboorg & Henry, 1941). Apparent insensitivity to pain and other unusual sensory phenomena may have resulted from hysterical states (Bromberg, 1954), which would be more likely under conditions of strict religious oppression typical of the period. This view then assumes a great upsurge of abnormality, towards the end of the Middle Ages, that was not recognized as such by the persecutors, and instead was seized upon as the excuse for theological tyranny.

Alternatively, Spanos (1978) has suggested that the presumption of epidemic mental illness is not necessary to explain the bizarre behavior of accused witches. Instead, it is argued that these apparent pathologies are what one would expect because of such factors as the atmosphere of panic, normal tensions between neighbors, prevalent anti-feminism and stereotyping of women as both lustful and tempting as well as morally weak, the torture and brutality with which many confessions were elicited, pervasive beliefs in witchcraft and sorcery, and the fact that some of the accused ac-

Fig.10.3   Witches concoting an ointment to be used for flying to the sabbat. By Hans Baldung
Grien, Strasbourg, 1514.

tually believed they were witches. Thus, confessions of diabolical and impossible feats and anomalies, such as apparent insensitivity to pain, may have, resulted as the enactment of the role associated with the widespread and intensive expectations regarding witchcraft. For example, in addition to torture, Spanos points to important characteristics of the situation that would be expected to lead to false confessions, such as isolation from social support, relentless pressure to confess from authority figures, false promises, leading questions, etc. Such pressures might lead to confessions even if the person were not disturbed.

However, even this interpretation assumes that behaviors related to witchcraft occurred as a function of social–psychological processes (although not pathological ones) that were erroneously judged by accusors and judges to be supernatural and indicative of a willful pact with the Devil. Also, original documents make it clear that when behaviors consistent with modern definitions of abnormality did occur, they were taken to be symptoms of witchcraft, even when torture was not applied to extract a confession. For example, Zilboorg and Henry (1941) report a case involving a delusion of grandeur in which a man openly and persistently claimed to be God. In this case, torture was used in an attempt to force the person to recant his heretical delusion, which he refused to do. As a result, he was beheaded and burned as a witch. Thus, although scholarly opinion now generally favors the interpretaton that most accused witches were not insane, it is also reasonable to conclude that during the period of time in question, the insane were often accused of being witches.

Old ideas die hard and the remnants of ancient and medieval concepts have persisted into the modern era. For example, Sebald (1978) has documented the continued belief in witchcraft in the peasant villages of Bavaria. Self-proclaimed witches exist in contemporary America, although the social and psychological determinants have undoubtedly changed. Indeed, the senior author of this volume was recently approached by a woman claiming to be a witch who wanted to be tested psychologically to authenticate her condition. Likewise, the idea that disordered behavior stems from something inside the individual that reflects moral weakness was not abandoned with the advent of the scientific age. Until very recently, accepted treatments and conditions of care for the insane have varied little from the standards of the Middle Ages. The use of restraints, punishment, and various remedies to shock the patient back to reality continued into this century in some locations. Some observers (e.g., Page, 1975) have even noted the conceptual similarity between ancient procedures such as exorcism and more modern treatment approaches like electroshock and lobotomy. Modern parents continue to ask their children "What's got into you?" when they misbehave, and psychiatric patients still claim that "the devil made me do it."

PSYCHOPATHOLOGY AND PSI

The supernatural–psychopathological connection has been preserved. But an additional element has been added by psychologists and psychiatrists who accept or favor parapsychological interpretations. In such approaches, characteristics of psychopathology are used to explain psi phenomena or the relationship between the two is explored. Some psychiatrists report frequent episodes of apparent paranormal phenomena such as prophetic dreams and telepathic anticipation of what someone was thinking or doing, and these occurrences are taken as suggesting a linkage between the conditions that lead patients to seek psychiatric services and psi abilities and experiences.

More directly, psychopathological states are seen as facilitating the emergence of telepathy and clairvoyance by some. For example, Ehrenwald (1948) has argued that a necessary condition for telepathy is the minus function, which is defined as some form of psychobiological dysfunction or inadequacy, whether permanent or transitory, e.g., brain defects, trance states, etc. Psychic ability in this view is seen as a form of primitive or regressive sensitivity that manifests itself particularly during the onset of psychological disturbances, such as schizophrenia. There is even the suggestion that *paranoia* (delusional ideas of persecution and importance) may represent the response to telepathically received threats, and *catatonia* (often involving a non-responsive, trance-like state) may be an attempt to block out the flood of information received through ordinary sensory channels as well as telepathic messages. Similarly, others have suggested that psi is associated with the greater vigilance of patients close to the "breaking-point" (Ullman, 1977); that hysteria facilitates but does not cause psi (Alberti, 1974); that somatic symptoms are analogous to telepathic messages (Stevenson, 1970); and that telepathic messages stimulate thoughts and actions just as external physical stimuli do (Eisenbud, 1970).

The problem with these speculations is that the reality of psychic phenomena is generally taken for granted or simply assumed to be true. If other explanations of the apparently psychic experiences of patients exist, then speculation regarding the influence of pathological states and behaviors on the manifestation of psi may be a groundless and superfluous exercise, and, of course, alternative explanations do exist. For example, Ellis (1970a, 1970b) has suggested that some of the instances of psychic phenomena in therapeutic situations emerge solely from the complex interpretations made by psychiatrists of the verbalizations of their patients. Some systems of psychotherapy, such as psychoanalysis, are highly interpretive and rely heavily upon the therapist's ability to understand the underlying and symbolic meaning of what may otherwise appear to be ordinary descriptions of everyday experiences and problems. Because the rules of interpretation are necessarily subjective, it is possible that therapists previously convinced of the reality of psi are simply more likely to attribute psychic properties to common experiences described by patients. In any case, Ellis notes that in many instances, the determination of the occurrence of a psychic event is to be found only in the interpretation and not directly in the content of what the patient said. Other interpretations of the same verbal material, Ellis notes, are equally, if not more, plausible.

Also, attempts to empirically establish the relationship between psychopathological states and various forms of psychic ability have been largely ineffective. For example, Ullman (1977), who favors the theory that psychopathology facilitates psychic phenomena, reviews several studies in which the psychic functioning of mental patients was tested experimentally. Generally, these studies have failed to establish a reliable relationship, and Ullman concludes that they have specifically failed to shed any light on the problem, perhaps due to various methodological and conceptual problems.

Writing in the same volume, Palmer (1977) reviews a different set of studies, which, curiously, were apparently intended to show that psychic abilities are more common among people who are better adjusted and healthier from a psychological point of view. Palmer cautiously concludes that two kinds of people are more likely to perform best on first-time laboratory tests of clairvoyance: the well adjusted and those who believe in psychic phenomena. He suggests that this occurs because both groups might be expected to be more relaxed or comfortable in the testing situation and thus presumably better able to be receptive. However, the evidence for these conclusions is not at all strong.

Concerning the personality dimension of *neuroticism* (i.e., mild, but troubling forms of psychological problems, usually not involving hospitalization), Palmer examines the results of 24 available studies. Studies involving group–testing situations were excluded from the analysis because, according to Palmer, group settings are more likely to arouse anxiety among certain individuals; studies using inappropriate or unusual statistical analyses were also excluded for obvious reasons. Of the remaining 24 studies, 18 produced results in the predicted direction (i.e., less neurotic subjects had better scores on the clairvoyance tasks), whereas only six studies yielded results in the opposite direction; that is a statistically significant proportion of anticipated results with 24 studies. However, only seven of the studies obtained statistically significant results (i.e., where neurotics scored significantly more poorly than non-neurotics), although all of these were in the predicted direction. Thus, in over two-thirds of the examined cases, a reliable relationship in either direction was not found, indicating that any differences between neurotics and non-neurotics might have been due to chance variation alone and suggesting that conclusions regarding the linkage between psychic ability and adjustment may be dubious. Palmer suggests that one reason for the inconsistency and lack of significance of these data may be the widely reported unreliability of psi phenomena. This is a crucial point in that such unreliability very possibly indicates that psi ability does not in fact exist and therefore statistical relationships between ESP and other variables would be spurious.

Box 10.2—The Case of Ilga K.

In 1935, the Director of the Forensic Institute of the Latvian State University in Riga, Dr. F. von Neureiter, published a monograph describing his experimental observations of a 9-year-old mentally retarded (I. Q. of 48) Latvian girl, Ilga Kirks, who supposedly was able to read the thoughts of her teacher and mother, as well as other individuals. Even though she had great difficulty reading Latvian from a book, she could read Latvian as well as foreign languages rather fluently if these were read silently by another person. Von Neureiter thought that the girl had genuine telepathic ability, and the case of Ilga K., as she is referred to in the literature, became well known both in Latvia and abroad. In 1936 and 1937, a specially formed commission, made up of 13 professionals representing psychology, physics, medicine, and speech and hearing disorders, conducted an extensive series of tests of Ilga K. Some of these were conducted in a soundproof room and in a Faraday cage (an insulated cubicle that keeps out electromagnetic waves).

In their report (Dahle, 1940), the Commission concluded that no paranormality was involved in Ilga's ability. When the agent was Ilga's mother, the word that the mother was thinking of was "sent" to her daughter by breaking it down into separate phonemes and tacking these onto the ends of the words of encouragement uttered by the mother. Ilga would pick them out and put them together into a whole word. When the mother was made to keep quiet or was isolated in a soundproof room, Ilga failed to receive, or else was only partly successful by using the highly expressive gestures and lip movements of the mother. Ilga was most successful with individuals who strongly moved their lips, tongue, and larynx while thinking or reading, which was the case with her teacher who had first brought Ilga's ability to the attention of the scientists. She could learn nothing from her mathematics teacher, whose subvocal speech was very weak, but a special teacher assigned by the Latvian Commission to tutor Ilga at home learned the communication method that Ilga and her mother were using and was able to replicate and even better the mother's performance. Ilga's ability was apparently one that she had developed on her own to compensate for her rather severe intellectual deficit. In spite of the fact that the Latvian Commission's work leaves not the slightest doubt as to the true nature of Ilga K.'s phenomenon, and the additional fact that von Neureiter was one of the Commission's members, some parapsychologists (Ehrenwald, 1977b) still present her case as a genuine case of telepathy, ignoring the Commission's report altogether.

THE ROLE OF PSYCHOPATHOLOGY IN MAGIC

Some theories of the origin of magical beliefs and practices, particularly those examining individuals as opposed to social causes (see Chapter 11), have stressed the importance of abnormal behavior in determining the apparent manifestation of these phenomena. As previously mentioned, psychiatric historians argue that people who believed they were witches and who self-consciously practiced black magic were actually hysterics or schizophrenics, two classical types of abnormality. Others have suggested that the behavior of the persecutors stemmed from paranoid fears and ruminations (see Sebald, 1978), and some have suggested that convictions of flying through the air, attending the sabbat, and sexual relations with demons were narcotically induced hallucinations caused by potentially psychotropic substances included in witches' brews and potions (e.g., Barnett, 1965).

Addressing the issue more generally, Field (1960) suggested that the delusions and other distorted views of reality common to schizophrenia (a type of psychosis often involving extremely bizarre behavior and gross distor-

Fig.10.4. Jimsonweed (Datura stramonium). One of a number of Old and New World plants of the genus Datura used in medicine and as hallucinogens since antiquity. The hallucinogenic agent in Jimsonweed is hyoscyamine. Supernatural properties have been attributed to the plant, which has been used for that reason in magical ceremonies, initiations, and witches' sabbats. (Leonard Zusne photo)

tions of reality) have historically been the original source of magical ideas. Schizophrenics often describe internal subjective reality (e.g., thoughts, fears, dreams, etc.) as if they were external, verifiable events. Because schizophrenia often goes unrecognized as such among ancient and tribal societies, such conceptions could be accepted and transmitted by others, who, although not sharing the distorted experiences, come to believe in them. Rawcliffe (1959), even though acknowledging that occult, mystical, and supernatural concepts are fundamental to human nature, also attributes them to anomalies of human psychology, particularly pathological states.

Prominent among theories of this type are the ideas of the early psychoanalysts. Freud (1960) believed that certain feelings, desires, and fears experienced by an individual might be so unacceptable by the standards of society that they are not experienced consciously. Instead, they exist on an unconscious level and are experienced only in symbolic and accidental ways such as in the content of dreams and slips of the tongue. According to the Freudian view, this is particularly true of sexual and aggressive ideas and impulses, which Freud believed were innate to all people. To reduce the anxiety associated with the presence of these features of the personality, they may be *projected* as external situations and events where they are less threatening in the sense that the person in question no longer feels responsible for them. For example, the premonition of the death of a loved one might represent the projection of the socially unacceptable hostility that a person feels towards the loved one. Similarly, the fear of ghosts may actually be the fear of one's own aggressive and self-destructive tendencies, symbolically represented by belief in the supernatural.

In subsequent formulations, Freud expanded these concepts to include the effects of human development. Freud argued that each child passes through a stage in which the power of one's own thought processes is narcissistically overestimated, and that one of the requirements of cognitive maturation is learning to distinguish between subjectively experienced desires and external reality. A child will initially put any object to the mouth, but eventually learns that only some objects taste good and satisfy hunger. Freud argued that some individuals (e.g., neurotics) do not learn this lesson as well as others and therefore continue to some extent to believe that their thoughts are omnipotent and can influence external events without mediating actions. More seriously disturbed persons known as *psychotics* may actually fixate at or regress to this stage of development, according to Freud. In fact, the ability to accurately perceive and respond appropriately to external reality as opposed to relying on the belief in magical wish fulfillment is a central concept in distinguishing normal from abnormal conditions in Freud's theory.

Jung's (1956) ideas on magic are more difficult to examine, although their influence has been major. This is partly because it is not always clear whether Jung is describing how magical ideas come about, or if he is suggesting that such phenomena are real (Jahoda, 1969). In any case, Jung argued that beliefs in the supernatural are deeply rooted in the unconscious and that the experience of emotional and pathological states increased the likelihood of believing and experiencing the paranormal. Jung also believed that there is no sharp distinction between beliefs that may be characterized as true versus those that are false, particularly with regard to how they function psychologically. The universality of superstitions is the product of the *collective unconscious*, according to Jung—that is, the influence of the unconscious memory of the common and significant experiences of our ancestors. Jung returned to the topic of magic and the supernatural often in his writings and generally argued for the maintenance of an open mind with regard to the reality of paranormal processes.

Although each of these theories undoubtedly reflects some aspects of the emergence of magical ideas, the important question at this point is, to what extent is psychopathology responsible for the development of magical beliefs and practices? There is no question that people experiencing severe or even mild problems of psychological functioning are more likely to exhibit behaviors suggesting magic causation and beliefs in magic. Most neurotic behaviors contain strongly superstitious themes. For example, a *phobia* is an intense fear and avoidance of an object or situation that either presents no actual danger or to which the avoidance response is out of proportion to the level of danger present. In certain *compulsions* that may be associated with neurosis a behavior will be avoided or performed to prevent a magical occurrence. For example, many people avoid stepping on cracks to keep from "breaking their mother's back," or knock on wood after self-laudatory comments to forestall negative outcomes. Lucky charms, coins, and numbers are also examples. These are, of course, widely known and common compulsions engaged in by many people. However, the differences between the superstitious behaviors widely shared and those of the neurotic concern the complexity and the degree to which the behavior is ritualized, as well as the consequences of violations of the compulsion. The more ingrained and complex the compulsive sequence, the more it tends to be associated with psychological problems. Others are haunted by persistent and unwanted thoughts, called *obsessions*, often of manifestly occult themes. Among the severely disturbed, allusions to magic and magical thinking are commonplace. The schizophrenic seems to live in a world of conceptual magic where thinking equals doing and in which the boundaries of time, space, and identity are easily crossed in fantasy. Of course, anyone can imagine the impossible, but the schizophrenic apparently fails to distinguish such fantasies from consensual reality to the same extent as others.

But the idea that magic in inherently linked to an underlying pathological state is a gross overgeneralization. As we have noted, entire cultures and periods of history have been characterized by the widespread belief in magic, and, as suggested in Chapter 7, things may not be much different in modern, scientifically oriented America. In Chapter 11, we discuss how, although beliefs are held by individuals, their content is most often generated in interactions with other people. Beliefs are certainly transmitted from one person to another and across generations socially. Also, available empirical evidence generally fails to support the hypothesis. Although mental patients almost invariably believe in magic in one form or another, the evidence that believers are more disturbed or neurotic is not conclusive (see Chapter 7). Data referring to the relationship between adjustment and psychic ability (see the earlier discussion) is particularly weak and unconvincing. Some of the theories suggesting a psychopathological cause for magic are difficult to evaluate themselves. For example, psychoanalytic theory is notoriously ambiguous, circular, and difficult to test, even though it has been a useful and important development in the emergence of modern psychology and psychiatry. Similarly, Jung's theory of the collective unconscious is very close to the notion of the inheritance of acquired characteristics, which has been discredited in biology, whereas his concept of synchronicity (see Chapter 13) itself borders on assuming magical causation.

The relationship between psychopathology and magic is thus real but circumscribed and limited. Extreme psychological problems are associated with magical thinking. This probably results because of the reduction of one's ability to function rationally under the influence of strong emotional stress. It is also possible that some of the remarkable behaviors associated with disturbance may have contributed to the acceptance of magical ideas in the absence of alternative explanations, as suggested by some theorists. Moreover, this effect could have occurred numerous times throughout history and may even persist today. However, the importance of psychopathological explanations is limited by other considerations.

First, as discussed at the beginning of the chapter, the relationship between abnormality and magic is due, in part, to the impression of abnormality. Psychotics say that they have been reincarnated, that they have traveled to distant parts of the universe, or that they can read another person's mind, but there is no reason to accept such claims at face value any more than one should accept statements that the patient's insides are being eaten away by maggots or that the patient caused the death of Jesus. It is generally assumed that mental patients have difficulty distinguishing fact from fancy. But that does not mean that other people who believe in magic do so for the same reasons. One major theme of this book is that attributions of the paranormal may result as a function of a wide variety of quite natural psychological processes. Also, in a psychological disturbance, many aspects of experience change and become exaggerated, including overt behavior, speech, thought processes, etc. It is common, for example, for psychotics to indicate excessive and obsessional concern regarding various religious and philosophical matters—e.g., one's relationship to God or what happens at death. These are simply psychotic expressions of the more general concern and questions most people have regarding such issues. But it would be ludicrous to suggest that psychological disturbance has caused the emergence of the world's great religions, although again, psychopathological and other anomalous psychological states may have influenced some religious experiences (e.g., religious visions). Finally, strict adherence to a psychopathological theory of magic leads to the conceptually strained conclusion that entire cultures and historical periods were populated by deranged people. This is not only improbable, but also ignores the possibility that anything so common and persistent as magic is likely to be fundamental to human nature and a product of forces beyond the inability of some to adequately function psychologically.

Far from being exclusively pathological, magic may have served very important social and psychological functions, particularly among ancient and tribal societies. Seligmann, (1948) has put forth a version of this idea:

> But a system that prevailed in society for thousands of years hardly needs an apology. The fact remains that magic upheld the great civilizations of the ancient world. Its predominance did not prevent man from leaving behind him works of continuing value, from tolerating his neighbor, cherishing his family, doing the adequate things at the right time. Magic was a stimulus to thinking. It freed man from fears, endowed him with a feeling of his power to control the world, sharpened his capacity to imagine, and kept alive his dreams of higher achievement [p. 322].

11

The Social Psychology
of the Extraordinary

*Ancient superstitions, after being steeped in human hearts, and em-
bodied in human breath, and passing from lip to ear, in manifold
repetition, through a series of generations, become imbued with an
effect of homely truth.*

Nathaniel Hawthorne

Box 11.1—*Mankind United*: An Illustration

In 1934, a book entitled *Mankind United* appeared for sale in the San Francisco Bay Area. The book purported to reveal how on December 25th, 1875, a
small group of farsighted men dedicated their lives and fortunes to an enterprise that would appropriately commemorate the birth of Jesus Christ.
Originally the group numbered 60 and committed $60,000,000 to the
endeavor. Called the "Sponsors," they recruited enlightened experts in
various fields including agriculture, mining, manufacturing, banking, and
education, and created the "International Institute of Universal Research and
Administration," whose purpose was to discover and implement any
mechanism by which the Golden Rule could be used in everyday human relationships as a means of preventing all poverty and war. The "Institute" in
turn allegedly organized secret research laboratories that produced not only a
plan for a new world order, but also a wide variety of amazing inventions and
secret devices. There were special attachments for the radios of the followers
to listen to secret messages, and a suspended animation device capable of stopping automobiles, airplanes, and even human behavior without pain or
damage to the target. More amazing still, these research laboratories were supposedly located many miles underground and the occupants had not appeared
on the surface of the Earth for several years and were not expected to do so
again for at least another 100 years!

The "Sponsors" also created what was called the "International Legion of
Vigilantes," a group of highly dedicated volunteers who undertook a 15–year
training course in order to prepared themselves for the task of acting as the

326

emissaries of the "Sponsors." A new world order was to be initiated beginning with a "30-day Program" at which time 60 years' worth of remarkable discoveries and recommendations would be offered to the human race. At the end of the "30-day Program," a democratic world-wide election was to be held and, if 200 million people voted their approval of the plan, a utopian "Universal Service Corporation" was to be established internationally.

Although the "Universal Service Corporation" had as its basic purpose the implementation of the Golden Rule in everyday human experience, numerous concrete benefits were anticipated as well. For example, guaranteed immediate employment was to be instituted with all workers receiving an equal but adequate salary ($3000 per year in 1934 dollars); a labor week consisting of only 4 hours per day, 4 days per week, for 8 months out of the year; paid vacation for all time not spent working; and pensions beginning at age 40 for those who chose to retire. Moreover, the plan called for salary increases for all workers, regardless of the type of employment, of up to $30,000 per year within 10 years of the advent of the plan. Changes in productive systems and capacities were envisioned such that every year, 100 times more food would be produced than could be consumed by the world's population, and other necessities, such as clothing, were to be manufactured in great abundance. A new currency was anticipated based on service and children would be taught a second, universal, auxiliary language creating better communication among all people. The end result of the program was expected to be an attractive world in which everyone lived in comparative luxury with beautiful homes furnished with the latest appliances and plush landscaping—hence, a generally comfortable existence. The plan also called for disbanding all military forces throughout the world and the total destruction of all armaments and war-making machinery. Consequently, it was expected that there would be no more war nor human conflict.

As luck would have it, however, one major obstacle stood in the way of the realization of the "Sponsors'" magnificent blueprint for world peace and happiness. The obstacle was a group of unidentified people known collectively as the "Hidden Rulers." In fact, the "Hidden Rulers" were conceived as such a threat that the "Sponsors" organized themselves and acted only with the utmost secrecy, vowing never to divulge even to their trusted lieutenants, the 'Vigilantes," their identities or activities. The proof of this claim was that after 60 years of protracted struggle with the "Hidden Rulers," the "Sponsors" remained undetected and unidentified. The danger of the "Hidden Rulers" was judged sufficient that, although the "Institute of Universal Research and Administratiin" had conceived its program as early as 1919, the "Sponsors" decided not to release it because the world was not yet prepared to accept it and because of the danger that the power and miraculous inventions of the "Sponsors" would fall into the hands of the "Hidden Rulers" and thus cvilization as well as all educated and religious people would be doomed, As a consequence, the "30-day Program" was indefinitely postponed until the public's cooperation was strong enough to guarantee its success.

According to the book, the "Hidden Rulers" were no small threat. They were described as a small, self-perpetuating group of fabulously wealthy families, in essence a group of conspirators, who by virtue of their control of money, particularly gold and silver, were able to exert almost total control over governments and other important and influential institutions in societies of varying political orientation. Because of their avarice, they had deliberately precipitated depressions and wars simply to increase their profits. Their methods for inhibiting those who worked for a better, more equitable world varied from intimidation to assassination and they maintained a cadre of 10,000 highly trained and richly rewarded spies to oppose the forces of good. So extensive was their influence that the "Hidden Rulers" had divided the world into "40,000 Principalities" for future domination. More sinister still, they deliberately planned and were prepared to execute two world wars, the first of which was to field test new weapons and armaments, but the second had as its purpose an Armageddon-like end to all good and religious people, followed by the enslavement of one billion survivors. The new world order envisioned by the "Hidden Rulers" was the diametric opposite of the plan of the "Sponsors." The "Hidden Rulers" themselves would enjoy undreamed-of wealth and power (including the pick of the most attractive female slaves for their harems), while the remainder of humanity would wither in incredible poverty, enslavement, drug-induced stupidity, and degradation. Perhaps most frightening of all was the menace of a radio-controlled device allegedly in the possession of the "Hidden Rulers" that was capable of setting off vibrations of such intensity that it would cause eyeballs to vibrate out of their sockets! Such was the specter of the "Hidden Rulers."

This brief synopsis may sound like the plot of a futuristic fiction thriller, yet it was presented as if true and served as the source of spiritual and political inspiration for several thousand adherents to the cult Mankind United. The group was studied by H. T. Dohrman and his investigation was reported in *California Cult* (1958). Dohrman collected his information through a series of interviews with members and former members of the cult, and from publicly available records such as court and legislative hearing transcripts. Although Mankind United was primarily a "world-saving," political–religious movement (it was eventually incorporated as a church), many of its followers were drawn from the network of interrelated occult groups that seem to thrive in California, and several of the manifest beliefs of both the group's leadership as well as the rank-and-file members were occult in content and metaphysical in origin. Thus, it provides an excellent source of illustrative material from which perspective occult groups may be examined and better understood.

The theory of society just outlined was the invention of Arthur L. Bell, a mysterious and charismatic Christian Science practitioner who wrote the basic text for the movement Mankind United and who served as the group's effective and only leader, although he claimed to be but one of several "Vigilantes" and the "Pacific Coast Supervisor of the Mankind United Registration Bureau." Bell made numerous grandiose claims for himself and the Mankind United movement. For example, he claimed to have seven "doubles"—that is, seven men with faces and fingerprints identical to his—that the "Sponsors" had given to him in order that he might accomplish more in behalf of the Mankind United cause. Regarding the movement itself, in 1939 Bell told an audience of followers that up to that time, 173 million people around the world had applied for membership in the mankind United organization, but that only 75 million had actually qualified. As early as 1934, he had claimed that Mankind United branches were active in 16 or 17 different countries.

Although his written and oral presentations were repetitious, and he often spoke in vague generalities, there is no doubt that Bell was a dynamic and persuasive leader who made a powerful impression on his followers. Often deliberately arriving late for meetings, he would make a dramatic entrance after the audience had been seated with anticipatory tension building, thereby giving the appearance of a busy and energetic disciple of the "Sponsors." Bell was also described as good looking and a fashionable dresser, and gossip among the cultists themselves suggested that the primary motive of several female members in the cult was more amorous than idealistic. Bell enhanced the air of mystery that surrounded him by disappearing for periods of time, using different names in interactions with different cult members, and claiming amazing occult abilities. For example, his meetings with the "Sponsors" were mostly accomplished, so he claimed, by the mechanism of translevitation (what would be called astral projection today) while asleep. In fact, to a California State Legislative Committee investigating Bell and the cult's activities, he said that there was no place on Earth that he could not reach within a period of a few hours. He also testified that he had the power of precognition and the ability to pass through a wall if he so desired. As proof of the latter contention, he indicated that he often left auditoriums following cult meetings by ascending through the roof.

There is little doubt that committed members of the cult took Bell's assertions seriously, although mostly on the flimsiest of evidence. For example, one follower indicated that Bell used to put one of his "doubles" on the phone in order to test the comparability of their voices. Because she could not tell the difference, this episode was apparently taken as proof that the "doubles" were both real and effective. Another cultist told the story of buying seven identical ties for Mr. Bell in the apparent belief that this was how the wardrobes of Bell and his identical counterparts were coordinated to confuse the evil "Hidden Rulers" and multiply the work of the "Pacific Coast Supervisor." Interestingly, in several cases, such beliefs persisted even after a particular member became disaffected and left the cult.

Dohrman's research revealed a different picture of the Mankind United movement, however. Although membership estimates were difficult to generate, in part because of Bell's grandiose claims and because of the cloak of secrecy that surrounded Mankind United affairs, indirect estimates suggested that the faithful membership was at times impressive, but hardly as large as Bell often claimed. For example, a printer testified that he printed less that 1300 copies of *Mankind United* (required reading for members) in 1936, but that the total grew to 41,182 in 1938, and peaked at over 75,000 in 1939. In 1940, after the beginning of the cult's difficulties with the government, the number of copies dropped to only 2000. The California State Attorney estimated that prior to 1939, approximately 250,000 people had at some time and to some degree been involved in the Mankind United cult. Thus, although impressive, Mankind United was hardly the far-reaching, world-wide secret organization that Bell led people to believe.

This is not to suggest that Mankind United was a figment of Bell's imagination. Beginning as simply one of several hundred fringe, quasi religious, and occult movements, the cult grew from a small, "store-front" organization to a vital, dynamic group commanding audiences of over 5000 at some of the larger meetings. Nor was the effect of the group minor on those who became deeply involved in its activities. For example, although later many members complained that the work assignments were often trivial and miniscule, the true believers were kept exceptionally busy conducting meetings, raising money for the organization, engaging in repeated study of the cult's literature (authored mostly by Bell), selling copies of the book *Mankind United*, and meeting endless deadlines and quotas. In fact, Bell often stated that the promised "30-day Program" that was to usher in the new age of utopian idealism would begin as soon as the "Pacific Coast Division of Mankind United" met certain quotas of membership and finances. Thus, considerable pressure was exerted by Bell and the upper echelons of the organization to get the rank-and-file members to produce in order to realize the widely shared goal of a new age, free from poverty and war.

In fact, the level of commitment required of the membership eventually exceeded even frantic exhortations to raise money and recruit new members. For example, in 1943, the membership was asked to pledge 50% of their income to keep the organization solvent. After reorganization of the cult as a religion called Christ's Church of the Golden Rule, with former "Supervisor" Bell as the sole Church Trustee holding absolute authority, the group initiated what was called "Statistical Project 11A," in which the membership was requested to give all of its money, property, and other worldly possessions, including their clothes, to the group and to work for nothing on commercial church projects such as hotels, restaurants, farms, laundries, etc. Approximately 850 dedicated members undertook this new life and gave up from $200 to $32,000 worth of possessions. More importantly, they were forced to cut off all relations with outside influences from their jobs, homes, relatives, and friends. Most members were sent to locales some distance from their original homes, and often did not know their eventual destination or assignment until they actually arrived. On many of the projects, the work was long and arduous, including 12–hour days, 6 days per week, with only 1 hour for meals. This did not include the time required for obligatory writing of digests and sermons, special meetings, and the never-ending study of cult literature with which they were inundated and that they were required to read and reread many times.

Thus, the cult members lived in an isolated world in which their principal contact was with other members who shared their hopes, beliefs, and anticipations for the new age. Therefore, the discrepancy between their actual living conditions and the ideal of the "Universal Service Corporation" could be collectively rationalized as the price that the small group of enlightened individuals had to pay in order to show the way to a slothful and ungrateful world. Not everyone endured these sacrifices with equal magnanimity, however. Several former members became quite embittered when, upon leaving the fold, they attempted to regain their property. They took their legal challenges to the California State Attorney, which led to some of the legal difficulties that finally dissipated the movement.

Before reviewing these developments, however, it is interesting to examine estimates of the amount of money that actually changed hands during the development of the Mankind United movement. For example, it was calculated that between 1934 and 1944, Mankind United realized $4,000,000. In 1944, the assets of the organization were fixed at $3,500,000. After incorporation as a Church, the group bought many properties including auditoriums, hotels, restaurants, residences, beach clubs, warehouses, bakeries, garages, an iron works, farms, etc. Many of the Church's projects were located on these properties and although some projects apparently lost money, several earned money and continued to do so into the 1950s. Because during the Legislative Committee hearings it was established that only 5% of the group's funds went for operating expenses for the organization, the question arose as to what, in addition to the purchase of property, happened to the several million dollars raised by Mankind United during its years of organizational life?

The answer lay with Bell. Legal and legislative testimony indicated that most of the remainder of the money found its way, often mysteriously, to headquarters and Bell. It was further revealed that although he paid no income tax because he had no visible income, Bell owned several fashionable apartments in Los Angeles and San Francisco, and more than one home valued at over $75,000 with lavish furnishings, swimming pools, and sumptuous landscaping.

Moreover, it turned out that although he preached vegetarianism and abstinence from alcohol and tobacco, he was apparently well known in the best hotels, restaurants, and night clubs on the West coast. At times, he labeled allegations to this effect as slander; on another occasion, he offered the explanation that his excursions into night life were but "research missions" for the "Sponsors" in order to monitor the extent of degradation of society.

The beginning of the end of Mankind United movement coincided with its peak in membership, in 1939. Bell and his group were investigated by the Tenney Committee of the California State Legislature for alleged seditious activities associated with the group's stand against World War II, in particular their opposition to American involvement in the war because of their belief that the war was simply a plot of the "Hidden Rulers" to increase their power and profits. Although the investigation resulted in negative publicity, Bell himself remained steadfast in his assertions before the Committee and was openly contemptuous of the Committee's incredulity at his claims and ideas. It is also apparent that the investigations did little to shake the faith of the more highly committed membership, who apparently viewed it as simply a sign of the "Hidden Ruler's" displeasure with the group and hence the power, influence, and importance of their mission. Because of the group's ideological opposition to the war, they became even more secretive after 1939, but still drew the attention of the F. B. I., which began surveillance and, subsequently, infiltration in that same year. On December 18, 1942, the F. B. I. arrested Bell and 15 of the cult's leaders for alleged violation of the Wartime Sedition Act and in May, 1943, 11 of the defendants were found guilty, six of whom, including Bell, were sentenced to 5 years in a federal prison. The sentences were never carried out, however, because on appeal the convictions were reversed on the grounds that the jury that convicted the Mankind United leadership had consisted of all males. More damaging still was the dissention among the rank-and-file membership over involvement in the war effort and complaints of dissenters to the California State Attorney of an atmosphere of fear, bullying, and dire threats. Finally, in mid-1945, the California Attorney General filed a complaint asking the court to oust Bell, terminate Christ's Church of the Golden Rule, and appoint a Receiver for bankruptcy for the organization's funds because of alleged financial irregularities. Although the bankruptcy proceedings dragged on for 6 years, the courts finally sold off most of the property in order to pay debts previously incurred by the cult, and by 1951, the group membership and original fervor was largely dissipated. By 1956, Mankind United consisted of less than 100 members.

On December 21, 1951, Bell indicated in a communiqué to the remaining members that the "Sponsors" had changed their minds and the promised new order was not to be established. The "Sponsors," it seems, decided that the world consisted of too many lazy and selfish people who were not worth saving, so Earth was to be abandoned to the evil forces that would inevitably bring the total destruction of mankind via atomic bombs, poison gasses, and deathrays. To escape the impending holocaust, Bell claimed that he had explored other planetary systems, one of which yielded identical plant and animal life, except that disease was unknown. This system was inhabited with superior beings capable of telepathic and psychokinetic powers. Most importantly, this world knew no social evil nor physical limitations: no ignorance, no greed, no poverty, no disease, no brutality, no war, no old age, not even death.

Thus, Mankind United's wonderful vision of a better world was not to be found on this Earth, but in another solar system, and the new vision was thereby enhanced. Hope for the faithful was to be found in the promise that in the underground laboratories, the scientists of Mankind United had been monitoring the thoughts of members and those found worthy would settle the new intergalactic promised land, The faithful were to be "beamed" there by a device capable of modifying one's "personal vibration rate" and atomic structure. Unfortunately, Bell explained that this was possible only in the fraction of a second immediately prior to one's death. Finally, Bell indicated that new and increased responsibilities placed upon him by the "Sponsors" required that he curtail his terrestrial Mankind United activities, and according to Dohrman, he quietly withdrew from the cult scene.

SOCIAL GROUPS

Although their beliefs were eccentric and their behavior unusual, much of what happened in the Mankind United movement resulted from common group processes that are inherent in the nature of all social groups, occult or conventional in orientation. To a degree, all groups exert pressure towards allegiance, loyalty, and personal sacrifice, whether the group is the local Lions Club, the Baptist Church, or Hare Krishna. That is, certain changes in behavior result from the very act of behaving in situations along with others who share common beliefs and a sense of belonging. Even the simple presence or absence of other people has an effect on the performance of certain behaviors. Although an in-depth examination of the phenomenon of social groups is beyond the scope of this book, we review some of the basic characteristics of groups that influence individual behavior and norms.

Group Structure

A group exists whenever two or more people interact with a common goal in mind. Groups are distinguished from simple collections of individuals by several characteristics, including identification of the members with the group, the development of a group structure, and strong pressures towards conformity (i.e., internal agreement). Although groups may form for a variety of reasons, some of the more common causes of group formation include the effects of common goals, competition with outsiders, physical proximity of individuals, similarity of members, and being in stressful situations. In Mankind United, for example, most members shared a sense of disenchantment with society and endorsement of the ideals of the "new order," and they faced the stress of legal and financial challenges to the organization together, thereby strengthening their degree of interdependence and the motivation to remain loyal to the group. Once the members of a group have interacted for a period of time, a group structure begins to emerge that develops a "life of its own" and operates somewhat independently of the behavior and desires of any single member of the group. Group structure refers to several types of beliefs held by the members of the groups.

Norms. The most important aspect of group structure is the development of social norms. Norms are ideas and beliefs shared by members of the group defining the proper behavior and attitudes of group members, particularly regarding group–relevant activities. Norms are a sort of uncodified law or rules of conduct. They define what the group stands for, what the members value, and how the members should behave. All functioning groups have norms, whether they recognize them as such or not, and there may be a difference between formally recognized rules, such as a group charter, and the norms that actually govern the behavior of participating members on a day-by-day basis. Norms of the Mankind United cult included, among other things, subscription to the lofty ideals of the "Sponsors" and the dire threat of the "Hidden Rulers" as well as more mundane values such as striving to meet the deadlines and quotas imposed by "Supervisor" Bell.

The importance of group norms derives from three processes. First, successful membership in a group depends on appropriate manifestation of the group's norms and, in fact, failure to do so will ultimately result in exclusion from the group, ie., *ostracism*. Imagine, for instance, someone attracted to Mankind United because of the ideas regarding a "new age" of peace and brotherhood, who failed, however, to be convinced of the reality of the "Sponsors," the underground laboratories, and all the rest. In order to remain in good standing with other cultists, the prospective member would have to at least publicly withhold doubts about the organization. Failure to do so would sooner or later arouse suspicion and hostility from other members of the group. However, even to feign belief in the group's norms and ideas might eventually convince the person in question that the claims are bona fide. This is particularly likely the greater the sacrifice the individual makes to remain a member of the organization, as is discussed later. It occurs because we tend to believe in what we do and because continued participation results in continued contact with people who do sincerely believe and who, with or without awareness, reinforce outward manifestations of that belief. Thus, the second reason that norms are important is that although they are initially mechanisms of control that are external to the individual, group members will, in most cases, internalize the group's norms. Internalization means that the members will accept the norms as their own and come to believe that they represent not the working rules of a social organization, but instead, the truth, the only right way to think, behave, and so on. Thus, group participation, particularly over a period of time, effectively defines the individual group member's point of view, at least on matters of relevance to the group. This process tends to occur whether the group is formally organized, such as a business, a school, or the military, or an informally organized group, such as a cult, a bridge club, or a street gang. Third, norms are also important because they define the life of the group. By rewarding members who conform to the group's values and sanctioning or excluding those who dissent, disagree, or deviate, the group "purifies" its membership, leaving only those who share a basic set of convictions and who are prepared to make personal investments in the group's cause. In fact, a group exists only so long as its members agree upon, at least in general, the basic values and goals of the group. Once this consensus is lost, the group breaks up into factions or disbands.

Cohesiveness. Group structure emerges because it tends to facilitate group interactions and to perpetuate the life of the group. Cohesiveness refers to the degree of interrelatedness among the members of the group, or more simply, the average degree of attraction of each individual member for the group as indicated by the extent to which individual members show a consensus regarding the basic norms and values of the group. Cohesiveness of a group tends to be high under certain conditions, such as when the initiation process into the group is severe or costly, and in the presence of external threats. The consequences of group cohesiveness are important to the life span of the group. For example, a high degree of cohesiveness is generally associated with more communication and cooperation among members and a greater degree of social influence of the members on one another.

Consequences of Group Membership. As has been suggested, people join and participate in social groups for a variety of social and psychological reasons, including boredom relief, fellowship, and expanded social activities, and to gain prestige, security, and identity. Participation in groups also creates the opportunity to act on one's beliefs. Regardless of initial motivations, however, active and persistent group participation typically results in more or less permanent consequences. For example, group norms serve as a principal source of individual beliefs and hence the source of the frame of reference from which reality, truth and falsity, goodness and evil, are evaluated. Also, group participation tends to foster what is known as *ethnocentrism*—i.e., the idea that one's beliefs are not only acceptable and right for oneself, but also that they constitute the only true and acceptable set of beliefs. This results from the group processes that reinforce group norms and punish deviations, and, as such, are to some extent characteristic of all groups. However, in some groups, the degree of ethnocentrism is such that it creates genuine hostility, anger, and even violence towards outgroup members—that is, those who do not belong to the group nor share its values. Another important consequence of group participation is the influence that fellow group members come to have on behavior and judgments, called the social-influence process, which is a pervasive and powerful determinant of individual behavior and beliefs.

Social Influence

Social influence refers to the extent to which one is affected by the beliefs, values, and judgments of others and it is involved in the process by which groups ensure that their members will adhere to a basic set of beliefs. For example, *indoctrination* (or socialization) denotes the procedure by which a group trains prospective members into its ways of thinking. Some groups have elaborate, extensive and formalized rituals of indoctrination (e.g., the family socialization of a child). Indoctrination works by making the individual feel less competent, placing him or her in a stressful situation the outcome of which is uncertain, making the individual more dependent on the group for structure, approval, and even survival, severing ties or reducing the importance of previous group affiliations, and reducing the person's sense of individuality. In the socialization of a child, of course, these conditions are not created; they are inherent in the child's situation. The child is naturally dependent on his or her parents for physical, emotional, and social survival. Under these conditions of dependence, the group then systematically rewards manifestations of the group's norms and punishes deviations from acceptable behavior. By making the individual feel less competent at meeting individual needs, the group enhances its own image, which results in increasing the probability that the individual's acceptance and internalization of the group's values and norms will occur. As the individual begins to conform to the group's norms, the more stringent requirements of indoctrination are lifted; when the person can be reasonably trusted to consistently abide by the norms, full acceptance into the group occurs.

One interesting aspect of the indoctrination process is that more difficult and costly forms of indoctrination often lead to more complete and enduring forms of allegiance and loyalty to the group, at least for those who successfully complete the indoctrination phase of group membership. In other words, the more one gives up in behalf of the group and the more difficult it is to gain admittance, the more one prizes the membership, and the more one will do to live up to the group's expectations. Thus, for the previously committed members of Mankind United, the request that they give all of their possessions to the cult and immerse themselves into a total cult existence probably strengthened their commitment rather than weakened it. The more they had committed, the more they had to lose by the cult's possible failure; thus, the more they were willing to do to ensure its success. Of course, there are limits to these processes. However, the finding that intensive indoctrination usually equals a greater degree of loyalty suggests how cults such as Mankind United are able to command what appears to outsiders to be extreme forms of loyalty.

The basic psychological process underlying indoctrination is called *conformity*—i.e., the tendency to agree with the judgments of others. In a series of classic studies, Sherif (1936) examined this process using what is known as the *autokinetic effect*. The autokinetic effect refers to the fact that for most people, a small, single, stationary light will appear to move in an otherwise totally darkened room because there is no standard against which the lack of movement of the light may be judged. Sherif had subjects make judgments about the distance of movement while they were alone. It must be noted that these judgments were totally subjective because the light was not actually moving, a fact of which the subjects were unaware. Later, several subjects would make such judgments together. What Sherif and numerous other researchers have found is that the judgments of the subjects will eventually converge (i.e., become similar). The convergence effect is even stronger when the subjects in the experiment are members of the same group. Sherif conceived of this experiment as an analogue of the process of norm formation in small social groups. In this experiment, there genuinely is no right or objectively determinable correct answer regarding the amount of movement because the light is not moving at all. Similarly when considering appropriate modes of dress and behavior, or answers to political, religious, social, and philosophical questions, what is judged to be the right answer is a highly subjective matter, and as Sherif's experiment suggests, easily influenced by the judgments of others. However, in some circumstances, the judgment need not be totally arbitrary and subjective for the influence of others to occur.

For example, Solomon Asch (1952) had subjects make judgments regarding which of three lines were most similar in length to a standard line in a series of comparisons. The dimensions of the lines were such that in sessions where subjects made the judgments alone, almost no one ever made a mistake in choosing which of the three comparison lines was closest in length to the standard. However, in the actual experiment, the subject was joined by several others who had agreed to give erroneous judgments on certain trials in order to assess the influence of group pressure on individual behavior. In the basic experiment, Asch found that approximately 80% of the subjects tested would conform to the erroneous judgments of the majority at least once, even though they were clearly incorrect, and that on one-third of the trials conformity occurred.

What are the consequences of social influence? One practical effect is liking; that is, members of a group tend not to like the individual who does not go along with group judgments (Schachter, 1951). Secondly, it has been shown that some individuals will conform even when the effect of their conformity is not trivial. For example, Stanley Milgram (1963) has demonstrated that obedience to authority will occur even if the end result of the conformity appears to be potentially damaging or harmful to someone else. In this case, obedience occurred despite the fact that what subjects were asked to do was to shock a victim at levels beginning at 15 volts but increasing to 450 volts. In fact, studies have shown that a person may conform to the behavior of others even when it is clear that the failure to act independently may result in actual injury to others or to oneself (Darley & Latane, 1968; Latane & Darley, 1968). Also, an authority figure is not always required to create conformity. Sometimes it is sufficient for an individual simply to see others acting in a certain way.

But why do we conform, particularly when it appears to be against our best interests to do so, such as when members of Mankind United gave up their worldly possessions to help perpetuate the group? Basically, there are two answers to this question, or more specifically, there are two processes of conformity. The first is *normative conformity* (e.g., Deutsch & Gerard, 1955), which occurs when we go along with the group because we desire to avoid some form of punishment (e.g., rejection, ridicule, criticism, or even the fear of looking foolish) or to gain a reward (e.g., praise, recognition, acceptance, affection, etc.). On other occasions, however, we may conform because the behavior of other people has informational value—that is, it suggests the proper, appropriate, or socially acceptable manner in which to behave. This is called *informational conformity* and is particularly relevant in ambiguous social situations where the appropriate behaviors and attitudes may not be known to some people. Social groups tend to work out their own solutions to questions of appropriateness of behavior, and there may be no universally right answer. Thus, the individual may conform because the behavior of others reveals the socially accepted way to act in the group in question. Both types of conformity reflect the powerful influence that others exert on our behavior and the degree to which incurring the displeasure of others is avoided. It is important to note that individuals ordinarily do not consider their own behavior as conformity, even when it appears to be so to others. Instead, one's own behavior is typically viewed as logical or the right thing to do. There is no evidence, however, that such beliefs make one less vulnerable to the influence of others.

The concept of conformity is relevant to the study of anomalistic experience for two reasons. First, many of the events that eventually receive a paranormal interpretation are ambiguous and, hence, the individual's judgment as to what exactly took place is to a large extent determined by how other people respond in that situation. The séance and UFO sightings are classic examples of situations in which the influence of others is apt to be strongly felt because of the ambiguity of the stimulus situation. Second, conformity also suggests how occult group members come to believe in some of the concepts to which they subscribe. Participation in occult groups results in conformity to the views of the group just as membership in any social organization does. Thus, what may appear to be individually generated occult beliefs are in many cases simply the internalization of the norms and judgments that emerge in the group context.

For example, Raven and his colleagues (Raven, Anthony, & Mansson, 1960; Raven, Mansson, & Anthony, 1962) have demonstrated the effects of social influence in the area of ESP, although this was not the primary purpose of their experiments. In one study, subjects were asked to receive an ESP image (not actually sent) and some subjects were led to believe that their coparticipants had actually received such a message. Results indicated that social influence (i.e., indications that fellow subjects had received a message) led to a greater number of reported receptions of the ESP image and greater belief in the existence of ESP. In a subsequent study, Raven (1962) demonstrated that reported reception and belief in the existence of ESP could be independently manipulated. What is termed *referent influence* was established by telling some subjects that their coparticipants were especially high in perceptual ability, telling others that they were average, and leading the remainder to believe that their coparticipants were unusually fallible in perceptual ability. *Expert influence* was created by attributing to the coparticipants various levels of ESP ability. Again, subjects were asked to attempt to receive a bogus ESP message and were led to believe that their coparticipants received an ESP image on some trials. Results indicated that referent influence (i.e., the influence ability associated with being similar to the subject) affected the rate of reported receptions of ESP messages, whereas expert influence (i.e., being knowledgeable or skillful with regard to a particular endeavor) had the greatest amount of influence on the degree of belief in the existence of ESP.

One implication of these results is that although experts in the various areas of occult phenomena would be expected to have a strong effect on what is believed regarding the existence or lack of existence of that phonomenon, one's friends and fellow group members would be expected to exert a stronger influence on the direct experience of the phenomenon. It is not surprising, therefore, that when believers join together in cults and other organizations they lead one another into believing that some occult phenomenon has taken place. Also, the facts that believers more often attempt manifestations of the paranormal and that some occult groups are organized specifically for the purpose of attempting and validating occult experiences simply increase the probability that unusual or unfamiliar events will receive occult interpretations. It is important to remember that the essential properties of many occult phenomena, such as the reception of ESP images (without controls or the determination of the actual rate of accuracy) are quite subjective and ephemeral. It is precisely on such judgments in which a correct answer is difficult to determine that we are most vulnerable to influence by others.

Similarly, in their field study of a small occult group that had predicted the end of the world, Festinger et al. (1956) found evidence for the powerful role of experiencing belief-relevant phenomena in the context of the group. As indicated in Chapter 7, the leader of the group received "messages" from outer space that were interpreted as indicating the precise date on which the world was to be flooded. At the appointed hour, some members of the group waited together, but others (mostly college students home on vacation) either faced the event alone or in the company of disbelieving family members. When the prophecy failed, those members waiting together eventually worked out the solution that the prophecy had been a test and thus the flood was averted because of their faith and efforts. Consequently, this portion of the group rejoiced at what was now judged to be a confirmation of the prediction, and began efforts to convince others of its accuracy. By contrast, those who awaited the end without the supportive atmosphere of the group were more inclined to conclude that the prophecy had indeed failed, thereby creating doubts in the authenticity of the leader's messages and the group's specific beliefs. Incidentally, even the members who lost faith in the group and the prophecy did not in most cases abandon their beliefs in other occult and extraterrestrial phenomena.

One important aspect of social influence is that these effects can occur with or without the individual's awareness or beliefs in their own vulnerabilities to them. For example, surveys have shown that most people believe that they (and most others as well) would not submit to the conformity effect such as that contained in Milgram's (1963) studies of obedience. And yet, repeated replications of the experiment itself suggest that around two-thirds of the subjects continue to obey up to the highest and most dangerous levels. Thus, what is believed to be true about human nature and the ways in which people actually behave in various situations may be entirely different.

OCCULTISM IN CULTURAL CONTEXT

In the chapter on beliefs, we discussed several explanations of why certain people might be personally attracted to paranormal ideas. The reasons for occultism are not solely an individual matter, however. Part of the impetus for occultism is to be found in the characteristics, history, and norms of the society in which occult beliefs appear. Occult believers do not generally discover anew the ideas to which they subscribe, although new varieties and combinations are occasionally invented. Similarly, beliefs do not exist in a vacuum, unaffected by the social context in which they emerge. Instead, the believer is exposed to and taught the occult ideology as it exists in a society. For example, some people are socialized into occultism in the same manner that they acquire religious beliefs, political views, language, prejudices, etc. Indeed, there is hardly any aspect of individual experience and behavior that is not profoundly influenced by the values of our cultural ancestors and the expectations of our social contemporaries. The fact that paranormal ideas are culturally transmitted from one generation to the next like other basic cultural values explains in part, their amazing permanence and resistance to change.

Social norms tend to outlive the conditions that produced them in the first place, a phenomenon known as *cultural lag*, and because of this, occult beliefs may be the residual of past social conditions. On the other hand, because there are indications that occultism is in some ways as strong and pervasive as ever, it may be that it reflects contemporary social conditions and trends.

The Occult Subculture

A wide variety of occult and pseudoscientific groups are available to the active believer, from Theosophy to the Flat Earth Society. And these are but two of the better-known organizations. In addition, there are literally hundreds of smaller regional and local groups organized around one or more occult themes. Several more groups like Mankind United have sprung into existence, enjoyed a period of growth and expansion and impressive membership, only to decline or die out entirely due to internal dissention, loss of enthusiasm, external interference, or other disruptive influences. Such groups vary in nature and structure from highly committed cults, the members of which have forsaken conventional life styles in order, for example, to prepare for being taken away by flying saucers, to university clubs, psychic–research organizations, and informal discussion groups.

At this point, a theoretical distinction is useful in defining the nature of the occult subculture. Bainbridge (1978a) has noted in this connection that there are two distinct ways in which the concept of a subculture is used in the social sciences. First, subcultures are groups of people who share common values, opinions, behaviors, heritage, language, and life styles, such as an ethnic group. Second, the concept of a subculture may be used to identify a set of ideas subscribed to by many people. Bainbridge further argues that the occult subculture more closely resembles the latter definition. That is, no single ethnic, religious, social, or demographic group exclusively subscribes to occult ideas. Furthermore, occultism is not entirely comprised of any single cohesive group in which believers have daily face-to-face contact with other believers. Instead, the occult subculture is a complex mixture of generalized ideas distributed by the media, books, word-of-mouth, and casual social interchange, and a wide variety of large and small, international and local organizations, groups, and cults. Indeed, it is difficult to imagine a time at which greater numbers of presentations of the paranormal have ever been available, leading skeptic Dennis Rawlins (1977) to wonder how believers can subscribe to the notion of the occult as being "ancient and secret wisdom" because it is available at every supermarket and bookstore.

In any case, the typical occult believer has several sources of ideas that may influence his or her beliefs and behavior. The sources tend to fall into one of two categories: occult groups and occult literature. Often, for example, an individual's first adventure into occultism is through one of the several best-selling books promoting occult or pseudoscientific views such as von Däniken's *Chariots of the Gods*. With their interest stiumlated by the wonderful and exciting ideas in such a book, the believer may be subsequently led into membership in any occult organization dealing with the same or a similar idea, followed perhaps by disenchantment, leading to a shift of loyalty to a competing organization or a return to privately held, informal belief. Many cultists believe that an amalgamation of many types of occult belief is possible, borrowing bits and pieces from several different systems and creating individualized ideologies. For some, such an amalgamation is also an overt reality, as is suggested by the belief of some cultists that the various paranormal organizations will join forces forming a "sixth race" that, with the special powers attributed to occult believers, will change the world accordingly (Dohrman, 1958). For those who directly participate in occult organizations however, it must be concluded that to the exciting and attractive ideas of the occult ideology are added powerful group influences such as conformity, which, although characteristic of all social groups, help to explain how some people, once active in such a group, can subscribe to wild and fanciful ideas and devote their fortunes, time, energies, liberties, and even their lives to the cause.

It is difficult if not impossible to establish the number of people influenced by the occult subculture either directly or indirectly. Dohrman (1958) estimated that five million people in the United States had at one time or another belonged to a cult. That number has undoubtedly increased since that time and many more people are affected in less extreme and drastic ways. Because there is a great variety of occult ideas, it is safe to conclude that everyone is to some degree affected by the occult subculture either by virtue of their own beliefs and participation or as a result of the interest and activity of someone they know.

Motives for Cult Participation.   From the perspective of an outsider, the motives of people who adopt cult ideologies and make personal sacrifices of time, energy, and money to such organizations seem perplexing. Not sharing the cultist's beliefs and expectations, the disbeliever wants to know how so many people can be so easily "misled." Often, in the absence of an adequate explanation, many people subscribe to a notion of the cult member as an irrational, easily swayed, if not insane, crackpot. But this stereotype adds nothing to the understanding of the cultist's motivation, and, in fact, is not supported by the evidence. According to Dohrman's research, for example, most of the Mankind United faithful were anything but weird cranks. The majority were White, middle-class descendents of Northwestern European ancestors, and at least second-generation Americans. Although women predominated, perhaps due to fewer occupational commitments and hence greater opportunity, 40.8% of one sample of members were men. Excluding children, over 50% of the membership were 40 to 60 years of age and almost one-third were over 60. Almost half were white-collar workers and skilled workers, with even a sizable proportion of professionals, particularly chiropractors, teachers, nurses, and ex-ministers. Finally, although frequently a sore point with cultists, the average level of formal education was approximately at the 9th to 10th grades, not far from the average for that period. These findings are generally consistent with those reported by Wallis (1976), who studied the Dianetics movement, the forerunner of Scientology. Similarly, Lynch (1977) described the members of one occult group as predominately "white, middle-aged, middle-class and middle-of-the-road [p. 97]" politically and socially. Thus, despite what differences might exist between the ardent cult follower and the disbelieving non-joiner, in many respects, the "average" Mankind United member and the members of many other similar cults differ little from the population as a whole demographically, and certainly are not typically the through-going social deviants often portrayed.

As observed earlier regarding beliefs in the paranormal, the reasons for joining a cult are undoubtedly complex and vary to some degree from one group to the next and from one individual to another. However, four important elements seem especially relevant: the cult, its ideology, the leader, and the cultist.

Some of the impetus for becoming involved in a cult emerges from the appeal of *the cult* itself and the group's basic ideas and ideals. Cults, along with all social groups, provide for their members a sense of purpose, fellowship with like-minded individuals, something to do, and hence relief from the boredom, isolation, and alienation felt by many people. For example, as noted earlier, Mankind United members were kept exceedingly busy meeting quotas and deadlines and preparing for meetings. Such activity takes place within a social context of other believers who share the individual member's values and goals and who therefore reinforce manifestations of the group's purpose with praise, attention, and friendship. Moreover, there is no doubt that followers of Mankind United came to believe that they were engaged in a momentous enterprise of earth-shaking importance and profound, world-wide implications that made almost any sacrifice seem unimportant. It is also likely that the mystery and secrecy inherent in Mankind United activities, as well as the threat of both real and imagined intervention and interference from outside the group, kept the membership in a relatively constant state of frenzied activity and excitement. Thus, cults provide for their members something to do that is important and meaningful. Similarly, a cult offers its members the opportunity for status and prestige, which may be unavailable from the larger community. For example, participation in Mankind United offered what appeared to be an important outlet for the intelligence, talents, and energies of many of the women members—opportunities not always available to women, particularly during the period of time in question. Another example of this effect, suggested by Dohrman (1958), was the role of the several chiropractors who were members of Mankind United. Scorned by the medical community and generally responded to with indifference by the public, the chiropractors were afforded special status and importance in Mankind United, where the principles of chiropractic manipulation and mistrust of conventional medicine interfaced easily with the metaphysical and conspiratorial thinking of the cultists.

The *ideology* of the cult is also responsible for part of the appeal of the group. For example, the cult ideology is often a complex blend of high-minded ideals, occult ideas, and practical, how-to suggestions on self-improvement, relations with others, and success and happiness. In Mankind United could be found not only the generally attractive notions of world peace and prosperity, but also special appeals to social groups often ignored and underserved (particularly in the 1930s and 1940s) by conventional institutions such as the middle class, women, the elderly, and the poor. Cult literature often offers vague slogans and promises that may be so general as not to mean very much but that somehow still sound appealing and positive. Members attending a large Mankind United meeting were once greeted by a large sign asserting "We are not cattle," for example. Cult ideologies also offer simple, easy-to-understand solutions to persistent and annoyingly complex problems, such as the meaning of life. Who would not be interested in what appeared to be answers to age-old paradoxes like wealth and poverty, health and disease, war and peace, good and evil, and so on? Often, the general paranoia experienced by many people is exploited by the cult ideology in the suggestion that such problems could be solved except for the interference of small groups of powerful, wealthy, and incredibly selfish conspirators. Similarly, the "Sponsors" of Mankind United may have satisfied the members' desire for enlightened, trustworthy, dedicated, and infallible leaders who would solve the problems of the world, making it safe and secure. Most groups also offer their prospective members a manufactured and packaged ideology that may require little contemplation or original thought, but that also paradoxically emphasizes the inherent wisdom, rationality, enlightenment, and high ideals of its followers by contrast with the rest of humanity. Brent (1979) has argued that westernized versions of eastern religions are tailored to fit the social values and realities of their new disciples and as a consequence are so greatly simplified and altered that they hardly resemble the original discipline. Many historical and contemporary paranormal cults have been secretive in nature. This serves the dual purpose of avoiding examination of the group's ideas by a skeptical and often hostile society, and it also enhances the idea that the cult is the reservoir of special "ancient knowledge," unavailable in conventional philosophies and systems of thought. Finally, cults offer a smorgasbord of occult and metaphysical ideas that are attractive to many people, as is discussed later. Some authors have suggested that the metaphysical occult world view serves as an "alternative reality" (e.g., Ellwood, 1973) that, even though its ideas have been around for centuries, has only recently become accessible and acceptable as a middle-class system of belief (Marty, 1970).

The *leader* of occult groups also usually plays a large and decisive role in the development of allegiance towards the group. Whether male or female, such individuals are often described as being physically attractive, charismatic, forceful, dynamic, mysterious, powerful, and perhaps most importantly of all, knowledgeable (e.g., Evans, 1973)—not necessarily knowledgeable in the usual sense of formal education, but rather, knowledgeable regarding the deepest, most enigmatic secrets of life and the universe. The influence of the cult leader is often so great that his or her active involvement effectively defines the life span of the cult, with the cult disbanding with the leader's departure, as happened with the withdrawal of "Superintendent" Bell from the Mankind United movement. In addition, cult leaders or their followers often promote the idea that the leader has special occult abilities (e.g., telepathy, astral projection, psychic healing and/or surgery), which lends an added dimension to the perception of the leader as an important and gifted person. Whether these claims are deliberate deceptions on the part of the leader, sincere beliefs, or misinterpretations matters little in terms of the effects of such apparent skills of the leader on the faithful.

In some cases, the leader takes on an almost Messianic stature whose authority is unquestioned and absolute (Wallis, 1976). Perhaps such leaders serve as surrogate parents, satisfying the desire of many to be free of the vexing problems of adulthood, with its responsibilities, disappointments, and conflicts. For example, Deutsch (1975) reported that the followers of one "sidewalk mystic" were primarily teenagers and young adults who expressed difficulty in relating to their parents and the expectations of modern living. A wise, powerful, and benevolent leader can protect the interests and safety of the group members while dispensing precious commodities of attention, affection, and acceptance. One of the most interesting patterns associated with cults is the tendency of sizable proportions of the members of such groups to continue to believe in the leader's sincerity and high ideals, even after the leader has been discredited in the eyes of others for violating the group's norms or becoming wealthy at the expense of the membership, as sometimes happens. Such loyalty exemplifies the power cult leaders exercise with their followers. Whatever the specific effects and personality characteristics of the cult leader, it is clear that in many, if not most, cases, a primary motive for participation in the cult is the magnetic appeal of the leader and that for some of the most highly committed members, the leader is revered as the embodiment of the cult's ideals. In some circumstances, cult leaders may even hold virtually total control over their members, as was apparently the case in the mass suicide of 900 of the People's Temple religious cult in Jonestown, Guyana, in November, 1978.

The personality and previous experiences of the *cult member* also seem to determine, to some extent, the probability of eventual cult participation. A central motive for cultism is a constellation of traits and experiences that centers around dissatisfaction with modern life and society (Evans, 1973). The loneliness and alienation induced by the interplay of complex social forces create impulses to action; in particular, the search for stable, comprehensible, and meaningful alternatives to existential chaos. Suzanne Gordon (1976) has observed that one strategy for finding answers for millions of lonely people is what she calls "the loneliness business" consisting of the faddish, quasi therapeutic self-improvement movements that proliferated in the 1960s and 1970s and that often mix concepts such as authenticity and self-actualization with parapsychology and traditional occultism. She also suggests that more manifestly metaphysical and occult groups, such as the Krisha Consciousness Movement, undoubtedly prosper from the interest, participation, and support of the disaffected, particularly those who are looking for something special, different, and mysterious.

By the same token, cultists appear to be cut off from conventional institutions such as the family, school, church, government, and the business community. Lacking a keen sense of purpose and direction in their lives, their frustration may be compounded by the belief that events that affect them are out of control because such institutions are often too large, unresponsive, bureaucratic, and self-motivated. Thus, the cultist is estranged from the conventional sources of purpose, activity, and truth. For example, the cultist is often defensive about his or her level of education and yet disparages formal education and expertise in favor of "deeper knowledge" and "profound wisdom." To such people, established science may be bewildering, too technical, as well as frightening in its implications. Similarly, classical philosophy, literature, and the humanities require a disciplined scholarship and patience beyond the intellectual habits and abilities of some. Most importantly, the "truths" of conventional scholarship are altogether too tentative, uncertain, and complex, and hence are not satisfying, particularly to those desperately searching for the final answer and absolute truth. By contrast, with such self-perceived intellectual and personal inadequacy, the cult stands as a vital, active, self-certain group of people who appear to have discovered a purposeful and meaningful life and who are doing something concrete and immediate about their problems.

Perhaps the most important source of dissatisfaction for the cultist is that concerning conventional religion. Although deeply religious ruminations are common in occult and pseudoscientific writings (e.g., Story, 1977) and often a close analogy exists between theology and cult ideology, there is also typically a mistrust and disenchantment with the everyday church. Dohrman (1958) found that many Mankind United members were disgusted with modern religions, believing them to be sanctimonious, otherworldly, self-righteous, and hypocritical. Specifically, many were put off by the so-called "negativism" of such concepts as sin, hell, and the devil. Apparently, they preferred the more positive, hopeful, here-and-now theology of Mankind United. Evidence for such dissatisfaction cited by Dohrman included the finding that although many denominations and faiths were represented in a survey of previous religious memberships among a sample of Mankind United members, over 37% of the sample had joined the movement while followers of one of several unconventional faiths such as the Rosicrucians, Theosophy, or other metaphysical sects. Thus, participation in Mankind United was preceded in many cases by excursions into other "fringe" religions and cultish movements, suggesting that the disenchantment with socially approved religion was persistent and well entrenched in the thinking of these Mankind United participants.

In fact, Evans (1973) has argued that the simultaneous decline of religion and the dramatic advancement of science and technology in the 20th century have combined to create a spiritual void fueling the development of such movements as Scientology, flying-saucer organizations, and westernized mystical groups. According to Evans, these groups bridge for their adherents a conceptual gap between the values of traditional belief systems and the realities of a scientifically altered and rapidly changing social structure. As Evans (1973) puts it:

> the cults, while revealing themselves as insubstantial and occasionally eccentric to the point of being purely funny, nevertheless do their level best to fill a serious vacuum—a vacuum which man has created by his own diligence and scientific curiosity. The truth is that we have been too clever for our own good, and have let our technical mastery of science move far, far ahead of our philosophical and social expertise. With contemptuous ease Man has kicked away from under his feet the bases of his age-old truce with the unknown—the multiple belief systems which we know of as religion. Now the Universe and the enigma of Man's existence and purpose are revealed only too clearly. It is little wonder that millions of uncertain souls, appalled by this, have striven to make peace again. Many have succeeded, but the terms of the truce have of course been changed [pp. 252-253].

A somewhat different view of the cultist has emerged from recent studies of occult groups. Balch and Taylor (1977) studied members of a cult that gained national recognition in 1975 when over 30 people from Oregon disappeared after attending a lecture on flying saucers by two individuals identifying themselves as Bo and Peep. From their investigation of this particular movement, Balch and Taylor offer two conclusions at variance with the standard characterization of the cultist. First, those individuals who left their homes and life styles to take up the regimen prescribed by Bo and Peep for obtaining eternal life in the heavens did so willingly. The reason for this apparently stems from the fact that those who were receptive to the message were generally committed to an occult view in the first place and because they defined themselves as "seekers" of spiritual and ideological truth. Second, having made the commitment, there was very little indoctrination and, in fact, the presentations of Bo and Peep were not high-pressure persuasion attempts. Thus, the image of the cultist being kidnapped and brainwashed often portrayed in the media was not in fact the case for this group. The generality of these findings to other cults is, of course, a matter for further research.

Similarly, Lynch (1977) concluded that most members of the occult group that he studied were neither deviant nor passive recipients of the occult ideology. Instead, members became involved because they had become acquainted with occult ideas through reading, had experienced what they took to be an occult phenomenon, were drawn by the new and exciting ideas of the group, and because the group served as a social support and source of emotional ties.

The Issue of "Brainwashing".   The term brainwashing has been used to refer to an intensive indoctrination experience such as that used by the Chinese during the Korean conflict. The term is something of a misnomer, because it suggests a mysterious, almost occult phenomenon. Instead, it is simply the use of tactics of persuasion and indoctrination in a more intensive form, over longer periods of time, and in circumstances in which greater social control over the individual may be exercised. The method involves several tactics including assaulting the self, removal or reduction of signs of identity and past allegiances, physical and psychological abuse, and very strong pressures to conform (Lifton, 1963). Other mechanisms of intensive indoctrination may involve the use of personal information to embarrass the individual and to manipulate guilt, the use of sensory deprived environments, removal of social support, and tension–relieving activities, physical discomfort, and the use of various kinds of distortion (e.g., Zimbardo, 1970).

Because of the intensity of the tactics, a "breaking point" is eventually reached at which the individual is sufficiently exhausted, depressed, confused, frightened, and disoriented that he or she is willing to "confess" or say virtually anything requested by the group. As is common with other forms of indoctrination, manifestations of conformity are rewarded with social rewards such as acceptance and by a reduction of the severity of the indoctrination procedures. Perhaps the essential qualities of the so-called "brainwashing" effect and what distinguishes it from more conventional forms of indoctrination are the extent to which the individual is made to feel dependent on the group and its ideology for survival and identity, and the extent to which the individual's sense of certainty, regularity, and predictability are disrupted. As was noted earlier, feelings of uncertainty and unpredictability are both highly stressful as well as likely to make an individual more receptive to external influences that promise to reinstate the condition of predictability and control over one's fate.

There is evidence that some extremist political groups use intensive indoctrination procedures, especially with kidnapped victims (Hacker, 1976).

Many people apparently believe that occult and religious cults use such indoctrination tactics, as is evidenced by legal actions brought by parents of adult cult members to have their children removed from the cult and its influence and the emergence of so-called deprogramming centers. There appears to be little evidence of "brainwashing" in the sense of involuntary and unwilling manipulation of members' beliefs, and, in fact, the closest thing to "brainwashing" may be the attempts at involuntary deprogramming (Shupe, Spielmann, & Stigall, 1977). Also, as previously indicated, available studies suggest that cult members are usually more than willing participants. This does not mean that the cults do not encourage indoctrination of their members in various ways nor that cult participation is something other than conformity to group norms.

The issue is one of choice. To the extent that cultists choose to become involved with occult groups, "brainwashing" is not the issue. However, to the extent that the group employs rituals of submission, deprivation, emotional propaganda, coercive pressure, and isolation from outside sources of social and ideological support, we may say that intensive indoctrination is being used. It is also important to keep in mind that people are apt to label any indoctrination or persuasion attempt that promotes ideas with which they disagree as "brainwashing" even though viewing propaganda consonant with their own beliefs as "education."

Characteristics of the Occult Literature. In addition to cult participation, people are influenced by the occult subculture through exposure to the many and varied presentations of occult ideas in books, magazines, and the media. As Bainbridge (1978a) has observed, this is probably the most common form of contact with the occult subculture for the average individual. But, what are the characteristics of the occult and pseudoscientific literature that distinguish it from other readily available sets of ideas, and in particular, what is it about occult ideas that make them so attractive to so many people? Also, what makes occult ideas so interchangeable? There are, of course, several perspectives from which these questions might be addressed, some of which have been previously discussed. In addition, a survey of the relevant literature suggests five characteristics of the occult subculture as a set of ideas that contribute to its appeal and that make possible the functional comparability of occult ideas.

First the idea of *problematic urgency*. Occult and pseudoscientific groups often begin by postulating the existence of a dramatic problem, need, or impending catastrophe that needs to be solved or answered. The problem may be real (e.g., the threat of nuclear war, or the need for meaning and purpose in one's life) or imagined (e.g., the "Hidden Rulers"' conspiracy); it may be global or personal; it may be historical or contemporary; it may be an impending disaster or the promise of a new opportunity. The paranormal literature is full of terms that suggest the urgency, importance, uniqueness, and timeliness of its revelations. Proclamations of newness and importance abound (e.g., "new breakthrough," "new revelations," "the discovery of the century," etc.) along with indications of sinister threats and profound enigmas (e.g., "the phenomena science cannot explain," "the plot against psychics," etc). Frequently, the urgent claim has to do with an aspect of human experience of ability supposedly unexplained by conventional scientific theory or the "discovery" of a new interpretation of historical events. Ironically, such momentous promises are usually followed by dreary accounts of the same occult theories found in hundreds of other treatments of the subject (Rawlins, 1977).

No doubt, the theme of problematic urgency is to some extent a promotional gimmick of publishers and authors to create the impression that there is something new and exciting about the latest book on occultism. But there is something more than advertising to the atmosphere of emergency. The existence of the theme, we suspect, also reflects the expression of a deeply felt condition of the occult reader. That is, the occultist senses the urgent need for answers and, more specifically, answers that are unique and creative. It is the occultist who is not only searching for the truth and seeking to solve problems, but who feels that conventional strategies are lacking and are not up to the task. It is the occultist who sees the problem as looming so large and immediate that patient, step-by-step analysis and problem solving is hopeless. Thus, appeals to the sense of urgency strike a resonant chord with many people because it is often implied that a final and absolute answer is at hand.

The second characteristic of occult literature might be called the concept of *pervasive reality*, captured by the idea that everything is possible. It may be argued that even dispositionally skeptical scientists might allow that anything is possible. However, this statement usually subsumes some unstated assumptions for the scientist. For example, one might propose that anything is possible until adequate evidence is available indicating what is and what is not possible. Similarly, scientists recognize that even the most recent and most thoroughly validated theories are in some way incomplete and must be altered in the light of new, and as yet undiscovered evidence. In this sense, too, anything may be possible. By contrast, much of the literature of the occult subculture promotes the idea that occult phenomena are real quite apart from the evidence. Indeed, the failure of conventional scientific investigation to support the existence of an occult phenomenon is sometimes taken as proof in favor of its existence, and one of the central characteristics of occultism is the tenacious tendency to accept as genuine any paranormal claim despite the amount or logic of proof to the contrary (Scheibe & Sarbin, 1965). Thus, no matter how remote the possibility, the assumption is often made that everything that is conceivable is, in fact, true.

Furthermore, unlike many religious beliefs, which may posit the existence of phenomena that contradict scientific theories, but which are usually more exacting and specific regarding which "miracles" are endorsed, occultism often assumes that anything that sounds interesting and wonderful is real.

In essence, this is unrestrained and undisciplined generalization. Often the conclusion that one remarkable event is an instance of the paranormal serves to validate a second similar conclusion, and so on, throughout the entire spectrum of occult ideas. It might also be thought of as a kind of individual projection or anthropomorphism of the universe in which personal beliefs are assumed to be universal reality. Some observers have argued that this tendency results from a general reduction of critical ability (e.g., Kusche, 1977), whereas others have suggested that it stems from an inherent desire to believe (e.g., Story, 1977). In either case, however, occult ideas often become highly interdependent and interchangeable. Truzzi (1977) has cautioned against treating all forms of occultism and eccentric belief as the same, noting that followers of one system may reject the beliefs of another, and in fact, intramural disagreements in the occult subculture may be a source of some of the best "debunking" literature. However, we suspect that specificity of belief is mostly characteristic of deeply involved occult believers such as professional occultists rather than the "average" believer, as is suggested by the high degree of correspondence among occult ideas found in general populations such as college students (e.g., Bainbridge, 1978a) and the common tendency of believers to easily move from one brand of occultism to another. It is not unusual to find even relatively sober parapsychologists discussing the possibilities of ghosts, levitation, and reincarnation. As is discussed later in this chapter, the unifying dimension for the idea that the conceivable is always real is probably popular metaphysics in which the unlimited properties of the soul make possible what otherwise appear to be impossible processes.

A related characteristic of occultism is the concept of *absolute certainty*. This is dogma in the place of evidence, logic, proof, or even speculation or faith. Although any system of beliefs, including scientific theories, may be held dogmatically, there often exists a generally agreed-upon method of arriving at the truth, whether the method is faithfully followed or not. The method may be the rules of evidence, the scientific method, logic, or the trials of faith. The point is that many belief systems assume such a method, requiring the believer to adhere to a set of principles and assumptions for the extrapolation of beliefs. By contrast, occultism does not have an established epistimology, and more frequently relies on several methods and assumptions, some of which may be internally inconsistent. For example, even those sympathetic to the notion of parapsychology have noted the tendency of believers to become impatient with questions regarding proof of the phenomenon despite the widespread aspirations of parapsychologists for their field to be accepted as a science and to use the scientific method (Beloff, 1978). Wallis (1976) has used the phrase "assertive claims of infallibility" to refer to this tendency within Dianetics. Bronowsky (1979) has argued that magic is a technology without a science—an attempt to exercise power to influence and control people and events, without an understanding of people and events.

A paradoxical feature of the occult subculture is that although the ideas promulgated are often illogical, improbable, and obscure, there is nonetheless a very strong expectation that they will be accepted, not as interesting ideas, hypotheses, alternative explanations, or even speculations, but as matter-of-fact reality, and often as the best possible explanation. Many systems of knowledge are complex and often difficult to comprehend, and even religious faith frequently involves trials and uncertainties, but occultism promises instant knowledge, ultimate truth, and infallible solutions.

Occultism also assumes *universal egocentric meaning*—that is, that all events and processes have special meaning for the individual (Rawlins, 1977). For example, nothing is taken to be simply random or natural without implications for one's life. Winer (1972) has amply documented the fact that the concept of chance is a poorly conceptualized and infrequently used category of explanation, even though it might often apply. By the same token, in the occult world, coincidences are not viewed as the inevitable combination of many randomly distributed events, but rather as important signs and oracles. Similarly, even natural events are characterized as signaling an underlying hidden message as opposed to the end product of processes that may or may not portend anything for the future of humankind. It is perhaps a uniquely human and productive tendency to search for and find meaning and structure in one's social and physical environment. However, occultism distorts this tendency by applying an ethical, individual-relevant interpretation to all processes, even when the application is strained, if not misleading. For example, Humphrey (1978) has argued that magic derives from the use of moral strategies of influence that are learned in social exchange in attempts to influence the physical universe where they are inappropriate. It is, of course, a question of value as to whether humanity is "better off" believing that the Earth revolves around the sun or that humans evolved from lower forms of animal life according to the principles of natural selection and mutation. There can be little doubt, however, that a central function of occultism and the paranormal is to reassure individuals of their unique and significant place in the cosmos and a restoration of their central function in the universal scheme of things.

Finally, at the heart of the occult subculture are the loosely woven tenets of what might be called *popular metaphysics* as distinct from formal philosophical metaphysics (Dohrman, 1958). The basic idea is that the human soul is a very real thing that is concrete, eternal, and measurable. Most forms of belief in the paranormal derive from this basic assumption. To the believer and the cultist, various phenomena, such as reincarnation, communication with the dead, astral projection, and others are possible because of the concrete reality of the soul. Perhaps most important, however, is the central implication of this kind of metaphysical thinking—that is, because the reality of the soul is taken for granted and either implicitly or explicitly assumed to be superior to other kinds or levels of reality, the apparent limitations of life and the physical universe are but illusions, effective only for those who choose to believe in them. Thus, by implying a possible escape from the dreaded inevitabilities of human life, such as limits on locomotion, time and space, and sickness, aging, and death, the occult subculture indirectly offers redemption from an evil and imperfect world in favor of something better, often a "new age" or a sort of "heaven on Earth" where happiness, prosperity, peace, and freedom from strife abound and good finally triumphs over evil.

Contributing Social Factors

Compatible Ideologies and Movements.   Modern occultism has emerged in conjunction with several related social phenomena that have affected its growth and widespread appeal. Although numerous examples of cross-fertilization with occultism have undoubtedly occurred, three contemporary social phenomena are particularly relevant: utopianism, fundamentalist religion, and the human consciousness movement. Many of the concepts found in the literature dealing with the paranormal bear a striking resemblance to the basic ideas of these movements, and as such may help to shed light on the development of occultism.

The concept of *utopianism* or an ideal community free from the common problems of everyday living and able to put into practice the social theories of some group or individual has been around for a long time and remains popular. For example, several well-known books have dealt with the subject, including Plato's *Republic*, Thomas More's *Utopia*, and Edward Bellamy's *Looking Backward*. According to Schneider (1976), the concept of an intentional community probably draws its appeal from several sources including the desire to escape oppression, the "pull" of the future, and the common idea that a community of like-minded people with similar values equals a good and satisfying existence. Utopian visions are often directly or indirectly a part of occult ideologies as well. For example, Edward Bellamy was believed by the members to be one of the original "Sponsors" of the Mankind United movement, and it is possible that Bell's activities were an attempt to make Bellamy's ideas a practical reality, or at least he may have been influenced by them (Dohrman, 1958).

Several well-known attempts to start utopias have ended as dismal failures, such as the community of New Harmony founded by Robert Dale Owen, which lasted a couple of years, after which Owen retired, bankrupted. On the other hand, the Shaker communities, whose members believed in communication with the spirits of the dead and that spirits attended their meetings, lasted 150 years, and a remnant of one group is still in existence, even though they also believed in and practiced complete celibacy (Schneider, 1976). It has been estimated that from 1965 to 1970, between 2000 and 3000 communes were established in the United States (Houriet, 1971), which may be interpreted as an indication of the staying power and mass appeal of the utopian concept. Kanter (1972) has suggested that there are basically two types of intentional communities; the retreat commune, which is ordinarily rural and emerges from the desire of many people to return to the simpler, more self-sufficient life styles of the past, and communes with missions, which have specific and well-developed ideologies and which seek to reform an errant society by serving as an example or an alternative social structure. It would appear that occult-related utopias more often fall into the latter category.

Utopianism has influenced occultism in several ways. First, many occult groups eventually take up a more or less isolated, commune-like existence either by residing in remote areas or by restricting the interaction between group members and the rest of society. Reliance on a commune life style can serve several purposes that would tend to increase the life span of the occult group by minimizing interference from hostile authorities and a skeptical public, reducing members' dependence on alternative sources of information, opinion, and social identity, creating the possibility of exercising greater control over members by group leaders, and intensifying indoctrination procedures. Similarly, a commune existence provides the opportunity for the occult group to, as Kanter puts it, serve as an example to society of its theory of social relations and human behavior by putting that theory into practice, unencumbered by social cross-pressures and commitments. Perhaps most important, however, is the influence that utopianism may have had on the occultist's view of society. By emphasizing the negative aspects of existing social organization and implying that a "perfect" society free from such negative influences is immediately and easily available, utopianism may have served as a model for social isolation, encouraging occult groups to abandon efforts to compromise with disbelievers and consequently widening the gap between occultists and others and intensifying the alienation of occult group members from the mainstream of society. It is also likely that to some degree both occultism and utopianism stem from the failure of conventional groups and institutions such as the family to satisfy certain individual's need for social interchange and a sense of belonging.

The relationship between religion and occultism is quite complex. On the one hand, it may be argued that most, if not all, religious experience contributes to occultism because of its emphasis on a subjective–ethical interpretation of life as well as beliefs based on faith and revelation. On the other hand, it was noted earlier that Mankind United members were particularly disenchanted with conventional religion, which is often the case with occult followers. Moreover, religious leaders have sometimes led the fight against occultism and parapsychology, believing them to be examples of devil worship. But these factors may not be as incompatible as they intitially appear. First, the simple act of overtly severing ties with the church in which one was raised does not necessarily mean that one will not continue to be influenced by the rejected faith, particularly in terms of basic theological teachings regarding the nature of the universe and truth. Thus, occultists may hold to the essential world view of their religious upbringing while forsaking the overt manifestations of beliefs such as membership, attendance, and worship, just as many Mankind United members continued to believe in the "Sponsors" and the "new world order" even after leaving the group itself. There is evidence (see Chapter 7) that occult believers hold to a subjective view of the world. Second, there are certain religious groups that themselves appear to be a reaction to what is called the mainline church— that is, the major denominations. In particular, *fundamentalistic religion*, like occultism, stems in part from a dissatisfaction with conventional religion.

There are many forms of fundamentalism. For example, evangelical religion refers to those churches and denominations that subscribe to public professions of faith and rituals such as daily Bible reading and prayers; witnessing and proselyting; emotional, subjective, and personalized religious experiences (e.g., being "born again"); personal salvation and conversion; and a conservative theology such as the literal interpretation of the Bible, a belief in an impending Apocalypse, and the view that the world is an evil place. Even though once considered a minority trend in American religion, recently, Evangelicalism has grown in size and influence to be a major force.

Another fundamentalistic phenomenon in American religion has been the so-called Charisma movement, a modern version of pentecostal beliefs and practices that often involves an intensive conversion experience associated with what is described as the "gift of the holy spirit." Charismatic theology is similar to the evangelical outlook, but in practice includes even more intensive religious expressions such as "talking in tongues" or glossolalia. "Fringe" religion refers to numerous sects and non-denominational churches that are also ordinarily conservative theologically, holding to a literal inter-pretation of the Bible and emphasizing religious experiences not generally found in the mainline denominations. In addition, however, the so-called "fringe" groups often engage in one or more of a wide variety of religious practices ranging from mass-directed prayers, to exorcism, faith healing, and snake handling as a form of religious ritual. Although many such groups exist only on a local level, others are able to support efficient and sophisticated organizations by their unique ability to raise large amounts of funds. Another phenomenon of fundamentalism is revivalism, which often overlaps with the previously described three. From the "hell fire and dam-nation" sermons of Billy Sunday to the Four Square Gospel of Aimee Sem-ple McPherson in the 1930s to the slick and theatrically orchestrated pro-ductions of radio and television ministries, many people have walked the "saw-dust trail" in response to the special call of revival preachers. The revival has been a powerful influence in the personal lives of many people and a driving force in the service of fundamentalism.

Fundamentalism has probably contributed more than other religious ap-proaches to the development and maintenance of occultism. For example, many of the extraordinary phenomena of fundamentalism are practiced, albeit in a more secular fashion, in occultism also, as is exemplified by faith healing, glossolalia, or possessions. There are philosophical similarities be-tween the two, such as the belief of fundamentalism in personal survival after death and of occultism in reincarnation. Perhaps such similarities are one of the reasons that many paranormal cults eventually reorganize themselves as churches or religions, e.g., Scientology, Mankind United, and Witchcraft. Also, many of the leading exponents of various occult and pseudoscientific doctrines have been professional clergy or deeply religious lay people, often attempting to resolve the inconsistencies between science and religion. This has been a powerful and persistent influence in the paranormal world.

A more basic similarity, however, is the reliance in both fundamentalism and occultism on emotional, simplistic, and personalized forms of belief. The term emotion is not meant to convey a pejorative connotation; rather, it is used to refer to the fact that with both systems of belief, it is assumed that the experience of belief-relevant phenomena involves deeply held feelings in emotionally charged situations. The term conversion often used to describe subscription to beliefs in both areas is an example, because it suggests a drastic, complete, and compelling change in direction, purpose, and belief. Lofland and Stark (1965) studied the conditions that encourage conversion to cults, and found that for conversion, a person must experience enduring and acute tensions within a religious perspective. If the person then en-counters the cult at this critical point in life, a conversion experience becomes more probable. An interesting aspect of these findings is that it appears to be descriptive of conversions to both fundamental religious groups as well as some cults. Similarly, both systems are relatively simplistic in the sense that a set of complex, highly interrelated and organized concepts are not generally required. Simple terms with a high degree of associated imagery and strong emotional connotations are used to distinguish the preferred system of beliefs from alternatives. Terms and phrases such as "enlightenment," "a new age for mankind" of occultism are, after all, not that far removed in meaning and symbolism from those of salvation and the Kingdom of God. Thus, both popular traditions of American culture share ideological similarities, with particular reliance upon metaphysical conceptualization regarding the composition of life and the nature of the universe. This ideological similarity probably derives from the believers' and the cultists' basic world view, which is committed to the subjective, symbolic, and idealistic. Another similarity between fundamental religion and occultism is evangelistic fervor, including conversion and attempts to convert others. Such highly committed behaviors probably derive from the fact that both groups originate from attempts to solve the most basic issues of human existence and both are to some degree removed from the mainstream of secular society. As Evans (1973) suggests, it may well be that fundamental religions and occult groups are both attempts to respond to the loss of faith many people have experienced with respect to conventional religion.

Another social phenomenon that has contributed to the growth of occultism is what has been called the *human consciousness movement*, which refers to a diverse and wide-ranging set of theories of behavior and therapeutic techniques stressing such concepts as introspection, self-actualization, self-help and improvement, discovery of the "true self," greater sensitivity and awareness, and particularly the predominance of inner experience over rational, cognitive processes. A common theme in the movement is the idea that ordinary consciousness and awareness are somehow less than real or are an illusion. Many examples of self-improvement systems might be categorized as belonging to the human consciousness movement, including Transactional Analysis, Gestalt therapy, some encounter and sensitivity groups, Silva Mind Control, Transcendental Meditation, EST, and rebirth therapy. As was the case with fundamental religion, some of the contributions to occultism are direct in that many participants in the human consciousness movement are also followers of the occult, and there are some examples in which an interest in human potential movement ideas has led to the endorsement of patently occult ideas—for instance, the acceptance of reincarnation within what is called transpersonal psychology. More important, however, is the correspondence between occultism and the human potential movement in terms of the idea of self-improvement. The argument here is not against the idea of self-improvement or even the value of unique, emotional, and peak experiences sought by the participants in such therapies. The claims, however, of some of these systems have been so thoroughly exaggerated and the experiences of some adherents so intensive that it has led to the expectation that any sort of personality and behavior change is possible if the right technique and persistent effort are applied. "You can be whatever you want to be" is a commonly used phrase that expresses the essential nature of this element in the human consciousness movement. Although there may be some merit in this concept (or perhaps, even more merit in believing it whether it is verifiable or not), it nonetheless fails to take into account other sources of influence on human behavior, such as the multitude of other environmental influences and heredity. Thus, by stressing that the ideal is real, by implying that ecstatic and peak experiences are the normal state of affairs, and by suggesting that inner and emotional reality is more real than external and rational reality, the human consciousness movement has reinforced the idea that everything is possible and the assumption that what might be desirable is obtainable by sheer force of will, regardless of other factors that impinge upon behavior.

This discussion is not meant to suggest that utopianism, fundamental religion, or self-improvement groups have exclusively caused the development of occultism or that they are all one and the same, although in certain instances it would be difficult to draw a distinction between occultism and these related movements, such as in the case of transcendental meditation. Instead, our thesis is that occultism is influenced and encouraged by such popular movements because they familiarize, legitimize, and indoctrinate people into a mode of thinking and behaving that is consistent with occultism whether experienced as active occult-group participation or simply through the ideas to be found in occult literature.

Occult groups and the broader phenomenon of the occult subculture exist because many people are (and apparently always have been) dissatisfied with conventional sources of certainty and truth, and thus seek more unique systems of belief. Regardless of the specific content of such beliefs, however, the mechanisms by which this happens are largely ordinary social-psychological processes that guide interpersonal and intellectual behavior as we interact with goal-oriented groups of people and subscribe to their concepts of reality. Thus, the main distinction between an occult believer or group member and anyone else is the content of what is believed, and not the specific mechanisms by which belief and group participation occurs.

Magic as Social Control.   In some cases, occult beliefs and practices function as a form of social control or a mechanism by which social problems can be alleviated avoiding the development of divisive forces such as violence (Jahoda, 1969). In many tribal societies, for example, sorcery, divination, exorcism, witchcraft, and other forms of magic are used to explain and rectify interpersonal tensions in such a way that the social status quo is restored and social functioning continues without significant disruption. For example, a quarrel between relatives that threatens to erupt into a serious feud may be brought to the shaman or sorcerer by one of the parties involved. The sorcerer, who in small face-to-face societies already knows of the dispute, engages in some form of magic ritual to determine the origin of the problem, the person responsible for initiating the problem, and the steps to be taken to solve the problem. In a way, it does not matter who is designated as the victim and who the guilty party, how the sorcerer arrives at these decisions, or even if the sorcerer's revelations reflect only self interest and prejudice. Because both victim and offender believe in the system and the sorcerer's power, the solution is accepted. Thus, magic provides an explanation that can be consensually validated for divisive social problems and a prescription for regaining the reciprocity and equilibrium necessary for social relationships.

Such forms of occultism are, of course, deeply imbedded in such a society's entire view of everything and hence may also be used to explain and guard against naturally occurring processes, such as illness and disasters. By serving social functions, occult ideas comprise part of the shared beliefs that help to create group cohesiveness and cultural stability over time and across generations.

The social–control analysis probably applies best to the occult thinking of small, self-contained societies, the members of which have daily contact, share a basic belief system, and face common environmental and social contingencies. In larger, more pluralistic and technological societies, these factors are less prevalent. However, this kind of analysis does reveal an important aspect of occultism as it is experienced by members of cults and certain subcultural groups, even in this country. The power of magic in tribal societies derives in part from the lack of ideological and social alternatives for the individual. That is, to reject such beliefs would be tantamount to rejecting the society on which the individual is dependent for social contact, identity, protection, and so on. Even though alternative social opportunities may, in reality, be greater for the member of a western cult, as compared to tribespeople, the cultist may not believe that this is true. Thus, occult ideas as encountered in cults like Mankind United are accepted because they are inextricably a part of the group that, in turn, has the power to reward or sanction the individual.

Uncertainty and Social Change. Another social explanation of occultism is that it occurs under conditions of uncertainty where the regularity and predictability necessary for psychological and social stability are somehow lacking. This is not to suggest that complete regularity is required, because pleasant surprises are valued, as is variety. However, a degree of regularity is associated with psychological stability and its absence may result in irrational problem-solving strategies in which individuals who experience a lack of control in one situation may generalize that experience and adopt self-defeating behaviors even in situations in which they do have control (e.g., M. Seligman, 1975).

In this regard, anthropologist Bronislaw Malinowski (1954) observed that magic associated with fishing was most prevalent among groups in which the conditions for fishing were more uncertain and hazardous. From this observation, Malinowski proposed a theory that magical practices will be engaged in only in circumstances in which knowledge is insufficient or does not allow for control of the situation. As Jahoda (1969) has observed, Malinowski's theory may have been overstated, but the essential idea of uncertainty increasing the frequency of occult beliefs and practices has been supported by several sources of evidence. For example, Jahoda argues that Malinowski's theory would lead one to expect magical practices to be associated with professions and activities in which uncertainty is particularly high, such as among soldiers and athletes, and during times of great stress and upheaval, such as the historical plague epidemics, and there is ample evidence of an anecdotal and observational nature to suggest that this is so. A more directly empirical test of this hypothesis is available in a study reported by Hyman and Vogt (1967). They reasoned from Malinowski's theory that the practice of dowsing or water witching should be greatest in those areas of the United States where water is known to be scarce and difficult to locate. They compared an index of the difficulty of finding water in a sample of U. S. counties with the number of dowsers practicing in those counties and found a statistically significant degree of association between the two. Similarly, Padgett (1978) compared economic indicators in Germany from 1918-1940 with the number of astrology and occultism articles appearing in selected German magazines and found that the more negative the economic data, the greater the interest in astrology, as evidenced by the number of articles. The concept of knowledge uncertainty may also explain the relationships between the degree of belief in the paranormal and certain personality and demographic variables (e.g., external locus of control and life change, education, socioeconomic status, etc.). The person who believes that events are beyond his or her control, or who has experienced relatively more change and trauma, or who faces social bigotry and disadvantage may turn to occult beliefs and practices as a means of restoring a sense of predictability and control.

Such factors as locus of control and life change refer to individuals. There may be a sense in which the uncertainty analysis applies to an entire culture or society and thus may account for the recent widespread interest in occultism. Uncertainty at a social level might derive from those factors that disrupt normative patterns of social interaction. In particular, any force or process that challenges or invalidates existing beliefs and norms would lead to a sense of uncertainty because the members of that society would no longer be confident regarding the appropriate way to act and think. Many features of modern American life might contribute to uncertainty, such as the extensive social mobility and a high degree of urbanization, which create depersonalized life styles; a real or perceived decline in the influence and effectiveness of conventional social institutions including government, education, the family, and religion; a rapidly changing social structure (e.g., the status and role of women and minorities); disturbing social upheavals (e.g., violence, crime, and riots); persistent social problems (e.g., poverty, prejudice, etc.); and ecological and political threats (environmental problems, threat of nuclear war or accident). To a degree, these factors combine to render the values of the past obsolete and passé.

There is probably no greater threat to a society than rapid social change or encountering a situation that renders its norms obsolete. This is because norms comprise the social fabric that creates and facilitates social exchange and gives people the sense that they understand what is right, and what is going to happen. The public and many social observers apparently agree that the root cause of rapid norm change is the unprecedented growth of technology, and this is probably why science is often viewed with fear, mistrust, and scorn, particularly by occultists. In any case, uncertainty at a societal level due to the disillusionment associated with social transition would be expected to increase the appeal of occultism because it restores the individual's, and hence the society's, sense of purpose and control (Tiryakian, 1974). For example, *revitalization* movements that occur in response to the frustration of being dominated by an alien culture have been described as attempts to replace a deteriorating social system by generating a new one based on magical ideas (Wallace, 1970). Such movements or religious cults often hold to supernatural ideas decidedly removed from reality in an attempt to regain control over the group's destiny. One such example was the Ghost Dance of American Indians, which was supposed to protect the participants from the bullets of White men.

12

Parapsychology: I

The knavery and folly of men are such a common phenomenon that I should rather believe the most extraordinary events to arise from their concurrence, than admit of a single violation of the laws of nature.

David Hume, *An Inquiry Concerning Human Understanding,* 1776 (Chapter *On Miracles*)

Gentlemen, I would rather believe that those two Yankee Professors would lie than to believe that stones fell from heaven."

Thomas Jefferson, 1807 (reacting to the report of Professors Silliman and Kingsley of Yale that the meteorite shower that fell in Weston, Connecticut, was stones from the sky)

In 1909, just a year before his death, William James wrote the following concerning psychical research (James, 1909/1960):

When imposture has been checked off as far as possible, when chance coincidence has been allowed for, when opportunities for normal knowledge on the part of the subject have been noted, and skill in "fishing" and following clues unwittingly furnished by the voice or face of bystanders have been counted in, those who have the fullest acquaintance with the phenomena admit that in good mediums *there is a residuum of knowledge displayed* [James' italics] that can only be called supernormal: the medium taps some source of information not open to ordinary people [pp. 316-317].

James then notes that Frederick Myers calls the medium's tapping of the unknown source of information "telepathy." We have pointed out in the preceding chapters that many paranormal phenomena can be reduced to information that is acquired in some unknown manner: unorthodox diagnosis of physical disorders, information obtained during an out-of-the-body experience, unusual memories, including memories of previous lives, information from the "spirit world" obtained by way of mediums, psychometry, clairvoyance, and precognition are examples. Some of these instances can be explained by nothing more extraordinary than cryptomnesia and information obtained in the usual, sensory way. Some claim an ability, called psi, to explain the unexplained residual of such cases, an ability that transcends time and space and allows its possessor to have information that is not normally available because the source is far away, or it lies in the unascertainable past or the unknown future. There are researchers, the parapsychologists, who specialize in studying this alleged ability. Should it

362

be possible to demonstrate the reality of psi, such a demonstration would not only verify the claims of parapsychology and put it on the map as an empirical field of enquiry, but it would also considerably alter our outlook on the nature of other anomalistic phenomena. This and the next chapter are concerned with the empirical studies of parapsychology and its theories.

THE EXPERIMENTAL METHOD IN PARAPSYCHOLOGICAL RESEARCH

Research on nonsensory information-processing phenomena and psychokinesis has formed the core of parapsychology since the 1930s when J. B. Rhine almost singlehandedly set the pattern for such research in the following decades. Experiments in thought transmission had been done since the founding of the Society for Psychical Research, albeit only sporadically. Some of these had involved card guessing, which was to become Rhine's preferred research tool. The new elements in Rhine's work were his single-minded dedication to the proposition that anomalistic phenomena could be studied scientifically in the laboratory, his introduction of systematicity and of the standard experimental paradigm from psychology in parapsychological research, his use of statistics to evaluate the results, and the fact that the research was conducted within an academic setting, the Psychology Department of Duke University. Psychical research became parapsychology (so named by Rhine around 1930, following the German use of the term *Parapsychologie*), although as practiced by Rhine, it excluded the problem of discarnate survival. Rhine was definitely interested in evidence concerning life after death, but he gradually came to the conclusion that such evidence could not be obtained with the experimental method and that survival was basically a hypothesis that could not be tested scientifically. Rhine's research centered on the phenomena of extrasensory perception and psychokinesis.

The Subject Matter of Parapsychology

As a group, parapsychologists study the same phenomena that were being studied by the psychical researchers of the SPR and the ASPR, as well as other phenomena that have been added more recently. Parapsychological laboratory experiments have been concerned mostly with extrasensory perception and psychokinesis, however.

Terminology. *Extrasensory perception* (ESP) is the awareness of information from an external source that is not mediated by the sense organs. The fact that this definition of ESP (as well as all other variants of it) is stated in terms of what it is not rather than what it is reflects one of the main problems with this concept: It fails to show the direction in which research on ESP should proceed. At first, no hypotheses as to the nature of ESP were advanced. The hypotheses that have been formulated over the past 20 years have been either untestable or have failed to receive any empirical support, and the negative form of the definition of ESP still stands. The three specific forms of ESP—telepathy, clairvoyance, and precognition—are defined in terms of ESP and therefore suffer from the same deficiency.

Telepathy is defined as the ESP of the mental activities of another person. Mind reading was the older term, and it is still being used to describe the act of the entertainer who pretends to tell us what we are thinking of. The mind-reading act also suggests that it is quite possible to read another person's mind without the help of telepathy. The mind reader (called the *percipient* or subject in a telepathy experiment) uses muscle reading (slight, involuntary muscular contractions, perceived by touch, in the person whose thoughts are being read, called the *agent* or sender in a telepathy experiment), facial expressions, information obtained beforehand, signaling systems, including miniature radios, to communicate with a shill in the audience, as well as many other ruses and devices to produce sometimes quite spectacular results. Telepathy implies that no such means are being used. *Remote viewing* is a form of telepathy in which the percipient is said to be able to see the randomly selected place to which the agent has gone. The percipient is presumably viewing the site as if through the agent's eyes.

Clairvoyance is the ESP of objects and events. It involves only one person, the percipient. "Second sight" has been and still is the popular name for this alleged ability. Telepathy may be considered a special case of clairvoyance, because there is in principle no difference between being aware of, for instance, what one does and what one intends to do, if the knowledge of either event is obtained by non-sensory means. The distinction between telepathy and clairvoyance is made mostly in terms of the procedures and operations by which these phenomena are tested. Some procedures fail to differentiate the two. Thus, if I am looking at a card and it is on my mind, the percipient may be reading my mind telepathically or the card clairvoyantly. Studies in which no attempt is made to separate telepathy from clairvoyance are designated as general ESP or GESP studies.

Precognition is the ESP of future events that could not be rationally inferred. Prophecy, psychic predictions, divination, premonitions, augury, scrying, and fortunetelling are terms that express the same idea. The sheer number and variety of methods bear witness to the age-old desire to look into the future. Yet, scientifically the idea is an unacceptable one because it reverses the cause-effect relationship and allows us to experience now the effects of a cause that is yet to occur.

Psi, the 23rd letter of the Greek alphabet, is a term suggested by the British psychologist Robert Thouless to designate the hypothetical ability that underlies all manifestations of ESP as well as psychokinesis. Psi is thus the subject matter of parapsychology.

Psychokinesis (PK), formerly called telekinesis, is the direct physical influence exerted on objects or events by mental effort or intention and without the mediation of known physical energies or instrumentation. Psychokinesis, like precognition, also places a great strain on the scientist's capacity to believe, because the current view of the physical world has no room for physical consequences whose antecedents are not physical also. We first consider experimentation with ESP, and treat PK in a separate section in Chapter 13.

Materials and Apparatus

One important innovation in parapsychological experimentation that was introduced by Rhine was a standard set of materials that was to serve as the targets in ESP tests. Playing card symbols were of too many different kinds. Rhine replaced the playing cards with a deck of 25 cards that contained only five symbols (shown in Fig. 12.1), each repeated five times. The cards were named Zener cards, after a Duke University psychologist, Carl Zener, who worked briefly with Rhine, or ESP cards. By far the most ESP experiments

Fig.12.1.   The five symbols of the Zener cards.

have been done with Zener cards, but lately they have been replaced by other types of targets.

The Zener symbols are not very interesting and create boredom over long runs of trials. Some researchers, such as S. G. Soal, have substituted animal pictures for the ESP symbols. Robert Van de Castle used such pictures in ESP tests with Panamanian Indians. Other ESP targets have included pictures of different kinds, ranging from simple outline drawings to color reproductions of paintings.

When ESP cards are used, the experiment is described as a *forced-choice* experiment because the response is forced on the subject: He or she is limited to only five kinds of responses, and the nature of these responses is predetermined. When artwork or photographs are used, the number of responses available to the percipient is much larger. Unless the general nature of the target objects is specified, the choices may be practically limitless. The experiment is then called a *free-response* experiment. Although the latter is much more interesting than the forced-choice type, it presents the very problem that the introduction of the ESP cards was designed to avoid. That problem is the decision that has to be made whether a response is on target, close to target, or has nothing to do with the target. Several judges must be used who should agree closely on the verdict. This introduces a large amount of uncertainty and subjectivity in the evaluation of the experimental results. An additional problem is to determine the odds that a correct guess did not occur by chance alone, because targets like famous paintings have no calculable probabilities associated with their occurrence (see the section *Data Analysis* later in this chapter).

The shuffling of the cards and the recording of both the sequence of the target cards and the subject's calls has been done by the experimenter or experimenters, but human record keepers make errors. To avoid conscious and unconscious falsification of data, electronic devices are being used to perform all of the functions normally performed by the human experimenter that are subject to error: the generation of random sequences of the targets, the recording of these sequences, the presentation of the targets, and the recording of the subject's calls. Examples are the VERITAC computer system developed at the Air Force Cambridge Research Laboratories (Hansel, 1966), the Aquarius ESP Teaching Machine, developed by Russell Targ and David B. Hurt (Gardner, 1975), and Charles Tart's ESPATESTER (Tart, 1976). When cards are used, precautions against erroneous recording are taken in the form of having a third person (besides the agent and the percipient), the experimenter, do the recording of the calls and not allowing that person to see the sequence of the cards, having more than one person check the card sequence against the subject's calls, and recording the calls on magnetic tape against which the written record may be checked later.

Procedures

One procedure to test for pure telepathy is for the agent to think of a card symbol at stated intervals and for the percipient to call the symbols at the same rate. The agent writes down his or her symbol after the percipient has made the call. In the GESP test using the Zener cards, the cards are shuffled, the agent looks at them, one by one, signaling to the percipient when the next card is turned, and the percipient attempts to identify the symbol that the agent is looking at (and thus has in his or her mind). The percipient's responses are recorded on a call sheet. In a clairvoyance test, the procedure may be the same except that the agent merely touches each card but does not turn it over. The agent's role is thus minimal. In the "down-through" procedure, the deck of cards is not touched, and the percipient simply calls the cards in the order in which he or she thinks they lie in the deck.

Tests for precognition are conducted in the following manner: The subject calls the order of the cards in which they will lie after shuffling, the deck is then shuffled and the order checked against the calls. Alternately, the procedure may be as in a GESP experiment, except that the subject's calls are compared with the cards one ahead of those the agent is actually looking at. In this procedure, precognition cannot be distinguished from clairvoyance, however.

In all cases, the agent and the percipient must be effectively isolated from each other. Rhine's early experiments (which were also the most successful) were conducted with the agent and percipient in a face-to-face situation or separated only by a small, thin partition placed in the middle of the table at which both of them were sitting. This situation provides multiple sensory cues that can be utilized by the percipient. In informal testing situations between friends or in mind-reading demonstrations on stage, voluntary and involuntary clues supplied by the agent including involuntary whispering, ideomotor movements and muscle reading, shifts in body posture, shuffling of feet, coughs, sighs, voice inflections, and many other visual and auditory clues have been shown repeatedly to be effective conveyors of information from agent to percipient. Tests performed under these conditions have no scientific validity. Placing the agent and the percipient in the same room cannot be permitted under any circumstances. They must each be placed in a separate room, preferably rooms that do not adjoin. Furthermore, care must be taken that sound does not travel between the rooms—for instance, through heating or ventilation ducts, spaces above the ceiling, or directly through the walls. Gilbert Murray, the classical scholar and twice president of the SPR, played a telepathy game with his friends for many years. He would leave the room in which his friends had gathered and go to another room or down the hall, while one of the friends would think of a mental image that Murray, upon his return, would try to describe. He was remarkably successful. What reports of these games (e.g., Koestler, 1972) fail to note is that Murray knew that on these occasions he would go into a "state" that heightened his auditory acuity so that he could hear some of the things that were being said down the hall and behind closed doors (Thompson, 1936). Auditory hyperacuity is rare, but hearing can be sharpened through concentration as well as through hypnosis and self-hypnosis.

Further care must be taken that neither the agent nor the percipient leave their respective rooms during the experiment. Additional precautions include assuring that the card sequences to be used by the agent are kept in a safe place and are not known to anyone until the agent looks at them. Because no place is completely secure, the best procedure is to generate the sequences on the spot. If a signalling system is used for the agent to signal the percipient that he is about to look at the next card, the system cannot involve voice communication because the tone of voice, inflections, and rate of speech can carry information. If light or sound signals are used, these must be activated by a switch that makes all signals the same length so that the possibility of both conscious and unconscious transmission of information about the cards is prevented. The percipient's calls should be transmitted to the recording experimenter via a public address system, which also makes it possible to tape-record them for a further check on the accuracy of the written record.

A *trial* is a single attempt by the percipient to use ESP in the experiment. In GESP tests it consists of the agent looking at the target and the percipient attempting to identify the target. In clairvoyance tests only the percipient's behavior is involved. Twenty-five trials constitute a *run* with the Zener cards. Typically, more than one run is used to establish whether ESP Zener cards. Typically, more than one run is used to establish whether ESP is operating or not. When J. B. Rhine was testing Duke University students, 10 runs were given to a prospective subject for screening purposes, and 20 runs were given to test a claim of telepathy or some new hypothesis. Regardless of how many runs are given, the number must be established beforehand—that is, it is not permissible to stop testing at any arbitrarily decided point. The purpose of this is to prevent the artificial increase in a subject's score if the experiment is terminated during a particularly successful run.

The order of the cards in the deck must be random, which means that any card must have the same chance of appearing in any position as any other card. Randomization is achieved by different means. One is simply to shuffle the cards well. Hand shuffling, however, is imperfect. A mechanical shuffler does a much better job. An alternate method is to arrange the cards following a random sequence of numbers obtained from a table of random numbers.

Usually, the subject does not learn how well he or she has done until the experiment is over. To study the effect of feedback, subjects are told, after each trail, whether they were right or wrong. In this case, it is inappropriate to use the so-called *closed deck* of cards—that is, to give separate runs of 25 cards in which the five symbols are repeated five times each, for then the chances of guessing a card correctly will continue to improve from the beginning to the end of each run. Instead, after determining the total number of trials to be given, of which the subject is not informed, the cards are randomized within the total sequence, so that it becomes quite unlikely that within any subset of 25 cards, the number of times a given symbol is represented will be five. The deck thus becomes an *open deck*.

Data Analysis

All data obtained in an experiment must be analyzed. The reason for this is obvious: Selective discarding of data will lead to the experimenter's obtaining precisely the results that he or she wants. It was known that J. B. Rhine, in testing a subject over a period of days, would discard the data for a given day if he decided that it happened to be a "bad" day for the subject. The rationale for this was the assumption that ESP cannot be turned on and off on demand, and that ignoring the subject's performance on an "off" day was justified because the purpose of the experiment was to study ESP when it was present and not when it was absent. This procedure, of course, makes it impossible to distinguish between an ebb in performance and genuine absence of ESP.

Any event, including the correct identification of ESP card symbols, can occur by chance alone. In experiments, it is therefore essential to be able to estimate how likely it is that the results did so occur. What are the chances that, without the help of ESP, you will be right guessing "cross" when you look at the first card of a well-shuffled ESP card deck? Because there are five crosses and a total of 25 cards, the chances (or probability) are 5 in 25, of 1 in 5, or .2. Because this probability is the same for any of the five symbols, one can expect, on the average, to make five correct guesses by chance alone. Five correct guesses or hits is the *mean chance expectation* (MCE) for a run of 25 cards.

How many hits are necessary to be able to say that something else besides chance is involved? That depends on how widely chance hits will vary around the MCE value. Clearly, even if chance alone is operating, the number of hits will not be five in every run. It may be more, or it may be less. The difference between the MCE and the actual score obtained is therefore compared with (divided by) the mean value of the expected variation in the MCE, which is called *standard deviation*. The standard deviation is computed as $\sqrt{npq}$, where n is the number of trials, p the probability of a hit on a trial, and $q = 1 - p$. For example, if the score in 100 trials (four runs) is 31 hits, the MCE is 20, or 1/5 of 100, the deviation score is $31 - 20 = 11$, and the standard deviation is $\sqrt{100 \times 1/5 \times 4/5} = 4$. The obtained number of hits therefore exceeds the average variation in the mean chance score $11/4 = 2.75$ times. The ratio of the deviation score and the standard deviation is known as the *critical ratio*. To establish the probability that the critical ratio of 2.75 could have occurred by chance alone, a table (the table of the t statistic) is entered with the value of 2.75. It will be found that 31 hits could have occurred by chance alone in only one case out of a hundred. This is a statistically significant result, which means that we can be fairly confident that some other factor or factors rather than chance were responsible for this result. The statistical procedure may be simplified by looking up the number of hits in special tables that have been prepared to evaluate ESP and PK experiments, such as those in the book *Parapsychology* (Rhine & Pratt, 1957).

The statistical computations just illustrated do not exhaust the statistical methodology used in parapsychology. Other and newer methods are available and are being employed as required by variations in the experimental design. Special works on statistical methodology applicable to this area of research, such as the review by Donald Burdick and Edward Kelly (1977) are available to those who intend to do serious experimental research.

Evaluation of the Results

In the card-guessing situation, the psi ability cannot be observed in the same way as a physical phenomenon is observed. The sequence of cards and the sequence of the subject's calls are physical enough, but by themselves they do not constitute ESP. ESP may be inferred from the size of the critical ratio, but it is only one possible inference. A large critical ratio can also be obtained if the subject utilizes sensory information available about the target cards, if deception is practiced, as well as by chance alone. It is necessary to eliminate or reduce the likelihood of these alternative explanations before the explanation that ESP was responsible for the high score can be accepted. Experimental controls are instituted to achieve that purpose. All this is no different from what takes place in any psychological experiment in which the existence of a phenomenon must be based on a statistical inference. What distinguishes the ESP experiment from other experiments is that the hypothesis being tested, that of the existence of psi, is so highly improbable in comparison with the alternative hypotheses that even extremely long odds against them may not be accepted as sufficient evidence. From the scientist's point of view, ESP and PK simply do not fit into the world picture. The scientist is extremely reluctant to abandon this view on the basis of only one or two kinds of apparent anomaly. The scientist therefore requires much more stringent controls in the ESP-testing situation and the elimination of the influence of any conceivable ordinary factor before admitting that the computed million-to-one odds were produced by something as improbable as ESP rather than sensory information, deception, artifact, or chance. This attitude of the scientist is illustrated by the oft-cited quotation from an article by the eminent psychologist D. O. Hebb (1951):

> Why do we not accept ESP as a psychological fact? Rhine has offered enough evidence to have convinced us on almost any other issue where we could make some guess as to the mechanics of the disputed process. Some of his evidence has been explained away, but as far as I can find out, not all of it . . . Personally, I do not accept ESP for a moment, because it does not make sense. My external criteria, both of physics and physiology, say that ESP is not a fact despite the behavioral evidence that has been reported. I cannot see what other basis my colleagues have for rejecting it; and if they are using my basis, they and I are allowing psychological evidence to be passed on by physical and physiological censors. Rhine may still turn out to be right, improbable as I think that is, and my rejection of his views is—in the literal sense—prejudice [p. 45].

Hermann von Helmholtz, the 19th-century scientific genius, said in 1880 in a speech delivered to the British Association of Physicists (quoted in Heywood, 1961) that: "Neither the testimony of all the Fellows of the Royal Society, nor even the evidence of my own senses, would lead me to believe in the transmission of thought from one person to another independently of the recognized channels of sense [p. 11]."

C. E. M. Hansel (1966), who wrote a very thorough and very critical book evaluating the scientific status of ESP, stated three principles that should be considered in evaluating an ESP study:

1. Each experiment must be considered solely on its own merits.

2. An experiment that has any defects that may lead to results attributable to causes other than ESP cannot be used to prove ESP.

3. An experiment is only as strong as its weakest part. Weakness of controls at one point cannot be compensated by strong controls at another. Furthermore, all factors that could possibly affect the result must be controlled.

Hansel particularly stresses the possibility of fraud and deception, going so far as to insist that even when no actual fraud has been demonstrated, an experiment remains suspect if the possibility of fraud has not been eliminated. If this attitude appears unreasonable, it must be remembered that it is the improbability of ESP that forces the scientist to adopt this attitude. To many scientists, any explanation, including fraud, is a more parsimonious explanation than ESP. This stance is not born out of sheer dogmatism or the refusal to accept new facts for fear that they may shatter a cherished view of the universe, although these attitudes may be observed in some. Two other factors nourish it. One is the failure of parapsychologists to produce any kind of testable hypothesis concerning the nature of ESP. For a long time, there were no hypotheses at all, except such statements as Rhine's that ESP did not obey the laws of physical nature. There are now quite a number of more specific hypotheses. They are, unfortunately, couched in a language that does not permit an empirical test. None of the characteristics of ESP are described in positive terms, and therefore, any characteristic can be ascribed to it. Thus, if it is found that the same conditions that facilitate ESP, such as relaxed controls, also facilitate fraud, both the proponents and opponents of ESP are still left with nothing but an undecidable argument. This has not helped to advance research on the nature of ESP.

The other factor is the high incidence of fraud, deception, self-deception, and gullibility that has characterized psychical research in the past. It cannot be expected that the scientist will ignore the history of psychical research and parapsychology and put ordinary scientific research and parapsychological research on the same footing, because fraudulent cases have been recorded in the former also. The very first study of telepathy conducted by Barrett of the SPR and reported to the Society in 1882 was hailed by Sidgwick as a conclusive demonstration of it. Six years later, the five girls who had been the subjects in this study were caught using a code and confessed their deception.

A further principle to be adhered to in the evaluation of ESP test results may be derived from the consideration of fraud cases: Nothing may be assumed about an experiment that is not explicitly stated in the experimental report. One very significant problem in parapsychological research has been the incompleteness of research reports. Even seemingly thorough and detailed reports may fail to disclose crucial experimental details that become apparent only upon visiting the laboratory in person and examining the experimental set-up firsthand. Such visits may disclose glaring inadequacies in the control of experimental variables (see, for instance, the exchange between Diaconis, 1978a, 1978b, and Puthoff & Targ, 1978).

ESP EXPERIMENTATION IN HISTORICAL PERSPECTIVE

J. B. Rhine and Parapsychology at Duke University

Statistics and cards were used in psychical research as early as 1884 (by Charles Richet), and Rhine's Parapsychology Laboratory was not the first such laboratory; it was an endowed laboratory for psychical research established at Stanford University as early as 1911. William McDougall, who was mentioned in Chapter 9 in connection with psychical research, assumed the chairmanship of the Psychology Department at Duke University in 1927. J. B. Rhine and his wife, Louise E. Rhine, both of whom had been teaching biology after graduating from the University of Chicago doctoral program in 1925 and 1923, respectively, saw the opportunity to do psychical research at Duke, a subject they were already interested in. J. B. Rhine secured an appointment in the Duke Psychology Department and proceeded with his research. It dealt initially with the question of survival. The first doctorate in parapsychology in the USA was awarded in 1933 on the subject of mediumship. It was granted by the Duke Psychology Department. It was not until 1934 that a Parapsychology Laboratory was established at Duke and Rhine published his first parapsychological monograph, *Extrasensory Perception*, describing the first years' work. By that time, however, Rhine had already begun to think that testing the survival hypothesis was not a profitable line of research, and he had turned to the study of ESP using the Zener cards. These were introduced in 1930, and *Extrasensory Perception* described the early ESP experiments using these cards.

Quite a number of the experiments yielded chance results; some, however, produced results that were highly significant. In fact, the odds against obtaining the results that came from some of Rhine's subjects were astronomical. Over a series of 100 runs, a subject may obtain 8 and 9 hits on some of the runs and even more, including 12 and 13. Fourteen hits in any run would not be very likely. A Duke student, Hubert Pearce, averaged 8 hits over 690 runs. Although in absolute numbers this is not a very great achievement, the odds against such a result are enormous. If Pearce had averaged only 5.3 hits per trials over the total of 17,250, that performance alone would have yielded odds against chance of more than a million to one. Such odds arise from the statistical principle that is well known but not well appreciated. It has to do with large numbers. When the number of observations is small, large differences (many hits) are necessary to obtain statistically significant results. Thus, 5.3 hits in a single run of ESP cards (25 observations) is not a statistically significant result, and 10 to 11 hits are required to achieve the odds against chance of 100 to 1. When the number of trials reaches into the tens or hundreds of thousands, just about any deviation from mean chance expectation will be statistically significant. Thus, when Rhine combined the results obtained with the best eight subjects tested during the period described in *Extrasensory Perception*, it gave odds greater than 10^{1000} to 1 against their having been obtained by chance. That very small deviations from chance results should yield astronomical odds against it when the number of observations is very large may at first not appear to make much sense. In terms of a subject's performance, it translates into a trade-off between the strength of performance and its consistency. A subject's performance may be statistically significant if it is very strong (large difference scores) on a few trials, or if it is weak but sustained over many trials. It is the consistency of above-chance performance, however low in absolute terms, that produces the high statistical significance when the number of observations is very large.

Chance was clearly not producing Rhine's results. It was opportunities to establish the identity of the cards by sensory means. These were so numerous and so readily available that much of Rhine's work during the 1930s may be safely ignored. Testing often occurred in a face-to-face situation, with minimal screening between the agent and the percipient or none at all. When an agent sits across the table from the percipient, the latter can see the backs of the cards. At one time, the ESP cards had been printed with such a heavy pressure that the symbols became embossed in the card material and could be read from the back. In 1938, it was discovered that the symbols could also be seen through the cards. In some experiments, the subject was allowed to touch the cards, which, of course, allows room for fingertip reading of the backs of the cards and, if they are marked, of their sides.

The instructions that accompany the ESP cards, which were made available to the public in 1937, indicate that an 18 × 24 inch piece of plywood would be sufficient for screening purposes. It is decidedly not. A small screen still allows the percipient to see the faces of the cards if the agent wears glasses, and even if the agent does not, because the card faces are also reflected from the agent's corneas. Changes in facial expression give away clues that are not concealed by small screens. Larger screens still allow the percipient to hear the agent's voice. If the agent also serves as the recorder, which was routine in Rhine's experiments, voice inflections are as useful a source of information as are facial expressions. Furthermore, the sound of the pen or pencil wielded by the agent as he or she records the calls can be also utilized by a person who is skilled at it or learns the skill when tested over a sufficiently large number of trials. Involuntary whispering on the part of the recording agent cannot be excluded as an additional source of information. When the distance between the percipient and the cards was increased, scores dropped. In the pure telepathy experiments, no cards were used, but the agent thought of a card symbol, the percipient called it, and the agent then recorded both the symbol and the call. Distance did not affect scores when this technique was being used because the subject's calls must have clearly influenced the generation of symbols by the agent, from which the percipient benefited. This technique worked best when the subject and agent knew each other well.

The keeping of records in Rhine's experiments was inadequate. Sometimes, the subject would help with the checking of his or her calls against the order of the cards. In some long-distance telepathy experiments, the order of the cards passed through the hands of the percipient before it got from Rhine to the agent.

Extrasensory Perception created great interest and attempts to repeat Rhine's results were made by other investigators. Thirty-six experimental reports were published between 1934 and 1940 (Hansel, 1966). Some of these told of success, others did not. Six different researchers, using some 500 subjects in experiments totaling almost half a million trials demonstrated nothing but chance scores. British parapsychologists were particularly unable to replicate Rhine's results. It took years, many subjects, and thousands of trials before the best-known British parapsychologist, S. G. Soal, was finally able to find one successful subject, Gloria Stewart. This is another property of large numbers that has played a role in parapsychological research. The discovery of Gloria Stewart or anyone else with seemingly high ESP ability after many rounds of testing was to be expected. Let us assume that we are screening people for ESP ability and that we are starting with an unselected sample of 128 volunteers. Let us further assume that there is no ESP and only chance factors are operating. All subjects are given 10 runs of ESP cards. If chance alone is operating, one-half of the 128 subjects will be expected to yield scores that are above mean chance expectation, the other half yielding scores that are below it. The second group is not tested further, and the first is given 10 more runs. Again, one-half of them scores above, the other below the chance level. The procedure is continued six more times, leaving in the end a single individual who has now scored at an above-chance level eight times in a row with nothing else but chance being responsible for the success. This case, however, may be written up and presented as evidence for ESP, with the other 99.22% of cases left out of the account. Very few concrete samples of 128 individuals are expected to yield results exactly like these, of course. The example represents what the results are likely to be on the average if many samples of 128 individuals are tested.

In 1939, J. L. Kennedy reviewed the experiments done between 1934 and 1938, and concluded that there had been only three whose results could not be explained in terms of insufficient experimental contols, such as the availability of sensory clues, mental habits and preferences, and recording errors (Kennedy, 1939b). Hansel (1966), using information that became available later, shows that in one of the three experiments, clues may have become available to the subject from the way light signals were presented and the characteristics of the cards used. In the second experiment, which showed hits from 17 to 21 per run on 10 consecutive days and then dropped to chance level, deception was very likely practiced, possibly involving a servant in the experimenter's home who had access to the drawer in which the card orders were kept. The third experiment was the famous Pearce-Pratt series that all parapsychologists have agreed was one of the incontrovertible demonstrations of ESP. Because this experiment was done under well-controlled conditions, Hansel (1966) made a detailed study of it in an effort to explain the exceptional results.

The Pearce-Pratt Experiments.   The subject in these experiments was Hubert Pearce, a divinity student at Duke University, and the agent J. G. Pratt, a Duke parapsychologist. The experiments were run in 1933 and 1934, the most detailed description of them appearing only 20 years later (Rhine & Pratt, 1954). Agent and percipient were at a distance of 100 yards from each other during some of the sessions and 250 yards apart in others. A day's session consisted of two runs of 25 trails each. In each trial, Pratt picked up a card and, without turning it up, placed it separately and kept it there for 1 minute. Pearce, who had his watch synchronized with Pratt's, would try to identify the card. A total of 75 runs made up the Pearce-Pratt series. It was divided into four subseries that differed in terms of the agent's location and distance from the percipient, number of sessions, and the presence of J. B. Rhine in the agent's room. Pearce obtained a score of 13 (the highest score in the series) in three runs, and nine scores of 12, but there were also three runs of score zero as well as runs with scores of 1, 2, and 3. Nevertheless, the overall odds against obtaining results like these by chance alone were 10^{22} to 1. Both Pearce and Pratt each placed their record of the day's session in an envelope and delivered them immediately to Rhine for evaluation. The order of the cards was not known to anyone until the session was over and Pratt had recorded the card sequence.

If the ESP hypothesis is not accepted, what extrachance factors could have been at work in the Pearce-Pratt series to have produced the results of the kind indicated? First, besides the 1954 complete review by Rhine and Pratt, there were eight additional items of literature in which the series had been described earlier. The various accounts of the experiments differ, sometimes widely, on a number of essential details, including the exact scores obtained by Pearce. It is impossible to determine to what extent reporting and recording errors might have affected the results of the experiment as reported in 1954, but there is good evidence that such an effect must have been present and working in favor of the ESP hypothesis. It has been demonstrated that belief alone produces unconscious biases that result in believers recording more hits than there actually are and nonbelievers erring in the other direction. R. S. Kaufman (Sheffield, Kaufman, & Rhine, 1952) at Yale University had four believers and four nonbelievers in PK score a PK experiment. The believers recorded more hits and the nonbelievers fewer hits than a concealed camera, which recorded hits at a chance level. The believers' scores were sufficiently biased to make for statistically significant results. Likewise, in an ESP experiment (Kennedy & Uphoff, 1939), 28 observers were asked to record the guesses made by the investigator of the symbols being sent by the observers. Of a total of 11,125 calls, 126 were recorded incorrectly, all observers making at least one error. Almost one-half of the errors (45.4%) increased the ESP scores, 21.4% decreased them, and 33.4% had no effect. Believers in telepathy made 71.5% more errors that increased ESP scores than did nonbelievers. On the other hand, nonbelievers made 100% more errors that decreased ESP scores than did believers. In the Pearce-Pratt series, Pearce and Pratt each made their own record and delivered it to Rhine, who was the only evaluator of the results. There is no indication in the reports of these experiments that the data were checked several times by noninvolved individuals. Because both Pratt and Rhine were believers, there was ample opportunity for recording errors to have crept in.

Second, in 1960, Hansel inspected the rooms where the Pearce-Pratt series had been conducted and realized that in 1933 and 1934, there had been the opportunity, for one who wished to do so, to observe Pratt going through the cards and recording them by watching him through a window or through a trapdoor to the attic, situated above Pratt's table. Both Pratt and Rhine saw Pearce enter the library where Pearce did his guessing, but they had no assurance that he could not have left the library during the 50-minute period of the daily session. Fig. 12.2 shows the distribution of scores among the 75 runs of the Pearce-Pratt series. The distribution has two clear maxima (dotted lines), each corresponding to a separate distribution. About one-half of the runs follow the shape of a distribution that would be expected if the results were produced by chance, the mean being around five hits. The other distribution containing the higher scores has more of a rectangular shape, characteristic of artificial, nonchance distributions. This is not inconsistent with Hansel's hypothesis that information on the order of cards was obtained by Pearce for some runs and inserted at various points in the four series.

The Pratt-Woodruff Experiments. There are few other experiments about which parapsychologists are unanimous that they are well controlled and constitute evidence for the ESP hypothesis. One such experiment was

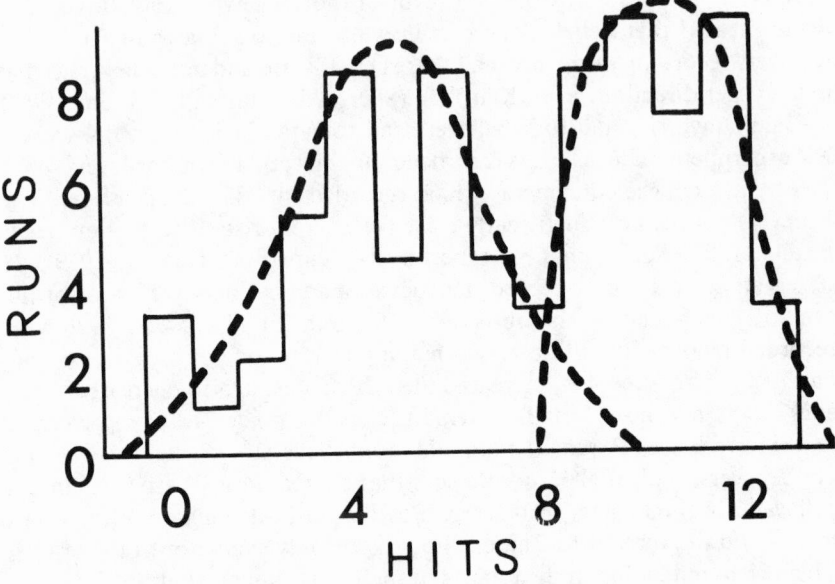

Fig.12.2. Distribution of scores in the Pearce-Pratt experiments, based on data in Rhine and Pratt, 1954.

done by J. G. Pratt and J. L. Woodruff (1939). Even 15 years later, Rhine claimed that no other psychological experiment had ever been carried out that had had more elaborate safeguards against error.

In this series of experiments, carried out in 1938 and 1939, Woodruff served as the agent and Pratt acted as a second experimenter or observer, seeing to it that all controls were maintained. Thirty-two individuals served as percipients. The experimenter-agent and the percipient sat at the ends of a table, separated by an 18 × 24 inch screen. A 2 × 20 inch opening was cut in the bottom of the screen. Five blank cards were placed under the screen so that both the experimenter and the subject could see them. On the subject's side, five cards, the "key" cards, each showing one of the ESP symbols, were hung from pegs, each above one of the blank cards. The experimenter gave the signal, and the subject attempted to identify the top card in the experimenter's deck. The cards were kept face down until the end of the run. Upon identifying it, the subject touched with a pencil the blank card above which hung the appropriate symbol. The experimenter then placed the card next to the blank card that had been touched. The procedure was repeated 24 more times, at the end of which all three participants checked the number of hits and recorded them on score sheets and in their personal notebooks. A total of 60,000 trials were run, yielding 5.204 hits per run. This result, nevertheless, yielded odds of more than a million to one against chance. What tipped the scale of an otherwise indifferent experiment towards statistical significance was the performance of five subjects, but especially one of them who in three out of eight sittings produced scores so high that her overall performance yielded odds of 20 million to one against chance. Hansel (1966) also analyzed this experiment, deciding that it cannot be taken as conclusive evidence of ESP. The main problem lies in the fact that subject and agent were in close proximity, which could have allowed the experimenter-observer to "help" the subject. Hansel, by duplicating the physical set-up of the Pratt-Woodruff experiment in his own laboratory, was able to demonstrate that even a person naive to the experiment could learn to ascertain, as the experimenter, the position of at least the first or the last key card, except for the first run. After each run and after the experimenter had made a record, the screen was taken down and the performance of the subject was checked. The experimenter could then learn the identity of the key cards in positions 1 or 5. When the screen was put back and the subject removed the key cards in order to rearrange them for the next run, the experimenter could assume that the last card that would be replaced would be the card that was in position 1 or 5 in the previous run. This depended on whether the cards were removed from the pegs going from left to right or from right to left, which was easy to establish from the noises made and the shadows cast by the subject. If this trick was employed, it would have led to an increased number of hits for symbols that had occupied positions 1 or 5 on the previous run. Hansel, on checking the data for the highest scoring subject, P. M., established that, considering all 4025 trials of this subject (the first run was disregarded), the odds against the subject's score arising by chance on symbols that occupied positions 2, 3, and 4 on previous runs were 2 to 1, whereas the odds for symbols that had occupied positions 1 and 5 were greater than 100 billion to 1. Similar results were obtained by Hansel for the other four high scoring subjects, although the odds were not quite as high.

S. G. Soal and Parapsychological Experimentation in England

J. B. Rhine's English counterpart had been S. G. Soal, who began doing parapsychological research at about the same time as Rhine. All through the 1930s, he tried to replicate Rhine's findings with ESP cards, but failed to obtain a single successful subject. In 1939, however, Soal, upon rechecking the record sheets of his unsuccessful subjects, discovered that two of them, Basil Shackleton and Gloria Stewart, had scored significantly, not on the target cards, but on the cards that came just before or just after the target cards (-1 and $+1$ hits). Both subjects were retested by Soal. The 40 sittings with Shackleton conducted in 1941, 1942, and 1943 by Soal and a member of the SPR, Mrs. Goldney, the Soal-Goldney experiment, became the most extensive and most often-cited British ESP experiment. The cards used by Soal bore the pictures of five animals instead of the ESP symbols. Shackleton and an observer sat in one room. The experimenter and the agent were seated in an adjoining room, with the door between the two rooms slightly ajar. The experimenter used either the numbers between 1 and 5 in a random sequence or colored markers to signal to the agent, through an opening in a screen, which of the five animal cards the agent was to look at on the next trial, then called out to Shackleton to record his guess. The five animal cards were hidden from everybody's view except the agent's, who would turn one of them over and look at it upon the experimenter's signal. Additional observers were present from time to time. The recording of the order of the targets and of Shackleton's calls was done while additional observers were present. The score sheets were placed in an envelope and mailed, in the presence of three witnesses, to the philosophy professor C. D. Broad at Cambridge. In some of the sittings, the clairvoyance procedure was used in that the agent only touched a card instead of looking at it, and some of the random-number series were prepared by people other than Soal himself. Shackleton was successful with only three of the 12 agents who worked with him. With these, however, his success rate was astronomical. For instance, he obtained 1101 hits out of 3789 trials with one agent. Because the expected chance score was only 776 hits, the odds against obtaining such results by chance alone were 10^{35} to one. The hits, however, were of the $+1$ type. Shackleton was also phenomenally successful with -1, -2, and $+2$ hits, but not with the direct targets. Although the experiment appears to have been conducted taking every possible precaution against error, the availability of sensory cues and deception and the possibility of trickery was not completely eliminated. Hansel (1966) and Price (1955) both discuss the possibilities of how trickery, of necessity involving either Soal or both him and Shackleton, could have been effected, but without producing any definite proof of it. As indirect evidence, Hansel presents data that show that Shackleton's scores were at the chance level on trials 5, 10, 15, and 20, and above chance on other trials, and relates this finding to a possible deceptive means that would produce such an unusual result. Hansel could have used as a further argument the circumstance that 38 of the 40 sessions with Shackleton, who was a professional photographer, were conducted in Shackleton's own studio, and that he could well have prepared it in some way so as to obtain information about the cards that the agent was looking at. Recently, Betty Markwick (1978) has reported on evidence that extra digits were inserted in the number sequences that Soal prepared to determine the sequence of targets. Shackleton guessed correctly on these trials, and they contributed to his high scores. She also notes that

Soal was present at the experiment every time Shackleton obtained high scores and that he scored at the chance level when Soal was absent.

Deception, however, need not be invoked in Shackleton's case. It is important to note that none of the high-scoring subjects discussed so far ever achieved very high absolute scores—that is, scores higher than 13 or 14. Because card shuffling and manually prepared lists of random sequences are human activities, they preclude the achievement of true randomness. When two nonrandom sequences are juxtaposed, such as the sequence of targets and the sequence of the subject's calls in an ESP test, for instance, more matches may be obtained than are expected by chance alone. This phenomenon is discussed in more detail in Chapter 13. This could well have been a contributing factor at least in the Shackleton experiment, and it was demonstrated to have been that in the experiment conducted by Soal with Gloria Stewart.

Soal conducted a series of 130 experimental sessions with Gloria Stewart in 1945. Of these, 120 took place in her home. Of a total of 37,100 trials, 9410 were straight hits, or 1990 more than expected by chance, which makes the odds against having obtained such a result by chance alone greater than 10^{70} to 1. The experiments were conducted under conditions similar to the Shackleton experiment, but the controls were somewhat more relaxed because Soal's purpose was not so much to demonstrate ESP as it was to study its working under various conditions, such as long distance, type of symbol used, and the employment of two agents.

Although Mrs. Stewart's discovery was due to her having shown above-chance ability to guess − 1 and + 1 targets, on this occasion she failed to do so, and her success was dependent entirely on her straight hits. Because the testing conditions were similar to those under which Shackleton had been tested, Hansel was able to show that the same possibility of deception on the part of Soal, Mrs. Stewart, or both, existed. His indirect evidence for this was the fact that Soal had either produced the lists of random numbers that governed the presentation of targets or else had control over them when they had been prepared by others. Although fraud may have been involved, it is not necessary to invoke that explanation here either. J. Fraser Nicol of the ASPR discovered, upon checking the lists of random numbers used in the Stewart tests, that they were not truly random (Nicol, 1959). The non-randomness consisted in the deficiency of numbers occurring in patterns of the type 121, 545, 353, 313, or, in general, ABA. Such groups are expected to occur about 16% of the time in a truly random sequence. The odds against a deficiency of this magnitude found in the Stewart series were calculated to be about 10^{200} to 1. The non-randomness of the Stewart number series provides a clue as to how the statistically significant results could have arisen. As already indicated, unless a series of numbers is generated by a truly random process, it will not be random. Subjects' calls are not random either. Deviations from randomness tend to produce more matches when two non-random series are compared than the laws of chance would predict. Computer-performed matching of two series of 37,100 digits one through five (which was the number of trials in the Stewart series) using an ESP experiment simulator program (Gaither & Zusne, 1978) yielded 529 more hits than would have been expected by chance, the odds against such a result being better than 10^{10} to one. The only non-chance factor operating in this situation was the non-random structure of the digit series.

In the 1950s, Soal conducted studies of two allegedly telepathic Welsh boys, Glyn and Ieuan Jones. The 2-year study was described by Soal in a book (Soal & Bowden, 1959). The book does not figure very prominently in reviews of parapsychological experiments in spite of the boys' having obtained many scores of 20 and even a couple of 25: They were caught signaling to each other at least once. They did so directly or through family members who were observing the tests. Soal never quite believed that it was all fraud and collusion among relatives. The Jones case deserves mention for one reason, which is an ingenious method of signaling that the Jones boys probably used, although no one bothered to check them to see if they did. It is the ultrasonic or Galton whistle. A piece of tubing 1/16 inch in diameter and 1/2 inch long will produce a sound above the threshold of hearing for most adults but audible to young children and dogs (hence also sometimes called the dog whistle). It can be activated by a small rubber bulb, such as that used in eye droppers, and can be easily concealed because of its small size. The ability to hear high-pitched tones decreases with age. Because the investigators were middle-aged and the boys were around 13, the Galton whistle would have worked perfectly. This was demonstrated in 1960 by a man and his wife who used the Galton whistle while being tested for telepathy by an elderly stage magician (Scott & Goldney, 1960). The magician, who had participated earlier in testing the Jones boys and had declared that no trickery was involved, was likewise impressed by the performance of Christopher Scott and his wife. The sound of the Galton whistle is a subliminal stimulus to many people, but not to those who have the required hearing ability. It cannot be dismissed as a possible means of information transmission whenever the agent and the percipient are under conditions where normal information transmission is also possible.

Parapsychology After 1940

In 1940, the Duke researchers published *Extrasensory Perception After 60 Years* (Pratt, Rhine, Smith, Stuart, & Greenwood, 1940). Although the book reviewed psychical research since the founding of the SPR, it dealt mainly with the work of the Duke laboratory. By now, the Duke parapsychologists considered ESP to be an established fact. Rhine believed that

ESP was probably present in everybody, and that only personality characteristics interfered with the full manifestation of the ability. The evaluation of his ESP experiments by others was not as sanguine. Surveys conducted among scientists kept showing only a very small percentage believing ESP to be a fact, with the majority either disbelieving it or considering it only a remote possibility.

The most disconcerting characteristic of ESP was its unpredictability. It clearly could not be produced upon demand. Those who scored highly with one experimenter failed with others. Everybody's performance, even that of the high scorers, eventually declined. As criticism of lax controls rose and these were tightened, scores declined and good subjects became rare if not nonexistent. Since Hubert Pearce, only one or two consistent high scorers have appeared, such as the Czech Pavel Stepanek (Pratt, 1973).

Persisting in their efforts, parapsychologists began to accumulate a substantial body of experiments in which ESP appeared to be demonstrated. Few papers were published with negative results, prompting the charge that, because parapsychologists were apt to pool their results to demonstrate the statistical significance of their findings, the exclusion of negative results biased the findings in the desired direction. It was particularly stressed that those who run an ESP test and fail to find ESP do not bother to publish their results, and that if all such experiments were considered as a whole, the case for ESP would evaporate. This argument is only partly valid. One of the reasons is that positive ESP results may be due to causes other than the operation of ESP, and the solution to the significance problem must therefore be sought not in sheer numbers but somewhere else. The other reason is this: Assuming that the positive instances of ESP tests are due to nothing but chance, it follows that for every five experiments that turn out to be statistically significant, at least 95 other experiments must be performed showing negative results in order for the entire body of ESP experiments to show nothing but chance effects. This assumes the usual odds of 100 to 5 as the lowest acceptable level of statistical significance. This also assumes that whenever positive results were achieved, the level of significance was only .05 and no higher, which is not true. Even then, if the whole body of scientifically acceptable ESP literature that found positively for ESP were only 100 experiments, one would have to expect 2000 negative experiments to have been performed and not published in order for the preceding argument to be true. Such an assumption is not very realistic.

Even so, parapsychologists kept feeling uncomfortable about their inability to identify any factors that could be shown reliably to have an effect on ESP and thus lead to repeatable experiments. One phenomenon that was noted early at the Duke laboratory was the drop in the number of hits over successive runs of ESP trials. This phenomenon was observed so often that it was considered to be the most reliable ESP phenomenon (Pratt, 1949).

The explanations for this *decline effect* ranged from boredom and fatigue to desensitization due to increasing experimental complexity, as well as completely ad hoc hypotheses, such as unhappy love affairs (an explanation used by Rhine to account for the decline in Hubert Pearce's ESP ability). Fatigue, boredom, and lack of feedback of performance are well-known factors that affect both learning and performance by affecting the learner's or performer's motivation. But motivation can affect ESP performance only if ESP is a real phenomenon. The decline effect was thus taken as indirect evidence of ESP. There are other, or at least additional, explanations. One is that many of the ESP subjects at Duke began their tests after having gone through a screening procedure, which means that at least at the end of the screening tests, their performance was high enough to warrant further testing. The decline in their scores upon such further testing was what is known as the regression to the mean. Simply stated, anything that goes up must come down, and vice versa. In other cases, the decline effect could have arisen from the gradual tightening of experimental controls. Finally, even though the decline effect is observed often enough, it is not always observed, especially if the number of trials is not very large. Thus, five or six runs of 25 cards may produce a split among subjects where one-third of them show the decline effect, one-third show improvement, and one-third keep performing at about the same level. This was the case, for instance, in the GESP experiment performed by the authors in 1978, which is described in the next section.

Convinced of the reality of ESP, parapsychologists began to study how it works—that is, what variables may affect its manifestations. A number of such variables were explored by various investigators. Type of personality, hypnosis, motivation and attitudes, drugs, internal attention states, and physiological factors were among them. In addition, group tests of ESP were conducted in schools, animals were tested for the presence of ESP, and the possibility of influencing dreams telepathically was explored. With the exception of the sheep-goat phenomenon (see the next section) and possibly the ESP learning experiments, all of these attempts may be considered inconclusive, which is admitted by the parapsychologists themselves (e.g., Beloff, 1977; Rhine, 1977).

Much interest has been generated by tests of animal ESP ("anpsi"). Anecdotes of dogs and cats finding their way home from a distance of many miles have been quite popular. It has been assumed that the animals are guided by ESP because the new location and the terrain between it and the old home is entirely unfamiliar to them. Somehow, the ads in the Lost Animals columns in newspapers all over the world telling the story of pets who got lost within their own neighborhood, unable to find their way home, are ignored. Humans have always been willing to attribute human qualities to their pets, including those they are not quite sure they themselves possess, such as ESP. Animal trainers, knowing that animals would take very slight cue from their masters to do a trick, capitalized on the public's willingness to believe in the superior abilities of domestic animals. Sometimes, no conscious training was involved, and the owner and exhibitor of the animal did not even know that the animal had acquired such marvelous ability from the owner.

Perhaps the most celebrated mind-reading animal was the horse Clever Hans, owned by a Mr. von Osten, a German mathematics teacher. Clever Hans could perform the four arithmetic operations and give answers to problems by tapping with his hoof. He could also read and spell. Von Osten did not make any money off the horse, and he swore that he did not cue him. The horse was investigated by a German psychologist, Oskar Pfungst (Pfungst, 1911), who found that the horse could not perform when the owner was absent or when the horse could not see the questioner. Pfungst discovered that the way to start the horse tapping was to incline one's head. The deeper was the inclination, the faster did the horse tap his hoof. When the horse approached the correct number of taps, straightening up would slow the horse down, and a slight upward motion of the head stopped the tapping. Raising the eyebrows or flaring one's nostrils also worked. Clever Hans also responded to slight auditory cues. Eventually, Pfungst taught himself how to act like Clever Hans, and became quite successful in giving answers that questioners were thinking of.

In 1928, a female counterpart of Clever Hans on this side of the ocean, Lady Wonder, was shown by a magician to perform upon cues supplied her by her master, who ascertained what the questioner was thinking of by having that person write it on a pad with a long pencil. The owner watched the movements of the tip of the pencil, then cued the horse (Gardner, 1957).

Research in animal psi and parapsychology in general received a blow when Dr. Walter J. Levy, Jr., director of research of Rhine's laboratory, was discovered tampering with the automated equipment used in experiments on ESP in animals (Rhine, 1974a, 1975b). The disclosure, as well as the subsequent discovery of data fabrication in Levy's earlier experiments and the resignation of Dr. Levy, destroyed the work that he had done between 1969 and 1974.

Group Tests of Unselected Subjects. One finding in parapsychological research that has been repeated, although not always, is the differential scoring or the *sheep-goat effect*. On ESP tests, the scores of subjects who believe in ESP (the "sheep") tend to be higher than the scores of those who disbelieve it (the "goats"). The effect was first described by Gertrude Schmeidler and was confirmed by her in subsequent investigations (Eilbert & Schmeidler, 1950; Schmeidler, 1943a, 1943b, 1945, 1975; Schmeidler & McConnell, 1958). The finding has been confirmed by other investigators as well (e.g., Bevan, 1947; Bhadra, 1966; Casper, 1951; Kahn, 1952; Moss & Gengerelli, 1968). Belief alone does not produce statistically significant ESP performance. In a group of subjects, one-half of whom are believers and other half nonbelievers, the overall performance of the whole group may be at a chance level. However, when the group is divided according to belief (on the basis of a belief-in-ESP questionnaire or question), the believers may be found to have scored at an above-chance level whereas the nonbelievers may have scored below it. Often, there is only a statistically nonsignificant deviation in this direction in each group, but the combined difference—that is, the difference between the mean scores of the two groups—is statistically significant.

The fact that an individual or group may score significantly below the chance level is interpreted by the parapsychologist in the sense that the subjects have ESP, but they use it to avoid the targets, then deny to themselves and others that they used it. Significant scoring below the chance level is called *psi missing*. The sheep-goat phenomenon and psi missing are also related in the sense that both appear to have something to do with motivation and emotion, both of which are components of attitudes. Furthermore, under the proper circumstances, the attitudes, motives, expectancies, and emotions of the experimenter are also conveyed to the subjects and affect their performance. In psychological experiments and test situations, subject motivation and attitudes clearly affect the results, and no special demonstration is needed. The intention to do poorly on any test is easily achieved, and the intention to do better also works, although not as well. Experimenter effects in behavioral research have been amply documented (Rosenthal, 1976). How the experimenter affects the attitudes and motives of the subjects is known: the experimenter conveys expectations and attitudes either overtly, although not necessarily verbally, or covertly. Very slight signals, of which the experimenter may not even be aware, may be given to the subjects, who perceive them and act accordingly—for instance, in ways that would confirm the experimenter's hypothesis and therefore make him or her happy. There is a difference between a psychological and a parapsychological experiment, however. In the former, the subject's task is a clearly specified, objective bit of behavior that is voluntary and conscious in nature and has been well rehearsed in other situations. In card guessing, even when an individual obtains a strong impression of a symbol, the individual does not know how it comes about—it just happens. As has been repeatedly pointed out by parapsychologists, instead of being the actor, in a parapsychological experiment psi happens *to* the subject. Under these circumstances, it is difficult to hypothesize about the mechanism whereby one's own beliefs and attitudes, and especially those of others, may affect ESP scores. If one does not know how to affect ESP scores consciously, the only possibility remaining is that they may be affected unconsciously. If this is so, the ESP hypothesis unexpectedly receives a boost from experiments that show no sign of ESP in the overall performance of a group of subjects, such as in some of the sheep-goat experiments cited earlier. In a previously unpublished series of experiments, the authors of this volume tested for the presence of GESP in several different groups of subjects and, although finding no positive evidence for GESP, unexpectedly saw that the degree of psi missing was perfectly correlated with what could be interpreted as the degree of motivation. (Zusne & Jones, 1978). The purpose of the experiment had been to apply the theory of signal detection to ESP data analysis in order to establish the degree to which above-chance scores, if such were obtained, could be attributed to the subjects' sensitivity, either sensory or extrasensory, or to other factors, the so-called response bias. The basic signal-detection approach to sensory information transmission was discussed in Chapter 4. We obtained measures of sensitivity, the d' statistic, and measures of response bias, the beta statistic, on 40 student volunteers, seven pairs of individuals who felt a strong link of empathy existed between them, and nine "sensitives" recruited through a newspaper advertisement. In order to use the signal-detection methodology, eight blank cards were added to the regular deck of ESP cards. The student volunteers also filled out an ESP belief questionnaire, and, for the purpose of data analysis, were divided into a group of 23 believers and 17 nonbelievers. The seven dyads were believers in ESP, and so were, of course, the nine sensitives. In addition to belief, the other variable tested in the experiments was information concerning the presence or absence of the blank cards. One-half of the 40 student subjects were told about the blank cards, the other half was not. All were told that they could use the response "Nothing" if on a given trial nothing came to mind. The dyads and the sensitives were all informed about the blank cards. The agent working with the student volunteers was a graduate student and a believer in ESP, one of the pair in the dyads group served as the agent, and one of the authors (LZ) was the agent with the nine sensitives. All subjects were given 132 trials.

No subject reached a level of performance significantly above the chance level. Four of the 40 students performed significantly below that level, however, as did four of the seven subjects in the dyads group and five of the nine sensitives. The d' measures of sensitivity were negative for all subjects and all groups. Because only a d' of zero indictes no sensitivity, all d' measures of less than 0 mean avoidance of the target. The absolute size of d' was largest in the nonbelievers who had not been told about the blank cards, followed by informed nonbelievers, noninformed believers, informed believers, dyads, and the sensitives. Having been told about a certain dimension of the experiment, such as the presence of blank cards, is a motivational factor. Holding a belief that is pertinent to the experiment also constitutes motivation. If these two sources of motivation are assumed to be additive in their effect, then the six subject groups just mentioned may be seen arranged in order of the degree of motivation they possessed to do well in the experiment, and the differential scores may be considered an analogue of the sheep-goat effect.

Not every study that has assessed the effect of attitudes on ESP has been able to show it. For instance, in a very carefully conducted study, Layton and Turnbull (1975) were able to show, by manipulating belief, its effect on ESP in one experiment, but they failed to replicate their own results in a second one. The effect is nevertheless there, for the number of studies that show positive results exceeds the number of negative studies by a substantial margin.

Another factor whose effect on ESP has been tested successfully with subject groups has been learning. The psychologist Charles Tart has been the main proponent of the learning approach to ESP (Tart, 1976). Because virtually every experimenter has supplied the subjects with performance feedback only after each run or even after a complete series of runs, Tart interprets the decline phenomenon as a form of extinction. In conditioning, presenting the conditioned stimulus without reinforcement leads to a decline in response strength, which is called extinction. If an ESP subject continues to guess cards many times in a row without receiving any information on how he or she is doing, decline in motive strength—that is, boredom—sets in, leading to a corresponding decline in ESP. The logical remedy is to give the subject feedback (reinforcement) on the performance. In his book on learning and ESP, Tart cites 28 studies, including his own, in which feedback in ESP tests had been given. Of the 748 subjects tested in these studies, only one showed a decline in performance, with all others performing at a steady rate or showing improvement in performance. The stabilization of performance is one of the significant effects of feedback in ESP tests. A considerable number of the subjects showed learning besides, with the greatest gains being associated with greater initial ESP ability. As in the case of the sheep-goat experiments, here, too, there have been studies in which there has been a complete failure to demonstrate the effect of learning on ESP. Gardner (1975) presents a detailed analysis of one such study.

By postulating extinction as a factor in ESP, Tart has also implied that ESP is at least a partly learned ability. Innate responses, such as the reflexes, do not extinguish, whereas learned ones do. If ESP does indeed suffer extinction, it must be at least in part a learned response, subject to increase in strength when reinforced. It could well be an ability that, like intelligence, combines both innate and learned components. The most important aspect of Tart's attempt to bring ESP to learning is the recognition that well-tested psychological methods and concepts can be used to study ESP.

When Rhine retired in 1965, Duke University severed its connection with the Parapsychology Laboratory. Rhine continued his work privately as the head of an independent organization at Durham, the Foundation for Research on the Nature of Man. Long before that time, Rhine had already arrived at the conclusion that psi, whatever it was, was not a physical phenomenon. Rhine (1977) used the following points as evidence for the non-physical nature of psi: (1) whereas physical energies obey the inverse square law of distance, ESP does not; (2) precognition runs counter to the principle of cause and effect; (3) and electromagnetic screening has no effect on ESP. To these may be added: the arguments, also used by Rhine and others, that the ESP subject is unpredictable in his or her ability; the decline effect, which is uncharacteristic of either energy or information transmission systems; psi missing; and the unconscious nature of psi. Unfortunately, these facts also characterize chance events. Rhine, however, did not choose to describe ESP as the product of the operation of chance factors. What he did decide was that physical methods were inadequate to test for psi ability (Rhine, 1975a). In view of the fact that all along psychology has been using physical methods to measure non-physical—that is, mental—events, Rhine's terminology was somewhat inadequate. What he meant, however, becomes clear from the example he held up as illustrative of the "non-physical" method he preferred. It was Schmeidler's sheep-goat experiments, in which a non-physical—that is, mental—factor (belief) affected ESP. It is interesting that one of the most severe critics of ESP experiments, C. E. M. Hansel, also favors the group experiment on factors that affect ESP over testing high-scoring subjects individually. The single outstanding subject sooner or later either loses his or her ability or simply disappears never to be heard of again. By contrast, if psi is present to whatever degree in substantial portions of the general population, it is possible to draw subject samples from that population time and again and expect to obtain similar results repeatedly. An additional advantage of the group experiment is that variation of the experimental variables becomes possible by exposing different subject groups to different amounts or kinds of such variables. Impressive odds against chance are meaningless by themselves. What makes a scientific experiment is showing that the experimental results can be affected by varying some experimental variable, such as the presence, absence, or difference in beliefs, or making an effort, not making an effort, or making an opposite effort.

NOTES

The best historical reviews of psychical and parapsychological research are found in Hansel (1966) and Moore (1977), even though Hansel's main purpose was to offer a critique of ESP experiments. The two should be read in conjunction, because Moore's perspective is that of a social historian whereas Hansel writes as a psychologist and scientific critic. The two historical reviews of parapsychology by two parapsychologists that appear in Wolman's *Handbook of Parapsychology*, (1977) Beloff (1977) and Rhine (1977), are briefer, but very useful reviews written from the insider's point of view. The autobiography of Rhine and his wife (Rhine & Rhine, 1978) is also valuable because it offers interesting personal glimpses of the history of parapsychology, written by the man whose name has become identified with it.

The latest, most comprehensive (almost 1000 pages) overview of the entire field of parapsychology is the *Handbook of Parapsychology* (Wolman, 1977). It contains reviews of experimental work, theories, and papers on the relationship between parapsychology and other fields, such as anthropology, religion, physics, and philosophy. Given the nature of parapsychology, it is unfortunate that all the contributions to this volume have been penned by Sheep. Hence, selectivity of data and bias in their interpretation are present throughout and must be kept in mind when using this work. An inevitable drawback is that the amount of literature reviewed is prodigious and each study is summarized only briefly, so that no evaluation of their adequacy is possible.

Mind reading, ESP, and precognition in the style of Jeanne Dixon are seen through the eyes of a professional magician in Christopher (1970).

The problem of attitudes and personality traits in experimental ESP research is well treated by John Palmer (1977), and a related paper on how the experimenter's motives and attitudes influence psi test results appears in the same publication (White, 1977).

On animal psi, see Morris (1977), and, for a somewhat more jaded look at it, Christopher (1970).

13 Parapsychology: II

The basic difficulty inherent in any investigation of phenomena such as those of psychic research or of UFOs is that it is impossible for science ever to prove a universal negative. There will be cases which remain unexplained because of lack of data, lack of repeatability, false reporting, wishful thinking, deluded observers, rumors, lies, and fraud. A residue of unexplained cases is not a justification for continuing an investigation after overwhelming evidence has disposed of hypotheses of supernormality, such as beings from outer space or communications from the dead. Unexplained cases are simply unexplained. They can never constitute evidence for any hypothesis.

Hudson Hoagland, 1969.

EXPLANATIONS, MODELS, AND THEORIES OF ESP

Explanations of the First Kind

The first kind of explanation of ESP reduces the psi phenomena to some well-known physical phenomenon or phenomena:

1. Fraud, deception, trickery.
2. Available sensory information, including the operation of sensory hyperacuity, unintentional clues, etc.
3. Recording errors.
4. Faulty experimental design, such as nonrandomness of target sequences.

Instances of these explanations, used singly or in combination, have been mentioned in the preceding chapter. A fifth instance of this type of explanation, which is an attitude more than an explanation, is to declare that psi phenomena do not fit the existing scientific scheme of things and to ignore the results of parapsychological experiments altogether. The quotation from D. O. Hebb in the section *Evaluation of the Results* in Chapter 12 illustrates this attitude.

Explanations of the Second Kind

Explanations of this type stem mostly from those who believe in ESP or are about to be converted to a belief in it and are seeking to justify their act. Others are the product of audacious speculation by creative minds who seek to subsume one more unexplained phenomenon in some general theoretical scheme. Some instances of this kind of explanation are:

1. Biological (ESP as an evolutionary remnant or an evolutionary hope; bioenergetic explanations).
2. Physical (invoking the concepts of particle physics, quantum mechanics, relativity theory, electromagnetism, or multidimensionality of time and space).
3. Metaphysical (the postulation of different realities, distinct from physical reality).
4. Psychological and information-theoretical.

There are two biological explanations that contradict each other. One holds that ESP is an evolutionary remnant, a primitive ability that was once present in all members of the human species but was superseded by sensory communication and is therefore only marginally present in a few individuals. Sigmund Freud was one important individual who held such a view. The other view is that ESP is an evolutionary development that is only now beginning to appear in humanity, but that it will become the preferred mode of communication in the future. This view is held by the occultists who consider telepathy a "higher" faculty whose development will parallel the spiritual development of humankind. Both views imply some organ or structure that mediates psi. No such structure has ever been discovered, although the pineal gland has been proposed as a candidate.

The bioenergetic theories have been favored by Soviet scientists, especially after S. D. Kirlian photographed the corona discharges of living tissues. "Bioplasm," an unspecified "fourth state of matter," is the supposed medium of psi phenomena.

Experiments with electromagnetic shields have practically eliminated the hypothesis that ESP might have something to do with electromagnetic forms of energy generated by the nervous system and transmitted to other nervous systems. The shields seem to do nothing to ESP. Besides, electromagnetic energy obeys the inverse square law of distance, whereas ESP does not.

The theories that invoke concepts of particle physics, relativity, and quantum theory appear to be very sophisticated. At least the physics part of them does, but the theorists are getting a free ride from the tremendous theoretical and experimental work of many physicists over the past 75 years or so, for parapsychological work itself has hardly supplied either the theoretical or the empirical grounds for such theorizing. A similarity between the behavior of subatomic particles and psi phenomena is seen, and a theory couched in the language of theoretical physics arises. For instance, there are few parapsychologists who have not referred to Heisenberg's principle of uncertainty. The principle states that the act of observing subatomic particles leads to uncertainty in the observation; if the mass and velocity of a particle are measured, its location becomes uncertain and can be expressed only as a probability. If its location and mass are determined, its velocity becomes uncertain, and so on. More often than not, this principle is used as a rationalization: If the physicist can afford to be uncertain in his or her observations, why not the parapsychologist? The elusiveness of psi phenomena thus becomes a virtue rather than a vice. The error that is sometimes made is to equate the physical world of the subatomic particle with the everyday physical world and apply the principles that govern the former to the latter. Determinism may break down in the world of mesons, neutrinos, and quarks, but in the world of gross objects and events, the law of cause and effect still rules. The same goes for relativity theory: It applies to events that take place at speeds approximating the speed of light, but has no bearing on events involving earthly physical bodies rather than energy quanta. Thus, the principle of uncertainty and relativity theory have hardly anything to offer to explain psi phenomena.

Some theorizing in this area goes along the following lines. Albert Einstein demonstrated that matter is convertible into energy and energy into matter. Matter is thought to consist of particles, and energy propagates in waves. On the subatomic level, however, matter-energy is at once particles and waves. This is the principle of complementarity. This principle forces one to look at the same event from two different frames of reference, both of which mutually exclude and complement each other. Energy comes in packets (quanta), and there are matter waves. A complete view of matter-energy is afforded only by considering it simultaneously as particles and as waves. This has prompted physicists like Heisenberg and Pauli to draw a parallel between this view of modern physics and the dualism of philosophy. The father of modern philosophy, René Descartes, was a complete dualist; to him, the body was physical and obeyed physical laws mechanically. The soul, on the other hand, belonged to a different realm. It was "unextended substance," not subject to the laws of physical nature, but it did interact with the body. This interaction took place in the pineal gland, but that was an ad hoc device that Descartes was not very satisfied with. How could an unextended substance interact with extended substance, either in the pineal gland or elsewhere? The Cartesian philosophers never solved this problem, in spite of valiant attempts to do so. The problem that beset them also besets the modern physicist and possibly for the same reason. If waves are movement, but are at the same time also waves of matter, the medium within which such waves move cannot be a medium with physical attributes. The carrier of these waves must be immaterial. An immaterial substrate of matter has been postulated, called the psi field or psi function, designated by physicists by the same Greek letter as the undefinable, nonmaterial phenomena of the parapsychologist. It is on this level of matter-energy, wave-particle interaction that an explanation of ESP phenomena is sought by some theorists.

Among the numerous subatomic particles now recognized in physics is the neutrino. The neutrino has no mass and no charge, and it passes with the greatest of ease through any amount of solid matter. The existence of neutrinos, demonstrated in 1956, led to speculations about particles of the same nature that would provide the link between mind and matter that Descartes sought 300 years ago. "Mindons" (V. A. Firsoff), "psychons" (Whatley Carington, Cyril Burt), and "psitrons" (Adrian Dobbs) are some of the candidates. Dobbs' psitrons operate in a second dimension of time and have an imaginary (in the mathematical sense) mass.

All such attempts at theorizing about psi and the relationship between mind and body disregard the basic working hypothesis of the psychologist concerning the nature of mind. The psychologist has long ceased to regard the mind as a thing, a substance, or a collection of particles. The mind is looked at as a process, an activity that arises from the brain's activity and is experienced by the perceiving subject. If mind is the name for a process that is indistinguishable from the material substrate from which it arises, there is no need to postulate a medium that intervenes between the mind and the brain. The mindons, psychons, and psitrons are the equivalents of Descartes's pineal gland and the "vital spirits" that the gland was supposed to push through the nerves to produce behavior. There is no solution to the problem of the interaction between the physical and the non-physical if the solution postulates a medium in which such interaction takes place. If the medium has physical properties, it belongs to the world of particles, and the problem has not begun to be solved. If it is not, it belongs to the world of mind and the same situation obtains. If it is both, it becomes unnecessary because in a monistic view, mind and matter on the ultimate level of analysis should be the same. This is the view taken by Benjamin Wolman (1965, 1977). His theory of monistic transitionism is based on the proposition of Heraclitus (540-475 B. C.) that the only reality is change, that the notion of identity is therefore untenable (one cannot bathe in the same river twice, because the second time, both the river and the bather have changed), and that apparent identity reduces to the perception of continuity in change. Continuity in change is the principle that reconciles monism and dualism. Although there is only one substance in the universe, continuous changes lead gradually to states that look quite different from the original state, yet are part of the same reality because of the transitionistic link. Thus, mind arose from matter in the course of evolution, and both are linked by the universal process of transition. Parapsychological phenomena arise in the area where mind and brain transform into each other.

Some of the metaphysical and mystical explanations invoke concepts used in specific metaphysical, mystical, and occult systems. Thus, an occultist may speak of energies associated with the etheric or astral levels of existence, or of activity on these levels of existence by the corresponding bodies, as did, for instance, Madame Blavatsky. To obtain clairvoyant information, one leaves the physical body, goes to the required place in one's astral body, and looks it up. Others postulate additional dimensions or realities. Lawrence LeShan, for example, (1974) elaborates upon the distinction between rational and intuitive knowledge, or direct and indirect knowing. He speaks of a sensory reality and a clairvoyant reality. Both are valid modes of knowing, but they are governed by different rules. When one is in a mental state ruled by clairvoyant reality (intuitive or direct knowing), psi phenomena make sense, and one engages in telepathy, mental healing, psychokinesis, and the like. The one who observes these phenomena but is governed by sensory awareness (rational, scientific, or indirect knowing), fails to understand them, dismisses them, or ignores them.

No purely psychological explanation of ESP has been advanced. One can, nevertheless, use concepts from psychology and present a model of psi that conforms to some current psychological model. One such model that has received its inspiration from communications engineering is the information-processing model. The idea of ESP as information processing has been broached by several individuals in spite of the difficulties created by the fact that information transmission in ESP does not seem to follow the laws that govern ordinary transmission of information. Charles Tart's model of telepathy is one example that combines information theory, perceptual psychology, and parapsychological notions. The model is shown in Fig. 13.1. ESP is treated here as an information transmission process, except that the nature of the signals as they travel in the communications

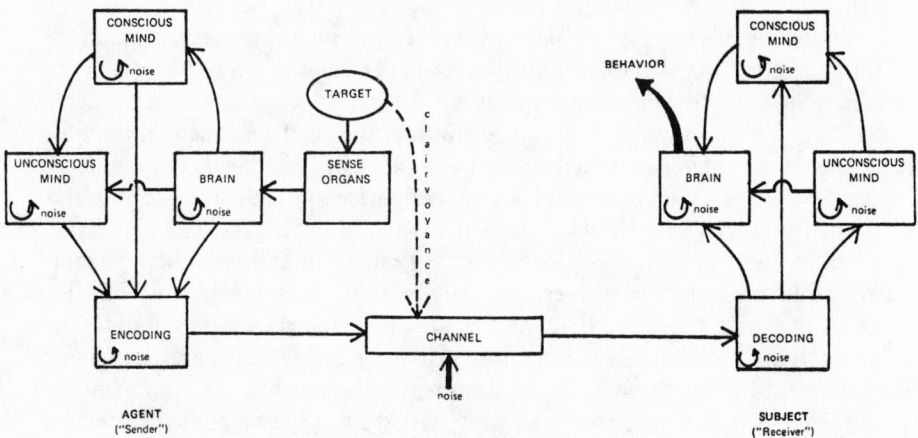

Fig.13.1.   Charles Tart's model of GESP. (From Tart, 1976. ©1976 by the University of Chicago. Used by permission of The University of Chicago Press.)

channel between the agent and the percipient is not known. Neither is the nature of the communications channel or the processes whereby ESP signals are encoded by the agent and decoded by the percipient. In this model, the terms channel, encoding, and decoding hide hypothetical parapsychological phenomena. As long as these remain unidentified, the model will not be much more than an attempt to define telepathy by analogy using information-theoretical and psychological concepts. It is not a theory—that is, a statement that organizes a reasonable number of empirical observations and offers testable hypotheses. The parapsychologist Karlis Osis has made an effort to specify some of the channel characteristics of ESP (Osis, 1976). For instance, his review of long-distance experiments with ESP shows an attenuation of the ESP effect over distance, which, however, is much slower than the rate predicted by the inverse square law of distance for physical energies.

Explanations of the Third Kind

Explanations of ESP of the third kind are more homogeneous, and could possibly be reduced to a single explanatory mechanism. Some of the terms that have been applied to this mechanism in non-parapsychological contexts are: self-organizing tendency; Gestaltung (in Gestalt psychology); the integrative tendency (Koestler, 1972); information creation (Gatlin, 1977); negative entropy; "order from disorder" principle (Schrödinger, 1969); anamorphosis; morpholysis or morphic principle; and emergentism. Two related terms that specifically refer to the surprising, anomalous results of the operation of this principle are the law of seriality (Kammerer, 1919) and synchronicity (Jung, 1973).

Following are some examples of the self-organizing tendency: An amorphous, unorganized amount of oil will organize itself into a perfect sphere if placed in water (the oil has to have about the same specific gravity as water). The way atoms come together to form molecules is determined entirely by chance. Yet, when a certain degree of complexity of chemical compounds is reached they will further combine strictly by necessity. Jacques Monod, the French biologist and Nobel prize winner, has suggested that life emerged when the originally pure chance events of chemical compounding became events governed by the strictest necessity, such as the self-replication of the DNA molecule (Monod, 1972). An analogous process can be simulated in an inorganic and purely mechanical system. At MIT, Stewart Kauffman (1969) studied the behavior of random networks made up of simple binary elements, analogues of switches, that existed in only two states, closed or open. The network was simulated on a computer. All connections among network elements were randomly determined. Each element responded to two other elements, but affected only one other element. Systems consisting of between 15 and 2000 elements showed an unexpectedly restricted pattern of behaviors (patterns of closed and open switches). Instead of displaying all possible 2^N states at random, the systems cycled through a very small number of states, and the number of variations in states achieved by arbitrarily changing the initial state was also very small. Constructed on a random plan, the networks showed order, patterning of behavior, and stability. Static collections of random elements also show organization and patterning that were not designed into them. The blank spaces between words in a large block of solidly printed text may come together to look like an object, such as a person's profile, a large block letter, or the outline of some common object. It is thought that the so-called canals on the planet Mars originated in the same fashion. Due to the poor resolution of the telescopes available at the time of Schiaparelli, the Italian astronomer who first saw the canals in 1877, fine Martian features that were in themselves invisible, produced, from large arrangements of such features, lines that appeared straight and therefore man-made.

In all of these examples, the emergence of patterns—that is, of meaningful forms—is determined by the fact that there is a perceiver and that this perceiver attributes meaning to the pattern. The objective, physical structure of the pattern is there, but it takes past experience of a certain kind in order for a given person to decide that the emerging pattern looks like, say, the big letter A, an irrigation canal, or even that a form is spherical and therefore has a special meaning. As we see later, the factor of meaning attribution is a crucial one in considering meaningful coincidences.

At the heart of the self-organizing tendency lies the presumed randomness of the elements from which the observed structure emerges. Groups of such elements can be called the *formants*. The words whose ends on a printed page form the outlines of the blank spaces that look like the slanting sides of a large letter A are its formants. It is the nonrandomness of the elements of the formants that leads to the emergence of structure.

In statistics, randomness refers to the manner in which items (elements) that are to make up a sample are selected from the entire population of such items. In a so-called random sample, every element has had the same chance of being selected from the population. This means that, if many such samples are considered together: (1) there will be approximately the same number of elements of each kind (e.g., ESP card decks will have about equal numbers of the five symbols), i.e., the samples will be equiprobable; and (2) they will not show any consistent regularities in the way sample elements follow each other. The frequencies with which each kind of element can follow or precede another kind or any combination of them are known. Strictly speaking, only infinitely long series of elements can show a truly random sequence. However, for practical purposes a well-shuffled

deck of ESP cards with all five symbols represented five times may be considered to be randomly sequenced most of the time. The nonequiprobable
deck, such as an open deck, will show a bias or patterning that will have important consequences for ESP.

To illustrate what happens when two biased formants come together, let
us look at a simpler example than the case of the ESP cards, the tossing of
two coins. If the coins are true, the sequencing of heads and tails from the
tosses of one coin may be considered to be a random formant, as can the
tosses of the other coin. If the two coins are tossed simultaneously many
times, two heads (HH) will come up about one-fourth of the time, two tails
(TT) will also come up one-fourth of the time, and tails-heads (TH) and
heads-tails (HT) will also each come up one-fourth of the time. In other
words, the two coins will match half of the time and will not match half the
time. If the coins are biased, this will no longer be the case. Let us assume
that the first coin comes up heads two times out of three and tails one-third
of the time, and that the second coin is also biased in favor of heads—three-
fourths of the time, with tails coming up only one-fourth of the time. Now,
the chances for HH is increased considerably; the probability of this happening is the product of the probabilities for heads of the two coins: 2/3
times 3/4, or 6/12. Tails (TT), however, will come up only 1/12 of the time
(1/3 times 1/4). The HT combination will occur 2/12 of the time (2/3 times
1/4), and TH will occur 3/12 of the time (1/3 times 3/4). Thus, matches will
occur 7/12 of the time (6/12 + 1/12) and mismatches 5/12 of the time
(2/12 + 3/12). If the direction of the bias of one of the coins is reversed
while remaining numerically the same, the symmetrically opposite results
are obtained: Now the coins match 5/12 of the time and fail to match 7/12
of the time.

The mechanics of an ESP experiment with cards are no different from
those just described. Instead of only two symbols (H and T), there are five
(the five Zener symbols), but otherwise the procedure is the same: Two random sequences of these symbols, one representing the sequence of cards,
the other the sequence of the percipient's calls, are placed side by side and
the matches across the two sequences noted. If digits are used instead of
graphic symbols, the ESP experiment may be simulated by using sequences
of digits obtained from tables of random numbers. How would a bias occur
in the sequence that represents the random sequence of ESP cards?

In 1953, the mathematician Spencer Brown reported that he had matched
pairs of digits at random in a simulation of card guessing, and had obtained
more matches than was expected by chance. Tables of random numbers
prepared before the age of the electronic computer are apt to show nonrandomness both in terms of patterning of sequences of the digits and in terms
of nonequiprobability of digits over quite extended segments of the tables.
For example, the tables of random digits of Kendall and Smith (1939) that

have been reprinted in various collections of statistical tables and have been used to determine orders in numerous experiments show the same pattern of nonequiprobability for the digits 1 through 5 as was obtained by one of the authors of this volume (LZ) by punching these digits on an electronic adding machine very rapidly and following his own idea of what a random sequence might be like. Any method of generating random sequences that does not exclude the influence of the human mind or the built-in biases of machines and mechanical devices is apt to produce sequences that are not truly random.

In 1967, the marine biologist Alister Hardy and Robert Harvie, a psychology graduate of London University, conducted a group experiment on GESP in which 200 individuals participated. In several sessions, up to 20 of the participants would be randomly selected to act as percipients. They sat in cubicles while the rest, the agents, were located around them in a large hall. The agents watched various visual targets being displayed on a stage before them, and they attempted to "send" these targets to the percipients telepathically (Hardy, Harvie, & Koestler, 1975). Although there were a number of apparent hits, the most striking result was the coincidence of similar drawings made by two, three, or more percipients. These, however, had nothing to do with the targets that the agents saw. Hardy and Harvie then matched targets and response drawings or written ideas that had not occurred together in the experiment as targets and responses to these targets—that is, they compared them in random combinations—and they found that coincidences still occurred and could not be statistically distinguished from the coincidences that had been observed in the genuine experiment. They then proceeded to conduct mock experiments using digits 0 through 9 in series obtained from random number tables, and checked for matching pairs in a total of 49,600 comparisons. The number of matches was significantly below mean chance expectation, the odds against chance being 1250 to 1. Hardy and Harvie also observed the decline effect, although not invariably. The experimenters concluded that the results they had obtained, both with the participation of human subjects and without them, were due to nothing but chance.

Manual matching of a large number of digit series is an extremely tedious and time-consuming task. A computer program that simulates the mechanics of the ESP card-guessing situation has been written (Gaither & Zusne, 1978). It takes two series of 25 digits and notes the matches across pairs. In one study, four kinds of sequences of the digits 1 through 5 were generated and compared: equiprobable sequences (each digit appeared five times); nonequiprobable sequences obtained from tables of random numbers; spontaneous sequences, generated with the adding machine, as previously described; and contrived sequences, in which the frequency with which each digit was to appear in the sequence was determined beforehand.

The results are shown in Fig. 13.2. Each data point is the mean number of matches per 250 trials, computed on the basis of 62,500 trials, or 2500 "runs." The 250-trial figure was chosen for purposes of comparison because this was the number of trials given a prospective ESP subject in the Duke Laboratory. It is clear that the number of matches increases in proportion to the degree of nonequiprobability found in the two series compared. The odds against 51.75 matches in 10 runs occurring by chance alone are 100 to 5 ($p < .05$), the odds against 55.90 matches (the spontaneous/contrived comparison), however, are 10^{11} to 1. Because the pro-

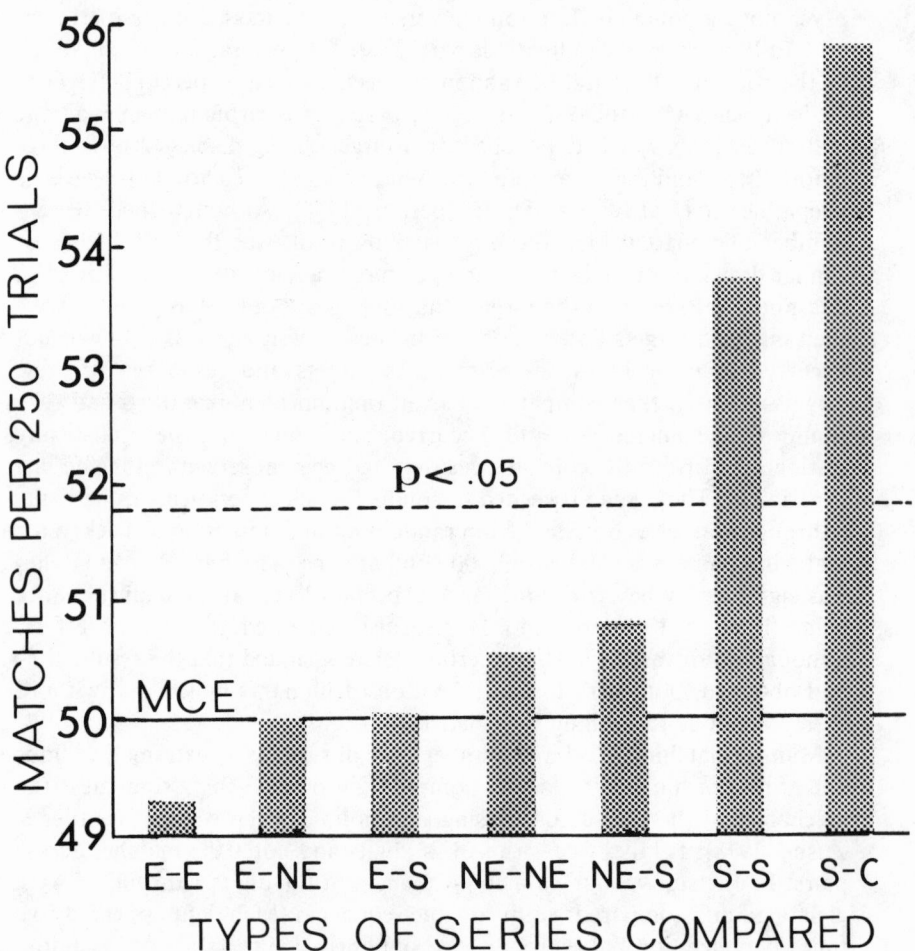

Fig.13.2.   Mean number of matches per 250 computer-made comparisons of nonsystematic series of five digits. E: equiprobable series; NE: non-equiprobable series; S: spontaneous series; C: contrived frequency distribution series.

cedure of comparison is an entirely mechanical one, the only non-chance factor that can produce these deviations from MCE is the non-random structure of the series compared.

The numbers shown in Fig. 13.2 are arithmetic means of many runs. Even in the case in which equiprobable series were compared, chance alone yielded on occasion 61, 62, 63, and 64 matches per 250 comparisons, sometimes one after another, which is equivalent to a successful screening of subjects for further ESP experiments. Of the 250 blocks of 250 trials each that comprised the spontaneous/contrived series, 71 yielded 60 matches or more. There were two scores of 70 and one of 71.

In an actual ESP experiment with cards, the decks of cards are equiprobable formants. Shuffling, however, does not guarantee that a random order of cards will be produced every time. It is quite possible to produce highly non-random series this way. The subject's responses are for the most part non-equiprobable. In some cases, the instructions given the subject explicitly say not to worry about making the number of calls for each symbol the same. Thus, even in the worst case, at least one of the formants of what might become a meaningful event is nonequiprobable. The importance of all this is that the very nature of the variables that produce the result in an ESP experiment, the order of the cards and the order of the subject's calls, is bound to affect the results so that they deviate from chance expectation, whether ESP is, in fact, in operation or not. Whether the deviation is upward or downward makes no difference because a downward deviation can be interpreted as psi missing, which is also significant.

This is not to say that ESP is nothing but an artifact of the way numbers in non-random series behave. The fact that they do behave non-randomly does not mean that ESP does not exist, or, for that matter, that sensory information transmission is not taking place. It only means that any deviation from randomness in either the order of the cards or the order of the subject's calls makes the interpretation of any significant deviation of the results from chance very difficult because the operation of ESP or anything else is completely confounded with the operation of non-randomness. The only solution is to establish the limits of variation in the number of matches that can be expected in two series of a particular probability structure. The only time a safe conclusion can be drawn that non-randomness probably did not play a role is when the number of matches obtained exceeds these limits. To our knowledge, this has never been done in any parapsychological study.

Real-Life Situations. Real-life situations that may appear to involve extrasensory perception are analogous to the digit-matching studies described in the preceding section. The formants of the phenomena described as telepathy, precognition, and all other meaningful coincidences are for the most part human lives, series of events set in motion by humans, and, in general, any causally related sequences of events. A human life may be considered a line of nonequiprobable events, a line within which each event is causally determined. There are also causal connections between the life lines of persons who interact as family members, coworkers, and so on, but the vast majority of human lives are not directly and causally connected. Such life lines run in parallel. They also run in parallel because the fundamental features of all human lives are the same—we are born, we live in dwellings, we take food, we work, play, go to school, have dreams, mate, and die. The similarities are great enough for two events in two life lines to coincide once in a while.

Schopenhauer (1891) compared the parallel life lines to the meridians on a globe, each being a causally determined sequence, and the acausal coincidences in two or more of them to the parallel circles. Paul Kammerer (1919) set out to collect cases of interesting coincidences in his own life and those of others, and produced a large collection of them, a taxonomy for systematizing them, and a principle that underlies them, which he called the law of seriality. It states that coincidences tend to occur periodically. His cases ranged from the trivial, such as finding on the same day that a streetcar ticket and a ticket to a concert bear the same number, to precognitive dreams and two people thinking of the same thing at the same time. Kammerer, however, rejected telepathy as a special phenomenon, and stated that the law of seriality subsumed it. Jung's idea of synchronicity (Jung, 1973), although basically similar to Kammerer's notion of the series, was more ambitious. To Jung, (1973) synchronicity was the "simultaneous occurrence of two meaningfully but not causally connected events [p. 25]." He sought an explanation of parapsychological phenomena in terms of synchronicity. But synchronicity was a much broader concept than just a principle to explain telepathy or astrological predictions. It was to be assigned the same place of importance among natural principles as the law of causality. In Jung's thinking, synchronicity and archetypes were connected because each coincidence that appeared meaningful to a person was also associated with the manifestation of some archetype.

Kammerer's law of seriality, a universal acausal principle, acted like the law of gravity, except that instead of attracting mass, this principle resulted in the attraction of form and function on the basis of their affinity ("like attracts like"). This is not too far removed from the principle of sympathetic magic. As we saw, however, meaningful coincidences can be produced by the simple expedient of bringing together two sequences of events of the same type, sequences that have some nonrandomness in them. Even though they may have no causal connection with each other, meaningful coincidences (synchronistic events) will be observed. It is therefore questionable whether affinity or archetypes need to be invoked to explain them.

Three facts must be borne in mind when considering cases of meaningful coincidence. One is that they are not an either-or phenomenon. Consider the following hypothetical example: A carpenter named Tracy Spencer is working on a construction site, hammering some nails two floors up from the street. A lawyer named Spencer Tracy passes the site on his way to the office. As he does, the carpenter accidently lets go of his hammer, which falls to the street, killing the lawyer. The story, prominently featuring the strange parallelism of names, naturally gets into the papers and such publications as FATE magazine. Now consider the same scenario again, except with the timing such that the hammer hits the ground a foot behind Spencer Tracy, without harming him. Spencer Tracy is startled, looks up and establishes where the hammer came from, but does nothing further about it. Chances are that this time, the story will not get written up in the papers, and much less so if the hammer falls after Spencer Tracy has already passed the fateful site so that he does not even hear it fall. The basic situation is still the same, except that the drama, the meaning of it all, has been all but removed. We are left by the construction site pondering on the implications of the fact that coincidences are not discrete, discontinuous phenomena. One is the problem of simultaneity and what it does to the meaningfulness of chance coincidences. If I dream of an accident, wake up, note the time, and then learn the next morning that an accident did indeed happen just the way I saw it in my dream and at the exact time noted, then I have a very meaningful coincidence, and may well enter it in my log book of precognitive dreams or synchronistic events. But, what if the accident happens just a few days later? What about a year later? What if the details are not quite the same? One could say that the meaningfulness of synchronistic events decreases directly with the passage of time between the two events that coincide, as well as with the degree of similarity or correspondence between them.

The second important fact that has a bearing on synchronistic events is one that Jung does not seem to mention. It is a truism that for a coincidence to be meaningful it must be observed by a person, and that person must attribute meaning to it. Meaning is an entirely psychological phenomenon and does not exist independently of an observer. The same event in one circumstance may appear as a meaningful coincidence, but not in another, or it may appear as meaningful to one person, but not to another. Meaning arises only from past experiences. If this is recognized, the persuasive power (and occult connotations) of many a story about "weird" coincidences is greatly diminished. One can think of meaningful coincidences that would be meaningful to only one or very few persons. The story told by Dr. Alvarez in Box 13.1 is a case in point.

Dr. Alvarez's story also illustrates the third factor that must be taken into account in connection with meaningful coincidences. They occur much more

---

Box 13.1—A Pseudo Experience in Parapsychology

The popular literature of parapsychology abounds in stories of the following kind: A person is dreaming of a friend he hasn't seen or thought of in 30 years. He is awakened by a call from a telegraph operator, telling him of the death of that friend several thousand miles away. Most scientists attribute such pairs of events to pure coincidence, but they offer no comparable stories to show that such apparently improbable coincidences do in fact occur. In the absence of such demonstrations, it is not surprising that the general public feels that there must be a causal relation between the two events, as, for example, by thought transference.

On 16 May 1965, reading the San Francisco *Sunday Chronicle* I noticed an article on page 22 entitled "Ancient men on the Nile." In scanning this story, I saw the phrase ". . . the expert appraisal of Philadelphia anthropologist Dr. Carleton S. Coon." To anyone who had been an undergraduate student at the University of Chicago in the early 1930's, this unusual name would call up nostalgic memories of another Carleton Coon and his partner, Joe Sanders, whose popular Coon-Sanders dance band was then playing at the Blackhawk. So I found myself thinking about Joe Sanders, very probably for the first time in 30 years.

Less than five minutes later, having turned the pages of the paper to page 33, I saw an obituary notice headed "Joe Sanders." It read, ". . . died Friday. . . .with the late Carleton Coon . . . organized the Coon-Sanders band." These two closely spaced recollections of a person forgotten for 30 years, with the second event involving a death notice, is in the classical pattern; but it is obvious that no causal relationship could have existed between the two events.

The probability of a coincidental recollection of a known person in a 5-minute period just before learning of that person's death can easily be calculated, to within a factor of 10. Let us take a 30-year period, and assume that an average person would recognize the names of 3000 different people who might die in that period of time (3000 is taken as a geometrical mean of 10^3 and 10^4, the probable extremes of a population of "known persons"). We assume that our subject will learn of the death of each of these persons at some time in the 30 years. If we restrict our attention to the time when our subject learns of the death of a particular person, we can then ask how probable it is, that in the 5 minutes just preceding that exact time of learning of the death, an unrelated recollection that is unique to the 30-year period will occur. This probability, to within a factor of 2, is the ratio of a 5-minute interval to a 30-year interval, or 3×10^{-7}. (It is clear that if one thinks of the particular person once a year rather than once every 30 years, the probability will rise by a factor of 30, to about 10^{-5}.) The probability that one will have such an experience when learning of the death of any one of the 3000 recognizable persons is clearly 10^{-3} in a 30-year period, or approximately 3×10^{-5} per year. If we take the sample of 10^8 adults in the United States, 3×10^3 experiences of the sort related above should occur per year, or about 10 per day. (For the average person 3000 recognizable names is probably an overestimate, but the postulated single recollection in 30 years is certainly much too low. These two departures from realistic assumptions have opposite effects on the computed rate, so 10 per day is still a reasonable estimate.) With such a large sample to draw from, it is not surprising that some exceedingly astonishing coincidences are reported in the parapsychological literature as proof of extrasensory perception in one form or another (Alvarez, 1965).

frequently than is thought. Popular ideas of the frequency of meaningful coincidences are usually gross underestimates. Precognitions acquire much of their paranormal flavor from the fact that the individual who experiences them believes them to be rare. This also goes for streaks of luck and similar events. Consider the case of Charles Wells, a gambler and confidence man (Wallechinsky & Wallace, 1978). In July of 1891, Wells, while gambling on a roulette wheel at Monte Carlo, broke the bank—that is, won all the money at that gaming table. He gamed for 11 hours straight and broke the bank 12 times that day. He broke it again the next day, and made big winnings that day and the next. He returned to England with over one million francs. Wells went back to Monte Carlo in a few months, broke the bank again, and again won a million francs in 3 days. In the winter of 1892, Wells broke the bank six times, but then began to lose without respite. He took up swindling money from people, went to jail, and died penniless. At the height of his fame, he claimed to be using a system, but nobody else who tried to copy it succeeded. In the end, Wells confessed that it had all been just a streak of luck. The odds against Well's incredible winning streak are incalculable, and yet it happened, with Wells claiming no paranormal powers.

As Dr. Alvarez's example shows, rather precise calculations may be made of the expected frequencies of at least some of these events. They turn out to be unexpectedly high. The formants of synchronistic events, human lives, include not only items of behavior, but events and circumstances in the person's immediate environment. Considering the basic similarity of human life patterns, the sheer numbers involved—of events, objects, circumstances, people—the only thing that is surprising is that life lines do not touch synchronistically more often or, rather, that such coincidences are not reported more often. One only has to think of the enormous number of dreams that are experienced every night just by people we are acquainted with to realize that precognitive dreams are bound to happen because each dream is made of the same components that constitute human lives, and the number of types of these components, although large, is not limitless. The formants of precognitive dreams—the dream events and real life events—are like segments from two series of digits that happen to match.

To avoid the special connotations of the terms "law of seriality" and "synchronicity," Koestler (1972) proposes that a neutral term, *confluential events*, be used to describe the acausal manifestations of the integrative tendency. The formants of these manifestations come together in time and space and give the appearance of a causal connection; a distant event seems to cause the clairvoyant dream, the dice thrower's will seems to make the dice roll in a certain way, and belief in ESP seems to cause higher ESP scores. To repeat the point made earlier, confluential events are not "just" coincidences, but coincidences brought about by the nonrandom structure of their causally unrelated formants.

PSYCHOKINESIS

Of all the imaginable forms of interaction between the mental and the physical, psychokinesis is the most direct and conceptually simplest. You roll a die wishing for a 6-spot, and it comes up. You wish for a matchbox to move across the table by itself, and it does. You wish for anything, and it happens. This is magic. Obtaining changes in accordance with one's will is the definition of magic given by Szandor la Vey, the high priest of the Church of Satan, Los Angeles. In the early stages of cognitive development, the child's thinking has also been described as magical (Piaget, 1930). The child's magic takes mostly the psychokinetic form: The clouds move because the child makes them move; the child wills things to happen and they do. Because the idea of psychokinesis sounds so much like magic, it has been received by scientists with even greater reluctance than ESP.

Psychokinesis, or PK, is a term relatively recently coined by para-psychologists to designate phenomena that in popular language are referred to as "mind over matter." The moving of objects by the sheer act of will is a standard feature of legends and fairy tales, and is ascribed to witches, sorcerers, and yogins as one of their powers. Broadly used, the term covers the setting in motion of stationary objects or their deformation by the mind or some paranormal means, influencing the course of an object already in motion, the production of sounds, voices, or writing without muscular or other physical intervention, influencing photographic emulsion mentally, and levitation. The so-called poltergeist phenomena and the physical phenomena of the medium are specific forms of psychokinesis.

Moving-Target PK

Although the alleged influence of mind over stationary objects is by far the oldest PK phenomenon reported, parapsychologists began the scientific study of PK by using targets in motion. The moving-target studies are at a distinct disadvantage in comparison to tests with stationary targets. Static targets either move or they do not move. In the dice-rolling experiment, on the other hand, a person attempts to make the dice roll in such a way as to produce a certain score. Because any score is possible by chance alone, it becomes a matter of establishing whether the scores obtained differed from chance in a statistically significant manner or not. The situation is therefore identical to that of the card-guessing experiment in that the existence of the phenomenon is determined on the basis of a statistical evaluation of whether two sequences of events—the die faces and the subject's calls—have produced sufficient matches.

J. B. Rhine began the study of PK in 1934. The reason for his not choosing static targets can only be surmised. One conceivable reason for the parapsychologists' choice of moving targets could have been to allow PK to show itself if it turned out to be a relatively weak force in spite of the alleged ability of mediums (or spirits) to levitate heavy furniture. Hansel (1966) reports that as late as 1950, when asked why he had not used a sensitive balance to test for PK, Rhine replied that it was a good suggestion and that he might get around trying it sometime. It does not appear that he ever did.

The early tests were informal, not well controlled, and yielded ambiguous results. Later, the dice were rolled by tilting a wire mesh cage that contained them instead of throwing them by hand or cup, the dice were checked for bias (using a control series of throws, with no PK influence present), and two experimenters were used to record the subject's calls and the actual scores obtained. It was not until 1942 that the results of these early studies, some 19 of them, were published. Also in 1942, the decline effect was discovered by Rhine in the records of these experiments. It was the decline effect rather than the statistical significance of the PK hits that convinced Rhine that he had a phenomenon that was worth investigating further.

In the *target-face* PK experiment, the die or dice are placed in a transparent cage that tilts about its midpoint. The subject states the score he or she will try to achieve, the dice are released, and the score is recorded. In the *placement* variety of the tests, several dice or other suitable objects are released to roll down an incline. The subject predicts whether most of the objects will roll to the right or the left side of the field at the bottom of the incline. The mean chance expectation and standard deviation are computed as in the ESP card case, except that the probability of a die face coming up is 1/6, and the probability of the objects rolling to one or the other side in the placement test is 1/2.

The biases that can affect the results of PK tests are recording errors and nonequiprobability of dice rolls and subjects' calls. Unless a photographic method of recording the rolls of dice is used and the subject's calls are taped, two experimenters are necessary to keep the record, one to record the subject's calls, the other the actual rolls of the dice. If a die has recessed spots, the faces with the larger number of spots, especially the 6-spot, will be lighter, and these will tend to come up more often than the other sides.

This may combine with the well-known tendency to wish for the 6-spot to come up, increasing the number of hits for the 6-side. For this reason, the number of times each face is to be selected by the subject must be determined before the experiment begins, as must the total number of runs to be made (a PK run consists of 24 throws).

In a review of PK experiments, Girden (1962) noted that of the 19 early PK experiments carried out at Duke University and published between 1942 and 1946, only one showed negative results, whereas two other experiments conducted elsewhere and under much better control conditions both yielded negative results. Of the 30 studies conducted after 1946, only 13 supported the PK hypothesis, and only one study demonstrated the decline effect. In *Parapsychology*, Rhine and Pratt (1957) state that in order for a PK test to be conclusive, it is necessary to employ two experimenters, randomize the target sequence and use equiprobable sequences of the six target faces, and record independently all targets and all hits and misses. In Girden's evaluation, none of the 13 positive tests satisfied all three conditions, whereas several of the 17 negative tests did.

In the 1960s, PK research methodology changed considerably. Experiments with dice were replaced by experiments with the random event generator (REG), and the dice experiments are rarely conducted now. The REG, an electronic device, not only generates truly random series of events, but can do so at differing rates, display the events to the subject, provide feedback, and record the results automatically. The most often used source of random events is a random natural process, the decay of radioactive material. The emission of particles from a radioactive source, such as the beta rays from strontium-90, is a process that is intrinsically unpredictable. A weak source of strontium-90 is placed next to a Geiger counter that registers the arriving particles at an average rate of, for instance, 10 events per second. Connected to the Geiger counter is a high-speed electronic switch with two or more positions. The arrival of a particle stops the switch in one of these positions, each position being equally likely. The switch then generates a current that can activate a light or an auditory signal that is displayed to the subject. The display may consist of a green and a red light or of several lights arranged in a circle. With the latter display, when the switch is stopped in position 1, it lights a bulb in the circle. Every time this happens, the light moves to the next lamp in the circle in a clockwise direction. When the switch stops in position 2, the movement of the light occurs counterclockwise. Normally, the directions of the movement of the lights or the turning on of the red and green light should occur randomly but an equal number of times in the long run. Electronic counters count the frequency of each event. The subject's task is to change the 50-50 relationship in the frequency of the binary event, presumably by PK, because the only other way to alter the output of the REG is to open it and make adjustments in its components. Adding another radioactive source from the outside does nothing but increase the rate at which particles arrive at the Geiger counter.

The first experiment with an radioactive REG was done by Beloff and Evans (1961). The results were negative. However, in 1965, Chauvin and Genthon, two German investigators, obtained positive results with subjects who tried to increase the counting rate of a Geiger counter. Most experiments with the electronic REG have been done by the physicist Helmut Schmidt. He has obtained positive results with the REG set in either the precognition or PK mode (e.g., Schmidt, 1967, 1969a, 1969b, 1971, 1975). There has been confirmation of Schmidt's results by several different investigators (e.g., André, 1972; Honorton & Barksdale, 1972; Kelly & Kanthamani, 1972) but others have not been able to replicate his results (e.g., Wadhams & Farrelly, 1968). Of all the studies conducted, about three-fourths show positive results. The effect that the human agent seems to exert on the radioactive decay process is very small, the best performers producing a deviation of 2% from the chance 50% level at most. However, in view of the very large number of trials (each lasts only a second or less), the odds against such deviations arising by chance alone range from 1000 to 1 to several billions to 1.

Stationary-Target PK

Perhaps the first scientific study of stationary-target PK was done by Michael Faraday (1853), described earlier (Chapter 8) in connection with table tilting, where we also discussed the "physical phenomena" of the séance room. The phenomena of levitation, raps, knocks, and other noises, musical instruments playing by themselves, paraffin casts of spirit hands, "direct voice" (voice that presumably originates not in the medium but from a point outside or near her), psychography (slate writing, or the appearance of spirit messages written on the inside of two slates tied together), the setting in motion of pendulums, and the teleportation of objects can all be considered instances of static object psychokinesis. In a review of studies of these phenomena in the *Handbook of Parapsychology* J. Fraser Nicol (1977) of the SPR states that "for a hundred years the subject has been infected with frauds beyond counting." One may wonder why, if PK is a genuine phenomenon, countless fraudulent attempts are necessary to prove its existence. The answer lies in Nicol's surprising conclusion that in spite of error and "frauds beyond counting," it is possible to make "a surprisingly impressive case" for the genuineness of "telekinesis, percussive sounds, and possibly other reported occurrences." It is James' "will to believe" at work. Nicol, after presenting one description after another of how fraud was perpetrated in ostensible displays of PK, seems to be saying, nevertheless, that as long as one unexplained case is left, its claim to genuineness must be honored.

As Nicol notes, PK phenomena outside the laboratory are difficult to investigate. They either take place spontaneously, such as the poltergeist phenomena, where the investigator is unprepared or unequipped to do a creditable job, or else there are public demonstrations, such as TV and stage appearances of individuals with alleged PK powers, or private demonstrations at the home of the sponsor where controls are impossible to maintain. Laboratory tests of stationary-object PK have uniformly failed to show any positive results. When objects have moved or have been deformed (bent, broken), they have done so because of some uncontrolled physical factor: shaky floor boards, air currents, static electricity, radiant heat, vibration of the support of the target object due to different causes—heavy trucks going by, underground railroads, underground streams, explosions—as well as threads and filaments attached to the mover's hands and simple sleight of hand whereby a to-be-bent object, for instance, is exchanged for a similar one that has already been bent. To these may be added the simple expedient of deforming the target object when no one is looking. This and the substitution ploy are resorted to by the 20th-century counterpart of Daniel Dunglas Home, the Israeli magician Uri Geller (Randi, 1975). The British physicist and PK enthusiast John Taylor allowed his subjects, who were young children and therefore presumably incapable of guile and deceit, to take metal samples home for unsupervised psychokinetic bending on the theory that watched metals do not bend (the "shyness effect") (Morrison, 1976). Even then, somehow, only metal rods in poorly sealed containers would bend.

When the operation of physical energies is effectively excluded, stationary objects do not move, bend, crack, or break when acted upon psychokinetically. One of the authors of this volume (LZ) once tested a woman who alleged that when she was around things were moving by themselves in her house and who felt that she had psychokinetic power. The initiative to be tested came from her. The test took place in the evening when no vibrations from trucks, pneumatic hammers, and so on, could affect the apparatus. The test took place on the first floor of a reinforced concrete building. The floor was a concrete slab in direct contact with the ground. The apparatus consisted of a short piece of an aluminum knitting needle balanced on its midpoint on the tip of a plastic needle set in a wooden base. The base had a circular scale marked in degrees. The device was enclosed in the glass bell of a vacuum pump used for physics demonstrations of the properties of a vacuum. The pump was set on the floor and the air removed from the bell. The subject sat on a chair several feet away from the needle. During a period of 1 hour, the subject made two attempts to move the needle, each attempt lasting about 1 minute. She expressed satisfaction with the atmosphere of the experiment (it took place in a comfortable and well-appointed office of a clinical psychologist), but her PK did not seem to work that night. The needle never moved.

Paranormal Photography. Paranormal photography refers to all those images on photographically sensitive materials that are presumed to have been achieved not by the light reflected from an object or other known radiation (such as infrared rays or X rays), but by means unknown or presumed to be mental or occult. This includes photographs of spirits of the dead, fairies, leprechauns, guardian angels, and other legendary beings, and the photographer's own thoughts or mental images.

Images of dead people ("extras") began to appear alongside the main subject of photographic portraits soon after the introduction of photography, which coincided with the beginning of spiritualism. The first spirit photographer, William Mumler, was forced to move his studio from Boston to New York when it was discovered that one of his "extras" was alive and living in Boston. The rest of the history of spirit photography is clad in murky fraudulence, so much so that any bits of genuine phenomena, if there were any, are hopelessly entangled with trick photography, double exposures, and doctored cameras. The fairy photographs taken in 1917 by two English girls turned out to be photographs of cardboard cutouts (see Notes for Chapter 9). By 1933, spirit photography was dead. Its reincarnation as psychophotography occurred in the 1960s when the "thought photography" of Ted Serios was brought to the attention of Dr. Jules Eisenbud, a psychiatrist at the University of Colorado Medical School. Serios would produce images on Polaroid camera film by simply thinking of them. Eisenbud tested Ted Serios at Denver over a period of 3 years (Eisenbud, 1977). In June of 1967, Ted Serios suddenly stopped producing structured images, causing Martin Gardner (1976) to surmise that the change had been brought about by an article written by two magicians, published in *Popular Photography* (Eisendrath, 1967; Reynolds, 1967), in which an explanation was offered as to how Serios did his photographs.

The mental photographs by Ted Serios were of poor quality, ambiguous, and suspicious in terms of their degree of correspondence with the targets Serios was attempting to put on film. In his review of paranormal photography, Eisenbud (1977) states, however, that the photographs cannot be explained in terms of any known energetic processes, and that even invoking "mind" is not of much help. That trickery might have been involved has occurred to Eisenbud, although he has been unable to detect it in his investigations. To those who know that thought and even mental images are not things but subjectively experienced processes of the brain, the idea that such processes may impress themselves upon photographic film in the form of their physical referents strikes as a fantasy, and they keep seeking evidence that the images get somehow impressed upon the Polaroid film pack by the unglamorous process of light waves. How this is probably accomplished is described by Scott and Hutchinson (1979) in their report of an investigation of the Japanese thought photographer Masuaki Kiyota, who claims to project mental images onto unexposed film under very tight conditions. Most of his attempts failed, although he produced a few blurred images when both the film and the camera had been in his possession overnight. Scott and Hutchinson were able to replicate the method by which a Polaroid film pack may be exposed without leaving traces of tampering.

The Poltergeist.   Poltergeist is a German word meaning a boisterous, noisy spirit. Poltergeist phenomena involve knocks and other noises of unknown origin, the inexplicable moving around of furniture and household objects, breakage of glass and crockery, the popping of corks and stoppers from bottles, and, less frequently, flying rocks, spontaneous fires, and the appearance of water from unknown sources. It is not thought that a spirit or spirits are actually involved. Rather, the activity usually centers on a living person whose "spirit" seems to be involved in the disturbance. If that person moves to another location, the disturbance may follow. It may last from a few days to several months.

Poltergeist phenomena, which parapsychologists have termed *recurrent spontaneous psychokinesis*, or RSPK, are a relatively rare occurrence. William G. Roll, one of the principal contemporary investigators of poltergeists, has counted only 116 cases between 1612 and 1974 that have appeared in print and have been witnessed by the author or reliable informants who were witnesses themselves (Roll, 1977). In 25 of these cases, the poltergeist events were witnessed by parapsychological investigators. Roll himself has investigated several of these cases and has made observations under controlled conditions. In a Miami, Florida, case that focused on a young warehouse employee (Roll, 1976; Roll & Pratt, 1971), Roll was able to chart over 200 displacements of objects and other events and to experiment with the placement of objects in areas where poltergeist activity seemed to be concentrated, relating it to the location of persons in the warehouse area.

RSPK phenomena have three significant aspects: sociological, psychological, and metaphysical. Roll (1977) notes that the largest block of cases, 31, comes from the United States, followed by 26 cases from Great Britain and Ireland, and 21 from the German-speaking parts of Europe. Only five cases are reported from outside of Europe and the United States. Although both the name poltergeist and the first observations of poltergeist phenomena came from Europe, the fact that the United States has yielded the largest number of incidents fits the tendency of Americans to seek and make effective the connection between ideas and their realization, between religion and science, the subjective and the objective. They produced not only the philosophy of pragmatism in which the worth of ideas is evaluated by whether they work or not, but also spiritualism, which tried to show that the invisible world of the spirits could be made the object of empirical observations, and the method of positive thinking whereby wishes, whether for health, wealth, or happiness, were turned into reality. Psychokinesis, as has been noted, is the most direct expression of the idea that mind can act directly upon matter. All of these ideas have arisen and have also existed elsewhere, but they have flourished in the United States.

The empirically most solid aspect of RSPK is psychological. Apart from its visible manifestations, the most notable thing about RSPK is that in most cases it centers on a living person. Of Roll's 116 cases, 92 were so centered. The characteristics of the focal person that have been studied involve both easily observable ones, such as age and sex, and personality traits ascertained through the administration of psychological tests, the observation of the physiological correlates of RSPK activity, and of the individual's physical and mental health. The following profile of the RSPK focal person emerges: He or she (both sexes are about equally represented) is apt to be a young person. The median age in Roll's 116 cases was between 13 and 14 years. Thus, the phenomenon appears to have some connection with puberal changes. Of the 92 RSPK agents studied by Roll, 49 had some more or less severe physical or psychological problem. Of these, 22 were prone to seizures, convulsions, fainting spells, or dissociation. Psychokinetic agents exhibit strong conflicts and hostilities that center on authority figures, such as parents or employers. Overtly, however, they may appear to have a mild disposition and a nonaggressive, withdrawn personality. Tests reveal, however, that they use such ego defense mechanisms as repression, denial, and sublimation to deal with the conflict arising from anger and aggression and their control. Because the individual finds it impossible to give direct expression to his or her frustration and anger, one may theorize that the inner conflict finds an indirect avenue through the poltergeist phenomena. This, of course, can take the form of the individual's causing the disturbance secretly, but deliberately. A number of teenagers in conflict with their families have been caught staging poltergeist episodes. Christopher (1970) describes a number of such cases that are not found in Roll's book. The moving and breaking of things is accomplished in various ways. Threads may be attached to objects so that when the threads are jerked the objects fly in different directions. The threads may be easily concealed and disposed of. Long sticks that are invisible to the myopic person who happens to be the target of the prank may be used to upset objects. Holes have been drilled through walls to upset brickabrack on shelves by poking them with a slender rod from the other side of the wall. Diversionary tactics allow one to create a disturbance directly while everybody's attention is on something else.

A number of psychokinetic agents have been found to exhibit dissociative tendencies. It can be assumed that such individuals could also topple furniture or arrange for the movement of objects quite unconsciously when in a dissociated state. Not all cases or all phenomena in a given case can be explained as the intentional or unintentional physical acts of a resentful adolescent. This is where metaphysics joins natural explanations. Diagnosing the presence of a dynamic pattern in a person's psyche is one thing; to prove that subjective phenomena can produce physical transformations in the environment is another. The problem is again one of the "externalization of sensitivity," of how does the subjective become the objective, if indeed it does. Attempts at providing non-naturalistic explanations of poltergeists suffer visibly from the same defect as do all dualistic explanations of paranormal phenomena: A phenomenon that is formulated in dualistic terms is solved using monistic ideas, either of the idealistic or materialistic kind. For example, Roll (1977), noting that some psychokinetic agents (only 20 in his sample) exhibit epilepsy or epileptoid convulsions, hypothesizes that the bursts of central nervous system energy involved in the convulsions may act as energy beams to effect the poltergeist phenomena. He even postulates the existence of two beams on the basis of the observation that objects near the focal person move shorter distances and away from the person, whereas objects farther away move longer distances and towards the person.

Theorizing about poltergeists is further complicated by the reported bizarre behavior of objects set in motion during poltergeist activity. They supposedly follow zigzag and other trajectories that physics fails to predict for falling objects, and they carefully avoid causing injury to the observers. Seldom, if ever, do observers see the beginning of a movement; it always begins when one's back is turned, or when nobody is watching. If, in addition, one is to take seriously the reports that on occasion objects moved by poltergeists, such as stones, appear to pass through walls and in and out of closed rooms, no reasonable theory can possibly account for all aspects of the poltergeist phenomena, and magic remains the only explanation. The psychophysiological profile of the psychokinetic agent in RSPK cases is real enough and it fits the hypothesis, as well as actual observations, that at least some of the poltergeist cases are pranks played by children. Much of the rest can be attributed to poor observation, memory lapses, and wishful thinking. The remainder is just unexplained phenomena, no paranormality implied.

The Nature of Psychokinesis

In an exhaustive review of experimental psychokinesis, Stanford (1977) examines some 20 psychological aspects of PK that have been studied, such as personality, drugs, and social factors, as well as a number of physical factors, such as the size of dice. Physical factors do not appear to play an important role in PK experiments, in spite of such findings as that small dice thrown upon a hard surface tend to produce the greatest amount of deviation from chance. PK seems to operate regardless of the distances involved, and the size, material, and number of the dice. Findings concerning the psychological factors are either weak or inconclusive, except one. From a variety of studies of the sheep-goat effect and of the role of motivation, incentives, intention, and conscious effort, it appears that the proper attitude for a PK subject to take to ensure success is not to make an effort to "make it happen." It seems that a deliberate effort of the will not only fails to bring about the desired results, but may actually work against PK. Robert Thouless (1951), a British parapsychologist, describes the proper attitude as one of "effortless intention to succeed" (p. 123). Mere intention, as compared to conscious effort, leads to a passive "allowing it to happen." Some studies suggest that the PK effect occurs not while the agent is making an effort to succeed, but afterwards, when he or she may be relaxing or engaging in an irrelevant task. This factor appears to be related to another aspect of the successful attitude in PK experiments, as well as in alleged spontaneous cases of PK, such as poltergeist cases. It may be referred to as the externalization of responsibility (Stanford, 1974). The PK effect, when it occurs, is felt to be ego-alien. Although it is the subject who has the intention, the effective agency is outside the subject and is responsible for the psychokinetic happening. It is as if the process starts within the person, but winds up outside the person, another instance that illustrates Rochas's apt phrase, "the externalization of sensitivity."

The failure to produce macro-PK phenomena under laboratory conditions, the successes of efforts to produce micro-PK effects with the random event generator, and the impossibility of distinguishing conceptually between telepathy, clairvoyance, precognition, and PK have defined the position of most parapsychologists on the question of PK along the following lines:

1. Although quantum processes may be affected psychokinetically, PK of objects is probably not possible.
2. ESP and PK are probably the same phenomenon, to be called psi.
3. Psi is not a physical, and therefore causally determined, phenomenon.

Concerning this last conclusion, it was indicated earlier that J. B. Rhine had reached it quite some time ago. Helmut Schmidt, known for his REG work, holds the same opinion (Schmidt, 1975), as does Rex Stanford (1974), an active ESP and PK researcher. Stanford's theory of PK is as follows: PK, like ESP, does not involve either information or energy transfer. Although an agent is involved, the agent does not cause PK in the same way as he or she causes a billiard ball to roll by striking it with a cue stick. Stanford proposes to substitute a new name for PK phenomena, "conformance behavior."

Conformance behavior involves four elements. One is a disposed system, such as a living organism. A disposed system changes, over time, when a need, such as hunger, gives rise to the motive to seek food and satisfy the hunger. The second element is a favorable event. If such an event is met by a disposed system, it will lead to changes that are favored by the disposed system, such as the satisfaction of hunger when food is eaten. The third element is a source of incompletely determined alternative states, such as a random event generator or a nervous system. The fourth element is a contingent relationship between favorable events and REG output, so that some outputs of the REG, if selected, will increase the probability of the favorable event. In the case of Schmidt's experiments with the electronic REG, the subject is told or not told that a hit has occurred, depending on the kind of event that the REG has generated on a given trial.

When these four elements come together and the REG output controls the probability of the favorable event, conformance behavior is said to occur. It is clear that this formulation of PK also applies to ESP, and thus is a model of psi in general. It is also clear that Stanford's model is closely related to Jung's synchronicity concept, although the terminologies differ. In Jung's synchronistic event, the disposed system is the individual who supplies meaning to the confluence of events. The formants of synchronistic events are a psychological state and a physical event. In Stanford's theory, the formants of conformance behavior are the REG and the disposed system. What Stanford adds to the idea of self-organization is the notion of reinforcement, although he does not refer to it as such. The favorable event is clearly a reinforcer. In learning theory, reinforcer and learned behavior are causally linked, but Stanford's conformance behavior is not causally determined. Jung uses meaning in lieu of reinforcement (or favorable event)—the confluence of events is not experienced as anything special unless meaning is attached to it. It can be assumed that neither Schmidt nor Stanford would attribute any special significance to the coincidence between their predictions or PK efforts and the behavior of the REG if the experiment did not take place in a highly meaningful context, with the special meaning of PK supplied by the culture. But meaning may be said to be an association between stimulus and response that has been previously reinforced. Reinforcement (or contingent relationship between the behavior of the disposed system and the occurrence of favorable events) and meaning are thus closely related, and so are the concepts of conformance behavior and synchronicity. Both approaches unfortunately postulate an acausal relationship between the subject and the psi event. Jung's notion of synchronicity is untestable. Although Stanford's theory is clothed in scientific terminology, its element of acausality places it outside the realm of science and makes it equally untestable.

PARAPSYCHOLOGY: AN ART OR A SCIENCE?

If ESP and PK are present in virtually everybody (e.g., Schmeidler, 1975), in a sizable portion of the population (40%, according to one estimate of Rhine's), or even in a relatively few individuals, why are they not used to perform all kinds of tasks and solve all kinds of problems of a practical nature? One should think that if, for example, the United States and the USSR each had just one powerful clairvoyant, there would be no more room for military and political secrets. Rhine at one time suggested as much (Rhine, 1957). If heavy furniture was lifted by D. D. Home and other mediums psychokinetically and if things are slung forcibly by poltergeists, why isn't PK used to lift furniture when vacuuming the floor or to pitch baseballs? Other desirable uses of psi would be winning at cards or the roulette, not to speak of crap games and group bingos.

Claims of the successful use of psi in playing the stockmarket or helping police solve crimes cannot be separated from the skillful use of information available by ordinary means. There is a vast discrepancy between belief in one's psi ability and its exercise. According to a survey conducted by the National Opinion Research Center (Greely, 1975), in a stratified sample of 1467 persons representing the USA population, 58% had experienced GESP, and 24% had experienced clairvoyance. Yet, in a mass telepathy experiment performed over the BBC radio in England in 1927 (Hansel, 1966), 24,659 listeners who sent in responses trying to identify the objects that were being looked at by agents in the studio failed to show any sign of psi. In spite of exceptional winners, such as Charles Well, the year-after-year records of Monte Carlo and Las Vegas casinos and of Chicago dice girls show nothing but the winnings being predictable from probability theory.

Parapsychologists have no good answer to the question about the application of psi except that psi cannot be turned on and off at will or that the conditions have to be right before it can be applied. Others take the question into the realm of metaphysics and join the occultists in declaring that the selfish use of psi is unlawful and leads to its loss or the moral deterioration of its user. This argument overlooks the money-making public appearances of alleged wielders of psi, which do not seem to diminish their "powers" at all, and leaves out of consideration the many opportunities that there exist for using psi for the benefit of one's fellow beings. In short, as an art or skill, psi does not receive very high marks.

The outstanding event in the history of parapsychology was the admission of the Parapsychological Association to the American Association for the Advancement of Science as a member organization in 1969. The Parapsychological Association had been founded by Rhine in 1957 to engage in parapsychological research, and counted as members professionals who held advanced degrees in their respective fields. Margaret Mead, the internationally known anthropologist who served as President of the AAAS at the time, was a supporter of parapsychology and played an important part in the admission of the Parapsychological Association. As she urged the admission of this organization into the AAAS, she cited in support of its candidacy the fact that parapsychologists use statistics and such devices as the blind and double-blind procedures. If Mead's purpose in invoking the use of statistics was to show that parapsychology was scientific, she showed only a dim awareness of the nature of science. The error of confounding the tools of science with science itself is an old one and goes back at least to Immanuel Kant, who asserted that a discipline was scientific only to the extent that it used mathematics. Because mathematics (and the applied branch of mathematics, statistics) is not a science but a system of logic, its use in a discipline only indicates that a particular form of logical reasoning is being used. It says nothing about how scientific that discipline is.

A science has two elements, a systematic body of knowledge and the use of the scientific method. Both must be present for a discipline to qualify as a science. Parapsychology does use the scientific method, which is basically controlled observation. Experimentation is one form of the scientific method. There is also a body of knowledge in parapsychology, although one may argue how systematic it is. The parapsychological literature counts hundreds of experimental studies and many studies of other kinds, as well as numerous works that survey the field and particular aspects of it or present theories and models of psi phenomena. Works like the *Handbook of Parapsychology* (Wolman, 1977), attest to the fact that there is a body of knowledge called parapsychology. Why then are scientists so hesitant to accept parapsychology, especially scientists in the academic world? A number of surveys have been conducted tabulating the number of scientists who believe and do not believe in ESP. Although there has always been a sizable number of those who have thought that ESP was "a remote possibility" or that it was a legitimate area of study, the number of those who have firmly believed in it has been small. Among psychologists, who are the most skeptical portion of the scientific community, the percentage has been under 10.

In addition to outright rejection of psi on a priori grounds, there have been numerous specific criticisms advanced against parapsychology, a number of which have been mentioned. Most of them are not unique to parapsychology, but can be directed at psychology and other disciplines as well. The critisim that psi cannot be produced upon demand and that parapsychological experiments are therefore not replicable, which make it unscientific, has been cited as parapsychology's most serious fault. Parapsychology, like psychology, deals with behavior, and behavioral phenomena cannot always be produced on demand. Well-known examples of areas of psychology in which the number of positive studies has been counterbalanced by about the same number of negative ones are the areas of the effect of internal states on perception (the "New Look" in perception studies) and studies on cognitive dissonance. Creativity, ego defense mechanisms, and social imitation cannot be produced upon demand either.

The argument of Price (1955) and many others that scientific laws do not fail in association with particular people (by contrast with psi, which seems to require a sympathetic investigator and fails to show when the investigator is hostile to the idea of psi) ignores the experimenter effect in psychological research (Rosenthal, 1976), a well-known phenomenon that, if used against psychology in a similar manner, would invalidate much of psychological research.

The demands for a definitive experiment in parapsychology, such as those presented by Price (1955) or Crumbaugh (1959), are likewise misplaced, for no science or scientific theory is ever proved, once and for all, by any crucial or definitive experiments or demonstrations. It is the accumulated weight of evidence produced by different practitioners of the discipline that gradually displaces old and erroneous notions, theories, and models.

Arguments and counterarguments about the repeatability of experiments, fraud, the nature of the decline effect, the influence of the experimenter on the experimental results, and the need for a congenial atmosphere for psi demonstrations to succeed have been repeated many times but without leading to any resolution of these issues. It appears that the problem lies not in an objective resolution of them, but in an entirely different area. There have been several well-known exchanges in scientific journals between prominent representatives of the sciences on the one side and parapsychologists on the other. The best-known exchange consists of an article by G. R. Price and a series of replies and comments on it that appeared in 1955 and 1956 in *Science*, the official organ of the American Association for the Advancement of Science (Bridgman, 1956; Meehl & Scriven, 1956; Price, 1955, 1956; Rhine, 1956a, 1956b; Soal, 1956). This exchange presents all the classical arguments for and against parapsychology, and it is as up to date today as it was in the 1950s. Similar, more recent exchanges that cover much of the same ground as well as new and additional points are those initiated by an article on the statistical aspects of ESP by Persi Diaconis (Diaconis, 1978a, 1978b; Puthoff & Targ, 1978; Tart, 1978) and one on ESP and credibility in science by R. A. McConnell (McConnell, 1969, 1978; Moss & Butler, 1978a, 1978b). It is abundantly clear from these exchanges that, after all the logical, psychological, and scientific arguments have been traded, the parties to the argument part without their beliefs having been affected one iota.

Belief is indeed the key to the controversy. The parapsychological experiment is in form and essence like any experiment in psychology. We may take as an example in psychology the study of the effect of political persuasion on voting behavior, and the effect of attitude towards ESP on clairvoyant behavior as an analogous example from parapsychology. In both cases, attitudes are measured, the dependent behaviors are measured, and a statistical test is made to see if a relationship between them exists. There is one difference between these two experiments, however, and it is a crucial one. Political behavior is only that that can be observed and nothing more. It may be quite complex, but all of its causes may be reduced to known empirical laws: reinforcement, sensory information, cognitions, muscular movements, and so on. ESP, on the other hand, is only partly an observable phenomenon. Although giving the response "circle" in a card-guessing experiment is a behavior, there is an unbridged gap between this response and the presumed stimulus for this response, the unseen card in the deck. How does the subject learn what the card is? This gap requires a leap of faith or belief in the reality of the unknown psi process. Until this gap is bridged, parapsychologists and non-parapsychologists, the believers and the non-believers, the sheep and the goats will continue their debate without arriving at a resolution.

NOTES

Review of theories of psi may be found in Chari (1974), Heywood (1971), Randall (1971), Rao (1961), and, of course, in the *Handbook of Parapsychology* (Wolman, 1977).

Arthur Koestler's small book on the roots of coincidence (Koestler, 1972) contains one of the more lucid and intelligent presentations of some of the difficult ideas from particle physics as they bear on psi phenomena. This book, the collection of essays by Hardy, Harvie, and Koestler (1975), and Lila Gatlin's paper on information creation (Gatlin, 1977) contain the most intelligent discussions of the ideas of chance and coincidence in relation to psi.

Although Uri Geller's feats are well publicized, the ways he works them are not. Charles Panati (1976) has prepared a collection of the scientific observations on Uri Geller. These, however, are marred by the inclusion of work that by the admission of Panati and the authors themselves does not meet scientific standards. Ten of the 18 experimental papers can be so classified. The remaining eight, although they show some degree of experimental control, are so flawed as to cast serious doubt on their usefulness as evidence for Geller's paranormal powers. A lengthy review and criticism of the book is provided by Hyman (1976). Marks and Kamman (1977) report on some detailed field observations of Geller's feats, and James Randi (1978a) on the confessions of his manager, Yasha Katz. Randi (1975) and Gardner (1976) show how Geller does his spoon and key bending trick. The latter article is particularly recommended as an essay on the incompetence of scientists, however brilliant or eminent, to detect fraud in "psychic" phenomena. It also has a series of photographs showing how a key may be bent á la Geller. There is an excellent summary of Geller's phenomena and all tests of his abilities in *The World Almanac Book of the Strange* (1977).

Sladek (1973) discusses the performance of Ted Serios in detail, including the possible construction of Serios's famed "gizmo" and how that device could have been used to produce his thought photographs.

14 The Psychology of Bad Science

There is no error to be named that has not its philosophers.

John Locke

In days of old
When Knights were bold
And science not invented
The Earth was flat
And that was that
With no man discontented.

English verse

There is no absolute knowledge. And those who claim it, whether they are scientists or dogmatists, open the door to tragedy. All information is imperfect. We have to treat it with humility.

Jacob Bronowsky, 1973

Many scientists take a dim view of occultism and many of the rest are highly skeptical. In part, this is because occult ideas contradict scientific conceptions of how the universe is organized and operates. In part, it is because so much of occultism is "superstitious"—i.e., subjective evaluations of reality held despite objective evidence to the contrary (Scheibe & Sarbin, 1965)—and objective evidence is the cornerstone of scientific thinking. But everyone adheres to certain cherished beliefs superstitiously, including scientists. The more critical issue has to do with the scientific claims made for paranormal concepts that imply that scientific procedures and methods have been used to substantiate their validity. Thus, the scientific objection is not so much to occultism as a personal belief system nor because its ideas are often improbable, fanciful, or transcendental, but because its advocates frequently attribute scientific verifiability to paranormal ideas. Scientific claims are not universal among occultists, as many are content to describe their beliefs as a matter of personal faith and preference. However, when scientific principles or methods are invoked to support paranormal concepts, as often happens, scientists in relevant fields have the obligation to examine those claims as they might any other scientific contention and, if need be, challenge their validity on strictly scientific grounds.

SCIENCE AND PSEUDOSCIENCE: A COMPARISON

Pseudoscience is false science because, as we discuss later, in it, the use of scientific procedures is haphazard and invalid and, as a consequence, the resulting conclusions are in error. Frequently, although not exclusively,

422

pseudoscience involves occult and other extraordinary ideas. But it should be noted at the outset that "truth" in science, as in other disciplines, can be an elusive matter. The latest and best scientific theories await revision in light of subsequent data, and even the most outlandish ideas often contain a grain of truth. New concepts on the frontiers of science, which may at present lack empirical and theoretical support but which nonetheless may be verifiable in the future, are obviously not pseudoscientific, and there is always the danger that such ideas will be incorrectly classified simply because they conflict with contemporary wisdom. Scientific theories inevitably change and thus it would be the epitome of "superstitiousness" and antiscience to rule out possible scientific advances simply because they are new, unusual, or not yet thoroughly documented. Truzzi (1977) has argued that a distinction may be drawn between those marginal disciplines and ideas that are not part of conventional science because they fail to make use of acceptable scientific methods and assumptions and those that are simply new and not yet accepted by the institution of science. Also, a discipline's acceptability or relation to ordinary science does not necessarily reveal whether or not it is a pseudoscience. As Truzzi has observed, pseudoscience can exist within the conventional sciences and among otherwise appropriately trained and qualified scientists (see insert on N-Rays later in the chapter) and it is at least conceivable that genuine science could occur outside of the mainstream laboratories.

On the other hand, as Gardner (1957) has noted, the existence of "borderline" theories where judgments of scientific merit cannot be made until sufficient data have been accumulated does not mean that the extremes of good versus bad science are indistinguishable. There are many instances for which it is clear that the term pseudoscience is an accurate description, as when scientific methods are consistently misapplied, or more often, simply claimed without being used at all. In part, science is a set of ideas that provides a means of discovering how nature works. Therefore, the danger of incorrectly challenging a valid but unfamiliar theory must be weighed against the equally misguided path of perpetuating the scientific status of concepts that have been thoroughly discredited.

Many people imagine science to be a sort of pristine and mathematically exact process. In principle, it may be described in this way. However, it is important to recognize that, as with any other human endeavor, preconceptions, moods, loyalties, prejudices, and underlying motives play an important, though typically not a decisive, role in science (e.g., Gould, 1978). Also, scientific activity and the almost inevitable technological changes it brings about create very real consequences, thereby raising social and moral questions of profound significance that must be addressed by the scientist and non-scientist alike. The following discussion is therefore not meant to imply that, in practice, science is perfect and antiseptic, nor that scientific issues should be left to scientists alone. But, the influence of human motives and the moral issues inherent to scientific activity also do not preclude drawing a relatively clear distinction between competing conceptualizations of nature in terms of their scientific acceptability. Again, this is particularly appropriate where scientific proof has been claimed for an esoteric theory.

Scientific Assumptions and the Scientific Method

A thorough discussion of the characteristics of science and its underlying philosophical assumptons is beyond the scope of this book. However, it is important to review at least some basic principles in order to illustrate the difference between science and pseudoscience. There are two components to any science. First, there is a body of knowledge—i.e., a set of facts combined in meaningful ways by theoretical explanations. Second, science is a set of principles, asumptions, and methods comprising a strategy for discovery. The scientific method is a general statement of this strategy.

The scientific method requires certain assumptions. For example, it assumes the appropriate subject matter of science to be phenomena that are subject to natural physical laws and that are discoverable by empirical methods. Thus, questions of meaning and purpose as well as transcendental issues (e.g., Is there a God?) are generally not considered to be questions to which the scientific method can be validly applied because they invoke processes and entities that lie beyond the physical reality of nature. This does not mean that other approaches to knowledge do not exist, nor that science is preferable to those other approaches in all instances. However, it does mean that to conduct acceptable scientific investigations and to draw valid scientific conclusions, one is limited in the subject matter that can be studied and the manner in which such investigations can proceed. For example, to assert that the weight of the soul can be measured, as has recently been claimed in Sweden, implicitly assumes that the soul is a physical entity governed by physical processes. This assumption is not sufficient however. The general criteria of the scientific method must also be satisfied.

The *scientific method* involves developing hypotheses that are empirically tested, leading to the construction of theories that are, in turn, evaluated by testing further hypotheses. An *hypothesis* is simply a guess regarding the outcome of a scientific investigation, and is usually based on an existing theory. The virtue of science is that the guess is not simply accepted as fact because it sounds reasonable, but instead, the hypothesis is subjected to testing—i.e., conditions specified by the hypothesis are observed to determine if they produce the anticipated results. Ideally, the observation is created experimentally, although other forms of observation are used when experiments are impractical. Observation in science involves two key elements, *control* and *measurement*. The concept of control refers to construction of the observation procedure in such a way as to eliminate or reduce the potential influence of extraneous factors. This may be accomplished by the use of control conditions (e.g., repeating the experiment exactly with the one exception that the experimental treatment is not applied) and randomization. For example, in scientific tests of telepathy, control procedures might include shuffling the deck of cards to be used (randomization) as well as ensuring that the participants do not have sensory contact (however subtle) with one another. Measurement refers to the application of independent means of observation and quantification. Measuring instruments of various types are preferred to casual subjective evaluations because such verbal reports are subject to a wide variety of extraneous processes—e.g., misperception, faulty memory, the influence of prior beliefs and expectations, etc. Two key issues in scientific measurement are validity (the extent to which an instrument measures what it was intended to measure) and reliability (the degree of stability in the results of the instrument). The important point is that observational techniques are not simply accepted at face value; instead, the techniques themselves are tested and calibrated against accepted criteria.

Analysis in science is the process whereby the results of an observation are evaluated. In many areas of science, this involves mathematical or statistical procedures designed to determine the likelihood that the results were due to the hypothesized factors as opposed to chance or extraneous factors. The important consideration in analysis is whether the appropriate test has been used. As everyone knows, statistics may be presented in a variety of ways to support virtually any conclusion. Less well-known is the fact that selective presentation or manipulation of data usually violates the underlying assumptions of the statistical method and thus is detectable.

Interpretation or *theory construction* is the most involved aspect of science and yet also the most creative. A theory is a conceptual device used to summarize and explain a set of known facts. As such, theories are neither really true nor false. Instead, they are useful or not useful. For example, useful theories are considered to be those that explain the greatest proportion of the available facts, using the fewest concepts, leading to subsequent useful research and applications.

Finally, incorporation of new data into a theory is followed by testing new hypotheses, requiring further observations, and so on. Thus, scientific activity does not follow a straight line leading to a static kind of truth. It is a dynamic, never-ending process, always in evolution, by which truth is approached or approximated in increments of ever-more useful theories tested against available evidence.

Some Illustrations of Bad Science

From anthropology to zoology, virtually every scientific discipline and allied technology has had its marginal ideas and pseudopractitioners. Lest the impression be created that what is typically labeled as pseudoscience is new ideas or the work of misunderstood geniuses, a few examples from Gardner's *Fads and Fallacies in the Name of Science* (1957) are presented here.

Scientific authenticity is still claimed for the idea that the Earth is flat and motionless. As recently as the 1930s, one flat-Earth cult commanded 10,000 or so followers. Another school of thought has offered hundreds of proofs that the Earth is hollow, with wide openings at the poles and habitable on the inside. Apparently unable to solve the childhood dilemma of how the universe could continue on without a boundary, Cyrus T. Reed created a boundary, generating elaborate proofs to show that the Earth is hollow and we are living on the inside. Reed's ideas attracted followers in both the United States and Europe. Alfred William Lawson, a self-proclaimed genius, reduced the actions of the physical universe to two ubiquitous principles called suction and pressure and zig-zag-and-swirl, respectively. Various researchers have observed amazing phenomena under their microscopes, from the spontaneous generation of life in inorganic materials to telepathically receptive salt crystals. Others have divined the future and discovered the secrets of the past by calculating every mathematical permutation of the dimensions of the Great Pyramid. Sir Isaac Babson spent a fortune encouraging inventors of anti-gravity and perpetual-motion machines. Charles Fort, perhaps the all-time champion of scientific hecklers, asserted the truth of virtually every whimsical notion except that of Santa Claus, which he rejected on the grounds of insufficient objective proof.

Pseudoscientific doctrines have not always been just harmless amusements, however. Theories of racial inferiority have been "proved" repeatedly with the questionable data and dubious procedures of pseudoscientists and have been used as the justification for discrimination, repression, and genocide. Pseudomedicine has also been a fertile field for the crank and every conceivable form of quackery, from colored lights to exotic diets to magical black boxes, have been used as the cure for ailments varying from the common cold to cancer. Thus, numerous patients in need of effective treatment have dangerously postponed or bypassed conventional scientifically based remedies in favor of magical cure-alls with undoubtedly catastrophic effects in some cases.

One of the recurrent themes of pseudoscience is the attempt to resolve conflicts between accepted scientific facts and some preconceived set of beliefs. Several attempts to prove the literal Biblical interpretation of creation have appeared. In one famous case, discredited genetic theories were resurrected and became official scientific dogma in the Soviet Union because they appeared to confirm Marxian ideological values. This resulted in crop failures and food shortages. One of the most influential and erudite theories of this type was proposed by Immanuel Velikovsky, a physician and psychoanalyst. In essence, he argued that a series of alleged interplanetary anomalies (e.g., a comet passing close to Earth, a near collision between Earth and Mars) had momentous effects, such as causing the Earth to slow its rate of rotation or to stop entirely. Although conventional scientific opinion argues strongly against the possibility of such a sequence of events, the more interesting point is that Velikovsky's catastrophies are made to appear to coincide in time with various milestones of religious history (e.g., the parting of the Red Sea during the Israelite Exodus) and, according to Velikovsky's reasoning, were the causes of such miracles.

Box 14.1—N-Rays

Pseudoscience has not always been the exclusive province of the unqualified outsider. One famous incident has been reported by Klass (1974) and others. In 1903, Professor R. Blondlot, head of the physics department of the University of Nancy, in France, announced the discovery of a new and amazing form of radiation, which he named N-rays. Blondlot reported that N-rays were emitted naturally by several different metals, but never by wood, and that they were faintly visible to the naked eye in a darkened room. Soon, other investigators, particularly in France, were replicating and extending Professor Blondlot's findings. Many other substances giving off N-rays were added to the list (e.g., human tissue, plants, and even a human corpse), but, again, never wood. The prestigious French Academy of Sciences published almost 100 papers on the topic within a year of Blondlot's original discovery, and it announced the decision to award Blondlot a medal and a cash prize for his accomplishment.

However, researchers outside of France were generally unable to replicate Blondlot's findings. Eventually, R. W. Wood, a scientist working in Great Britain, visited Blondlot in his laboratory at Nancy to observe directly the now famous N-rays. But, still unable to detect N-rays even in Blondlot's lab with Blondlot himself conducting the demonstrations, Wood decided that N-rays might be more imaginary than real. Wood proved this by surreptitiously altering some of Blondlot's apparatus. For example, he substituted a wooden roller for a metal file that Blondlot was using as the source of N-rays. When Blondlot reported that he could still see the N-rays, Wood had evidence that N-rays were non-existent because all investigators had reported that wooden objects did not produce N-rays. Several other tests also suggested self-delusion. When Wood's findings and conclusions were reported to the scientific community, the phenomenon of N-rays passed into the history of pseudoscience.

> Commentators have generally agreed that the phenomenon of N-rays was not a hoax of the usual sort. Apparently, Blondlot was sincere in his beliefs. He certainly was a qualified scientist in terms of training and expertise. What the saga of N-rays does sadly illustrate is the powerful influence that wishes and extrinsic motivation can have on judgments and reasoning. Blondlot's folly occurred at a time when other strange forms of radiation, such as X-rays, were being discovered. It is likely that Blondlot deluded himself (as did many others) because of the strong desire to participate in the exciting advancements in science being made at that time.

Gardner's examples were drawn primarily from the first half of this century. However, there is considerable evidence that questionable scientific notions have persisted unabated. Consider, for example, the widespread popularity today of such concepts as auras, biorhythms, astral projection, plant telepathy, pyramid power, and the Bermuda triangle, to name but a few.

Distinguishing Scientific Criteria

Specifying some ideas as scientifically unacceptable or false raises the central question regarding bad science: What criteria can be applied to assess the scientific authenticity of an idea? Methodological problems are the key to bad science. In some cases, the problems are relatively simple to detect and easy to understand. For example, regarding the question of plant sensitivity, follow-up studies have demonstrated the original idea to be simply in error (Kmetz, 1978). Similarly, recent studies on the ability of psychics in predicting earthquakes indicated a rate of accuracy below chance-level expectations (Fraser, 1979). In some cases, what is originally anomalous and considered by some to have an extraordinary explanation, eventually receives adequate scientific attention and subsequently a naturalistic explanation. For instance, the effects of Kirlian photography have been shown to be the effects of coronal discharges of moisture of the subject rather than some mysterious life force or aura (Pehek, Kyler, & Faust, 1976). An even simpler situation exists when a theory proposes to be scientific, but fails to use scientific methodology at all. For example, claims for the usefulness of dowsing rest primarily on personal testimony and self-evidence (e.g., "I've tried it and it works") without further specification of mechanisms or conditions (Hechinger, 1979). Similarly, Kusche (1977) notes several problems typical of accounts of the Bermuda Triangle mystery, including differences between sympathetic presentations and official records and what he calls "undue familiarity" (i.e., the inclusion of information that the author could not possibly have known, such as the dialogue between two crew members on a ship that allegedly disappeared moments later without a trace). If such basic facts as the time of day, prevailing weather conditions, and locations are in error, along with the inclusion of gratuitous information, one naturally wonders about the truth of the more basic assertions.

However, some pseudoscientific theories are so extensive and complicated that it might take an entire career just to document every way in which the theory is erroneous. Concerning von Däniken's ancient-astronauts theory, two articles have examined some of the fallacies and reasons for doubting the correctness of the basic thesis. For example, such problems as bad reasoning, reliance on argumentation, selective quotation, reliance on questionable testimony or witnesses, misrepresentation of facts, errors based on ignorance, logical fallacies, innuendo, reliance on rhetorical questions as proof, non-sequiturs, the lack of criteria for inclusion of evidence, misdating errors, facts taken out of context, omission of relevant evidence, and the lack of supporting data have been cited as objections to the theory (Omohundro, 1976; Story, 1977). The more interesting point, however, is that both of these authors acknowledge that the theory is too complex for a comprehensive refutation and they list these objections only as examples of some of the problems with the theory. Story also reminds us that something in print is not necessarily true, even if it is labeled by the publisher as nonfiction, and that the nonexistence of a refutation by a reputable scientist also does not mean a theory is true. It may simply not be worth the effort for the established scientist to challenge the more grandiose claims of pseudoscience. Therefore, criteria internal to questionable scientific works must often be applied in those cases where detailed and specific refutations do not exist.

Pseudoscience is science misapplied. Despite its volume and the variety of topics that fall into its domain, there is an essential commonality to most pseudoscientific thinking. Gruenberger (1964) emphasizes the idea that no single criterion is sufficient to detect all pseudoscience and that not all pseudoscientific works will contain every distinguishing characteristic in equal proportion. However, if a particular work purporting to be scientific contains several of the negative indicators and few of the positive criteria listed earlier in this chapter, there is a good chance that its conclusions cannot be verified using scientific methods and, thus, extensive claims of scientific merit are probably exaggerated if not fraudulent.

To be accepted, a scientific theory or method must be publicly as well as intersubjectively verifiable and replicable (e.g., Fraser, 1976; Gruenberger, 1964). *Public verifiability* refers to the necessity of stating the essentials of science in such a way that others may also confirm them. Thus, methods are clearly and explicitly described, raw data are placed in repositories or are available from individual researchers, and theories are not simply proclaimed to the public but are published in scholarly journals that exercise standards of scientific merit and rigor as a prerequisite for publication. By contrast, most occult and pseudoscientific works are exceedingly cryptic. Such works often contain few if any references, so that it is not only impossible to determine the source of the original information, but it is also impossible to determine if it is in any way true. For example, one book purporting to prove the existence of spirits begins with the blatant assertion that research in abnormal psychology supports the existence of spirits and suggests that they cause, in part, psychological disturbances (Harber, 1976). Except for Biblical quotations, the books contain no references whatsoever by which the reader could verify the truth of this statement.

Intersubjective reliability refers to the ability of both advocates and detractors of a particular scientific viewpoint to produce the same results. A continuing problem in the area of parapsychology, for example, is the inability of researchers skeptical of the extasensory hypothesis to find results supportive of ESP. One might object that scientists are always disagreeing with one another regarding scientific questions and therefore this proves nothing. However, scientific arguments ordinarily concern what a particular fact means—i.e., its theoretical interpretation—and not the reality of the phenomenon under investigation.

A related concept, and perhaps the key to the nature of pseudoscience is the idea of *replicability*. What gives scientists confidence in their results and interpretations is the ability to replicate key experiments—that is, to repeat them with essentially the same results. One of the principal reasons that parapsychology has not been accepted as a science is that no consistently replicable experiment exists in parapsychology (Kurtz, 1978).

Replicability cuts two ways. First, it is the means by which a researcher is protected against charges of fraud, poorly constructed experiments, and self-delusion; if others duplicate the experiments with analogous results, it suggests that there might be something there and thus the originator can be supported by colleagues. On the other hand, if the finding is a fluke, fraud, or the product of compromised procedures, the process of replication will eventually expose the problem as other researchers report conflicting results. It should be noted that the more important and timely the research question, the more likely others will attempt replications.

Another characteristic of genuine science is the concept of *falsifiability* (Fraser, 1976; Truzzi, 1977), which refers to the requirement that theories be stated in such a way that they can be proved wrong. A theory that contains circular reasoning or what amounts to excuses for those observations that fail to support it is not a very useful or explanatory theory. This is a relative matter, of course, but it can become a critical issue in terms of whether any progress can be made at explaining the phenomenon in question with the theory. Advocates of parapsychology, for example, argue that if a "psychic" is caught cheating or using conjurer's tricks, it does not mean that he or she is not genuine on other occasions, or that the presence of disbelievers spoils the atmosphere and therefore the psychic's abilities diminish (e.g., see Fraser, 1976). The problem with these assumptions, often included in positive presentations of parapsychology, is that they make it impossible to test the theory that ESP exists. For example, if a test is conducted and it produces positive results (which will happen occasionally even if ESP does not exist, because of chance variation), advocates will claim that an extrasensory process was at work, whereas if the test fails to produce positive results, the advocate may invoke one of the previously described ideas and thereby continue to claim the reality of ESP.

A related concept that contributes to much of the success of pseudoscientific ideas is the inability to prove a *universal negative* (e.g., Hoagland, 1969; Trefil, 1978). Advocates may claim that a particular phenomenon has an extraordinary interpretation, such as that UFO sightings represent extraterrestrial spacecraft. Skeptics then proceed to investigate reported sightings, finding natural explanations for, say, 95% of them. However, the advocate only needs one positive instance to be proved to support the extraordinary hypothesis (James' white crow) and thus the remaining 5% of still unexplained cases appears to swing the balance in favor of the advocate. The simple point is that you can never prove a universal negative because there will always remain those potential instances for which adequate information is unavailable or where doubts linger. Indeed, the advocate may assert that the proof is not yet available, but that it will be forthcoming in the future. It should be noted that the advocate has not really proved anything either and the unexplained cases are simply that, unexplained. Much of pseudoscience, however, rests on precisely this contention: If conventional science cannot explain or disprove all paranormal claims, they must be true. Genuine science generally avoids this kind of thing by stating hypotheses in such a way that they can unambiguously be supported or not supported by the evidence. Thus, as is noted later in this chapter, the burden of proof should be on the claimant, not the skeptic.

Much of pseudoscientific argument relies on *irrelevant* and *nonsequitur arguments* that do not logically support the claim but that may appear to some to do so (Asimov, 1979; Gruenberger, 1964). For example, Asimov has listed several types of argument often used to "prove" pseudoscientific claims but that are scientifically unacceptable, including appeals to authority (e.g., the Bible tells me so); internal conviction (i.e., personal faith); irrelevancies (e.g., they did not believe Galileo and he was right); personal abuse (e.g., only an idiot would disagree with me); anecdote (e.g., this happened to my Aunt Maude); and public opinion (e.g., most people agree with me). In addition, the possibility that something is mysterious, strange, or at present unexplainable is not proof in favor of a paranormal hypothesis. Pseudoscientific writing relies heavily on rhetorical questions with the implication that if the reader cannot answer the question, the basic thesis of the presentation must be true.

Another criterion of bona fide science is the concept of *parsimony* (or Ockham's razor; e.g., Gruenberger, 1964; Trefil, 1978). The idea is that, other things being equal, the best scientific theory is the one that uses the fewest explanatory principles. Many pseudoscientific ideas are not in themselves impossible, and yet they include such a complex, and often convoluted set of assumptions that other, simpler explanations become much more reasonable and therefore probable. For example, it is simpler to conclude that extrachance performance at ESP tasks is due to some combination of expected probabilities, fraud, poor controls, conjuring, and so on, that it is to assume that a mysterious, unknown, and indescribable force exists that invalidates many of the central principles of several areas of science, including physics, physiology, and psychology. Similarly, even in the absence of conclusive proof one way or another, such explanations for UFO sightings as the planet Venus, balloons, hoaxes, conventional aircraft, meteors, etc., are more parsimonious explanations than that of extraterrestrial visitors from other planets who would have had to travel for centuries at close to the speed of light, only to perform trivial actions (e.g., following and scaring people) when they reached Earth.

An important principle of science is that of *control*, which is often a sore point with pseudoscientists and occultists (Gruenberger, 1964). The standard complaint is that scientists insist on various kinds of control because they are hostile towards the kinds of phenomena that tend not to fare well under conditions of good scientific control. However, controls are extensively used in conventional science as well, and for a very good reason. Without controls, one never knows whether the outcome of one's research is due to the hypothesized factors or something else. Thus, rather than obstinance, the insistance upon the use of controls derives from the practical need to eliminate other possible explanations in order to be confident about the hypothesis one is testing. Without controls, an observed phenomenon could be due to anything, and there is literally no way to determine which of several alternative processes (whether extraordinary or natural) is operating. It is one of the curiosities of the paranormal that those who are most interested in adopting extraordinary explanations appear to be the least interested in making use of the characteristics of science, such as control, which would be most helpful in determining the true nature of occult phenomena.

Another criterion of the usefulness of a scientific concept is *predictability* (Gruenberger, 1964)—i.e., the ability of the researcher to anticipate research outcomes by extrapolation from the theory. If the theory can, in essence, predict the future, then it is more likely to be an accurate reflection of reality than a theory that can only be used after an event has taken place. For example, it is very common for psychics, astrologers, and other "seers" to explain their predictions (both failures and apparent successes) after the event in question has taken place (Rawlins, 1977). If such predictions were really generated from a theory containing some essential truth about nature, the explanations should be available prior to the events. As it stands, the predictions are worded in such a vague and fuzzy manner (e.g., see Hyman, 1977; Schwartz, 1978) that many possible events can be interpreted as fulfilling the prediction after the fact.

Another clue to the substance of a theory is known as *heuristic value* (Gruenberger, 1964)—i.e., the degree to which the theory generates useful research and applications. If the general theory of parapsychology is true, then one would expect that over time, parapsychological research would become cumulative, and increasingly more precise and explanatory. However, several observers (including some proponents) have noted that after years of research and hundreds of studies, the field of parapsychology is essentially in the same position in which it started—i.e., trying to come up with a replicable experiment and a plausible explanation of psi (e.g., Beloff, 1978). The same was also true of research into spiritualism after years of tests.

Anomalistic interpretations are not, and should not be, evaluated in a vacuum—free of the context provided by the explanations available in conventional scientific research and theory; this is particularly so when the claim involved is a scientific one, invokes a scientific principle or method, or is generalized beyond one's own meaningful interpretation of subjective experience. This in no way implies that the conventional explanation will be the best one eventually. But before one abandons the available natural explanation and the generally large body of empirical data and theoretical interpretation on which it is constructed for the paranormal explanation, one should be confident regarding its range of applicability, utility, and parsimony. Indeed, many scholars from the philosopher David Hume to the present have argued that the kind of evidence required to prove a magical or paranormal explanation would need to be stronger and more convincing, precisely because of its improbability, than a new interpretation less at variance with existing ideas. This amounts to saying that *better evidence* is needed to support a paranormal as opposed to a conventional explanation (Fraser, 1976). However, as a general rule, the kind of evidence used to support pseudoscientific claims is particularly weak. It is worth repeating at this point the idea that existing theories and paranormal explanations are not necessarily complementary; if a phenomenon cannot be explained at present, that alone does not support a paranormal explanation. Instead, there may be some third, quite natural, but as yet undeveloped explanation. Often, an occult or pseudoscientific theory is based on an apparent anomaly that is not yet explained, as in the case of the Kirlian photography effect. But the existence of an anomaly does not justify drawing the conclusion that scientific concepts must be abandoned in favor of the occult. Instead, the scientific approach requires the *suspension of judgment* until the phenomenon can be adequately explained. Although speculation may, of course, run ahead of available proof, a specific explanation cannot be claimed until evidence that rules out possible alternatives is available. Pseudoscience is usually speculation without explanation. This relates to another key issue of pseudoscience. In science, the *burden of proof* is on the claimant and not on the skeptics, and this rule should be particularly applied to theories that are extraordinary in character (Fraser, 1976). If someone wants to claim that UFOs represent extraterrestrial visitors, then it is their responsibility to provide the evidence that proves this hypothesis and rules out other, more mundane explanations and not the extraterrestrial skeptics. For a theory to be accepted, the originator must not only supply supportive evidence, but must also explain how the theory works. In fact, a theory without an explanation is not a theory at all; at best, it is an hypothesis. Without an explanation, nothing has been accomplished scientifically, except perhaps the generation of some interesting data. In conventional science, such an approach would be laughable, but in extraordinary science, it can be wildly successful and, in fact, is the norm.

It may appear that *anomalies* and science are antithetical, but this is not the case. Indeed, the discovery of anomalous facts not explained by existing theories is the principal mechanism by which science progresses, and the back-and-forth interplay between anomalies and established theories is what science is all about (Woodward, 1978). But there are differences between anomalous facts of science and those of pseudoscience. The anomalies of science are real in the sense of being verifiable, replicable, and so on, whereas the anomalies of pseudoscience are either manufactured, so inconsistent as to raise doubts about their authenticity, or essentially untestable. Second, the discovery of a genuine anomaly spurs scientific activity: Tests and experiments are conducted, tighter controls are applied, procedures are more finely tuned, and more sophisticated mathematical and analytical tools are applied, all in an attempt to discover the true nature of the anomaly and its relation to relevant conventional theories. In pseudoscience, the detection of an anomaly (real or imagined) often leads directly to the proclamation of an extraordinary explanation. If science cannot explain the anomaly immediately, it must be caused supernaturally, claims the pseudoscientist (Alcock, 1979). Moreover, when sufficient evidence has accumulated to generate a natural explanation, the pseudoscientist will continue to ignore it.

Some Related Issues

There are several criteria that, even though they do not directly address the scientific authenticity of a theory or idea, nevertheless provide clues to differentiating pseudoscience from genuine science. One such criterion is *ex-*

pertise. The vast majority of scientific and engineering advancements are made by trained and expert scientists and it almost never happens that an amateur, even a knowledgeable one, does so (Asimov, 1979). Indeed, it is also rare for the trained scientist to make a significant contribution outside of his or her own specialized area of expertise, because even the intelligent amateur ordinarily lacks the technical know-how. Historically, there have been scientific "heretics" who were eventually proved right, but for the most part, they also have been trained experts. Thus, if an idea or phenomenon has genuine scientific merit, it is natural to suppose that scientists would be studying it (Trefil, 1978) and if not, it could be that the idea is ill conceived.

A related issue in questionable science concerns the location of the information being offered to support an extraordinary conclusion. Articles on scientific issues can, of course, be found in popular magazines, for example, but these are ordinarily popular accounts of research or theories that have previously been widely circulated among relevant scientific circles. Thus, if authentic, it should be possible to find the original sources of information (in technical form) published in reputable scientific journals and as presentations at scholarly meetings. If, however, the source of information for the idea is found primarily or exclusively in periodicals appealing to the public, particularly those with dubious reputations for scientific accuracy, then the authenticity of the claim is in doubt. Needless to say, the *National Enquirer* is not a publication to which reputable scientists turn to inform the public of their latest innovation. For example, Kusche (1975) reports that the information supportive of the Bermuda Triangle idea was to be found in several books (mostly paperbacks), one film and one television program, and several popular magazine articles (e.g., in *Argosy, Saga, Male, Cosmopolitan, Fate, Flying Saucer Review*).

Another clue to pseudoscientific works concerns the *style, tone, and scope* of the writing. Scientific studies ordinarily involve rather specific and narrowly defined issues derived from some general theory. Major paradigmatic breakthroughs do occur from time to time, but they are relatively rare. As a consequence, any single scientific article is apt to be extremely limited in scope and generally cautious regarding the conclusions drawn. Scientific articles are also very technical and specific, some students might even say boring. By contrast, pseudoscientific proclamations are heralded in grandiose terms such as "discovery of the century," "astounding facts and ideas," "earth-shattering," "profound enigmas," etc. Claims of great accuracy are common. The gee-whiz and wide-eyed tone of pseudoscience is an attempt to impress the reader with the significance and reality of otherwise hackneyed clichés of science fiction. Similarly, much of pseudoscientific writing contains paranoid ruminations (see the discussion later in this chapter) of self-importance and persecution, as when the author rails against the "scientific establishment" for failing to breathlessly accept the profound insights contained therein (Trefil, 1978). Also, Gruenberger (1964) has noted tendencies towards ineffective communication, lack of humility, proclamations of stupendous importance, dogmatism, and compulsive, overinclusive explanations as symptomatic of the pseudoscientific treatise.

On the other hand, such factors as scientific authority and writing style are not criteria that directly pertain to the truth or falsity of an assertion; at best, they are clues for the reader unfamiliar with the methods and theories of a particular area of science. Scientists can be and have been wrong. As Trefil (1978) has noted, there is no idea so idiotic that all credential experts will refuse to support it. Several famous scientists were themselves believers in the paranormal—e.g., Alfred R. Wallace (the co-inventor of the theory of evolution) believed in the manifestations of mediums, Newton was apparently a mystic, and William Crookes (the discoverer of thallium) was a believer in spirits. Moreover, even established scientists professing verifiable theories can do so dogmatically, with arrogance and a closed mind towards alternative explanations.

An issue of central importance to extraordinary science is that of *fraud*, whether self-conscious or self-deceiving. Chicanery has been exposed so often among parapsychologists, psychics, UFO contactees, and other advocates of extraordinary science (e.g., see Klass, 1974; Randi, 1979) that some skeptics may conclude that all extraordinary science is self-conscious fraud. At the very least, magicians skilled in deception and legerdemain should occupy prominent roles in investigations of the paranormal because so often simple stage magic is involved. But some scientists are not above deceiving themselves and others, and there are suggestions that even the most eminent of scientists (e.g., Newton and Mendel) may have fudged some of their data (Gould, 1978). For example, Gould describes how Samuel G. Morton, a 19th-century physician and scientist, selectively treated his data on skull (and hence brain) size in order to reach the ethnocentric conclusions widely popular then as now that races of people are separate but unequal, with English and German Whites occupying the superior caste, followed by Jews, Hindus, Indians, and Blacks. More recent evidence of possible fraud in studies of intelligence as it relates to racial differences also demonstrates the power of deeply cherished stereotypes and prejudices to dictate the direction that scientific research takes and the conclusions drawn by supposedly sober and rational scientists. Indeed, even highly prestigious endeavors such as cancer research have not been immune from charges of deliberate manufacturing of data.

If cheating also occurs in conventional science, how can instances of fraud be used as an argument against the unusual conclusions of the extraordinary sciences? In conventional science, the tendency seems to be towards manipulation of data in the direction of self-evident conclusions that are consistent with other evidence as opposed to counterintuitive conclusions. The difference is that such conclusions can often be supported by genuine research, although perhaps not as clearly as the scientist who fudges would prefer. Cheating in extraordinary science is most often directed towards supporting ideas at variance with conventional theory and thus, in the absence of other forms of supportive evidence, whether or not fraud has occurred becomes the cental issue. Similarly, legitimate science remains so even with some finagling in its midst because its basic findings are replicable. Thus, as Gould noted, even if Newton fudged some of his data, Newtonian physics still stands because the essential components of his theory can and have been verified by others. Most pseudoscientific phenomena are of such an ephemeral nature that good results are highly suspect (e.g., who would believe the UFO enthusiast who reported a sighting every day or the ESP researcher whose subjects scored 100 correct hits out of every 100 trials?) and thus fudging could occur in very small amounts and still be successful. Thus, with pseudoscience, fraud that originally goes undetected may remain forever anomalous because poor replicability is one of the characteristics of the area.

Box 14.2—The Bermuda Triangle: What, When, Where, and How?

A very popular extraordinary idea of recent vintage is the Bermuda Triangle, examined extensively by Kusche (1975). The Triangle is the area within a line running from Bermuda to Puerto Rico to the tip of Florida and back to Bermuda. The Legend of the Triangle, as Kusche calls it, holds that many mysterious disappearances of ships and airplanes have occurred in this area. Also, derelict ships with crews missing (sometimes supposedly with their meals undisturbed on the table) have also alledgedly been found. Further, these mysteries are described as taking place in good weather for air and seaworthy craft with experienced pilots and captains. How could this be, unless there is an unusual explanation, such as the Legend of the Triangle, which intimates that the area may be a space station for UFOs that cause the disappearances?

Kusche researched each of the 68 supposed instances of a mysterious disappearance or derelict by examining records of reputable sources of information such as *Lloyd's Register of Shipping, Proceedings of Naval Inquiries, Nature,* the *Dictionary of Disasters at Sea,* and other reference works, and the present authors have prepared a summary of his findings. Of the 24 airplanes allegedly lost in the Bermuda Triangle, 20.8% were known or believed by authorities to have been lost somewhere else (sometimes thousands of miles away), and one airplane (4.2%) has no record of ever having existed. Of the remaining 75% that did apparently crash or go down in the Triangle, possible prosaic explanations are available in 83.3% of the cases—e.g., recorded maintenance problems, non-instrument rated and inexperienced pilots, bad weather, and visual sightings of debris and explosions. In some cases, identifying information has been recovered and thus the allegation that these airplanes disappear without a trace is unfounded. Kusche also points out that the disappearance of airplanes that go down over the ocean is no mystery, as they tend to sink.

Of the 44 sea vessels alleged to have disappeared mysteriously or have their crews vanish into thin air, 27.3% disappeared or sank outside the Bermuda Triangle (one in the Pacific), or the only connection between the Triangle and the missing vessel concerned the *intended* course of the vessel (in such cases, it is not known whether the vessel sank in the Triangle or elsewhere); 22.7% were at sea with, according to nautical and weather-service records, severe weather in the area, in some cases of gale or hurricane strength; 15.9% never sank, or if the ship did sink, the crew was rescued and told a story of the circumstances that differs from that of the Bermuda Triangle Legend; 13.6% never existed, or at least there is no record of their existence in the standard sources; and in 9.1% of the cases, the vessel was known to have been overloaded, improperly loaded for the cargo, or unseaworthy. In the remaining 11.4% of the alleged disappearances, other possible explanations apply—e.g., suspected sabotage by German U-boats during World War II, suspected hijackings to Cuba, etc. This classification by the authors, generated from Kusche's report, only concerns the most likely apparent cause of the missing or derelict ship. In several instances, more than one possible explanation would apply. Also, nearly half of the alleged mysteries (both air and sea) took place, if at all, prior to 1950, and thus records potentially explaining the disappearance are more difficult to locate or less likely to still exist. Thus, the Bermuda Triangle mystery is much less mysterious upon closer inspection. It has probably been manufactured by combining innuendo with insufficient records and accounts, and poor scholarship, in an attempt to make it appear that there is something truly anomalous about it when there is not. For example, during the period from 1964 to 1975, three times as many aircraft disappeared while flying over the continental United States as compared to the Bermuda Triangle (Klass, 1977).

THE PSYCHOLOGY OF BAD SCIENCE

As with occultism, there are probably two basic types of pseudoscience and, hence, two kinds of psychological motivation for it. First, the advocate of extraordinary science may consciously peddle fraudulent notions with the expectation of certain personal gains. Conversely, the pseudoscientist may sincerely believe in the authenticity of a discredited idea; this is surely true of the vast majority of supportive followers who do not engage in pseudoscientific activity directly but who strongly believe in it. In the case of the former, the expectation of financial, psychological, or social advantage is the obvious impetus, whereas the latter is undoubtedly more complicated and interesting, as it would appear to involve some sort of self-deception, and thus we focus on it.

The central feature of pseudoscience is belief; therefore, the concepts discussed in Chapter 7 would apply here as well. However, the pseudoscientist is rarely content to hold beliefs privately and informally. Instead, there is the additional attempt to clothe the extraordinary idea with the legitimacy of science and often an almost frantic effort to convince others of its accuracy, sometimes at great personal sacrifice.

Reactance, Commitment, and Mystery

One cause of pseudoscience is a process called *reactance* (Brehm, 1966). Reactance is the psychological response to a perceived loss of freedom to act and think. Thus, when a pleasant activity becomes obligatory, it is less satisfying than before because the exercise of choice and control is lost. By the same token, the discoveries and theories of science may be viewed by many as limiting conditions that somehow restrict one's intellectual freedom to think, and therefore create motivation to prove the reverse. As Gardner (1957) has noted, pseudoscientific thinking often occurs in diametric opposition to prevailing scientific thought and apparently as a counterpoint response to it. Gardner (1957) indicates that:

> When Newton was the outstanding name in physics, eccentric works in that science were violently anti-Newton. Today, with Einstein the father-symbol of authority, a crank theory of physics is likely to attack Einstein in the name of Newton. This same defiance can be seen in a tendency to assert the diametrical opposite of well-established beliefs. Mathematicians prove the angle cannot be trisected. So the crank trisects it. A perpetual motion machine cannot be built. He builds one. There are many eccentric theories in which the "pull" of gravity is replaced by a "push." Germs do not cause disease, some modern cranks insist. Disease produces germs. Glasses do not help the eyes, said Dr. Bates. They make them worse [p. 13].

No one likes to be told what to think and this is particularly true when one's mind is already set. Thus, many people, especially if they are hostile towards or generally ignorant of scientific matters, may perceive scientific explanations as intrusions into their own way of thinking. This process is further enhanced if misinformation creates the impression that scientific theories are somehow arrived at by the arbitrary actions of a "scientific establishment." By dismissing the rules and methods of science as limiting conditions, reactance thereby restores an individual's sense of control and freedom to think anything he or she chooses.

Reactance is closely related to the effects of psychological *commitment*. Considerable psychological research has established that taking a public stand on an issue enhances the individual's motivation to defend the position (Kiesler, 1971). Indeed, some attitude researchers have suggested that the best way to strengthen an attitude is to have a person take a public stand and then to argue strenuously against. People are often not swayed by counterattitudinal arguments, especially if a public commitment has been made, and this appears to be so regardless of the logic of such arguments or the initial reasons for taking the stand. This process may be involved in the persistence of pseudoscience. For example, it has been observed (e.g., Klass, 1974) that hoaxers tend to assert the truth of a hoax even when presented with overwhelming contradictory evidence. The importance of commitment is that once a public stand is taken, the psychological motivation for maintaining that position becomes very strong and thus may outweigh the logic of alternative explanations. People do not like to admit to having been wrong. Therefore, in pseudoscience, the goal of saving face is often more important than finding the truth.

In his investigation of responses to human freaks, Fiedler (1977) discusses the inconsistencies in the responses of many people to bearded ladies, dwarfs, giants, and so on. On the one hand, there is an almost universal fascination with the unusual, mysterious, and strange that draws our attention and interest towards abnormal people. On the other hand, there is also a sense of revulsion and rejection towards people who are dramatically different and from things that are unfamiliar. A similar paradox also applies to pseudoscience. Many people appear to derive comfort and satisfaction from believing in the existence of processes and entities that in another context would be unpleasant. UFO enthusiasts scan the skies for saucers, apparently confident that aliens would be friendly rather than bent on destruction and conquest. Psychics and parapsychologists rarely, if ever, discuss what it would really mean to lose the privacy of one's own inner experience. Despite these contradictions, there remains a strong, appealing quality to things that are strange and mysterious or simply unusual, as is exemplified by the appeal of Ripley's Believe It Or Not. Seligmann (1948) pointed out this feature of pseudoscience and occultism when discussing a 17th-century Rosicrucian novel, *The Chemical Wedding*:

> *The Chemical Wedding* satisfied man's longing for the marvelous, for the continuation of childhood dreams, and for a refuge from the banalities of daily life. In every man there is a child that yearns to play, and the most attractive game is occultation, mystery. The underground of the human psyche finds its counterpart in the meanderings of a mythical labyrinth, subterranean meetings by candlelight, secret passages hidden within the double walls of castles, treasures concealed in gullies [p. 294].

Science threatens the special world of the mysterious by providing mundane and natural explanations for what is unknown, and thus may, for many people, carry the risk of destroying the pleasures of amazement, fantasy, and wonder. A common theme in pseudoscientific and occult writings is the idea that the scientific world would be turned upside down if even one anomalous phenomenon could be proved to have an extraordinary or occult explanation. Thus, pseudoscience exists in part as an attempt to restore the magical and romantic aspects of human existence for those who somehow feel that these are on the verge of extinction.

Prior Beliefs, Science as Religion, and Antiscience

In extraordinary science, prior beliefs are an important source of motivation for challenging conventional scientific depictions of life and the universe. The most common example concerns attempts to resolve the apparent inconsistencies between science and religion. This conflict is centuries old and continues today. Originally, the principal issue concerned the place of Earth in the solar system, but the primary issue of the last 100 years has been Darwin's theory of evolution and its possible implications for the traditional religious teachings of creation. Several observers have pointed out the similarities between theories of extraterrestrial visitors and traditional beliefs in a Supreme Being from the heavens (e.g., Gardner, 1957; Omohundro, 1976; Story, 1977). The "we are not alone" theme of recent vintage suggests salvation from the sky and it is likely that the tremendous appeal of such extraordinary theories as von Däniken's ancient astronauts and Velikovsky's ancient catastrophies stem from the apparent, if superficial, reconciliation of scientific and historical fact with religious goals (e.g. the literal interpretation of scripture). However, the influence of existing beliefs on receptivity to pseudoscientific doctrines can apparently occur for other political and philosophical orientations as well.

Prior beliefs constitute the emotional commitment that makes pseudoscientific ideas, no matter how preposterous, appealing and satisfying. Believers are unconcerned about the scientific absurdities of pseudoscience, not because they are incapable of understanding them, nor because of emotional instability, but rather, because they have been previously committed to a world view in which meaning and purpose take precedence over precision and accuracy. Thus, extraordinary explanations persist because people want to believe them.

A case can be made for concluding that science and its allied technologies (e.g., medicine) have achieved a status in Western culture tantamount to that of a religion. One popular reference source even mockingly lists "scientism" among the world's religions (Wallechinsky & Wallace, 1975). Jahoda (1969) suggests that the 19th-century intellectual optimism originally led to the exaggerated and naive expectation that science would eventually solve all problems of physical need and social evil. But, given the widespread belief in the power and efficiency of science, how does pseudoscience come about? If science truly functions as a religion, should not its pretenders be particularly singled out for rejection and scorn? The answer seems to lie in the failure of science as a form of religion. Science does not satisfy religious needs because the expectations are too high; the sciences simply are not capable of solving all human problems, and even when a scientific approach is applicable, the result may be disappointingly tentative or damaging to other beliefs. Often, scientific theories have frightening implications, either in terms of what they reveal in terms of humanity's place in the scheme of things or the potential applications and consequences of scientific knowledge, such as nuclear proliferation.

But, some people hold on to the exaggerated promise of science, and because it is not forthcoming from conventional science, they turn to marginal sources of scientific information, such as the popular media and what appears therein to be scientific (e.g., Omohundro, 1976; Wallis, 1976). Pseudoscience and medical quackery satisfy the simultaneous desire of many people for the sophistication and precision of science along with the miraculous and magical. Science is not a good substitute for religion, but for those desiring such a substitution, pseudoscience is the nearest approximation.

Finally, *anti-scientific attitudes* and movements have had a continuing effect on the development of pseudoscience. There is often a strong opposition to new scientific theories because they disturb existing scientific views and challenge conventional wisdom. Scientific theories, especially new ones, are also often interpreted as contradicting traditional value systems. The heliocentric theory of the solar system, germ theory, and relativity are examples of theories that at least initially generated considerable opposition both within the scientific community and elsewhere. Anti-scientifically thinking individuals and groups contribute to occultism because they stress the idea that scientists are elitists, interested only in the narrow-minded defense of their own pet conceptualizations in which they have a vested interest, and the concept that the truth regarding the nature of things must necessarily be easy to understand and readily available (i.e., discoverable) to everyone. These factors combine to encourage those who are hostile towards science or disappointed at its failure to solve life's problems to look to scientifically marginal institutions, such as the media and occult literature, for answers to scientific questions (Wallis, 1976). Thus, critical judgment is sacrificed for the more satisfying and personal element of consistency with prior beliefs. Also, because of the typical lack of scientific background of those who adopt an anti-scientific viewpoint, they tend to neglect scientific methodology. The rejection of methodological issues as unimportant clears the way for virtually any conclusion to emerge on the basis of any sort of evidence or argument, and thus extraordinary interpretations may be reached by distortion of the data, groundless speculation, rhetorical questioning, and so on.

Misinformation

Another factor that contributes heavily to pseudoscience is the generally inadequate or erroneous information held by the public regarding many scientific issues. It is important to recognize that the impression that we are more knowledgeable than we really are is very compelling. We live in an environment containing numerous technological marvels, and yet how many people who use televisions, automobiles, computers, etc., actually know how they work? In fact, it is extremely difficult to be informed in an age of enormous scientific and technological complexity and specialization. Even Einstein has been described as naive and gullible in matters outside his special realm of genius (Clark, 1971). An anecdote by Abell (1978) illustrates the point. He recalls his reaction to Velikovsky's controversial book, *Worlds in Collision*. As an astronomer, Abell recognized the fallacies and absurdities in Velikovsky's arguments concerning astronomy and physics, but he was impressed, as others had been, with the treatment of such topics as archeology and mythology. Over lunch, Abell told an archeologist his appraisal of Velikovsky's archeological ideas and the response elicited is best described in Abell's (1978) own words: "To my surprise my companion, in considerable shock, announced that he felt Velikovsky was quite well versed in astronomy but that his archeology was complete bunk. My friend informed me that Velikovsky had badly garbled archeological data, and had even misplaced events by many centuries in time [p. 85]."

Thus, it is apparently easy for even knowledgeable scholars to be fooled in areas of research beyond their own expertise, and the magnitude of such effects probably increases as a direct function of the complexity and technical specificity of the issue. Paradoxically, in an age of universal education and mass media, most Americans cannot recite the Bill or Rights, let alone the subtleties of theory, instrumentation, or methodology of most areas of science. However, the real dilemma derives from the believers' inclination to uncritically accept as genuine the assertions of pseudoscientific advocates rather than relying on the judgments of scholarly experts or improving their own understanding of science. This process is, of course, exacerbated by the explicit disdain for scientific expertise and procedure of many occultist and fringe scientists (e.g., see Johnson, 1975).

Psychological research has suggested that our beliefs are not always supported by reliable and objective information. This is even true in areas of vital concern and strongly held beliefs, such as politics and sex (e.g., Hansson, Jones, & Chernovetz, 1979; Robinson, 1967). In fact, it may be that attitudes take the place of information for many of our beliefs, creating the illusion that we are well informed and rational on a certain topic, when in reality what is being experienced are strong feelings and deeply cherished

beliefs (e.g., Jones & Rambo, 1973). Indeed, studies have found that subjects will express strong opinions regarding non-existent groups of people
about which information is not even possible (Hartley, 1946). The amount
of information an individual possesses does affect several aspects of that individual's beliefs and actions, such as their vulnerability to attitude change
(e.g., Jones, Rambo, & Russell, 1978). However, the mere fact that someone possesses a strong attitude regarding a particular issue tells nothing
about how much the person knows concerning the issue in question. This is
particularly true for technical scientific issues involving such subjects as
methodology and probability.

Paranoia and Psychopathy

Sometimes, the psychological factors that contribute to pseudoscience combine to create a pattern of beliefs and behavior that is essentially
pathological. *Paranoia* is a psychological disturbance in which a fantastic
and unsubstantiated system of ideas called the *delusion* is the dominant
feature (see Chapter 10 for a more general discussion of occultism and
psychopathology). Paranoid delusions often take one of two forms: exaggerated assertions of one's own importance (i.e., the delusion of grandeur),
and the belief that one is the victim of a menacing conspiracy (i.e., the delusion of persecution). For example, in extreme and severely pathological
forms of paranoia (often associated with schizophrenia), the individual may
claim to be some notable personage from history, such as Napoleon,
Roosevelt, Churchill, and so on, who is the target of a massive conspiracy
on the part of Russians, men from Mars, or whomever. In less extreme
forms, where personal identity remains intact, the claim may simply be that
jealous enemies are thwarting one's rightful emergence to a status of
greatness.

One common paranoid delusional theme centers on assertions of great
scientific discoveries and inventions that have not been accepted by the
scientific community because of conspiratorial attempts to prevent the
originator from immediately achieving a position of scientific fame. Of
course, the discoveries and inventions prove to have little, if any, value, and
often are of the perpetual-motion machine variety. One interesting feature
of paranoia that is also common in occultism is that delusional beliefs are
interdependent and may be used to justify and reinforce one another. When
asked why he or she is being persecuted, the paranoiac will respond that it is
because of his or her (secret) greatness, and when asked for proof of the
remarkable accomplishments, he or she will point to the alleged persecution.

Gardner (1957) lists several characteristics of crank and pseudoscientific
activity that serve as clues to paranoid tendencies: a preference for working

in isolation completely outside the mainstream of conventional science; frequent accusations of scientific prejudice and persecution; self-proclaimed genius and wisdom, as well as grandiose assertions of accomplishment and discovery; derogation of scientific colleagues, particularly the great or famous ones, and often vicious attacks on skeptics (e.g., see Gardner's discussion of Wilhelm Reich's "Listen Little Man"); and reliance on unduly complex and idiosyncratic jargon, which is often incomprehensible to the uninitiated.

Despite their underlying disturbance, true paranoiacs (as opposed to paranoid schizophrenics) may at times appear to be quite reasonable because paranoid delusions can be specific and circumscribed. In other words, in areas unrelated to the delusional system, the individual may be essentially normal. The delusion itself may also be somewhat believable despite the fact that it is not true. This is particularly so when one accepts the basic premises from which it derives. For instance, for someone already committed to a metaphysical or anti-scientific point of view, the paranoiac's preposterous pronouncements of "secret" discoveries and scientific hostility may have the ring of truth. Also, paranoiacs tend to be more intelligent than the average mental patient, and this may contribute to the perception of the delusion as legitimate. In one famous case of a particularly intelligent an well-educated patient, Lindner (1955), a psychiatrist, describes how this patient invented an imaginary civilization on a fictitious planet, complete with a unique language, architecture, mathematics, social customs, and history. Because of the patient's intelligence and creativity, his delusional creations were quite ingenious.

Another form of psychopathology that contributes particularly to the application of pseudoscientific concepts such as those of quack medicine, is *psychopathy*. Contrary to popular opinion, the psychopath is not typically the homicidal maniac he or she is often depicted to be. Instead, the psychopathic personality is characterized by an inadequate development of conscience and an accompanying general lack of anxiety and guilt (Coleman, 1972). Psychopaths are also often described as friendly, likable and persuasive, at least in initial and casual interactions. The psychopaths' reduced sense of guilt and initial appeal combine to create the opportunity to dupe unsuspecting seekers of unusual medical treatments and magical technologies and inventions.

THE UFO PROBLEM

In June, 1947, a private pilot, Kenneth Arnold, who was flying near Mt. Rainier in Washington, sighted nine circular objects that appeared to be flying in formation at high speed. The wire services covered the story, and within weeks, "flying saucers" had been reported in every state and several foreign countries (Gardner, 1957). Thus began the modern furor concerning UFOs that has continued intermittently to the present. The central issue in the controversy centers around the extraterrestrial hypothesis—i.e., the conclusion that UFOs are spacecraft from another planet. Few issues have captured national attention so completely so many times. One Air Force pilot lost his life chasing UFOs, extensive government-sponsored studies were undertaken, hundreds of books and articles appeared, and numerous investigation groups and organizations for enthusiasts sprang into existence.

Between 1947 and 1974, over 10,000 UFO sightings were reported in the United States. Reports of such sightings have varied considerably across time. For example, in 1969 the average was less than 15 per month, whereas in one month alone, July, 1952, 536 sightings were reported (Klass, 1974). But, UFO sightings cannot simply be dismissed as hallucinations or human imagination. There is general agreement among advocates and opponents alike that many, if not most, are reported by sober, educated, emotionally stable people, often with impeccable reputations. Indeed, President Carter is reported to have seen a UFO, as have airline pilots, radar operators, police officers, and some astronomers. Therefore, there can be little doubt that UFOs are real in the sense that, in most cases, something is seen. In a relatively small number of cases, there are physical forms of evidence, such as depressions in the ground and charred vegetation, that some interpret as confirmation of actual UFO landings. Also, photographs have been presented purporting to show actual UFOs in flight. Most interesting are those 200 or so cases in which individuals claim to have made personal contact with the inhabitants of UFOs. Such accounts have varied from simply witnesssing a spacecraft and its occupants to communication (sometimes telepathic) and even abductions where the "abductees" have supposedly been taken aboard alien spacecraft. Also, some UFO accounts have unfolded incredible tales of being transported to space stations or other planets.

It is also clear that UFOs are viewed favorably by many people. In Chapter 7, several studies were cited suggesting that close to half of the adult population believe UFOs to be real. Whatever the exact rate of belief, however, it is clear that many people interpret UFO sightings as evidence in favor of extraterrestrial visitation. For example, in an extensive study of student attitudes, Saunders (1968) reported the following endorsement rates, among others: intelligent life exists elsewhere in the universe (92.9%); authentic photos of UFOs have been taken (71.9%); science has established the existence of UFOs (66.7%); the Earth has been visited by extraterrestrial beings at least once (47.9%); and UFOs have attempted communication with Earth (40.1%).

More recently, the UFO concept has spawned a number of new ideas and has been used as the explanation for further anomalies. For example, von Däniken's theory of ancient astronauts contends that we are not alone and never have been. Von Däniken claims that extraterrestrial astronauts visited the Earth at various times, enabling ancient civilizations to create their remarkable achievements (e.g., Egypt's pyramids and the great stone statues of Easter Island), leaving traces of their presence in the folklore and artistry of those civilizations and telltale signs of their technological superiority, such as landing strips for their space vessels. The concept of the UFOs has been used to explain an alleged wave of cattle mutilations in the 1970s (Stewart, 1977), and the ever-deepening mystery of the Bermuda Triangle area. Also, the extraterrestrial hypothesis in the form of "ancient astronauts" has been invoked to explain such diverse phenomena as a midair explosion over Siberia in 1908 (Oberg, 1978b); the meaning of inscriptions on a Bronze-Age Chinese pictograph (Keightley, 1978); and legends among the Dogon people of Africa (Ridpath, 1978). Every conceivable link between UFOs and occult phenomena has been suggested at one time or another, and even the more sober UFO enthusiasts have sometimes suggested they may be related to psychic abilities (Klass, 1979). In fact, the UFO has become a spiritual magnet attracting the full range of paranormal concepts and becoming inextricably woven together with them.

But the scientific community remains largely unconvinced of the extraterrestrial origins for UFOs. Even a recent attempt by the White House to have the National Aeronautics and Space Administration reopen government UFO investigations was declined by NASA (Klass, 1978). There are several reasons for the reluctance to accept the extraterrestrial hypothesis.

First, it is inconsistent with accepted scientific fact and requires some unlikely assumptions. For example, available evidence suggests that, with the exception of Earth, the planets of the solar system and their satellites are generally unsuitable for the development of life forms, let alone a race of superior intelligence. Even the "canals" of that extraterrestrial favorite Mars have faded upon closer scientific inspection, which has occurred in recent years. Thus, a more probable location for the extraterrestrial origins of UFOs is possible satellites of stars beyond our solar system. But, as the nearest star is over four light years away from the Earth, it would take a spacecraft with speeds comparable to those of Earth space probes thousands of years to traverse that distance. Thus, the extraterrestrial hypothesis for UFOs requires either the assumption of incredibly extended space journeys or speeds approaching that of light.

Second, there are a variety of alternative physical phenomena that could produce what are identified as UFO sightings, and in numerous cases, a connection has been conclusively demonstrated. Examples include heavenly bodies, particularly the planet Venus, comets, meteors, balloons, conventional aircraft, vapor trails, hang gliders, white owls, weather inversions, radar "angels," refracted light, space debris, electrical plasmas, flares, and a variety of other phenomena (Klass, 1974). The physical evidence interpreted as supporting the "flying-saucer" viewpoint has alternative natural explanations, and to date no conclusive physical evidence for the presence of extraterrestrial visitors has been forthcoming, whereas the photographic evidence appears to be largely fraudulent or unclear images of natural phenomena (e.g., Klass, 1974; Oberg, 1978a; Oberg & Sheaffer, 1977). Indeed, a 20-year study by the U. S. Air Force and a government-sponsored independent investigation conducted by University of Colorado scientists resulted in the conclusion that even though not every UFO report could be explained or assigned a natural cause, there was no evidence to support the extraterrestrial claim. Only 5% of the cases reported to the Air Force could not be classified as resulting from natural causes; this general figure has been confirmed by UFO advocates (Sheaffer, 1978).

Third, the psychology of UFOs suggest that specifics of UFO reports (e.g., seeing portholes on UFOs, so-called "intelligent movement") as well as the entirety of some UFO incidents, could be caused by psychological processes. For example, the perception of unfamiliar and unexpected objects (see Chapter 4), the influence of beliefs and expectations (Chapter 7), the influence of others on judgments (Chapter 11), emotional instability (Chapter 10), and memory (Chapter 6) can influence the nature and content of subsequent verbal reports to a major extent. Thus, there is a strong psychological component that could determine the specifics of UFO experiences. Similarly, some of the reports of contacts with extraterrestrial beings (often taken by the general public as the best evidence for the existence of extraterrestrial visitors) have emerged using the technique of hypnosis. Recent studies have demonstrated that individuals not claiming to have had contact with UFOs (and hence perhaps anyone) also yield testimony under hypnosis that corresponds closely to that of "genuine" UFO abduction victims (Lawson, 1978).

Fourth, the area of UFO investigation has been plagued by hoaxes, and in many ways appears to be similar to belief in bogus phenomena no longer in vogue. In the 1890s, many people reported sighting mysterious airships traveling at terrific speeds (Klass, 1974). As is true today, there were reports of close encounters with the occupants, but unlike today's reports, the craft were said to be balloons and the occupants mere earthlings. This, of course, preceded the introduction of large airships in the United States. Similarly, the current UFO craze corresponds closely to the enthusiasm for fairies in the last century (Sheaffer, 1977), complete with sightings, close encounters, and photographs. Hoaxing has played a prominent role in UFO sightings both in terms of bogus reports as well as in creating the impression that a

UFO has landed. Homemade balloons with trailing flares have been a common prank of school children and college students, for example. Perhaps the most revealing hoax was perpetrated by a high school sociology teacher and a group of students as an experiment in the social psychology of UFO reports (Klass, 1974). The important point is that once the hoaxers reported seeing the UFO and revealed a bogus landing site and it was reported by the media, the story was readily and widely believed. It is also common for even one bogus reporting of a UFO to lead to reports by others of strange sights in the sky.

The problem and confusion created by marginal science is epitomized by the UFO controversy. On the one hand, there is widespread belief among the general public that UFO sightings represent extraterrestrial spacecraft, whereas many, if not most, scientists dismiss the idea as clearly not supported by the evidence. Also, there are many cogent arguments against drawing the extraterrestrial conclusion. This uneasy and perpetual stalemate emerges from the differences between science and personal belief. The role of personal belief is to create a recognizable pattern out of the chaos of experience, and, one hopes, a pattern that is meaningful and provides direction. Science also seeks regularity, but the guiding principle is the reality of nature, whether it is personally satisfying or not. There is another difference. Science is primarily a social processs, the attempt of a society to apply its technological and analytical skills to the goal of understanding nature. Personal belief is private and self-fulfilling, unchecked by the requirements and limitations of public rules of evidence. Thus, despite the similarity, the scientist and believer are not really engaging in the same activity and therefore divergent conclusions should not be surprising.

The extraterrestrial hypothesis generally fails among scientists because it cannot pass the test; conclusive evidence in its favor simply has not been mustered. On the other hand, it succeeds as an article of faith because of the sheer psychological power of its imagery and implications. There is something about the idea that is appealing on a grand scale. There is something in it that creates immediate interest and excitement. Klass (1974) calls the UFO concept an adult fairy tale, the product of the human tendency to wish the world to be something more than it appears to be. Carl Gustav Jung (1959) says the UFO is the symbol of an archetype, which thus explains its potency. He has offered an entirely psychological explanation of UFOs. As the most common synonym of the UFOs—flying saucers—indicates, they are mostly round, round things in the sky. Round things have been seen in the sky for a long time, long before there were any manmade flying objects of any kind. They are also seen in dreams, visions, and modern paintings. Added to the fact that no material proof of actual extraterrestrial visitations has ever been produced, Jung concludes that the dreams and visions of the round, the *rotundum* of the medieval alchemist, is a projected image or symbol of an archetype (see *Real-Life Situations* in Chapter 13), the archetype of wholeness. The Eastern mandala, the circle divided into four or eight segments, is one widely used symbol of this archetype. Mandalas, Jung says, usually appear in situations of psychic confusion and perplexity, and represent order and wholeness. Superimposed on the confusion and disintegration, the circle brings about order, integrating the splintered psychic fragments. The reason why so many people see round things in the sky these days is that they represent the order and wholeness that is longed for in times of fragmentation, confusion, perplexity, depersonalization (and therefore threat to the ego), and threats to the very existence of humanity.

The UFO is a modern combination of the subjective and the objective. It is easy to see how the combination occurs. For example, the concept (as opposed to a sighting) of a UFO is usually a wonderful combination of both moral and scientific visions of the future. Thus, although often described as technologically advanced and masterfully engineered spacecraft, UFOs also usually contain creatures of superior intellect whose intentions towards earthlings vary from benign but curious to being prepared to directly intervene should our greatest faults and follies be realized through some major catastrophe, such as nuclear war. In this fashion, one has simultaneously the fruits of advanced technology that the best of futuristic science can offer, accompanied by the ancient reassurance of the existence of superior beings free from human frailties and age-old shortcomings. The enormous popularity of movies like "Close Encounters of the Third Kind" attests to the strong appeal of such ideas. Indeed, numerous "science fiction groupies" attend conventions, dress up as space characters and, in general, act out the fanciful story of a universe that, even though sufficiently exciting as a result of occasional "intergalactic emergencies," is nevertheless a safe, just, and meaningful world in which to live because good and justice always triumph while science solves all human problems of need, conflict, and physical comfort.

The problem with pseudoscience is not that it is not science. Literature, art, and philosophy are not sciences either, but they are nevertheless true. The problem of pseudoscience is that it distorts scientific knowledge by substituting the proposed for the proven, the desired for the demonstrable. Scientific knowledge is imperfect, and yet it is an important source of knowledge and forms part of the basis of understanding ourselves and the world we live in. Pseudoscience abandons that base of understanding without a compensatory gain. The choice between science and pseudoscience is not a choice between restrictive and reductionistic principles versus an open-minded freedom to explore the enigmas of life. It is the choice between knowledge, however tentative, and ignorance.

15

Anomalistic Psychology: Retrospect and Prospect

In the last 13 chapters, we have discussed anomalistic psychological phenomena, their characteristics, esoteric beliefs, and how psychological principles of everyday behavior can be used to understand them. We have argued that such behaviors, experiences, and beliefs are the products of the intricate relationships among natural processes that shape and affect us: physiological states, learning processes, perceptual processes, and personality dispositions. In doing so, we have implied that many anomalistic phenomena can be better explained in terms of human psychology and physiology than in terms of the various versions of occult beliefs and esoteric philosophies. This is not to suggest that this is the only way to look at paranormality. As any student of psychology knows, some of the very principles of behavior employed here to explain anomalistic phenomena are themselves the focus of considerable debate and controversy. However, we expect that such an approach will ultimately result in a more complete and functional theory of the paranormal for the "outsider" as continued research and analysis uncover even more links between anomalistic phenomena and psychological processes.

ANOMALISTIC PSYCHOLOGY: A SOCIO-PSYCHOLOGICAL RETROSPECT

One conclusion to be drawn from a review of the relevant literature is that, in a sense, esotericism often appears to work for the believer and hence is not the hollow, totally useless system of ideas it is often portrayed to be. As discussed earlier, such beliefs do seem to fulfill needs that are deeply felt, especially in relation to the interrelated issues of order, structure, predictability, meaning, and a sense of self-worth. In this regard, esotericism might best be thought of as a form of religion or mythology whose focus is not so much whether the beliefs are scientifically verifiable, but rather the psychological and social functions and processes that are enhanced by such beliefs.

Another important implication of this line of argument is that the processes that produce anomalistic experiences and occult beliefs do not appear to be fundamentally different from the processes that produce any other type of experience or belief, regardless of the content of the belief and quite apart from who has the experience. The British psychologist Gustav Jahoda (1969) has examined several theories proposed to account for the development of many of the occult beliefs and practices covered in this book. He considers the influences attributed to errors of description, observation, and memory, unconscious processes, non-contingent reinforcement, social organization and practices, and styles of thinking. His general conclusions are instructive. Although acknowledging the potential importance of all of the just-cited factors with regard to the explanation of paranormal beliefs, he also finds each to be limited in its explanatory value, applicable only to certain beliefs, and something less the one essential and conceptually clear idea that might explain all instances of esotericism and anomalistic experience. More importantly, Jahoda contends that previous theories have failed in particular to account for the frequency, normality, and functionality of paranormal beliefs and practices, and he further criticizes existing theories for failing to consider the possibility that such beliefs are directly linked to common and basic styles of thinking and feeling rather than exclusively to irrationality, emotional instability, or personal rigidity.

We agree with Jahoda that the most striking feature of esotericism may well be its prevalence and persistence rather than the ideation of its content. It only seems logical to conclude that any facet of human experience that is so resilient and found in such a variety of cultures and individuals must be serving some very basic psychological, biological, or social function. Similarly, it is probably a gross mistake to equate esoteric beliefs and practices exclusively or even primarily with irrationality, maladjustment, or chicanery as some disbelievers do. Even though there is no lack of documented cases in which fraud, self-delusion, or self-serving motives have been the heart of some paranormal claim, most believers appear to be rational, honest, sincere, and serious individuals. Indeed, it was noted earlier that the tendency to distort contradictory evidence may be typical of most or all strongly held beliefs rather than just occult beliefs. Although there may be negative intellectual and social consequences associated with paranormal beliefs, it is important to keep in mind that the occult believer is usually not deviant in either the psychopathological or the statistical sense of the term.

One interesting possibility is that esotericism as experienced by the "average" believer may represent little more than a preference for the more subjective, symbolic, metaphorical, and meaningful description and analysis of life to be found in art, literature, allegories, fantasy, and so on. Although this idea probably does not apply to the hard-boiled approach of many professional occultists who make specific claims of scientific authenticity, it may be that many believers are attracted to esoteric ideas not because they are seeking a scientifically accurate description of the universe, but because they are simply drawn by the essential underlying themes of occultism. It is even possible that many believers take esotericism figuratively rather than literally, although this possibility has not been empirically investigated. For example, it is not uncommon to find believers expressing the idea that what they really believe in is the potential for human improvement or the existence of transcendental principles, whether they are exactly embodied in such concepts as ESP and UFOs or not. This may strike the ardent disbeliever as a lame rationalization for the failures to verify occult claims scientifically, and perhaps that is precisely what it is. On the other hand, it may reflect the believer's commitment to the subjective, dialectic, and rational aspects of life as was suggested by our study of the relationship between belief in the paranormal and world view. To the extent that this is so, the disbeliever might want to rethink that typical response to esotericism that labels it as bunk and drivel. Although we still may wish to challenge occultism's scientific claims on purely scientific grounds, to reject its purpose and central themes mindlessly as having no relevance to the human condition may be analogous to rejecting, for instance, modern art because of inaccuracies in depicting the size and shape of objects.

It is also useful at this point to emphasize the distinction between experiencing and understanding. The possibility that an anomalistic experience has a logical, mundane or natural explanation does not by itself suggest that the person having that experience is insane, stupid, easily misled, dishonest, or irrational. Such experiences are usually not mundane because they often create considerable emotional upheaval in the experiencing individual. But experiences are not explanations, and there is no reason to accept the interpretation of someone who has experienced an allegedly paranormal occurrence as the sole basis for determining what precisely happened. This divergence between experience and explanation is inherent in the nature of explanations, which, by definition, are not experiences themselves but detached and simplified abstractions.

We noted on several occasions that most people (including psychologists) tend not to think of their own behavior in technical explanatory terms. It is significant that even though we may not be distressed at the difference between a scientific description of, say gustatory and digestive processes and the actual experience of consuming our favorite foods, many people become upset over what appears to them to be the trivialization and sterilization of anomalistic experiences. In the case of eating, we recognize that one's experience of the joys to be found in some favored delicacy is not really the same kind of thing as a dispassionate analysis of related physiological processes, but with unusual or meaningful experience, this distinction becomes blurred and obscure. The point is that even if every strange experience ever reported has a naturalistic explanation, it does not imply that the experience itself was not a powerful and meaningful one for the experiencer, or that such explanations are somehow more real than the experience.

Consequences of Esotericism

All this does not mean that esotericism is a neutral force for the society or for the individual. It may be argued that serious if not dire consequences stem from a reliance on unsubstantiated, arcane concepts. The frequently cited example of the person in need of effective and available medical attention who foregoes conventional treatments and procedures in favor of some preferred form of quackery, cure-all, or magical regimen exemplifies the very real possibility of negative effects deriving from subscription to and participation in esotericism. Occult themes have also been used to bilk considerable amounts of money from believers. Those most vulnerable to such schemes, such as the elderly and the poor, are typically those who are least able to afford the hard and cynical lessons of dealing with con artists.

Esoteric cults often drastically alter the lives of their members, in some cases affecting not only their wealth but their emotional stability and health as well. The frequency of these kinds of occult influences are difficult to establish for obvious reasons, however. Furthermore, to some extent, they may be beside the point in that all sorts of appealing concepts may be and have been used to relieve the gullible of their money (e.g., religious, philanthropic, and patriotic ideas), and even the failure to use adequate medical services can occur for a variety of reasons. The supposition that belief in paranormal happenings leads one astray and down the path of irrationality (e.g., Bok, 1975) is not well supported by facts. Individuals who believe in UFOs, pyramid power, or telepathy perform their everyday functions as normally and as efficiently as those who do not. Such dogmas of orthodox religion as the Catholic dogma of the bodily assumption of Mary are as irrational and untenable scientifically as most of the paranormal beliefs, yet belief in one or the other set of these notions seems to have little or no effect on how well an individual will function in situations where rationality is required. It is not unusual for people to believe simultaneously in materialistic and monistic scientific concepts and otherwordly and dualistic religious and philosophical ideas. This is possible because the incompatible beliefs are unconsciously compartamentalized or perhaps even consciously differentiated on the basis of applicability and purpose. When one ponders the meaning of life, one typically turns to philosophical, literary, artistic, political, religious social, or mythological creations and teachings of one's culture. However to build a bridge, to travel to the moon, or to explain the diversity of plant and animal species, one turns to the engineering technologies and theories of science. In sum, although not questioning the seriousness of problems when they do occur, one wonders if examples such as those cited earlier constitute the principal negative outcome of esoteric beliefs.

Paranormal beliefs contain elements of both science and religion in varying proportions. For example, the notions of reincarnation, astral projection, and demonic possession are related to the notions of life after death, the soul, and personified evil, and may be interpreted as being in support of such concepts as that life has a special meaning beyond the immediate and apparent reality, or that humankind's quest for purpose and meaning has a definite and reachable goal. The methods and technologies of science are also frequently invoked to substantiate paranormal ideas and practices and, to a greater or lesser degree, science is used as the ultimate criterion against which the reality of the esoteric is assessed, even by believers. Such assessments are often scientifically incorrect or unreliable, but that does not seem to matter to the believer. Rather, the important issue for believers would seem to be that science and technology can be used to support their beliefs. Thus, the metaphor of the occult, the hidden, provides the answer to the question of the relationship between the subjective and the objective that both science and religion, taken separately, fail to provide.

Paranormal Claims and Skepticism

Because of their frequency and variety, it would be impossible for any single individual to evaluate thoroughly and logically all the claims regarding anomalistic occurrences. Also, in many treatments of the subject, the "facts" of a paranormal phenomenon are taken for granted (either for or against the reality of it) and only the interpretation is presented, whether paranormal or naturalistic. In such a complex situation, how can the uninitiated evaluate the reality or even the nature of paranormal claims? Some specific criteria for judging pseudoscientific ideas were presented in Chapters 1 and 14, but there may be an even more general strategy that can be applied to this problem. It emphasizes the role of skepticism in the evaluation of any type of tentative conceptualization.

It is clear that sweeping generalizations that characterize unusual experiences or explanations as illusion or deception without sufficient corroboration or logic are misguided and, if practiced universally, would result in the stagnation and atrophy of scientific and other kinds of knowledge (see, for instance, Preuss, 1978). It is precisely this kind of "dogmatic orthodoxy" that rejects out of hand and without reason or evidence any anomaly that believers often attribute to nonbelievers. On the other side of things, it is equally clear that the data-free, all-embracing endorsement of the full range of paranormal ideas is what leads disbelievers to attribute gullibility to believers and also contributes to tension between these two groups. For example, the development of psychotherapeutic techniques for eliciting psychic abilities or treating their difficulties (e.g., Burg, 1975) seems not only premature but clearly ignores the fundamental questions associated with the reality of such abilities. It may also be argued that unselective and uncritical endorsement of anomalistic experiences and occult ideas and a refusal to address the central questions underlying them in a sober manner would also eventually lead to intellectual stagnation and atrophy because one of the ways, and perhaps the most important way, in which knowledge progresses is by the differentiation and discrimination between ideas, methods, and theories using agreed-upon criteria, such as, in the case of science, predictability, usefulness, and parsimony.

Although it should be patently obvious, it is nonetheless worth noting that ad hominem arguments (which may be found in both camps) that are intended primarily to attack the personality and motives of those holding the opposing view tell us little about the issues involved, except perhaps that they are emotional ones. The Committee for the Scientific Investigation of Claims of the Paranormal, a special committee recently created by the American Humanist Association, has been accused by detractors of setting up a scientific "inquisition" or engaging in a "witch-hunt" (Kurtz, 1976). Although we do not agree with this characterization, it is fair to say that any endeavor that did become more devoted to rooting out "erroneous thinking" than to the advancement of knowledge would not only tend to impede creative processes directed towards new and potentially useful ideas, but would also, in all probability, encourage such "errors" by polarizing and solidifying viewpoints, thereby reducing the flow of information and opinion between individuals of differing perspectives. Immovable and dogmatic rejection as well as non-resisting, uncritical acceptance would both appear to be counterproductive responses to anomalous claims.

A better approach to evaluating paranormal claims is suggested in the analogy to the practice of statistical analysis of research results. There is a conventional and widely agreed upon degree to which experimental results may be attributed to chance before they will be accepted as statistically significant. That degree is called the alpha level. There is always the danger that an alpha level that is too conservative may lead the researcher to miss important differences in the data, whereas liberal alphas increase the probability of deciding that a phenomenon is worth pursuing when in fact it is due to chance alone. One solution to this dilemma is to always use the same relatively conservative alpha level, which is what is usually done in practice (results are ordinarily not accepted as significant unless the probability that they are due to chance alone is less than 5%). Another solution would be to select (in advance of examining the data, of course) the level of significance appropriate to the nature and purpose of the study. For example, in the early stages of a research program, when the precise nature of the phenomenon under investigation is not yet clear, or when specific hypotheses cannot be generated, it may be advisable to select a relatively liberal alpha criterion to reduce the likelihood of overlooking some potentially meaningful relationship. Later in the same program of research, after methods and ideas have become more precise, one might want to use a more rigorous definition of significance to ensure that the observed relationships are strong and reliable. Similarly, with anomalistic ideas, claims, and theories, it would seem appropriate to be relatively more accepting with regard to the introduction of such concepts so as not to bypass some important phenomenon or type of explanation even if rare or in some ways strange, whereas a more conservative and discriminating attitude might best be used for a more complete acceptance. This is essentially the advice of William James when he suggested that we ought to be tender-minded with regard to accepting subjective experience as an appropriate domain for study while being tough-minded when deciding that an appropriate explanation has been offered.

Anomalistic Psychology as an Esoteric Field

In Chapter 1, a sixfold classificaiton of occult beliefs was presented: proto-scientific, quasi scientific, pragmatic, philosophical, mystical, and theistic occultism. It may not have escaped the reader's attention that these six types of occultism were presented in a certain order. If we add orthodox science and orthodox religion to the ends of this order, we obtain a continuum of belief systems that are characterized by the degree to which scientific and transcendental concepts enter into them. We conditionally call this continuum the esoteric field (Fig. 15.1).

The beliefs, practices, and institutions that constitute the esoteric field arise out of the need to reconcile two fundamental realities of human consciousness. We are aware of both an objective reality—things out there, the non-me—and of our mental life, ourselves, the subjective side of existence. At one time during the course of evolution humans, like all animals, were only conscious, but not self-conscious. Once self-consciousness and therewith the subjective-objective distinction arose in humans, it in turn gave rise to the idea that the subjective was more than just a state of the body, that it perhaps could function on its own, outside the body. The illusion of autonomy of the subjective is an extremely powerful one. In fact, most of our beliefs in the existence of incorporeal entities may be attributed to our ability to project inner, subjective events as external, autonomous processes or entities. What is in reality inside, our thoughts, images, feelings, are now experienced as being outside ourselves. The psychologist Julian Jaynes (1976) presents a convincing case of the ancients who, on hearing the subjective voices of their own right hemisphere of the brain, projected them outside and believed them to be those of the gods. The origin of a dualistic philosophy that postulates the existence of two kinds of substance, mind and matter, also lies in the recognition of the difference between the subjective and the objective. The other philosophy that concerns itself with the nature of the universe, monism, postulates only one kind of substance, either mind (idealistic monism) or matter (materialistic monism). The conflict between monism and dualism is at the core of every controversy between adherents of occult beliefs and the critics of such beliefs.

The inside-outside, subjective-objective distinction takes on various other guises and may be described by a variety of other contrasting terms. In Chapter 9, we described the evolution of the terms soul and mind and showed how the former term became associated with religion and other transcendental belief systems whereas the latter became the preferred term in the social and behavioral sciences, including psychology where it simply means an inference from behavior. Located between monistic science and dualistic religion, pluralistic theosophy speaks of mind, body, as well as other substances, each located on a different level of existence. Another dimension of this basic aspect of the esoteric field that we have shown in Fig. 15.1 is the well-known distinction between empirical and transcendental belief systems, because the essence of religion is subjective experiences of a certain kind and science is based on empirical, objective observations.

Science is often said to be opposed to or incompatible with religion. Attempts to reconcile or integrate the two have been numerous. They have ranged from a flat denial that there is any difference, through elaborate attempts of combining them, to a complete rejection of the possibility that there ever will be a time when the scientifc and the religious view will blend into a single world picture. Science and religion do represent two distinct ways of acquiring knowledge. In science, the acquisition of knowledge is mediated by the senses; there is something out there, the objective, the physical, that we learn about indirectly, mediately by the way of the senses. A consequence of mediated knowledge is that it is subject to error. On the other hand, the experiences of intuitive insight, ecstasy, or revelation have

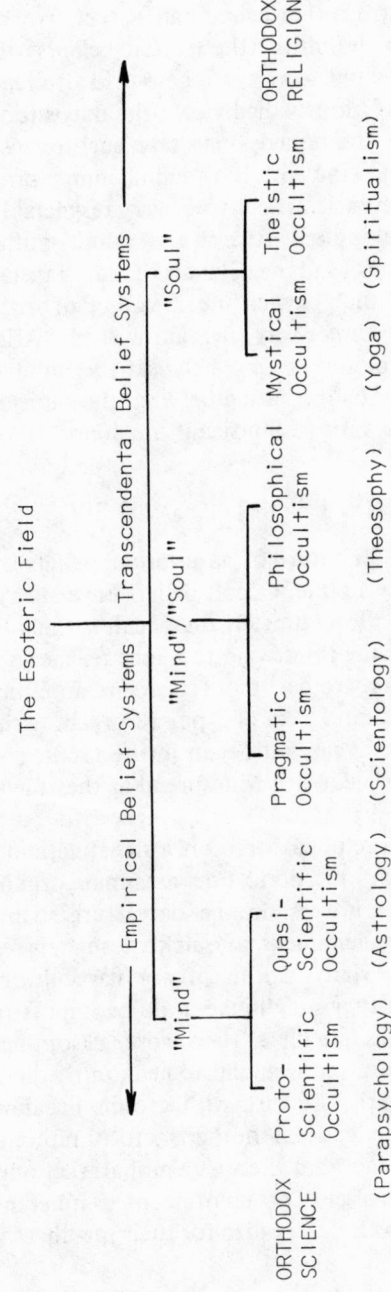

Fig.15.1. The esoteric field. The names of the groups in parentheses serve only as examples.

459

always been considered to be a direct way of knowing, not subject to error, at least not from the viewpoint of the experiencer, because the subjective feeling of certainty and truth that accompanies such experiences does not admit of such. Almost by definition, the esoteric belief systems arise out of dissatisfaction with the explanations of the world offered by the strictly scientific or the strictly religious world view. The one is too commonplace, the other too incredible. The remedy may take such forms as introducing faith healing or communication with the dead in church practice, taking up the scientific study of some scientifically not very respectable phenomenon, such as telepathy, or making an attempt at a grand synthesis of science, religion, and philosophy, as Madame Blavatsky did. A metaphor is literally and etymologically that that carries the meaning of one thing over to another when there is no direct way of relating them. Aristotle once said that a metaphor is the middle ground between the unintelligible and the commonplace. Occultism, by mediating between the subjective and the objective, may be humanity's most significant metaphor.

ANOMALISTIC PSYCHOLOGY: A PROSPECT

The question concerning the future of paranormal beliefs has two answers, a long-term and a short-term one. Occult beliefs have always been with us, and probably will be for a long time. If the occult is the metaphor that for many solves the riddle of the inside and the outside, the subjective and the objective, then it is not likely to pass from the scene. The short-term answer concerns temporary fluctuations in the popularity or visibility of occult ideas, such as the upward cycle that began in the 1960s, and whether they will continue ot be as prevalent and widespread as they have been in recent years.

Arguments could be developed for both a negative and an affirmative answer to the short-term question. For example, arguing against the unabated continuation of interest in the occult are such factors as the tendency of trendy social phenomena to quickly lose their relevance and, as a result, their following. Many aspects of popular culture are extremely short lived, and although they may make a major impact for a few years, they may decline and die as quickly as they arose. Also, there is a tendency for cults and popular religious movements to peak fairly quickly and then to dissolve. This is particularly the case with groups organized around the dynamic appeal of a single leader. Another factor limiting the life span of such organizations is the fact that the very emphasis on unusual ideas and consequently the appeal to a select group of people is inherently limiting. To the extent that such groups fail to realize for their members the promises of

the standard objections to, for example, parapsychological research.

By almost any criterion, transpersonal psychology is an improvement over the popularized and cultish versions of parapsychology, but whether it can solve the conceptual and empirical problems of the older version of parapsychology is uncertain. One reason for this if that although it is conceptually much more sophisticated, transpersonal psychology to some degree still rests on the same kind of parapsychological evidence as that about which there is so much debate. Until these shortcomings are removed, transpersonal psychology will probably fall short of its goal of scientific illumination of the essential characteristics of subjective experience. However, the debate between believer and disbeliever might be elevated by the emergence of new approaches.

Anomalistic Psychology

Regardless of the philosophical orientation one brings to the study of what we have called anomalistic experiences, it would seem that continued investigation, research, and analysis are clearly warranted. From a psychological point of view, much research is needed, particularly with regard to the nature and determinants of subjective experience and value-related behaviors. Considering only one aspect of the anomalous experience, the occult beliefs that often emerge in conjunction with them, there is considerable diversity of reasons for holding such beliefs and, consequently, several levels of analysis at which they may be examined. For example, occult beliefs vary in terms of origin, cognitive complexity, and the degree to which they are incompatible with scientific treatment of the same issue. There are differences associated with beliefs emerging from the cultures and philosophies of other societies as compared to those emanating from one's own culture. Some beliefs derive from personal and immediate experience whereas others are only verbally communicated, without additional experiential mediation. Some are idiosyncratic, whereas others are widely shared. The "superstitions" of childhood differ from the esoteric beliefs held later in life, despite their similarities. Care must be taken to distinguish the professional occultist from the avid amateur because of potential differences in motives and other personal factors. It is also possible that a given belief may result for different reasons in different persons, or even in the same person over time. For some, a given belief may have irrational and emotional origins, for others, it may simply reflect a desire for unique and exciting experiences, and yet for others, it may be a manifestation of some other, more central system of beliefs, such as anti-scientific attitudes. Such diversity underscores the need for more detailed specification regarding the types, origins, and motives underlying various paranormal beliefs.

By contrast with other areas of research, little is known about the relationship between brain functioning and subjective experience, in particular the relationship between states of consciousness and the varieties of subjective experience. The role of right and left hemisphere functioning would also seem worth pursuing in this regard. How often do unusual but quite natural perceptual abilities, such as hyperacuity, determine what appear to be anomalous effects? Less complex, but equally important would be the investigation of baseline rates for various kinds of allegedly paranormal experiences. How often, for example, do people experience what they take to be telepathy, UFOs, out-of-the-body states, and so on? Also, what kinds of people and what kinds of situations increase the probability of extraordinary happenings? For example, how often does telepathy appear to take place outside of parapsychological laboratories and among those previously opposed to parapsychological interpretations? To what extent does the human need for structure, purpose, and meaning influence judgments of randomly distributed events and how much of occultism can be attributed to the anxiety associated with social and value change?

Answers to these and many other related questions must be provided in order to generate a comprehensive theory of anomalistic experience. Unfortunately, two trends in American psychology and related disciplines make these questions difficult to research. These are the tendencies to avoid issues involving subjective, particularly meaningful experiences, and the tendency to focus on common, repetitive, and continuous aspects of behavior. Without such research, however, we will be left with only the various renderings of the occult ideology to explain the unusual and extraordinary events and processes in our lives, and to the extent that scientists ignore these questions, they help foster occult thinking.

In his thoughtful paper on the scientific and the transcendental world views, Jerome Frank (1977) concludes that these two disparate conceptualizations of life and the universe probably cannot be reconciled despite the fact that they share areas in common where the methods, assumptions, and terminology of both approaches seem to apply. However, he also concludes that perhaps the two world views can enrich each other, such as when scientific procedures are used to understand mystical experiences and when we look beyond strictly scientific conceptions of reality to ponder the meaning of life.

REFERENCES

Abell, G. O. Book review. *The Skeptical Inquirer*, Spring/Summer 1978, *2*(2), 84-90.

Achterberg, J., & Lawlis, G. F. *Imagery of cancer*. Chicago: Institute for Personality and Ability Testing, 1978.

Ader, R., & Cohen, N. Behaviorally conditioned immunosuppression. *Psychosomatic Medicine*, 1975, *37*, 333-340.

Adorno, T. W., Frenkel-Brunswik, E., Levinson, D. J., & Sanford, N. *The authoritarian personality*. New York: Harper, 1950.

Agricola, G. *De re metallica* (H. C. & L. H. Hoover, trans.). London: Mining Magazine, 1912. (Originally published, 1556).

Alberti, G. Psychopathology and parapsychology: Some possible contacts. In A. Angoff & B. Shapin (Eds.), *Parapsychology and the sciences*. New York: Parapsychology Foundation, 1974.

Alcock, J. E. Psychology and near-death experiences. *The Skeptical Inquirer*, Spring 1979, *3*(3), 25-41.

Alexander, F. G., & Selesnick, S. T. *The history of psychiatry*. New York: Harper & Row, 1966.

Allport, G. W. Attitudes. In C. Murchison (Ed.), *A handbook of social psychology*. Worcester, Mass.: Clark University Press, 1935.

Allport, G. W., & Pettigrew, T. F. Cultural influence on the perception of movement: The trapezoidal window illusion among Zulus. *Journal of Abnormal and Social Psychology*, 1957, *55*, 104-113.

Allport, G. W., & Postman, L. J. The basic psychology of rumor. *Transactions of the New York Academy of Science* (Series 2), 1945, *8*, 61-81.

Allport, G. W., Vernon, P. E., & Lindzey, G. *Study of values*. Boston: Houghton Mifflin, 1951.

Alvarez, L. W. Letter to the Editors. *Science*, June 18, 1965, *148*, 1541.

Anand, B. K., Chhina, G. S., & Singh, B. Some aspects of electroencephalographic studies in yogis. *Electroencephalography and Clinical Neurophysiology*, 1961, *13*, 452-456. (a)

Anand, B. K., Chhina, G. S., & Singh, B. Studies on Shri Ramanand Yogi during his stay in an air-tight box. *Indian Journal of Medical Research*, 1961, *49*(1), 82-89. (b)

André, E. Confirmation of PK action on electronic equipment. *Journal of Parapsychology*, 1972, *36*, 283-293.

Arehart-Treichel, J. The great pain plan. *Science News*, 1978, *114*(No. 16), 266-267.

Arieti, S., & Bemporad, J. R. Rare, unclassifiable, and collective psychotic syndromes. In S. Arieti & E. B. Brody (Eds.), *American handbook of psychiatry* (Vol. 3). New York: Basic Books, 1974.

Asch, S. E. *Social psychology*. Englewood Cliffs, N.J.: Prentice-Hall, 1952.

Aserinsky, E., & Kleitman, N. Regularly occurring periods of eye motility, and concomitant phenomena, during sleep. *Science*, 1953, *118*, 273-274.

Asimov, I. Asimov's corollary. *The Skeptical Inquirer*, Spring 1979, *3*(3), 58-67.

Averill, J. Personal control over aversive stimuli and its relationship to stress. *Psychological Bulletin*, 1973, *80*, 286-303.

Ayeroff, F., & Abelson, R. P. ESP and ESB: Belief in personal success at mental telepathy. *Journal of Personality and Social Psychology*, 1976, *34*, 240-247.

Bagchi, B., & Wenger, M. Electrophysiological correlates of some yogic exercises. *Electroencephalography and Clinical Neurophysiology*, 1957, *7*, 132-149.

Bailey, A. *A treatise on the seven rays* (Vol. 1) (2nd ed.). New York: Lucis, 1950.

Bailey, A. *The unfinished autobiography*. New York: Lucis, 1951.

Bailey, A. *A treatise on the seven rays* (Vol. 4). New York: Lucis, 1953.

Bainbridge, W. S. Biorhythms: Evaluating a pseudoscience. *The Skeptical Inquirer*, Spring/ Summer 1978, *2*(2), 40-56. (a)

Bainbridge, W. S. Chariots of the gullible. *The Skeptical Inquirer*, Winter 1978, *3*(2), 33-48. (b)

Balch, R. W., & Taylor, D. Seekers and saucers: The role of the cultic milieu in joining a UFO cult. In J. T. Richardson (Ed.), *Conversion careers: In and out of the new religions.* Beverly Hills, Cal.: Sage, 1977.

Bandura, A., & Walters, R. *Social learning and personality development.* New York: Holt, Rinehart & Winston, 1963.

Bannister, H., & Zangwill, O. L. Experimentally induced visual paramnesias. *British Journal of Psychology*, 1941, *32*, 30-51.

Barber, T. X. Hypnosis, suggestion, and psychosomatic phenomena: A new look from the standpoint of recent experimental studies. *Americal Journal of Clinical Hypnosis*, 1978, *21*, 13-27.

Barnett, B. Witchcraft, psychopathology, and hallucinations. *British Journal of Psychiatry*, 1965, *111*, 439-445.

Barth, J. R., & Bennett, J. T. Predicting human behavior. *Journal of Irreproducible Results*, June 20, 1973.

Bartlett, F. C. *Remembering.* Cambridge, Mass.: Cambridge University Press, 1932.

Bastedo, R. W. An empirical test of popular astrology. *The Skeptical Inquirer*, Fall 1978, *3*(1), 17-38.

Bateson, C. D. Rational processing or rationalization? The effect of disconfirmation on a stated religious belief. *Journal of Personality and Social Psychology*, 1976, *32*, 176-184.

Baudouin, C. *Suggestion and autosuggestion.* London: Allen & Unwin, 1920.

Behanan, K. T. *Yoga, a scientific evaluation.* New York: Dover, 1959.

Beloff, J. Historical overview. In B. B. Wolman (Ed.), *Handbook of parapsychology.* New York: Van Nostrand Reinhold, 1977.

Beloff, J. Why parapsychology is still on trial. *Human Nature*, 1978, *1*(12), 68-74.

Beloff, J., & Evans, L. A radioactivity test of psychokinesis. *Journal of the Society for Psychical Research*, 1961, *41*, 41-46.

Benassi, V. A., Sweeney, P. D., & Drevno, G. E. Mind over matter: Perceived success at psychokinesis. *Journal of Personality and Social Psychology*, 1979, *37*, 1377-1386.

Berkowitz, A. H. The effect of transcendental meditation on trait anxiety and self-esteem (Doctoral dissertation, University of Colorado, 1977). *Dissertation Abstracts International*, 1977, *38*(5-B), 2353-2354.

Bernstein, M. *The search for Bridey Murphy.* New York: Doubleday, 1956.

Besterman, T. The psychology of testimony in relation to paraphysical phenomena: Report of an experiment. *Proceedings of the Society for Psychial Research*, 1931-1932, *40*, 363-387.

Bevan, J. M. The relation of attitude to success in ESP scoring. *Journal of Parapsychology*, 1947, *11*, 296-309.

Bhadra, B. H. The relationship of test scores to belief in ESP. *Journal of Parapsychology*, 1966, *30*, 1-17.

Bharati, A. *The light at the center: Context and pretext of modern mysticism.* Santa Barbara, Cal.: Ross-Erikson, 1976.

Blackowski, S. The magical behavior of children in relation to school. *American Journal of Psychology*, 1937, *50*, 347-361.

Blatty, W. P. *The exorcist.* New York: Harper, 1971.

Bok, B. J. A critical look at astrology. *The Humanist*, September-October 1975, 6-9.

Bok, B. J. Jerome, L. E., & Kurtz, P. Objections to astrology. *The Humanist*, September-October 1975, 4-6.

Bok, B. J., & Mayall, M. W. Scientists look at astrology. *Scientific Monthly*, 1941, *52*, 233-244.

Bond, F. B. *The gate of remembrance*. Oxford: B. H. Blackwell, 1920.

Boshier, R. Conservatism and superstitious behavior. In C. Wilson (Ed.), *The psychology of conservatism*. New York: Academic Press, 1973.

Brehm, J. *A theory of psychological reactance*. New York: Academic Press, 1966.

Brent, P. Why the guru movement can't succeed here. *Human Nature*, 1979, *2*(2), 30-37.

Bridgman, P. W. Probability, logic, and ESP. *Science*, 1956, *123*, 15-17.

Broad, C. D. *Lectures on psychical research*. New York: Humanities Press, 1962.

Broadbent, D. E. *Perception and communication*. New York: Pergamon Press, 1958.

Brodie, B. B. Interaction of psychotropic drugs with physiological and biochemical mechanisms in the brain. *Modern Medicine*, 1958, *26*, 69-80.

Bromberg, W. *The mind of man: A history of psychotherapy and psychoanalysis*. New York: Lippincott, 1954.

Bronowsky, J. *Magic, science, and civilization*. New York: Columbia University Press, 1979.

Brosse, T. A psychophysiological study. *Main Currents in Modern Thought*, July 1946, 77-84.

Brosse, T. Contribution to the psychophysiological study of altruism. In P. Sorokin (Ed.), *Forms and techniques of altruistic and spirtual growth: A symposium*. Boston: Beacon Press, 1954.

Brown, G. B. A report on three experimental fire-walks by Ahmed Hussain and others. University of London Council for Psychical Investigation, Bulletin 4, 1938.

Brown, W. (Ed.), *Psychology and the science*. London: A. & C. Black, 1924.

Brownfield, A. C. *Isolation*. New York: Random House, 1965.

Bruner, J. S. & Goodman, C. C. Value and need as organizing factors in perception. *Journal of Abnormal and Social Psychology*, 1947, *42*, 33-44.

Bruner, J. S., Postman, L., & Rodrigues, J. Expectation and the perception of color. *American Journal of Psychology*, 1951, *64*, 216-227.

Bruner, J. S., & Potter, M. C. Interference in visual recognition. *Science*, 1964, *144*, 424-425.

Buchanan, J. R. *Manual of psychometry*. Boston: Author, 1885.

Bucke, R. *Cosmic consciousness* (19th ed.). New York: Dutton, 1959.

Buckhout, R. Eyewitness testimony. *Scientific American*, 1974, *231*(6), 23-31.

Burdick, D. S., & Kelley, E. F. Statistical methods in parapsychological research. In B. B. Wolman (Ed.), *Handbook of parapsychology*. New York: Van Nostrand Reinhold, 1977.

Burg, B. The puzzle of psyhic patients. *Human Behavior*, 1975, *4* (9), 24-39.

Burtt, H. E. An experimental study of early childhood memory: Final report. *Journal of Genetic Psychology*, 1941, *58*, 435-439.

Byrd, R. E. *Alone*. New York: Putnam's Sons, 1938.

Byrne, D. *The attraction paradigm*. New York: Academic Press, 1971.

Cabot, R. C. One hundred Christian Science cases. *McClure's Magazine*, August, 1908.

Caldwell, O. W., & Lundeen, C. E. Students' attitudes regarding unfounded beliefs. *Science Education*, 1931, *15*, 246-266.

Caldwell, O. W., & Lundeen, C. E. What can be done regarding unfounded beliefs? *School and Society*, 1932, *35*, 780-786.

Cannon, W. B. Voodoo death. *American Anthropologist*, 1942, *44*, 169-181.

Carrington, H. *The physical phenomena of spiritualism*. Boston: Small Maynard, 1908.

Carroll, L. *The annotated Alice*. Introduction and notes by Martin Gardner. New York: Clarkson N. Potter, 1960.

Casper, G. W. A further study of the relation of attitude to success in ESP scoring. *Journal of Parapsychology*, 1951, *15*, 178-184.

Cattell, R. B., Eber, H. W., & Tatsouka, H. M. *Handbook for the Sixteen Personality*

Factor Questionnaire (16PF). Champaign, Ill.: Institute for Personality and Ability Testing, 1970.

Cavendish, R. (Ed.). *Man, myth, and magic* (24 vols.). New York: Marshall Cavendish, 1970.

Chari, C. T. K. Recent research into Hélène Smith's "Hindoo cycle." In T. Flournoy, *From India to the planet Mars*. New Hyde Park, N.Y.: University Books, 1963.

Chari, C. T. K. The challenge of psi. *Journal of Parapsychology*, 1974, *38*, 1-15.

Chari, C. T. K. Reincarnation research: Method and interpretation. In M. Ebon (Ed.), *The Signet handbook of parapsychology*. New York: New American Library, 1978.

Chauvin, R., & Genthon, J. P. Eine Untersuchung über die Möglichkeit psychokinetischer Experimente mit Uranium und Geigerzähler. *Zeitschrift für Parapsychologie und Grenzgebiete der Psychologie*, 1965, *8*, 140-147.

Chaves, J. F., & Barber, T. X. Hypnotic procedures and surgery: A critical analysis with applications to "acupuncture analgesia." *American Journal of Clinical Hypnosis*, 1976, *18*, 217-236.

Chevreul, M. E. *De la baguette divinatoire, du pendule dit explorateur, et des tables tournantes, au point de vu de l'histoire, de la critique et de la méthode expérimentale*. Paris: Mallet-Bachelier, 1854.

Christopher, M. *Panorama of magic*. New York: Dover, 1962.

Christopher, M. *ESP, seers & psychics*. New York: Thomas Y. Crowell, 1970.

Clark, R. *Einstein. The life and times*. New York: World, 1971.

Clark, W. C., & Yang, J. C. Acupuncture analgesia? Evaluation by signal detection theory. *Science*, 1974, *184*, 1096-1097.

Clements, F. E. Primitive concepts of disease. *University of California Publications in American Archeology and Ethnology*, 1932, *2*, 185-252.

Coleman, J. *Abnormal psychology and modern life*. Glenview, Ill.: Scott, Foresman, 1972.

The Committee Para replies to Gauquelin. *The Humanist*, January-February 1976, 31-32. (a)

The Committee Para's reply to Gauquelin. *The Humanist*, May-June 1976, 32-33. (b)

Conklin, E. S. Superstitious beliefs and practices among college students. *American Journal of Psychology*, 1919, *30*, 83-102.

Converse, P. E. The nature of belief systems in mass publics. In D. Apter (Ed.), *Ideology and discontent*. New York: Free Press, 1964.

Coué, E. *My method, including American impressions*. Garden City, N.J.: Doubleday, Page, 1923.

Crowne, D., & Marlowe, D. *The approval motive*. New York: Wiley, 1964.

Crumbaugh, J. C. ESP and flying saucers: A challenge to parapsychologists. *American Psychologist*, 1959, *14*, 604-606.

Cunningham, R. J. From holiness to healing: The faith cure in America, 1872-1892. *Church History*, 1974, *43*, 499-513.

Cutten, G. B. *Speaking with tongues*. New Haven: Yale University Press, 1927.

Dahle, P. Experimentelle Untersuchungen über das "Gedankenlesen" des lettischen Mädchens Ilga K. *Zeitschrift für angewendte Psychologie und Charakterkunde*, 1940, *58*, 273-316.

Dakin, E. F. *Mrs. Eddy*. New York: Scribner's, 1930.

Darley, J. M., & Latane, B. Bystander intervention in emergencies: Diffusion of responsibility. *Journal of Personality and Social Psychology*, 1968, *8*, 377-383.

Dement, W. C. *Some must watch while some must sleep*. New York: Norton, 1976.

Deonna, W. *De la planète Mars en terre sainte*. Paris: E. de Boccard, 1932.

Deren, M. *Divine horsemen: The Voodoo gods of Haiti*. New York: Chelsea House, 1970.

Deutsch, A. Observations on a sidewalk ashram. *Archives of General Psychiatry*, 1975, *32*, 166-174.

Deutsch, M., & Gerard, H. B. A study of normative and informational influence upon individual judgment. *Journal of Abnormal and Social Psychology*, 1955, *51*, 629-636.

Diaconis, P. Letter to editor. *Science*, 1978, *202*, 1146. (a)

Diaconis, P. Statistical problems in ESP research. *Science*, 1978, *201*, 131-136. (b)

Dixon, N. F. *Subliminal perception: The nature of the controversy.* New York: McGraw-Hill, 1971.

Dohrman, H. T. *California cult.* Boston: Beacon Press, 1958.

Donahoe, J. J. Explaining mutual dreaming. *Psychic*, November-December 1975, 23-25.

Dresser, H. (Ed.) *The Quimby manuscripts* (2nd ed.). New York: Thomas Y. Crowell, 1921.

Dudycha, G. J. The superstitious beliefs of college students. *Journal of Abnormal and Social Psychology*, 1933, *19*, 503-520.

Duncker, K. The influence of past experience upon perceptual properties. *American Journal of Psychology*, 1939, *52*, 255-265.

Ebon, M. Telepathy and precognition in dreams. In M. Ebon (Ed.), *The Signet handbook of parapsychology.* New York: New American Library, 1978.

Eddy, M. B. *Science and health with a key to the scriptures.* Boston: Trustees of the Will of Mary Baker Eddy, 1934.

Edwards, M. *The dark side of history.* New York: Stein & Day, 1977.

Ehrenwald, J. *Telepathy and medical psychology.* New York: Norton, 1948.

Ehrenwald, J. Parapsychology and the healing arts. In B. B. Wolman (Ed.), *Handbook of parapsychology.* New York: Van Nostrand Reinhold, 1977. (a)

Ehrenwald, J. Psi phenomena and brain research. In B. B. Wolman (Ed.), *Handbook of parapsychology.* New York: Van Nostrand Reinhold, 1977. (b)

Eilbert, L., & Schmeidler, G. R. A study of certain psychological factors in relation to ESP performance. *Journal of Parapsychology*, 1950, *14*, 53-74.

Eisenbud, J. *Psi and psychoanalysis.* New York: Grune & Stratton, 1970.

Eisenbud, J. Paranormal photography. In B. B. Wolman (Ed.), *Handbook of parapsychology.* New York: Van Nostrand Reinhold, 1977.

Eisendrath, D. B. An amazing weekend with the amazing Ted Serios. Part 2. *Popular Photography*, October 1967, 85-89; 131-133; 136.

Ellenberger, H. F. *The discovery of the unconscious.* New York: Basic Books, 1970.

Ellis, A. Reanalysis of an alleged telepathic dream. In G. Devereux (Ed.), *Psychoanalysis and the occult.* New York: International Universities Press, 1970. (a)

Ellis, A. Telepathy and psychoanalysis: A critique of recent "findings." In G. Devereux (Ed.), *Psychoanalysis and the occult.* New York: International Universities Press, 1970. (b)

Ellis, A. J. *The divining rod.* Washington: Government Printing Office, 1957. (Originally published, 1917.)

Ellwood, R. S. *Religions and spiritual groups in modern America.* Englewood Cliffs, N.J.: Prentice-Hall, 1973.

Emme, E. E. Modification and origin of certain beliefs in superstition among 96 college students. *Journal of Psychology*, 1940, *10*, 279-291.

Engel, G. Sudden and rapid death during psychological stress: Folklore or folk medicine? *Annals of Internal Medicine*, 1971, *74*, 771-782.

Erdelyi, M. H., & Appelbaum, G. A. Cognitive masking: The disruptive effect of an emotional stimulus upon the perception of contiguous neutral items. *Bulletin of the Psychonomic Science*, 1973, *1*, 59-61.

Eriksen, C. W. Perceptual defense as a function of unacceptable needs. *Journal of Abnormal and Social Psychology*, 1951, *46*, 557-564. (a)

Eriksen, C. W. Some implications for TAT interpretation arising from need and perception experiments. *Journal of Personality*, 1951, *19*, 283-288. (b)

Eriksen, C. W. Psychological defenses and ego strength in the recall of completed and incompleted tasks. *Journal of Abnormal and Social Psychology*, 1954, *49*, 45-50.

Esdaile, J. Mesmerism in India. In D. N. Robinson (Ed.), *Significant contributions to the history of psychology 1750-1920* (Vol. 10). Washington, D.C.: University Publications of America, 1977. (Originally published, 1846.)

Evans, C. *Cults of unreason.* New York: Farrar, Straus, & Giroux, 1973.

Everson, T. C., & Cole, W. H. *Spontaneous regression in cancer.* Philadelphia: Saunders, 1966.

Faraday, M. Experimental investigation of table turning. *Atheneum*, July 1853. pp. 801-808.

Farnsworth, P. R. Aesthetic behavior and astrology. *Character and Personality*, 1937, *6*, 335-340.

Feigen, G. M. Bucky Fuller and the firewalk. *Saturday Review*, July 12, 1969.

Festinger, L. *A theory of cognitive dissonance.* New York: Harper & Row, 1957.

Festinger, L., Riecken, H. W., & Schachter, S. *When prophecy fails.* New York: Harper & Row, 1956.

Fiedler, L. The fascination of freaks. *Psychology Today*, August 1977, 56-82.

Field, M. J. *Search for security.* London: Faber, 1960.

Fields, H. L. Secrets of the placebo. *Psychology Today*, 1978, *12*(6), 172.

Fischer, R. A cartography of the ecstatic and meditative states. *Science*, 1971, *174*, 897-904.

Fischer, R. Cartography of inner space. In R. K. Siegel & L. J. West (Eds.), *Hallucinations.* New York: Wiley, 1975.

Fishbein, M., & Raven. B. H. The AB Scales: An operational definition of belief and attitude. *Human Relations*, 1962, *15*, 35-44.

Flournoy, T. *From India to the planet Mars.* New Hyde Park, N.Y.: University Books, 1963. (Originally published, 1900.)

Fodor, N. *Encyclopedia of psychic science.* London: Arthurs Press, 1933.

Forgus, R. H., & Melamed. L. E. *Perception* (2nd ed.). New York: McGraw-Hill, 1976.

Foulkes, D., Spear, P. S., & Symonds, J. D. Individual differences in mental activity at sleep onset. *Journal of Abnormal Psychology*, 1966, *71*, 280-286.

Frank, J. Superstitions and science teaching. *Social Science and Mathematics*, 1930, 277-282.

Frank, J. D. *Persuasion and healing.* Baltimore: Johns Hopkins Press, 1961.

Frank, J. D. Nature and function of belief systems. *American Psychologist*, 1977, *32*, 555-559.

Fraser, K. Science and the parascience cults. *Science News*, 1976, *109*, 346-349.

Fraser, K. Earthquakes and psychics. *The Skeptical Inquirer*, Spring 1979, *3*(3), 7-8.

Frazer, J. G. Magic and religion. In V. F. Calverton (Ed.), *The making of man: An outline of anthropology.* New York: Modern Library, 1931.

Freeman, J. M. Trial by fire. *Natural History*, 1974, *83* (1), 55-63.

Freud, S. *The interpretation of dreams.* London: Hogarth, 1953. (Originally published, 1900.)

Freud, S. *Collected works* (Vol. 6). London: Hogarth Press, 1960.

Fuller, J. G. *Arigó: Surgeon of the rusty knife.* New York: Thomas Y. Crowell, 1974.

Funderburk, J. *Science studies yoga: A review of physiological data.* Glenview, Ill.: Himalayan International Institute, 1977.

Gaither, D. M., Jr., & Zusne, L. Simulation of the telepathy experiment with Zener cards. *Behavior Research Methods and Instrumentation*, 1978, *10*, 78-80.

Gardner, M. *Fads and fallacies in the name of science.* New York: Dover, 1957.

Gardner, M. Dermo-optical perception: A peek down the nose. *Science*, 1966, *151*, 654-657.

Gardner, M. Concerning efforts to demonstrate extrasensory perception by machine. *Scientific American*, 1975, *233*(4), 114-118.

Gardner, M. Magic and paraphysics. *Technology Review*, June 1976, 42-51.

Garret, H. E., & Fisher, T. R. The prevalence of certain popular misconceptions. *Journal of Applied Psychology*, 1926, *10*, 411-420.

Gatlin, L. L. Meaningful information creation: An alternative interpretation of the psi phenomenon. *Journal of the American Society for Psychical Research*, 1977, *71*, 1-18.

Gauld, A. *The founders of psychical research*. London: Routledge & Kegan Paul, 1968.

Gauld, A. Discarnate survival. In B. B. Wolman (Ed.), *Handbook of parapsychology*. New York: Van Nostrand Reinhold, 1977.

Gauquelin, M. Die planetare Heredität. *Zeitschrift für Parapsychologie und Grenzgebiete der Psychologie*, 1962, *5*(2/3), 168-193.

Gauquelin, M. *The scientific basis of astrology*. New York: Stein & Day, 1970.

Gauquelin, M. The influence of planets on human beings: Facts versus fiction. *The Humanist*, January-February 1976, 29-31. (a)

Gauquelin, M. The influence of planets on human beings: Facts versus fiction. *The Humanist*, March-April 1976, 53. (b)

Gauquelin, M. Book review. *The Skeptical Inquirer*, Spring/Summer 1978, *2*(2), 118-128.

Gellhorn, E. The emotions and the ergotropic and trophotropic systems. *Psychologische Forschung*, 1970, *34*, 68-94.

Gettings, F. *Ghosts in photographs*. New York: Harmony Books, 1978.

Gibson, W. B., & Young, M. N. (Eds.) *Houdini on magic*. New York: Dover, 1953.

Gidro-Frank, L., & Bowersbuch, M. K. A study of the plantar response in hypnotic age regression. *Journal of Nervous and Mental Disease*, 1948, *107*, 443-458.

Gilliland, A. R. A study of the superstitions of college students. *Journal of Abnormal and Social Psychology*, 1930, *24*, 472-479.

Girden, E. A review of psychokinesis (PK). *Psychological Bulletin*, 1962, *59*, 353-388.

Gmelch, G. Baseball magic. *Human Nature*, 1978, *1*(8), 32-39.

Goldstein, L., Murphree, H., Sugerman, A., Pfeiffer, C., & Jenney, E. Quantitative electroencephalographic analysis of naturally occurring (schizophrenic) and drug-induced psychotic states in human males. *Clinical Pharmacology and Therepeutics*, 1963, *4*, 10-21.

Goodman, F. *Trance, healing, and hallucinations*. New York: Wiley, 1974.

Gordon, S. *Lonely in America*. New York: Simon & Schuster, 1976.

Gorer, G. *Exploring English character*. London: Cresset, 1955.

Gould, R. Superstitions among Scottish college girls. *Pedagogical Seminary*, 1921, *28*, 203-248.

Gould, S. The finagle factor. *Human Nature*, 1978, *1*(7), 80-87.

Graef, H. C. *The case of Therese Neumann*. Westminster, Md.: Newman Press, 1951.

Gralnick, A. Folie à deux—the psychosis of association: A review of 103 cases and the entire English literature, with case presentations. *Psychiatric Quarterly*, 1942, *14*, 230-263.

Greeley, A. M. *The sociology of the paranormal*. Sage Research Papers in the Social Sciences (Studies in Religion and Ethnicity Series, No. 90-023). Beverly Hills: Sage Publications, 1975.

Green, C. *Out-of-the-body experiences*. New York: Ballantine, 1968.

Green, E. E., Green, A., & Walter, E. D. *A demonstration of voluntary control of bleeding and pain*. Unpublished manuscript. Menninger Foundation, 1972.

Greenwald, A. G., & Sakamura, J. S. Attitude and selective learning: Where are the phenomena of yesteryear? *Journal of Personality and Social Psychology*, 1967, *7*, 387-397.

Gruenberger, F. A measure for crackpots. *Science*, 1964, *145*, 1413-1415.

Gurney, E., & Myers, F. W. H. Visible apparitions. *Nineteenth Century*, July 1884, *16*, 89-91.

Gurney, E., Myers, F. W. H., & Podmore, F. *Phantasms of the living* (2 vol.). London: Trübner, 1886.

Hacker, F. J. *Crusaders, criminals, crazies.* New York: Norton, 1976.

Hadfield, J. A. The influence of suggestion on body temperature. *The Lancet,* July 1920, *199,* 68.

Hansel, C. E. M. *ESP: A scientific evaluation.* New York: Scribner's, 1966.

Hansen, C. *Witchcraft at Salem.* New York: George Braziller, 1969.

Hansson, R. O., Jones, W. H., & Chernovetz, M. E. Contraceptive knowledge: Antecedents and implications. *Family Coordinator,* 1979, *28,* 20-34.

Harber, F. *Schizophrenia, obsession, exorcism, reincarnation, and mediums.* New York: Vantage, 1976.

Hardy, A., Harvie, R., & Koestler, A. *The challenge of chance.* New York: Vintage Books, 1975.

Hardyck, J., & Braden, H. Prophecy fails again: A report of a failure to replicate. *Journal of Abnormal and Social Psychology,* 1962, *65,* 136-141.

Harlow, H. F. The nature of love. *American Psychologist,* 1958, *13,* 673-685.

Harper, R. S. The perceptual modification of colored figures. *American Journal of Psychology,* 1953, *66,* 86-89.

Hartley, E. *Problems in prejudice.* New York: King's Crown, 1946.

Hastings, J. (Ed.) *Encyclopedia of religion and ethics* (Vol. 11). New York: Scribner's, 1922.

Hebb, D. O. The role of neurological ideas in psychology. *Journal of Personality,* 1951, *20,* 39-55.

Hechinger, N. Discovering human nature. *Human Nature,* 1979, *2*(1), 18-21.

Heider, F. Attitudes and cognitive organization. *Journal of Psychology,* 1946, *21,* 107-112.

Heider, F. *The psychology of interpersonal relations.* New York: Wiley, 1958.

Heron, W. The pathology of boredom. *Scientific American,* 1957, *196*(1), 52-56.

Hess, W. R. *The biology of mind.* Chicago: University of Chicago Press, 1964.

Heywood, R. *Beyond the reach of sense.* New York: Dutton, 1961.

Heywood, R. *The sixth sense.* London: Pan Books, 1971.

Hilgard, E. R. *Divided consciousness: Multiple controls in human thought and action.* New York: Wiley, 1977.

Hilgard, E. R., & Hilgard, J. R. *Hypnosis in the relief of pain.* Los Altos, Cal.: William Kaufmann, 1975.

Hoagland, H. Beings from outer space—corporeal and spiritual. *Science,* 1969, *163,* 3868.

Hodgson, R. Mr. Davey's imitations by conjuring of phenomena sometimes attributed to spirit agency. *Proceedings of the Society for Psychical Research,* 1892, *8,* 253-310.

Hodgson, R., & Davey, S. J. The possibilities of mal-observation and lapses of memory from a practical point of view. *Proceedings of the Society for Psychical Research,* 1886-1887, *4,* 381-495.

Hodson, G. *The seven human temperaments* (3rd ed.). Adyar, Madras: Theosophical Publishing House, 1956.

Holzman, P. S., & Klein, G. S. Cognitive system-principles of leveling and sharpening: Individual differences in assimilation effects in visual time-error. *Journal of Psychology,* 1954, *37,* 105-122.

Honorton, C., & Barksdale, W. PK performance with waking suggestions for muscle tension versus relaxation. *Journal of the American Society for Psychical Research,* 1972, *66,* 208-214.

Hopewell-Ash, E. L. *Faith and suggestion.* London: Herbert & Daniel, 1912.

Horowitz, M. J. Hallucinations: An information-processing approach. In R. K. Siegel & L. J. West (Eds.), *Hallucinations.* New York: Wiley, 1975.

Horton, L. H. The illusion of levitation. *Journal of Abnormal Psychology,* 1918-19, *13,* 42-53.

Houdini, H. *A magician among the spirits.* New York: Harper & Brothers, 1924.

Houriet, R. *Getting back together*. New York: Coward, McCann & Geoghegan, 1971.

Humphrey, N. The origins of human intelligence. *Human Nature*, 1978, *1*(12), 42-47.

Hunt, J. M. *Personality and the behavior disorders*. New York: Ronald, 1944.

Huxley, A. *The devils of Loudun*. New York:Harper & Row, 1952.

Hyman, H. *Political socialization: A study of the psychology of political behavior*. New York: Free Press, 1969.

Hyman, R. Book review. *The Zetetic*, Fall/Winter 1976, *1*(1), 73-80.

Hyman, R. "Cold reading:" How to convince strangers that you know all about them. *The Zetetic*, Spring/Summer 1977, *1*(2), 18-37.

Hyman, R. Book review. *The Skeptical Inquirer*, Summer 1979, *3*(4), 51-58.

Hyman, R., & Vogt, E. Z. Water witching: Magic rituals in contemporary United States. *Psychology Today*, 1967, *1*(1), 34-42.

Indian fire-walk. *The Lancet*, 1935, *229*, 750.

Ivanov, A. Soviet experiments in "eye-less vision." *International Journal of Parapsychology*, 1964, *6*, 5-23.

Jahoda, G. *The psychology of superstition*. London: Allen Lane, 1969.

Jahoda, G. Supernatural beliefs and changing cognitive structures among Ghanian university students. *Journal of Cross-Cultural Psychology*, 1970, *1*, 115-130.

James, W. Report on Mrs. Piper's Hodgson-control. *Proceedings of the Society for Psychical Research*, 1909, *23*, 2-121.

James, W. *The principles of psychology* (Vol. 1). New York: Dover, 1950. (Originally published, 1890.)

James, W. What psychical research has accomplished. In G. Murphy & R. O. Ballou (Eds.), *William James on psychical research*. New York: Viking Press, 1960. (Reprinted from W. James, *The will to believe and other essays*, 1897).

James, W. The final impressions of a psychical researcher. In G. Murphy & R. O. Ballou (Eds.), *William James on psychical research*. New York: Viking Press, 1960. (Reprinted from *The American Magazine*, October 1909.)

James, W. *Pragmatism*. Cambridge, Mass.: Harvard University Press, 1978. (Originally published, 1907).

Janet, P. *L'automatisme psychologique*. Paris: Felix Alcan, 1889.

Janet, P. *Psychological healing: A historical and clinical survey*. London: Allen & Unwin, 1925.

Jastrow, J. *Error and eccentricity in human belief*. New York: Dover, 1962. (Originally published, 1935.)

Jaynes, J. *The origin of consciousness in the breakdown of the bicameral mind*. Boston: Houghton Mifflin, 1976.

Jennings, M., & Niemi, R. The transmission of political values from parent to child. *American Political Science Review*, 1968, *62*, 169-184.

Jerome, L. E. Astrology: Magic or science? *The Humanist*, September-October 1975, 10-16.

Jerome, L. E. Planetary 'influence' versus mathematical realities. *The Humanist*, January-February 1976, 52-53.

Jerome, L. E. *Astrology disproved*. New York: Prometheus, 1977.

Johnson, K. *Photographing the nonmaterial world*. New York: Hawthorn, 1975.

Jones, W. H., & Rambo, W. W. Information and the level of constraint in a system of social attitudes. *Experimental Study of Politics*, 1973, *2*, 25-38.

Jones, W. H., Rambo, W. W., & Russell, D. W. The effect of prior information on attitude change. *Journal of Social Psychology*, 1978, *106*, 203-205.

Jones, W. H. & Russell, D. W. The selective processing of belief disconfirming information. *European Journal of Social Psychology*, 1980, *6*, 83–88.

Jones, W. H., Russell, D. W., & Nickel, T. W. *Personality and behavioral correlates of superstitious beliefs.* Paper presented at the meeting of the Midwestern Psychological Association, Chicago, 1976.

Jones, W. H., Russell, D. W., & Nickel, T. W. Belief in the paranormal scale: An objective instrument to measure belief in magical phenomena and causes. *JSAS Catalog of Selected Documents in Psychology*, 1977, *7*, 100. (Ms. No. 1577)

Jung, C. G. The psychological foundation of belief in spirits. *Proceedings of the Society for Psychical Research*, Part 79, May 1910.

Jung, C. G. *Collected works* (Vol. 5) (Eds. H. Read, M. Fordham, & G. Adler). London: Kegan Paul, 1956.

Jung, C. G. On the psychology and pathology of so-called occult phenomena. In *The Collected Works* (Vol. 1) (Eds. H. Read, M. Fordham, & G. Adler). New York: Pantheon, 1957.

Jung, C. G. *Flying saucers*. New York: Harcourt, Brace, 1959.

Jung, C. G. *Synchronicity: An acausal connecting principle*. Princeton, N.J.: Princeton University Press, 1973.

Kahn, S. D. Studies in extrasensory perception: Experiments utilizing an electronic scoring device. *Proceedings of the American Society for Psychical Research*, 1952, *25*, 1-49.

Kammerer, P. *Das Gesetz der Serie*. Stuttgart-Berlin: Deutsche Verlangsanstalt, 1919.

Kant, I. *Dreams of a spirit-seer*. London: S. Sonnenschein, 1900. (Authorized xerographic reprint, University Microfilms, Ann Arbor, Michigan, 1969.) (Originally published, 1766.)

Kanter, R. *Commitment and community: Communes and utopias in sociological perspective.* Cambridge, Mass.: Harvard University Press, 1972.

Kantor, J. R. *The scientific evolution of psychology* (2 vols.). Chicago: Principia Press, 1963.

Kasamatsu, A., & Hirai, T. The electroencephalographic study on the Zen meditation (Zazen). *Folia Psychiatrica et Neurologica Japonica*, 1966, *20*, 315-336.

Katz, D. The functional approach to the study of attitudes. *Public Opinion Quarterly*, 1960, *24*, 163-204.

Kauffman S. Metabolic stability and epigenesis in randomly constructed genetic nets. *Journal of Theoretical Biology*, 1969, *22*, 437-467.

Keefe, F. J. Biofeedback vs. instructional control of skin temperature. *Journal of Behavioral Medicine*, 1978, *1*(3).

Keightley, D. Space travel in bronze age China? *The Skeptical Inquirer*, Winter 1978, *3*(2), 58-63.

Kelly, E. F., & Kanthamani, B. K. A subject's efforts toward voluntary control. *Journal of Parapsychology*, 1972, *36*, 185-197.

Kelly, G. A. *The psychology of personal contructs*. New York: Norton, 1955.

Kendall, M. G., & Smith, B. B. *Tables of random sampling numbers*, Tracts for Computers XXIV. London: Cambridge University Press, 1939.

Kennedy, J. L. Changes in attitude toward telepathy and clairvoyance during a 25-year period. *Psychological Bulletin*, 1939, *36*, 649-650. (a)

Kennedy, J. L. A methodological review of extrasensory perception. *Psychological Bulletin*, 1939, *36*, 59-103. (b)

Kennedy, J. L., & Uphoff, H. F. Experiments on the nature of extra-sensory perception: 3. The recording error criticism of extra-chance scores. *Journal of Parapsychology*, 1939, *3*, 226-245.

Kiesler, C. *The psychology of commitment: Experiments linking behavior to belief.* New York: Academic Press, 1971.

Kiev, A. *Magic, faith, and healing*. New York: Free Press, 1974.

Killen, P., Wildman, R. W., & Wildman, R. W., II. Superstitiousness and intelligence. *Psychological Reports*, 1974, *34*, 1158.

Kisker, G. W. *The disorganized personality*. New York: McGraw-Hill, 1972.

Klass, P. *UFOs explained*. New York: Random House, 1974.

Klass, P. Book review. *The Zetetic*, Fall/Winter 1977, *2*(1), 97-102.

Klass, P. NASA, the White House, and UFOs. *The Skeptical Inquirer*, Winter 1978, *2*(2), 72-81.

Klass, P. The conversion of J. Allen Hynek. *The Skeptical Inquirer*, Spring 1979, *3*(3), 49-57.

Klein, D. B. *The unconscious: Invention or discovery?* Santa Monica, Cal.: Goodyear, 1977.

Kline, M. V. Hypnosis and age progression: A case report. *Journal of Genetic Psychology*, 1951, *78*, 195-206.

Kline, M. V. Hypnotic retrogression: A neuropsychological theory of age regression and progression. *Journal of Clinical and Experimental Hypnosis*, 1953, *1*, 21-28.

Kline, M. V. (Ed.) *A scientific report on the search for Bridey Murphy*. New York: Julian Press, 1956.

Kmetz, J. Plant primary perception: The other side of the leaf. *The Skeptical Inquirer*, Spring/Summer 1978, *2*(2), 57-61.

Knox, V. J., Crutchfield, L., & Hilgard, E. R. The nature of task interference in hypnotic dissociation: An investigation of hypnotic behavior. *International Journal of Clinical and Experimental Hypnosis*, 1975, *23*, 305-323.

Koestler, A. *The roots of coincidence*. London: Hutchinson, 1972.

Krafft, K. E. *Traité d'astrobiologie*. Paris: A. Legrand, 1939.

Krech, D., Crutchfield, R. S., & Ballachey, E. *Individual in society*. New York: McGraw-Hill, 1962.

Krippner, S., & Greene, G. *Transpersonal experiences and psi phenomena*. Paper presented at the meeting of the American Psychological Association, Toronto, 1978.

Krippner, S., & Villoldo, A. *The realms of healing*. Millbrae, Cal.: Celestial Arts, 1976.

Krishna, G. *Kundalini, the evolutionary energy in man*. Berkeley, Cal.: Shambala, 1971.

Kubler-Ross, E. *On death and dying*. New York: Macmillan, 1968.

Kuhlman, K. *I believe in miracles*. Englewood Cliffs, N.J.: Prentice-Hall, 1962.

Kupper, H. I. Psychic concomitants in wartime injuries. *Psychosomatic Medicine*, 1945, *7*, 15-21.

Kurtz, P. The aims of the Committee for the Scientific Investigation of Claims of the Paranormal. *The Zetetic*, Fall/Winter 1976, *1*(1), 6-7.

Kurtz, P. Is parapsychology a science? *The Skeptical Inquirer*, Winter 1978, *3*(2), 14-32.

Kusche, L. *The Bermuda triangle mystery solved*. New York: Warner, 1975.

Kusche, L. Critical reading, careful writing, and the Bermuda triangle. *The Zetetic*, Fall/Winter 1977, *2*(1), 36-40.

Langer, E. J. The illusion of control. *Journal of Personality and Social Psychology*, 1975, *32*, 311-328.

Latane, B., & Darley, J. M. Group inhibition of bystander intervention in emergencies. *Journal of Personality and Social Psychology*, 1968, *10*, 215-221.

Lawson, A. *Hypnosis of imaginary UFO "abductees."* Paper presented at the meeting of the American Psychological Association, Toronto, 1978.

Layton, B. D., & Turnbull, B. Belief, evaluation, and performance on an ESP task. *Journal of Experimental Social Psychology*, 1975, *11*, 166-179.

Lehman, H. C., & Fenton, N. The prevalance of certain misconceptions and superstitions among college students before and after a course in psychology. *Education*, 1929, *50*, 485-494.

Lerner, M., & Simmons, C. Observer's reaction to the "innocent victim:" Compassion or rejection? *Journal of Personality and Social Psychology*, 1966, *4*, 302-310.

LeShan, L. *The medium, the mystic, and the physicist*. New York: Viking Press, 1974.

Levine, R., Chein, I., & Murphy, G. The relation of intensity of a need to the amount of perceptual distortion. *Journal of Psychology*, 1942, *13*, 283-293.

Levinson, B. W. States of awareness during general anesthesia. In J. Lassner (Ed.), *Hypnosis and psychosomatic medicine*. New York: Springer Verlag, 1967.

Levitt. E. E. Superstitions: Twenty-five years ago and today. *American Journal of Psychology*, 1952, *65*, 443-449.

Lifton, R. *Thought reform and the psychology of totalism: A study of "brainwashing" in China*. New York: Norton, 1963.

Lindner, R. *The fifty-minute hour*. New York: Holt, Rinehart & Winston, 1955.

Littig, L. Affiliation motivation and belief in extraterrestrial UFOs. *Journal of Social Psychology*, 1971, *83*, 307-308.

Litvag, I. *Singer in the shadows: The strange case of Patience Worth*. New York: Macmillan, 1972.

Lofland, J. "Becoming a world-saver" revisited. In J. T. Richardson (Ed.), *Conversion careers: In and out of the new religions*. Beverly Hills, Cal.: Sage, 1977.

Lofland, J., & Stark, R. Becoming a world saver: A theory of conversion to a deviant perspective. *American Sociological Review*, 1965, 862-875.

Long, J. K. (Ed.) *Extrasensory ecology: Parapsychology and anthropology*. Metuchen, N.J.: Scarecrow Press, 1977.

Lord, E. The impact of education on non-scientific beliefs in Ethiopia. *Journal of Social Psychology*, 1958, *47*, 339-353.

Lundeen, G. E., & Caldwell, O. W. A study of unfounded beliefs among high school seniors and college students. *Journal of Educational Research*, 1930, *22*, 257-273.

Luthe, W. (Ed.) *Autogenic therapy* (6 vols.). New York: Grune & Stratton, 1969-1973.

Lynch, F. R. Toward a theory of conversion and commitment to the occult. In J. T. Richardson (Ed.), *Conversion careers: In and out of the new religions*. Beverly Hills, Cal.: Sage, 1977.

MacHovec, F. J., & Man, S. C. Acupuncture and hypnosis compared: Fifty-eight cases. *American Journal of Clinical Hypnosis*, 1978, *21*, 45-47.

Makous, W. L. Cutaneous color sensitivity: Explanation and demonstration. *Psychological Review*, 1966, *73*, 280-294.

Malinowski, B. *Magic, science, and religion*. Garden City, N.Y.: Doubleday, 1954.

Maller, J. B., & Lundeen, C. E. Sources of superstitious beliefs. *Journal of Educational Research*, 1932, *26*, 321-343.

Maller, J. B., & Lundeen, C. E. Superstition and emotional maladjustment. *Journal of Educational Research*, 1933, *27*, 592-617.

Marks, D., & Kamman, D. The non-psychic powers of Uri Geller. *The Zetetic*, Spring/ Summer 1977, *1*(2), 9-17.

Markwick, B. The Soal-Goldney experiments with Basil Shackleton: New evidence of data manipulation. *Proceedings of the Society for Psychical Research*, 1978, *56*, 250-278.

Marty, M. The occult establishment. *Social Research*, 1970, *37*, 212-230.

Maslach, C., Marshall, G., & Zimbardo, P. G. Hypnotic control of peripheral skin temperature: A case report. *Psychophysiology*, 1972, *2*, 600-605.

McBurney, D. H. ESP in the psychology curriculum. *Teaching of Psychology*, 1976, *3*, 66-69.

McConnell, J. V., Cutler, R. L., & McNeill, E. B. Subliminal stimulation: An overview. *American Psychologist*, 1958, *13*, 229-242.

McConnell, R. A. ESP and credibility in science. *American Psychologist*, 1969, *24*, 531-538.

McConnell, R. A. ESP and the credibility of critics. *Perceptual and Motor Skills*, 1978, *47*, 875-878.

McGervey, J. D. A statistical test of sun-sign astrology. *The Zetetic*, Spring/Summer 1977, *1*(2), 49-54.

McGinnies, E. Emotionality and perceptual defense. *Psychological Review*, 1949, *56*, 244-251.

McGuire, W. J. The nature of attitudes and attitude change. In C. Lindzey & E. Aronson (Eds.), *The handbook of social psychology* (Vol. 3). Reading, Mass.: Addison-Wesley, 1969.

McKellar, P. *Imagination and thinking*. London: Cohen & West, 1957.

McKellar, P. Imagery from the standpoint of introspection. In P. W. Sheehan (Ed.), *The function and nature of imagery*. New York: Academic Press, 1972.

Medhurst, R. G. (Ed.) *Crookes and the spirit world*. New York: Taplinger, 1972.

Meehl, P. E., & Scriven, M. Compatibility of science and ESP. *Science*, 1956, *123*, 14-15.

Melzack, R. The perception of pain. *Scientific American*, 1961, *204*(2), 41-49.

Melzack, R. How acupuncture works. *Psychology Today*, June 1971, 28-38.

Melzack, R., & Wall, P. D. Pain mechanisms: A new theory. *Science*, 1965, *150*, 971-979.

Merrien, J. *The lonely voyagers*. New York: Putnam's, 1954.

Messerschmidt, R. A quantitative investigation of the alleged independent operation of conscious and subconscious processes. *Journal of Abnormal and Social Psychology*, 1927-28, *22*, 325-340.

Meth, J. M. Exotic psychiatric syndromes. In S. Arieti & E. E. Brody (Eds.), *American handbook of psychiatry* (Vol. 3). New York: Basic Books, 1974.

Meyer, D. *The positive thinkers*. New York: Doubleday, 1965.

Milgram, S. Behavioral study of obedience. *Journal of Abnormal and Social Psychology*, 1963, *67*, 371-378.

Moberly, C. A. E., & Jourdain, E. F. *An adventure* (5th ed.). London: Feber & Feber, 1955.

Monod, H. *Chance and necessity*. New York: Vintage Books, 1972.

Moody, R. A., Jr. *Life after life*. New York: Bantam Books, 1975.

Moody, R. L. Bodily changes during abreaction. *The Lancet*, 1948, *254*, 964.

Moore, R. L. *In search of white crows*. New York: Oxford University Press, 1977.

Morris, R. L. Parapsychology, biology, and ANPSI. In B. B. Wolman (Ed.), *Handbook of parapsychology*. New York: Van Nostrand Reinhold, 1977.

Morrison, P. Uri Geller: International Pied Piper of the credulous, and other matters. *Scientific American*, 1976, *234*(2), 134-135.

Moss, L. *Acupuncture and you*. Secaucus, N.J.: Citadel Press, 1964.

Moss, S., & Butler, D. C. Comments on McConnell's paper. *Perceptual and Motor Skills*, 1978, *47*, 992. (a)

Moss, S., & Butler, D. C. The scientific credibility of ESP. *Perceptual and Motor Skills*, 1978, *46*, 1063-1079. (b)

Moss, T., & Gengerelli, J. A. ESP effects generated by affective states. *Journal of Parapsychology*, 1968, *32*, 92-100.

Mühl, A. M. *Automatic writing*. Dresden and Leipzig: Theodor Steinkopf, 1930.

Müller, M. (Ed.) *The sacred books of the East* (Vol. 43). Oxford: Clarendon Press, 1897.

Münsterberg, H. *On the witness stand*. New York: Doubleday, Page, 1915.

Murphy, G., & Ballou, R. O. (Eds.) *William James on psychical research*. New York: Viking Press, 1960.

Murray, H. A. Some basic psychological assumptions and conceptions. *Dialectica*, 1951, 266-292.

Myers, F. W. H. *Human personality and its survival of bodily death* (2 vols.). London: Longmans, Green, 1903.

Naranjo, C., & Ornstein, R. E. *On the psychology of meditation*. New York: Viking, 1971.

Neureiter, F., von. *Wissen um fremdes Wissen auf unbekanntem Wege erworben*. Gotha: Verlag Leopold Klotz, 1935.

Newbrough, J. B. *Oahspe* (12th ed.). Montrose, Colorado: Essenes of Kosmon, 1950.

Nicol, J. F. The statistical controversy in quantitative research. *International Journal of Parapsychology*, 1959, *1*(1), 56-61.

Nicol, J. F. Historical background. In B. B. Wolman (Ed.), *Handbook of parapsychology*. New York: Van Nostrand Reinhold, 1977.

Nixon, H. K. Popular answers to some psychological questions. *American Journal of Psychology*, 1925, *36*, 418-423.

Nolen, W. A. *Healing: A doctor in search of a miracle*. Greenwich, Conn.: Fawcett, 1975.

Oberg, J. Astronaut "UFO" sightings. *The Skeptical Inquirer*, Fall 1978, *3*(1), 39-46. (a)

Oberg, J. Tunguska echoes. *The Skeptical Inquirer*, Winter 1978, *3*(2), 49-57. (b)

Oberg, J., & Sheaffer, R. Pseudoscience at *Science Digest*. *The Skeptical Inquirer*, Fall/Winter 1977, *2*(1), 41-44.

Okeima, T., Kogu, E., Ikeda, K., & Sugiyama, H. The EEG of yoga and Zen practitioners. *Electroencephalography and Clinical Neurophysiology*, 1957, *9*, 51.

Oleski, J. M., & Munz, D. C. *Inside vs. outside perspective in psychology: Measurement of psychological metatheory*. Paper presented at the meeting of the Midwestern Psychological Association, Chicago, 1978.

Omohundro, J. Von Däniken's chariots: A primer in the art of a cooked science. *The Skeptical Inquirer*, Fall/Winter 1976, *1*(1), 58-68.

Orne, M. T. The nature of hypnosis: Artifact and essence. *Journal of Abnormal and Social Psychology*, 1959, *58*, 277-299.

Ornstein, R. E. *The psychology of consciousness*. San Francisco: Freeman, 1972.

Ornstein, R. E. *The nature of human consciousness*. San Francisco: Freeman, 1973.

Osis, K. Channel characteristics of ESP. *Proceedings of the Third International Conference on Computer Communication*, August 1976, 25-27.

Osis, K., & Haraldsson, E. *At the hour of death*. New York: Avon, 1977.

Osgood, C. E., & Tannenbaum, P. H. The principle of congruity in the prediction of attitude change. *Psychological Review*, 1955, *62*, 42-55.

Oskamp, S. *Attitudes and opinions*. Englewood Cliffs, N.J.: Prentice-Hall, 1977.

Otis, L. Selective exposure to the film Close Encounters. *Journal of Psychology*, 1979, *101*, 293-295.

Owen, I. M., & Sparrow, M. *Conjuring up Philip*. New York: Harper & Row, 1976.

Padgett, V. *Astrology and economic threat*. Paper presented at the Western Psychological Association meeting, San Francisco, 1978.

Page, J. D. *Psychopathology: The science of understanding deviance*. Chicago: Aldine, 1975.

Palmer, J. A. Attitudes and personality traits in experimental ESP research. In B. B. Wolman (Ed.), *Handbook of parapsychology*. New York: Van Nostrand Reinhold, 1977.

Palmer, J. A. The out-of-the-body experience: A psychological theory. *Parapsychology Review*, 1978, *9*, 19-22.

Panati, C. (Ed.) *The Geller papers*. Boston: Houghton Mifflin, 1976.

Patanjali. *The Yoga-Sutras of Patanjali* (M. N. Dvivedi, trans.). Adyar, Madras: Theosophical Publishing House, 1947.

Pavlov, I. P. Les sentiments d'emprise et la ultraparadoxical phase. *Journal de Psychologie*, 1933, *30*, No. 9-10.

Pavlov, I. P. *Lectures on conditioned reflexes* (Vol. 2). Conditioned reflexes and psychiatry (W. Horsley Gantt, ed. and trans.). New York: International Publishers, 1941.

Pehek, J. O., Kyler, H., & Faust, D. Image modulation in corona discharge photography. *Science*, 1976, *194*, 263-270.

Pelletier, K. R. Neurological, psychophysiological, and clinical differentiation of the alpha and theta altered states of consciousness (Doctoral dissertation, University of California, Berkeley, 1974). *Dissertation Abstracts International*, 1974, *35*, 520-B.

Pfungst, O. *Clever Hans (the horse of Mr. von Osten): A contribution to experimental, animal, and human psychology* (C. L. Rahn, trans.). New York: Holt, 1911.

Piaget, J. *The child's conception of the world.* New York: Harcourt, Brace, 1929.

Piaget, J. *The child's conception of physical causality.* London: Kegan Paul, 1930.

Polzella, D., Popp, R., & Hinsman, M. *ESP?* Paper presented at the meeting of the American Psychological Association, Chicago, 1975.

Postman, L., Bruner, J. S., & McGinnies, E. Personal values as selective factors in perception. *Journal of Abnormal and Social Psychology*, 1948, *43*, 142-154.

Powell, A. E. *The etheric double.* London: Theosophical Publishing House, 1925.

Powell, L. P. *Mary Baker Eddy.* New York: Macmillan, 1930.

Pratt, J. G. The meaning of performance curves in ESP and PK test data. *Journal of Parapsychology*, 1949, *13*, 9-22.

Pratt, J. G. A decade of research with a selected ESP subject: An overview and reappraisal of the work with Pavel Stepanek. *Proceedings of the American Society for Psychical Research*, 1973, *30*, 1-78.

Prat, J. G., Rhine, J. B., Smith, B. M., Stuart, C. E., & Greenwood, J. A. *Extrasensory perception after 60 years.* New York: Holt, 1940.

Pratt, J. G. & Woodruff, J. L. Size of stimulus symbols in extrasensory perception. *Journal of Parapsychology*, 1939, *3*, 121-158.

Preuss, P. Does Don Juan live on campus? *Human Behavior*, 1978, *7*(11), 52-61.

Price, G. R. Science and the supernatural. *Science*, 1955, *122*, 359-367.

Price, G. R. Where is the definitive experiment? *Science*, 1956, *123*, 17-18.

Price, H. *A report on two experimental fire-walks.* University of London Council for Psychical Investigation, Bulletin 2, 1936.

Prince, M. Experiments to determine co-conscious (subconscious) ideation. *Journal of Abnormal Psychology*, 1909, *3*, 33-42.

Prince, M. *The unconscious.* New York: Macmillan, 1914.

Prince, R. (Ed.) *Trance and possession states.* Montreal: R. M. Bucke Memorial Society, 1968.

Puthoff, H. E., & Targ, R. Letter to editor. *Science*, 1978, *202*, 1145-1146.

Ralya L. F. Some surprising beliefs concerning human nature among pre-medical psychology students. *British Journal of Educational Psychology*, 1945, *15*, 70-75.

Randall, J. L. Psi phenomena and biological theory. *Journal of the Society for Psychical Research*, 1971, *46*, 151-165.

Randi, J. *The magic of Uri Geller.* New York: Ballantine Books, 1975.

Randi, J. "Levitation" for fun and profit. *The Zetetic*, Fall/Winter 1977, *2*(1), 7-9.

Randi, J. Tests and investigations of three psychics. *The Skeptical Inquirer*, Spring/Summer 1978, *2*(2), 25-39. (a)

Randi, J. The "psychic" and the museum. *The Skeptical Inquirer*, Spring/Summer 1978, *2*(2), 15-16. (b)

Randi, J. Examination of the claims of Suzie Cottrell. *The Skeptical Inquirer*, Spring 1979, *3*(3), 16-21.

Rao, K. R. Consideration of some theories in parapsychology. *Journal of Parapsychology*, 1961, *25*, 32-54.

Rappoport, L. *Personality development.* Glenview, Ill.: Scott, Foresman, 1972.

Raudive, K. *Breakthrough.* New York: Taplinger, 1971.

Raven, B. H., Anthony, E., & Mansson, H. H. Group norms and dissonance reduction in belief, behavior, and judgment (Tech. Rep. No. 4, Nonr. 233(547)). University of California, Los Angeles, 1960.

Raven, B. H., Mansson, H. H., & Anthony, E. The effect of attributed ability upon expert and referent influence (Tech. Rep. No. 10, Nonr. 233(547)). University of California, Los Angeles, 1962.

Rawcliffe, D. H. *Illusions and delusions of the supernatural and the occult.* New York: Dover, 1959.

Rawlins, D. What they aren't telling you: Suppressed secrets of the psychic world, astrological universe, and Jeanne Dixon. *The Zetetic,* Fall/Winter 1977, *2*(1), 62-83.

Reed, G. *The psychology of anomalous experience.* London: Hutchinson University Library. 1972.

Rehder, H. Wunderheilungen, ein Experiment. *Hippokrates,* 1955, *26,* 577-580.

Reiff, G., & Scheerer, M. *Memory and hypnotic age regression.* New York: International Universities Press, 1959.

Reyna, R. *Reincarnation and science.* New Delhi: Sterling, 1973.

Reynolds, C. An amazing weekend with the amazing Ted Serios. Part 1. *Popular Photography,* October 1967, 81-83; 136-140; 158.

Rhine, J. B. *Extrasensory perception.* Boston: Bruce Humphries, 1934.

Rhine J. B. Comments on "Science and the supernatural." *Science,* 1956, *123,* 11-14. (a)

Rhine, J. B. The experiment should fit the hypothesis. *Science,* 1956, *123,* 19. (b)

Rhine, J. B. Why national defense overlooks parapsychology. *Journal of Parapsychology,* 1957, *21,* 245-258.

Rhine, J. B. A new case of experimenter unreliability. *Journal of Parapsychology,* 1974, *38,* 218-225. (a)

Rhine, J. B. Telepathy and other untestable hypotheses. *Journal of Parapsychology,* 1974, *38,* 137-153. (b)

Rhine, J. B. Psi methods re-examined. *Journal of Parapsychology,* 1975, *39,* 38-58. (a)

Rhine, J. B. Second report on a case of experimental fraud. *Journal of Parapsychology,* 1975 *39,* 323-324. (b)

Rhine, J. B. History of experimental studies. In B. B. Wolman (Ed.), *Handbook of parapsychology.* New York: Van Nostrand Reinhold, 1977.

Rhine, J. B., & Pratt, J. G. A review of the Pearce-Pratt distance series of ESP tests. *Journal of Parapsychology,* 1954, *18,* 165-177.

Rhine, J. B., & Pratt, J. G. *Parapsychology: Frontier science of the mind.* Springfield, Ill.: Charles C. Thomas, 1957.

Rhine, J. B., & Rhine, L. A. A search for the nature of the mind. In T. S. Krawiec (Ed.), *The psychologists* (Vol. 3). Brandon, Vt.: Clinical Psychology, 1978.

Rice, W. A. A "surgeon's" magic touch that's too good to be true. *Today's Health,* 1974, *52*(6), 54-59.

Richards, J. *But deliver us from evil.* New York: Seabury Press, 1974.

Richter, C. P. On the phenomenon of sudden death in animals and man. *Psychosomatic Medicine,* 1957, *19,* 191-198.

Ridpath, I. Investigating the Sirius mystery. *The Skeptical Inquirer,* Fall 1978, *3*(1), 56-62.

Ritter, C. *A woman in the polar night.* New York: Dutton, 1954.

Robbins, R. H. *The encyclopedia of witchcraft and demonology.* New York: Crown, 1959.

Roberts, O. *The call.* Garden City, N.J.: Doubleday, 1972.

Robinson, J. *Public information about world affairs.* Ann Arbor, Mich.: Survey Research Center, Institute for Social Research, University of Michigan, 1967.

Rochas d'Aiglun, E. A. A. *L'extériorisation de la sensibilité.* Paris: Chamnel, 1899.

Rochas d'Aiglun, E. A. A. *Les vies succesifs.* Paris: Charconac, 1911.

Rodewyk, A. *Possessed by Satan.* Garden City, N.J.: Doubleday, 1975.

Rogers, C. The necessary and sufficient conditions of therapeutic personality change. *Journal of Consulting Psychology,* 1957, *21,* 95-103.

Roll, W. G. *The poltergeist.* Metuchen, N.J.: Scarecrow Press, 1976.

Roll, W. G. Poltergeists. In B. B. Wolman (Ed.), *Handbook of parapsychology.* New York: Van Nostrand Reinhold, 1977.

Roll, W. G., & Pratt, J. G. The Miami disturbances. *Journal of the American Society for Psychical Research*, 1971, *65*, 409-454.

Romains, J. *La vision extra-rétinienne et le sens paroptique*. Paris: Nouvelle Revue Française, 1920.

Rose, L. *Faith healing*. London: Gollancz, 1968.

Rosenthal, R. *Experimenter effects in behavioral research*. New York: Irvington, 1976.

Rosenthal, R., & Jacobson, L. *Pygmalion in the classroom: Teachers' expectations and pupils' intellectual development*. New York: Holt, Rinehart & Winston, 1968.

Rosenthal, T. L., Hendersen, R., Hobson, A., & Hurt, M. Social strata and perceptions of magical and folk-medical child-care practices. *Journal of Social Psychology*, 1969, *77*, 3-13.

Rosett, J. *The mechanism of thought, imagery, and hallucination*. New York: Columbia University Press, 1939.

Rubenstein, R., & Newman, R. The living out of "future" experiences under hypnosis. *Science*, 1954, *119*, 472-473.

Russell, D. W., & Jones, W. H. When superstition fails: Differential reactions to the disconfirmation of paranormal beliefs. *Personality and Social Psychology Bulletin*, in press.

Rychlak, J. F. *A philosophy of science for personality theory*. Boston: Houghton Mifflin, 1968.

Saint Augustine. *Confessions*. (R. S. Pine-Coffin, trans.). Baltimore, Md.: Penguin Books, 1961.

Samarin, W. J. *Tongues of men and angels*. New York: Macmillan, 1972.

Sargant, W. *Battle for the mind*. New York: Harper & Row, 1959.

Saunders, D. Factor analysis of UFO-related attitudes. *Perceptual and Motor Skills*, 1968, *27*, 1207-1218.

Schachter, S. Deviation, rejection, and communication. *Journal of Abnormal and Social Psychology*, 1951, *46*, 190-208.

Schafer, R., & Murphy, G. The role of autism in a visual figure-ground relationship. *Journal of Experimental Psychology*, 1943, *32*, 335-343.

Scheibe, K. E., & Sarbin, T. K. Towards a theoretical conceptualization of superstition. *British Journal for the Philosophy of Science*, 1965, *16*, 143-158.

Scheidt, R. J. Belief in supernatural phenomena and locus of control. *Psychological Reports*, 1973, *32*, 1159-1162.

Schmeidler, G. R. Predicting good and bad scores in a clairvoyance experiment: A preliminary report. *Journal of the American Society for Psychical Research*, 1943, *37*, 103-110. (a)

Schmeidler, G. R. Predicting good and bad scores in clairvoyance experiments: A final report. *Journal of the American Society for Psychical Research*, 1943, *37*, 210-221. (b)

Schmeidler, G. R. Separating the sheep from the goats. *Journal of the American Society for Psychical Research*, 1945, *39*, 47-50.

Schmeidler, G. R. Personality differences in the effective use of ESP. *Journal of Communication*, Winter 1975, *25*(1), 133-141.

Schmeidler, G. R., & McConnell, R. A. *ESP and personality patterns*. New Haven, Conn.: Yale University Press, 1958.

Schmidt, H. New correlation between a human subject and a quantum mechanical random number generator. *Boeing Scientific Research Laboratories Document DI-82-0684, November, 1967*.

Schmidt, H. Clairvoyance tests with a machine. *Journal of Parapsychology*, 1969, *33*, 300-306. (a)

Schmidt, H. Quantum processes predicted? *New Scientist*, October 16, 1969, 114. (b)

Schmidt, H. Mental influence on random events. *New Scientist and Science Journal*, June 24, 1971, 757.

Schmidt, H. Toward a mathematical theory of psi. *Journal of the American Society for Psychical Research*, 1975, *69*, 301-319.

Schneider, D. J. *Social psychology*. Reading, Mass.: Addison-Wesley, 1976.

Schopenhauer, A. Parerga und Paralipomena. In (E. Grisebach (Ed.)), *Sämtliche Werke* (Vol. 4). Leipzig: Philipp Reclam, 1891.

Schrödinger, E. *What is life?* Cambridge, England: Cambridge University Press, 1969.

Schwartz, R. Sleight of tongue. *The Skeptical Inquirer*, Fall 1978, *3*(1), 47-55.

Scott, C., & Goldney, K. M. The Jones boys and the ultrasonic whistle. *Journal of the Society for Psychical Research*, 1960, *40*, 249-260.

Scott, C., & Hutchinson, M. Television tests of Masuaki Kiyota. *The Skeptical Inquirer*, Spring 1979, *3*(3), 42-48.

Scott, L. J. Transcendental meditation: Effect of pretreatment personality and prognostic expectancy upon degree of reported personality change (Doctoral dissertation, George Washington University, 1977). *Dissertation Abstracts International*, 1977, *38*(5-B), 2383.

Sebald, H. *Witchcraft*, New York: Elsevier, 1978.

Secord, P. F., Bevan, W., & Katz, B. The negro stereotype and perceptual orientation. *Journal of Abnormal and Social Psychology*, 1956, *53*, 78-83.

Seligman, M. E. *Helplessness*. San Francisco: Freeman, 1975.

Seligmann, K. *Magic, supernaturalism, and religion*. New York: Pantheon, 1948.

Shadowitz, A., & Walsh, P. *The dark side of knowledge*. Menlo Park, Cal.: Addison-Wesley, 1976.

Sheaffer, R. Do fairies exist? *The Skeptical Inquirer*, Fall/Winter 1977, *2*(1), 45-52.

Sheaffer, R. NBC's "Project UFO": Just the facts ma'am, please. *The Humanist*, 1978, *35*(5), 46-48.

Sheffield, F. D., Kaufman, R. S., & Rhine, J. B. A PK experiment at Yale starts a controversy. *Journal of the American Society for Psychical Research*, 1952, *46*, 111-117.

Shepard, L. (Ed.). *Encyclopedia of occultism and parapsychology* (2 vols.). Detroit: Gale Research, 1978.

Sherif, M. *The psychology of social norms*. New York: Harper, 1936.

Shupe, A. D., Spielmann, R., & Stigall, S. Deprogramming: The new exorcism. In J. T. Richardson (Ed.), *Conversion careers: In and out of the new religions*. Beverly Hills, Cal.: Sage, 1977.

Sidis, B. *The psychology of suggestion*. New York: Appleton, 1910.

Siegel, R. K. Hallucinations. *Scientific American*, 1977, *237*(10), 132-140.

Siegel, R. K., & West, L. J. (Eds.) *Hallucinations*. New York: Wiley, 1975.

Singer, B. Course on scientific examinations of paranormal phenomena: Resources and suggestions for educational approaches. *JSAS Catalog of Selected Documents in Psychology*, 1977, *7*, 1. (Ms. No. 1404)

Skinner, B. F. Superstition in the pigeon. *Journal of Experimental Psychology*, 1948, *38*, 168-172.

Sladek, J. T. *The new apocrypha*. New York: Stein & Day, 1973.

Slocum, J. *Sailing around the world*. New York: Century, 1900.

Smith, V. Science method and superstition. *School and Society*, 1930, *31*, 66-68.

Snyder, C. R., Larsen, D. L., & Bloom, L. J. Acceptance of general personality interpretations prior to and after receipt of diagnostic feedback supposedly based on psychological, graphological, and astrological assessment procedures. *Journal of Clinical Psychology*, 1976, *32*, 258-265.

Snyder, C. R. & Shenkel, R. J. The P. T. Barnum effect. *Psychology Today*, March 1975, 52-54.

Soal, S. G. On "Science and the supernatural." *Science*, 1956, *123*, 9-11.

Soal, S. G., & Bowden, H. T. *The mind readers*. London: Faber & Faber, 1959.

Spanos, N. P. Witchcraft in histories of psychiatry: A critical analysis and an alternative conceptualization. *Psychological Bulletin*, 1978, *85*, 417-439.

Spencer Brown, G. Statistical significance in psychical research. *Nature*, 1953, *167*, 154-156.

Spranger, E. *Types of men* (trans. from 5th German ed.). Halle (Saale): Max Niemayer Verlag, 1928.

Stace, W. T. *The teachings of the mystics*. New York: New American Library, 1960.

Stanford, R. G. An experimentally testable model for spontaneous psi events. 2. Psychokinetic events. *Journal of the American Society for Psychical Research*, 1974, *68*, 321-356.

Stanford, R. G. Experimental psychokinesis: A review from diverse perspectives. In B. B. Wolman (Ed.), *Handbook of parapsychology*. New York: Van Nostrand Reinhold, 1977.

Staudenmaier, L. *Die Magie als experimentelle Naturwissenschaft* (2nd ed.). Leipzig: Akademische Verlagsgesellschaft, 1922.

Stein, M., Schiavi, R. C., & Camerino, M. Influence of brain and behavior on the immune system. *Science*, 1976, *191*, 435-440.

Stern, J. *The search for a soul*. Greenwich, Conn.: Fawcett, 1973.

Stevenson, I. Telepathic impressions: A review and report of thirty-five new cases. *Proceedings of the American Society for Psychical Research*, 1970, *29*, 1-198.

Stevenson, I. *Twenty cases suggestive of reincarnation* (2nd ed.). Charlottesville: University Press of Virginia, 1974.

Stevenson, I. Reincarnation: Field studies and theoretical issues. In B. B. Wolman (Ed.), *Handbook of parapsychology*. New York: Van Nostrand Reinhold, 1977.

Stevenson, J. H. The effect of posthypnotic dissociation on the performance of interfering tasks. *Journal of Abnormal Psychology*, 1976, *85*, 398-407.

Stewart, J. R. Cattle mutilations: An episode of collective delusion. *The Zetetic*, Spring/Summer 1977, *1*(2), 55-66.

Story, R. D. Von Daniken's golden gods. *The Zetetic*, Fall/Winter 1977, *2*(1), 22-35.

Strauch, I. Medical aspects of "mental" healing. *International Journal of Parapsychology*, 1963, *5*, 135-165.

Sugi, Y., & Akutsu, K. *Science of Zen-energy metabolism*. Tokyo: 1964.

Surwit, R. S. Warming thoughts for a cold winter. *Psychology Today*, December 1978, 112-115.

Tart, C. T. A psychophysiological study of out-of-the-body experiences in a selected subject. *Journal of the American Society for Psychical Research*, 1968, *62*, 3-27.

Tart, C. T. *Altered states of consciousness*. New York: Wiley, 1969.

Tart, C. T. (Ed.) *Transpersonal psychologies*. New York: Harper & Row, 1975.

Tart, C. T. *Learning to use extrasensory perception*. Chicago: University of Chicago Press, 1976.

Tart, C. T. Letter to editor. *Science*, 1978, *202*, 1145.

Taylor, S. E. L. (Ed.) *Fox-Taylor automatic writing, 1869-1892*. Minneapolis: Tribune-Great West Printing, 1932.

Taylor, W. S., & Martin, M. F. Multiple personality. *Journal of Abnormal and Social Psychology*, 1944, *39*, 281-300.

Teodorowicz, J. *Mystical phenomena in the life of Theresa Neumann*. St. Louis: B. Herder, 1940.

Ter Keurst, A. J. Comparative differences between superstitious and non-superstitious children. *Journal of Experimental Education*, 1939, *7*, 261-267.

Thompson, J. J. *Recollections and reflections*. London: G. Bell, 1936.

Thompson, W. R., & Melzack, R. Early environment. *Scientific American*, 1956, *194*(1), 38-42.

Thouless, R. H. A report on an experiment in psychokinesis with dice, and a discussion on psychological factors favoring success. *Proceedings of the Society for Psychical Research*, 1951, *49*, 107-130.

Thurston, H. The phenomena of stigmatization. *Proceedings of the Society for Psychical Research*, 1922, *32*, 185-187.

Thurston, H. Article in *The Month*, December 1930. In H. C. Graef, *The case of Therese Neumann*. Westminister, Md.: Newmann Press, 1951.

Tietze, T. R. *Margery*. New York: Harper & Row, 1973.

Tiryakin, E. A. *On the margin of the visible: Comparative sociology, the esoteric, and the occult*. New York: Wiley, 1974.

Torrey, E. F. *The mind game: Witchdoctors and psychiatrists*. New York: Bantam Books, 1973.

Trefil, J. A consumer's guide to pseudoscience. *Saturday Review*, March 29, 1978, 16-21.

True, R. M., & Stephenson, C. W. Controlled experiments correlating electroencephalogram, pulse, and plantar reflexes with hypnotic age regression and induced emotional states. *Personality*, 1951, *1*, 252-263.

Truzzi, M. Definition and dimensions of the occult: Toward a sociological perspective. *Journal of Popular Culture*, 1971, *5*, 635-646.

Truzzi, M. Parameters of the paranormal. *The Zetetic*, Spring/Summer, 1977, *1*(2), 4-8.

Tuch, L. *Superstition as related to security*. Unpublished Master's thesis, University of Tulsa, 1968.

Turnbull, C. M. Some observations regarding the experiences and behavior of the Ba Mbuti pygmies. *American Journal of Psychology*, 1961, *74*, 304-308.

Turner, F. *Between science and religion*. New Haven: Yale University Press, 1974.

Tylor, E. B. Animism. In V. F. Calverton (Ed.), *The making of man: An outline of anthropology*. New York: Modern Library, 1931.

Ullman, M. Psychopathology and psi phenomena. In B. B. Wolman (Ed.), *Handbook of parapsychology*. New York: Van Nostrand Reinhold, 1977.

Ullman, M., & Krippner, S. Experimental dream studies. In M. Ebon (Ed.), *The Signet handbook of parapsychology*. New York: New American Library, 1978.

Ullman, M., & Krippner, S., with Vaughan, A. *Dream telepathy*. New York: Macmillan, 1973.

Underhill, E. *Mysticism: A study in the nature and development of man's spiritual consciousness*. New York: Meridian, 1955.

Urantia Foundation. *The Urantia book*. Chicago: Urantia Foundation, 1955.

Valentine, W. L. Common misconceptions of college students. *Journal of Applied Psychology*, 1936, *20*, 633-658.

Van de Castle, R. L. Sleep and dreams. In B. B. Wolman (Ed.), *Handbook of parapsychology*. New York: Van Nostrand Reinhold, 1977.

Van Deusen, E. *Astrogenetics*. New York: Doubleday, 1976.

Vogt, E. Z., & Hyman, R. *Water witching USA*. Chicago: University of Chicago Press, 1959.

A vote for sasquatch. *Newsweek*, June 26, 1978, 32.

Wadhams, P., & Farrelly, B. A. The investigation of psychokinesis using p-particles. *Journal of the Society for Psychical Research*, 1968, *44*, 281-289.

Wagner, M. E. Superstitions and their social and psychological correlates among students. *Journal of Educational Sociology*, 1928, *2*, 26-36.

Walker, J. The amateur scientist. *Scientific American*, 1977, *237*(2), 126-131.

Wall, P. M. *Eyewitness identification in criminal cases*. Springfield, Mass.: C. C. Thomas, 1965.

Wallace, A. F. *Culture and personality*. New York: Random House, 1970.

Wallace, R. K. Physiological effects of transcendental meditation. *Science*, 1970, *167*, 1751-1754.

Wallechinsky, D., & Wallace, I. (Eds.) *The people's almanac*. Garden City, N. Y.:

Doubleday, 1975.

Wallechinsky, D., & Wallace, I. (Eds.) *The people's almanac no. 2.* New York: Bantam Books, 1978.

Wallis R. "Poor man's psychoanalysis?" Observation on dianetics. *The Zetetic,* Fall/Winter 1976, *1*(1), 9-24.

Warburton, F. W. Beliefs concerning human nature in a university department of education. *British Journal of Educational Psychology,* 1956, *26,* 156-162.

Warren, D. I. Status inconsistency theory and flying saucer sightings. *Science,* 1970, *170,* 599-603.

Wescott, R. Paranthropology: A nativity celebration and a communion commentary. In J. K. Long (Ed.), *Extrasensory ecology: Parapsychology and anthropology.* Metuchen, N.J.: Scarecrow Press, 1977.

Wesley, J. *The works.* Vols. 1-4, *The Journal.* London: Wesleyan Conference Office, 1872-78.

West, D. J. *Eleven Lourdes miracles.* London: Duckworth, 1957.

White, R. A. The influence of experimenter motivation, attitudes, and methods of handling subjects on psi test results. In B. B. Wolman (Ed.), *Handbook of parapsychology.* New York: Van Nostrand Reinhold, 1977.

Williams, G. M. *Priestess of the occult.* New York: Knopf, 1946.

Winer, B. *Theories of motivation.* Chicago: Markhous, 1972.

Witkin, H. A., Lewis, H. B., Hertzman, M., Machover, K., Meissner, P. B., & Wapner, S. *Personality through perception.* New York: Harper, 1954.

Wolman, B. B. Principles of monistic transitionism. In B. B. Wolman & E. Nagel (Eds.), *Scientific psychology: Principles and approaches.* New York: Basic Books, 1965.

Wolman, B. B. (Ed.) *Handbook of parapsychology.* New York: Van Nostrand Reinhold, 1977.

Wolman, B. B. Mind and body: A contribution to a theory of parapsychological phenomena. In B. B. Wolman (Ed.), *Handbook of parapsychology.* New York: Van Nostrand Reinhold, 1977.

Wood, E. *The seven rays* (4th ed.). Adyar, Madras: Theosophical Publishing House, 1952.

Woodward, W. *A case study of scientific revolutions: Kuhn, Popper, Lakatos, and psychophysics.* Paper presented at the meeting of the American Psychological Association, Toronto, 1978.

The world almanac book of the strange. New York: New American Library, 1977.

Worrall, A. A., & Worrall, O. N. *The gift of healing.* New York: Harper & Row, 1965.

Youtz, R. P. Can fingers see color? *Psychology Today,* 1968, *1*(9), 37-41.

Zapf, R. M. Comparison of responses to superstitions on a written test and in actual situations. *Journal of Educational Research,* 1945, *39,* 13-24.

Zelen, M. Astrology and statistics: A challenge. *The Humanist,* January-February 1976, 32-33.

Zilboorg, G. *The medical man and the witch during the Renaissance.* Baltimore: Johns Hopkins Press, 1935.

Zilboorg, G., & Henry, G. W. *A history of medical psychology.* New York: Norton, 1941.

Zimbardo, P. G. The psychology of police confessions. In *Readings in social psychology today.* Del Mar, Calif.: CRM Books, 1970.

Zusne, L. Entoptically perceived retinal circulation: A method for classroom demonstration of the circulatory phenomenon. *The American Biology Teacher,* 1963, *25,* 621-625.

Zusne, L. Metaphysical parallels of the *Study of Values. Psychological Record,* 1965, *15,* 537-543.

Zusne L., & Jones, W. H. *ESP, belief, and signal detection theory.* Unpublished manuscript, University of Tulsa, 1978.

Subject and Name Index